Introduction to the Philosophy of Law

Readings and Cases

Jefferson White
Dennis Patterson

New York • Oxford
OXFORD UNIVERSITY PRESS
1999

Oxford University Press

Oxford New York
Athens Auckland Bangkok Bogotá Buenos Aires Calcutta
Cape Town Chennai Dar es Salaam Delhi Florence Hong Kong Istanbul
Karachi Kuala Lumpur Madrid Melbourne Mexico City Mumbai
Nairobi Paris São Paulo Singapore Taipei Tokyo Toronto Warsaw

and associated companies in
Berlin Ibadan

Copyright © 1999 by Oxford University Press, Inc.

Published by Oxford University Press, Inc.
198 Madison Avenue, New York, New York 10016

Oxford is a registered trademark of Oxford University Press

Grateful acknowledgment to the following publishers for their kind permission to reprint:

Aristotle, *Physics*, trans. R. Hardie and R. Gaye in *The Oxford Translation of Aristotle, Vol. II*, ed. W. D. Ross. Copyright © 1930 by Oxford
University Press. Used by permission of Oxford University Press.
Aristotle, *Politics*, trans. B. Jowett in *The Oxford Translation of Aristotle, Vol. X*, ed. W. D. Ross. Copyright © 1921 by Oxford University Press.
Used by permission of Oxford University Press.
Aristotle, *Nicomachean Ethics*, trans. W. D. Ross in *The Oxford Translation of Aristotle, Vol. IX*, ed. W. D. Ross. Copyright © 1925 by Oxford
University Press. Used by permission of Oxford University Press.
Reprinted by permission of the publishers and the Loeb Classical Library from *Cicero: Philosophical Treatises, Vol XVI*, translated by Clinton
W. Keyes, Cambridge, Mass.: Harvard University Press, 1928.
An Aquinas Reader by Mary Clark, Ed. Copyright © 1972 by Mary T. Clark. Reprinted by permission of Doubleday, a division of Bantam
Doubleday Dell Publishing Group, Inc.
Hugo Grotius, *De Jure Belli ac Pacis Libri Tres* in *Classics of International Law*, trans. F. Kelsey, ed. J. Scott. Copyright © 1925 by Claredon Press.
Used by permission of the Carnegie Endowment for International Peace.
William Blackstone, *Commentaries on the Laws of England* Vol I Copyright © 1807 by Thomas B. Wait and Company.
The Concept of Law, 2nd ed. by H.L.A. Hart, edited by Joseph Raz and Penelope Bulloch. Copyright © 1994 by Oxford University Press.
Reprinted by permission of publisher.
Taking Rights Seriously by Ronald Dworkin. Copyright © 1977 by Ronad Dworkin. Reprinted by permission of Harvard University Press.
Law's Empire by Ronald Dworkin. Copyright © 1986 by Ronald Dworkin. Reprinted by permission of Harvard University Press.
Problems of Jurisprudence by Richard Posner. Copyright © 1990 by the President and Fellows of Harvard College. Reprinted by permission
of Harvard University Press.
"Legal Realism, Critical Legal Studies and Dworkin" by Andrew Altman in *Philosophy and Public Affairs*. Copyright © 1986 by Princeton
University Press. Reprinted by permission of publisher.
Knowledge and Politics by Roberto Mangabeira Unger. Copyright © by Roberto Mangabeira Unger. Reprinted by the permission of The Free
Press, a Division of Simon and Schuster.
"Justice Engendered" by Martha Minow in *Harvard Law Review*. Copyright © 1987 by Harvard Law Review Association. Reprinted by per-
mission of publisher.
Constitutional Interpretation by Philip Bobbitt. Copyright © 1991 by Blackwell Publishers, Oxford. Reprinted by permission of Blackwell Pub-
lishers.
Law and Truth by Dennis Patterson. Copyright © 1996 by Dennis Patterson. Reprinted by permission of Oxford University Press, Inc.
Natural Law and Natural Rights by John Finnis. Copyright © 1980 by Oxford University Press. Reprinted by permission of publisher.
Nuclear Deterrence, Morality, and Realism by John Finnis, Joseph Boyle, and Germain Grisez. Copyright © 1987 by Oxford University Press.
Reprinted by permission of publisher.

Library of Congress Cataloging-in-Publication Data

White, Jefferson, 1930–
Introduction to the philosophy of law : readings and cases / by
  Jefferson White & Dennis Patterson.
      p. cm.
    ISBN 0-19-511975-4 (hardcover : alk. paper)
    1. Law—Philosophy.   I. Patterson, Dennis M. (Dennis Michael),
1955–   . II. Title.
K235.W55   1998
340'.1—DC21   98-12815
                                                         CIP

9 8 7 6 5 4 3 2 1

Printed in the United States of America
on acid-free paper

Contents

Preface   **v**

Selection Authors   **ix**

Part I: TYPES OF LEGAL PHILOSOPHY

Chapter 1:   **Classical Natural Law Jurisprudence**   **3**
Readings from Aristotle, Cicero, Aquinas, Grotius, and Blackstone

Chapter 2:   **Positivism**   **41**
Readings from H.L.A. Hart

Chapter 3:   **Constructivism**   **65**
Readings from Ronald Dworkin

Chapter 4:   **Consequentialism**   **94**
Readings from Richard Posner

Chapter 5:   **Critical Legal Theory**   **119**
Readings from Andrew Altman, Roberto Unger, and Martha Minow
Part I: Critical Legal Studies   119
Part II: Feminist Jurisprudence   140

Chapter 6:   **Practice Theory**   **160**
Readings from Phillip Bobbitt and Dennis Patterson

Chapter 7:   **New Natural Law Theory**   **184**
Readings from John Finnis

Part II: CASES IN STATUTORY INTERPRETATION, CONTRACT LAW, TORT LAW, AND PUBLIC LAW

Chapter 8:   **Statutory Interpretation**   **207**
Riggs v. Palmer   207
Church of the Holy Trinity v. United States   215
United Steelworkers of America, AFL-CIO v. Weber.   219
Lujan v. Defenders of Wildlife   235

Chapter 9:   **Contract Law**   **258**
Hamer v. Sidway   259
C & J Fertilizer, Inc. v. Allied Mutual Insurance Company   265

Williams v. Walker-Thomas Furniture Company 274
In the Matter of Baby M 278

Chapter 10: **Tort Law** **296**
Palsgraf v. The Long Island Railroad Company 296
Dillon v. Legg 306
Thing v. LaChusa 315
Hymowitz v. Eli Lilly and Company 343
Vincent et al. v. Lake Erie Transportation Company 356

Chapter 11: **Public Law** **361**
Texas v. Johnson 361
Home Building & Loan Ass'n v. Blaisdell 377
Meyer v. State of Nebraska 406
Everson v. Board of Education of Ewing TP. 410

Glossary **421**

Index **429**

Preface

A multitude of philosophical perplexities arise in the course of legal practice and in the reflective thought that accompanies it. Textbooks in philosophy of law typically include discussions of a score or so of such perplexities; for example, what are the appropriate limits to freedom of expression? Under what circumstances is legal paternalism justified? How should "insanity" be defined for purposes of law? How should the justification of punishment be understood in legal contexts? Selected readings usually focus attention on discussion of such topics by a variety of philosophers and legal theorists, and disagreements between and among various discussions are often useful as a means to engage a student's own critical assessment of the issues under consideration.

The word "introduction" in the title of this book reflects a conviction that while study of specialized topics is altogether appropriate at advanced stages of philosophical and legal study, it is not the most effective way to introduce undergraduates to legal philosophy. Rather than organize materials along numerous and varied topical lines, we focus attention on fundamental differences in the *conception* of law exemplified in both early and more contemporary legal theory and practice, differences in system-atic ways of thinking about the nature of law. In Part I we include texts representing seven fairly distinct types of legal philosophy: classical natural law theory, positivism, constructivism, economic analysis of law, critical legal philosophy, feminist legal studies, practice theory and "new" natural law jurisprudence. This group does not represent the full range of general jurisprudential options, of course, but it does include some of the more well-developed and influential of these.

One reason for emphasis on general approaches to legal theory and practice is the strength of recent legal philosophy in augmenting distinct lines of traditional jurisprudence. In our view recent advocates of several types of jurisprudence have carried articulation of the perspectives they represent to remarkable levels of clarity and coherence—one thinks, for example, of the outstanding contribution of H.L.A. Hart, Ronald Dworkin, or Richard Posner to their respective jurisprudential traditions. Part I includes a number of such advocates, and in selecting from their work we have tried to provide these authors an opportunity to explain their positions at some length and in their own voice. As a consequence, many of the readings are more extensive in scope than in other textbooks—a full section here, a full chapter there, and in some places an article almost in its entirety. The payoff for including some degree of "bulk" in the treatment of various jurisprudential types is, we believe, substantial gain in appreciation of the types in question. Such appreciation can have a triple effect: (1) it can increase appreciation of the power inherent in the set of ideas in question; (2) it can enable more ready identification of fragments of these systems of jurisprudential thought when they occur in legal writing; and (3) it can highlight significant historical dimensions of the various positions represented. With regard to this third effect, it is important to note that the readings in Part I provide both taxonomical description and materials for understanding relationships between and among various jurisprudential types. Of particular importance are the reactions of one and another of the authors to different, often opposing, doctrines and points of view. In understanding the historical fate of Aristotle's conception of final cause, for example, we come to understand better both Unger's critical legal theory and Dworkin's constructivism.

The introductory agenda developed here is not confined to study of jurisprudential types, however; equally important is legal case-analysis. Selections from cases are frequently included in philosophy of law textbooks, often as illustrations of some special issue or topic under consideration; this textbook differs from most others in the extent and variety of cases provided. So far as extent is concerned, it is worth noting that cases constitute more than one-half of the material selected for study. With respect to variety, we note that most textbooks in legal philosophy include only or mostly "public law" cases, that is, cases concerned with questions about the degree to which our lives may properly be subject to governmental regulation and control. In this context, specific legal issues (privacy issues, for example) implicate larger questions of political and philosophical theory (autonomy, for example). "Private law," by contrast, addresses the obligations we owe to one another simply by virtue of our status as persons. The cases in Part II divide about equally between public and private law because: (1) at least so far as undergraduates are concerned, philosophical issues in private law such as the nature of "good faith" and "reasonable care" evoke as much interest as those connected with public law and (2) cases in contract and tort law bring the study envisioned here closer to that which is undertaken in law school, especially during the first year.

More important than either the extent or the variety of case analysis is its *function* in relation to the study of jurisprudential types. Adjudication is an eclectic enterprise in which the best law a jurist can muster is combined with the best admissible evidence of fact she or he can find in the most legally convincing way possible for that particular jurist. But inherently eclectic as it is, adjudication is far from arbitrary. What blocks arbitrariness is the presence of normative thought, that is, articulation of priorities and principles of value capable of binding law and fact together in a coordinated way. Knowledge of the priorities and values which *divide* representatives of one jurisprudential type from another can play an important role in case analysis. For one thing, it can enable us to recognize the primary arguments which comprise these comprehensive theories. While these arguments are best understood and supported in the systematic context supplied by jurisprudential thought, they are not confined to it. Indeed they typically occur in legal discourse as theory-independent considerations, detached from any kind of coordinated expression of legal norms and values as such. It is not uncommon in close reading of a legal opinion, for example, to observe segments of characteristic positivist or consequentialist or natural law reasoning. It is important to recognize that where such reasoning can be clearly identified, a direct and possibly significant connection between philosophy and legal practice may be at work. The point of philosophical case study is analysis of the effect of connections of this kind on the overall pattern of argument in a legal opinion. Especially important in this regard is the

reading from Philip Bobbitt in Chapter 6 where a classification scheme for legal argument is developed in some detail. Though confined to an account of constitutional law, this scheme has obvious connections to legal argument generally, and it can prove very useful in analysis of many, if not all, of the cases in Part II. We recommend study and class discussion of this reading early in a course of study since it provides both a useful method of approaching analysis of legal cases and some conceptual tools with which it can be carried out. Reflection informed by such analysis is a natural and effective way to open up for undergraduate scrutiny some of the genuinely philosophical dimensions of legal decision-making.

The authors are grateful to Daffodil Tyminski for preparation of the Index and Table of Cases.

Orono, Maine
Voorhees, New Jersey
September 1998

J. W.
D. P.

Selection Authors

Altman, Andrew (b. 1950). Professor of Philosophy, The George Washington University. He is the author of *Critical Legal Studies: A Liberal Critique* (Princeton University Press, 1990) and *Arguing About Law: An Introduction to Legal Philosophy* (Wadsworth Publishing Company, 1996).

Aquinas, Thomas (1226–1274). A member of the Dominican order, born near Naples. Aquinas was canonized in 1323. His *Summa Theologica* (1265–1274) is the most important treatise on law produced during the medieval period.

Aristotle (384–322 B.C.). Arguably the most important ancient philosopher after Plato. Aristotle's work *The Nicomachean Ethics* contains some of the most important work on ethics and legal theory in the western tradition.

Blackstone, William (1723–1780). Author of *Commentaries on the Laws of England*, perhaps the most important legal treatise in the English language.

Bobbitt, Philip Chase (b. 1948). Baker & Botts Professor of Law, University of Texas. Bobbitt is the author of two important books in constitutional theory. The first of these, *Constitutional Fate* (Oxford University Press, 1982), introduced the notion of the modalities of constitutional argument. In *Constitutional Interpretation* (Blackwell, 1991), Bobbitt shows how his position explains not only constitutional argument but congressional debate and political controversy (specifically the Iran-Contra affair) as well.

Cicero, Marcus Tullius (106–43 B.C.). In addition to being a lawyer, Cicero was a politician and orator. Murdered in 43 B.C., Cicero left a large collection of important works, including *De Oratore*. Cicero's view of law was much influenced by Stoicism. In Cicero's view, for positive law to be true law it must realize external and changing rules of justice and reason.

Dworkin, Ronald (b. 1931). Dworkin is the author of several important books in legal philosophy. He is best known for his critique of legal positivism in *Taking Rights Seriously* (Harvard University Press, 1977). In *Law's Empire* (Harvard University Press, 1986), Dworkin defends the view that law is best understood as an interpretive practice.

Finnis, John M. (b. 1940). Born in Australia, Finnis is the leading modern proponent of natural law theory. His book *Natural Law and Natural Rights* (Oxford University Press, 1980) is already a classic.

Grotius, Hugo (1583–1645). A famous Dutch jurist, Grotius enjoyed a distinguished career, which included a stint as ambassador to London. His book *De Jure Belli ac Pacis* is generally regarded as establishing modern public international law.

Hart, H.L.A. (b. 1907–1992). In his career, Hart was a barrister as well as the most important postwar figure in legal philosophy. He was appointed Professor of Jurisprudence at Oxford in 1955, a position he held until 1968. His classic work is *The Concept of Law* (Oxford University Press, 1961).

Minow, Martha (b. 1954). Professor of Law, Harvard Law School. Minow is regarded as a leading author in feminist legal theory. She is the author of *Making All The Difference: Inclusion, Exclusion, and American Law* (Cornell University Press, 1990).

Patterson, Dennis (b. 1955). Distinguished Professor of Law at Rutgers University, School of Law (Camden). He is the author of *Law and Truth* (Oxford University Press, 1996) and the editor of *The Blackwell Companion to Legal Theory and Legal Philosophy*. In addition to his interests in legal philosophy, Patterson is a commercial lawyer and the author of several books in commercial law.

Posner, Richard (b. 1939). Chief Judge for the Federal Court of Appeals, Seventh Circuit. Before joining the Court of Appeals, Posner was a Professor of Law at the University of Chicago Law School. He is best known for his work in the economic analysis of law. His book *Economic Analysis of Law* (Little, Brown and Company, 4th ed., 1992) is a classic.

Unger, Roberto Mangabeira (b. 1947). Professor of Law, Harvard Law School. Included among his best known works are *Knowledge and Politics* (The Free Press, 1975), *Law and Modern Society: Towards a Criticism of Social Theory* (The Free Press, 1976), and *The Critical Legal Studies Movement* (Harvard University Press, 1986).

Part I

Types of Legal Philosophy

Chapter 1

Classical Natural Law Jurisprudence

Readings from Aristotle, Cicero, Aquinas, Grotius, and Blackstone

Readings in Part I introduce students to several different "types" of legal philosophy—sometimes referred to as "schools" or "positions" or "traditions." We understand a type of legal theory or philosophy as a framework of interrelated belief that recurs with some frequency in the history of jurisprudence. Legal positivism, for example, includes among other beliefs (1) that the existence of a law depends on its having been established through some socially recognized decision-making process and (2) that the existence of that law in no way depends on whether some moral standard—any moral standard—is applicable to it. These claims are part of a larger "set" or "network" of belief about the nature of law.

It is important to recognize that beliefs and claims characteristic of a type do not constitute a checklist of defining features applicable as a test for determining the "legal philosophy" of any particular author—whether she or he is a natural law theorist or a positivist, for example. We assume a "family resemblance"[1] conception of types of legal theory; that is, individual expressions of positivism or natural law jurisprudence are alike in the way that members of a family are alike: no two members are similar in all respects, and there are few, if any, important family likenesses that are shared by all members of the family.

The sources of natural law jurisprudence are ancient and venerable, and they illustrate especially well the idea that it is impossible to formulate a set of necessary and sufficient conditions for attribution of belief in "natural law." What will be evident in the readings here from Aristotle, Cicero, Aquinas, Grotius, and Blackstone is that while their views vary greatly in

---

1. In his later work Wittgenstein stressed that the objects referred to by a term like *legal type* are held together not by a feature shared by all the objects of that type but rather by a series of characteristic resemblances among members of the type, e.g., resemblances among facial features of the members of a family. See Ludwig Wittgenstein, *Philosophical Investigations*, eds. G.E.M. Anscombe and R. Rhees, tr. G.E.M. Anscombe, 3rd ed. (New York: The Macmillan Company, 1971), pp. 31, 32.

detail, they share, nonetheless, some features that mark them as representatives of a single tradition in legal philosophy. For one thing, they stand in firm opposition to the idea that human nature is basically indifferent to concern for justice except as a survival value. Such concern, they say, is deeply rooted in the social nature of persons. Human nature is variously understood within the tradition, but the idea persists throughout that people share a capacity for special kinds of cognition and communication and that among the kinds of knowledge they possess is moral understanding. This accounts for what is generally regarded as a salient feature of natural law theory: the claim that there is a necessary connection between law and morality. Evidence for this connection is thought to reside in the capacity of human beings to "reason correctly" about what is just and unjust: moral truth, in other words, is "objective" in nature, and the truth value of both moral and legal judgments can be determined by reason. Exactly how such determination is made is a large question, of course, especially with regard to legal judgments, but the important point in this regard is that natural law advocates can be counted on to reject the idea that human laws are basically adventitious and that legal truth is always relative in nature, that is, merely the product of particular lawmaking in different historically situated communities. For natural law theorists, what blocks the claim that legal truths are relative in nature is recognition of their essential connection to—their foundation in—moral principles that are universal.

Aristotle

As a foundation for the idea that morality is necessarily related to law, Aristotle argues that there is only one alternative to belief that events are related "by necessity," and that is belief that they are related "by accident." The passages below are taken from Book II of his *Physics*, and they contain his explanation of the concepts "by necessity" and "by accident." Earlier in that book he advances his famous analysis of four different ways in which the origin or cause of natural events can be explained, and since his concept of the "four causes" sets the context for discussion of "accidental" and "necessary" relations, it will be well to review this concept briefly. First, he says that anything that happens may be explained by reference to what it is *made out of*, what he calls its "material cause." Second, he says, we may refer to the *power or agency that brought it into existence*, its "efficient cause." Third, explanation may refer to *a structure*, which is shared by other things of the same type: its "formal cause." And finally we may explain things by reference to an *end or purpose toward which the completion or fulfillment as a natural kind is directed*—its "final cause."

In the passages to follow Aristotle discusses the idea of final cause in terms of several connected observations and reflections: (1) While some events are "for the sake of something," some are not, that is, some things happen accidentally, by chance; (2) nature belongs to the class of causes that act for the sake of something; (3) the chief obstacle to belief in final causes is the possibility that everything happens by accident; (4) there is an argument for the existence of final causes; and finally (5) there are natural "monstrosities," that is, instances in which nature fails to realize or fulfill a purpose or "end in view." The idea of nature as purposeful sets the stage for a naturalist account of law in the following way: law is rooted in an innate tendency of human beings toward social life and societal development. Such development is impossible without law, so law is natural in the way that breathing and other vital functions are natural—it is an indispensable element in human well-being.

~

Reading 1

From Aristotle,
PHYSICS, BOOK II, CHAPTER 8

We must explain then . . . that Nature belongs to the class of causes which act for the sake of something. . . . A difficulty presents itself: why should not nature work, not for the sake of something, nor because it is better so, but just as the sky rains, not in order to make the corn grow, but of necessity? What is drawn up must cool, and what has been cooled must become water and descend, the result of this being that the corn grows. Similarly if a man's crop is spoiled on the threshing-floor, the rain did not fall for the sake of this—in order that the crop might be spoiled—but that result just followed. Why then should it not be the same with the parts in nature, e.g., that our teeth should come up of necessity—the front teeth sharp, fitted for tearing, the molars broad and useful for grinding down the food—since they did not arise for this end, but it was merely a coincident result; and so with all other parts in which we suppose that there is purpose? Wherever then all the parts came about just what they would have been if they had come to be for an end, such things survived, be-

ing organized spontaneously in a fitting way; whereas those which grew otherwise perished and continue to perish. . . .

Such are the arguments (and others of the kind) which may cause difficulty on this point. Yet it is impossible that this should be the true view. For teeth and all other natural things either invariably or normally come about in a given way; but of not one of the results of chance or spontaneity is this true. We do not ascribe to chance or mere coincidence the frequency of rain in winter, but frequent rain in summer we do; nor heat in the dog-days, but only if we have it in winter. If then, it is agreed that things are either the result of coincidence or for an end, and these cannot be the result of coincidence or spontaneity, it follows that they must be for an end; and that such things are all due to nature even the champions of the theory which is before us would agree. Therefore action for an end is present in things which come to be and are by nature.

Further, where a series has a completion, all the preceding steps are for the sake of that. Now surely as in intelligent action, so in nature; and as in nature, so it is in each action, if nothing interferes. Now intelligent action is for the sake of an end; therefore the nature of things also is so. Thus if a house, e.g., had been a thing made by nature, it would have been made in the same way as it is now by art; and if things made by nature were made also by art, they would come to be in the same way as by nature. Each step then in the series is for the sake of the next; and generally art partly completes what nature cannot bring to a finish, and partly imitates life. If, therefore, artificial products are for the sake of an end, so clearly also are natural products. The relation of the later to the earlier terms of the series is the same in both.

This is most obvious in the animals other than man: they make things neither by art nor after inquiry or deliberation. Wherefore people discuss whether it is by intelligence or by some other faculty that these creatures work—spiders, ants, and the like. By gradual advance in this direction we come to see clearly that in plants too that is produced which is conducive to the end—leaves, e.g., grow to provide shade for the fruit. If then it is both by nature and for an end that the swallow makes its nest and the spider its web, and plants grow leaves for the sake of the fruit and send their roots down (not up) for the sake of nourishment, it is plain that this kind of cause is operative in things which come to be and are by nature. . . .

Now mistakes come to pass even in the operations of art: the grammarian makes a mistake in writing, and the doctor pours out the wrong dose. Hence clearly mistakes are possible in the operations of nature also. If then in art there are cases in which what is rightly produced serves a purpose, and if where mistakes occur there was a purpose in what was attempted, only it was not attained, so must it be also in natural products, and monstrosities will be failures in the purposive effort. . . .

Those things are natural which, by a continuous movement originated from an internal principle, arrive at some completion—the same completion is not reached from every principle; nor any chance completion, but always the tendency in each is towards the same end, if there is no impediment.

The end and the means towards it may come about by chance. We say, for instance, that a stranger has come by chance, paid the ransom, and gone away, when he does so as if he had come for that purpose, though it was not for that he came. This is incidental, for chance is an incidental cause, as I remarked before. But when an event takes place always or for the most part, it is not incidental or by chance. In natural products the sequence is invariable, if there is no impediment. . . .

It is plain then that nature is a cause, a cause that operates for a purpose.

Further connections between Aristotle's general understanding that all natural processes are goal directed and his understanding of human law are made clear in the following passage from the *Politics* where he discusses the development of human communities. In Chapter 1 of that work he says that social and political life are derived from the "union of those who cannot exist without each other." The first such union is between male and female, without which the race could not continue to exist. Out of this union the family develops in accordance with its natural purpose which is to supply essential everyday needs. Families are not always sufficient to provide such needs, however, and wider communities are formed—first villages and later the state. The formation of social life is purposeful in that it originates in the "bare needs of life" and continues to develop in service of the "goods of human life."

Reading 2

From Aristotle, *POLITICS*, BOOK I, CHAPTER 2

... The state is a creation of nature, and ... man is by nature a political animal. ... He who by nature and not by mere accident is without a state, is either a bad man or above humanity; he is like the "tribeless, lawless, heartless one," which Homer denounces. The natural outcast is forthwith a lover of war; he may be compared to an isolated piece (in a game of) draughts.

That man is more of a political animal than bees or any other gregarious animals is evident. Nature, as we often say, makes nothing in vain, and man is the only animal whom she has endowed with the gift of speech. And whereas mere voice is but an indication of pleasure or pain, and is therefore found in other animals ... the power of speech is intended to set forth the expedient and the inexpedient, and therefore likewise the just and the unjust. And it is characteristic of man that he alone has any sense of good and evil, of just and unjust, and the like, and the association of living beings who have this sense makes a family and a state. ...

The proof that the state is a creation of nature and prior to the individual is that the individual, when isolated, is not self-sufficing; and therefore he is like a part in relation to a whole. But he who is unable to live in society, or who has no need because he is sufficient for himself, must be either a beast or a god. ... A social instinct is implanted in all men by nature. ... Man, when perfected, is the best of animals, but when separated from law and justice, he is the worst of all. ... Wherefore, if he have not virtue, is the most unholy and the most savage of animals, and the most full of lust and gluttony. But justice is the bond of men in states, for the administration of justice, which is the determination of what is just, is the principle of order in a political society.

In the next two readings from Aristotle's *Nicomachaean Ethics* we encounter a refinement of his concept of justice. The refinement consists in two qualifications of what has been said about the understanding of human law. The first is a qualification of the idea that justice is universal: human law, he says, is "natural" and "universal" only in part. Normally the content of natural law is expressed in general terms, for example, as the duty to keep one's promises or as the principle that no person should benefit from his or her own crime. However, often the content of justice in particular cases escapes capture by general statements of legal rules and principles, a point made earlier by Plato.

> Law can never issue an injunction binding on all which really embodies what is best for each; it cannot prescribe with perfect accuracy what is good and right for each member of the community at any one time. . . . The variety of man's activities and the inevitable unsettlement attending all human experience make it impossible for any art whatsoever to issue unqualified rules holding good on all questions at all times.[2]

A significant consequence of this understanding of the limitations of general rules is that for a rule to be applicable to some concrete situations something must be *added to* the rule. In the following passage Aristotle explores this "added" element briefly, but importantly, arguing (1) that when application of general legal rules and principles is unable to determine justice in particular cases, a "decree" is necessary and (2) that since "decrees" are conventional in nature we must conclude that law is natural, unchanging, and universal only "in part": in toto it is both natural and conventional.

∼

Reading 3

From Aristotle,
NICHOMACHEAN ETHICS, BOOK V, CHAPTER 6

Of political justice part is natural, part legal—natural, that which everywhere has the same force and does not exist by people's thinking this or that; legal, that which is originally indifferent, but when it has been laid down is not indifferent, e.g., that a prisoner's ransom shall be a mina, or that a goat and not two sheep shall be sacrificed. . . . Now some think that all justice is of this sort, because that which is by nature is unchangeable and has everywhere the same force (as fire burns both here and in Persia), while they see change in the things recognized as just. This is not true, however, in this unqualified way. . . . It is evident which sort of thing, among things capable of being otherwise, is by nature and which is not but is legal and conventional, assuming that both are equally changeable. . . . The things which are just by virtue of convention and expediency are like measures; for wine and corn measures

---

2. Plato, "Statesman," *The Collected Dialogues of Plato*, E. Hamilton and H. Cairns eds., tr. J.B. Skemp (New York: Bollinger Foundation, 1961), p. 1063.

are not everywhere equal, but larger in wholesale and smaller in retail markets. Similarly, the things which are just not by nature but by human enactment are not everywhere the same. . . .

Of things just and lawful each is related as the universal to its particular; for the things that are done are many, but of them [i.e., the things that are just] each is one, since it [i.e., justice] is universal.

~

In a second qualification of his general account of justice, Aristotle advances a somewhat stronger claim: that there are cases in which justice requires not conventional adaptation or extension of some universal principle, but decision *inconsistent* with established legal principle. Such decisions, he says, involve *epieikeia*—equity—a short definition of which is given in the following passage from the *Nichomachaen Ethics*.

~

Reading 4

From Aristotle, *NICHOMACHEAN ETHICS*, BOOK V, CHAPTER 10

Our next subject is equity and the equitable and their respective relations to justice and the just. . . . These are the considerations that give rise to the problem about the equitable. . . . The equitable is just, but (it is) not *legally* just—(it is, rather,) a correction of justice. The reason is that all law is universal but about some things it is not possible to make a universal statement which shall be correct. In those cases, then, in which it is necessary to speak universally, but not possible to do so correctly, the law takes the usual case, though it is not ignorant of the possibility of error. And it is . . . correct (in this), for the error is not in the law nor in the legislator but in the nature of the thing, since the matter of practical affairs is of this kind from the start.

When the law speaks universally, then, and a case arises in it which is not covered by the universal statement, it is right, where the legislator fails us and has erred by oversimplicity, to correct the omission—to say what the legislator himself would have said had he been present, and would have put into his law if he had known. Hence the equitable is just, and better than one kind of justice—not better than absolute justice, but better than the error that arises from the absoluteness of the [universal] statement. And this is the nature of the equitable: a correction of law where it is defective owing to its universality. In fact, this is the reason why all things are not determined by law, viz. that about some things it is impossible to lay down a law, so that a decree is needed. For when the thing is indefinite the rule is also indefinite, like the leaden rule used in making the Lesbian moulding; the rule adapts itself to the shape of the stone and is not rigid—so too the decree is adapted to the facts.

An even more extensive discussion of equity than what we find in the *Nichomachaean Ethics* occurs in the *Rhetoric*.[3] While his basic understanding of this concept remains unchanged in that work, he modifies it in one respect. Throughout the *Ethics* equity is understood entirely with reference to legislative intent: equity is doing what a legislator would have done had she or he been confronted with the case at hand. In the *Rhetoric* Aristotle points out that equity is partly a matter of legislative intent but partly not. "Not intended, where they have noticed no defect in the law; intended, where they find themselves unable to define things exactly . . . or where it is not easy to be complete owing to the endless possible cases presented, such as the kinds and sizes of weapons used to inflict wounds—a lifetime would be too short to make out a complete list of these."

In these passages from the *Ethics* and the *Rhetoric* Aristotle recognizes a central problem in jurisprudence, which is the impossibility of stating the applicable meaning of any legal rule abstractly. This problem, perplexing to legal philosophers generally, is especially acute for those within the natural law tradition because, as we remarked earlier, the content of natural law is normally expressed abstractly, that is, in general rules, principles, and maxims. An important question for any practicing lawyer or judge is the following: in cases where justice can be achieved only by "adding something to" the general rules and principles that naturally govern human affairs, how is what should be added determined? Is the conventional or added element arbitrary? Or can it be "objectively just" in some sense of that term? Aristotle clearly wants to affirm the latter; as he says, "The equitable is the just." But how is the "decree" to be determined? Aristotle is less than clear on this point, but what he does say has considerable significance for future developments in the natural law tradition. He emphasizes that a decree is a "practical affair" and that practical affairs are to some degree indeterminate from the start. This observation takes us to a final point about Aristotle's version of natural law jurisprudence: the determination of justice for him is the product of "practical," not "theoretical," reasoning and judgment.[4] We will have more to say on this subject when we discuss Aquinas's conception of natural law, but since it is Aristotle who first develops the distinction between these modes of reasoning, a brief comment on his concept of practical reason is in order.

Aristotle distinguishes between (1) knowledge involved in the creation of drama and poetry, for example—what he calls "productive" knowledge; and (2) knowledge involved in ethical decision-making, including law—which he calls "practical" knowledge. Both of these are

---

3. Aristotle, *Rhetoric, The Oxford Translation of Aristotle,* trans. W. Roberts (Oxford: Oxford University Press), Bk. I, Ch. 13, 1374a. 29–33.

4. Cf. *Ethics,* Id., Bk. VI, Ch. 1.

distinguished from (3) factual or descriptive cognition—which he calls "theoretical" knowledge. These distinctions reflect roughly the difference between the product of demonstrative and presumably value-neutral reasoning such as is involved in mathematical and scientific inquiry and the kind of value-laden or normative reasoning involved in both the production of works of art and in ethical and legal practice. Aristotle's account of law, especially his account of the content of law, depends in an important way on the concept of practical reasoning. This is less true, if it is at all true, of other natural law advocates. The readings that follow from Cicero, Grotius, and Blackstone, for example, make little, if anything, of the distinction between practical and theoretical reasoning and knowledge. Natural law advocates like Aquinas, on the other hand, follow Aristotle in making the content of law dependent specifically on practical reason. This is one among several important differences within the diverse tradition of natural law theory, one that has considerable importance for contemporary legal philosophy.

Cicero

One legal philosopher who does *not* employ a distinction between theoretical and practical reasoning is Cicero. One of the most learned men of his time, he studied philosophy in Athens, and his political and philosophical works have special historical significance for the role they play in the application of Greek philosophical ideas to Roman law. These works are unremarkable for their philosophical originality: Cicero's conception of law is derived largely from the Stoics who held (1) that there is a "true law," discoverable by "right reason," that is univeral and unchanging and (2) that knowledge of this law is shared by all persons. In an effort to give the idea of true law a meaning applicable to his own time, he employs many Platonic and Stoic arguments in the interpretation of Roman law. He distinguishes, for example, both the "law of nature" and "positive law" from true law, and he argues that if positive law is to be true law it must embody the universal principles of justice and reason and not merely express the desires of a dominant political class. Justice, he says, is the the supreme virtue because it is the foundation of social solidarity. These and other themes emphasized by Cicero are taken up by later jurists who give the language of Roman law a foundation in Greek, and particularly in Stoic, philosophical argument and conception. The historical significance of this work is reflected in the opinion of some historians that his conception of natural law was the most well known and the most influential of all the ancient versions of natural law, including those of Plato and Aristotle. The following passages express in brief compass a few of Cicero's main themes, especially his unwavering faith in the universally distributed power of moral perception as expressed in law.

Reading 1

From Cicero,
DE LEGIBUS, BOOK I, CHAPTERS X–XIII

Out of all the material of the philosophers' discussions, surely there comes nothing more valuable than the full realization that we are born for Justice, and that right is based, not upon men's opinions, but upon Nature. This fact will immediately be plain if you once get a clear conception of man's fellowship and union with his fellow-men. For no single thing is so like another, so exactly its counterpart, as all of us are to one another. Nay, if bad habits and false beliefs did not twist the weaker minds and turn them in whatever direction they are inclined, no one would be so like his own self as all men would be like all others. . . . This is a sufficient proof that there is no difference in kind between man and man: for if there were, one definition could not be applicable to all men; and indeed reason, which alone raises us above the level of the beasts and enables us to draw inferences, to prove and disprove, to discuss and solve problems, and to come to conclusions, is certainly common to us all, and though varying in what it learns, at least in the capacity to learn it is invariable. For the same things are invariably perceived by the senses, and those things which stimulate the senses, stimulate them in the same way to all men; and those rudimentary beginnings of intelligence to which I have referred, which are imprinted on our minds, are imprinted on all minds alike; and speech, the mind's interpreter, though differing in the choice of words, agrees in the sentiments expressed. In fact, there is no human being of any race who, if he finds a guide, cannot attain to virtue. . . .

Troubles, joys, desires and fears haunt the minds of all men without distinction, and even if different men have different beliefs, that does not prove, for example, that it is not the same quality of superstition that besets those races which worship dogs and cats as gods, as that which torments other races. But what nation does not love courtesy, kindliness, gratitude and remembrance of favors restored? What people does not hate and despise the haughty, the wicked, the cruel and the ungrateful? Inasmuch as these considerations prove to us that the whole human race is bound together in unity, it follows . . . that knowledge of the principles of right living is what makes men better. . . .

We are so constituted by Nature as to share the sense of Justice with one another and to pass it on to all men. . . . What I shall call Nature is [that which is implanted in us by Nature]. . . . The corruption caused by bad habits is so great that the sparks of fire, so to speak, which Nature has kindled in us are extinguished by this corruption, and the vices, which are their opposites, spring up and are established. But if the judgments of men were in agreement with Nature, so that, as the poet says, they considered "nothing alien to them which concerns mankind," then Justice would be equally observed by all. For those creatures who have received the gift of reason from Nature have also received right reason, and therefore they have also received the gift of Law, which is right reason applied to command and prohibition. And if they have received Law, they have received Justice also. . . .

Now all this is really a preface to what remains to be said in our discussion, and its purpose is to make it more easily understood that Justice is inherent in Nature.

~

Reading 2

From Cicero,
THE REPUBLIC, BOOK III, CHAPTER XXII

True law is right reason in agreement with nature; it is of universal application, unchanging and everlasting; it summons to duty by its commands, and averts from wrongdoing by its prohibitions. And it does not lay its commands or prohibitions upon good men in vain, though neither have any effect on the wicked. It is a sin to try to alter this law, nor is it allowable to attempt to repeal any part of it, and it is impossible to abolish it entirely. We cannot be freed from its obligations by senate or people, and we need not look outside ourselves for an expounder or interpreter of it. And there will not be different laws at Rome and at Athens, or different laws now and in the future. But one eternal and unchangeable law will be valid for all nations and all times, and there will be one master and ruler, that is, God, over us all, for he is the author of this law, its promulgator, and its enforcing judge. Whoever is disobedient is fleeing from himself and denying his human nature, and by reason of this very fact, he will suffer the worst penalties, even if he escapes what is commonly considered punishment.

~

Reference at the beginning of the foregoing passage to "true law" as distinct from law that is somehow less than or otherwise than true law is developed briefly in Book II Chapter V of *De Legibus*. In this passage Cicero advances a claim often repeated in the literature of natural law: unjust laws are not really laws. The implications of this claim for our duty to obey the law have been the subject of much controversy, as we shall see in the next chapter. Here, as his contribution to discussion of the subject, is Cicero's argument.

~

Reading 3

From Cicero,
DE LEGIBUS, BOOK IV, CHAPTERS IV–VI

M. Once more, then, before we come to the individual laws, let us look at the character and nature of Law, for fear that, though it must be the standard to which we refer everything, we may now and then be led astray by an incorrect use of terms, and forget the rational principles on which our laws must be based.

Q. Quite so, that is the correct method of exposition.

M. Well, then, I find that it has been the opinion of the wisest men that Law is not a product of human thought, nor is it any enactment of peoples, but something eternal which rules the whole universe by its wisdom in command and prohibition. Thus they have been accustomed to say that Law is the primal and ultimate mind of God, whose reason directs all things either by compulsion or restraint. Wherefore that Law which the gods have given to the human race has been justly praised; for it is the reason and mind of a wise lawgiver applied to command and prohibition.

Q. You have touched upon this subject several times before. But before you come to the laws of peoples, please make the character of this heavenly Law clear to us, so that the waves of habit may not carry us away and sweep us into the common mode of speech on such subjects.

M. Ever since we were children, Quintus, we have learned to call, "If one summon another to court," and other rules of the same kind, laws. But we must come to the true understanding of the matter, which is as follows: this and other commands and prohibitions of nations have the power to summon to righteousness and away from wrong-doing; but this power is not merely older than the existence of nations and States, it is coeval with that God who guards and rules heaven and earth. For the divine mind cannot exist without reason

and divine reason cannot but have this power to establish right and wrong. No written law commanded that a man should take his stand on a bridge alone, against the full force of the enemy, and order the bridge broken down behind him; yet we shall not for that reason suppose that the heroic Cocles was not obeying the law of bravery and following its decrees in doing so noble a deed. Even if there was no written law against rape at Rome in the reign of Lucius Tarquinius, we cannot say on that account that Sextus Tarquinius did not break that eternal Law by violating Lucretia, the daughter of Tricipitinus! For reason did exist, derived from the Nature of the universe, urging men to right conduct and diverting them from wrong-doing, and this reason did not first become Law when it was written down, but when it first came into existence; and it came into existence simultaneously with the divine mind. Wherefore the true and primal Law, applied to command and prohibition, is the right reason of supreme Jupiter.

Q. I agree with you, brother, that what is right and true is also eternal, and does not begin or end with written statutes.

M. Therefore, just as that divine mind is the supreme Law, so, when [reason] is perfected in man, [that also is Law; and this perfected reason exists] in the mind of the wise man; but those rules which, in varying forms and for the need of the moment, have been formulated for the guidance of nations, bear the title of laws rather by favour than because they are really such. For every law which really deserves that name is truly praiseworthy, as they prove by approximately the following arguments. It is agreed, of course, that laws were invented for the safety of citizens, the preservation of States, and the tranquillity and happiness of human life, and that those who first put statutes of this kind in force convinced their people that it was their intention to write down and put into effect such rules as, once accepted and adopted, would make possible for them an honourable and happy life; and when such rules were drawn up and put in force, it is clear that men called them "laws." From this point of view it can be readily understood that those who formulated wicked and unjust statutes for nations, thereby breaking their promises and agreements, put into effect anything but "laws." It may thus be clear that in the very definition of the term "law" there inheres the idea and principle of choosing what is just and true. I ask you then, Quintus, according to the custom of the philosophers: if there is a certain thing, the lack of which in a State compels us to consider it no State at all, must we consider this thing a good?

Q. One of the greatest goods, certainly.

M. Then Law must necessarily be considered one of the greatest goods.

Q. I agree with you entirely.

M. What of the many deadly, the many pestilential statutes which nations put in force? These no more deserve to be called laws than the rules a band of robbers might pass in their assembly. For if ignorant and unskillful men have prescribed deadly poisons instead of healing drugs, these cannot possibly be called physicians' prescriptions; neither in a nation can a statute of any sort be called a law, even though the nation, in spite of its being a ruinous regulation, has accepted it. Therefore Law is the distinction between things just and unjust, made in agreement with that primal and most ancient of all things, Nature; and in conformity to Nature's standard are framed those human laws which inflict punishment upon the wicked but defend and protect the good.

Q. I understand you completely, and believe that from now on we must not consider or even call anything else law.

M. Then you do not think the Titian or Apuleian Laws were really laws at all?

Q. No; nor the Livian Laws either.

M. And you are right, especially as the Senate repealed them in one sentence and in a single moment. But the Law whose nature I have explained can neither be repealed nor abrogated.

Q. Then the laws you intend to propose will, of course, be the kind that will never be repealed?

M. Certainly, if only they are accepted by both of you. But I think that I should follow the same course as Plato, who was at the same time a very learned man and the greatest of all philosophers, and who wrote a book about the Republic first, and then in a separate treatise described its Laws. Therefore, before I recite the law itself, I will speak in praise of that law. I note that Zaleucus and Charondas did the same thing, though they wrote their laws, not for the interest and pleasure of doing so, but for actual use in their own States. Clearly Plato agreed with their opinion that it was also the function of Law to win some measure of approval, and not always compel by threats of force.

Aquinas

While Cicero's treatment of natural law has great historical significance, most intellectual historians regard Aquinas as the most important among classical natural law philosophers. Writing in the thirteenth century, he developed a conception of natural law that, by reason of its detail and sophistication, has become the centerpiece of natural law jurisprudence, extending in influence to the present day.

In the first passage for study here, Aquinas follows Aristotle in relating natural law to natural desires for and inclinations toward human goods, and he redevelops Aristotle's distinction between theoretical and practical reason. (The term that in Aristotle is translated as "theoretical" is translated here as "speculative.") The relevance of this distinction for determination of the "good" of justice can be explained in the following way: reasoning about justice can be either speculative or practical. If it is speculative then it is directed toward determining necessary truths: that is to say, truths like logical and mathematical truths that cannot possibly be regarded as otherwise than true. Practical reasoning, on the other hand, is directed to determination of truth that is contingent, that is, that might have been otherwise. Of special importance here is the concern of practical reason with circumstances that may constitute exceptions to a general rule or principle—the kind of situation Aristotle was concerned about in developing his concept of equity. Construing practical reason in this way allows Aquinas to provide an account of change and development in natural law that he discusses briefly toward the end of the passage below. The importance of this account can hardly be overestimated, adding as it does a strong and much needed temporal dimension to natural law jurisprudence.

speculative = theoretical

Reading 1

From Aquinas,
SUMMA THEOLOGICA, QUESTION 94

Natural Law

The order of the precepts of natural law is the order of our natural inclinations. For there is in man a primary and natural inclination to good, which he has in common with all things, inasmuch as every thing desires the preservation of its own being (esse) according to its nature. Through this inclination the natural law pertains to everything that makes for the preservation of human life and all that impedes its death. There is in man a second inclination to more specific ends according to the nature he has in common with other animals. According to this inclination, those things are said to be of natural law "that nature has taught all animals," instincts such as the union of husband and wife, the education of children, and so forth. Third, there is in man a certain inclination to good according to his rational nature, and this is proper to man alone: thus man has a natural inclination to know the truth about God and to live in society. And in respect to this, there come under the natural law all actions pertaining to such inclinations: notably that a man should avoid ignorance, that he must not offend those with whom he deals, and all other actions of this kind.

Universality and/or Particularity of Natural Law

As was said above, the actions to which man is naturally inclined pertain to the natural law; among these it is proper to man that he should be inclined to act according to reason. Reason, however, proceeds from general principles to concrete particulars, as made clear in [Aristotle's] *Physics*. The speculative reason of man does this in one way, the practical reason in another way. For the speculative reason is chiefly used in respect to necessary truths, which are impossible to be other than they are; so that truth is found just as surely in the particular conclusions as in the general principles themselves. But practical reason is used in respect to contingent matters in which human actions are located; hence, although there is a certain necessity in the general principles, the more one descends to the particulars, the more is the conclusion open to exception.

So therefore it is clear that as far as the general principles of reason are concerned, whether speculative or practical, there is one standard of truth or uprightness for all and it is equally known by all. With regard to the particular conclusions of speculative reason, there is again one standard of truth for all, but this is not equally known to all; it is universally true, for example, that the three interior angles of a triangle are equal to two right angles; but this conclusion is not known by all people.

When we come to the particular conclusions of the practical reason, however, there is neither the same standard of truth or uprightness for all, nor are these conclusions equally known to all. All people realize that it is right and true to act according to reason. And from this principle it follows as a particular conclusion that debts should be paid. And in most cases this is true; but it could happen in some special case that it would be injurious and therefore irrational to repay a debt (if, for example, the money were to be used for a war against one's own country). Such exceptions are all the more likely to occur the more we get down to concrete cases, as when it is said that debts are to be paid with such a precaution or in such a way. The more specialized the conditions stated, the greater is the possibility of an exception arising so that it might not be upright to return or not to return the payment.

So it must be said that the natural law, as far as general first principles are concerned, is the same for all, both as a norm of uprightness and as equally knowable. But as to certain concrete cases that are conclusions from the general principles, it is the same for all only in the majority of cases, both as a norm and as knowable. So in special cases it can admit of exceptions, both with regard to uprightness because of certain impediments (just as in nature the generation and change of bodies is subject to accidents caused by some impediment), and with regard to knowability. This can also happen because in some persons reason is depraved by passion or by some evil habit, as Caesar says in *The Gallic War of the Germans*, that once upon a time they did not think robbery to be wrong (although it is obviously against natural law).

Immutability and Development of Natural Law

Natural law can be understood to change in two ways. One is in that certain additions are made to it. And nothing stops natural law from changing in this way, for much that is useful to human life is added to natural law by divine law as well as by human laws.

In another way, natural law can be understood to change by having something subtracted from it, as though something might cease to be of natural law that formerly was of natural law. . . . As far as the first principles of natural law are concerned, natural law is entirely unchangeable. Moreover, as far as the secondary precepts, which we have said to be certain particular conclusions following upon the first principles, natural law again does not change, in the sense that it remains a general law for the majority of cases that what the natural law prescribes is right. It can nevertheless change in some particular case or a small number of cases on account of some special causes preventing the observance of such precepts, as was said above. . . .

Changeability of Human Law

Human law, as was said above, is a certain dictate of reason by which human actions are directed. And for this reason, there can be two causes for changing human law justly. The first is on the part of reason; the second is on the part of men whose acts are regulated by law. On the part of reason, because it seems to be natural to human reason to proceed gradually from the imperfect to the perfect. So we see in the speculative sciences that those who first philosophized arrived at an inadequate view of things, which their successors later developed into something more perfect. It is the same likewise in practical affairs. For the first who intended to arrive at something useful to the human community, not able to consider everything themselves, established certain regulations, imperfect and deficient in many ways; these regulations were later modified by their successors so that those best adapted to promote the public interest were retained.

On the part of the men whose actions are regulated by law, the law can be rightly changed on account of altered human conditions, for different laws are required for different conditions. So, Augustine proposed this example in *On Free Choice* 1, 6: "If a people is well-ordered, serious, and a very vigilant guardian of the public interest . . . a law allowing them to elect their own magistrates to administer public affairs is justified. . . . But if that people should gradually become dishonest and the elections corrupt, and the government in the hands of dishonorable and criminal men, the power of appointing to office is rightly taken from such people, and the choice should be limited to the few and honest."

Limits of Changeableness

As was said, a change in human law is justified only insofar as it benefits the public interest. Now, the very change of law is itself somewhat harmful to the general safety, because in the observance of law custom has great value—so much so that any action that is opposed to general custom, even if it should be itself inconsequential, seems more serious. Hence when law is changed, its coercive power is diminished by the setting aside of custom. Thus human law should never be changed unless the benefits accruing to the public interest are able to compensate for the harm done. . . .

Law, General Definition

From the preceding we may gather the definition of law. It is nothing other than a reasonable direction of beings toward the common good, promulgated by the one who is charged with the community.

The subject addressed in the next reading is the status of positive laws that by natural law standards are unjust. Cicero, remember, claimed that only just laws deserve the attribution of "law." But how exactly should we regard duly established positive laws that fail to measure up to those standards? In Aquinas's view this is a question to which Cicero and early natural law theorists never provided a satisfactory answer. The following discussion of this issue attempts to advance beyond Cicero's claim that unjust laws are not "truly" law by exploring in some detail the implications of this claim for one's obligation to obey the law.

Reading 2

From Aquinas, *SUMMA THEOLOGICA*, QUESTION 95

Human Laws Subordinated to Natural Law

. . . St. Augustine says in *On Free Choice*: "There is no law unless it be just." Whence in proportion to its justice a law has the force of law. But in human affairs something is called just insofar as it is right or accords with the rule of reason. But the first rule of reason is natural law, as was evident from the above. Hence all humanly enacted laws are in accord with reason to the extent that they flow from natural law. And if a human law disagrees in any particular with natural law, it will not be a law but a corruption of law.

But we should be aware that something may flow from natural law in two ways. First, as a conclusion from more general principles; second, as a determination from certain general principles.

The first way is close to the scientific method, by which demonstrative conclusions are derived from first principles. The second way is like that of the arts, in which some common form is determined to a particular instance (as, for instance, when an architect, starting from the general idea of a house, then goes on to design the particular plan of this or that house). So, therefore, some derivations are made from the general principles of the natural law by way of formal conclusions—such as the conclusion, "Murder should not be done," which is derived from the general principle, "Do no evil to anyone." Other conclusions are reached as determinations of special cases. Thus the natural law prescribes that whoever sins shall be punished, but that a specific penalty should be the punishment is a particular determination of the natural law.

Both types of derivation are found in human law. Those reached the first way are sanctioned not only by human law, but by natural law as well; but those reached the second way have the force of human law alone.

Obligation of Human Law

. . . Laws enacted by men are either just or unjust. If they are just, they have the power to oblige in conscience from the eternal law, from which they are derived; according to Prov. 8:15: "By me kings rule, and lawmakers decree just laws." Now, laws are called just either with respect to their end, as when they are directed to the common good; or with respect to their author, as when the law enacted does not exceed the power of the lawmaker; or with respect to their form, as when the burdens they impose are distributed eq-

uitably to promote the common good. For since every man is part of the community, that which he is and possesses belongs to the community, just as any part as a part belongs to the whole; whence nature allows harm to the part in order to save the whole. And according to this principle, laws of such a kind that they distribute the burdens equitably are laws both binding in conscience and legal.

However, laws are unjust for two reasons. In one way they are unjust when they go against the human good, as contrary to what was previously established: either with respect to the end (as when some ruler enacts laws burdensome to his subjects and not directed to the common good, but directed more to his own gain and vanity), or with respect to their author (as when someone without jurisdiction makes laws), or finally with respect to their form (as when the burdens are distributed inequitably throughout the community). Laws like this have more in common with violence than with legality. . . . Hence such laws do not oblige in conscience except perhaps to avoid scandal or disorder, for to avoid these a man may be obliged to yield his rights. . . .

Human Laws Coercive

Law, as has been previously explained, has two essential characteristics: first, that it is a rule of human action; second, that it has coercive power. There are, therefore, two ways of being subject to law. In one way as one who is ruled is subject to the rule. And in this way all who are subject to a power are subject to the rule made by that power. There are, however, two ways of being not subject to a power. In one way when someone is wholly absolved from such subjection, as when the citizens of one state or kingdom are not subject to the laws of another nor to its ruler. In another way as when persons are subject to a higher law. So, for instance, one who is subject to a proconsul must obey his command except when dispensed by the emperor, for in those matters wherein he is subject to higher commands, he is not bound by the orders of a subordinate. In this case it happens that one subject to a certain law in principle is in some matters exempt from it when in these matters he is subject to a higher law.

The second way in which anyone may be said to be subject to the law is as one coerced by force. And in this way virtuous and just men are not subject to the law but only evil men. For whatever is forced and violent is contrary to the will. But the will of good men agrees with the law, whereas the will of wicked men disagrees with the law. And so in this sense the good men are not under the law, but only the wicked.

Hugo Grotius

One attraction of natural law theory is that it has some conceptual resources particularly appropriate to an understanding of what we now call "international law" or the "law of nations." Cicero touched on this point briefly, but the most extensive development of these resources is undertaken by Hugo Grotius, the Dutch jurist whose masterwork *The Law of War and Peace* (*De Jure Belli ac Pacis*) deals with this subject. In the Prolegomena to this work Grotius outlines some of the main implications of natural law theory for international relations, in the process strengthening the theory of natural law in at least three important respects, each of which is a primary subject in the readings to follow.

First, he lays the groundwork for a purely secular conception of natural law: he claims that the law of nature would obtain even if (1) it turns out that there is insufficient reason to believe in the existence of God or (2) that a Divine Being exists who has no concern for the affairs of human beings. Either of these conditions seems unimaginable to Grotius, who like most natural law theorists of his time, was a devout theist, but the claim he makes is important because it asserts the independence of belief in natural law from religious, and especially theistic, belief of any sort.

Reading 1

From Hugo Grotius, *DE JURE BELLI AC PACIS LIBRI TRES*

The municipal law of Rome and of other states has been treated by many, who have undertaken to elucidate it by means of commentaries or to reduce it to a convenient digest. That body of law, however, which is concerned with the mutual relations among states or rulers of states, whether derived from nature, or established by divine ordinances, or having its origin in custom and tacit agreement, few have touched upon. Up to the present time no one has treated it in a comprehensive and systematic manner; yet the welfare of mankind demands that this task be accomplished.

Cicero justly characterized as of surpassing worth a knowledge of treaties of alliance, conventions, and understandings of peoples, kings and foreign nations; a knowledge, in short, of the whole law of war and peace. Such a work is all the more necessary because in our day, as in former times, there is no lack of men who view this branch of law with contempt as having no reality outside of an empty name. On the lips of men quite generally is the saying of Euphemus, which Thucydides quotes, that "In the case of a king or imperial city nothing is unjust which is expedient." Of like implication is the statement that "For those whom fortune favours might makes right," and that "The administration of a state cannot be carried on without injustice.". . . Among Christian writers a similar thought finds frequent expression. A single quotation from Tertullian may serve in place of many: "Deception, harshness, and injustice are the regular business of battles."

Since our discussion concerning law will have been undertaken in vain if there is no law, in order to open the way for a favourable reception of our work and at the same time to fortify it against attacks, this very serious error must be briefly refuted. In order that we may not be obliged to deal with a crowd of opponents, let us assign to them a pleader. And whom should we choose in preference to Carneades?[5] For he had attained to so perfect a mastery of the peculiar tenet of his Academy that he was able to devote the power of his eloquence to the service of falsehood not less readily than to that of truth. . . .

Carneades . . . having undertaken to hold a brief against justice, in particular against that phase of justice with which we are concerned, was able to muster no argument stronger than this, that, for reasons of expediency, men imposed upon themselves laws, which vary according to customs, and among the same peoples often undergo changes as times change; moreover that there is no law of nature because all creatures, men as well as animals, are impelled by nature toward ends advantageous to themselves; that, consequently, there is no justice, or, if such there be, it is supreme folly, since one does violence to his own interests if he consults the advantage of others. . . .

Man is, to be sure, an animal, but an animal of a superior kind, much farther removed from all other animals than the different kinds of animals are from one another; evidence on this point may be found in the many traits peculiar to the human species. But among the traits characteristic of man is an impelling desire for society, that is, for the social life— not of any and every sort, but peaceful, and organized according to the measure of his intelligence—with those who are of his own kind; this social trend the Sto-

---

5. One of the most well-known members of the so-called New Academy, noted for its skeptical opposition to the teaching of the Stoics. He was especially noted for a public adress in which he opposed the idea of natural justice, arguing that the true basis of justice was human expediency.

ics called "sociableness." Stated as a universal truth, therefore, the assertion that every animal is impelled by nature to seek only its own good cannot be conceded.

Some of the other animals, in fact, do in a way restrain the appetency for that which is good for themselves alone, to the advantage, now of their offspring, now of other animals of the same species. This aspect of their behaviour has its origin, we believe, in some extrinsic intelligent principle, because with regard to other actions, which involve no more difficulty than those referred to, a like degree of intelligence is not manifest in them. The same thing must be said of children. In children, even before their training has begun, some disposition to do good to others appears. . . . The mature man in fact has knowledge which prompts him to similar actions under similar conditions, together with an impelling desire for society, for the gratification of which he alone among animals possesses a special instrument, speech. He has also been endowed with the faculty of knowing and of acting in accordance with general principles. Whatever accords with that faculty is not common to all animals, but peculiar to the nature of man.

This maintenance of the social order, which we have roughly sketched, and which is consonant with human intelligence, is the source of law properly so called. To this sphere of law belong the abstaining from that which is another's, the restoration to another of anything of his which we may have, together with any gain which we may have received from it; the obligation to fulfill promises, the making good of a loss incurred through our fault, and the inflicting of penalties upon men according to their deserts. . . .

What we have been saying would have a degree of validity even if we should concede that which cannot be conceded without the utmost wickedness, that there is no God, or that the affairs of men are of no concern to Him. The very opposite of this view has been implanted in us partly by reason, partly by unbroken tradition, and confirmed by many proofs as well as by miracles attested by all ages. Hence it follows that we must without exception render obedience to God as our Creator, to Whom we owe all that we are and have. . . .

Herein, then, is another source of law besides the source in nature, that is, the free will of God, to which beyond all cavil our reason tells us we must render obedience. But the law of nature of which we have spoken, comprising alike that which relates to the social life of man and that which is so called in a larger sense, proceeding as it does from the essential traits implanted in man, can nevertheless rightly be attributed to God, because of His having willed that such traits exist in us. In this sense, too, Chrysippus and the Stoics used to say that the origin of law should be sought in no other source than Jupiter himself; and from the name Jupiter the Latin word for law (ius) was probably derived. . . .

The second and third respects in which Grotius advances natural law jurisprudence are reflected in Reading 2 below. The second has to do with his conception of the foundation of morality. In the fifth line of this reading he says that even the skeptic Carneades admits that a person who violates a law of his or her own country is foolish in that such violation "breaks down that by which the advantage of himself and his posterity are for all time assured." The implication of this admission is that obedience to law and morality serves self-interest. In time this doctrine exerts great influence on seventeenth-century political and legal thinkers, especially Thomas Hobbes. Part of the reason for this is that the doctrine provides the groundwork for claims to a "natural right" of self preservation.

Grotius's third advance in natural law jurisprudence is development of the idea that the foundation of relations between states is the principle of *pacta sunt servanda* (treaties are to be respected). In developing this idea Grotius is often cited as the "father of international law," a reputation due in large part to his insight into the scope and significance of this principle.

One final note on Grotius's conception of natural law: like Cicero, he lays no stress on the distinction between theoretical and practical reasoning. His version of natural law and its application to concrete cases stands squarely in the rationalist tradition: concrete justice is derived from axioms of natural law such as "we should abstain from what belongs to other persons"; "we should restore to another any goods of hers or his which we have"; "we should keep our promises and fulfill obligations agreed to in pacts"; "we should repay damages done to another through fault"; and "we should inflict punishment on people who deserve it." In his view many, if not most, of the rules of the law and their correct application to cases are derivations by reason *directly* from general precepts such as these.

～

Reading 2

From Hugo Grotius, *DE JURE BELLI AC PACIS LIBRI TRES*

Since it is a rule of the law of nature to abide by pacts (for it was necessary that among men there be some method of obligating themselves one to another, and no other natural method can be imagined), out of this source the bodies of municipal law have arisen. For those who had associated themselves with some group, or had subjected themselves to a man or to men, had either expressly promised, or from the nature of the transaction must be understood impliedly to have promised, that they would conform to that which should have been determined, in the one case by the majority, in the other by those upon whom authority had been conferred.

What is said, therefore, in accordance with the view not only of Carneades but also of others, that "Expediency is, as it were, the mother of what is just and fair," is not true, if we wish to speak accurately. For the very nature of man which, even if we had no lack of anything would lead us into the mutual relations of society, is the mother of the law of nature. But the mother of municipal law is that obligation which arises from mutual consent; and since this obligation derives its force from the law of nature, nature may be considered, so to say, the great-grandmother of municipal law. . . .

Just as the laws of each state have in view the advantage of that state, so by mutual consent it has become possible that certain laws should originate as between all states, or a great many states; and it is apparent that the laws thus originating had in view the advantage, not of particular states, but of the great society of states. And this is what is called the law of nations, whenever we distinguish that term from the law of nature.

This division of law Carneades passed over altogether. For he divided all law into the law of nature and the law of particular countries. Nevertheless if undertaking to treat of the body of law which is maintained between states—for he added a statement in regard to war and things acquired by means of war—he would surely have been obliged to make mention of this law.

Wrongly, moreover, does Carneades ridicule justice as folly. For since, by his own admission, the national who in his own country obeys its laws is not foolish, even though, out of regard for that law, he may be obliged to forgo certain things advantageous for himself, so that nation is not foolish which does not press its own advantage to the point of disregarding the laws common to nations. The reason in either case is the same. For just as the national, who violates the law of his country in order to obtain an immediate advantage, breaks down that by which the advantages of himself and his posterity are for all future time assured, so the state which transgresses the laws of nature and of nations cuts away also the bulwarks which safeguard its own future peace. Even if no advantage were to be contemplated from the keeping of the law, it would be a mark of wisdom, not of folly, to allow ourselves to be drawn towards that to which we feel that our nature leads. . . .

Least of all should that be admitted which some people imagine, that in war all laws are in abeyance. On the contrary war ought not to be undertaken except for the enforcement of rights; when once undertaken, it should be carried on only within the bounds of law and good faith. Demosthenes well said that war is directed against those who cannot be held in check by judicial processes. For judgments are efficacious against those who feel that they are too weak to resist; against those who are equally strong, or think that they are, wars are undertaken. But in order that wars may be justified, they must be carried on with not less scrupulousness than judicial processes are wont to be. . . .

Fully convinced, by the considerations which I have advanced, that there is a common law among nations, which is valid alike for war and in war, I have had many and weighty reasons for undertaking to write upon this subject. Throughout the Christian world I observed a lack of restraint in relation to war, such as even barbarous races should be ashamed of; I observed that men rush to arms for slight causes, or no cause at all, and that when arms have once been taken up there is no longer any respect for law, divine or human; it is as if, in accordance with a general decree, frenzy had openly been let loose for the committing of all crimes. . . .

Through devotion to study in private life I have wished . . . to contribute somewhat to the philosophy of the law, which previously, in public service, I practised with the utmost degree of probity of which I was capable. Many heretofore have purposed to give to this subject a well-ordered presentation; no one has succeeded. And in fact such a result cannot be accomplished unless— a point which until now has not been sufficiently kept in view—those elements which come from positive law are properly separated from those which arise from nature. For the principles of the law of nature, since they are always the same, can easily be brought into a systematic form; but the elements of positive law, since they often undergo change and are different in different places, are outside the domain of systematic treatment, just as other notions of particular things are.

If now those who have consecrated themselves to true justice should undertake to treat the parts of the natural and unchangeable philosophy of law, after having removed all that has its origin in the free will of man; if one, for example, should treat legislation, another taxation, another the administration of justice, another the determination of motives, another the proving of facts, then by assembling all these parts a body of jurisprudence could be made up.

Blackstone

So far as early American legal history is concerned Sir William Blackstone may be the most influential among all the classical natural law theorists: "In the history of American institutions, no other book—except the Bible—has played so great a role as Blackstone's _Commentaries on the Laws of England_."[6] The reason for this influence is that the core principles of American law either are taken directly from English law or are built on that law. In this regard it is important to understand that English law was and is a system of law quite different from most European legal systems. Most of those systems find their highest expressions in a legal "code" of one sort or another; English law, by contrast, is "common law" or "customary law" that is, law expressed not in a code but only in decisions of common law judges. The problem with such law, of course, is that it is judge-made law, handed down from generation to generation only in the form of reported cases. In Blackstone's day English law was very difficult to learn, much less to master; access to its rules and principles could be acquired only by immersion in a labyrinth of essentially unorganized judicial opinions. Taking his clue from continental legal scholarship Blackstone in his _Commentaries_ presents English law in a reasonably well organized and systematic form. More important for our purposes, the scheme of organization employed makes crucial use of a set of basic natural law principles. English law, as Blackstone presents it, far from being a massive collection of ad hoc and sometimes inconsistent legal opinions, consists of a fairly coherent body of rules whose

6. Daniel Boorstin, _The Mysterious Science of the Law_ (Boston, Mass.: Beacon Press, 1958), p. iii.

unity can be shown to reside in natural law precepts, especially in the idea that persons have "natural rights."

The *Commentaries* consists of four books dealing respectively with the Rights of Persons, the Rights of Things, Private Wrongs, and Public Wrongs. Reading 1 is taken from the introduction to this work, and it will be well to keep in mind the *organizational purpose* that informs what Blackstone says here. Unlike many of the readings so far, his primary concern is not to develop the theory of natural law, that is, to advance or improve or add to it in some way. Neither is he presenting yet another summary or exposition of its main doctrines. Rather he is laying the groundwork for a comprehensive view of English common law, one that has both scope and coherence and can embrace at least a large portion of the legal content resident in the opinions of common law judges. He finds such principles in natural law, and he begins his introduction by identifying what he regards as the five most basic and fundamental of these: (1) an account of the nature of laws in general, (2) the source of laws, (3) the univeral nature of law, (4) the role of reason in determining law, and (5) the relation between natural law and human law, including what is generally called "positive law" (or what he calls "municipal law"). Taken together these doctrines form the underlying structure of Blackstone's analysis of the content of English common law, a sort of unified "deep structure" in terms of which the variegated and diverse "surface structure" of common law rules and judicial opinions can be understood.

~

Reading 1

From William Blackstone, *COMMENTARIES ON THE LAWS OF ENGLAND I*

Of the Nature of Laws in General

Law, in its most general and comprehensive sense, signifies a rule of action, and is applied indiscriminately to all kinds of action, whether animate or inanimate, rational or irrational. Thus we say, the laws of motion, of gravitation, of optics, or mechanics, as well as the laws of nature and of nations. And it is that rule of action which is prescribed by some superior, and which the inferior is bound to obey.

Thus, when the Supreme Being formed the universe, and created matter out of nothing, he impressed certain principles upon that matter, from which it can never depart, and without which it would cease to be. When he put that matter into motion, he established certain laws of motion, to which all movable bodies must conform. And, to descend from the greatest operations to the smallest, when a workman forms a clock, or other piece of mechanism, he establishes, at his own pleasure, certain arbitrary laws for its direction, as that the hand shall describe a space in a given time to it, which law as long as the work conforms, so long, continues in perfection, and answers the end of its formation. If we farther advance, from mere inactive matter to vegetable and animal life, we shall find them still governed by laws, more numerous indeed, but equally fixed and invariable. The whole progress of plants, from the seed to the root, and from thence to the seed again; the method of animal nutrition, digestion, secretion, and all other branches of vital economy; are not left to chance, or the will of the creature itself, but are performed in a wondrous involuntary manner, and guided by unerring rules laid down by the great Creator.

This, then is the general signification of law: a rule of action dictated by some superior being, and, in those creatures that have neither the power to think, nor to will, such laws must be invariably obeyed, so long as the creature itself subsists, for its existence depends on that obedience. But laws, in their more confined sense, and in which it is our present business to consider them, denote the rules, not of action in general, but of action or conduct; that is the precepts by which man, the noblest of all sublunary beings, a creature endowed with both reason and freewill, is commanded to make use of those faculties in the general regulation of his behaviour.

Man, considered as a creature, must necessarily be subject to the laws of his Creator, for he is entirely a dependent being. A being, independent of any other, has no rule to pursue but such as he describes to himself; but a state of dependence will inevitably oblige the inferior to take the will of him on whom he depends as the rule of his conduct; not, indeed, in every particular, but in all those points wherein his dependence consists. This principle, therefore, has more or less extent and effect, in proportion as the superiority of the one and the dependence of the other is greater or less, absolute or limited. And consequently, as man depends absolutely upon his Maker for every thing, it is necessary that he should, in all points, conform to his maker's will.

Law of Nature

This will of his Maker is called the law of nature. For as God, when he created matter, and endowed it with a principle of mobility established certain rules for the perpetual direction of that motion, so, when he created man, and endued him with free will to conduct himself in all parts of life, he laid down certain immutable laws of human nature, whereby that freewill is in some degree regulated and restrained, and gave him also the faculty of reason to discover the purport of those laws.

Considering the Creator only, as a being of infinite power, he was able unquestionably to have prescribed whatever laws he pleased to his creature, man, however unjust or severe. But, as he is also a being of infinite wisdom, he has laid down only such laws as were founded in those relations of justice that existed in the nature of things antecedent to any positive precept. These are the eternal immutable laws of good and evil, to which the Creator himself, in all his dispensations, conforms; and which he has enabled human reason to discover, so far as they are necessary for the conduct of human actions. Such, among others, are these principles: that we should live honestly, should hurt nobody, and should render to every one his due; to which these three general precepts Justinian has reduced the whole doctrine of law.

But if the discovery of these first principles of the law of nature depended only upon the due exertion of right reason, and could not otherwise be obtained than by a chain of metaphysical disquisitions, mankind would have wanted some inducement to have quickened their inquiries, and the greater part of the world would have rested content in mental indolence, and ignorance, its inseparable companion. As, therefore, the Creator is a being not only of infinite power and wisdom, but also of infinite goodness, he has been pleased so to contrive the constitution and frame of humanity, that we should want no other prompter to inquire after and pursue the rule of right, but only our own self-love, that universal principle of action. For he has so intimately connected so inseparably interwoven the laws of eternal justice with the happiness of each individual, that the latter cannot be attained but by observing the former; and, if the former be punctually obeyed, it cannot but induce the latter. In consequence of which mutual connection of justice and human felicity, he has not perplexed the law of nature with a multitude of abstracted rules and precepts, referring merely to the fitness or unfitness of things, as some have vainly surmised, but has graciously reduced the rule of obedience to this one paternal precept, "that man should pursue his own true and substantial happiness." This is the foundation of what we call ethics, or natural law; for the several articles into which it is branched in our systems, amount to no more than demonstrating that this or that action tends to man's real happiness, and therefore, very

justly concluding that the performance of it is a part of the law of nature; or, on the other hand, that this or that action is destructive of man's real happiness, and therefore that the law of nature forbids it.

Human Law Must Not Contravene Nature

This law of nature, being coeval with mankind, and dictated by God himself, is of course superior in obligation to any other. It is binding over all the globe, in all countries, and at all times: no human laws are of any validity, if contrary to this; and such of them as are valid derive all their force, and all their authority, mediately or immediately, from this original.

But in order to apply this to the particular exigencies of each individual, it is still necessary to have recourse to reason, whose office it is to discover, as was before observed, what the law of nature directs in every circumstance of life, by considering what method will tend the most effectually to our own substantial happiness. And if our reason were always, as in our first ancestor before his transgression, clear and perfect, unruffled by passions, unclouded by prejudice, unimpaired by disease or intemperance, the task would be pleasant and easy; we should need no other guide but this. But every man now finds the contrary in his own experience; that his reason is corrupt, and his understanding full of ignorance and effort.

This has given manifold occasion for the benign interposition of divine Providence, which, in compassion to the frailty, the imperfection, and the blindness of human reason, hath been pleased, at sundry times and in divers manners, to discover and enforce its laws by an immediate and direct revelation. The doctrines thus delivered we call the revealed or divine law, and they are to be found only in the holy scriptures. These precepts, when revealed, are found upon comparison to be really a part of the original law of nature, as they tend in all their consequences to man's felicity. But we are not from thence to conclude that the knowledge of these truths was attainable by reason, in its present corrupted state; since we find that, until they were revealed, they were hid from the wisdom of ages. As then the moral precepts of this law are indeed of the same original with those of the law of nature, so their intrinsic obligation is of equal strength and perpetuity. Yet undoubtedly the revealed law is of infinitely more authenticity than that moral system which is framed by ethical writers, and denominated the natural law; because one is the law of nature, expressly declared so to be by God himself; the other is only what, by the assistance of human reason, we imagine to be that law. If we could be as certain of the latter as we are of the former, both would have an equal authority; but, till then, they can never be put in any competition together.

Upon these two foundations, the law of nature and the law of revelation, depend all human laws; that is to say, no human laws should be suffered to contradict these. There are, it is true, a great number of indifferent points in which both the divine law and the natural leave a man at his own liberty, but which are found necessary, for the benefit of society, to be restrained within certain limits. And herein it is that human laws have

their greatest force and efficacy; for, with regard to such points as are not indifferent, human laws are only declaratory of, and act in subordination to, the former. To instance in the case of murder: this is expressly forbidden by the divine, and demonstrably by the natural law; and, from these prohibitions, arises the true unlawfulness of this crime. Those human laws that annex a punishment to it do not at all increase its moral guilt, or superadd any fresh obligation, *in foro conscientiae* (in the court of conscience), to abstain from its perpetration. Nay, if any human law should allow or enjoin us to commit it, we are bound to transgress that human law, or else we must offend both the natural and the divine. But, with regard to matters that are in themselves indifferent, and are not commanded or forbidden by those superior laws—such, for instance, as exporting of wool into foreign countries—here the inferior legislature has scope and opportunity to interpose, and to make that action unlawful which before was not so.

The State of Nature

If man were to live in a state of nature, unconnected with other individuals, there would be no occasion for any other laws than the law of nature and the law of God. Neither could any other law possibly exist: for a law always supposes some superior who is to make it; and, in a state of nature, we are all equal, without any other superior but Him who is the author of our being. But man was formed for society; and, as is demonstrated by the writers on this subject, is neither capable of living alone, nor indeed has the courage to do it.

Origin of Nations

However, as it is impossible for the whole race of mankind to be united in one great society, they must necessarily divide into many, and form separate states, commonwealths, and nations entirely independent of each other, and yet liable to a mutual intercourse, called "the Law of nations," which, as none of these states will acknowledge a superiority in the other, cannot be dictated by any, but depends entirely upon the rules of natural law or upon mutual contacts, treaties, leagues, and agreements between these several communities; in the construction also of which compacts we have no other rule to resort to but the law of nature; being the only one to which all the communities are equally subject; and therefore the civil law very justly observes *quod naturalist ratio inter omnes homines constituit, vocatur jus gentium* (that rule which natural reason has dictated to all men, is called the law of nations).

Municipal Law

Thus it [was] necessary to premise concerning the law of nature, the revealed law, and the law of nations, before I proceeded to treat more fully of the principal subject of this section, municipal or civil law; that is, the rule by which particular districts, communities or nations, are governed; being thus defined by Justinian, "*jus civile est quod quisque sibi populus constituit*" (the civil law is that which every nation has established for its own government). I call it municipal law, in compliance with common speech; for, though strictly that expression denotes the particular customs of one single mu-

nicipium or free town, yet it may with sufficient propriety be applied to any one state or nation, which is governed by the same laws and customs.

Definition

Municipal law, thus understood, is properly defined to be "a rule of civil conduct prescribed by the supreme power in a state, commanding what is right and prohibiting what is wrong." Let us endeavor to explain its several properties, as they arise out of this definition. And, first it is a rule: not a transient sudden order from a superior to or concerning a particular person; but something permanent, uniform, and universal. Therefore a particular act of the legislature to confiscate the goods of Titius, or, to attain him of high treason, does not enter into the idea of a municipal law: for the operation of this act is spent upon it only, and has no relation to the community in general; it is rather a sentence than a law. But an act to declare that the crime of which Titius is accused shall be deemed high treason: this has permanency, uniformity, and universality, and therefore is properly a rule. It is also called a rule to distinguish it from advice or counsel, which we are at liberty to follow or not, as we see proper, and to judge upon the reasonableness or unreasonableness of the thing advised: whereas our obedience to the law depends not upon our approbation, but upon the maker's will. Counsel is only matter of persuasion, law is matter of injunction; counsel acts only upon the willing, law upon the unwilling also.

It is also called a rule to distinguish it from a compact or agreement; for a compact is a promise proceeding from us law is a command directed to us. The language of a compact is, "I will, or will not, do this"; that of a law is, "thou shalt, or shalt not, do it." It is true there is an obligation which a compact carries with it, equal in point of conscience to that of a law; but then the original of the obligation is different. In compacts, we ourselves determine and promise what shall be done, before we are obliged to do it; in laws, we are obliged to act without ourselves determining or promising anything at all. Upon these accounts law is defined to be "a rule."

Municipal Law (Again)

Municipal law is "a rule of civil conduct." This distinguishes municipal law from the natural, or revealed; the former of which is the rule of moral conduct, and the latter not only the rule of moral conduct, but also the rule of faith. These regard man as a creature, and point out his duty to God, to himself, and to his neighbour, considered in the light of an individual. But municipal or civil law regards him also as a citizen, and bound to other duties towards his neighbour than those of mere nature and religion; duties, which he has engaged in by enjoying the benefits of the common union; and which amount to no more than that he do contribute, on his part, to the subsistence and peace of the society.

It is likewise "a rule prescribed." Because a bare resolution, confined in the breast of the legislator, without manifesting itself by some external sign, can never be properly a law. It is requisite that this resolution be notified to the people who are to obey it. But the manner in which this notification is to be made, is

matter of very great indifference. It may be notified by universal tradition and long practice, which supposes a previous publication, and is the case of the common law of England. It may be notified *viva voce* (by word of mouth), by officers appointed to be publicly read in churches and other as it may lastly be notified by writing, printing, or the like; which is the general course taken with all our acts of Parliament. Yet, whatever way is made use of, it is incumbent on the promulgators to do it in the most public and perspicuous manner, not like Caligula who (according to Dio Cassius) wrote his laws in a very small character, and hung them upon high pillars, the more effectually to ensnare the people. There is still a more unreasonable method than this, which is called making of laws *ex post facto* (after the fact); when after an action (indifferent in itself) is committed, the legislature then for the first time declares it to have been a crime, and inflicts a punishment upon the person who has committed it. Here it is impossible that the party could foresee that an action innocent when it was done, should be afterwards converted to guilt by a subsequent law; he had therefore no cause to abstain from it; and all punishment for not abstaining must of consequence be cruel and unjust. All laws should be therefore made to commence *in futuro* (at a future period), and be notified before their commencement; which is implied in the term "prescribed." But when this rule is in the usual manner notified or prescribed, it is then the subject's business to be thoroughly acquainted therewith; for if ignorance, of what he might know, were admitted as a legitimate excuse the laws would be of no effect, but might always be eluded with impunity. . . .

Definition Continued—Right and Wrong Clause

From what has been advanced, the truth of the former branch of our definition, is (I trust) sufficiently evident; that "municipal law is a rule of civil conduct prescribed by the supreme power in a state." I proceed now to the latter branch of it; that it is a rule so prescribed, "commanding what is right, and prohibiting what is wrong."

Now in order to do this completely, it is first of all necessary that the boundaries of right and wrong be established and ascertained by law. And when this is once done, it will follow of course that it is likewise the business of the law, considered as a rule of civil conduct, to enforce these rights, and to restrain or redress these wrongs. It remains therefore only to consider in which manner the law is said to ascertain the boundaries of right and wrong; and the methods which it takes to command the one and prohibit the other.

Species of Laws

For this purpose every law may be said to consist of several parts; one declaratory; whereby the rights to be observed, and the wrongs to be eschewed, are clearly defined and laid down: another, directory; whereby the subject is instructed and enjoined to observe those rights, and to abstain from the commission of those wrongs: a remedial; whereby a method is pointed out to recover a man's private rights, or redress his private wrongs: to which may be added a fourth, usually termed the sanction or vindicatory branch of the law; whereby it is signified what evil or penalty shall be incurred by such as commit any public wrongs, and transgress or neglect their duty. . . .

Acts Malum Prohibitum Et Malum in Se (Crimes Wrong Because Forbidden as Distinct From Wrong in Themselves)

It is true, it hath been holden and very justly, by the principal of our ethical writers, that human laws are binding upon men's consciences. But if that were the only or most forcible obligation, the good only would regard the laws, and the bad would set them at defiance. And, true as this principle is, it must still be understood with some restriction. It holds, I apprehend, as to rights; and that, when the law has determined the field to belong to Titius, it is matter of conscience no longer to withhold or to invade it. So also in regard to natural duties, and such offenses as are *mala in se* (wrong in themselves); here we are bound in conscience; because we are bound by superior laws, before those human laws were in being, to preform the one and abstain from the other. But in relation to those laws, which enjoin only positive duties, and forbid only such things as are not *mala in se* (wrong in themselves), but *mala prohibita* (crimes, because forbidden), merely, without any intermixture of moral guilt, annexing a penalty to non-compliance, here I apprehend conscience is no farther concerned, than by directing a submission to the penalty, in case of our breach of those laws: for otherwise the multitude of penal laws in a state would not only be looked upon as an impolitic, but would also be a very wicked thing; if every such law were a snare for the conscience of the subject. But in these cases the alternative is offered to every man;

"either abstain from this, or submit to such a penalty": and his conscience will be clear, which ever side of the alternative he things proper to embrace. Thus, by the statutes for preserving the game, a penalty is denounced against every unqualified person that kills a (hare) and against every person who possesses a partridge in August. And so, too, by other statutes, pecuniary penalties are inflicted for exercising trades without serving an apprenticeship thereto, for not burying the dead in woolen, for not performing the statute-work on the public roads, and for innumerable other positive misdemeanors. Now these prohibitory laws do not make the transgression a moral offense, or sin: the only obligation in conscience is to submit to the penalty, if levied. It must however be observed, that we are here speaking of laws that are simply and purely penal, where the thing forbidden or enjoined is wholly a matter of indifference, and where the penalty inflicted is an adequate compensation for the civil inconvenience supposed to arise from the offence. But where disobedience to the law involves in it also any degree of public mischief or private injury, there it falls within our former distinction, and is also an offence against conscience.

Rules of Interpretation

I have now gone through the definition laid down of a municipal law and have shown that it is " a rule of civil conduct prescribed by the supreme power in a state, commanding what is right, and prohibiting what is wrong"; in the explication of which I have endeavored to interweave a few useful principles concerning the nature of civil government,

and the obligation of human laws. Before I conclude this section, it may not be amiss to add a few observations concerning the interpretation of laws.

Roman Method

When any doubt arose upon the construction of the Roman laws, the usage was to state the case to the emperor in writing and take his opinion upon it. This was certainly a bad method of interpretation. To interrogate the legislature to decide particular disputes is not only endless, but affords great room for partiality and oppression. The answers of the emperor were called his rescripts, and these had in succeeding cases the force of perpetual laws; though they ought to be carefully distinguished by every rational civilian from those general constitutions which had only the nature of things for their guide. The emperor Macrinus, as his historian Capitolinus informs us, had once resolved to abolish these rescripts, and retain only the general edicts: he could not bear that the hasty and crude answers of such princes as Commodus and Caracalla should be reverenced as laws. But Justinian thought otherwise, and he has preserved them all. In like manner the canon laws, or decretal epistles of the popes are, all of them, rescripts in the strictest sense. Contrary to all true forms of reasoning, they argue from particulars to generals.

Intent as Expressed

The (fairest) and (most rational) method to interpret the will of the legislator is by exploring his intentions at the time when the law was made, by signs the most natural and probable. And these signs are either the words, the context, the subject matter, the effects and consequence, or the spirit and reason of the law. Let us take a short view of them all:

1. Laws are generally to be understood in their usual and most known signification; not so much regarding the propriety of grammar, as their general and popular use. Thus the law mentioned by Puffendorf which forbade a layman to lay hands on a priest, was adjudged to extend to him, who had hurt a priest with a weapon. Again terms of art, or technical terms, must be taken according to the acceptation of the learned in each art, trade, and science. So in the act of settlement, where the crown of England is limited "to the princess Sophia, and the heirs of her body, being Protestants," it becomes necessary to call in the assistance of lawyers, to ascertain the precise idea of the words "heirs of her body," which, in a legal sense, comprise only certain of her lineal descendants.

2. If words happen to be still dubious, we may establish their meaning from the context, with which it may be of singular use to compare a word or a sentence, whenever, they are ambiguous, equivocal or intricate. Thus the proeme, or preamble is often called in to help the construction of an act of parliament. Of the same nature and use is the comparison of a law with other laws, that are made by the same legislator, that have some affinity with the subject, or that expressly relate to the same point. Thus, when the law of England declares murder to be felony without benefit of clergy, we must resort to the same law of England to learn what the benefit of clergy is; and, when the common law

censures simoniacal contracts, it affords great light to the subject to consider what the canon law has adjudged to be simony.

3. As to the subject matter, words are always to be understood as having a read thereto, for that is always supposed to be in the eye of the legislator, and all his expressions directed to that end. Thus, when a law of our Edward III forbids all ecclesiastical persons to purchase provisions at Rome, it might seem to prohibit the buying of grain and other victuals; but, when we consider that the statute was made to repress the usurpations of the papal see, and that the nominations to benefices by the pope were called provisions, we shall see that the restraint is intended to be laid upon such provisions only.

4. As to the effects and consequence, the rule is, that where words bear either none, or a very absurd signification, if literally understood, we must a little deviate from the received sense of them. Therefore the Bolognian law, mentioned by Puffendorf, which enacted "that whoever drew blood in the streets should be punished with the utmost severity," was held after long debate not to extend to the surgeon, who opened the vein of a person that fell down in the street with a fit.

5. But, lastly, the most universal and effectual way of discovering the true meaning of a law, when the words are dubious is by considering the reason and spirit of it or the cause which moved the legislator to enact it. For when this reason ceases, the law itself ought likewise to cease with it. An instance of this is given in a case put by Cicero, or whoever was the author of the treatise inscribed to Herennius. There was a law, that those who in a storm for-

sook the ship should forfeit all property therein; and that the ship and lading should belong entirely to those who stayed in it. In a dangerous tempest all the mariners forsook the ship, except only one sick passenger, who, by reason of his disease, was unable to get out and escape. By chance the ship came safe to port. The sick man kept possession, and claimed the benefit of the law. Now here all the learned agree that the sick man is not within reason of the law; for the reason of making it was, to give encouragement to such as should venture their lives to save the vessel; but this is a merit which he could never pretend to, who neither stayed in the ship upon that account, nor contributed anything to its preservation.

From this method of interpreting laws, by the reason of them, arises what we call equity, which is thus defined by Grotius as "the correction of that wherein the law, by reason of its universality, is deficient." For, since in laws all cases cannot be foreseen or expressed, it is necessary that, when the general decrees of the law come to be applied to particular cases, there should be somewhere a power vested of defining those circumstances, which (had they been foreseen) the legislator himself would have expressed. And these are the cases which according to Grotius, *"lex non exacte definit, sed arbitrio boni viri permittit."* (The law does not define exactly, but leaves something to the discretion of a just and wise judge.)

Equity thus depending, essentially, upon the particular circumstances of each individual case, there can be no established rules and fixed precepts of equity laid down, without destroying its very essence, and reducing it to a positive law. And, on the other hand, the liberty of considering all cases in an equitable light must not be indulged too far, lest thereby we destroy all law, and leave the decision of every question entirely in the breast of the judge. And law, without equity, though hard and disagreeable, is much more desirable for the public good than equity without law; which would make every judge a legislator, and introduce most infinite confusion; as there would then be almost as many different rules of action laid down in our courts as there are differences of capacity and sentiment in the human mind.

Having identified the deep structure of English law with certain principles of natural law, Blackstone turns to his main subject: exemplification of these principles in common law rules of adjudication. If his idea about the fundamental coherence of these rules is correct it should be possible to connect specific legal doctrines employed in deciding common law cases with the kind of universal, underlying principles described in his introduction. Reading 2 is designed to show Blackstone at work in this task. The kind of law in question here is property law and the topic is the legal doctrine of "nuisance." Notice Blackstone's method in this discussion: he comments on several eighteenth-century applications of the law of nuisance with a view to revealing the underlying rationality and morality of the applications. With regard to the nuisance rule governing corruption or poison of a stream used by another he says that England enforces that excellent rule of gospel-morality, of "doing to others as we would they should do unto ourselves." And with regard to adjudication which rules it *not* a nuisance to set up any trade or school in competition with another he says, "Where reason ceases, the law ceases also with it." Noteworthy also in this reading is reference to the Latin maxims, "Use your own property in such a manner as not to injure that of another," and "The owner of the soil owns to the sky." These are often identified as fundamental principles of Blackstonian property law, and their use in the passage below exemplifies his natural law-based, structural interpretation of eighteenth-century English common law.

~

Reading 2

From William Blackstone, *COMMENTARIES ON THE LAWS OF ENGLAND III*

Nuisance, *nocumentum*, or annoyance, signifies any thing that worketh hurt, inconvenience, or damage. And nuisances are of two kinds; public or common nuisances, which affect the public, and are an annoyance to all the king's subjects; for which reason we must refer them to the class of public wrongs, or crimes and misdemeanors: and private nuisances, which are the objects of our present consideration, and may be defined as any thing done to the hurt or annoyance of the lands, tenements, or hereditaments of another. . . .

I. *In discussing the several kinds of nuisances, we will consider, first, such nuisances as may affect a man's corporeal hereditaments, and then those that may damage such as are incorporeal.*

1. First, as to corporeal inheritances. If a man builds a house so close to mine that his roof overhangs my roof, and throws the water off his roof upon mine, this is a nuisance, for which an action will lie. Likewise to erect a house or other building so near to mine, that it obstructs

my ancient lights and windows, is a nuisance of a similar nature. But in this latter case it is necessary that the windows be *ancient*; that is, have subsisted there time out of mind; otherwise there is no injury done. For he hath as much right to build a new edifice upon his ground, as I have upon mine: since every man may erect what he pleases upon the upright or perpendicular of his own soil, so as not to prejudice what has long been enjoyed by another; and it was my folly to build so near another's ground. Also, if a person keeps his hogs, or other noisome animals, so near the house of another, that the stench of them incommodes him and makes the air unwholesome, this is an injurious nuisance, as it tends to deprive him of the use and benefit of his house. A like injury is, if one's neighbour sets up and exercises any offensive trade; as a tanner's, a tallow-chandler's or the like; for though these are lawful and necessary trades, yet they should be exercised in remote places; for the rule is, "*sic utere tuo, ut alienum non laedas*" (use your own property in such a manner as not to injure that of another): this therefore is an actionable nuisance. So that the nuisances which affect a man's dwelling may be reduced to these three: 1. Overhanging it: which is also a species of trespass, for *cujus est solum ejus est usque ad coelum* (the owner of the soil owns to the sky); 2. Stopping ancient lights; and, 3. Corrupting the air with noisome smells: for light and air are two indispensable requisites to every dwelling. But depriving one of a mere matter of pleasure, as of a fine prospect, by building a wall, or the like; this, as it abridges nothing really convenient or necessary, is no injury to the sufferer, and is therefore not an actionable nuisance.

As to nuisance to one's lands: if one erects a smelting house for lead so near the land of another, that the vapor and smoke kills his corn and grass, and damages his cattle therein, this is held to be a nuisance. And by consequence it follows, that if one does any other act, in itself lawful, which yet being done in that place necessarily tends to the damage of another's property, it is a nuisance: for it is incumbent on him to find some other place to do that act, where it will be less offensive. . . .

With regard to other corporeal hereditaments: it is a nuisance to stop or divert water that used to run to another's meadow or mill or to corrupt or poison a water-course, by erecting a dye-house or a lime-pit for the use of trade, in the upper part of the stream; or in short to do any act therein, that in its consequences must necessarily tend to the prejudice of one's neighbour. So closely does the law of England enforce that excellent rule of gospel-morality, of "doing to others, as we would they should do unto ourselves."

2. As to incorporeal hereditaments, the law carries itself with the same equity. If I have a way, annexed to my estate, across another's land, and he obstructs me in the use of it, either by totally stopping it, or putting logs across it, or ploughing over it, it is a nuisance: for in the first case I cannot enjoy my right at all, and in the latter I cannot enjoy it so commodiously as I ought. Also, if I am entitled to hold a fair or market, and another person sets up a fair or market so near mine that he does me a prejudice, it is a nuisance to the freehold which I have in my market or fair. But in order to make this out to be a nuisance, it is necessary: 1. that my market or fair be the elder, otherwise the nuisance lies at my own door; 2. that the market be erected within the third part of twenty miles from mine. For sir Matthew Hale construes the dieta, or reasonable day's journey mentioned by Bracton, to be twenty miles. So that if the new market be not within seven miles of the old one, it is no nuisance: for it is held reasonable that every man should have a market within one-third of a day's journey from his own home that the day being divided into three parts, he may spend one part in going, another in returning, and the third in transacting his necessary business there. If such market or fair be on the same day with mine, it is prima facie a nuisance to mine, and there needs no proof of it, but the law will intend it to be so; but if it be on any other day, it may be a nuisance; though whether it is so or not, cannot be intended or presumed, but I must make proof of it to the jury. If a ferry is erected on a river, so near another ancient ferry as to draw away its custom, it is a nuisance to the owner of the old one. For where there is a ferry by prescription, the owner is bound to keep it always in repair and readiness, for the ease of all the king's subjects; otherwise he may be grievously amerced: it would be therefore extremely hard, if a new ferry were suffered to share his profits, which does not also share his burden. But where the reason ceases, the law also ceases with it: therefore it is no nuisance to erect a mill so near mine, as to draw away the custom unless the miller also intercepts the water. Neither is it a nuisance to set up any trade, or a school, in neighbourhood or rivalship with another: for by such emulation the public are like to be gainers; and, if the new mill or school occasion a damage to the old one, it is *damnum absque injuria* (harm without legal injury).

II. *Let us next attend to the remedies, which the law has given for this injury of nuisance. . . .*

The remedies by suit are, 1. By action on the case for damages; in which the party injured shall only recover a satisfaction for the injury sustained; but cannot thereby remove the nuisance. Indeed every continuance of a nuisance is held to be a fresh one; and therefore a fresh

action will lie, and very exemplary damages will probably be given, if, after one verdict against him, the defendant has the hardiness to continue it. Yet the founders of the law of England did not rely upon probabilities merely in order to give relief to the injured. They have therefore provided two other actions; the assize of nuisance, and the writ of *quod permittat prosternere* (that he permit to abate): which not only give the plaintiff satisfaction for his injury past, but also strike at the root and remove the cause itself, the nuisance that occasioned the injury. . . .

Both these actions, of assize of nuisance, and of *quod permittat prosternere*, are now out of use, and have given way to action on the case. . . . The effect will be much the same, unless a man has a very obstinate as well as an ill-natured neighbour who had rather continue to pay damages than remove his nuisance. For in such a case, recourse must at last be had to the old and sure remedies, which will effectually conquer the defendant's perverseness, by sending the sheriff with his *posse comitatus*, or power of the county, to level it.

QUESTIONS

1. What does Aristotle mean by "equity"?

2. Aristotle says that things come to be either "by necessity" or "by accident." Are these the only possibilities?

3. Define Aquinas's three kinds of law. Give examples of each.

4. Why, according to Aquinas, are each of the three kinds of law needed? Do you agree? Why or why not?

5. Explain the connection(s) between the three kinds of laws.

6. Would Aquinas's theory be significantly weakened if God does not exist?

7. Does the existence of widespread disagreement on legal (and moral) questions and answers undermine natural law jurisprudence in any way? How does a natural law advocate explain such disagreement? Give two examples from the readings above.

8. Plato and Aristotle and some Stoics accepted the institution of slavery and offered arguments in its support based on natural law. So did some early American political writers. Does such divergence on this issue undermine the theory of natural law in a serious way?

9. Think of one example of what you regard as an unjust law. Then think of a situation in which you would have to choose between obeying that law or not obeying it. What would a natural law advocate say about this issue? Would you agree with that analysis?

10. Some contemporary students of legal theory regard the readings in this section as either (1) uninteresting and unimportant or (2) of merely historical interest and significance. Why do you think they regard them in this way? In what sense is their attitude correct and/or incorrect, in your view?

Chapter 2

Positivism
Readings from H.L.A. Hart

Belief in "natural" law and "natural" rights has had a decisive influence on social and political thought and practice. Think, for example, of the importance of these doctrines for framers of the American Constitution and their continuing significance in the defense of human rights and principles of international law. Notwithstanding this influence, however, there are serious objections to this belief. Criticism has taken many different forms, but three of these can serve as an introduction to our second general type of legal theory, positivism.

First, the "classical" understanding of natural law is deeply at variance with modern conceptions of nature. The reason for this is the demise of the so-called "final cause" in the modern explanation of natural occurrences. Aristotle and other premodern proponents of natural law have an animistic conception of nature; they understand all natural processes as controlled by an internal *nissus* or striving to develop in a prescribed way. Individuals are thought of as "wired into" the cosmic scheme of things through a tendency to become some particular sort-of-thing (e.g., a carrot, an eagle, a gnat). As a result of being hard-wired in this way, that is, as a natural kind, individuals are conceived as living out their lives under a certain charter of existence, a charter that determines necessary conditions for growth and well-being. The fact of existence—that a cat or a human being exists—is understood as necessarily giving rise to particular existential values: what is *natural*, they say, is connected with what it is *good to become.*

Like these early natural law advocates, most legal theorists today understand everything that happens as part of a single cosmic order, but they do not understand nature animistically. Instead they view nature as a causal order: everything that happens does so in accordance with causal laws that operate in a purely mechanical way, devoid of purpose and point. Of course, nature and natural objects are useful for human purposes—people fashion sticks into furniture and stones into retaining walls. But purpose here is *given* to natural objects by people; it is not something preexisting in nature.

The question whether it makes sense to think of "immanent ends or purposes" as determining the life-history of a fish or a bird is a sensible question in one respect. It is certainly the case that life histories are under the control of patterns we call "natural" rather than "artificial" kinds. But to say that nature is a causal order is to say that even if there are natural kinds, the kinds in question have come to be in exactly the same way that other things have come to be: through the inexorable and essentially purposeless operation of causal laws.

From a modern perspective, then, concepts of purpose, along with concepts of value generally, are detached from any metaphysical mooring outside human beings. This is not to say that explanation in terms of purposes and values is illogical in any way. It is interesting to note that many of those most responsible for the demise of "final cause" in the explanation of natural events—Galileo, Kepler, and Newton, for example—believed in cosmic purposes: they were religious people who did not doubt God's purposeful creation of the world. What they doubted was the usefulness of inquiry into final causes as a means to natural or scientific knowledge: as Darwin put it, the question of the ultimate purpose of evolution is a subject of inquiry "beyond the human intellect," like "predestination and free will" or the "origin of evil."[1] Thus while there is nothing logically incoherent about belief in cosmic purposes, even purposes that extend to natural events, it is clear that the truth of such belief is not susceptible to confirmation in the modern, that is, the scientific, sense of that term.

A second, and connected, criticism—sometimes referred to as the "Is-Ought Objection"—is based on the assumption that there is a categorical distinction between (1) factual assertions, that is, assertions to the effect that "something is the case," and (2) normative assertions, that is, assertions to the effect that "something ought to be the case" or that "something ought to be done." Making use of this distinction, G. E. Moore developed the "open question argument," the conclusion of which was that it is *always* an open question whether—given some naturally derived matter of fact—something *ought* to be the case or *ought* to be done.[2] To believe that what ought to be the case can be derived from what is naturally the case involves what he called the "naturalistic fallacy." Philosophers writing after Moore have made clear that the form of reasoning employed by the natural law theorists is not really a fallacy, that is, there is no logical problem in reasoning as natural law advocates do. If, for example, certain natural attitudes are "built in" to the structure of human thinking, for example, positive attitudes toward keeping promises and negative attitudes toward lying, *and* if these attitudes invariably find expression in human choice and action, then natural law arguments can go through. The problem with such reasoning is with the assumptions about "built-in natural attitudes." If, for example, there are "natural moral tendencies" in human beings, then how does one account for the apparent

---

1. See *The Life and Letters of Charles Darwin*, ed. F. Darwin (New York: D. Appleton and Company, 1893), vol. II, p. 98.

2. See G.E. Moore, *Principia Ethica* (Cambridge: Cambridge University Press, 1959), pp. 5–27.

ubiquity of moral disagreement, especially across cultures and over time? And even granted the existence of such attitudes, how can their applicable legal content be identified? Classical natural law theory was notably unclear about the answer to these questions, and Jeremy Bentham went so far as to say that, all things considered, the theory amounts to "nonsense on stilts."

The third general line of criticism challenges claims by natural law theorists that a law that stands in violation of clear and evident moral principle is not "really" law. We encountered this claim in the selection from Cicero and it is repeated throughout the literature on natural law—by Blackstone, for example: "No human laws are of any validity, if contrary to 'natural law.'" Exactly what is implied in this claim is difficult to determine. Clearly one has no *moral* duty to obey such laws, but what about legal duty? Do all morally incorrect laws lose their *legal* standing? One striking weakness of classical natural law jurisprudence is the failure of many writers in this tradition to distinguish sharply between issues having to do with the nature of law and those having to do with one's duty to obey *positive* law. Knowledge that one has no moral duty to obey a law does not entail that one has no legal duty to obey it: whether one does depends on logically separable considerations.

One effective response to these objections to natural law theory has been adoption of a dualistic understanding of law and morality. We can know what the law *is*—there being well-defined ways of finding out what has been established as such—and we can know what the law *ought to be*—there are ways of finding that out as well. But in a dualistic understanding, the two kinds of knowledge—descriptive and normative—should not be confused. One advantage of this response is the opportunity it affords for accommodation of normative disagreement. As long as we are clear (1) that judicial decisions should be made "according to established law" and (2) that reliable methods of identifying "established law" are available, then we have at least a staging ground for legal practice. The only cognitive claims to which a legal positivist need be committed are claims about what the law is. These claims are necessary for legal practice in a way that claims about what the law should be are not. On this view individuals and groups can— and indeed should—criticize "established law" and promote legal change based on normative judgment, including moral judgment. But law is not dependent on normative agreement in the way that it is dependent on agreement about positive law.

The most influential representative of this type of legal philosophy is H.L.A. Hart from whom the following selections are taken. Among other features of his work that make it attractive is his distinction between a "regime of primary rules" and a "legal regime." It is worth noting that his account of primary rules is based on something like the moral content of natural law; however, he describes this content as "minimal" and he shows why any organization of society must fail if it is based strictly on rules of this kind.

Reading 1

From H.L.A. Hart,
THE CONCEPT OF LAW

It is, of course, possible to imagine a society without a legislature, courts or officials of any kind. Indeed, there are many studies of primitive communities which not only claim that this possibility is realized but depict in detail the life of a society where the only means of social control is that general attitude of the group towards its own standard modes of behaviour. . . . A social structure of this kind is often referred to as one of "custom"; but we shall not use this term, because it often implies that the customary rules are very old and supported with less social pressure than other rules. To avoid these implications we shall refer to such a social structure as one of primary rules of obligation. If a society is to live by such primary rules alone, there are certain conditions which, granted a few of the most obvious truisms about human nature and the world we live in, must clearly be satisfied. The first of these conditions is that the rules must contain in some form restrictions on the free use of violence, theft, and deception to which human beings are tempted but which they must, in general, repress, if they are to coexist in close proximity to each other. Such rules are in fact always found in the primitive societies of which we have knowledge, together with a variety of others imposing on individuals various positive duties to perform services or make contributions to the common life. Secondly, though such a society may exhibit the tension, already described, between those who accept the rules and those who reject the rules except where fear of social pressure induces them to conform, it is plain that the latter cannot be more than a minority, if so loosely organized a society of persons, approximately equal in physical strength, is to endure: for otherwise those who reject the rules would have too little social pressure to fear. This too is confirmed by what we know of primitive communities where, though there are dissidents and malefactors, the majority live by the rules seen from the internal point of view.

More important for our present purpose is the following consideration. It is plain that only a small community closely knit by ties of kinship, common sentiment, and belief, and placed in a stable environment, could live successfully by such a regime of unofficial rules. In any other conditions such a simplistic form of social control must prove defective and will require supplementation in different ways. In the first place, the rules by which the group lives will not form a system, but will simply be a set of separate standards, without any identifying or common mark, except of course that they are the rules which a particular group of human beings accepts. They will in this respect resemble our own rules of etiquette. Hence if doubts arise as to what the rules are or as to the precise scope of some given rule, there will be no procedure for settling this doubt, either by reference to an authoritative text or to an official whose declarations on this point are authoritative. For, plainly, such a procedure and the acknowledgement of either authoritative text or persons involve the existence of rules of a type different from the rules of obligation or duty which ex hypothesi are all that the group has. This defect in the simple social structure of primary rules we may call its uncertainty.

A second defect is the static character of the rules. The only mode of change in the rules known to such a society will be the slow process of growth, whereby courses of conduct once thought optional become first habitual or usual, and then obligatory, and the converse process of decay, when deviations, once severely dealt with, are first tolerated and then pass unnoticed. There will be no means, in such a society, of deliberately adapting the rules to changing circumstances, either by eliminating old rules or introducing new ones: for, again, the possibility of doing this presupposes the existence of rules of a different type from the primary rules of obligation by which alone the society lives. In an extreme case the rules may be static in a more drastic sense. This, though never perhaps fully realized in any actual community, is worth considering because the remedy for it is something very characteristic of law. In this extreme case, not only would there be no way of deliberately changing the general rules, but the obligations which arise under the rules in particular cases could not be varied or modified by the deliberate choice of any individual. Each individual would simply have fixed obligations or duties to do or abstain from doing certain things. It might indeed very often be the case that others would benefit from the performance of these obligations; yet if there are only primary rules of obligation they would have

no power to release those bound from performance or to transfer to others the benefits which would accrue from performance. For such operations of release or transfer create changes in the initial positions of individuals under the primary rules of obligation, and for these operations to be possible there must be rules of a sort different from the primary rules.

The third defect of this simple form of social life is the inefficiency of the diffuse social pressure by which the rules are maintained. Disputes as to whether an admitted rule has or has not been violated will always occur and will, in any but the smallest societies, continue interminably, if there is no agency specially empowered to ascertain finally, and authoritatively, the fact of violation. Lack of such final and authoritative determinations is to be distinguished from another weakness associated with it. This is the fact that punishments for violations of the rules, and other forms of social pressure involving physical effort or the use of force, are not administered by a special agency but are left to the individuals affected or to the group at large. It is obvious that the waste of time involved in the group's unorganized efforts to catch and punish offenders, and the shouldering of vendettas which may result from self help in the absence of an official monopoly of "sanctions," may be serious. The history of law does, however, strongly suggest that the lack of official agencies to determine authoritatively the fact of violation of the rules is a much more serious defect; for many societies have remedies for this defect long before the other.

The remedy for each of these three main defects in this simplest form of social structure consists in supplementing the primary rules of obligation with secondary rules which are rules of a different kind. The introduction of the remedy for each defect might, in itself, be considered a step from the prelegal into the legal world; since each remedy brings with it many elements that permeate law: certainly all three remedies together are enough to convert the regime of primary rules into what is indisputably a legal system. We shall consider in turn each of these remedies and show why law may most illuminatingly be characterized as a union of primary rules of obligation with such secondary rules. Before we do this, however, the following general points should be noted. Though the remedies consist in the introduction of rules which are certainly different from each other, as well as from the primary rules of obligation which they supplement, they have important features in common and are connected in various ways. Thus they may all be said to be on a different level from the primary rules, for they are all about such rules in the sense that while primary rules are concerned with the actions that individuals must or must not do, these secondary rules are all concerned with the primary rules themselves. They specify the ways in which the primary rules may be conclusively ascertained, introduced, eliminated, varied, and the fact of their violation conclusively determined.

The simplest form of remedy for the uncertainly of the regime of primary rules is the introduction of what we shall call a "rule of recognition." This will specify some feature or features possession of which by a suggested rule is taken as a conclusive affirmative indication that it is a rule of the group to be supported by the social pressure it exerts. The existence of such a rule of recogni-

tion may take any of a huge variety of forms, simple or complex. It may, as in the early law of many societies, be no more than that an authoritative list or text of the rules to be found in a written document or carved on some public monument. No doubt as a matter of history this step from the prelegal to the legal may be accomplished in distinguishable stages, of which the first is the mere reduction to writing of hitherto unwritten rules. This is not itself the crucial step, though it is a very important one: what is crucial is the acknowledgement of reference to the writing or inscription as authoritative, i.e. as the proper way of disposing of doubts as to the existence of the rule. Where there is such an acknowledgement there is a very simple form of secondary rule: a rule for conclusive identification of the primary rules of obligation.

In a developed legal system the rules of recognition are of course more complex; instead of identifying rules exclusively by reference to a text or list they do so by reference to some general characteristic possessed by the primary rules. This may be the fact of their having been enacted by a specific body, or their long customary practice, or their relation to judicial decisions. Moreover, where more than one of such general characteristics are treated as identifying criteria, provision may be made for their possible conflict by their arrangement in an order of superiority, as by the common subordination of custom or precedent to statute, the latter being a "superior source" of law. Such complexity may make the rules of recognition in a modern legal system seem very different from the simple acceptance of an authoritative text: yet even in this simplest form, such a rule brings with it many elements distinctive of law. By providing an authoritative mark it introduces, although in embryonic form, the idea of a legal system: for the rules are now not just a discrete unconnected set but are, in a simple way, unified. Further, in the simple operation of identifying a given rule as possessing the required feature of being an item on an authoritative list of rules we have the germ of the idea of legal validity.

The remedy for the static quality of the regime of primary rules consists in the introduction of what we shall call "rules of change." The simplest form of such a rule is that which empowers an individual or body of persons to introduce new primary rules for the conduct of the life of the group, or of some class within it, and to eliminate old rules. As we have already argued . . . it is in terms of such a rule, and not in terms of orders backed by threats, that the ideas of legislative enactment and repeal are to be understood. Such rules of change may be very simple or very complex: the powers conferred may be unrestricted or limited in various ways: and the rules may, besides specifying the persons who are to legislate, define in more or less rigid terms the procedure to be followed in legislation. Plainly, there will be a very close connexion between the rules of change and the rules of recognition: for where the former exists the latter will necessarily incorporate a reference to legislation as an identifying feature of the rules, though it need not refer to all the details of procedure involved in legislation. Usually some official certificate or official copy will, under the rules of recognition, be taken as a sufficient proof of due enactment. Of course if there is a social structure so simple that the only "source of law" is legislation, the rule of recognition will simply specify enact-

ment as the unique identifying mark or criterion of validity of the rules. . . .

We have already described in some detail the rules which confer on individuals power to vary their initial positions under the primary rules. Without such private power-conferring rules society would lack some of the chief amenities which law confers upon it. For the operations which these rules make possible are the making of wills, contracts, transfers of property, and many other voluntarily created structures of rights and duties which typify life under law, though of course an elementary form of power-conferring rule also underlies the moral institution of a promise. The kinship of these rules with the rules of change involved in the notion of legislation is clear, and . . . any of the features which puzzle us in the institutions of contract or property are clarified by thinking of the operations of making a contract or transferring property as the exercise of limited legislative powers by individuals.

The third supplement to the simple regime of primary rules, intended to remedy the inefficiency of its diffused social pressure, consists of secondary rules empowering individuals to make authoritative determinations of the question whether, on a particular occasion, a primary rule has been broken. The minimal form of adjudication consists in such determinations, and we shall call the secondary rules which confer the power to make them "rules of adjudication." Besides identifying the individuals who are to adjudicate, such rules will also define the procedure to be followed. Like the other secondary rules these are on a different level from the primary rules: though they may be reinforced by further rules imposing duties on judges to adjudicate, they do not impose duties but confer judicial powers and a special status on judicial declarations about the breach of obligations. Again these rules, like the other secondary rules, define a group of important legal concepts: in this case the concepts of judge or court, jurisdiction and judgment. Besides these resemblances to the other secondary rules, rules of adjudication have intimate connexions with them. Indeed, a system which has rules of adjudication is necessarily also committed to a rule of recognition of an elementary and imperfect sort. This is so because, if courts are empowered to make authoritative determinations of the fact that a rule has been broken, these cannot avoid being taken as authoritative determinations of what the rules are. So the rule which confers jurisdiction will also be a rule of recognition, identifying the primary rules through the judgments of the courts and these judgments will become a "source" of law. It is true that this form of rule of recognition, inseparable from the minimum form of jurisdiction, will be very imperfect. Unlike an authoritative text or a statute book, judgments may not be couched in general terms and their use as authoritative guides to the rules depends on a somewhat shaky inference from particular decisions, and the reliability of this must fluctuate both with the skill of the interpreter and the consistency of the judges.

It need hardly be said that in few legal systems are judicial powers confined to authoritative determinations of the fact of violation of the primary rules. Most systems have, after some delay, seen the advantages of further centralization of social pressure; and have partially prohibited the use of physical punishments or violent self help by private individuals. Instead they have supplemented the primary rules of obligation by further secondary rules, specifying or at least limiting the penalties for violation, and have conferred upon judges, where they have ascertained the fact of violation, the exclusive power to direct the application of penalties by other officials. These secondary rules provide the centralized official "sanctions" of the system. If we stand back and consider the structure which has resulted from the combination of primary rules of obligation with the secondary rules of recognition, change and adjudication, it is plain that we have here not only the heart of a legal system, but a most powerful tool for the analysis of much that has puzzled both the jurist and the political theorist. Not only are the specifically legal concepts with which the lawyer is professionally concerned, such as those of obligation and rights, validity and source of law, legislation and jurisdiction, and sanction, best elucidated in terms of this combination of elements. The concepts (which bestride both law and political theory) of the state, of authority, and of an official require a similar analysis if the obscurity which still lingers about them is to be dissipated. The reason why an analysis in these terms of primary and secondary rules has this explanatory power is not far to seek. Most of the obscurities and distortions surrounding legal and political concepts arise from the fact that these essentially involve reference to what we have called the internal point of view: the view of those who do not merely record and predict behaviour conforming to rules, but use the rules as standards for the appraisal of their own and others' behaviour. This requires more detailed attention in the analysis of legal and political concepts than it has usually received. Under the simple regime of primary rules the internal point of view is manifested in its simplest form, in the use of those rules as the basis of criticism, and as the justification of demands for conformity, social pressure, and punishment. Reference to this most elementary manifestation of the internal point of view is required for the analysis of the basic concepts of obligation and duty. With the addition to the system of secondary rules, the range of what is said and done from the internal point of view is much extended and diversified. With this extension comes a whole set of new concepts and they demand a reference to the internal point of view for their analysis. These include the notions of legislation, jurisdiction, validity and, generally, of legal powers, private and public. There is a constant pull towards an analysis of these in the terms of ordinary or "scientific," fact-stating or predictive discourse. But this can only reproduce their external aspect: to do justice to their distinctive, internal aspect we need to see the different ways in which the law-making operations of the legislator, the adjudication of a court, the exercise of private or official powers, and other "acts-in-the-law" are related to secondary rules. . . .

~

In the next selection Hart treats a series of issues that arise from his conception of law as a union or combination of primary rules of obligation and secondary rules of recognition, change, and adjudication. The first point developed was mentioned briefly above: his distinction between an *internal* and an *external* attitude or point of view. The difference between the two is that the internal point of view presupposes an acceptance of and commitment to the legal rules of a community. An external point of view, on the other hand, is the kind of attitude a stranger would normally have toward the rules and regulations of a foreign community—a strictly observer's point of view. Hart makes clear that law depends on adoption of an internal point of view.

~

Reading 2

From H.L.A. Hart,
THE CONCEPT OF LAW

. . . In the day-to-day life of a legal system its rule of recognition is very seldom expressly formulated as a rule; though occasionally, courts in England may announce in general terms the relative place of one criterion of law in relation to another, as when they assert the supremacy of Acts of Parliament over other sources or suggested sources of law. For the most part the rule of recognition is not stated, but its existence is shown in the way in which particular rules are identified, either by courts or other officials or private persons or their advisers. There is, of course, a difference in the use made by courts of the criteria provided by the rule and the use of them by others: for when courts reach a particular conclusion on the footing that a particular rule has been correctly identified as law, what they say has a special authoritative status conferred on it by other rules. In this respect, as in many others, the rule of recognition of a legal system is like the scoring rule of a game. In the course of the game the general rule defining the activities which constitute scoring (runs, goals, etc.) is seldom formulated; instead it is used by officials and players in identifying the particular phases which count towards winning. Here too, the declarations of officials (umpire or scorer) have a special authoritative status attributed to them by other rules. Further, in both cases there is the possibility of a conflict between these authoritative applications of the rule and the general understanding of what the rule plainly requires according to its terms. This, as we shall see later, is a complication which must be catered for in any account of what it is for a system of rules of this sort to exist.

The use of unstated rules of recognition, by courts and others, in identifying particular rules of the system is characteristic of the internal point of view. Those who use them in this way thereby manifest their own acceptance of them as guiding rules and with this attitude there goes

a characteristic vocabulary different from the natural expressions of the external point of view. Perhaps the simplest of these is the expression, "It is the law that... ," which we may find on the lips not only of judges, but of ordinary men living under a legal system, when they identify a given rule of the system. This, like the expression "Out" or "Goal," is the language of one assessing a situation by reference to rules which he in common with others acknowledges as appropriate for this purpose. This attitude of shared acceptance of rules is to be contrasted with that of an observer who records ab extra the fact that a social group accepts such rules but does not himself accept them. The natural expression of this external point of view is not "It is the law that . . ." but "In England they recognize as law ... whatever the Queen in Parliament enacts. . . ." The first of these forms of expression we shall call an internal statement because it manifests the internal point of view and is naturally used by one who, accepting the rule of recognition and without stating the fact that it is accepted, applies the rule in recognizing some particular rule of the system as valid. The second form of expression we shall call an external statement because it is the natural language of an external observer of the system who, without himself accepting its rule of recognition, states the fact that others accept it.

A second point developed in this chapter concerns the issues raised earlier in connection with how one's duty to obey the law should be understood. Here the distinction Hart develops is between the *validity* and the *efficacy* of laws. Validity is a function in part of the internal point of view: a law is valid if it passes all the tests provided by the rule of recognition. The criteria for efficacy is different, however: a law is efficacious if it is obeyed more often than not. That a law is valid is no guarantee that it is efficacious, and that it is *not* efficacious is no proof that it is invalid.

Reading 3

From H.L.A. Hart,
THE CONCEPT OF LAW

If this use of an accepted rule of recognition in making internal statements is understood and carefully distinguished from an external statement of fact that the rule is accepted, many obscurities concerning the notion of legal "validity" disappear. For the word "valid" is most frequently, though not always, used, in just such internal statements, applying to a particular rule of a legal system, an unstated but accepted rule of recognition. To say that a given rule is valid is to recognize it as passing all the tests provided by the rule of recognition and so as a rule of the system. We can indeed simply say that the statement that a particular rule is valid means that it satisfies all the criteria provided by the rule of recognition. This is incorrect only to the extent that it might obscure the internal character of such statements; for, like the cricketers' "Out," these statements of validity normally apply to a particular case a rule of recognition accepted by the speaker and others, rather than expressly state that the rule is satisfied.

Some of the puzzles connected with the idea of legal validity are said to concern the relation between the validity and the "efficacy" of law. If by "efficacy" is meant that the fact that a rule of law which requires certain behaviour is obeyed more often than not, it is plain that there is no necessary connexion between the validity of any particular rule and its efficacy, unless the rule of recognition of the system includes among its criteria, as some do, the provision (sometimes referred to as a rule of obsolescence) that no rule is to count as a rule of the system if it has long ceased to be efficacious.

From the inefficacy of a particular rule, which may or may not count against its validity, we must distinguish a general disregard of the rules of the system. This may be so complete in character and so protracted that we should say, in the case of a new system, that it had never established itself as the legal system of a given group, or, in the case of a once-established system, that it had ceased to be the legal system of the group. In either case, the normal context or background for making any internal statement in terms of the rules of the system is absent. In such cases it would be generally pointless either to assess the rights and duties of particular persons by reference to the primary rules of a system or to assess the validity of any of its rules by reference to its rules of recognition. To insist on applying a system of rules which had either never actually been effective or had been discarded would, except in special circumstances mentioned below, be as futile as to assess the progress of a game by reference to a scoring rule which had never been accepted or had been discarded.

One who makes an internal statement concerning the validity of a particular rule of a system may be said to presuppose the truth of the external statement of fact that the system is generally efficacious. For the normal use of internal statements is in such a context of general efficacy. It would however be wrong to say that statements of validity "mean" that the system is generally efficacious. For though it is normally pointless or idle to talk of the validity of a rule of a system which has never established itself or has been discarded, none the less it is not meaningless nor is it always pointless. One vivid way of teaching Roman Law is to speak as if the system were efficacious still and to discuss the valid-ity of particular rules and solve problems in their terms; and one way of nursing hopes for the restoration of an old social order destroyed by revolution, and rejecting the new, is to cling to the criteria of legal validity of the old regime. This is implicitly done by the White Russian who still claims property under some rule of descent which was a valid rule of Tsarist Russia.

The notion that law consists of "internal statements" allows Hart to distinguish his account of law from what is sometimes called the "prediction theory of law," an understanding of law associated most directly with Justice Oliver Wendell Holmes. In a famous essay titled "The Path of the Law," Holmes argued that both the practice of law and the work of legislators should be understood as predictions of what courts will do. Clients consult lawyers to obtain information of this sort, and lawyers are judged good and/or bad at what they do precisely in terms of their predictions. Hart thinks this conception of law is seriously mistaken, and in the following passage he identifies the most important respect in which this is so.

Reading 4

From H.L.A. Hart,
THE CONCEPT OF LAW

A grasp of the normal contextual connexion between the internal statement that a given rule of a system is valid and the external statement of fact that the system is generally efficacious, will help us see in its proper perspective the common theory that to assert the validity of a rule is to predict that it will be enforced by courts or some other official action taken. . . . The motive for advancing this predictive theory is the conviction that only thus can metaphysical interpretations be avoided: that either a statement that a rule is valid must ascribe some mysterious property which cannot be detected by empirical means or it must be a prediction of future behaviour of officials. In both cases also the plausibility of the theory is due to the same important fact: that the truth of the external statement of fact, which an observer might record, that the system is generally efficacious and likely to continue so is normally presupposed by anyone who accepts the rules and makes an internal statement of obligation or validity. The two are certainly very closely associated. In both cases alike the mistake of the theory is the same: it consists in neglecting the special character of the internal statement and treating it as an external statement about official action.

This mistake becomes immediately apparent when we consider how the judge's own statement that a particular rule is valid functions in judicial decision; for, though here too, in making such a statement, the judge presupposes but does not state the general efficacy of the system, he plainly is not concerned to predict his own or others' official action. His statement that a rule is valid is an internal statement recognizing that the rule satisfies the tests for identifying what is to count as law in his court, and constitutes not a prophecy but part of the reason for his decision. There is indeed a more plausible case for saying that a statement that a rule is valid is a prediction when such a statement is made by a private person; for in the case of conflict between unofficial statements of validity or invalidity and that of a court in deciding a case, there is often good sense in saying that the former must then be withdrawn. . . .

A final topic of discussion rounds out Hart's conception of law in chapters 5 and 6 of his *Concept of Law*: the legal "ultimacy" of the "rule of recognition." According to Hart, we can say of a "rule of recognition" what cannot be said of any other rule, namely, that the question of its validity does not arise. More exactly, it cannot arise because the attitude of commitment that constitutes the internal point of view is directed toward the rule of recognition: it is the source of validity for all other rules of the legal system. He compares the status of the rule of recognition in a legal system with the status of the standard meter bar in a metric system—there is no further standard against which to check validity.

At the beginning of the following passage he distinguishes between the *ultimacy* of the rule of recognition and the *supremacy* of one among two or more criteria of legal validity supplied by the rule of recognition. The idea is this: a rule of recognition—a constitution, for example—may supply several distinct ways of providing for legal validity— legislative enactment and administrative decree, for example—and it may rank them hierarchically such that legislative enactment *has supremacy over*, that is, has the capacity to override an administrative decree. Hart wants to make clear that a rule of recognition cannot be overridden in this way; it has a kind of ultimacy attached to it that no primary rule of obligation has nor has any other secondary rule, for example, of change or adjudication.

Reading 5

From H.L.A. Hart,
THE CONCEPT OF LAW

The sense in which the rule of recognition is the ultimate rule of a system is best understood if we pursue a very familiar chain of legal reasoning. If the question is raised whether some suggested rule is legally valid, we must, in order to answer the question, use a criterion of validity provided by some other rule. Is this purported by-law of the Oxfordshire County Council valid? Yes: because it was made in exercise of the powers conferred, and in accordance with the procedure specified, by a statutory order made by the Minister of Health. At this first stage the statutory order provides the criteria in terms of which the validity of the by-law is assessed. There may be no practical need to go farther; but there is a standing possibility of doing so. We may query the validity of the statutory order and assess its validity in terms of the statute empowering the minister to make such orders. Finally when the validity of the statute has been queried and assessed by reference to the rule that what the Queen in Parliament enacts is law, we are brought to a stop in inquiries concerning validity: for we have reached a rule which, like the intermediate statutory order and statute, provides criteria for the assessment of the validity of other rules; but it is also unlike them in that there is no rule providing criteria for the assessment of its own legal validity.

There are, indeed, many questions which we can raise about this ultimate rule. We can ask whether it is the practice of courts, legislatures, officials, or private citizens in England actually to use this rule as an ultimate rule of recognition. Or has our process of legal reasoning been an idle game with the criteria of validity of a system now discarded? We can ask whether it is a satisfactory form of legal system which has such a rule at its root. Does it produce more good than evil? Are there prudential reasons for supporting it? Is there a moral obligation to do so? These are plainly very important questions; but, equally plainly, when we ask them about the rule of recognition we are no longer attempting to answer the same kind of question about it as those which we answered about other rules with its aid. When we move from saying that a particular enactment is valid, because it satisfies the rule that what the Queen in Parliament enacts is law, to saying that in England this last rule is used by courts, officials, and private persons as the ultimate rule of recognition, we have moved from an internal statement of law asserting the validity of a rule of the system to an external statement of fact which an observer of the system might make even if he could not accept it. So too when we move from the statement that a particular enactment is valid, to the statement that the rule of recognition of the system is an excellent one and the system based on it is one worthy of support, we have moved from a statement of legal validity to a statement of value.

Some writers, who have emphasized the legal ultimacy of the rule of recognition, have expressed this by saying that, whereas the legal validity of other rules of the system can be demonstrated by reference to it, its own validity cannot be demonstrated but is "assumed" or "postulated" or is a "hypothesis." This may, however, be seriously misleading. Statements of legal validity made about particular rules in the day-to-day life of a legal system whether by judges, lawyers, or ordinary citizens do indeed carry with them certain presuppositions. They are internal statements of law expressing the point of view of those who accept the rule of recognition of the system and, as such, leave unstated much that could be stated in external statements of fact about the system. What is thus left unstated forms the normal background or context of statements of legal validity and is thus said to be "presupposed" by them. But it is important to see precisely what these presupposed matters are, and not to obscure their character. They consist of two things. First, a person who seriously asserts the validity of some given rule of law, say a particular statute, himself makes use of a rule of recognition which he accepts as appropriate for identifying the law. Secondly, it is the case that this rule of recognition, in terms of which he assesses the validity of a particular statute, is not only accepted by him but is the rule of recognition actually accepted and employed in the general operation of the system. If the truth of this presupposition were doubted, it could be established by reference to actual practice: to the way in which courts identify what is to count as law, and to the general acceptance of or acquiescence in these identifications.

Neither of these two presuppositions are well described as assumptions of a "validity" which cannot be demonstrated. We only need the word "validity," and commonly only use it, to answer questions which arise within a system of rules where the status of a rule as a member of the system depends on its satisfying certain criteria provided by the rule of recognition. No such question can arise as to the validity of the very rule of recognition which provides the criteria; it can neither be valid nor invalid but is simply accepted as appropriate for use in this way. To express this simple fact by saying darkly that its validity likely says it is "assumed but cannot be demonstrated," is like saying that we assume, but can never demonstrate, that the standard metre bar in Paris which is the ultimate test of the correctness of all measurement in metres, is itself correct.

Having developed his conception of law as an interlocking system of primary and secondary rules, Hart turns in our final selection to some important observations about how legal rules and standards are conveyed to a population, that is, how they are communicated. It is clear enough that the most significant means of communication is language, but that is not the only means: there is communication by example as well, and in law this is effected through appeal to precedent. In connection with his discussion of these two primary modes of legal communication Hart develops one of his most influential ideas—that legal concepts are "open-textured."

Reading 6

From H.L.A. Hart,
THE CONCEPT OF LAW

The Open Texture of Law

In any large group general rules, standards, and principles must be the main instrument of social control, and not particular directions given to each individual separately. If it were not possible to communicate general standards of conduct, which multitudes of individuals could understand, without further direction, as requiring from them certain conduct when occasion arose, nothing that we now recognize as law could exist. Hence the law must predominantly, but by no means exclusively, refer to classes of persons, and to classes of acts, things, and circumstances; and its successful operation over vast areas of social life depends on a widely diffused capacity to recognize particular acts, things, and circumstances as instances of the general classifications which the law makes.

Two principal devices, at first sight very different from each other, have been used for the communication of such general standards of conduct in advance of the successive occasions on which they are to be applied. One of them makes a maximal and the other a minimal use of general classifying words. The first is typified by what we call legislation and the second by precedent. We can see the distinguishing features of these in the following simple non-legal cases. One father before going to church says to his son, "Every man and boy must take off his hat on entering a church." Another baring his head as he enters the church says, "Look: this is the right way to behave on such occasions."

The communication or teaching of standards of conduct by example may take different forms, far more sophisticated than our simple case. Our case would more closely resemble the legal use of precedent, if instead of the child being told on the particular occasion to regard what his father did on entering the church as an example of the right thing to do, the father assumed that the child would regard him as an authority on proper behavior, and would watch him in order to learn the way to behave. To approach further the legal use of precedent, we must suppose that the father is conceived by himself and others to subscribe to traditional standards of behavior and not to be introducing new ones.

Communication by example in all its forms, though accompanied by some general verbal directions such as "Do as I do," may leave open ranges of possibilities, and hence of doubt, as to what is intended even as to matters which the person seeking to communicate has himself clearly envisaged. How much of the performance must be imitated? Does it matter if the left hand is used, instead of the right, to. remove the hat? That it is done slowly or smartly? That the hat is put under the seat? That it is not replaced on the head inside the church? These are all variants of general questions which the child might ask himself: "In what ways must my conduct resemble his to be right?" "What precisely is it about his conduct that is to be my guide?" In understanding the example, the child attends to some of its aspects rather than others. In so doing he is guided by common sense and knowledge of the general kind of things and purposes which adults think important, and by his appreciation of the general character of the occasion (going to church) and the kind of behavior appropriate to it.

In contrast with the indeterminacies of examples, the communication of general standards by explicit general forms of language ("Every man must take off his hat on entering a church") seems clear, dependable, and certain. The features to be taken as general guides to conduct are here identified in words; they are verbally extricated, not left embedded with others in a concrete example. In order to know what to do on other occasions the child has no longer to guess what is intended, or what will be approved; he is not left to speculate as to the way in which his conduct must resemble the example if it is to be right. Instead, he has a verbal description which he can use to pick out what he must do in the future and when he must do it. He has only to recognize instances of clear verbal terms, to "subsume" particular facts under general classificatory heads and draw a simple syllogistic conclusion. He is not faced with the alternative of choosing at his peril or seeking further authoritative guidance. He has a rule which he can apply by himself to himself.

Much of the jurisprudence of this century has consisted of the progressive realization (and sometimes the exaggeration) of the important fact that the distinction between the uncertainties of communication by authoritative example (precedent), and the certainties of communication by authoritative general language (legislation) is far less firm than this naive contrast suggests. Even when verbally formulated general rules are used, uncertainties as to the form of behavior required by them may break out in particular concrete cases. Particular fact-situations do not await us already marked off from each other, and labelled as instances of the general rule, the application of which is in question; nor can the rule itself step forward to claim its own instances. In all fields of experience, not only that of rules, there is a limit, inherent in the nature of language, to the guidance which general language can provide. There will indeed be plain cases constantly recurring in similar contexts to which general expressions are clearly applicable ("If anything is a vehicle a motor-car is one") but there will also be cases where it is not clear whether they apply or not. (Does "vehicle" used here include bicycles, airplanes, roller skates?) The latter are fact-situations, continually thrown up by nature or human invention, which possess only some of the features of the plain cases but others which they lack. Canons of "interpretation" cannot eliminate, though they can diminish, these uncertainties; for these canons are themselves general rules for the use of language, and make use of general terms which themselves require interpretation. They cannot, any more than other rules, provide for their own interpretation. The plain case, where the general terms seem to need no interpretation and where the recognition of instances seems unproblematic or "automatic," are only the familiar ones, constantly recurring in similar contexts, where there is general agreement in judgments as to the applicability of the classifying terms.

General terms would be useless to us as a medium of communication unless there were such familiar, generally unchallenged cases. But the variants on the familiar also call for classification under the general terms which at any given moment constitute part of our linguistic resources. Here something in the nature of a crisis in communication is precipitated: there are reasons both for and against our use of a general term, and no firm convention or general agreement dictates its use, or, on the other hand, its rejection by the person concerned to classify. If in such cases doubts are to be resolved, something in the nature of a choice between open alternatives must be made by whoever is to resolve them.

At this point, the authoritative general language in which a rule is expressed may guide only in an uncertain way much as an authoritative example does. The sense that the language of the rule will enable us simply to pick out easily recognizable instances, at this point gives way; subsumption and the drawing of a syllogistic conclusion no longer characterize the nerve of the reasoning involved in determining what is the right thing to do. Instead, the language of the rule seems now only to mark out an authoritative example, namely that constituted by the plain case. This may be used in much the same way as a precedent, though the language of the rule will limit the features demanding attention both more permanently and more closely than precedent does. Faced with the question whether the rule prohibiting the use of vehicles in the park is applicable to some combination of circumstances in which it appears indeterminate, all that the person called upon to answer can do is to consider (as does one who makes use of a precedent) whether the present case resembles the plain case "sufficiently" in "relevant" respects. The discretion thus left to him by language may be very wide; so that if he applies the rule, the conclusion, even though it may not be arbitrary or irrational, is in effect a choice. He chooses to add to a line of cases a new case because of resemblances which can reasonably be defended as both legally relevant and sufficiently close. In the case of legal rules, the criteria of relevance and closeness of resemblance depend on many complex factors running through the legal system and on the aims or purpose which may be attributed to the rule. To characterize these would be to characterize whatever is specific or peculiar in legal reasoning.

Whichever device, precedent or legislation, is chosen for the communication of standards of behavior, these, however smoothly they work over the great mass of ordinary cases, will, at some point where their application is in question, prove indeterminate; they will have what has been termed an open texture. So far we have presented this, in the case of legislation, as a general feature of human language; uncertainty at the borderline is the price to be paid for the use of general classifying terms in any form of communication concerning matters of fact. Natural languages like English are when so used irreducibly open textured. It is, however, important to appreciate why, apart from this dependence on language as it actually is, with its characteristics of open texture, we should not cherish, even as an ideal, the conception of a rule so detailed that the question whether it applied or not to a particular case was always settled in advance, and never involved, at the point of actual application, a fresh choice between open alternatives. Put shortly, the reason is that the necessity for such choice is thrust upon us because we are men, not gods. It is a feature of the human predicament (and so of the legislative one) that we labor under two connected handicaps whenever we seek to regulate, unambiguously and in advance, some sphere of conduct by means of general standards to be used without further official direction on particular occasions. The first handicap is our relative ignorance of fact: the second is our relative indeterminacy of aim. If the world in which we live were characterized only by a finite number of features, and these together with all the modes in which they could combine were known to us, then provision could be made in advance for every possibility. We could make rules, the application of which to particular cases never called for a further choice. Everything could be known, and for everything, since it could be known, something could be done and specified in advance by rule. This would be a world fit for "mechanical" jurisprudence.

Plainly this world is not our world; human legislators can have no such knowledge of all the possible combinations of circumstances which the future may bring. This inability to anticipate brings with it a relative indeterminacy of aim. When we are bold enough to frame some general rule of conduct (e.g., a rule that no vehicle may be taken into the park), the language used in this context fixes necessary conditions which anything must satisfy if it is to be within its scope, and certain clear examples of what is certainly within its scope may be present to our minds. They are the paradigm, clear cases (the motor-car, the bus, the motor-cycle); and our aim in legislating is so far determinate because we have made a certain choice. We have ini-

tially settled the question that peace and quiet in the park is to be maintained at the cost, at any rate, of the exclusion of these things. On the other hand, until we have put the general aim of peace in the park into conjunction with those cases which we did not, or perhaps could not, initially envisage (perhaps a toy motor-car, electrically propelled) our aim is, in this direction, indeterminate. We have not settled, because we have not anticipated, the question which will be raised by the unenvisaged case when it occurs: whether some degree of peace in the park is to be sacrificed to, or defended against, those children whose pleasure or interest it is to use these things. When the unenvisaged case does arise, we confront the issues at stake and can then settle the question by choosing between the competing interests in the way which best satisfies us. In doing so we shall have rendered more determinate our initial aim, and shall incidentally have settled a question as to the meaning, for the purposes of this rule, of a general word.

Different legal systems, or the same system at different times, may either ignore or acknowledge more or less explicitly such a need for the further exercise of choice in the application of general rules to particular cases. The vice known to legal theory as formalism or conceptualism consists in an attitude to verbally formulated rules which both seeks to disguise and to minimize the need for such choice, once the general rule has been laid down. One way of doing this is to freeze the meaning of the rule so that its general terms must have the same meaning in every case where its application is in question. To secure this we may fasten on certain features present in the plain case and insist that these are both necessary and sufficient to bring anything which has them within the scope of the rule, whatever other features it may have or lack, and whatever may be the social consequences of applying the rule in this way. To do this is to secure a measure of certainty or predictability at the cost of blindly prejudging what is to be done in a range of future cases, about whose composition we are ignorant. We shall thus indeed succeed in settling in advance, but also in the dark, issues which can only reasonably be settled when they arise and are identified. We shall be forced by this technique to include in the scope of a rule cases which we would wish to exclude in order to give effect to reasonable social aims, and which the open textured terms of our language would have allowed us to exclude, had we left them less rigidly defined. The rigidity of our classifications will thus war with our aims in having or maintaining the rule.

The consummation of this process is the jurists' "heaven of concepts"; this is reached when a general term is given the same meaning not only in every application of a single rule, but when ever it appears in any rule in the legal system. No effort is then ever required or made to interpret the term in the light of the different issues at stake in its various recurrences.

In fact all systems, in different ways, compromise between two social needs: the need for certain rules which can, over great areas of conduct, safely be applied by private individuals to themselves without fresh official guidance or weighing up of social issues, and the need to leave open, for later settlement by an informed, official choice, issues which can only be properly appreciated and settled when they arise in a concrete case. In some legal systems at some periods it may be

that too much is sacrificed to certainty, and that judicial interpretation of statutes or of precedent is too formal and so fails to respond to the similarities and differences between cases which are visible only when they are considered in the light of social aims. In other systems or at other periods it may seem that too much is treated by courts as perennially open or revisable in precedents, and too little respect paid to such limits as legislative language, despite its open texture, does after all provide. Legal theory has in this matter a curious history; for it is apt either to ignore or to exaggerate the indeterminacies of legal rules. To escape this oscillation between extremes we need to remind ourselves that human inability to anticipate the future, which is at the root of this indeterminacy, varies in degree in different fields of conduct, and that legal systems cater for this inability by a corresponding variety of techniques.

Sometimes the sphere to be legally controlled is recognized from the start as one in which the features of individual cases will vary so much in socially important but unpredictable respects, that uniform rules to be applied from case to case without further official direction cannot usefully be framed by the legislature in advance. Accordingly, to regulate such a sphere the legislature sets up very general standards and then delegates to an administrative, rule-making body acquainted with the varying types of case, the task of fashioning rules adapted to their special needs. Thus the legislature may require an industry to maintain certain standards: to charge only a fair rate or to provide safe systems of work. Instead of leaving the different enterprises to apply these vague standards to themselves, at the risk of being found to have violated them ex post facto, it may be found best to defer the use of sanctions for violations until the administrative body has by regulation specified what, for a given industry, is to count as a "fair rate" or a "safe system." This rule-making power may be exercisable only after something like a judicial inquiry into the facts about the particular industry, and a hearing of arguments pro and con a given form of regulation.

Of course even with very general standards there will be plain indisputable examples of what does, or does not, satisfy them. Some extreme cases of what is, or is not, a "fair rate" or a "safe system" will always be identifiable ab initio. Thus at one end of the infinitely varied range of cases there will be a rate so high that it would hold the public up to ransom for a vital service, while yielding the entrepreneurs vast profits; at the other end there will be a rate so low that it fails to provide an incentive for running the enterprise. Both these in different ways would defeat any possible aim we could have in regulating rates. But these are only the extremes of a range of different factors and are not likely to be met in practice; between them fall the difficult real cases requiring attention. The anticipatable combinations of relevant factors are few, and this entails a relative indeterminacy in our initial aim of a fair rate or a safe system, and a need for further official choice. In these cases it is clear that the rule-making authority must exercise a discretion, and there is no possibility of treating the question raised by the various cases as if there were one uniquely correct answer to be found, as distinct from an answer which is a reasonable compromise between many conflicting interests.

A second similar technique is used where the sphere to be controlled is such that it is impossible to identify a class of specific actions to be uniformly done or forborne and to make them the subject of a simple rule, yet the range of circumstances, though very varied, covers familiar features of common experience. Here common judgments of what is "reasonable" can be used by the law. This technique leaves to individuals, subject to correction by a court, the task of weighing up and striking a reasonable balance between the social claims which arise in various unanticipatable forms. In this case they are required to conform to a variable standard before it has been officially defined, and they may learn from a court only ex post facto when they have violated it, what, in terms of specific actions or forbearances, is the standard required of them. Where the decisions of the court on such matters are regarded as precedents, their specification of the variable standard is very like the exercise of delegated rule-making power by an administrative body, though there are also obvious differences.

The most famous example of this technique in Anglo-American law is the use of the standard of due care in cases of negligence. Civil, and less frequently criminal, sanctions may be applied to those who fail to take reasonable care to avoid inflicting physical injuries on others. But what is reasonable or due care in a concrete situation? We can, of course, cite typical examples of due care: doing such things as stopping, looking, and listening where traffic is to be expected. But we are all well aware that the situations where care is demanded are hugely various and that many other actions are now required besides, or in place of, "stop, look, and listen"; indeed these may not be enough and might be quite useless if looking would not help to avert the danger. What we are striving for in the application of standards of reasonable care is to ensure (1) that precautions will be taken which will avert substantial harm, yet (2) that the precautions are such that the burden of proper precautions does not involve too great a sacrifice of other respectable interests. Nothing much is sacrificed by stopping, looking, and listening unless of course a man bleeding to death is being driven to the hospital. But owing to the immense variety of possible cases where care is called for, we cannot ab initio foresee what combinations of circumstances will arise nor foresee what interests will have to be sacrificed or to what extent, if precaution against harm is to be taken. Hence it is that we are unable to consider, before particular cases arise, precisely what sacrifice or compromise of interests or values we wish to make in order to reduce the risk of harm. Again, our aim of securing people against harm is indeterminate till we put it in conjunction with, or test it against, possibilities which only experience will bring before us; when it does, then we have to face a decision which will, when made, render our aim pro tanto determinate.

Consideration of these two techniques throws into relief the characteristics of those wide areas of conduct which are successfully controlled ab initio by rule, requiring specific actions, with only a fringe of open texture, instead of a variable standard. They are characterized by the fact that certain distinguishable actions, events, or states of affairs are of such practical importance to us, as things either to avert or bring about, that very few concomitant circumstances incline us to regard them differently. The crudest example of this is the killing of a human being. We are in a position to make a rule

against killing instead of laying down a variable standard ("due respect for human life"), although the circumstances in which human beings kill others are very various: this is so because very few factors appear to us to outweigh or make us revise our estimate of the importance of protecting life. Almost always killing, as it were, dominates the other factors by which it is accompanied, so when we rule it out in advance as "killing," we are not blindly prejudging issues which require to be weighed against each other. Of course there are exceptions, factors which override this usually dominant one. There is killing in self-defence and other forms of justifiable homicide. But these are few and identifiable in relatively simple terms; they are admitted as exceptions to a general rule.

It is important to notice that the dominant status of some easily identifiable action, event, or state of affairs may be, in a sense, conventional or artificial, and not due to its "natural" or "intrinsic" importance to us as human beings. It does not matter which side of the road is prescribed by the rule of the road, nor (within limits) what formalities are prescribed for the execution of a conveyance; but it does matter very much that there should be an easily identifiable and uniform procedure, and so a clear right and wrong on these matters. When this has been introduced by law the importance of adhering to it is, with few exceptions, paramount; for relatively few attendant circumstances could outweigh it and those that do may be easily identifiable as exceptions and reduced to rule. The English law of real property very clearly illustrates this aspect of rules.

The communication of general rules by authoritative examples brings with it, as we have seen, indeterminacies of a more complex kind. The acknowledgement of precedent as a criterion of legal validity means different things in different systems, and in the same system at different times. Descriptions of the English "theory" of precedent are, on certain points, still highly contentious: indeed even the key terms used in the theory, "ratio decidendi," "material facts," "interpretation," have their own penumbra of uncertainty. We shall not offer any fresh general description, but merely attempt to characterize briefly, as we have in the case of statute, the area of open texture and the creative judicial activity within it.

Any honest description of the use of precedent in English law must allow a place for the following pairs of contrasting facts. First, there is no single method of determining the rule for which a given authoritative precedent is an authority. Notwithstanding this, in the vast majority of decided cases there is very little doubt. The head-note is usually correct enough. Secondly, there is no authoritative or uniquely correct formulation of any rule to be extracted from cases. On the other hand, there is often very general agreement, when the bearing of a precedent on a later case is in issue, that a given formulation is adequate. Thirdly, whatever authoritative status a rule extracted from precedent may have, it is compatible with the exercise by courts that are bound by it of the following two types of creative or legislative activity. On the one hand courts deciding a later case may reach an opposite decision to that in a precedent by narrowing the rule extracted from the precedent, and admitting some exception to it not before considered, or, if considered, left open. This process of "distinguishing" the earlier case involves finding some legally

relevant difference between it and the present case, and the class of such differences can never be exhaustively determined. On the other hand, in following an earlier precedent the courts may discard a restriction found in the rule as formulated from the earlier case, on the ground that it is not required by any rule established by statute or earlier precedent. To do this is to widen the rule. Notwithstanding these two forms of legislative activity, left open by the binding force of precedent, the result of the English system of precedent has been to produce, by its use, a body of rules of which a vast number, of both major and minor importance, are as determinate as any statutory rule. They can now only be altered by statute, as the courts themselves often declare in cases where the 'merits' seem to run counter to the requirements of the established precedents.

The open texture of law means that there are, indeed, areas of conduct where much must be left to be developed by courts or officials striking a balance, in the light of circumstances, between competing interests which vary in weight from case to case. Nonetheless, the life of the law consists to a very large extent in the guidance both of officials and private individuals by determinate rules which, unlike the applications of variable standards, do not require from them a fresh judgment from case to case. This salient fact of social life remains true, even though uncertainties may break out as to the applicability of any rule (whether written or communicated by precedent) to a concrete case. Here at the margin of rules and in the fields left open by the theory of precedents, the courts perform a rule-producing function which administrative bodies perform centrally in the elaboration of variable standards. In a system where stare decisis is firmly acknowledged, this function of the courts is very like the exercise of delegated rule-making powers by an administrative body. In England this fact is often obscured by forms: for the courts often disclaim any such creative function and insist that the proper task of statutory interpretation and the use of precedent is, respectively, to search for the 'intention of the legislature' and the law that already exists.

QUESTIONS

1. What for Hart is the difference between "being obliged" and "being obligated"?

2. How does Hart distinguish between primary and secondary rules?

3. What defects exist in a regime of primary rules?

4. How do secondary rules remedy these defects?

5. What functions has a rule of recognition in our legal system?

6. What does Hart mean by mechanical jurisprudence?

7. What is the main point of Hart's discussion of the "vehicle in the park" case?

8. Can you explicate what Hart means by the internal point of view?

9. Can Hart accommodate Dworkin's arguments about the role of principles in legal reasoning?

10. What do you think the natural law thinkers (both old and new) might say in response to Hart's claims about the minimal natural content of law?

Chapter 3

Constructivism
Readings from Ronald Dworkin

A much discussed reservation about positivist legal theory can be traced to Lon Fuller. In an important article he argues that the legal process requires a particular kind of normative content that is given insufficient recognition in positivist accounts of law, including the version developed by H.L.A. Hart. He identifies this content in the following passage.

> We may see this . . . in the case of an employee who desires an increase in pay. If he asks his boss for a raise, he may, of course, claim a "right" to the raise. He may argue the fairness of the principles of equal treatment and call attention to the fact that Joe, who is not better than he, recently got a raise. But he does not have to rest his plea on any ground of this sort. He may merely beg for generosity, urging the needs of his family. Or he may propose an exchange, offering to take on extra duties if he gets the raise. If, however, he takes his case to an arbitrator he cannot, explicitly at least, support his case by an appeal to charity or by proposing a bargain. He will have to support his demand by a principle of some kind, and a demand supported by principle is the same thing as a claim of right.[1]

In accord with Fuller's emphasis on the normative content of law, Ronald Dworkin develops a rights-based conception of law which he intends both as a challenge and as an alternative to the rule-based conception advanced by Hart. The readings that follow deal with three fairly distinct subject matters, each of which forms an essential part of Dworkin's jurisprudential program. The first deals with his criticism of positivism in general and with Hart's version in particular. In the second selection Dworkin presents an account of the rights-determining process of reasoning that judges employ in so-called "hard cases." In his view this process can best be described by what John Rawls calls the "method of reflective equilibrium," an understanding of which is essential to the meaning of "constructivism" in legal theory. Finally we consider some passages from *Law's Empire* that explain the constructive process by drawing an analogy between legal interpretation in hard cases and joint authorship of a chain novel. In developing this analogy

---

1. Lon Fuller, "The Forms and Limits of Adjudication," 369 *Harvard Law Review*, 92 (1978).

Dworkin clarifies, among other things, how historical considerations bear upon legal interpretation and especially how associations developed over time create social and legal obligations.

~

Reading 1

From Ronald Dworkin,
TAKING RIGHTS SERIOUSLY

Positivism

I want to examine the soundness of legal positivism, particularly in the powerful form that Professor H.L.A. Hart has given to it. I choose to focus on his position, not only because of its clarity and elegance, but because here, as almost everywhere else in legal philosophy, constructive thought must start with a consideration of his views. Positivism has a few central and organizing propositions as its skeleton, and though not every philosopher who is called a positivist would subscribe to these in the way I present them, they do define the general position I want to examine. These key tenets may be stated as follows:

(a) The law of a community is a set of special rules used by the community directly or indirectly for the purpose of determining which behavior will be punished or coerced by the public power. These special rules can be identified and distinguished by specific criteria, by tests having to do not with their content but with their *pedigree* or the manner in which they were adopted or developed. These tests of pedigree can be used to distinguish valid legal rules from spurious legal rules (rules which lawyers and litigants wrongly argue are rules of law) and also from other sorts of social rules (generally lumped together as "moral rules") that the community follows but does not enforce through public power.

(b) The set of the valid legal rules is exhaustive of "the law," so that if someone's case is not clearly covered by such a rule (because there is none that seems appropriate, or those that seem appropriate are vague, or for some other reason) then that case cannot be decided by "applying the law." It must be decided by some official, like a judge, "exercising his discretion," which means reaching beyond the law for some other sort of standard to guide him in manufacturing a fresh legal rule or supplementing an old one.

(c) To say that someone has a "legal obligation" is to say that his case falls under a valid legal rule that requires him to do or to forbear from doing something. (To say he has a legal right, or has a legal power of some sort, or a legal privilege or immunity, is to assert, in a shorthand way, that others have actual or hypothetical legal obligations to act or not to act in certain ways touching him.) In the absence of such a valid legal rule there is no legal obligation; it follows that when the judge decides an issue by exercising his discretion, he is not enforcing a legal right as to that issue.

This is only the skeleton of positivism. The flesh is arranged differently by different positivists, and some even tinker with the bones. Different versions differ chiefly in their description of the fundamental test of pedigree a rule must meet to count as a rule of law. . . .

Rules, Principles and Policies

I want to make a general attack on positivism, and I shall use H.L.A. Hart's version as a target, when a particular target is needed. My strategy will be organized around the fact that when lawyers reason or dispute about legal rights and obligations, particularly in those "hard cases" when our problems with these concepts seem most acute, they make use of standards that do not function as rules, but operate differently as principles, policies, and other sorts of standards. Positivism, I shall argue, is a model of and for a system of rules, and its central notion of a single fundamental test for law forces us to miss the important roles of these standards that are not rules.

I just spoke of "principles, policies, and other sorts of standards." Most often I shall use the term "principle" generically, to refer to the whole set of these standards other than rules; occasionally, however, I shall be more precise, and distinguish between principles and policies. Although nothing in the present argument will turn on the distinction, I should state how I draw it. I call a "policy" that kind of standard that sets out a goal to be reached, generally an improvement in some economic, political, or social feature of the community (though some goals are negative, in that they stipulate that some present feature is to be protected from adverse change).

I call a "principle" a standard that is to be observed, not because it will advance or secure an economic, political, or social situation deemed desirable, but because it is a requirement of justice or fairness or some other dimension of morality. Thus the standard that automobile accidents are to be decreased is a policy, and the standard that no man may profit by his own wrong a principle. The distinction can be collapsed by construing a principle as stating a social goal (i.e., the goal of a society in which no man profits by his own wrong), or by construing a policy as stating a principle (i.e., the principle that the goal the policy embraces is a worthy one) or by adopting the utilitarian thesis that principles of justice are disguised statements of goals (securing the greatest happiness of the greatest number). In some contexts the distinction has uses which are lost if it is thus collapsed.

My immediate purpose, however, is to distinguish principles in the generic sense from rules, and I shall start by collecting some examples of the former. The examples I offer are chosen haphazardly; almost any case in a law school casebook would provide examples that would serve as well. In 1889 a New York court, in the famous case of *Riggs v. Palmer*, had to decide whether an heir named in the will of his grandfather could inherit under that will, even though he had murdered his grandfather to do so. The court began its reasoning with this admission: "It is quite true that statutes regulating the making, proof and effect of wills, and the devolution of property, if literally construed, and if their force and effect can in no way and under no circumstances be controlled or modified, give this property to the murderer." But the court continued to note that "all laws as well as all contracts may be controlled in their operation and effect by general, fundamental maxims of the common law. No one shall be permitted to profit by his own fraud, or to take advantage of his own wrong, or to found any claim upon his own iniquity, or to acquire property by his own crime." The murderer did not receive his inheritance.

In 1960, a New Jersey court was faced, in *Henningsen v. Bloomfield Motors, Inc.*, with the important question of whether (or how much) an automobile manufacturer may limit his liability in case the automobile is defective. Henningsen had bought a car, and signed a contract which said that the manufacturer's liability for defects was limited to "making good" defective parts—"this warranty being expressly in lieu of all other warranties, obligations or liabilities." Henningsen argued that, at least in the circumstances of his case, the manufacturer ought not to be protected by this limitation, and ought to be liable for the medical and other expenses of persons injured in a crash. He was not able to point to any statute, or to any established rule of law, that prevented the manufacturer from standing on the contract. The court nevertheless agreed with Henningsen. At various points in the court's argument the following appeals to standards are made: (a) "We must keep in mind the general principle that, in the absence of fraud, one who does not choose to read a contract before signing it cannot later relieve himself of its burdens." (b) "In applying that principle, the basic tenet of freedom of competent parties to contract is a factor of importance." "Freedom of contract is not such an immutable doctrine as to admit of no qualification in the area in which we are concerned." (d) "In a society such as ours, where the automobile is a common and necessary adjunct of daily life, and where its use is so fraught with danger to the driver, passengers and the public, the manufacturer is under a special obligation in connection with the construction, promotion and sale of his cars. Consequently, the courts must examine purchase agreements closely to see if consumer and public interests are treated fairly." (e) "Is there any principle which is more familiar or more firmly embedded in the history of Anglo-American law than the basic doctrine that the courts will not permit themselves to be used as instruments of inequity and injustice?" "More specifically the courts generally refuse to lend themselves to the enforcement of a 'bargain' in which one party has unjustly taken advantage of the economic necessities of the other. . . ."

The standards set out in these quotations are not the sort we think of as legal rules. They seem very different from propositions like "The maximum legal speed on the turnpike is sixty miles an hour" or "A will is invalid unless signed by three witnesses." They are different because they are legal principles rather than legal rules.

The difference between legal principles and legal rules is a logical distinction. Both sets of standards point to particular decisions about legal obligation in particular circumstances, but they differ in the character of the direction they give. Rules are applicable in an all-or-nothing fashion. If the facts a rule stipulates are given, then either the rule is valid, in which case the answer it supplies must be accepted, or it is not, in which case it contributes nothing to the decision.

This all-or-nothing is seen most plainly if we look at the way rules operate, not in law, but in some enterprise they dominate—a game, for example. In baseball a rule provides that if the batter has had three strikes, he is out. An official cannot consistently acknowledge that this is an accurate statement of a baseball rule, and decide that a batter who has had three strikes is not out. Of course, a rule may have exceptions (the batter who has taken three strikes is not out if the catcher drops the third strike). However, an accurate statement of the rule would take it into account, and any that did not would be incomplete. If the list of exceptions is very large, it would be too clumsy to repeat them each time a rule is cited—there is, however, no reason why they could not all be added on, and the more that are, the more accurate is the statement of the rule.

If we take baseball rules as a model, we find that rules of law, like the rule that a will is invalid unless signed by three witnesses, fit the model well. If the requirement of three witnesses is a valid legal rule, then it cannot be that a will has been signed by only two witnesses and is valid. The rule might have exceptions, but if it does then it is inaccurate and incomplete to state the rule so simply, without enumerating the exceptions. In theory, at least, the exceptions could all be listed, and the more of them that are, the more complete is the statement of the rule.

But this is not the way the sample principles in the quotations operate. Even those which look most like rules do not set out legal consequences that follow automatically when the conditions provided are met. We say that our law respects the principle that no man may profit from his own wrong, but we do not mean that the law never permits a man to profit from wrongs he commits. In fact, people often profit, perfectly

legally, from their legal wrongs. The most notorious case is adverse possession: if I trespass on your land long enough, some day I will gain a right to cross your land whenever I please. There are many less dramatic examples. If a man leaves one job, breaking a contract, to take a much higher paying job, he may have to pay damages to his first employer, but he is usually entitled to keep his new salary. If a man jumps bail and crosses state lines to make a brilliant investment in another state, he may be sent back to jail, but he will keep his profits.

We do not treat these—and countless other counter-instances that can easily be imagined—as showing that the principle about profiting from one's wrongs is not a principle of our legal system, or that it is incomplete and needs qualifying exceptions. We do not treat counter-instances as exceptions (at least not exceptions in the way in which a catcher's dropping the third strike is an exception) because we could not hope to capture these counter-instances simply by a more extended statement of the principle. They are not, even in theory, subject to enumeration because we would have to include not only these cases (like adverse possession) in which some institution has already provided that profit can be gained through a wrong, but also those numberless imaginary cases in which we know in advance that the principle would not hold. Listing some of these might sharpen our sense of the principle's weight (I shall mention that dimension in a moment), but it would not make for a more accurate or complete statement of the principle.

A principle like "No man may profit from his own wrong" does not even purport to set out conditions that make its application necessary. Rather, it states a reason that argues in one direction, but does not necessitate a particular decision. If a man has or is about to receive something, as a direct result of something illegal he did to get it, then that is a reason which the law will take into account in deciding whether he should keep it. There may be other principles or policies arguing in the other direction—a policy of securing title, for example, or a principle limiting punishment to what the legislature has stipulated. If so, our principle may not prevail, but that does not mean that it is not a principle of our legal system, because in the next case, when these contravening considerations are absent or less weighty, the principle may be decisive. All that is meant, when we say that a particular principle is a principle of our law, is that the principle is one which officials must take into account, if it is relevant, as a consideration inclining in one direction or another.

The logical distinction between rules and principles appears more clearly when we consider principles that do not even look like rules. Consider the proposition, set out under "(d)" in the excerpts from the *Henningsen* opinion, that "the manufacturer is under a special obligation in connection with the construction, promotion and sale of his cars." This does not even purport to define the specific duties such a special obligation entails, or to tell us what rights automobile consumers acquire as a result. It merely states—and this is an essential link in the Henningsen argument—that automobile manufacturers must be held to higher standards than other manufacturers, and are less entitled to rely on the competing principle of freedom of contract. It does not mean that they may never rely on that principle, or that courts may rewrite automobile purchase contracts at will; it

means only that if a particular clause seems unfair or burdensome, courts have less reason to enforce the clause than if it were for the purchase of neckties. The "special obligation" counts in favor, but does not in itself necessitate, a decision refusing to enforce the terms of an automobile purchase contract.

This first difference between rules and principles entails another. Principles have a dimension that rules do not—the dimension of weight or importance. When principles intersect (the policy of protecting automobile consumers intersecting with principles of freedom of contract, for example), one who must resolve the conflict has to take into account the relative weight of each. This cannot be, of course, an exact measurement, and the judgment that a particular principle or policy is more important than another will often be a controversial one. Nevertheless, it is an integral part of the concept of a principle that it has this dimension, that it makes sense to ask how important or how weighty it is.

Rules do not have this dimension. We can speak of rules as being *functionally* important or unimportant (the baseball rule that three strikes are out is more important than the rule that runners may advance on a balk, because the game would be much more changed with the first rule altered than the second). In this sense, one legal rule may be more important than another because it has a greater or more important role in regulating behavior. But we cannot say that one rule is more important than another within the system of rules, so that when two rules conflict one supersedes the other by virtue of its greater weight.

If two rules conflict, one of them cannot be a valid rule. The decision as to which is valid, and which must be abandoned or recast, must be made by appealing to considerations beyond the rules themselves. A legal system might regulate such conflicts by other rules, which prefer the rule enacted by the higher authority, or the rule enacted later, or the more specific rule, or something of that sort. A legal system may also prefer the rule supported by the more important principles. (Our own legal system uses both of these techniques.)

It is not always clear from the form of a standard whether it is a rule or a principle. "A will is invalid unless signed by three witnesses" is not very different in form from "A man may not profit from his own wrong," but one who knows something of American law knows that he must take the first as stating a rule and the second as stating a principle. In many cases the distinction is difficult to make—it may not have been settled how the standard should operate, and this issue may itself be a focus of controversy. The first amendment to the United States Constitution contains the provision that Congress shall not abridge freedom of speech. Is this a rule, so that if a particular law does abridge freedom of speech, it follows that it is unconstitutional? Those who claim that the first amendment is "an absolute" say that it must be taken in this way, that is, as a rule. Or does it merely state a principle, so that when an abridgement of speech is discovered, it is unconstitutional unless the context presents some other policy or principle which in the circumstances is weighty enough to permit the abridgement? That is the position of those who argue for what is called the "clear and present danger" test or some other form of "balancing."

Sometimes a rule and a principle can play much the same role, and the differ-ence between them is almost a matter of form alone. The first section of the Sherman Act states that every contract in restraint of trade shall be void. The Supreme Court had to make the decision whether this provision should be treated as a rule in its own terms (striking down every contract "which restrains trade," which almost any contract does) or as a principle, providing a reason for striking down a contract in the absence of effective contrary policies. The Court construed the provision as a rule, but treated that rule as containing the word "unreasonable," and as prohibiting only "unreasonable" restraints of trade. This allowed the provision to function logically as a rule (whenever a court finds that the restraint is "unreasonable" it is bound to hold the contract invalid) and substantially as a principle (a court must take into account a variety of other principles and policies in determining whether a particular restraint in particular economic circumstances is "unreasonable").

Words like "reasonable," "negligent," "unjust," and "significant" often perform just this function. Each of these terms makes the application of the rule which contains it depend to some extent upon principles or policies lying beyond the rule, and in this way makes that rule itself more like a principle. But they do not quite turn the rule into a principle, because even the least confining of these terms restricts the kind of other principles and policies on which the rule depends. If we are bound by a rule that says that "unreasonable" contracts are void, or that grossly "unfair" contracts will not be enforced, much more judgment is required than if the quoted terms were omitted. But suppose a case in which some consideration of policy or principle suggests that a contract should be enforced even though its restraint is not reasonable, or even though it is grossly unfair. Enforcing these contracts would be forbidden by our rules, and thus permitted only if these rules were abandoned or modified. If we were dealing, however, not with a rule but with a policy against enforcing unreasonable contracts, or a principle that unfair contracts ought not to be enforced, the contracts could be enforced without alteration of the law.

Principles and the Concept of Law

Once we identify legal principles as separate sorts of standards, different from legal rules, we are suddenly aware of them all around us. Law teachers teach them, law books cite them, legal historians celebrate them. But they seem most energetically at work, carrying most weight, in difficult lawsuits like *Riggs* and *Henningsen*. In cases like these, principles play an essential part in arguments supporting judgments about particular legal rights and obligations. After the case is decided, we may say that the case stands for a particular rule (e.g., the rule that one who murders is not eligible to take under the will of his victim). But the rule does not exist before the case is decided; the court cites principles as its justification for adopting and applying a new rule.

Discretion

. . . Sometimes we use "discretion" in a weak sense, simply to say that for some reason the standards an official must apply cannot be applied mechanically but demand the use of judgment. We use this weak sense when the context does not already make that clear, when the background our audience assumes does not contain that piece of information. Thus we might say, "The sergeant's orders left him a great deal of discretion," to those who do not know what the sergeant's orders were or who do not know something that made those orders vague or hard to carry out. It would make perfect sense to add, by way of amplification, that the lieutenant had ordered the sergeant to take his five most experienced men on patrol but that it was hard to determine which were the most experienced.

Sometimes we use the term in a different weak sense, to say only that some official has final authority to make a decision and cannot be reviewed and reversed by any other official. We speak this way when the official is part of a hierarchy of officials structured so that some have higher authority but in which the patterns of authority are different for different classes of decision. Thus we might say that in baseball certain decisions, like the decision whether the ball or the runner reached second base first, are left to the discretion of the second base umpire, if we mean that on this issue the head umpire has no power to substitute his own judgment if he disagrees.

I call both of these senses weak to distinguish them from a stronger sense. We use "discretion" sometimes not merely to say that an official must use judgment in applying the standards set him by authority, or that no one will review that exercise of judgment, but to say that on some issue he is simply not bound by standards set by the authority in question. In this sense we say that a sergeant has discretion who has been told to pick any five men for patrol he chooses or that a judge in a dog show has discretion to judge airedales before boxers if the rules do not stipulate an order of events. We use this sense not to comment on the vagueness or difficulty of the standards, or on who has the final word in applying them, but on their range and the decisions they purport to control. If the sergeant is told to take the five most experienced men, he does not have discretion in this strong sense because that order purports to govern his decision. The boxing referee who must decide which fighter has been the more aggressive does not have discretion, in the strong sense, for the same reason.

If anyone said that the sergeant or the referee had discretion in these cases, we should have to understand him, if the context permitted, as using the term in one of the weak senses. Suppose, for example, the lieutenant ordered the sergeant to select the five men he deemed most experienced, and then added that the sergeant had discretion to choose them. Or the rules provided that the referee should award the round to the more aggressive fighter, with discretion in selecting him. We should have to understand these statements in the second weak sense, as speaking to the question of review of the decision. The first weak sense—that the decisions take judgment—would be otiose, and the third, strong sense is excluded by the statements themselves.

We must avoid one tempting confusion. The strong sense of discretion is not tantamount to license, and does not exclude criticism. Almost any situation in which a person acts (including those in which there is no question of decision under special authority, and so no question of discretion) makes relevant certain standards of rationality, fairness, and ef-

fectiveness. We criticize each other's acts in terms of these standards, and there is no reason not to do so when the acts are within the center rather than beyond the perimeter of the doughnut of special authority. So we can say that the sergeant who was given discretion (in the strong sense) to pick a patrol did so stupidly or maliciously or carelessly, or that the judge who had discretion in the order of viewing dogs made a mistake because he took boxers first although there were only three airedales and many more boxers. An official's discretion means not that he is free to decide without recourse to standards of sense and fairness, but only that his decision is not controlled by a standard furnished by the particular authority we have in mind when we raise the question of discretion. Of course this latter sort of freedom is important; that is why we have the strong sense of discretion. Someone who has discretion in this third sense can be criticized, but not for being disobedient, as in the case of the soldier. He can be said to have made a mistake, but not to have deprived a participant of a decision to which he was entitled, as in the case of a sports official or contest judge. . . .

I conclude that if we treat principles as law we must reject the positivist' first tenet, that the law of a community is distinguished from other social standards by some test in the form of a master rule. We have already decided that we must then abandon the second tenet, the doctrine of judicial discretion—or clarify it into triviality. What of the third tenet, the positivist' theory of legal obligation?

This theory holds that a legal obligation exists when (and only when) an established rule of law imposes such an obligation. It follows from this that in a hard case—when no such established rule can be found—there is no legal obligation until the judge creates a new rule for the future. The judge may apply that new rule to the parties in the case, but this is *ex post facto* legislation, not the enforcement of an existing obligation.

The positivist' doctrine of discretion (in the strong sense) required this view of legal obligation, because if a judge has discretion there can be no legal right or obligation—no entitlement—that he must enforce. Once we abandon that doctrine, however, and treat principles as law, we raise the possibility that a legal obligation might be imposed by a constellation of principles as well as by an established rule. We might want to say that a legal obligation exists whenever the case supporting such an obligation, in terms of binding legal principles of different sorts, is stronger than the case against it.

Of course, many questions would have to be answered before we could accept that view of legal obligation. If there is no rule of recognition, no test for law in that sense, how do we decide which principles are to count, and how much,

in making such a case? How do we decide whether one case is better than another? If legal obligation rests on an undemonstrable judgment of that sort, how can it provide a justification for a judicial decision that one party had a legal obligation? Does this view of obligation square with the way lawyers, judges and laymen speak, and is it consistent with our attitudes about moral obligation? Does this analysis help us to deal with the classical jurisprudential puzzles about the nature of law?

These questions must be faced, but even the questions promise more than Positivism provides. Positivism, on its own thesis, stops short of just those puzzling, hard cases that send us to look for theories of law. When we read these cases, the positivist remits us to a doctrine of discretion that leads nowhere and tells nothing. His picture of law as a system of rules has exercised a tenacious hold on our imagination, perhaps through its very simplicity. If we shake ourselves loose from this model of rules, we may be able to build a model truer to the complexity and sophistication of our own practices.

If principles can be shown to be legitimate sources of legal obligation generally and claims to right in particular, an obvious question is: How is our knowledge of principles acquired? As a first approximation Dworkin's answer to this question takes shape in *Taking Rights Seriously* where he argues that concepts of legal validity and what can be legally justified enter the process of adjudication through what he calls "conceptions" of justice. He acknowledges that in this early work his account of a conception is largely intuitive and less than clear and complete: "Earlier in this book I described a special kind of intellectual activity, which I called defending a particular conception of a concept. I do not pretend to have yet given an adequate or even a clear account of that activity. . . ."[2]

---

2. Ronald Dworkin, *Taking Rights Seriously* (Cambridge, Mass.: Harvard University Press, 1977), p. 315.

Notwithstanding its incompleteness, Dworkin's early discussion of "conceptions" plays an important role in his more mature account of adjudication. The substance of his argument in *Taking Rights Seriously* is expressed in the form of a thought-experiment. Imagine, he says, that a chess referee is faced with the problem of ruling on the behavior of a grandmaster of chess, one Cal, who continually smiles at his opponent, Fischer, in an important match. The referee must decide whether Cal's behavior counts as "unreasonable annoyance" under the forfeiture rule. If so, Fischer has a right to the match; otherwise Cal has a right to continue smiling, to the annoyance of Fischer.

Cal's decision, Dworkin reasons, is an example of decision under the condition of indeterminacy: "unreasonable annoyance," is open to various construals. For Dworkin deciding whether what Cal has done constitutes unreasonable annoyance under the forfeiture rule, the referee's main concern will not be with rules exclusively or even primarily, but rather with the "character" or "conception" or "theory" of the game. For example, since chess is intellectual in character, the referee might ask: what role does psychological intimidation play in chess compared with poker? Taking into account such considerations the referee's mind will "oscillate between the philosophy of mind and facts of the institution which he must elucidate." Dworkin is cognizant the fact that the referee might differ with other referees in his interpretation of "unreasonably annoying an opponent" but he cautions against the idea that he is exercising "discretion." Rather we must recognize that the referee's behavior is constrained as much as if it were determined by a prescriptive rule like "three strikes and you are out." What provides the constraint is the referee's theory or conception of the character of the game.

> Any official's sense of the game will have developed over a career, and he will employ rather than expose that sense in his judgments. (My) reconstruction enables us to see how the concept of the game's character is tailored to a special institutional problem. Once an autonomous institution is established, such that participants have institutional rights under distinct rules belonging to that institution, then hard cases may arise that must, in the nature of the case, be supposed to have an answer. If Cal does not have a right that the game be continued, it must be because the forfeiture rule, properly understood, justifies the referee's intervention. If it does, then Fischer has a right to win at once. It is not useful to speak of the referee's "discretion" in such a case. If some weak sense of discretion is meant, then the remark is unhelpful; if some strong sense is meant, such that Cal no longer has a right to win, then this must be, again, because the rule properly understood destroys the right he would otherwise have.[3]

Several points in this passage merit comment. First, Dworkin claims that the referee is not at liberty to decide this issue *merely* as he sees fit, that is,

---

3. *Id*. at 104.

subjectively. Second, he says that if Fischer has a right to win it is because the forfeiture rule, properly understood, *justifies* the referee's intervention. He says that competent referees from *different* chess cultures (say France or China) might construct equally impressive but different interpretations of "reasonable annoyance" which would produce *different outcomes* if applied to a single case. There is no way, he says, to determine the "soundest theory of reasonable annoyance" across chess cultures.

He emphasizes, however, that chess referees, like judges, perform their function in one culture at a time: there is, he notes, even a distinctive international chess culture. Dworkin's point is that within a *given* or established chess culture there is in principle a correct outcome for decisions such as the one the referee in this case must make. What controls the correct outcome is an adquate *conception* of the game. The same account of decision-making applies to law: "I insist that the process of adjudication, even in hard cases, can sensibly be aimed at discovering, rather than inventing, the rights of the parties concerned, and that the political justification of the process depends upon the soundness of that characterization."[4] He rejects the idea that judges have "discretion" in the sense that they are free to invent the outcome of a case. This would make legal outcomes subjective and arbitrary in a way he could not accept.

It seems clear that much is riding on Dworkin's idea that referees in chess and judges in law need to possess adequate "conceptions." But (1) what, more exactly, are conceptions? In the passage just cited Dworkin makes it clear that they are acquired through extensive experience. And more importantly, (2) how can we determine whether a conception—"reasonable annoyance," for example—is an adequate or correct conception? Dworkin answers these questions roughly as follows: (1) If we want to identify a conception we must look to how persons regard situations of a certain type: how they think about reasonable annoyance, for example. To have a conception is to have a way of *constructing* things of that sort in one's mind and thinking about or *interpreting* them. With respect to the adequacy of a conception Dworkin notes that people who engage in various practices like chess and law find that they often *agree* on what constitutes reasonable annoyance or "justice" in certain situations. It is not the case, of course, that they have interpretive agreement in all situations, but they do tend to agree about many situations, especially paradigm cases of one sort and another.

Following this general line of thought, Dworkin attempts to explain how judges reason about situations that are *not* paradigm cases—not situations about which interpretive agreement is not ready to hand. In these situations of this sort, we begin with *what can be agreed upon*, with paradigm cases and the like, and we *construct* or *build upon* this foundation. At this point, that is, the point of explaining how to proceed under conditions of uncertainty about what constitutes an "adequate" or "correct" conception, Dworkin draws on a technique described by John Rawls: the "method of reflective equilibrium."

---

4. *Id.* at 280.

In Reading 2, Dworkin discusses this technique and how it might be employed to explain how judges reason in hard cases. We should keep clearly in mind the purpose of reference to this Rawlsian technique: Dworkin is attempting to answer the question: How do we build an adequate or correct conception out of only fragmentary agreement in legal interpretation, that is, agreement about paradigm cases but not about this particular case?

Reading 2

From Ronald Dworkin,
TAKING RIGHTS SERIOUSLY

The technique [of reflective equilibrium] assumes that . . . readers have a sense, which we draw upon in our daily life, that certain particular political arrangements or decisions, like conventional trials, are just and others, like slavery, are unjust. It assumes, moreover, that we are each able to arrange these immediate intuitions or convictions in an order that designates some of them as more certain than others. Most people, for example, think that it is more plainly unjust for the state to execute innocent citizens of its own than to kill innocent foreign civilians in war. They might be prepared to abandon their position on foreign civilians in war, on the basis of some argument, but they would be much more reluctant to abandon their view on executing innocent countrymen.

It is the task of moral philosophy, according to the technique of equilibrium, to provide a structure of principles that supports these immediate convictions about which we are more or less secure, with two goals in mind. First, this structure of principles must explain the convictions by showing the underlying assumptions they reflect; second it must provide guidance—in those cases about which we have either no convictions or weak or contradictory convictions. If we are unsure, for example, whether economic institutions that allow great disparity of wealth are unjust, we may turn to the principles that explain our confident convictions, and then apply these principles to that difficult issue.

But the process is not simply one of finding principles that accommodate our more-or-less settled judgments. These principles must support, and not merely account for, our judgments, and this means that the principles must have independent appeal to our moral sense. It might be, for example, that a cluster of familiar moral convictions could be shown to serve an undeserving policy— perhaps, that the standard judgments we make without reflection serve the purpose of maintaining one particular class in political power. But this discovery would not vouch for the principle of class egoism; on the contrary, it would discredit our ordinary judgments, unless some other principle of a more respectable sort could be found that also fits our intuitions, in which case it would be this principle and not the class-interest principle that our intuitions would recommend.

It might be that no coherent set of principles could be found that has independent appeal and that supports the full set of our immediate convictions; indeed it would be surprising if this were not often the case. If that does happen, we must compromise, giving way on both sides. We might relax, though we could not abandon, our initial sense of what might be an acceptable principle. We might come to accept, for example, after further reflection, some principle that seemed to us initially unattractive, perhaps the principle that men should sometimes be made to be free. We might accept this principle if we were satisfied that no less harsh principle could support the set of political convictions we were especially reluctant to abandon. On the other hand, we must also be ready to modify or adjust, or even to give up entirely, immediate convictions that cannot be accommodated by any principle that meets our relaxed standards; in adjusting these immediate convictions we will use our initial sense of which seem to us more and which less certain, though in principle no immediate conviction can be taken as immune from reinspection or abandonment if that should prove necessary. We can expect to proceed back and forth between our immediate judgments and the structure of explanatory principles in this way, tinkering first with one side and then the other, until we arrive at what Rawls calls the state of reflective equilibrium in which we are satisfied, or as much satisfied as we can reasonably expect.

~

In the next reading Dworkin explores the philosophical underpinnings of the method of reflective equilibrium. He makes clear (1) that the assumptions and beliefs associated with its employment are inconsistent with belief in moral realism of any sort and (2) that in this respect his conception of the nature of law can be distinguished from classical natural law theory. In his view the moral intuitions about which there is agreement in "hard cases" are fragmentary at best. The procedure of reflective equilibrium assumes, however, that all things considered they are not fragmentary but coherent: the technique of reflective equilibrium, he says, relies on a "coherence theory of morality." There are, however, two very different ways of understanding this coherence: the natural model and the constructivist model. Dworkin's discussion of these in the passage below represents one of the clearest statements in the literature of the difference *in type* between classical natural law jurisprudence and constructivism.

~

Reading 3

From Ronald Dworkin, *TAKING RIGHTS SERIOUSLY*

I shall start by considering the philosophical basis of the technique of equilibrium I just described. I must spend several pages in this way, but it is important to understand what substantive features of Rawls's deep theory are required by his method. This technique presupposes, as I said, a familiar fact about our moral lives. We all entertain beliefs about justice that we hold because they seem right, not because we have deduced or inferred them from other beliefs. We may believe in this way, for example, that slavery is unjust, and that the standard sort of trial is fair.

These different sorts of beliefs are, according to some philosophers, direct perceptions of some independent and objective moral facts. In the view of other philosophers they are simply subjective preferences, not unlike ordinary tastes, but dressed up in the language of justice to indicate how important they seem to us. In any event, when we argue with ourselves or each other about justice we use these accustomed beliefs—which we call "intuitions" or "convictions"—in roughly the way Rawls's equilibrium technique suggests. We test general theories about justice against our own intuitions, and we try to confound those who disagree with us by showing how their own intuitions embarrass their own theories.

Suppose we try to justify this process by setting out a philosophical position about the connection between moral theory and moral intuition. The technique of equilibrium supposes what might be called a "coherence" theory of morality. But we have a choice between two general models that define coherence and explain why it is required, and the choice between these is significant and consequential for our moral philosophy. I shall describe these two models, and then argue that the equilibrium technique makes sense on one but not the other.

I call the first a "natural" model. It presupposes a philosophical position that can be summarized in this way. Theories of justice, like Rawls's, describe an objective moral reality; they are not, that is, cre-

ated by men or societies but are rather discovered by them, as they discover laws of physics. The main instrument of this discovery is a moral faculty possessed by at least some men, which produces concrete intuitions of political morality in particular situations, like the intuition that slavery is wrong. These intuitions are clues to the nature and existence of more abstract and fundamental moral principles, as physical observations are clues to the existence and nature of fundamental physical laws. Moral reasoning or philosophy is a process of reconstructing the fundamental principles by assembling concrete judgments in the right order, as a natural historian reconstructs the shape of the whole animal from the fragments of its bones that he has found.

The second model is quite different. It treats intuitions of justice not as clues to the existence of independent principles, but rather as stipulated features of a general theory to be constructed. . . . This "constructive" model does not assume, as the natural model does, that principles of justice have some fixed, objective existence, so that descriptions of these principles must be true or false in some standard way. It does not assume that the animal it matches to the bones actually exists. It makes the different, and in some ways more complex, assumption that men and women have a responsibility to fit the particular judgments on which they act into a coherent program of action, or, at least, that officials who exercise power over other men have that sort of responsibility.

This second, constructive, model is not unfamiliar to lawyers. It is analogous to one model of common law adjudication. Suppose a judge is faced with a novel claim—for example, a claim for damages based on a legal right to privacy that courts have not heretofore recognized. He must examine such precedents as seem in any way relevant to see whether any principles that are, as we might say, "instinct" in these precedents bear upon the claimed right to privacy. We might treat this judge as being in the position of a man arguing from moral intuitions to a general moral theory. The particular precedents are analogous to intuitions; the judge tries to reach an accommodation between these precedents and a set of principles that might justify them and also justify further decisions that go beyond them. He does not suppose, however, that the precedents are glimpses into a moral reality, and therefore clues to objective principles he ends by declaring. He does not believe that the principles are "instinct" in the precedents in that sense. Instead, in the spirit of the constructive model, he accepts these precedents as specifications for a principle that he must construct, out of a sense of responsibility for consistency with what has gone before.

I want to underline the important difference between the two models. Suppose that an official holds, with reasonable conviction, some intuition that cannot be reconciled with his other intuitions by any set of principles he can now fashion. He may think, for example, that it is unjust to punish an attempted murder as severely as a successful one, and yet be unable to reconcile that position with his sense that a man's guilt is properly assessed by considering only what he intended, and not what actually happened. Or he may think that a particular minority race, as such, is entitled to special protection, and be unable to reconcile that view with his view that distinctions based on race are inherently unfair to individuals. When an official is in this position the two models give him different advice.

The natural model supports a policy of following the troublesome intuition and submerging the apparent contradiction, in the faith that a more sophisticated set of principles, which reconciles that intuition does in fact exist though it has not been discovered. The official, according to this model, is in the position of the astronomer who has clear observational data that he is as yet unable to reconcile in any coherent account, for example, of the origin of the solar system. He continues to accept and employ his observational data, placing his faith in the idea that some reconciling explanation does exist though it has not been, and for all he knows may never be, discovered by men.

The natural model supports this policy because it is based on a philosophical position that encourages the analogy between moral intuitions and observational data. It makes perfect sense, on that assumption, to suppose that direct observations, made through a moral faculty, have outstripped the explanatory powers of those who observe. It also makes sense to suppose that some correct explanation, in the shape of principles of morality, does in fact exist in spite of this failure; if the direct observations are sound, some explanation must exist for why matters are as they have been observed to be on the moral universe, just as some explanation must exist for why matters are as they have been observed to be in the physical universe.

The constructive model, however, does not support the policy of submerging apparent inconsistency in the faith that reconciling principles must exist. On the contrary, it demands that decisions taken in the name of justice must never outstrip an official's ability to account for these decisions in a theory of justice, even when such a theory must compromise some of his intuitions. It demands that we act on principle rather than on faith.

Its engine is a doctrine of responsibility that requires men to integrate their intuitions and subordinate some of these, when necessary, to that responsibility. It presupposes that articulated consistency, decisions in accordance with a program that can be made public and followed until changed, is essential to any conception of justice. An official in the position I describe, guided by this model, must give up his apparently inconsistent position; he must do so even if he hopes one day, by further reflection, to devise better principles that will allow all his initial convictions to stand as principles.

The constructive model does not presuppose skepticism or relativism. On the contrary, it assumes that the men and women who reason within the model will each hold sincerely the convictions they bring to it, and that this sincerity will extend to criticizing as unjust political acts or systems that offend the most profound of these. The model does not deny, any more than it affirms, the objective standing of any of these convictions; it is therefore consistent with, though as a model of reasoning it does not require, the moral ontology that the natural model presupposes.

It does not require that ontology because its requirements are independent of it. The natural model insists on consistency with conviction, on the assumption that moral intuitions are accurate observations; the requirement of consistency follows from that assumption. The constructive model insists on consistency with conviction as an independent requirement, flowing not from the assumption that these convictions are accurate reports, but from the different assumption that it is unfair for officials to act except on the basis of a general public theory that will constrain them to consistency, provide a public standard for testing or debating or predicting what they do, and not allow appeals to unique intuitions that might mask prejudice or self-interest in particular cases. The constructive model requires coherence, then, for independent reasons of political morality; it takes convictions held with the requisite sincerity as given, and seeks to impose conditions on the acts that these intuitions might be said to warrant. If the constructive model is to constitute morality, in either of the senses I have distinguished, these independent reasons of political morality are at the heart of our political theories.

The two models, therefore, represent different standpoints from which theories of justice might be developed. The natural model, we might say, looks at intuitions from the personal standpoint of the individual who holds them, and who takes them to be discrete observations of moral reality. The constructive model looks at these intuitions from a more public standpoint; it is a model that someone might propose for the governance of a community each of whose members has strong convictions that differ, though not too greatly, from the convictions of others.

The constructive model is appealing, from this public standpoint, for an additional reason. It is well suited to group consideration of problems of justice, that is, to developing a theory that can be said to be the theory of a community rather than of particular individuals, and this is an enterprise that is important, for example, in adjudication. The range of initial convictions to be assessed can be expanded or contracted to accommodate the intuitions of a larger or smaller group, either by including all convictions held by any members, or by excluding those not held by all, as the particular calculation might warrant. This process would be self-destructive on the natural model, because every individual would believe that either false observations were being taken into account or accurate observations disregarded, and hence that the inference to objective morality was invalid. But on the constructive model that objection would be unavailable; the model, so applied, would be appropriate to identify the program of justice that best accommodates the community's common convictions, for example, with no claim to a description of an objective moral universe.

The passages above make clear two basic elements in Dworkin's conception of law: (1) In concert with "legal process" theorists like Lon Fuller he holds that the process of adjudication has a unity and structure provided by legal and moral principles, and (2) he understands the technique of reflective equilibrium as a method of determining choice among and application of these principles. Concepts of legal validity and justification thus enter the process of adjudication through *conceptions* or *theories* of justice, that is, as constructive interpretations, not as moral discoveries about which there can be universal agreement.

Reading 4 introduces a third major feature of Dworkin's constructivism: its incorporation of historical factors into the process of determining legal obligations. In the passage below from *Law's Empire,* he argues that at least some of the legal rights of parties to a case involve what he calls "associative or communal obligations," and he explores how it is that communal associations like friendship, for example, entail obligations that are formed not by one act of deliberate contractual commitment, the way one joins a club, but by development through a series of choices and events that are "never seen, one by one, as carrying a commitment."

In reading this passage it is well to keep in mind that most moral theory, including classical natural law theory, appeals to a test of morality in which history plays no essential role. According to Cicero and Grotius, for example, what is good for persons is good for all persons *wherever and whenever* they exist. Similarly, for a utilitarian like Jeremy Bentham, what is good is what produces the greater balance of happiness over unhappiness, *whenever and wherever* people exist. Dworkin's contribution to our understanding of the temporal dimension of justification in law is one of the most noteworthy features of his constructivism.

Reading 4

From Ronald Dworkin, *LAW'S EMPIRE*

We have friends to whom we owe obligations in virtue of a shared history, but it would be perverse to describe this as a history of *assuming* obligations. On the contrary, it is a history of events and acts that attract obligations, and we are rarely even aware that we are entering upon any special status as the story unfolds. People become self-conscious about the obligations of friendship in the normal case only when some situation requires them to honor these obligations, or when they have grown weary of or embarrassed by the friendship, and then it is too late to reject them without betrayal. Other forms of association that carry special responsibilities, of academic colleagueship, for example, are even less a matter of free choice: someone can become my colleague even though I voted against his appointment. And the obligations some members of a family owe to others, which many people count among the strongest fraternal obligations of all, are matters of the least choice. . . .

We have a duty to honor our responsibilities under social practices that define groups and attach special responsibilities to membership, but this natural duty holds only when certain other conditions are met or sustained. Reciprocity is prominent among these other conditions. I have special responsibilities to my brother in virtue of our brotherhood, but these are sensitive to the degree to which he accepts such responsibilities toward me; my responsibilities to those who claim that we are friends or lovers or neighbors or colleagues or countrymen are equally contingent on reciprocity. But we must be careful here: if associative concepts are interpretive—if it can be an open question among friends what friendship requires—then the reciprocity we demand cannot be a matter of each doing for the other what the latter thinks friendship concretely requires. Then friendship would be possible only between people who shared a detailed conception of friendship and would become automatically more contractual and deliberative than it is, more a matter

of people checking in advance to see whether their conceptions matched well enough to allow them to be friends.

The reciprocity we require for associative obligations must be more abstract, more a question of accepting a kind of responsibility we need the companion ideas of integrity and interpretation to explain. Friends have a responsibility to treat one another as friends, and that means, put subjectively, that each must act out of a conception of friendship he is ready to recognize as vulnerable to an interpretive test, as open to the objection that this is not a plausible account of what friendship means in our culture. Friends or family or neighbors need not agree in detail about the responsibilities attached to these forms of organization. Associative obligations can be sustained among people who share a general and diffuse sense of members' special rights and responsibilities from or toward one another, a sense of what sort and level of sacrifice one may be expected to make for another. I may think friendship, properly understood, requires that I break promises to others to help a friend in need, and I will not refuse to do this for a friend just because he does not share this conviction and would not do it for me. But I will count him a friend and feel this obligation only if I believe he has roughly the same concern for me as I thereby show for him, that he would make important sacrifices for me of some other sort.

Nevertheless, the members of a group must by and large hold certain attitudes about the responsibilities they owe one another if these responsibilities are to count as genuine fraternal obligations. First, they must regard the group's obligations as *special,* holding distinctly within the group, rather than as general duties its members owe equally to persons outside it. Second, they must accept that these responsibilities are *personal:* that they run directly from each member to each other member, not just to the group as a whole in some collective sense. My brother or my colleague may think he has responsibilities to the reputation of the family or the university he best acquits by concentrating on his own career and thus denying me help when I need it or company when I want it. He may be right about the best use of his time overall from the standpoint of the general good of these particular communities. But his conduct does not form the necessary basis for my continuing to recognize fraternal obligations toward him.

Third, members must see these responsibilities as flowing from a more general responsibility each has of concern for the well-being of others in the group; they must treat discrete obligations that arise only under special circumstances, like the obligation to help a friend who is in great financial need, as derivative from and expressing a more general responsibility active throughout the association in different ways. A commercial partnership or joint enterprise, conceived as a fraternal association, is in that way different from even a long-standing contractual relationship. The former has a life of its own: each partner is concerned not just to keep agreements hammered out at arm's length but to approach each issue that arises in their joint commercial life in a manner reflecting special concern for his partner as partner. Different forms of association presuppose different kinds of general concern each member is assumed to have for others. The level of concern is different—I need not act toward my partner as if I thought his welfare as important as my son's—and also its range: my concern

for my union "brother" is general across the economic and productive life we share but does not extend to his success in social life, as my concern for my biological brother does. (Of course my union colleague may be my friend as well, in which case my overall responsibilities to him will be aggregative and complex.) But within the form or mode of life constituted by a communal practice, the concern must be general and must provide the foundation for the more discrete responsibilities.

Fourth, members must suppose that the group's practices show not only concern but an equal concern for all members. Fraternal associations are in that sense conceptually egalitarian. They may be structured, even hierarchical, in the way a family is, but the structure and hierarchy must reflect the group's assumption that its roles and rules are equally in the interests of all, that no one's life is more important than anyone else's. Armies may be fraternal organizations if that condition is met. But caste systems that count some members as inherently less worthy than others are not fraternal and yield no communal responsibilities.

We must be careful to distinguish, then, between a "bare" community, a community that meets the genetic or geographical or other historical conditions identified by social practice as capable of constituting a fraternal community, and a "true" community, a bare community whose practices of group responsibility meet the four conditions just identified. The responsibilities a true community deploys are special and individualized and display a pervasive mutual concern that fits a plausible conception of equal concern. These are not psychological conditions. Though a group will rarely meet or long sustain them unless its members by and large actually feel some emotional bond with one another, the conditions do not themselves demand this. The concern they require is an interpretive property of the group's practices of asserting and acknowledging responsibities—these must be practices that people with the right level of concern would adopt—not a psychological property of some fixed number of the actual members. So, contrary to the assumption that seemed to argue against assimilating political to associative obligations, associative communities can be larger and more anonymous than they could be if it were a necessary condition that each member love all others, or even that they know them or know who they are.

Nor does anything in the four conditions contradict our initial premise that obligations of fraternity need not be fully voluntary. If the conditions are met, people in the bare community have the obligations of a true community whether or not they want them, though of course the conditions will not be met unless most members recognize and honor these obligations. It is therefore essential to insist that true communities must be bare communities as well. People cannot be made involuntary "honorary" members of a community to which they do not even "barely" belong just because earlier members are disposed to treat them as such. I would not become a citizen of Fiji if people there decided for some reason to treat me as one of them. Nor am I the friend of a stranger sitting next to me on a plane just because he decides he is a friend of mine. . . .

An important reservation must be made to the argument so far. Even genuine communities that meet the several conditions just described may be unjust or promote injustice. . . . Genuine communal obligations may be unjust in two ways. First, they may be unjust to the members of the group: the conception of equal concern they reflect, though sincere, may be defective. It may be a firm tradition of family organization in some community, for example, that equal concern for daughters and sons requires parents to exercise a kind of dominion over one relaxed for the other. Second, they may be unjust to people who are not members of the group. Social practice may define a racial or religious group as associative, and that group may require its members to discriminate against nonmembers socially or in employment or generally. If the consequences for strangers to the group are grave, as they will be if the discriminating group is large or powerful within a larger community, this will be unjust. In many cases, requiring that sort of discrimination will conflict, not just with duties of abstract justice the group's members owe everyone else, but also with associative obligations they have because they belong to larger or different associative communities. For if those who do not belong to my race or religion are my neighbors or colleagues or (now I anticipate the argument to follow) my fellow citizens, the question arises whether I do not have responsibilities to them, flowing from those associations, that I ignore in deferring to the responsibilities claimed by my racial or religious group.

In order to further explain associative obligations Dworkin says that two "companion ideas" are required: the idea of "interpretation" and the idea of "integrity." The four previous readings have been concerned with

Dworkin's understanding of constructive interpretation; in the reading to follow he sets out a more complete integration of his ideas about interpretation with the notion that morality in law has an irreducibly temporal dimension. The concept through which this integration takes place is the concept of integrity. Reading 5 begins with some general remarks on this subject and follows these with discussion of what it means for a legal interpretation to have integrity: his central claim in this regard is that interpretive integrity in law depends on history. One of the most striking features of this reading is its employment of an analogy between legal interpretation and the work of writers who compose a chain novel. The usefulness of this analogy for Dworkin's purposes derives from the way in which chain novel composition must incorporate a wide variety of concerns—with aesthetic principles, psychological principles, and moral principles, for example—in a context of composition constrained and in certain ways determined by history, that is, by the work of other authors.

~

Reading 5

From Ronald Dworkin,
LAW'S EMPIRE

Law as integrity denies that statements of law are either the backward-looking factual reports of conventionalism or the forward-looking instrumental programs of legal pragmatism. It insists that legal claims are interpretive judgments and therefore combine backward and forward-looking elements; they interpret contemporary legal practice seen as an unfolding political narrative. So law as integrity rejects as unhelpful the ancient question whether judges find or invent law; we understand legal reasoning, it suggests, only by seeing the sense in which they do both and neither.

The adjudicative principle of integrity instructs judges to identify legal rights and duties, so far as possible, on the assumption that they were all created by a single author—the community personified—expressing a coherent conception of justice and fairness. We form our . . . view of what rights and duties flow from past political decisions by restating this instruction as a thesis about the grounds of law. According to law as integrity, propositions of law are true if they figure in or follow from the principles of justice, fairness, and procedural due process that provide the best constructive interpretation of the community's legal practice. . . .

Law as integrity is therefore more relentlessly interpretive than either conventionalism or pragmatism. These latter theories offer themselves as interpretations. They are conceptions of law that claim to show our legal practices in the best light these can bear, and they recommend . . . distinct styles or programs for adjudication. But the programs they recommend are not themselves programs of interpretation: they do not ask judges deciding hard cases to carry out any further, essentially interpretive study of legal doctrine. Conventionalism requires judges to study law reports and parliamentary records to discover what decisions have been made by institutions conventionally recognized to have legislative power. No doubt interpretive issues will arise in that process: for example, it may be necessary to interpret a text to decide what statutes our legal conventions construct from it. But once a judge has accepted conventionalism as his guide, he has no further occasion for interpreting the legal record as a whole in deciding particular cases. Pragmatism requires judges to think instrumentally about the best rules for the future. That exercise may require interpretation of something beyond legal material: a utilitarian pragmatist may need to worry about the best way to understand the idea of community welfare, for example. But once again, a judge who accepts pragmatism is then done with interpreting legal practice as a whole.

Law as integrity is different: it is both the product of and the inspiration for comprehensive interpretation of legal practice. The program it holds out to judges deciding hard cases is essentially, not just contingently, interpretive; law as integrity asks them to continue interpreting the same material that it claims to have successfully interpreted itself. It offers itself as continuous with—the initial part of—the more detailed interpretations it recommends. We must therefore now return to the general study of interpretation. . . . We must continue the account given there of what interpretation is and when it is done well, but in more detail and directed more to the special interpretive challenge put to judges and others who must say what the law is.

History matters in law as integrity: very much but only in a certain way. Integrity does not require consistency in principle over all historical stages of a community's law; it does not require that judges try to understand the law they enforce as continuous in principle with the abandoned law of a previous century or even a previous generation. It commands a horizontal rather than vertical consistency of principle across the range of the legal standards the community now enforces. It insists that the law—the rights and duties that flow from past collective decisions and for that reason license or require coercion—contains not only the narrow explicit content of these decisions but also, more broadly, the scheme of principles necessary to justify them. History matters because that scheme of principle must justify the standing as well as the content of these past decisions. Our justification for treating the Endangered Species Act as law, unless and until it is repealed, crucially includes the fact that Congress enacted it, and any justification we supply for treating that fact as crucial must itself accommodate the way we treat other events in our political past.

Law as integrity, then, begins in the present and pursues the past only so far as and in the way its contemporary focus dictates. It does not aim to recapture, even for present law, the ideals or practical purposes of the politicians who first created it. It aims rather to justify what they did (sometimes including, as we shall see, what they said) in an overall story worth telling now, a story with a complex claim: that present practice can be organized by and justified in principles sufficiently attractive to provide an honorable future. Law as integrity deplores the mechanism of the older "law is law" view as well as the cynicism of the newer "realism." It sees both views as rooted in the same false dichotomy of finding and inventing law. When a judge declares that a particular principle is instinct in law, he reports not a claim about the motives of past statesmen, a claim a wise cynic can easily refute, but an interpretive proposal: that the principle both fits and justifies some complex part of legal practice, that it provides an attractive way to see, in the structure of that practice, the consistency of principle integrity requires. Law's optimism is in that way conceptual; claims of law are endemically constructive, "just" in virtue of the kind of claims they are. This optimism may be misplaced: the practice may, in the end, lead to nothing but a deeply skeptical interpretation. But that is not inevitable just because a community's history is one of great change and conflict. An imaginative interpretation can be constructed on morally complicated, even ambiguous terrain.

The Chain Novel

I argued . . . that creative interpretation takes its formal structure from the idea of intention, not (at least not only) because it aims to discover the purposes of any necessarily particular historical person or group but because it aims to impose purpose over the text or data or tradition being interpreted. Since all creative interpretation shares this feature, and therefore has a normative aspect or component, we profit from comparing law with other forms or occasions of interpretation. We can usefully compare the judge deciding what the law is on some issue not only with the citizens of cour-

tesy deciding what that tradition requires, but with the literary critic teasing out the various dimensions of value in a complex play or poem.

Judges, however, are authors as well as critics. A judge . . . adds to the tradition he interprets; future judges confront a new tradition that includes what he has done. Of course literary criticism contributes to the traditions of art in which authors work; the character and importance of that contribution are themselves issues in critical theory. But the contribution of judges is more direct, and the distinction between author and interpreter more a matter of different aspects of the same process. We can find an even more fruitful comparison between literature and law, therefore, by constructing an artificial genre of literature that we might call the chain novel.

In this enterprise a group of novelists writes a novel seriatum; each novelist in the chain interprets the chapters he has been given in order to write a new chapter, which is then added to what the next novelist receives, and so on. Each has the job of writing his chapter so as to make the novel being constructed the best it can be, and the complexity of this task models the complexity of deciding a hard case under law as integrity. The imaginary literary enterprise is fantastic but not unrecognizable. Some novels have actually been written in this way, though mainly for a debunking purpose, and certain parlor games for rainy weekends in English country houses have something of the same structure. Television soap operas span decades with the same characters and some minimal continuity of personality and plot, though they are written by different teams of authors even in different weeks. In our example, however, the novelists are expected to take their responsibilities of continuity more seriously; they aim only to create, so far as they can, a single unified novel that is the best it can be.

Each novelist aims to make a single novel of the material he has been given, what he adds to it, and (so far as he can control this) what his successors will want or be able to add. He must try to make this the best novel it can be construed as the work of a single author rather than, as is the fact, the product of many different hands. That calls for an overall judgment on his part, or a series of overall judgments as he writes and rewrites. He must take up some view about the novel in progress, some working theory about its characters, plot, genre, theme, and point, in order to decide what counts as continuing it and not as beginning anew. If he is a good critic, his view of these matters will be complicated and multifaceted, because the value of a decent novel cannot be captured from a single perspective. He will aim to find layers and currents of meaning rather than a single, exhaustive theme. We can, however, in our now familiar way give some structure to any interpretation he adopts, by distinguishing two dimensions on which it must be tested. The first is what we have been calling the dimension of fit. He cannot adopt any interpretation, however complex, if he believes that no single author who set out to write a novel with the various readings of character, plot, theme, and point that interpretation describes could have written substantially the text he has been given. That does not mean his interpretation must fit every bit of the text. It is not disqualified simply because he claims that some lines or tropes are accidental, or even that some events of plot are mistakes because they work against the literary ambitions the interpretation states. But the interpretation he takes up must nevertheless flow throughout the text; it must have general explanatory power, and it is flawed if it leaves unexplained some major structural aspect of the text, a subplot treated as having great dramatic importance or a dominant and repeated metaphor. If no interpretation can be found that is not flawed in that way, then the chain novelist will not be able fully to meet his assignment; he will have to settle for an interpretation that captures most of the text, conceding that it is not wholly successful. Perhaps even that partial success is unavailable; perhaps every interpretation is inconsistent with the bulk of the material supplied to him. In that case he must abandon the enterprise, for the consequence of taking the interpretive attitude toward the text in question is then a piece of internal skepticism: that nothing can count as continuing the novel rather than beginning anew.

He may find, not that no single interpretation fits the bulk of the text, but that more than one does. The second dimension of interpretation then requires him to judge which of these eligible readings makes the work in progress best, all things considered. At this point his more substantive aesthetic judgments, about the importance or insight or realism or beauty of different ideas the novel might be taken to express, come into play. But the formal and structural considerations that dominate on the first dimension figure on the second as well, for even when neither of two interpretations is disqualified out of hand as explaining too little, one may show the text in a better light because it fits more of the text or provides a more interesting integration of style and content. So the distinction between the two dimensions is less crucial or profound than it might seem. It is a useful analytical device that helps us give structure to any interpreter's working theory or style. He will form a sense of when an interpretation fits so poorly that it is unnecessary to consider its substantive appeal, because he knows that this cannot outweigh its embarrassments of fit in deciding whether it makes the novel better, everything taken into account, than its rivals. This sense will define the first dimension for him. But he need not reduce his intuitive sense to any precise formula; he would rarely need to decide whether some interpretation barely survives or barely fails, because a bare survivor, no matter how ambitious or interesting it claimed the text to be, would almost certainly fail in the overall comparison with other interpretations whose fit was evident.

We can now appreciate the range of different kinds of judgments that are blended in this overall composition: judgments about textual coherence and integrity, reflecting different formal literary values, are interwoven with more substantive aesthetic judgments that themselves assume different literary aims. Yet these various kinds of judgments, of each general kind, remain distinct enough to check one another in an overall assessment, and it is that possibility of contest, particularly between textual and substantive judgments, that distinguishes a chain novelist's assignment from more independent creative writing. Nor can we draw any flat distinction between the stage at which a chain novelist interprets the text he has been given and the stage at which he adds his own chapter, guided by the interpretation he has settled on. When he begins to write he might discover in what he has written a different, perhaps radically different, interpretation. Or he might find it impossible to write in the tone or theme he first took

up, and that will lead him to reconsider other interpretations he first rejected. In either case he returns to the text to reconsider the lines it makes eligible. . . .

Law is an interpretive concept. Judges should decide what the law is by interpreting the practice of other judges deciding what the law is. General theories of law, for us, are general interpretations of our own judicial practice. We rejected conventionalism, which finds the best interpretation in the idea that judges discover and enforce special legal conventions, and pragmatism, which finds it in the different story of judges as independent architects of the best future, free from the inhibiting demand that they must act consistently in principle with one another. I urged the third conception, law as integrity, which unites jurisprudence and adjudication. It makes the content of law depend not on special conventions or independent crusades but on more refined and concrete interpretations of the same legal practice it has begun to interpret.

These more concrete interpretations are distinctly legal because they are dominated by the adjudicative principle of inclusive integrity. Adjudication is different from legislation, not in some single, univocal way, but as the complicated consequence of the dominance of that principle. We tracked its impact by acknowledging the stronger force of integrity in adjudication that makes it sovereign over judgments of law, though not inevitably over the verdicts of courts, by noticing how legislation invites judgments of policy that adjudication does not, by observing how inclusive integrity enforces distinct judicial constraints of role. Integrity does not enforce itself—judgment is required. That judgment is structured by different dimensions of interpretation and different aspects of these. We noticed how convictions about fit contest with and constrain judgments of substance, and how convictions about fairness and procedural due process contest with one another. The interpretive judgment must notice and take account of these several dimensions; if it does not, it is incompetent or in bad faith, ordinary politics in disguise. But it must also meld these dimensions into an overall opinion: about which interpretation, all things considered, makes the community's legal record the best it can be from the point of view of political morality. So legal judgments are pervasively contestable.

That is the story told by law as integrity. I believe it provides a better account of our law than conventionalism or pragmatism on each of the two main dimensions of interpretation, so no tradeoff between these dimensions is necessary at the level at which integrity competes with other conceptions. Law as integrity, that is, provides both a better fit with and a better justification of our legal practice as a whole. I argued the claim of justification by identifying and studying integrity as a distinct virtue of ordinary politics, standing beside and sometimes conflicting with the more familiar virtues of justice and fairness. We should accept integrity as a virtue of ordinary politics because we should try to conceive our political community as an association of principle; we should aim at this because, among other reasons, that conception of community offers an attractive basis for claims of political legitimacy in a community of free and independent people who disagree about political morality and wisdom. . . .

Have I said what law is? the best reply is: up to a point. I have not devised an algorithm for the courtroom. No elec-

tronic magician could design from my arguments a computer program that would supply a verdict everyone would accept once the facts of the case and the text of all past statutes and judicial decisions were put at the computer's disposal. But I have not drawn the conclusion many readers think sensible. I have not said that there is never one right way, only different ways, to decide a hard case. On the contrary, I said that this apparently worldly and sophisticated conclusion is either a serious philosophical mistake, if we read it as a piece of external skepticism, or itself a contentious political position resting on dubious political convictions if we treat it, as I am disposed to do, as an adventure in global internal skepticism.

I described the nested interpretive questions a judge should put to himself and also the answers I now believe he should give to the more abstract and basic of these. I carried the process further in some cases, into the capillaries as well as the arteries of decision, but only as example and not in more detail than was needed to illustrate the character of the decisions judges must make. Our main concern has been to identify the branching points of legal argument, the points where opinion divides in the way law as integrity promises. . . .

The question how far I have succeeded in showing what law is, is a distinct question for each reader. He must ask how far he would follow me along the tree of argument, given the various interpretive and political and moral convictions he has after this reflection I have tried to provoke. If he leaves my argument early, at some crucial abstract stage, then I have largely failed for him. If he leaves it late, in some matter of relative detail, then I have largely succeeded. I have failed entirely, however, if he never leaves my argument at all.

What is law? Now I offer a different kind of answer. Law is not exhausted by any catalogue of rules or principles, each with its own dominion over some discrete theater of behavior. Nor by any roster of officials and their powers each over part of our lives. Law's empire is defined by attitude, not territory or power or process. We studied that attitude mainly in appellate courts, where it is dressed for inspection, but it must be pervasive in our ordinary lives if it is to serve us well even in court. It is an interpretive, self-reflective attitude addressed to politics in the broadest sense. It is a protestant attitude that makes each citizen responsible for imagining what his society's public commitments to principle are, and what these commitments require in new circumstances. The Protestant character of law is confirmed, and the creative role of private decisions acknowledged, by the backward looking, judgmental nature of judicial decisions, and also by the regulative assumption that though judges must have the last word, their word is not for that reason the best word. Law's attitude is constructive: it aims, in the interpretive spirit, to lay principle over practice to show the best route to a better future, keeping the right faith with the past. It is, finally, a fraternal attitude, an expression of how we are united in community though divided in project, interest, and conviction. That is, anyway, what law is for us: for the people we want to be and the community we aim to have.

QUESTIONS

1. Can you articulate Dworkin's distinctions between rules, principles, and policies?

2. Given what Dworkin says about positivism, is there any way for positivism to incorporate his criticism that the picture of law given by positivism is defective because it fails to take account of principles?

3. Summarize Dworkin's discussion of the logical character of legal rules. Can you think of any legal rules that seem not to fall under his account of rules as "all-or-nothing" norms?

4. Dworkin says that principles play a large and important role in cases like Riggs and Henningsen. What role is that?

5. Summarize Dworkin's discussion of discretion. Is this discussion accurate in the context of positivism?

6. With respect to the chain novel example, are you persuaded that law can profitably be compared with fiction writing, or is law just too different from such writing to make any comparison between the two illuminating?

7. How does Dworkin handle conflict among legal principles? Does the discussion of conflict among constitutional modalities in Bobbitt's work help us to understand conflict among principles?

8. To what degree do you think Dworkin's account of law is an accurate account of the reality of legal practice? Does it matter that it may or may not be completely accurate?

9. What is the role of the concept of "associative obligation" in Dworkin's theory?

10. What does Dworkin mean when he says that law is an "interpretive" concept? Given the discussion of interpretation in connection with Patterson's work, do you see any potential problems with the idea that all understanding of law is a matter of interpretation?

Chapter 4

Consequentialism
Readings from Richard Posner

In this chapter we turn to one of the most influential forms of modern jurisprudence: the consequentialist tradition. What accounts in large part for its persuasiveness is the fact that most philosophies of law take the well-being of society to be an overriding concern—and naturally so, for what, after all, is the purpose of law if not to advance the good for society? In typical versions of this tradition, advancing the good for society is understood as increasing the balance of happiness over unhappiness in society considered as a whole. Legally applied, this means that the norm that should govern legal decision-making is the *effect* or *consequence* of that decision in bringing about such a balance. As a jurisprudential type, *consequentialism* foregrounds a preoccupation of jurists with *assessment* of the consequences of judicial decisions. Assessment is important because it forges an all-important link between fact and legal value—to the degree that a decision in question can be shown as a matter of fact to increase social well-being, to that degree the decision has legal value for the consequentialist, that is, it is a candidate for justification.

Granted the appropriate concern of law with social good, difficult questions arise when we try to decide how this good is to be determined. Specifically, there is the problem of determining an exact reference for the term "society" and for the term "social good." For purposes of evaluating the worth of a legal decision, it makes a difference whether the good in question includes only the citizens of a particular nation state, or foreigners as well, or all sentient beings. As a normative theory of law, consequentialism is essentially incomplete in that it leaves open how we understand the term society, and sometimes this diminishes its effectiveness since there can be wide variation among reasonable people about how exactly society should be understood.

A related problem in assessing social consequences is that any assessment depends on some method of *aggregating* pleasure or happiness or well-being across the population of a given society. Some critics of utilitarianism have argued that only an omniscient being would be in a position to carry out such an assessment—otherwise how could unintended and unpredictable effects be taken into account? Closer to home is the fact that assessment of consequences frequently depends on making judgments about the effect of some action on one person *as compared* with another person, (the so-called problem of interpersonal comparisons); yet we have no reliable way of making such judgments.

These problems among others surfaced early in the development of consequentialist jurisprudence, but their existence has done little to diminish either the influence or the development of this tradition. We study next selections from the work of one of its most important representatives. Like Dworkin, Richard Posner rejects Hart's claims (1) that law is a body of rules established through authorized procedures by authorized lawgivers and (2) that when the rules break down in some way judges have "discretion" to modify them in ways that fit a case at hand. He also concurs with the view of Fuller and other so-called legal process scholars that while it is important to distinguish adjudication from other forms of lawmaking—legislation, for example—a *unity* within the lawmaking process can be demonstrated. He is in sharp disagreement, however, with Fuller and Dworkin who see this unity as a unity of principle. In fact, he questions whether a convincing case can be made that there is any meaningful distinction between a "principle" and a "policy."

> When law is defined to include, under the rubric of "principle," the ethical and political norms that judges use to decide the most difficult cases, decision according to law and decision according to political preference becomes difficult, sometimes impossible, to distinguish in a society as morally heterogeneous as ours. Dworkin does distinguish between policy and principle, and he argues that only the latter is a fit foundation for and limitation on judicially declared rights. The argument is unconvincing, the distinction arbitrary, the principles merely the policies that commend themselves to Dworkin's brand of political liberalism.[1]

For Posner the unity that marks adjudication, and indeed marks law as a whole, is the singular concern for social well-being—in this respect he thinks that utilitarianism is correct. It is easy to see that a significant difference between classical utilitarianism and Posner's account of law is the use he makes of analytical tools supplied by contemporary economic theory and analysis. This is not the only nor even the primary difference, however, for as we shall see, Posner is opposed to the central claims of utilitarianism for ethical and methodological reasons as well. With regard to the economic dimensions of his jurisprudence he is reluctant to think of himself as an adherent of the so-called "school of economic analysis" in legal decision-making: some of the more engaging and important passages in these readings have to do with criticism of this approach to the nature of law and adjudication. To distinguish his understanding of law from both utilitarianism

---

1. Richard Posner, *Problems of Jurisprudence*, (Cambridge, Mass.: Harvard University Press, 1990), p. 22.

and strict economic analysis, he describes his jurisprudence as "pragmatist," understood in a loose and somewhat idiosyncratic way:

> Not only is it difficult to tell when one has strayed across the boundaries that separate pragmatism from neighboring philosophical traditions, but the core of pragmatism, if there is such a thing, is too variform to make pragmatism a single philosophical school in the useful sense. . . . To say that one is a pragmatist is to say little. The brand of pragmatism that I like emphasizes the scientific virtues . . . elevates the process of inquiry over the results of inquiry, prefers ferment to stasis, dislikes distinctions that make no practical difference . . . is doubtful of finding "objective truth" in any area of inquiry, is uninterested in creating an adequate philosophical foundation for its thought and action, likes experimentation, likes to kick sacred cows, and—within the bounds of prudence—prefers shaping the future to maintaining the past. So I am speaking of an attitude rather than a dogma; an attitude whose "common denominator" is "a future-oriented instrumentalism that tries to deploy thought as a weapon to enable more effective action". . . .[2]

essence of Pragmatism

Given the pervasive skepticism reflected in this passage one might be inclined to wonder whether Posner is really a representative of the consequentialist tradition. Understandable as this question is, a close reading of Posner's work, including the selections that follow, make it clear that his version of pragmatism is consequentialist in nature. To the extent that the legal enterprise, including adjudication, has a unity all its own, that unity is, for Posner, concern for the well-being of society. In the passages below he clarifies his view that adjudication is distinct from legislation and that it has a fairly well-defined functional unity. Economic analysis is not a foundation of law in the sense that justifiable legal decisions can be reduced to this kind of analysis—for Posner law has no foundations—however, he argues forcefully that adjudication has an internal unity or core, and that given the present state of knowledge, "wealth maximization" is the best way to understand it. "The fact that wealth maximization . . . is instrumental rather than foundational is not an objection to its use in guiding law and public policy. It may be the right principle for that purpose, even though it is right only in virtue of ends that are not solely economic."[3] Use of the term *instrumental* here is the key to Posner's consequentialism: if we ask, instrumental to what?, the answer is, to the social good as defined by wealth maximization.

Reading 1 concerns Posner's conception of the unity of law. As noted above, he joins company with Fuller and Dworkin in rejecting the notion that the unity of law resides in a body of rules. He eschews, however, their

---

2. Posner, *Problems of Jurisprudence, Id.* at p. 28. The quotation in the last sentence is from Cornel West, *The American Evasion of Philosophy: A Geneaology of Pragmatism* (Madison, Wis.: University of Wisconsin Press, 1989), p. 5.

3. Posner, *Problems of Jurisprudence, Id.* at p. 387.

idea that it consists of a body of principles that underwrite and justify legal rules. For him the unity of law is supplied by the fact that it is created by rational people engaged in an effort to "maximize their satisfaction." Viewed in this light, the legal process should be understood as deal-making between and among individuals with the single goal of maximizing satifactions. The directness and simplicity of Posner's conception of the unity of law as deal-making opens the door to what in subsequent readings becomes a complex and sometimes controversial understanding of the significance of economic analysis for law.

~

Reading 1

From Richard A. Posner,
PROBLEMS OF JURISPRUDENCE

The Economic Approach to Law

The most ambitious and probably the most influential effort in recent years to elaborate an overarching concept of justice that will both explain judicial decision making and place it on an objective basis is that of scholars working in the interdisciplinary field of "law and economics," as economic analysis of law is usually called. . . .

The basic assumption of economics that guides the version of economic analysis of law that I shall be presenting is that people are rational maximizers of their satisfactions—all people (with the exception of small children and the profoundly retarded) in all of their activities (except when under the influence of psychosis or similarly deranged through drug or alcohol abuse) that involve choice. Because this definition embraces the criminal deciding whether to commit another crime, the litigant deciding whether to settle or litigate a case, the legislator deciding whether to vote for or against a bill, the judge deciding how to

cast his vote in a case, the party to a contract deciding whether to break it, the driver deciding how fast to drive, and the pedestrian deciding how boldly to cross the street, as well as the usual economic actors, such as businessmen and consumers, it is apparent that most activities either regulated by or occurring within the legal system are grist for the economic analyst's mill. It should go without saying that nonmonetary as well as monetary satisfactions enter into the individual's calculus of maximizing (indeed money for most people is a means rather than an end) and that decisions, to be rational, need not be well thought out at the conscious level—indeed, need not be conscious at all. Recall that "rational" denotes suiting means to ends, rather than mulling things over, and that much of our knowledge is tacit.

Since my interest is in legal doctrines and institutions, it will be best to begin at the legislative (including the constitutional) level. I assume that legislators are rational maximizers of their satisfactions just like everyone else. Thus nothing they do is motivated by the public interest as such. But they want to be elected and re-elected, and they need money to wage an effective campaign. This money is more likely to be forthcoming from well-organized groups than from unorganized individuals. The rational individual knows that his contribution is unlikely to make a difference; for this reason and also because voters in most elections are voting for candidates rather than policies, which further weakens the link between casting one's vote and obtaining one's preferred policy, the rational individual will have little incentive to invest time and effort in deciding whom to vote for. Only an organized group of individuals (or firms or other organizations—but these are just conduits for individuals) will be able to overcome the informational and free-rider problems that plague collective action. But such a group will not organize and act effectively unless its members have much to gain or much to lose from specific policies, as tobacco farmers, for example, have much to gain from federal subsidies for growing tobacco and much to lose from the withdrawal of those subsidies. The basic tactic of an interest group is to trade the votes of its members and its financial support to candidates in exchange for an implied promise of favorable legislation. Such legislation will normally take the form of a statute transferring wealth from unorganized taxpayers (for example, consumers) to the interest group. If the larger were another interest group, the legislative transfer might be effectively opposed. The unorganized are unlikely to mount effective opposition, and it is their wealth, therefore, that typically is transferred to interest groups.

On this view, a statute is a deal. . . . But because of the costs of transactions within a multi-headed legislative body,

and the costs of effective communication through time, legislation does not spring full-grown from the head of the legislature; it needs interpretation and application, and this is the role of the courts. They are agents of the legislature. But to impart credibility and durability to the deals the legislature strikes with interest groups, courts must be able to resist the wishes of current legislators who want to undo their predecessors' deals yet cannot do so through repeal because the costs of passing legislation (whether original or amended) are so high, and who might therefore look to the courts for a repealing "interpretation." The impediments to legislation actually facilitate rather than retard the striking of deals, by giving interest groups some assurance that a deal struck with the legislature will not promptly be undone by repeal. An independent judiciary is one of the impediments.

Judicial independence makes the judges imperfect agents of the legislature. This is tolerable not only for the reason just mentioned but also because an independent judiciary is necessary for the resolution of ordinary disputes in a way that will encourage trade, travel, freedom of action, and other highly valued activities or conditions and will minimize the expenditure of resources on influencing governmental action. Legislators might appear to have little to gain from these widely diffused rule-of-law virtues. But if the aggregate benefits from a particular social policy are very large and no interest groups' ox is gored, legislators may find it in their own interest to support the policy. Voters understand in a rough way the benefits to them of national defense, crime control, dispute settlement, and the other elements of the night watchman state, and they will not vote for legislators who refuse to provide these basic public services. It is only when those services are in place, and when (usually later) effective means of taxation and redistribution develop that the formation of narrow interest groups and the extraction by them of transfers from unorganized groups become feasible.

The judges thus have a dual role: to interpret the interest-group deals embodied in legislation and to provide the basic public service of authoritative dispute resolution. They perform the latter function not only by deciding cases in accordance with preexisting norms, but also—especially in the Anglo-American legal system—by elaborating those norms. They fashioned the common law out of customary practices, out of ideas borrowed from statutes and from other legal systems (for example from Roman law), and out of their own conceptions of public policy. The law they created exhibits, according to the economic theory that I am expounding, a remarkable (although not total. . .) substantive consistency. It is as if the judges wanted to adopt the rules, procedures, and case outcomes that would maximize society's wealth.

In the second reading we jump from the simple and direct analysis of lawmaking as "dealing" to the complex and sophisticated analysis of correct and proper "legal dealing" as "wealth-maximization." A few remarks may be helpful in making this conceptual jump. Dealing has to do, among other things, with allocation of resources, and a question of concern to all parties to a deal is: What should be the criteria governing allocation? One idea, which economists sometimes refer to as the "Pareto principle," is roughly this: one allocation is preferable to another if at least one person is better off and no one worse off. That criterion, which Posner refers to below, seems capable of generating considerable agreement among reasonable people, and it goes a long way toward explaining correct or proper—which is to say reasonable—legal outcomes.

Reading 2

From Richard A. Posner, *PROBLEMS OF JURISPRUDENCE*

I must pause to define "wealth maximization," a term often misunderstood. The wealth in wealth maximization refers to the sum of all tangible and intangible goods and services, weighted by prices of two sorts: offer prices (what people are willing to pay for goods they do not already own); and asking prices (what people demand to sell what they do own). If A would be willing to pay up to $100 for B's stamp collection, it is worth $100 to A. If B would be willing to sell the stamp collection for any price above $90, it would be worth $90 to B. So if B sells the stamp collection to A (say for $100, but the analysis is qualitatively unaffected at any price between 90 and 100—and it is only in that range that a transaction will occur), the wealth of society will rise by $10. Before the transaction A had $100 in cash and B had a stamp collection worth $90 (a total of $190); after the transaction A has a stamp collection worth $100 and B has $100 in cash (a total of $200). The transaction will not raise measured wealth—gross national product, national income, or whatever—by $10; it will not raise it at all unless the transaction is recorded, and if it is recorded it is likely to raise measured wealth by the full $100 purchase price. But the real addition to social wealth consists of the $10 increment in *nonpecuniary* satisfaction that A derives from the purchase, compared with that of B. This shows that "wealth" in the economist's sense is not a simple monetary measure, and explains why it is a fallacy (the Earl of Lauderdale's fallacy) to think that wealth would be maximized by encouraging the charging of monopoly prices. The wealth of producers would increase but that of consumers would diminish— and actually by a greater amount, since monopoly pricing will induce some consumers to switch to goods that cost society more to produce but, being priced at a competitive rather than a monopoly price, appear to the consumer to be cheaper. The fallacy thus lies in equating business income to social wealth.

Similarly, if I am given a choice between remaining in a job in which I work forty hours a week for $1,000 and switching to a job in which I would work thirty hours for $500, and I decide to make the switch, the extra ten hours of leisure must be worth at least $500 to me, yet GNP will fall when I reduce my hours of work. Suppose the extra hours of leisure are worth $600 to me, so that my full income rises from $1,000 to $1,100 when I reduce my hours. My former employer presumably is made worse off by my leaving (else why did he employ me?), but not more than $100 worse off; for if he were, he would offer to pay me a shade over $1,100 a week to stay—and I would stay. (The example abstracts from income tax.)

Wealth is *related* to money, in that a desire not backed by ability to pay has no standing—such a desire is neither an offer price nor an asking price. I may desperately desire a BMW, but if I am unwilling or unable to pay its purchase price, society's wealth would not be increased by transferring the BMW from its present owner to me. Abandon this essential constraint (an important distinction, also, between wealth maximization and utilitarianism—for I might derive greater utility from the BMW than its present owner or anyone else to whom he might sell the car), and the way is open to tolerating the crimes committed by the passionate and the avaricious against the cold and the frugal.

The common law facilitates wealth-maximizing transactions in a variety of ways. It recognizes property rights, and these facilitate exchange. It also protects property rights, through tort and criminal law. (Although today criminal law is almost entirely statutory, the basic criminal protections—for example, those against murder, assault, rape, and theft—have, as one might expect, common law origins.) Through contract law it protects the process of exchange. And it establishes procedural rules for resolving disputes in these various fields as efficiently as possible.

The illustrations given thus far of wealth-maximizing transactions have been of transactions that are voluntary in the strict sense of making everyone affected by them better off, or at least no worse off. Every transaction has been assumed to affect just two parties, each of whom has been made better off by it. Such a transaction is said to be Pareto superior, but Pareto superiority is not a necessary condition for a transaction to be wealth maximizing. Consider an accident that inflicts a cost of $100 with a probability of .01 and that would have cost $3 to avoid. The accident is a wealth-maximizing "transaction" (recall Aristotle's distinction between voluntary and involuntary transactions) because the expected accident cost ($1) is less than the cost of avoidance. (I am assuming risk neutrality. Risk aversion would complicate the analysis but not change it fundamentally.) It is wealth maximizing even if the victim is not compensated. The result is consistent with Learned Hand's formula,[4] which defines negligence as the failure to take cost-justified precautions. If the only precaution that would have averted the accident is not cost-justified, the failure to take it is not negligent and the injurer will not have to compensate the victim for the costs of the accident.

If it seems artificial to speak of the accident as the transaction, consider instead the potential transaction that consists of purchasing the safety measure that would have avoided the accident. Since a potential victim would not pay $3 to avoid an expected accident cost of $1, his offer price will be less than the potential injurer's asking price and the transaction will not be wealth maximizing. But if these figures were reversed— if an expected accident cost of $3 could be averted at a cost of $1—the transaction would be wealth maximizing, and a liability rule administered in accordance with the Hand formula would give potential injurers an incentive to take the measures that potential victims would pay them to take if voluntary transactions were feasible. The law would be overcoming transaction-cost obstacles to wealth-maximizing transactions—a frequent office of liability rules.

The wealth-maximizing properties of common law rules have been elucidated at considerable length in the literature of the economic analysis of law. Such doctrines as conspiracy, general average (admiralty), contributory negligence, equitable servitudes, employment at will, the standard for granting preliminary injunctions, entrapment, the contract defense of impossibility, the collateral-benefits rule, the expectation measure of damages, assumption of risk, attempt, invasion of privacy, wrongful interference with contract rights, the availability of punitive damages in some cases but not others, privilege in the law of evidence, official immunity, and the doctrine of moral consideration have been found—at least by some contributors to this literature—to conform to the dictates of wealth maximization. . . . It has even been argued that the system of precedent itself has an economic equilibrium. Precedents are created as a by-

---

4. First formulated in *U.S. v. Carroll Towing* (1947), 159 F.2d 169 the formula reads B < PL where B stands for "burden of precautions," P for the "probability that a certain type of accident will occur," L for the "magnitude of the loss if the accident did occur" and < for "is less than." In other words, negligence is understood as the failure to take care when the cost of taking care is less than the expected loss.

product of litigation. The greater the number of recent precedents in an area, the lower the rate of litigation will be. In particular, cases involving disputes over legal as distinct from purely factual issues will be settled. The existence of abundant, highly informative (in part because recent) precedents will enable the parties to legal disputes to form more convergent estimates of the likely outcome of a trial, and . . . if both parties agree on the outcome of trial they will settle beforehand because a trial is more costly than a settlement. But with less litigation, fewer new precedents will be produced, and the existing precedents will be obsolescent as changing circumstances render them less apt and informative. So the rate of litigation will rise, producing more precedents and thereby causing the rate of litigation again to fall.

This analysis does not explain what drives judges to decide common law cases in accordance with the dictates of wealth maximization. Prosperity, however, which wealth maximization measures more sensitively than purely monetary measures such as GNP, is a relatively uncontroversial policy, and most judges try to steer clear of controversy: their age, method of compensation, and relative weakness vis-à-vis the other branches of government make the avoidance of controversy attractive. It probably is no accident, therefore, that many common law doctrines assumed their modern form in the nineteenth century, when laissez-faire ideology, which resembles wealth maximization, had a strong hold on the Anglo-American judicial imagination. . . .

It may be objected that in assigning ideology as a cause of judicial behavior, the economist strays outside the boundaries of his discipline; but he need not

rest on ideology. The economic analysis of legislation implies that fields of law left to the judges to elaborate, such as the common law fields, must be the ones in which interest-group pressures are too weak to deflect the legislature from pursuing goals that are in the general interest. Prosperity is one of these goals, and one that judges are especially well equipped to promote. The rules of the common law that they promulgate attach prices to socially undesirable conduct, whether free riding or imposing social costs without corresponding benefits. By doing this the rules create incentives to avoid such conduct, and these incentives foster prosperity. In contrast, judges can, despite appearances, do little to redistribute wealth. A rule that makes it easy for poor tenants to break leases with rich landlords, for example, will induce landlords to raise rents in order to offset the costs that such a rule imposes, and tenants will bear the brunt of these higher costs. Indeed, the principal redistribution accomplished by such a rule may be from the prudent, responsible tenant, who may derive little or no benefit from having additional legal rights to use against landlords—rights that enable a tenant to avoid or postpone eviction for non-payment of rental—to the feckless tenant. That is a capricious redistribution. Legislatures, however, have by virtue of their taxing and spending powers powerful tools for redistributing wealth. So an efficient division of labor between the legislative and judicial branches has the legislative branch concentrate on catering to interest-group demands for wealth distribution and the judicial branch on meeting the broadbased social demand for efficient rules governing safety, property, and transactions. Although there are other possible goals of judicial action besides efficiency and redistribution, many of these (various conceptions of "fairness" and "justice") are labels for wealth maximization, or for redistribution in favor of powerful interest groups; or else they are too controversial in a heterogeneous society, too ad hoc, or insufficiently developed to provide judges who desire a reputation for objectivity and disinterest with adequate grounds for their decisions.

Finally, even if judges have little commitment to efficiency, their inefficient decisions will, by definition, impose greater social costs than their efficient ones will. As a result, losers of cases decided mistakenly from an economic standpoint will have a greater incentive, on average, to press for correction through appeal, new litigation, or legislative action than losers of cases decided soundly from an economic standpoint—so there will be a steady pressure for efficient results. Moreover, cases litigated under inefficient rules tend to involve larger stakes than cases litigated under efficient rules (for the inefficient rules, by definition, generate social waste), and the larger the stakes in a dispute the likelier it is to be litigated rather than settled; so judges will have a chance to reconsider the inefficient rule.

Thus we should not be surprised to see the common law tending to become efficient, although since the incentives of judges to perform well along any dimension are weak (this is a by-product of judicial independence), we cannot expect the law ever to achieve perfect efficiency. Since wealth maximization is not only a guide in fact to common law judging but also a genuine social value and the only one judges are in a good position to promote, it provides not only the key to an accurate description of what

the judges are up to but also the right benchmark for criticism and reform. If judges are failing to maximize wealth, the economic analyst of law will urge them to alter practice or doctrine accordingly. In addition, the analyst will urge—on any legislature sufficiently free of interest-group pressures to be able to legislate in the public interest—a program of enacting only legislation that conforms to the dictates of wealth maximization.

Besides generating both predictions and prescriptions, the economic approach enables the common law to be reconceived in simple, coherent terms and to be applied more objectively than traditional lawyers would think possible. From the premise that the common law does and should seek to maximize society's wealth, the economic analyst can deduce in logical—if you will, formalist—fashion (economic theory is formulated nowadays largely in mathematical terms) the set of legal doctrines that will express and perfect the inner nature of the common law, and can compare these doctrines with the actual doctrines of common law. After translating from the economic vocabulary back into the legal one, the analyst will find that most of the actual doctrines are tolerable approximations to the implication for economic theory and so are formalistically valid. Where there are discrepancies, the path to reform is clear—yet the judge who takes the path cannot be accused of making rather than finding law, for he is merely contributing to the program of realizing the essential nature of the common law.

The project of reducing the common law—with its many separate fields, its thousands of separate doctrines, its hundreds of thousands of reported decisions—to a handful of mathematical formulas may seen quixotic, but the economic analyst can give reasons for doubting this assessment. Much of the doctrinal luxuriance of common law is seen to be superficial once the essentially economic nature of the common law is understood. A few principles, such as cost-benefit analysis, the prevention of free-riding, decision under authority, risk aversion, and the promotion of mutually beneficial exchanges, can explain most doctrines and decisions. Tort cases can be translated into contract cases by recharacterizing the tort issue as finding the implied pre-accident contract that the parties would have chosen had transaction costs not been prohibitive, and contract cases can be translated into tort cases by asking what remedy if any would maximize the expected benefits of the contractual undertaking considered ex ante. The criminal's decision whether to commit a crime is no different in principle from the prosecutor's decision whether to prosecute; a plea bargain is a contract; crimes are in effect torts by insolvent defendants because if all criminals could pay the full social costs of their crimes, the task of deterring antisocial behavior could be left to tort law. Such examples suggest not only that the logic of the common law really is economics but also that the teaching of law could be simplified by exposing students to the clean and simple economic structure beneath the particolored garb of legal doctrine.

If all this seems reminiscent of Langdell, it differs fundamentally in being empirically verifiable. The ultimate test of a rule derived from economic theory is not the elegance or logicality of the derivation but the rule's effect on social wealth. . . .

Having advanced what he calls the "economic thesis" in Reading 2, Posner turns in the next selections to criticism of what he calls the "positive theory" of economic analysis. This theory, developed in a large body of recent literature, claims that economic analysis *explains* why courts have decided cases as they have. This is a descriptive theory, that is, a theory about how best to account for legal decisions when those decisions were reasonable. Positive theories of economic analysis are similar in some ways to natural law theories of common law adjudication of the sort exemplified in Blackstone: they attempt to show that legal outcomes in typical cases are controlled by an underlying structure of rationality of which the court may not itself have been explicitly aware but which, nonetheless, best explains the outcome in question. The "underlying structure of reasoning" in English common law cases is understood very differently by Blackstone and by Posner, of course, but their accounts have in common the assumption of an underlying structure of rationality independent of the language of the legal opinions per se. In Reading 3, Posner identifies what he regards as the most important criticisms of the positive theory of economic analysis, and he concludes that, by his lights at least, some of these criticisms are difficult, if not impossible, to refute.

Reading 3

From Richard A. Posner,
PROBLEMS OF JURISPRUDENCE

Criticisms of the Positive Theory

Stated as boldly, as provocatively, as I have stated it, the economic thesis invites attack from a variety of quarters. . . . It will be convenient to divide the attackers into two camps: those who attack the positive aspect of the economic theory of law (law can best be understood in wealth-maximizing and rent-seeking terms, the former being the domain of common law, the latter of statute law), and those who attack the normative aspect (law should be made to conform as closely as possible to the dictates of wealth maximization). Of course often the same people attack on both fronts.

Two criticisms of the positive theory are fundamental. The first is that the economic model of human behavior is wrong, and economic science phony. The second is that the proper study of economics is markets rather than nonmarket activity, the latter being the category that includes crime, adjudication, and other characteristic concerns of the legal system.

Economists pride themselves on being engaged in a scientific endeavor. From the basic premise that people are rational maximizers of their satisfactions the economist deduces a variety of hypotheses, of which the best known is the "law of demand"—a rise in the relative price of a product will, other things held constant, cause a reduction in the quality of the product demanded. These hypotheses are confirmed or refuted by studies of actual economic behavior. Usually the studies are statistical in nature, though much of the evidence that actually persuades people that there is "something to" economics is of a more casual sort—for example, observing that nonprice rationing leads to queuing. Although many positive economists are followers of Karl Popper and therefore believe that falsifiability is the defining characteristic of a scientific theory, empirical economists in practice place far greater emphasis on confirmation than on falsification. In part this is because economic theory has become so rich, so complex, that almost any hypothesis, even one that appeared to deny a fundamental implication of the theory such as the law of demand, could be made to conform to the theory. For example, a finding that the demand for a product had risen in response to an increase in its price could be rationalized by arguing either that the product was a Giffen good[5] or that consumers had been fooled by the price increase into thinking that the quality of the product had improved; consumers often take prices as an index of quality and often are warranted in doing so. In fact, the law of demand seems robust; but it is distressingly easy to explain away empirical findings that appear to conflict with the basic theoretical

---

5. A good the demand for which rises when people's income falls.

assumptions and propositions of economics.

Falsifiability is placed still farther beyond the economist's reach by the infeasibility in most areas of economic inquiry of performing controlled experiments. The normal method of seeking to confirm or falsify an economic hypothesis is by conducting a "natural" experiment: an economic model is used to predict a relationship between statistical variables (for example, between price data and quantity data) and the reliability of the prediction is evaluated by applying tests of statistical significance. The problems with this methodology include the tedium, expense, and sometimes impossibility of obtaining the data that the model implies are relevant, and as a result of these obstacles the low ratio of empirical to theoretical work; the absence of professional rewards for negative findings, or, what amounts to the same thing, career pressures to come up with positive results by hook or by crook; the large, sometimes indefinite number of omitted independent variables that may be correlated with the independent variables the researcher is trying to test for; the typically very low percentage of the variance in the observations that is explained by the model, suggesting either that the data are poor or that the economic model is able to capture only a small part of the social phenomenon being investigated; the ease of explaining away poor results as being due to problems with data; and the fact that the results being predicted are known in advance which creates both pressure and opportunity to tinker with the model in order to make it conform better to the data—and the complexity of economic theory makes such tinkering easy to do. The last two points may explain why negative findings are likely to be ascribed to lack of imagination on the part of the researcher.

A theory that is not effectively falsifiable, but only confirmable, is tenuously grounded. One can never be certain whether observations that confirm (that is, are consistent with) theory A are not really confirming theory B instead, which overlaps with or includes A. The low percentage of variance explained by most econometric studies makes this a lively possibility. This is a less serious problem for sciences that do not only generate insights into natural phenomena, such as the origin of the universe or of species, but also enable dramatic interventions. The atomic bomb is proof (not conclusive, but then no proof is) that modern atomic theory is more than just another clever speculation about invisible entities; and so with biotechnology and genetic theory. Although economics, too, has its technological side as well as its academic side, economic theory can take credit for some new trading strategies in securities markets, some new methods of pricing, and some new public policies, such as the deregulation of transportation and banking—these interventions are less dramatic, and more ambiguous in their results and interpretation, than the interventions of natural science in such areas as weaponry and medicine.

There is a further problem. The basic assumption of economics—that people are rational maximizers—seems not only counterintuitive (a common feature of scientific theory, however, well illustrated by the heliocentric theory of the solar system and by evolution, not to mention by quantum theory) but also seriously incomplete. People have difficulty in dealing with low-probability events, which are important in many areas of behavior studied by economists; and much human behavior appears to be impulsive, emotional, superstitious—in a word, irrational. These are reasons for concern that observations which confirm theory A (economics) may in fact be confirming a more inclusive, more realistic, theory B.

These points suggest that economics is weak in comparison with the natural sciences, although it is the strongest of the human sciences. But the discussion has not shown, and it would be a mistake to believe, that it is a false science, like astrology, or an ideology, like Marxism. On the contrary, it seems to capture an important part, though possibly only a small part, of the phenomena it seeks to explain. In this respect as well as in its heavy reliance on calculus for the formulation of its models, economics resembles Newtonian physics. This resemblance points up the confusion in the common criticism of economics as "reductionist" in seeking to use mathematical models to describe human social behavior. All science involves abstraction. Newton's law of falling bodies abstracts from many of the particulars of such bodies (for example, was the apple red?) in an effort to discover a law of nature— specifically, a law to describe the behavior of a variety of bodies, from apples to tides to cannonballs to stars, that differ in many of their particulars. . . . We do not describe this process as reductionism; we reserve, or should reserve, that word for unsuccessful efforts to explain one thing in terms of another, for example, ideas in terms of molecular changes in the brain.

We should not forget that an important branch of physics, astrophysics, is for the most part not an experimental science; that there are other nonexperimen-

tal natural sciences as well, including geology and paleontology; that some of the most important theories in science, notably theories of evolution in biology and geology, cannot as a practical matter be falsified; that experiments are highly fallible, since an excluded variable may be the real cause that the experiment is trying to test for, and the variable that the experimenter finds to be the cause merely a correlate of the real cause; that much of science is a breathtakingly counterintuitive offense to common sense (quantum theory, for example, or the evolution of the human eye); that scientists often make arbitrary, unprovable assumptions (such as that the laws of physics as we know them hold throughout the universe); and that because of the impossibility of ever really "confirming" a scientific hypothesis it might be best to view all scientific knowledge as conjectural. In short, some of the most salient methodological weaknesses, real or apparent, of economic science are shared with natural science—to which it should be added that economists and other social scientists do on occasion conduct controlled experiments.

Should the weaknesses of economics discourage attempts to apply economics to nonmarket behavior? Surely not. Although much non-market behavior is indeed baffling, this is so whether one approaches it from the standpoint of economics, which assumes that human beings behave rationally, or from the standpoint of other human sciences, which do not make that assumption but have nothing to put in its place. The economics of law may well be a weak field, partaking of the general weakness of economics and of additional weaknesses specific to itself. But is the psychology of law strong? The sociology of law? Legal anthropology? Jurisprudence as a positive theory of law? These fields of interdisciplinary legal studies, and others that could be named, are older than economic analysis of law yet are weaker candidates for a leading role in fashioning a positive theory of law. . . .

The last important criticism of the positive economic theory of law, and the bridge to the criticisms of the normative theory, is that wealth maximization is so incoherent and repulsive a social norm that it is inconceivable that judges would embrace it. Let me defer consideration of this criticism for a moment and ask the reader to accept provisionally the conclusion of the next section: that as a universal social norm wealth maximization is indeed unsatisfactory, but that it is attractive or at least defensible when confined to the common law arena. With this stipulation, let us see where the positive theory stands. Plainly it has many weaknesses; legal theory has not yet had its Isaac Newton or its Adam Smith. Nor can these weaknesses be waved away with the observation that one can beat a theory only with a better theory. This observation is true—what else could one *beat* a theory with?—but trivial. If the only theoretical explanation that has been offered for a phenomenon is unconvincing despite the absence of a competing explanation, one is entitled to regard the phenomenon as unexplained. Maybe *compelled* to do so: an absence of competing expla-

nations is one reason for believing an explanation, and if nevertheless you do not believe it the proponent cannot force you to do so merely by pointing out that there are no competing explanations. There is much about society (as about nature) that we do not yet understand.

But this would be the wrong note on which to end discussion of the positive economic theory of law. Apart from its pedagogical merit in enabling the jumble of common law rules and doctrines to be arranged in a coherent system, the theory has alerted legal scholars to the possibilities of scientific theorizing about law and has challenged them to seek competing theories, although so far the search has been pretty barren. Moreover, in its weakest form the positive economic theory can claim some empirical support. It seems that intuitions about wealth maximization *have* shaped to a significant degree the doctrines of the common law and that statute law *does* reflect to a much greater degree the pressure of interest groups. Although it would be a gross overstatement to conclude from the evidence gathered to date that the logic of the economic law has been wealth maximization and the logic of statute law wealth redistribution, the statement contains some truth—and . . . undermines suggestions that law is an autonomous field of social thought and action. . . .

∽

Posner addresses a second type of criticism leveled at economic theory: one aimed at what he calls the normative thesis: the claim that economic principles not only have been but *should* be determinative in legal decision-making. One way to understand the impetus for this thesis is to note that in the readings so far a great part of the attractiveness of Posner's sketch of wealth maximization derives from its appeal to the Pareto principle, that is, the principle that it is reasonable to prefer allocations of wealth in which at least one person is made better off and no one less well off. Only a little reflection is required to recognize that this principle is very limited in its range of applicability: in many, if not most, legal situations there is no way to avoid loss to someone, and when this is the case the following normative question is raised: How, if at all, can such loss be justified? And especially, does economic analysis have the resources for justification? In Reading 4 Posner discusses, among other objections to normative economic legal theory, the claim that economic theory per se lacks such resources.

∿

Reading 4

From Richard A. Posner,
PROBLEMS OF JURISPRUDENCE

Criticisms of the Normative Theory

The question whether wealth maximization *should* guide legal policy, either in general or just in common law fields (plus those statutory fields where the legislative intent is to promote efficiency—antitrust law being a possible example), is ordinarily treated as separate from the question whether it *has* guided legal policy, except insofar as the positive theory may be undermined by the inadequacies of the normative theory. Actually the two theories are not as separable as this, illustrating again the lack of a clear boundary between "is" and "ought" propositions. One of the things judges ought to do is follow precedent, although not inflexibly; so if efficiency is the animating principle of much common law doctrine, judges have some obligation to make decisions that will be consistent with efficiency. This is ordinarily the reason why the positive economic theory of the common law is so contentious.

The normative theory has been highly contentious in its own right. Most contributors to the debate over it conclude that it is a bad theory, and although many of the criticisms can be answered, several cannot be, and it is those I shall focus on.

The first is that wealth maximization is inherently incomplete as a guide to social action because it has nothing to say about the distribution of rights—or at least nothing we want to hear. Given the distribution of rights (whatever it is), wealth maximization can be used to derive the policies that will maximize the value of those rights. But this does not go far enough, because naturally we are curious about whether it would be just to start off with a society in which, say, one member owned all the others. If wealth maximization is indifferent to the initial distribution of rights, it is a truncated concept of justice.

Since the initial distribution may dissipate rapidly, this point may have little practical significance. Nor is wealth maximization completely silent on the initial distribution. If we could compare two otherwise identical nascent societies, in one of which one person owned all the others and in the other of which slavery was forbidden, and could repeat the comparison a century later, almost certainly we would find that the second society was wealthier and the first had abolished slavery (if so, this would further illustrate the limited effect of the initial distribution on the current distribution). Although it has not always and everywhere been true, under modern conditions of production slavery is an inefficient method of organizing production. The extensive use of slave labor by the Nazis during World War II may seem an exception but only if we disregard the welfare of the slave laborers.

This response to the demand that wealth maximization tell us something about the justice of the initial distribution of rights is incomplete. Suppose it were the case—it almost surely *is* the case— that some people in modern American society would be more productive as slaves than as free persons. These are not antisocial people whom we want to punish by imprisoning (a form of slavery that is tolerated); they are not psychotic or profoundly retarded; they just are lazy, feckless, poorly organized, undisciplined people—people incompetent to manage their own lives in a way that will maximize their output, even though the relevant output is not market output alone but also leisure, family associations, and any other sources of satisfaction to these people as well as to others. Wealth would be maximized by enslaving these people, provided the costs of supervision were not too high—but the assumption that they would not be too high is built into the proposition that their output would be greater as slaves than as free persons, for it is net output that we are interested in. Yet no one thinks it would be right to enslave such people, even if there were no evidentiary problems in identifying them, the slave masters could be trusted to be benign, and so on; and these conditions, too, may be implicit in the proposition that the net social output of some people would be greater if they were slaves.

It is no answer that it would be inefficient to enslave such people unless they consented to be enslaved, that is, unless the would-be slave-master met the asking price for their freedom. The term "*their* freedom" assumes they have the property right in their persons, and the assumption is arbitrary. We can imagine assigning the property rights in persons (perhaps only persons who appeared likely to be unproductive) to the state to auction them to the highest bidder. The putative slave could bid against the putative master, but would lose. His expected earnings, net of consumption, would be smaller than the expected profits to the master; otherwise enslavement would not be efficient. Therefore he could not borrow enough—even if capital markets worked without any friction (in the present setting, even if the lender could enslave the borrower if the latter defaulted!)—to outbid his master-to-be.

This example points to a deeper criticism of wealth maximization as a norm or value: like utilitarianism, which it closely resembles, or nationalism, or Social Darwinism, or racialism, or organic theories of the state, it treats people as if they were the cells of a single organism; the welfare of the cell is important only insofar as it promotes the welfare of the organism. Wealth maximization implies that if the prosperity of the society can be promoted by enslaving its least productive citizens, the sacrifice of their freedom is worthwhile. But this implication is contrary to the unshakable moral intuitions of Americans, and as I stressed in the last chapter, conformity to intuition is the ultimate test of a moral (indeed of any) theory.

Earlier chapters provide illustrations of collisions between, on the one hand, moral intuitions that have been influential in law and, on the other hand, wealth maximization. Recall, first, that the idea of corrective justice may well include the proposition that people who are wronged are entitled to some form of redress, even in cases when from an aggregate social standpoint it might be best to let bygones be bygones. Such an idea has no standing in a system powered by wealth maximization. Second, the prohibition of involuntary confessions rests on a notion of free will that has no standing in a system of wealth maximization, even though the particular notion of free will that the law uses equates free will with capacity for rational choice, and rational choice is fundamental to economics. The lawfulness of confessions in a system single-mindedly devoted to wealth maximization would depend entirely on the costs and benefits of the various forms of coercion, which range from outright torture to the relatively mild psychological pressures that our legal system tolerates. Cost-benefit analysis might show that torture was rarely cost-effective under modern conditions, being a costly method of interrogation (especially for the victim, but perhaps also for the torturer) that is apt to produce a lot of false leads and unreliable confessions. Nevertheless, even the most degrading forms of torture would not *necessarily* be ruled out, even in the investigation of ordinary crimes. . . .

Or suppose it were the case—it may be the case—that some religious faiths are particularly effective in producing law-abiding, productive, healthy citizens. Mormonism is a plausible example. Would it not make sense on purely secular grounds, indeed on purely wealth-maximizing grounds, for government to subsidize these faiths? Practitioners of other religious faiths would be greatly offended, but from the standpoint of wealth maximization the only question would be whether the cost to them was greater than the benefits to the country as a whole.

Consider now a faith that both has few adherents in the United States and is feared or despised by the rest of the population. (The Rastafarian faith is a plausible example.) Such a faith will by assumption be imposing costs on the rest of the community, and given the fewness of its adherents, the benefits conferred by the faith may, even when aggregated across all its adherents, be smaller than the costs. It could then be argued that wealth maximization warranted or even required the suppression of the faith. This example suggests another objection to wealth maximization, one alluded to in the discussion of slavery: its results are sensitive to assumptions about the initial distribution of rights—a distribution that is distinct from the initial distribution of wealth (which is unlikely to remain stable over time), but about which wealth maximization may again have relatively little to say. If Rastafarians are conceived to have a property right in their religion, so that the state or anyone else who wants to acquire that right and suppress the religion must meet their asking price, probably the right will not be sold. Asking prices can be very high—in principle, infinite: how much would the average person sell his life for, if the sale had to be completed immediately? But if rights over religious practices are given to the part of the populace that is not Rastafarian, the Rastafarians may find it impossible to buy the right back; their offer price will be limited to their net wealth, which may be slight.

No doubt in this country, in this day and age, religious liberty is the cost-justified policy. The broader point is that a system of rights—perhaps the system we have—may well be required by a *realistic* conception of utilitarianism, that is, one that understands that given the realities of human nature a society dedicated to utilitarianism requires rules and institutions that place checks on utility-maximizing behavior in particular cases. For example, although one can imagine specific cases in which deliberately punishing an innocent person as a criminal would increase aggregate utility, one has trouble imagining a system in which government officials could be trusted to make such decisions. "Wealth maximizing" can be substituted for "utilitarian" without affecting the analysis. Religious liberty may well be both utility maximizing and wealth maximizing, and this may even be why we have it. And if it became *too* costly, probably it would be abandoned; and so with the prohibition of torture, and the other civilized political amenities of a wealthy society. If our crime rate were much lower than it is, we probably would not have capital punishment—and if it gets much higher, we surely will have fewer civil liberties.

But at least in the present relatively comfortable conditions of our society, the regard for individual freedom appears to transcend instrumental considerations; freedom appears to be valued for itself rather than just for its contribution to prosperity, at least to be valued for reasons that escape the economic calculus. Is society really better off in a utilitarian or wealth-maximizing sense as a result of the extraordinarily elaborate procedural safeguards that the Bill of Rights gives criminal defendants? This is by no means clear. Are minority rights welfare maximizing—when the minority in question is a small one? That is not clear either, as the Rastafarian example showed. The main reasons these institutions are valued seem not to be utilitarian or even instrumental in character. What those reasons are is far from clear; indeed, "noninstrumental reason" is almost an oxymoron. And as I have suggested, we surely are not willing to pay an infinite price, perhaps not even a very high price, for freedom. While reprobating slavery we condone similar (but more efficient) practices under different names—imprisonment as punishment for crime, preventive detention, the authority of parents and school authorities over children, conscription, the institutionalization of the insane and the retarded. The Thirteenth Amendment has been read narrowly. Although the only stated exception is for punishment for crime ("neither slavery nor involuntary servitude, except as a punishment for crime whereof the party shall have been duly convicted, shall exist within the United States, or any place subject to their jurisdiction"), laws requiring jury service, military service, and even working on the public roads have been upheld. We reprobate the infliction of physical pain as a method of extracting confessions or imposing punishment but, perhaps in unconscious tribute to the outmoded dualism of mind and body, condone the infliction of mental pain for the same purposes.

Still, hypocritical and incoherent as our political ethics may frequently be, we do not permit degrading invasions of individual autonomy merely on judgment that, on balance, the invasion would make a net addition to the social wealth. And whatever the philosophical grounding of this sentiment, it is too deeply entrenched in our society at present for wealth maximization to be given a free rein. The same may be true of the residue of corrective justice sentiment. . . .

The strongest argument for wealth maximization is not moral, but pragmatic. Such classic defenses of the free market as chapter 4 of Mill's *On Liberty* can easily be given a pragmatic reading. We look around the world and see that in general people who live in societies in which markets are allowed to function more or less freely not only are wealthier than people in other societies but have more political rights, more liberty and dignity, are more content (as evidenced, for example, by their being less prone to emigrate)—so that wealth maximization may be the most direct route to a variety of moral ends. The recent history of England, France, and Turkey, of Japan and Southeast Asia, of East versus West Germany and North versus South Korea, of China and Taiwan, of Chile, of the Soviet Union, Poland, and Hungary, and of Cuba and Argentina provides striking support for this thesis. . . .

A sensible pragmatism does not ignore theory. The mounting evidence that capitalism is more efficient than socialism gives us an additional reason for believing economic theory (not every application of it, to be sure). The theory in turn gives us greater confidence in the evidence. Theory and evidence are mutually supporting. From the perspective of economic theory, brain drain . . . is the rational response to leveling policies by those whose incomes are being leveled downward.

I said that Mill's defense of free markets in *On Liberty* is most persuasive when viewed in pragmatic terms. This suggestion will jar some readers, for whom pragmatism is associated with socialism. Many leading pragmatists have been socialists, such as Dewey, Habermas, and Wittgenstein. But Holmes was a pragmatist, and he was not a socialist; ditto with Sidney Hook. If there is a correlation between pragmatism and socialism, it tells us more about academic fashions than about the allure of pragmatism. . . .

My pragmatic judgment is . . . a qualified one. All modern societies depart from the precepts of wealth maximization. The unanswered question is how the conditions in these societies would change if the public sector could somehow be cut all the way down to the modest dimensions of the night watchman state that the precepts of wealth maximization seem to imply. That is a difficult counterfactual question (it seems that no society's leadership has both the will and the power to play the guinea pig in an experiment with full-fledged wealth maximization). . . . Until it is answered, we should be cautious in pushing wealth maximization; incrementalism should be our watchword.

The fact that wealth maximization, pragmatically construed, is instrumental rather than foundational is not an objection to its use in guiding law and public policy. It may be the right principle for that purpose even though it is right only in virtue of ends that are not solely economic. At least it may be the right default principle, placing on the proponent of departures from wealth maximization the burden of demonstrating their desirability.

Even if my observations on comparative economic performance in the Third World and elsewhere are correct, do such matters belong in a book on jurisprudence? They do. The object of pragmatic analysis is to lead discussion away from issues semantic and metaphysical and toward issues factual and empirical. Jurisprudence is greatly in need of such a shift in direction. Jurisprudence needs to become more pragmatic.

In the final reading here Posner describes in more detail his own pragmatic approach to normative questions and further explains how the principles of wealth maximization fit into his notion of what normative legal theory should be. The approach can be described roughly as follows: If we ask, what should determine rational allocation of resources in circumstances that involve inevitable loss?, the answer is that we need not rely entirely on the Pareto principle. We have in addition what is sometimes referred to as the "hypothetical compensation principle." Roughly speaking, this is the principle that one allocation is preferable to another if some people are *so much better off* under one allocation than another in question, that the advantaged could *compensate* those who were *not* better off. As with the Pareto principle, the problem with application of the hypothetical compensation principle is in justifying any losses suffered under it *to which people do not consent*. At the end of this reading Posner deals with this problem by appealing to the notion of "ex ante compensation," that is, the idea that losses that *seem* to be imposed on people without their consent have sometimes been compensated in advance. His discussion of the difference between the ex post and the ex ante perspectives is important for an understanding of what he means by losses having been compensated in advance (i.e., ex ante). When they have been so compensated—and he believes that in many cases ex ante compensation can be demonstrated—Posner argues that the losses suffered can be justified. Cases in which a legal decision is based on wealth maximization *without* ex ante compensation *cannot* be justified, however, unless insurance, whether social or private, is available. Wealth maximization thus fails to be self-sufficient as a normative principle for Posner: it requires backing in order to be justified—backing either by ex ante compensation or by the availability of insurance.

Reading 5

From Richard A. Posner,
PROBLEMS OF JURISPRUDENCE

The case for using wealth maximization as a guiding principle in common law adjudication is particularly strong. The common law judge operates within a framework established by the Constitution, which, by virtue of a number of the amendments, not only rules out of bounds the ethically most questionable applications of wealth maximization but largely eliminates the problems of incompleteness and indeterminacy that result from the uncertain relationship between wealth maximization and the initial distribution of rights. That initial distribution is more or less a given for the common law judge. A related point is that such a judge operates in a domain where distributive or egalitarian considerations can play at best only a small role. The judge whose business is enforcing tort, contract, and property law lacks effective tools for bringing about an equitable distribution of wealth, even if he thinks he knows what such a distribution would be. He would be further handicapped in such an endeavor by the absence of consensus in our society on the nature of a just distribution, an absence that undermines the social acceptability of attempts to use the judicial office to achieve distributive goals. A sensible division of labor has the judge making rules and deciding cases in the areas regulated by the common law in such a way as to maximize the size of the social pie, and the legislature attending to the sizes of the slices.

The case is strongest in those common law areas where the relevant policies are admitted to be economic. Suppose the idea of an implied warranty of habitability—which entitles a tenant to sue his landlord if the premises fall below the standards of safety and comfort specified in the local housing code—is defended, as normally it is defended, on the ground that it is needed to protect tenants from deception and overreaching by landlords and will not lead to a reduction in the stock of housing available to poor people or to higher rentals than the poor are willing and able to pay. If research demonstrates that these assumptions are incorrect, the proponent,

if fair-minded, will have to withdraw the proposal. In this example, in principle (for the necessary research is difficult to conduct), legal questions can be made determinate by the translation of a legal question into a social-scientific one in a setting of common ends, and therefore the valid Benthamite project of placing law on a more scientific basis can be advanced without injury to competing values.

If it could be shown or if it is conceded that common law decision making is indeed not an apt field for efforts to redistribute wealth, then it may be possible to ground wealth maximization (as used to guide such decision making) in a more powerful normative principle of economics, the Pareto principle. A transaction is Pareto superior when it makes at least one person better off and no one worse off. A simple contract approximates a Pareto-superior transaction. Neither party would sign the contract unless he thought he would be better off as a result. So, assuming adequate information (which does not mean assuming omniscience) and no adverse effects on third parties, the contract will be Pareto superior. At least this will be so on an ex ante basis, for as things turn out one of the parties (perhaps both) may be made worse off by the contract. This possibility is inevitable if there is uncertainty, and uncertainty is inevitable.

The ethical appeal of the Pareto principle is similar to that of unanimity. If everyone affected by a transaction is better off, how can the transaction be socially or ethically bad? There are answers to this question, yet a Pareto-superior transaction makes a powerful claim for ethical respect because it draws on intuitions that are fundamental to both utilitarianism and Kantian individualism—

respect for preferences, and for persons, respectively. It may seem paradoxical to derive a norm of wealth maximization from the principle of Pareto superiority, when the hallmark of the latter is compensation of all potential losers (for remember that no one must be made worse off by the transaction if it is to be Pareto superior), while wealth maximization requires only that the winners' gains exceed the losers' losses. But if, as in the contract example, compensation is permitted to be cx ante, the paradox disappears.

The difference between the ex ante and ex post perspectives is fundamental, and failure to attend to it underlies much confused thinking about markets and transactional competence. Because many choices are made, unavoidably, under conditions of uncertainty, a fair number *must* turn out badly. Ex post, they are regarded as mistaken and engender regret, yet ex ante they may have been perfectly sensible. Suppose I have a choice between two jobs. One would pay me $50,000 every year with certainty, the other either $500,000 a year (with a 90 percent probability) or nothing (with a 10 percent probability). The expected income in the first job is $50,000 and in the second $450,000. (Notice the use of Bayesian probability. . . .) The second, however, involves uncertainty. If I am risk averse—and let us assume I am—I will value an uncertain expectation at less than its actuarial equivalent. Hence the second job will not really be worth $450,000 to me, and let us suppose it will be worth only one-third as much—$150,000. Still, that is more than $50,000, so I will take the second job. But I am unlucky, the 10 percent chance materializes, and my income is zero. I would be less (or more) than human if I did not regret

my choice, rail against my fate, berate myself for having chosen stupidly. But in fact I made the right choice—and would make it again, given the same uncertainty as before.

Consider now the case where negligence is the more efficient principle, in a wealth-maximizing sense, than strict liability because when all the costs and benefits are toted up the negligence regime turns out to produce the greater excess of benefits over costs. If so, the sum of liability and accident insurance premiums will be lower in the negligence regime and all drivers will be better off ex ante, although ex post, of course, some may do better in a regime of strict liability. Actually, not all will be better off even ex ante. Some people who are more prone to be injured than to injure will be worse off, since negligence favors injurers relative to strict liability, and some who are more prone to injure than to be injured will be better off. The "losers" will lose little, though—a matter of slightly higher insurance premiums. And both the "winners" and the vast majority of drivers who are neither disproportionately likely to injure than to be injured nor vice versa will be better off. Complete unanimity will be unattainable, but near unanimity can be presumed and the few losers will hardly be degraded, their autonomy wrecked, or their rights destroyed by having to pay a few dollars a month more in automobile insurance premiums.

I am painting with slightly too rosy a palette. Some people will lack the knowledge, intelligence, and foresight to buy insurance (I am putting to one side the deliberate risk takers); some may not be able to afford adequate insurance; and insurance that pays off as generously as common law damages may not be available in the market. When a person becomes a victim of a serious accident in which the injurer is not at fault, it may spell a financial disaster not attributable to the choices or the deserts of the victim—a disaster that strict liability could have avoided. An alternative, of course, is social insurance—the famous safety net. If cases of catastrophic uninsured nonnegligent accidental injury are rare, social insurance may be a better solution than a strict liability system that would require compensation through the tort system in all accident cases.

The essential point is that the availability of insurance, private or social, is necessary to back wealth maximization with the ethical weight of the Pareto principle. Once it is so backed, however, wealth maximization provides an ethically adequate guide to common law decision making—indeed a superior guide to any other that has been suggested. And the adequacy of private and public insurance markets, on which this conclusion depends, is an empirical, a studiable, issue.

No doubt most judges (and lawyers) think that the guiding light for common law decision making should be either an intuitive sense of justice or reasonableness, or a casual utilitarianism. But these may all be the same thing, and if pressed such a judge would probably have to admit that what he called utilitarianism was what I am calling wealth maximization. Consider whether a thief should be permitted to defend himself at trial on the ground that he derived greater pleasure from the stolen item than the pain suffered by the owner. The answer obviously is no, but it is offered more confidently by the wealth maximizer than by the pure utilitarian. The former can point out that the thief is bypassing the market system of exchange and that the pleasure he derives from the

good he has stolen has no social standing because his desire for the good is not backed by willingness to pay. These are separate points. The thief might be willing to pay if he had to—that is, he might value the good more than its owner—yet prefer theft because it is a cheaper way for him to acquire the good. So theft might be utility maximizing, although this is unlikely because a *practice* of theft results in enormous, utility-reducing expenditures on protection of property.

Since utility is more difficult to estimate than wealth, a system of wealth maximization may seem a proxy for a utilitarian system, but it is more; its spirit is different. Wealth maximization is an ethic of productivity and social cooperation—to have a claim on society's goods and services you must be able to offer something that other people value, while utilitarianism is a hedonistic, unsocial ethic, as the last example showed. And an ethic of productivity and cooperation is more congruent with the values of the dominant groups in our society than the pure utilitarian ethic would be. Unfortunately, wealth maximization is not a pure ethic of productivity and cooperation, not only because even lawful efforts at maximizing wealth often make some other people worse off, but more fundamentally because luck plays a big role in the returns to market activities. What is worse, it is always possible to argue that the distribution of productivity among a population is itself the luck of the genetic draw, or of upbringing, or of where one happens to have been born, and that these forms of luck have an ethical charge. There are counterarguments, of course, but they are not decisive. So, once again, the foundations of an overarching principle for resolving legal disputes are rotten, and one is driven back to the pragmatic ramparts.

QUESTIONS

1. What is "equal bargaining power"? Posner maintains (elsewhere) that contracting parties have equal bargaining power because both can exit, that is, walk away from, the deal. Do you agree? Why or why not?

2. Bobby buys a baseball card from a hobby shop for $5 knowing it was worth $500 and that the card was mistakenly priced by a clerk. Is this an enforceable contract? Defend your answer.

3. Is Posner correct to endorse "efficient" breaches? Why or why not?

4. Are fraudulent exchanges ever efficient? If so, must Posner endorse them just as he endorses efficient breaches? Defend your answers.

5. What should happen when a breach results because performance is impossible? In answering discuss some specific examples.

6. Elsewhere Posner has argued that laissez-faire capitalism is the most efficient system and therefore the one that the law ought to provide and protect. Critics have urged, however, that such a system is unacceptable since it permits, at least in principle, sale of everything: sex, favors by public officers, children, exemptions from jail, even people as slaves. With which position do you agree, and why?

7. In a discussion of Dworkin[6], Posner presents the example of a suit by homeowners against an airline that lowers the value of their property through the noise of its planes. Suppose that noise abatement by the airline would cost much more than the lowered value of the homes. How might your decision, as judge, be formed or influenced by such calculations and by the notion of maximizing utility?

---

6. *Ronald Dworkin and Contemporary Jurisprudence*, ed. M. Cohen (Totowa, New Jersey: Rowman and Allanheld, 1984), p. 239.

Chapter 5

Critical Legal Theory

Readings from Andrew Altman,
Roberto Unger, and Martha Minow

Part I: Critical Legal Studies

All the types of jurisprudence studied so far share a common characteristic: they are cognitive theories of law in one way or another. Each one claims (1) that some particular kind of knowledge is possible that bears directly upon legal decision-making (whether knowledge of natural law, knowledge of positive law, knowledge of principles, or knowledge of what makes for an increase in the good for society) and (2) that legal judgments derived from that knowledge are objective in nature—that is, they are neither purely subjective nor arbitrary, but rooted in intersubjective understanding. As expressions of knowledge, legal propositions are understood as arguably either true or false, independent of whether any particular lawyer or judge thinks them so. As we have seen, various accounts of determining legal truth have been developed, and their adequacy has been the subject of controversy, but even these disagreements have been informed by cognitive assurances of one kind and another. Recall Posner's characterization of his brand of pragmatism: he is doubtful of finding objective truth in any area of inquiry; he elevates the process of inquiry over the results of inquiry[1]; and he advocates a skeptical conception of the legal process.[2] But his skepticism is far from wholesale. The same passages in which various forms of philosophical and legal doubt are expressed reveal confidence in various forms of knowledge. His position is "skeptical, but decidedly not cynical," and his normative jurisprudence relies on empirical knowledge in combination with economic analysis. One of the main reasons why pragmatism is attractive to Posner is its emphasis on scientific virtues and empirical knowledge.

---

1. Posner, *Problems of Jurisprudence*, Id. at p. 28.
2. Ibid., p. 26.

A distinguishing mark of critical legal theory is the absence of any central cognitive claim; its predominent theme is doubt about legal knowledge. The reasons for skepticism and the degree to which it is partial or wholesale vary considerably among its representatives, but all of the accounts of law studied in this chapter are remarkably non-cognitive, both with respect to the character of their claims and their theoretical underpinnings.

The first vigorous expression of non-cognitivism in American legal history is evident as early as the 1920s when a group of American lawyers and jurists developed cogent arguments against two prevailing ideas: (1) that established law is an identifiable body of knowledge and (2) that an adequate understanding of the law when combined with an adequate understanding of the facts produces a correct legal outcome. Realists argued, from personal experience, that careful observation plainly reveals that often considerations *additional to* legal and factual judgments enter into and determine legal outcomes. Their insights were based on what lawyers and judges *actually do*, thus winning for this group of jurists the label "realist."

It is now widely appreciated that American legal realists are responsible for recording an impressive phenomenology of adjudication—their collective work shows that in many instances, especially in appellate litigation, law is essentially indeterminate. The indeterminacy in question is a direct result of the fecundity of legal thinking, which, over a fairly long period, generates a plethora of rules, precedents, interpretations of rules, variations in procedure and the like, making it entirely possible for opposite sides of many legal cases to be equally correct under the law. In all but the easiest of cases, they argue, it is extra-legal considerations that finally determine legal outcomes. Which among many possible extra-legal factors (sociological, ideological, political, economic, or psychological) is determinative for adjudication can be a matter of disagreement; but notwithstanding this disagreement, realists hold firm to the conviction that established law is intrinsically indeterminate.

In the first set of readings in this chapter Andrew Altman argues that insufficient attention has been paid to the work of realists, especially to their arguments for legal indeterminacy. He traces this neglect directly to the influence of H.L.A. Hart's *The Concept of Law*, which is widely regarded as diminishing realist doctrine in two rather different ways. First, Hart advances arguments against what he considers realist "excesses," among them a "strong indeterminacy" claim. Second, he "absorbs" much realist insight into the phenomenology of adjudication through discussion of how jurists deal with the "open texture" of legal concepts. In the first reading Altman argues that neither aspect of Hart's work deals sufficiently with the most important source of legal indeterminacy recognized by realists.

Reading 1

From Andrew Altman,
"LEGAL REALISM, CRITICAL LEGAL STUDIES
AND DWORKIN" IN *PHILOSOPHY AND
PUBLIC AFFAIRS*

One of the now familiar theses defended by Hart in *The Concept of Law* is that there are some cases in which the rules of a legal system do not clearly specify the correct legal outcome. Hart claims that such cases arise because of the ineliminable open-texture of natural language: all general terms have a penumbral range in which it is unclear and irresolvably controversial as to whether the term applies to some particular. Yet, this penumbral range of extensional indeterminacy is necessarily much smaller than the core extension in which the terrn's application is clear and uncontroversial. For Hart, then, the indeterminacy of law is a peripheral phenomenon in a system of rules which, by and large, does provide specific outcomes to cases.

The realist analysis of indeterminacy sees it as both more pervasive and deeper than the indeterminacy Hart attributes to the legal order. For the realist, there is no way to confine indeterminacy to some peripheral region of the law. For my purposes here, I shall be concerned mainly with the realist analysis of common-law adjudication. It should not be forgotten, however, that the realists could and did extend their analysis to all types of adjudication found in our legal system, including those involving statutory and constitutional issues.

The realist analysis of indeterminacy can be presented in two stages. The first stage proceeded from the idea that there was always a cluster of rules relevant to the decision in any litigated case. Thus, deciding whether an uncle's promise to pay his nephew a handsome sum of money if he refrained from smoking, drinking, and playing pool was enforceable brought into play a number of rules, for example, rules regarding offer, acceptance, consideration, revocation, and so on. The realists understood that the vagueness of any one of these rules could affect the outcome of the case. In any single case, then, there were multiple potential points of indeterminacy due to rule vagueness, not a single point as Hart's account sometimes seems to suggest.

The second stage of the realist analysis began with the rejection of a distinction central to the doctrine of precedent, namely, that between holding and dictum. The holding in a case referred to the essential grounds of the decision and thus what subsequent judges were bound by. The dicta were everything in an opinion not essential to the decision, for example, comments about points of law not treated as the basis of the outcome. The realists argued that in its actual operation the common-law system treated the distinction as a vague and shifting one. Even when the judge writing an opinion characterized part of it as "the holding," judges writing subsequent opinions were not bound by the original judge's perception of what was essential for the decision. Subsequent judges were indeed bound by the decision itself, that is, by the finding for or against the plaintift, and very rarely was the decision in a precedent labeled as mistaken. But this apparently strict obligation to follow precedent was highly misleading, according to the realists. For later judges had tremendous leeway in being able to redefine the holding and the dictum in the precedential cases. This leeway enabled judges, in effect, to rewrite the rules of law on which earlier cases had been decided. The upshot was that in almost any case which reached the stage of litigation, a judge could find opinions which read relevant precedents as stating one legal rule and other opinions which read the precedents as stating a contrary rule. The common-law judge thus faced an indeterminate legal situation in which he had to render a decision by choosing which of the competing rules was to govern the case. In other words, while the realists claimed that all cases implicated a cluster of rules, they also contended that in any cluster there were competing rules leading to opposing outcomes.

It is this second form of indeterminacy which the realist saw as the deepest and most pervasive. Depending upon how a judge would read the holdings in the cases deemed to be precedents, she would extract different rules of law capable of generating conflicting outcomes in the case before her. In the common-law system, it was left undetermined as to which rules, of a number of incompatible rules, were to govern a case. This type of indeterminacy cuts a much deeper and wider path than the kind Hart was willing to acknowledge. For Hart, the cases afflicted with indeterminacy are the ones in which we know

which rule applies but are uncertain over the outcome because the rule contains some vague general term. This second type of realist indeterminacy stems from the fact that the choice of which rules to apply in the first place is not dictated by the law and that competing rules will be available in almost any case which reaches the stage of litigation.

In discussing realism, Hart makes three concessions to realist indeterminacy claims, while at the same time coupling each claim with a major qualification designed to show that actual indeterminacy is far less radical than realism suggests. First, Hart concedes that "there is no single method of determining the rule for which a given authoritative precedent is an authority." But he quickly adds: "Notwithstanding this, in the vast majority of decided cases, there is very little doubt. The headnote is usually correct enough." It is simply question begging, though, for Hart to assert that the headnote usually provides a sufficiently accurate statement of the correct rule. The realist point is that there is nothing that can be thought of as "the correct rule" for which a precedent stands, and so there is no standard against which one can say that a given rule is "correct enough." On the realist analysis, the headnote, or indeed a later opinion, states only one of any number of competing rules which may, with equal legitimacy, be said to constitute the holding of a case. Hart's assertions do nothing to show that this analysis is wrong; they merely presuppose that it is wrong.

Hart's second concession to realism is that "there is no authoritative or uniquely correct formulation of any rule to be extracted from cases." But then he adds that "there is often very general agreement, when the bearing of a precedent on a later case is in issue, that a given formulation is adequate." Hart seems to be saying here that lawyers may disagree on the precise formulation of a rule but still agree on the correct outcome of a case and so be able to accept, for the purposes of the case, a formulation which, in the given instance, straddles the different versions of the rule. This claim may very well be accurate, but it fails to defeat the realist indeterminacy claims for two reasons. It assumes that the problem of being able to extract conflicting rules from the same line of precedents has been resolved, and, as I argued in connection with Hart's first pair of points, that assumption is question begging. Second, even if there is general agreement on the outcome of a case and on some rough statement of the governing rule (and this, of course, ignores the disagreement which will always be found between the attorneys for the litigants), it does not follow that they agree on the outcome because they agree (roughly) on the legal rule which is said to govern the case. In other words, it does not follow that the law determines the outcome. Agreement on the outcome and on the rough statement of the rule used to justify the outcome may both be the result of some

more fundamental political value choice which is agreed upon. Indeed, this is exactly what the realist analysis would suggest by way of explaining broad agreement on outcomes and rules. Realism is not committed to denying broad agreement. It is simply committed to the view that the agreement cannot be explained by the determinacy of the law. Thus, Hart's invocation of agreement here does nothing to defeat the realist's indeterminacy thesis.

Hart's third concession to realism is that courts invariably engage in narrowing and widening the rules which precedents lay down. Yet he says that, despite this, the doctrine of precedent has produced "a body of rules of which a vast number, of both major and minor importance, are as determinate as any statutory rule." The problem with this claim, though, is that it misses the crucial realist point regarding the availability of competing rules: let each legal rule be as precise as is humanly possible, the realists insist that the legal system contains competing rules which will be available for a judge to choose in almost any litigated case. The claims made by Hart in his effort to domesticate the realist notion of legal indeterminacy all systematically fail to deal with this crucial realist point.

In Altman's view, realist's arguments for indeterminacy stand up well not only when compared with Hart's treatment of them, but also when compared with Dworkin's conception of legal indeterminacy. Reading 2 is a three-way comparison: of Hart's opposition to the realists, of Dworkin's opposition to Hart, and of Dworkin's differences with realism. As a result of this comparison Altman raises the possibility that Dworkin may have succeeded where Hart failed, that is, in defeating realist arguments for radical indeterminacy in law.

Reading 2

From Andrew Altman, "LEGAL REALISM, CRITICAL LEGAL STUDIES AND DWORKIN" IN *PHILOSOPHY AND PUBLIC AFFAIRS*

To this point, I have portrayed the realists as focusing upon the choice of competing legal rules which judges in common-law cases must make. This may seem to leave the realist open to one of the principal criticisms which Dworkinians have made of Hart: the law is more than just legal rules. It is also the ethical principles and ideals of which the rules are an (albeit imperfect) expression, and it is these principles and ideals which help to guide judges to a determinate outcome. Indeed, the Dworkinian might try to use the realist indeterminacy analysis to his advantage: if the law were simply a collection of rules, as Hart thinks, it would be afflicted by exactly the kind of deep and pervasive indeterminacy which the realist posits. Yet, if the law were indeterminate to the degree suggested by the realist analysis, it would not be much more than a pious fraud: judges would be "legislating" not only in penumbral cases, but in all cases. Judges would always be creating law, in flagrant violation of their institutional duty to apply preexisting law. The Dworkinian may conclude that we face this choice: either include principles and ideals as part of the law in order to contain (and, perhaps, eliminate) the indeterminacy it would have were it simply a collection of rules or admit that common-law adjudication is a fraud. Although the latter choice is logically possible, assumptions shared by both Dworkin and his positivist critics make it an entirely implausible one from their point of view. The only plausible al-

ternative may thus seem to be the acceptance of Dworkin's important idea that ethical principles be understood as part of the law even when they are not explicitly formulated in some authoritative legal text or clearly identifiable by the application of some noncontroversial, positivist rule for specifying authoritative legal norms in terms of their source. Thus, Dworkin argues that adjudication requires the invocation of principles which take judges "well past the point where it would be accurate to say that any 'test' of pedigree exists. . . ." Moreover, such principles are, on Dworkin's view, binding on judges and so we must realize that "legal obligation . . . [is] . . . imposed by a constellation of principles as well as by an established rule." Indeed, it is this constellation of principles which must guide the judge to a determinate outcome when the relevant legal rules are in competition with one another. For instance, the principles could indicate to the judge the proper scope of application of each of the competing rules and thus resolve any apparent conflict by showing that just one of the rules was properly applicable in the case at hand.

Yet, which principles are legally binding? Dworkin's answer is that they are those which belong to the "soundest theory of the settled law." The settled law consists of those legal rules and doctrines which would be accepted as authoritative by the consensus of the legal community. The soundest theory is the most defensible ethical and political theory which coheres with and justifies those legal rules and doctrines. The coherence does not have to be perfect, for Dworkin allows that the soundest theory may characterize some rules and legal outcomes as mistakes, but coherence with most of the settled law is demanded. In principle, the soundest theory is to encompass every area of law: every branch of the common law, all statutes, the whole body of administrative law, and the entire range of constitutional law. Of course, Dworkin recognizes that no merely human judge could ever formulate and defend such a theory. But his character, Hercules, is intended to show us that, in principle, such a theory could be formulated and defended by a sufficiently great intelligence. Even though the fictional, judicial Hercules has powers far beyond those of mortal judges, Dworkin tells us that mortal judges are committed both to the logical possibility of such a character and to the task of trying to arrive at the outcome he would arrive at were he to be hearing their cases. Mortal judges thus can and do appeal to principles in reaching determinate outcomes, and, in doing so, they are giving force to preexisting legal obligations, and not simply making a political choice among competing legal rules.

It should be noted that the realists were not blind to seeing legal rules as expressions of ethical principles. Nonetheless, there are tremendous differences between the way in which a realist such as Thurman Arnold viewed these principles and the way in which Dworkin and his followers see them. Arnold was thoroughly cynical about the ethical ideals in terms of which the law was understood: they were high-sounding phrases which appealed to people's emotions and satisfied their need to

think of the legal order as more than just some arbitrary and contingent setup. But they had no meaning other than this emotive one and could not be the subject of any rational discussion or defense. Other realists, such as Felix Cohen, were not at all cynical and believed that ethical principles were amenable to rational discussion. Yet they did little to analyze carefully the ethical principles embedded in law or to examine the implications of the existence of such principles for the problem of indeterminacy.

In this section, I have raised the possibility that Dworkin's jurisprudential project succeeds where Hart failed in defeating the radical realist indeterminacy thesis. However, it would be premature to make a judgment regarding the success of Dworkin's project in this respect, for scholars in the Critical Legal Studies movement have picked up and elaborated realist ideas in a way that seriously threatens the foundations of Dworkinian jurisprudence. It is to CLS that I shall turn presently. One important point should be made before I do that, however. For the most part, proponents of CLS and Dworkinians have ignored one another's positions. There are some passing references to CLS in some pieces by avowed Dworkinians, such as Charles Fried. And there is some treatment of Dworkin in the CLS literature. Yet, neither side seems to do anything more than make very superficial, highly polemical points against the other. The interchange of ideas between Dworkinians and CLSers is one which I have constructed with the deliberate aim of avoiding the superficial polemics which have thus far characterized the few occasions on which the one side has deigned in print to deal with the position of the other.

We pause now in our review of Altman's account of legal indeterminacy for a brief legal and philosophical interlude made appropriate by several factors. First, Altman bases his defense of realist views on what he calls elaborations developed within the CLS movement. It turns out that these elaborations are part and parcel of a comprehensive and fairly systematic interpretation of contemporary social and political thought. While this interpretation has had considerable influence, from a student's point of view it is difficult to understand; its central claims are sometimes counterintuitive and it challenges several deep-seeded assumptions and beliefs.

The CLS movement began in the 1970s when a group of scholars, many of them connected with Harvard Law School, advanced the idea that law, as currently practiced, is the expression of an identifiable set of intellectual commitments specific to modern culture, beliefs about nature, and about the relation between persons and the rest of nature. This scheme of commitments is radically different from pre-modern beliefs. One example, mentioned in Chapter 2, involves the modern rejection of final cause as an explanation of natural processes. Other differences involve ways of thinking about social and political life, and these have particular relevance to an understanding of law.

At the center of CLS understanding of these differences is the work of Roberto Unger who, in *Knowledge and Politics* argues that what passes as modern understanding is in fact not as distinct from pre-modern understanding as we normally assume. Contemporary thought, including moral, political, and legal thought, turns out to be a blend or amalgam of beliefs and attitudes whose sources can be traced *both* to pre-modern and to modern cultures. Unger finds quite understandable the fact that contemporary thinkers are neither willing nor able to abandon pre-modern ways of thinking—modern, and especially scientific, conceptual schemes are inadequate for many purposes, especially those having to do with human aims and goals. It is thus useful, perhaps even necessary, to employ premodern ideas, but problems arise when we do because ancient and modern conceptions of nature and human experience are not only different but clearly inconsistent. For Unger the uncertainties of modern political and legal thought can be traced directly to its incorporation of contrasting elements of pre-modern thought. "Traced directly" in the sense that (1) modern and ancient conceptions of nature and human experience cannot both be true at the same time and in the same way; and that (2) incompatible as these conceptual schemes are, we are both unable and unwilling to give up either in its entirety.

Unger provides an example of how this general understanding of modern culture applies to law in *The Critical Legal Studies Movement*.[3] First, he

---

3. Roberto Unger, *The Critical Legal Studies Movement* (Cambridge, Mass.: Harvard University Press, 1983), see especially pp. 66–88.

draws attention to the fact that modern moral and political thought is based on an "individualistic" vision of social life; that is, it accords priority to individual freedom, self-reliance, and other essentially individual norms and values. Second, however, he observes that this *same* moral and political thought is "altruistic" in the sense that it accords priority to social solidarity, stability, and communal norms and values. Considered as ultimate sources of social and legal value, individualism and altruism are mutually exclusive and contradictory in their implications for legal decision-making. In Unger's view the content of any area of law harbors an essentially antithetical structure; that is, its content consists of a series of principles and counterprinciples derived from conflicting priorities of value like those inherent in individualistic and altruistic visions of social life.

In contract law, for example, he invites us to examine two different explanatory models of how we decide whether a contract has been formed. On one model, this issue is determined by reference to the principle that no one has assumed any obligation to anyone else until there has been an offer and an overtly communicated acceptance of the offer. According to Unger this principle is derived from assumptions about individuality and freedom; that is, the idea that one is free to contract with whomever, under whatever conditions one chooses. However, on another, equally established model, a decision on this issue is determined by reference to a different principle, namely that once a party has begun to negotiate with another party about possible terms of a contract, she or he incurs a duty to negotiate in "good faith." For Unger this way of thinking about the existence of a contract can be traced to communal values rooted in an altruistic rather than an individualistic vision of social life.

What Unger seeks to demonstrate in this example is that the law as such does not decide a case at bar. It cannot because the content of law is essentially indeterminate with respect to questions such as exactly how and under what conditions a contract is formed. The problem in answering such questions is not that law is vague in the way all abstract and general statements are vague with respect to their application—Aristotle had pointed this out. Nor is it merely that legal concepts are "open-textured" in Hart's sense. The problem is more serious than this: law is internally conflicted and inconsistent. If this state of affairs can be shown to exist in the way Unger claims, the jurisprudential implications are large. Among other things it entails an account of legal decision-making fundamentally different from the accounts reviewed in previous chapters. Any given instance of adjudication will turn out to involve a *forced* choice between plausible, but conflicting, principles for justifying the decision made in a case at hand. And what will determine this choice? Not "the law," because "the law" is nothing but an amalgam of conflicting visions.

It is important to recognize that Unger declines to recommend any moral or social vision over any other. Nor does he see the possibility of some reconciling synthesis among them: we are, as it were, "conceptually stuck" where we are. In an early work, *Knowledge and Politics*, he discusses an important conclusion which follows from recognition of our plight: *just because legal theory is inherently conflicted to the core, objectivity in legal judgment is something beyond our conceptual reach.* According to Unger the kind of legal indeterminacy brought to attention by American legal realists is symptomatic of our legal-theoretic condition. Given this indeterminacy, judges and law-makers have no alternative but to rely on something far short of legal objectivity. But upon what should they rely? Unger cannot say because strictly speaking his legal theory lacks positive normative content. The point of his writing is enlightenment, that is, recognition and acknowledgement of the protean forms which theoretical inconsistency and conflict take in law. When successful, such enlightenment results in what he calls "total criticism," and in the following passage he explains how his legal studies forced him beyond the usual idea of criticism to something more comprehensive and radical.

> Total criticism arises from the inability of partial critiques of a system of thought to achieve their objectives and from the desire to deal with the difficulties the partial critiques themselves produce. It was in just such a manner that the present work was conceived. Having turned my mind to some familiar matters of jurisprudence, I soon found that these were so closely tied to one another that the answer to any of them would be the answer to all. Then I discovered that the solutions generally offered to each of the problems fall into a small number of types, none adequate by itself, yet none capable of reconciliation with its contenders. Thus the house of reason in which I was working proved to be a prison-house of paradox whose rooms did not connect and whose passageways led nowhere.[4]

Unger's jurisprudence is a paradigm case of critical legal theory—no knowledge claims are advanced to resolve outstanding problems in legal philosophy; the only claims defended are that these problems have not been properly understood and that as properly understood they are both unavoidable and intractable.

When grasped for the first time, the non-cognitive, thoroughly critical feature of Unger's thought can have a defamiliarizing effect on typical legal readers. He challenges us to think about adjudication absent any supposed legal objectivity, a thoroughly *unfamiliar* way of thinking. Reading 3 is particularly important in this regard because it helps make plausible this unusual way of thinking about law. In this reading Unger presents the staging-ground for a *thoroughly critical* jurisprudence, that is, the philosophical and epistemological presuppositions upon which it depends. Briefly put, the staging ground consists of three interconnected claims. Unger's originality consists neither in originating these claims nor in devel-

---

4. Roberto Unger, *Knowledge and Politics* (New York: Free Press, 1975), pp. 2–3.

oping arguments for their support (he considers them well-established). It consists, rather, in appreciating their *combined* implication for law and legal decision-making. The claims are: (1) that all concepts are theory-laden and theory-determined, including the concept of fact; (2) that all theories contain antinomies, paradoxes, and other kinds internal inconsistency; and (3) that while it is true that theories are what make all understanding possible, any such understanding must be regarded as partial and limited *just because* its theoretical underpinning contains some form of incoherence. When combined in the way Unger suggests, these claims support his main conclusion: that total understanding is never possible, only total criticism.

In studying the passage that follows notice how important the idea of theory-determination is for thoroughgoing criticism as a general framework of thought. In the final paragraph Unger asks why the tensions at work in contemporary thought are so often overlooked or ignored. His answer is that we do not attend to theoretical strain and inconsistency because we believe *falsely* that, when these aspects of thought are encountered, we can step outside the theory wherein the conflict resides and assess it from some "neutral" or "objective" point of view. But if we have seen to the theory–relative core of knowledge and understanding, we recognize that this is impossible. Any assessment of theoretical conflict must itself be theoretical; there is no theory-independent realm for us to enter.

∽

Reading 3

From Roberto Unger,
KNOWLEDGE AND POLITICS

Imagine the world as a field of space and a continuum of time that are the scene of facts or objects-events. An object exists through time as a succession of events. The world constituted by space, time, and objects-events has the following characteristics. There are an indefinite number of objects-events. Events succeed one another constantly and objects collide with each other in certain ways. The occurrence of a set of events will be followed by the occurrence of another set. The regularities that exist or that we suppose exist among events are different from the events themselves, or from the objects whose temporal aspect those events represent. A causal law of nature is distinct from the phenomena it joins together. Regularities are general; object-events particular. Object-events exist independently of our perception of what they are or of what they should be. Either we assume that everything that happens in nature happens necessarily, or we say that we do not know why things happen. The latter conception, however, implies unintelligible chance, which is also a kind of necessity. So, in either case, the field of object-events is given to us as a necessity. We call this necessity experience.

It is possible to divide the world in an indefinite number of ways. No one way of dividing it describes what the world is really like. That is because things lack intelligible essences. Something has an intelligible essence if it has a feature, capable of being apprehended, by virtue of which it belongs to one category of things rather than to another category. According to such a view, a stone is different from a plant because it has a quality of stoneness, if you like, which we can grasp immediately. Some say that the essence can be understood directly as an abstract category, quite apart from concrete things that exemplify it. Others claim that it can only be inferred or induced from its particular instances. On the latter view, we learn to distinguish the quality of stoneness by looking at particular stones.

Many, though not all, of the metaphysical systems of ancient and medieval Europe accepted the view of knowledge whose keynote is the idea that all things in nature have intelligible essences. Hence they taught that the mind can understand what the world is really like. Now this doctrine is truly a master principle, for its friends have drawn from it conclusions about language, morals, and politics. They have reasoned that because everything has an essence, everything can be classified under the word which names its category. And the supporters of the doctrine of intelligible essences have gone on to hold that the standards of right and wrong must also have essences which thought can comprehend. Plato's ethics and Aquinas' theory of natural law exemplify this line of argument.

The modern conception of nature and of the relation of thought to nature that I am describing rejects the doctrine of intelligible essences. It denies the existence of a chain of essences or essential qualities that we could either infer from particular things in the world or perceive face to face in their abstract forms. And it therefore insists that there are numberless ways in which objects and events in the world might be classified.

We cannot decide in the abstract whether a given classification is justified. The only standard is whether the classification serves the particular purpose we had in mind when we made it. Every language describes the world completely, though in its own way. On the modern view of nature, there is no basis for saying that one language portrays reality more accurately than another, for the only measure of the "truth" of language is its power to advance the ends of the communities of men who speak it. The theories of science are partial languages because they classify things in the world. Their claims to acceptance must therefore rest on their ability to contribute to particular ends, like the prediction or control of events, rather than on their fidelity to a true world of essences.

This simple idea, the denial of intelligible essences, leaves no stone of the preliberal [i.e. premodern] metaphysic standing. Its consequences for our moral and political views are as far-reaching as they are paradoxical. . . .

If there are no intelligible essences, there is no predetermined classification of the world. We can distinguish among objects-events only by reference to a standard of distinction implicit in a theory. It is the theory that determines what is to count as a fact and how facts are to be distinguished from one another. In other words, a fact becomes what it is for us because of the way we categorize it. How we classify it depends on the categories available to us in the language we speak, or in the theory we use, and on our ability to replenish the fund of categories at our disposal. In whatever way we view the play of tradition and conscious purpose in the manipulation of the categories, there is no direct appeal to reality, for reality is put together by the mind.

Yet we also believe that the history of science is progressive and that ultimately one can make a rational choice among conflicting theories about the world. Some theories describe the world more accurately than others. This belief is just as firmly grounded in the traditional conception of nature as the principle that insists we can never step outside the categories of a particular language or theory to see the world naked. Its basis is the proposition that things are what they are no matter what we think they are or ought to be. How can we sustain confidence in the possibility of an ultimate comparison of theory and fact unless we are willing to qualify the principle that the world of facts is constructed by the mind according to its purposes? The conception that there is a realm of things, independent of the mind, and capable at some point of being perceived as it truly is, seems necessary to the notion of science. Yet this

conception also appears to rely on the doctrine of intelligible essences or of plain facts, assumed to be inconsistent with the modern idea of science.

In its simplest form, the antinomy of theory and fact is the conflict of the two preceding ideas: the mediation of all facts through theory and the possibility of an independent comparison of theory with fact. Each of the principles seems plausible in its formulation and absurd in its consequences. They contradict one another, but to qualify either of them would seem to require a drastic revision of the view of nature and thought from which both are drawn. Here is a conundrum that appears to imply the incoherence of our idea of science, indeed of knowledge in general.

Why then are we not struck by the incoherence? Why are we not more frequently disturbed by the antinomy of theory and fact? Perhaps the reason for our misguided assurance is that the theories with which we work are always partial theories. They are not, like languages, descriptions of the whole world. Consequently, it always seems possible to stand apart from the particular theory we are considering. We forget that when we do this we are stepping into another theory rather than into the realm of plain facts.

In Reading 2 Altman suggested that Dworkin's conception of indeterminacy and its role in adjudication might be capable of defeating realist claims of radical legal indeterminacy. In the section to follow Altman follows up on this possibility. He argues that in light of the particular development of those arguments by critical legal studies scholars, the doctrine of radical indeterminacy holds up in ways which, so far at least, resist the criticism of positivists like Hart, constructivists like Dworkin, or for that matter conventional legal philosophers "of any stripe."

Reading 4

From Andrew Altman,
"LEGAL REALISM, CRITICAL LEGAL STUDIES AND DWORKIN" IN *PHILOSOPHY AND PUBLIC AFFAIRS*

CLS scholars accept the Dworkinian idea that legal rules are infused with ethical principles and ideals. Moreover, they take such principles as seriously as Dworkinians in that they conceive of the articulation and examination of such principles to be one of the major tasks of legal theory. Thus, Duncan Kennedy has analyzed the role in the form and content of legal doctrine of what he characterizes as "individualist" and "altruist" ethical conceptions. And Roberto Unger has examined the normative principles which he takes to be embodied in the common law of contracts. Yet, one of the main themes of CLS work is that the incorporation of ethical principles and ideals into the law cuts against Dworkinian efforts to rescue legal determinacy. The operative claim in CLS analysis is that the law is infused with irresolvably opposed principles and ideals. Kennedy writes that the opposing ethical conceptions which inform legal doctrine "reflect a deeper level of contradiction. At this deeper level, we are divided, among ourselves and also within ourselves, between irreconcilable visions of humanity and society, and between radically different aspirations for our common future." While the realists stress competing rules, CLSers stress competing, and indeed irreconcilable, principles and ideals. Yet, the basic theme is the same: the judge must make a choice which is not dictated by the law. In the CLS analysis, the choice is one of several competing principles or ideals to be used in guiding her to a decision. Different choices lead to different outcomes. Thus, from the CLS perspective, the jurisprudential invocation of principles only serves to push back to another stage the point at which legal indeterminacy enters and judicial choice takes place.

The Dworkinian response would be to deny that legal indeterminacy follows from the fact that the law contains principles which pull in opposing directions. One of Dworkin's major points in his account of principles is that they have differing weights. Thus, even if we have a case in which two competing principles appear applicable, for example, "A person should not be held liable unless she was at fault" versus "As between two innocents, the one who caused the harm should pay," Dworkin will argue that, in all likelihood, one of those principles will carry greater weight in the case at hand and it is that principle which determines the correct legal outcome. Dworkin does allow for the possibility that there may be a case in which the weights of all applicable principles are exactly equal, leaving the legal outcome truly indeterminate, but goes on to claim that such cases will be extremely rare in any developed legal system.

It must be noted here that Dworkin's conception of the soundest theory of the settled law assumes that there is some metalevel principle for determining the appropriate weights to be assigned to the different principles which may be applicable in a given case. This assumption becomes clear once we see that Dworkin's conception of the soundest theory rejects intuitionism, according to which relative weights are intuited in each case without there being any higher order standard in virtue of which each principle has its particular weight. Dworkin's position is that there is a legal fact of the matter regarding the weight of a given principle in a given case, and this fact is determined by the weight that principle receives according to the standards of the soundest theory of the settled law. Moreover, this rejection of intuitionism is firmly rooted in a commitment to the rule of law ideal. That ideal requires that legal decisions be the outcome of reasoning that can be reconstructed according to principles which can be articulated and understood. To use a term which has been popular among legal theorists, judicial decision must be "principled." This means that the judge cannot simply appeal to his inarticulate sense that a particular principle is weightier than some competing principle in the case before him. He must believe that there is some higher order principle which makes the one weightier than the other, and he must at least try to figure out and articulate what that higher order principle is.

Now, one line of CLS attack against Dworkin is to argue that there is no discoverable metaprinciple for assigning weights. Duncan Kennedy suggests this line in discussing the possibility of using moral theory to justify legal doctrine. Kennedy admits that, in the context of the fact situation of a particular case, opposing principles do not necessarily carry the same weight: "We are able to distinguish particular fact situations in which one side is more plausible than the other. The difficulty, the mystery, is that there are no available metaprinciples to explain just what it is about these particular situations that make them ripe for resolution." Actually, Kennedy's point should be put in a less sweeping way: no one has come up with such metaprinciples, and it is implausible to think that it can be done. When put in these terms, the CLS position becomes an essentially reactive one which awaits Dworkinian efforts and then reacts against them: Dworkinians put forth their rational/ethical reconstructions of the law (or some portion of it), complete with metaprinciples for assigning weights to principles, and then CLSers and others attempt to show that the reconstruction is inadequate and incoherent. The burden of production thus seems to be on the Dworkinians. What have they produced? . . . .

There are within CLS distinct and more powerful lines of reasoning against the viability of the Dworkinian project. . . . The additional lines of reasoning are premised on the idea that the settled law is the transitory and contingent outcome of ideological struggles among social factions in which conflicting conceptions of justice, goodness, and social and political life get compromised, truncated, vitiated, and adjusted. The point here is not simply that there are competing principles embodied in settled doctrine, although that is a starting point for the statement of the problem. More fundamentally, the point is that these principles have their weight and scope of application in the settled law determined, not by some metalevel philosophical principle which imposes order and harmony, but by an ideological power struggle in which coherent theories become compromised and truncated as they fit themselves into the body of law. The settled law as a whole, and each field within it, represents the (temporary) outcome of such an ideological conflict. This is, to be sure, a causal claim about the genesis of legal doctrines and principles, rather than a logical one regarding the lack of amenability of such doctrines and principles to rational reconstruction. But the CLS position can be interpreted as linking the logical claim to the causal one. The position is that it is implausible to believe that any system of norms generated by such a process of struggle and compromise will be capable of an ethically principled reconstruction. Unger summarizes the CLS view this way:

> . . . it would be strange if the results of a coherent, richly developed normative theory were to coincide with a major portion of any extended branch of law. The many conflicts of interest and vision that lawmaking involves, fought out by countless minds and wills working at cross purposes, would have to be the vehicle of an immanent moral rationality whose message could be articulated by a single cohesive theory. This daring and implausible sanctification of the actual is in fact undertaken by the dominant legal theories.*

This idea that the law is a patchwork quilt, as it were, of irreconcilably opposed ideologies is tied to CLS's version of the repudiation of the distinction between law (adjudication) and politics. Sometimes CLS scholars suggest that the distinction unravels principally because of the fact that controversial normative and descriptive judgments are just as much an ineliminable part of adjudication as they are of politics. Yet, I think that there is a more important, though related, way in which the distinction is thought to unravel. The idea is this: all of those ideological controversies which play a significant part in the public debate of our political culture are replicated in the argument of judicial decision. In other words, the spectrum of ideological controversy in politics is reproduced in the law. Of course, CLS recognizes that in legal argument the controversies will often be masked or hidden by talk of the intent of the framers, the requirements of stare decisis, and so on. The point is that the same ideological debates which fragment political discourse are replicated in one form or another in legal argument. As a patchwork quilt of irreconcilable ideologies, the law is a mirror which faithfully reflects the fragmentation of our political culture. Such, at least, is a principal CLS theme.

How is it possible to parlay these CLS ideas regarding the patchwork-quilt character of doctrine and the unraveling of the law/politics distinction into a cogent argument against Dworkinian jurisprudence? I think there are two principal lines of argument. The first seeks to show that it makes no sense to think there is any soundest theory of the settled law. The second seeks to show that the Dworkinian theory fails on its own terms to provide a satisfactory account of the legitimacy of judicial decision making. Let us explore each of these lines of argument in turn. . . .

One possible line of CLS argument is that legal doctrine is so internally inconsistent that it is implausible to believe

---

*Roberto Unger, "The Critical Legal Studies Movement," 571 *Harvard Law Review* 96 (1983).

that there is any single, coherent theory capable of justifying enough of it to satisfy the Dworkinian fit requirement. Consistently applying any of the theories embodied in some significant portion of the law across the entire body of doctrine would, the argument goes, involve such substantial doctrinal reconstruction that it would violate the Dworkinian mandate that any theory invoked to decide cases fit or cohere with the bulk of the settled law. Thus, ethically principled reconstruction of any substantial portion of doctrine is ruled out by the law's internal contradictions, such contradictions being symptomatic of the law's conception in ideological compromise and struggle and of its tendency to reflect the range of political conflict present in the culture. This means that there simply is no soundest theory of the settled law, and so the Dworkinian efforts to rescue legal determinacy by appealing to such a notion fail. . . .

In this respect the CLS position may be usefully analogized with Alasdair MacIntyre's diagnosis of the ethical thought of modern culture. MacIntyre argues that such thought is internally incoherent. This state of incoherence is due to the fact that modern ethical thought amounts to an amalgam of fragments of irreconcilable ethical views. Conventional philosophers not only fail to perceive the utter incoherence of modern ethical thought, but operate on the assumption that it is largely in good order. For them the issue is the best way to systematize that thought, not whether it is so self-contradictory that systematization is impossible. The result is that the debates fought out among conventional ethical philosophers, such as Rawls and Nozick, do not join the issue with MacIntyre's position. He repudiates the assumptions which the conventional antagonists share. In a very similar way, the debate between Dworkin and his conventional critics fails to join the issue with CLS. They assume a doctrinal coherence which CLS repudiates, and so the conventional debate takes place in terms which are largely irrelevant to the CLS position.

Duncan Kennedy makes the CLS position on doctrinal incoherence plain in his description of a private law field which he takes to be representative of doctrine in general:

> In contract law, for example, there are two principles: there is a reliance, solidarity, joint enterprise concept, and there is a hands-off, arms length, expectancy-oriented, "no flexibility and no excuses" orientation. They can be developed very coherently, but only if one accepts that they are inconsistent. There are fifteen or twenty contract doctrines about which there is a conflict. . . . That is the structure of contract doctrine, and it's typical. Doctrine is not consistent or coherent. The outcomes of these conflicts form a patchwork, rather than following straight lines.*

Given the terms in which the CLS position has been stated, it is clear what the Dworkinian reply must be in order to join the issue: that doctrine is not as internally contradictory as CLS claims. The main argument would have to be that any internal inconsistencies in legal doctrine are merely marginal, capable of characterization as "mistakes" without any substantial rupture to the fabric of

---

*Duncan Kennedy, "The Political Significance of the Structure of the Law School Curriculum," 15 *Seton Hall Law Review* (1983).

doctrine. This argument would be supplemented, I think, by one to the effect that CLS exaggerates the degree to which theory must fit the settled law in order to be said to fit well enough. To make out these arguments would not be at all easy. CLS analyses have sought to exhibit the deep and pervasive incoherence of doctrine in such areas as constitutional law, labor law, contract law, administrative law, and criminal law, to name only a few. Indeed, I think it is accurate to say that CLS has, through these analyses, made a much more thorough and stronger case for the incoherence of legal doctrine than MacIntyre has made for the incoherence of ethical thought. Meanwhile, Dworkinians have done little to respond to these CLS analyses. . . .

Dworkin is concerned to defend the legitimacy of judicial decision making that invokes controversial principles of ethical or political philosophy. The Dworkinian judge is licensed to rely on such principles because, as Dworkin well realizes, it is inevitable that a judge who, in a hard case, seeks to enunciate and invoke the principles embodied in the settled law will fail to find principles on which everyone can agree. If the judge is to guide her decision by the principles she thinks are embodied in the law, then the reliance of adjudication on controversial principles is inescapable, at least for many cases. In this sense, Dworkin is willing to acknowledge that adjudication is "political." Yet, he thinks that such an acknowledgment does nothing to impugn the legitimacy of the adjudication.

Dworkin's arguments in favor of the legitimacy of such admittedly "political adjudication" are not entirely clear. Let me suggest the following as the principal Dworkinian argument on this point. The invocation of controversial ethical or political principles in adjudication is constrained by the judicial duty to decide a hard case according to the dictates of the soundest theory of the settled law. Thus, the "political" reasoning and choice of the judge take place within much narrower confines than if she were a legislator deciding what sort of legislative enactment was best. As Dworkin says in his discussion of a judge deciding an abortion case, it is one thing for her to decide whether political philosophy dictates that government should acknowledge a right to an abortion, and it is quite another for her to decide whether the settled law of our legal/political system is best accounted for by a theory incorporating a conception of dignity which entails such a right. The former decision is, of course, appropriate for a legislature, not a court. Yet, it is the latter decision, not the former, which the Dworkinian judge is under a duty to make, and it is a decision which is made within much narrower confines than the former. Thus, it is misguided to think that the kind of "political adjudication" endorsed by Dworkinian jurisprudence constitutes an illegitimately broad exercise of judicial power and is tantamount to judicial legislation. Such adjudication is inevitably controversial, but it is substantially constrained by the duty under which judges, but not legislators, act.

Certain CLS claims regarding the law/politics distinction can be parlayed into an argument against this Dworkinian defense of the legitimacy of adjudication in hard cases. What makes this CLS argument particularly interesting for current purposes is that it does not hinge on the adequacy of the patchwork-quilt argument examined in the preceding section. Indeed, it can be construed as granting, arguendo, that there is a unique soundest theory of the law which does dictate the correct legal outcomes in hard cases. Let us set the stage for such a CLS argument.

In trying to undo the law/politics distinction, CLS claims that the spectrum of ideological controversy in the political arena is replicated in the legal forum. The claim means that all of the arguments and ideologies which are a significant part of political debate in our culture are to be found, in one form or another, in legal argument and doctrine. It is undoubtedly true that certain ideological viewpoints are foreclosed from the legal arena. Thus, the ideology of Islamic theocracy is to be found embodied nowhere in our legal doctrine. But such ideologies also play no significant role in the internal political debates of our polity.

It is also undeniable that the canons of legal argument place certain formal constraints on the ideological controversies which manifest themselves within judicial decision making. Judges cannot ignore the authoritative texts of the legal culture: the Constitution, statutes, case law, and so on. And legal argument is constrained by the need to phrase itself in terms of the framer's intent, stare decisis, and so on. Controversy in the political arena is not bound as strongly by such formal constraints, even though the language of legal opinion does often spill over into the political arena. CLS does not deny any of these distinctive, formal marks of legal argument. What they do claim is that beneath these legal forms one can find all of the significant ideological controversies of the political culture. The substance of the political debates is replicated in judicial argument, even if the form of the debates is distinctive. Legal form fails to screen out or significantly reduce the range of ideo-

logical conflict present within the general political culture.

CLS supports these contentions regarding the range of ideological conflict within legal doctrine and argument by analyses of doctrinal principles and the kinds of arguments found in judicial decisions. Consider again Kennedy's description of the structure of contract law. Doctrines from the "solidarity" side of contract law, for example, those of duress, unconscionability, and reasonable reliance, are taken to embody the principles of the political left: welfare-state liberals and, to some extent, left-wing egalitarians. Doctrines from the "individualist" side, such as those of consideration, the revocability of an offer until there is acceptance, and the demand that acceptance be a mirror image of the offer, are taken to embody the principles of the political right: free-marketeers and libertarians. The political middle is represented by attempts to mix the two sides of doctrine in varying proportions (attempts which, in CLS eyes, are doomed to logical incoherence for reasons made clear in the patchwork-quilt argument). A hard case emerges when the two sides of doctrine collide in a single fact situation: there was no consideration, but there was reliance; or there was consideration, but it was quite disproportionate in value to what was received in exchange. The CLS view is that such cases implicate doctrinal materials and arguments representing the spectrum of conflicting political viewpoints.

The CLS claim that the range of ideological conflict in the political arena is replicated in legal doctrine and argument can be viewed in two ways. On the first, it is taken as reinforcing the patchwork-quilt argument against Dworkin. To the extent that one documents the claim, one lends support to the idea that doctrine is a patchwork quilt of inconsistent political ideologies of which no single, coherent political theory could ever capture very much. Take Kennedy's account of contract law. The CLS argument can be put this way: to the extent that we have no reason to believe that the political philosophy of a welfare-state liberal can be reconciled with that of a libertarian, we have no reason to think that the opposing doctrines of contract law can be logically reconciled with one another, for those doctrines are the legal embodiment of just those opposing political philosophies (or something close to them). The position is then generalized to cover all fields of law. This way of setting up the CLS argument is, at bottom, another effort to show that the law is too internally incoherent for there to be any soundest theory of it and thereby to discredit Dworkin's attempts to defend judicial legitimacy by invoking a judicial duty to decide according to the dictates of the soundest theory. . . .

It should be noted that the CLS view on this point is not the same as a view often expressed by mainstream critics of Dworkin and against which Dworkin has directed several arguments. That view consists of the idea that in a hard case, the law "runs out" and the judge makes her decision in a kind of legal vacuum. Dworkin has argued quite forcefully that this gives us a false picture of how judges should and characteristically do go about deciding hard cases. It leads us to think that judges first consult the authoritative materials, find that there is no unambiguous answer there, and then proceed to forget the legal materials and decide by some wholly extralegal criterion. Dworkin counters with a picture of judges who search for the most cogent principles and theories which can be thought of as embodied in the relevant authoritative materials and who decide according to such principles and theories. This is, in Dworkin's eyes, the search for (the relevant portion of) the soundest theory of the settled law.

CLS can agree with Dworkin's important point that judges do not leave the authoritative materials behind when they make a decision in a case where those materials fail to dictate unambiguously an answer to the case. It can also agree with Dworkin that in such cases judges look for the most convincing principles and theories embodied in the materials. The point of the present CLS argument is that, even though judges typically do decide in such Dworkinian fashion and even if there happens to be a soundest theory dictating the correct legal outcome, the existence of such a theory makes no practical difference because a judge will typically see her favored ideology as constituting that theory. The soundest theory is not some brooding omnipresence in the sky, but rather a brooding irrelevance in the sky (assuming it is anywhere at all). . . .

Let me hasten to add that CLS does not accept an important assumption shared by both Dworkinians and their positivist critics, namely, that the exercise of judicial power, even in hard cases, is largely legitimate and that the issue is over how to account for that legitimacy. For CLSers, the legitimacy of the exercise of judicial power is not something that can be assumed but is deeply problematic. Thus, they are no more persuaded by the positivist's efforts to wrap judicial decision in the cloak of legislative legitimacy than they are by Dworkin's invocation of the duty to decide by the soundest theory of law. From the CLS perspective, the positivist injunction to decide according to the will of the legislature leaves as much room for judges to make their favored ideology the basis of decision as does the Dworkinian injunction to decide according to the soundest theory. . . .

In this article, I have not aimed at providing the last word on the points of contention between CLS and Dworkinian jurisprudence. I have tried to locate some of the more important issues within a frame that recognizes the influence of legal realism on contemporary legal thought. CLS has picked up and elaborated upon the realist contention that the law largely fails to determine the outcome in cases which are brought to litigation. Among the important advances of the CLS analysis over that of their realist forerunners are: the effort to take seriously and to analyze the conflicting ethical visions and principles which infuse legal doctrine; the painstaking attempts to display doctrinal inconsistencies and incoherencies; and the effort to show how debates in the political arena are replicated in unsuspected corners of private-law doctrine. I believe that these are substantial advances on the realist position and that they can be parlayed into powerful arguments which are thus far unmet by Dworkinians or indeed by conventional legal philosophers of any stripe. It is well past the time when legal philosophers can justifiably ignore the body of work associated with the Critical Legal Studies movement.

QUESTIONS

1. Is Hart's view on indeterminacy adequate? Why or why not?

2. In what sense, if any, does Unger acknowledge the superiority of Dworkin's theory over Hart's? On what do Dworkin and Unger agree and disagree?

3. What danger is there in allowing judges openly and candidly to follow their feelings and hunches? What if their feelings lead to evil decisions?

4. It has been suggested that the realist insistence on the almost complete indeterminacy of the law resulted from a distorted or skewed perspective, one explained by the so-called selection hypothesis: Those cases that reach the appellate court level, and upon which legal scholars (like the realists) tend to focus, are just those cases in which the law is uncertain and in which the opposing arguments are fairly equally balanced. The great bulk of the law, however, the argument continues, is far more stable and determinate than the realists would admit. Does this explanation undermine legal realism?

5. Does the realist indeterminacy thesis express a necessary feature of law or legality? Or is it simply a contingent claim about a specific legal system or legal culture, namely, our own?

6. What exactly does Altman mean when he says that Dworkin's jurisprudential project may be understood as succeeding where Hart's project fails?

7. What does Unger mean by the antinomy of rules and values?

Part II: Feminist Jurisprudence

Critical legal theory does not depend, of course, on acceptance of the "internal inconsistency" claim advanced by Unger and others. Legal realism, for example, does not depend on that claim and neither does most feminist legal theory. In the readings to follow, Martha Minow is concerned with an assumption tacitly operative throughout legal history to the disadvantage of women: that the experience of men can and should serve as the standard for individual rights. She says that feminist scholars have done much to reveal the persistence and influence of this assumption, and in her view that revelation is a good thing. Her own approach to the problem of legal discrimination against women differs markedly from some feminist writers, however. She is concerned that in elaborating the idea of "women's experience" as a mode of experience distinct from that of men, some feminist analyses have recreated the primary problem they set out to address, that is, the problem of discrimination. In "Justice Engendered," from which these selections are taken, she claims no special mode of knowledge gained through the experience of women upon which to build a feminist-specific jurisprudence. Rather her arguments are directed toward analysis and critique of concepts such as objectivity and neutrality in legal judgment—a critique that links her argument to those of Unger and the critical legal studies movement as well as to legal realism.

Minow's central question is: What exactly would it *mean* to take feminist theory seriously in law? Her answer is that feminist issues belong to a class of issues that arise from the general problem of "difference" in law—difference between individuals, difference in religion, difference in race, difference in handicapping conditions, as well as difference in gender. She asks: What differences should matter in law? And how are litigators to give them their proper significance? Until we have greater insight into how such questions should be answered as a practical matter, she thinks little progress can be made in resolution of the issues with which feminist legal scholars are concerned. The passages below are directed toward increasing such insight.

In the first reading Minow conducts an analysis of the concept of difference and how it enters into adjudication. She is particularly concerned with what she calls the "dilemma of difference," presenting, as it turns out, difficult choices in the legal domain. There are, she says, three versions or forms the dilemma can take, but they all converge on a single point: in cases involving differences of various sorts the Court is faced with a choice between two alternative decisions against *both* of which convincing legal arguments can be made. How that dilemma was dealt with in the 1986 term of the Supreme Court and how, more generally, it should be dealt with is the subject in what follows.

∼

Reading 1

From Martha Minow, "JUSTICE ENGENDERED"

What's the Difference?

The use of anesthesia in surgery spread quickly once discovered. Yet the nineteenth-century doctors who adopted anesthesia selected which patients needed it and which deserved it. Both the medical literature and actual medical practices distinguished people's need for painkillers based on race, gender, ethnicity, age, temperament, personal habits, and economic class. Some people's pain was thought more serious than others; some people were thought to be hardy enough to withstand pain. Doctors believed that women, for example, needed painkillers more than men and that the rich and educated needed painkillers more than the poor and uneducated. How might we, today, evaluate these examples of discrimination? What differences between people should matter, and for what purposes?

The endless variety of our individualism means that we suffer different kinds of pain and may well experience pain differently. But when professionals use categories like gender, race, ethnicity, and class to presume real differences in people's pain and entitlement to help, I worry. I worry that unfairness will result under the guise of objectivity and neutrality. I worry that a difference assigned by someone with power over a more vulnerable person will become endowed with an apparent reality, despite powerful competing views. If no one can really know another's pain, who shall decide how to treat pain, and along what calculus? These are questions of justice, not science. . . .

The Problem and the Argument

Each term, the Supreme Court and the nation confront problems of difference in this heterogeneous society. The cases that present these problems attract heightened media attention and reenact continuing struggles over the meanings of subgroup identity in a nation committed to an idea called equality. The drama of these cases reveals the enduring grip of "difference" in the public imagination, and the genuine social and economic conflicts over what particular differences come to mean over time. During the 1986 term, litigators framed for the Court issues about the permissible legal meanings of difference in the lives of individuals, minority groups, and majority groups in cases involving gender, race, ethnicity, religion, and handicap.

Uniting these questions is the dilemma of difference. The dilemma of difference has three versions. The first version is the dilemma that we may recreate difference either by noticing it or by ignoring it. Decisions about employment, benefits, and treatment in society should not turn on an individual's race, gender, religion, or membership in any other group about which some have deprecating or hostile attitudes. Yet refusing to acknowledge these differences may make them continue to matter in a world constructed with some groups, but not others, in mind. If women's biological differences from men justify special benefits for women in the workplace, are women thereby helped or hurt? Are negative stereotypes reinforced, and does that matter? Focusing on differences poses the risk of recreating them. Especially when used by decision makers who award benefits and distribute burdens, traits of difference can carry meanings uncontrolled and unwelcomed by those to whom they are assigned. Yet denying those differences undermines the value they may have to those who cherish them as part of their own identity.

The second version of the dilemma is the riddle of neutrality. If the public schools must remain neutral toward religion, do they do so by balancing the teaching of evolution with the teaching of scientific arguments about divine creation—or does this accommodation of a religious view depart from the requisite neutrality? Governmental neutrality may freeze in place the past consequences of differences. Yet any departure from neutrality in governmental standards uses governmental power to make those differences matter and thus symbolically reinforces them.

The third version of the dilemma is the choice between broad discretion, which permits individualized decisions, and formal rules that specify categorical decisions for the dispensing of public—or private—power. If the criminal justice system must not take the race of defendants or victims into account, is this goal achieved by granting discretion to prosecutors and jurors, who can then make

individualized decisions but may also introduce racial concerns, or should judges impose formal rules specifying conditions under which racial concerns must be made explicit to guard against them? By granting discretion to officials or to private decision makers, legislators and judges disengage themselves from directly endorsing the use of differences in decisions; yet this grant of discretion also allows those decision makers to give significance to differences. Formal rules constrain public or private discretion, but their very specificity may make differences significant.

I believe these dilemmas arise out of powerful unstated assumptions about whose point of view matters and about what is given and what is mutable in the world. "Difference" is only meaningful as a comparison. I am no more different from you than you are from me. A short person is different only in relation to a tall one. Legal treatment of difference tends to take for granted an assumed point of comparison: Women are compared to the unstated norm of men, "minority" races to whites, handicapped persons to the able-bodied, and "minority" religions to "majorities." Such assumptions work in part through the very structure of our language, which embeds the unstated points of comparison inside categories that bury their perspective and wrongly imply a natural fit with the world. The term *working mother* modifies the general category *mother*, revealing that the general term carries some unstated common meanings (that is, a woman who cares for her children full time without pay), which, even if unintended, must expressly be modified. Legal treatment of difference thus tends to treat as unproblematic the point of view from which difference is seen, assigned, or ignored, rather than acknowledging that the problem of difference can be described and understood from multiple points of view.

Noticing the unstated point of comparison and point of view used in assessments of difference does not eliminate the dilemma of difference; instead, more importantly, it links problems of difference to questions of vantage point. I will argue that what initially may seem to be an objective stance may appear partial from another point of view. Furthermore, what initially appears to be a fixed and objective difference may seem from another viewpoint like the subordination or exclusion of some people by others. Regardless of which perspective ultimately seems persuasive, the possibility of multiple viewpoints challenges the assumption of objectivity and shows how claims to knowledge bear the imprint of those making the claims.

Difference may seem salient not because of a trait intrinsic to the person but instead because the dominant institutional arrangements were designed without that trait in mind. Consider the difference between buildings built without considering the needs of people in wheelchairs and buildings that are accessible to people in wheelchairs. Institutional arrangements define whose reality is to be the norm and make what is known as different seem natural. By asking how power influences knowledge, we can address the question of whether difference was assigned as an expression of domination or as a remedy for past domination. In so doing, we can determine the risks of creating a new pattern of domination while remedying unequal power relationships.

The commitment to seek out and to appreciate a perspective other than one's own animates the reasoning of some Supreme Court justices, some of the time. It is a difficult commitment to make and to fulfill. Aspects of language, social structure, and political culture steer in the opposite direction: toward assertions of absolute categories transcending human choice or perspective. It is not only that justice is created by, and defeated by, people who have genders, races, ethnicities, religions—people who are themselves situated in relation to the differences they discuss. It is also the case that justice is made by people who live in a world already made. Existing institutions and language already carve the world and already express and recreate attitudes about what counts as a difference and who or what is the relevant point of comparison. Once we see that any point of view, including one's own, *is* a point of view, we will realize that every difference we see is seen in relation to something already assumed as the starting point. Then we can expose for debate what the starting points should be. The task for judges is to identify vantage points, to learn how to adopt contrasting vantage points, and to decide which vantage points to embrace in given circumstances. . . .

In the next reading Minow deals with a series of cases before the Supreme Court during the 1986 term. What these cases show, she argues, is that dealing with problems of difference presents the Court with exactly the set of problems identified in the first reading. Discussion of the cases here is very brief, and students should read her account of each case carefully in order to understand clearly how each of the cases exemplifies one of the three versions or forms of the dilemma of difference.

Reading 2

From Martha Minow, "JUSTICE ENGENDERED"

A Case of Differences

Arguments before the Supreme Court engage all three versions of the difference dilemma and cut across cases otherwise differentiated by doctrine and contexts. The dilemma arises in both equality and religion cases, and in statutory and constitutional contexts. This section explicitly draws connections across these seemingly disparate cases and explores the dilemma in cases decided in the 1986 term.

The Dilemma of Recreating Difference Both by Ignoring It and by Noticing It

California Federal Savings & Loan Association v. *Guerra (Cal Fed)* presented in classic form the dilemma of recreating difference through both noticing and ignoring it. Petitioners, a collection of employers, argued that a California statute mandating a qualified right to reinstatement following an unpaid pregnancy disability leave amounted to special preferential treatment, in violation of Title VII's prohibition of discrimination on the basis of pregnancy. Writing an opinion announcing the judgment for the Court, Justice Marshall transformed the question

presented by the plaintiffs: instead of asking whether the federal ban against discrimination on the basis of pregnancy precluded a state's decision to require special treatment for pregnancy, the majority asked whether the state could adopt a minimum protection for pregnant workers while still permitting employers to avoid treating pregnant workers differently by extending similar benefits to nonpregnant workers. Framing the problem this way, the majority ruled that "Congress intended the PDA [Pregnancy Discrimination Act] to be 'a floor beneath which pregnancy disability benefits may not drop—not a ceiling above which they may not rise.' " The majority acknowledged the risk that recognizing the difference of pregnancy could recreate its stigmatizing effects, but noted that "a State could not mandate special treatment of pregnant workers based on stereotypes or generalizations about their needs and abilities." Thus, despite the federal antidiscrimination requirement, the majority found that states could direct employers to take the sheer physical disability of the pregnancy difference into account, but not any stereotyped views associated with that difference. The majority gave two responses to the problem of difference: first, accommodating pregnant workers would secure a workplace that would equally enable both female and male employees to work and have a family; second, the federal and state statutes should be construed as inviting employers to provide the same benefits to men and women in comparable situations of disability.

Writing for the dissenters, Justice White maintained that the California statute required disability leave policies for pregnant workers even in the absence of similar policies for men. It thus violated the PDA, which "leaves no room for preferential treatment of pregnant workers." In the face of this conflict, the federal statute must preempt the state law. The commands of nondiscrimination prohibit taking differences into account, Justice White argued, regardless of the impact of this neglect on people with the difference. Justice White acknowledged the majority's argument that preferential treatment would revive nineteenth-century protective legislation, perpetuating sex role stereotypes and "imped[ing] women in their efforts to take their rightful place in the workplace." For Justice White, however, such arguments were irrelevant, because the Court's role was restricted to interpreting congressional intent and thus would not permit consideration of the arguments about stereotyping. Yet to some extent, the issue of stereotypes was unavoidable: the dilemma in the case, from one point of view, was whether women could secure a benefit that would eliminate a burden connected with their gender, without at the same time reactivating negative meanings about their gender.

In two other cases in the 1986 term, the Court confronted the dilemma of recreating difference in situations in which individuals claimed to be members of minority races in order to obtain special legal protections. By claiming an identity in order to secure some benefit from it, the individuals faced the dilemma that they might fuel negative meanings of that identity, meanings beyond their control. Although racial identification under federal civil rights statutes provides a means of legal redress, it also runs the risk of recreating stigmatizing associations, thereby stimulating prejudice.

In *Saint Francis College* v. *Al-Khazraji*, a man from Iraq who had failed to secure tenure from his employer, a private college, brought a claim of racial discrimination under 42 U.S.C. section 1981. His case foundered, however, when the lower courts rejected his claim that his Arab identity constituted racial membership of the sort protected by the federal statute.

In *Shaare Tefila Congregation* v. *Cobb*, members of a Jewish congregation whose synagogue was defaced by private individuals alleged violations of the federal guarantee against interference with property rights on racial grounds. The difference dilemma appeared on the face of the complaint: the petitioners argued that Jews are not a racially distinct group, and yet they claimed that Jews should be entitled to protection against racial discrimination because others treat them as though they were distinct. The petitioners thus demonstrated their reluctance to have a difference identified in a way that they themselves could not control, while simultaneously expressing their desire for protection against having that difference assigned to them by others. To gain this protection, the petitioners had to identify themselves through the very category they rejected as a definition of themselves. Both the district court and the court of appeals refused to allow the petitioners to be included in the protected group on the basis of the attitudes of others, without some proof of well-established traits internal to the group. The court of appeals reasoned: "although we sympathize with appellant's position, we conclude that it cannot support a claim of racial discrimination solely on the basis of defendants' perception of Jews as being members of a racially distinct group. To allow otherwise would permit charges of racial discrimination to arise out of nothing more than the subjective, irrational perceptions of defendants."

In contrast, one member of the appeals panel, dissenting on this point, argued: "Misperception lies at the heart of prejudice, and the animus formed of such ignorance sows malice and hatred wherever it operates without restriction."

Is the cause of individualized treatment advanced by allowing groups to claim legal protections by dint of group membership, however erroneously assigned by others? Conversely, may denying these claims of legal protection against assigned difference allow the Supreme Court to avoid addressing the dilemma and thereby reenact it? In both *Shaare Tefilala* and *Saint Francis*, the Court asked only whether the legislators adopting the anti-discrimination legislation shortly after the Civil War viewed Jews and Arabs as distinct races. The Court answered the question affirmatively in both cases but based its conclusion on a review of the legislative histories and contemporaneous dictionaries and encyclopedias instead of tackling the difference dilemma directly.

The Court's historical test for membership in a minority race effectively revitalized not just categorical thinking in general, but the specific categorical thinking about race prevailing in the 1860s, despite considerable changes in scientific and moral understandings of the use of abstract categories to label people and solve problems. Whether the issue is gender, religion, or race, reviving old sources for defining group difference may reinvigorate older attitudes about the meanings of group traits. Denying the presence of those traits, however, and their significance in society, deprives individuals of protection against discrimination due to outmoded or unsubstantiated conceptions of group difference.

Neutrality and Nonneutrality: The Dilemma of Government Embroilment in Difference

The dilemma of difference appears especially acute for a government committed to acting neutrally. Neutral means might not produce neutral results, given historic practices and social arrangements that have not been neutral. For example, securing neutrality toward religious differences is the explicit goal of both the First Amendment's ban against the establishment of religion and its protection of the free exercise of religion. Thus to be truly neutral, the government must walk a narrow path between promoting or endorsing religion and failing to make room for religious exercise. Accommodation of religious practices may look nonneutral, but failure to accommodate may also seem nonneutral by burdening the religious minority whose needs were not built into the structure of mainstream institutions.

The "creation science" case, *Edwards v. Aguillard*, raised the question of how the government, in the form of public schools, can respect religious differences while remaining neutral toward them. In *Edwards*, parents and students claimed that a Louisiana statute requiring public schools to teach creation science whenever they taught the theory of evolution violated the establishment clause. Community members subscribing to fundamentalist religious beliefs, however, have argued that public school instruction in evolution alone is not neutral, because it gives a persuasive advantage to views that undermine their own religious beliefs. Relying on similar arguments, the state avowed a neutral, nonreligious purpose for its statute.

The majority, in an opinion by Justice Brennan, concluded that the legislation was actually intended to "provide persuasive advantage to a particular religious doctrine that rejects the factual basis of evolution in its entirety." By contrast, the dissenting opinion by Justice Scalia, which was joined by Chief Justice Rehnquist, expressly tangled with the neutrality problem, noting the difficult tensions between antiestablishment and free exercise concerns and between neutrality through indifference and neutrality through accommodation. In the end, the dissent was moved by the state's attempt to avoid undermining the different views of fundamentalist Christian students, while the majority was persuaded that the statute gave an illegal preference to a particular religious view. For both sides, however, the central difficulty was how to find a neutral position between these two risks.

In a second case, *Hobbie* v. *Unemployment Appeals Commission*, the neutrality problem arose when the Court reviewed a state's decision to deny unemployment benefits to a woman under an apparently neutral scheme. Hobbie was discharged from her job when she refused to work during her religious Sabbath. The state argued that Hobbie's refusal to work amounted to misconduct related to her work and rendered her ineligible for unemployment benefits under a statute limiting compensation to persons who become "unemployed through no fault of their own." The Court rejected this emphasis on the cause of the conflict, because the "salient inquiry" was whether the denial of unemployment benefits unlawfully burdened Hobbie's free exercise right. The Court also rejected the state's claim that making unemployment benefits available to Hobbie would unconstitutionally establish religion by easing eligibility requirements for religious adherents. By requiring accommodation for free exercise, despite charges of establishing religion, the Court's solution thus framed a dilemma of neutrality: How can the government's means be neutral in a world that is not itself neutral?

A facially neutral state policy on unemployment compensation also figured in *Wimberly* v. *Labor & Industrial Relations Commission*. Wimberly had taken a pregnancy leave from her job with no guarantee of reinstatement, and upon her return the employer told her that there were no positions available. Her application for unemployment benefits was denied under a state law disqualifying applicants unless their reasons for leaving were directly attributable to the work or to the employer. Wimberly argued that a federal statute forbidding discrimination in unemployment compensation "solely on the basis of pregnancy or termination of pregnancy" required accommodation for women who leave work because of pregnancy.

The Supreme Court unanimously rejected Wimberly's claim that this denial of benefits contravened the federal statute. The Court found that the state had not singled out pregnancy as the reason for withholding unemployment benefits; instead, pregnancy fell within a broad class of reasons for unemployment unrelated to work or to the employer. The Court interpreted the federal statute to forbid discrimination but not to mandate preferential treatment. In the Court's eyes, then, it was neutral to have a general rule denying unemployment benefits to anyone unemployed for reasons unrelated to the workplace or the employer.

In essence, the Court interpreted the federal statutory scheme as granting discretion to state legislatures to define their own terms for disqualification from eligibility for benefits. Although many states provide unemployment benefits for women who leave their jobs because of pregnancy, subsuming it under terms like "good cause," along with other compelling personal reasons, injury, illness, or the federal ban against refusing benefits "solely on the basis of pregnancy" does not, according to the Court, compel such coverage. A state choosing to define its unemployment eligibility narrowly enough to disqualify not just those who leave work due to pregnancy but also those who leave work for good cause, illness, or compelling personal reasons may thus do so without violating federal law.

The Court in *Wimberly* rejected the argument that ignoring the difference of pregnancy produces illicit discrimination under an apparently neutral unemployment benefits rule. In *Hobbie*, on the other hand, the Court embraced the view that ignoring a religious difference produces illicit discrimination under an apparently neutral unemployment benefits rule. In both cases, the Court grappled with the dilemma of whether to give meaning to neutrality by recognizing or not recognizing difference.

Discretion and Formality: The Dilemma of Using Power to Differentiate

The Court's commitment to the rule of law often leads it to specify, in formal terms, the rules that govern the decisions of others. This practice can secure adherence to the goals of equality and neutrality by ensuring that differences are not taken into account except in the manner explicitly specified by the Court. Although likely to promote accountability, this solution of formal rules has drawbacks. Making and enforcing specific rules engages the Court in the problem of reinvesting differences with significance by noticing them. Specifically requiring the Court to articulate permissible and impermissible uses of difference may enshrine categorical analysis and move further away from the ideal of treating persons as individuals. One way for the Court to resolve the difference dilemma is to grant or cede discretion to other decision makers. Then the problems from both noticing and ignoring difference, and from risking nonneutrality in means and results, are no longer problems for the Court but, instead, matters within the discretion of other private or public decision makers. This approach simply moves the problem to another forum, allowing the decision maker with the discretion to take difference into account in an impermissible manner. The tension between formal, predictable rules and individualized judgments under discretionary standards thus assumes heightened significance in dilemmas of difference.

This dilemma of discretion and formality most vividly occupied the Court in

McCleskey v. *Kemp*, in which the Court evaluated charges of racial discrimination in the administration of the death penalty in Georgia's criminal justice system. A statistical study of over two thousand murder cases in Georgia during the 1970s, submitted by the defendant and assumed by the Court to be valid, demonstrated that the likelihood of a defendant's receiving the death sentence was correlated with the victim's race and, to a lesser extent, the defendant's race. According to the study, black defendants convicted of killing white victims "have the greatest likelihood of receiving the death penalty." Should the Court treat a sentencing "discrepancy that appears to correlate with race" as a defect requiring judicial constraints on prosecutorial and jury discretion, or as an unavoidable consequence of such discretion? In making this choice, the majority and the dissenters each latched onto opposing sides of the dilemma about discretion and formality.

Justice Powell, for the majority, began by asserting that the discretion of the jury is critical to the criminal justice system and operates to the advantage of criminal defendants because it permits individualized treatment rather than arbitrary application of rules. Because of the importance of discretion, unexplained racial discrepancies in the sentencing process should not be assumed to be invidious or unconstitutional. In the majority's view, recognizing claims such as McCleskey's would open the door "to claims based on unexplained discrepancies that correlate to membership in other minority groups, and even to gender" or physical appearance. This argument, perhaps meant in part to trivialize the dissent's objections by linking physical appearance with race, sex, and ethnicity, implied that discrepancies in criminal sentences are random and too numerous

to control. Furthermore, in the majority's view, any attempt to channel discretion runs the risk of undermining it altogether: "It is difficult to imagine guidelines that would produce the predictability sought by the dissent without sacrificing the discretion essential to a humane and fair system of criminal justice."

Justice Brennan, in dissent, approached the problem of discretion and formality from the other direction. Like the majority, Justice Brennan asserted that imposition of the death penalty must be based on an "individualized moral inquiry." To Justice Brennan, however, the statistical correlation between death sentences and the race of defendants and victims showed that participants in the state criminal justice system had, in fact, considered race and produced judgments "completely at odds with [the] concern that an individual be evaluated as a unique human being." Justice Brennan argued that "discretion is a means, not an end" and that, under the circumstances, the Court must monitor the discretion of others. Justice Brennan also responded to the majority's fear of widespread challenges to all aspects of criminal sentencing: "Taken on its face, such a statement seems to suggest a fear of too much justice.... The prospect that there may be more widespread abuse than McCleskey documents may be dismaying, but it does not justify complete abdication of our judicial role."

Justice Stevens, also in dissent, argued that there remains a middle road between forbidding the death penalty and ignoring, in the name of prosecutorial and jury discretion, the correlation between the death penalty and the defendant's and victim's races. He urged a specific rule: The class of defendants eligible for the death penalty should be narrowed to the category of cases, identified by the study, in which "prosecutors consistently seek, and juries consistently impose, the death penalty without regard to the race of the victim or the race of the offender."

For the majority in *McCleskey*, constricting prosecutorial and jury discretion would push toward so regulated a world that the criminal justice system would no longer produce particularized, individualized decisions about defendants. For the dissenters, the Court's acquiescence in unmonitored prosecutorial and jury discretion, in the face of sentencing disparities correlated with race, condoned and perpetuated racial discrimination and thereby allowed racial stereotyping to be substituted for individualized justice.

Debate among the justices last term in an entirely different context exposed a similar tension between rules and discretion. In *Corporation of the Presiding Bishop of the Church of Jesus Christ of Latter-Day Saints* v. *Amos (Presiding Bishop)*, the Court considered whether the federal statute exempting religious organizations from nondiscrimination requirements in their employment decisions arising out of nonprofit activities violated the establishment clause. The Court's majority endorsed the legislative grant of discretion to religious organizations while rejecting the discharged engineer's claims that such state accommodation unconstitutionally promotes religion.

The opinions in the case clearly illustrate the dilemma of discretion. The majority reasoned that under the exemption the preference for religion was not exercised by the government but, rather, by the church. Justice O'Connor, however, pointed out in her concurring opinion that allowing discretion to the private decision maker to use religion in his decisions inevitably engaged the government in that differentiation. The Court could not, simply by protecting the discretion of religious organizations, escape consideration of the tension between the constitutional command against promoting religion and the constitutional demand for free exercise of religion. Instead, Justice O'Connor argued, in distinguishing constitutional accommodation of religion from unconstitutional assistance to religious organizations, the Court must evaluate the message of the government's policy as perceived by an "objective observer."

Justice Brennan's separate opinion also treated this tension as unavoidable. Yet Justice Brennan focused on the risk that case-by-case review by the Court would chill the very freedom assured to religious organizations. He therefore endorsed a categorical exemption from the ban against religious discrimination in employment for the nonprofit activities of religious organizations but argued for reserving judgment as to profit-making activities. Like Justice Stevens in *McCleskey*, Justice Brennan searched for a formal rule that could preserve discretion for other decision makers while also implementing the Court's special commitment to protect individuals from categorical, discriminatory treatment.

The Dilemmas in Sum

Other cases before the Court have raised one or more aspects of the difference dilemma. The Court's voluntary affirmative action cases, during the 1986 term and earlier, directly present dilemmas about recreating difference, risking non-neutral means to transform nonneutral ends, and choosing between rules and discretion in an effort to avoid categorical decisions. Decisions about handicapped persons also raise perplexing issues about when the Court should permit public and private decision makers to make the difference of handicap matter. The Court comes down one way or another in each case, but the splits between majority and minority views persist and recreate the dilemmas. . . .

In a portion of her work not included here, Minow argues that the difference dilemma in one or another of its forms appears both inescapable and unresolvable. The reason it appears so is that we make certain false assumptions about the nature of difference. She lists five of these.

Assumption 1: Difference Is Intrinsic, not Relational.
The legal analyst tends to treat the difference question as one of discovery rather than of one made by choice. The judge asks, "Into what category does a given person or feature belong?" The distinguishing features we employ in critical perception and classification themselves appear natural rather than chosen.[1]

Assumption 2: The Unstated Norm.
When women argue for rights, the implicit reference point often used in discussions of sameness and difference is the privilege accorded some males. This reference point can generate powerful arguments for overcoming the exclusion of women from activities and opportunities available to men. For example, reform efforts on behalf of women during both the nineteenth and the twentieth centuries asserted women's fundamental similarities to privileged, white men as a tactic for securing equal treatment. Unfortunately for the reformers, embracing the theory of "sameness" meant that any sign of difference between men and women could be used to justify treating women differently from men. Men remained the unstated norm.[2]

Assumption 3: The Observer Can See Without a Perspective.
Judges often see difference in relation to some unstated norm or point of comparison and fail to acknowledge their own perspective and its influence on the assignment of difference. This failure prevents us from discovering who is doing the labeling, but it does not negate the effect of the labeling itself. Veiling the standpoint of the observer conceals its impact on our perception of the world.[3]

Assumption 4: The Irrelevance of Other Perspectives.
Some justices, on some occasions, have tried to see beyond the dominant perspective and reach an alternative construction of reality. In many instances, however, the justices presume that the perspective they adopt is either universal or superior to others. A perspective may go unstated because it is so powerful and pervasive that it may be presumed without defense; it may also go unstated because it is so unknown to those in charge that they do not recognize it as a perspective.[4]

---

1. Martha Minow, "Justice Engendered," 10 *Harvard Law Review* (1987), p. 227.
2. Ibid., p. 228.
3. Ibid., p. 229.
4. Ibid.

Assumption 5: The Status Quo Is Natural, Uncoerced and Good.
From this assumption follow three propositions: first, the goal of governmental neutrality demands the status quo because existing societal arrangements are assumed to be neutral. Second, governmental actions that change the status quo have a different status than omissions, or failure to act, that maintain the status quo. Third, prevailing social and political arrangements are not forced on anyone.[5]

Minow's point in exposing these false assumptions is to encourage, promote, and develop better ways of making the inescapable choices, by acknowledging the fact that no truly "neutral" point of view is possible. Her program of "engendering justice" depends on such recognition. In the final section below she discusses the problem of "choice among divergent demands;" she argues that understanding differences, important as this is, does not by itself determine legal outcomes: judges must still decide which differences are important, which differences should control the outcome of a case. So far as legal outcomes are concerned, judges make decisions in a way or ways "committed to meaning" and this is the most we can hope for in adjudication since there are no such things as impartial and neutral points of view. It should be obvious that Minow's reasoning comports well with some key ideas of critical jurisprudence presented in this chapter: no normative theory is advanced, no source of knowledge is identified that can assure justification of legal decisions, and there is no way to avoid loss of some kind when dilemmas of difference are addressed and resolved by courts—we must acknowledge the "tragedy" of nonneutrality. Her position also accords well with Unger's notion that choice based on theory is "partial" since theories are inevitably "partial" in the sense of being essentially selective and incomplete.

∽

Reading 3

From Martha Minow,
"JUSTICE ENGENDERED"

The dissenting justices in *McCleskey* asked how defendants would react to the statistical disparity in capital sentencing by race, breaking out of the tendency to see the challenge only as a threat to the discretion and manageability of the criminal justice system. In *Saint Francis College, Shaare Tefila,* and *Arline,* members of the Court struggled over whose perspective should count for purposes of defining a race and a handicap, reaching conclusions that refused to take the usual answers for granted.

Efforts to adopt or imagine alternate perspectives are also reflected in opin-

---

5. Ibid.

ions from previous terms. For example, Justice Stevens assessed an equal protection challenge to a zoning restriction burdening mentally retarded people by expressing sensitivity to a point of view other than his own: "I cannot believe that a rational member of this disadvantaged class could ever approve of the discriminatory application of the city's ordinance in this case." Still earlier, Justice Douglas invited inquiry into the experience of non-English-speaking students sitting in a public school classroom conducted entirely in English. Similarly, litigants have sometimes tried to convince the Court to adopt their perspective. Justice Harlan's dissent in *Plessy* v. *Ferguson* may have been assisted by Homer Plessy's attorney, who had urged the justices to imagine themselves in the shoes of a black person:

> Suppose a member of this court, nay, suppose every member of it, by some mysterious dispensation of providence should wake to-morrow with a black skin and curly hair . . . and in traveling through that portion of the country where the "Jim Crow Car" abounds, should be ordered into it by the conductor. It is easy to imagine what would be the result. . . . What humiliation, what rage would then fill the judicial mind!

It may be ultimately impossible to take the perspective of another completely, but the effort to do so may help us recognize that our perspective is partial and that the status quo is not inevitable or ideal. After shaking free of these unstated assumptions and developing a sense of alternative perspectives, judges must then choose. The process of looking through other perspectives does not itself yield an answer, but it may lead to an answer different from the one that

the judge would otherwise have reached. Seen in this light, the difference dilemma is hard but not impossible. . . .

Engendering Justice

The nineteenth-century American legal system recognized only three races: "white," "Negro," and "Indian." Californian authorities faced an influx of Chinese and Mexicans and were forced to confront the now complicated question of racial categorization. They solved the problem of categorizing Mexicans by defining them as "whites" and by according them the rights of free white persons. Chinese, however, were labeled "Indian" and denied the political and legal rights of white persons. Similarly, in 1922, a unanimous Supreme Court concluded that Japanese persons were not covered by a federal naturalization statute applicable to "free white persons," "aliens of African nativity," and "persons of African descent."

In retrospect, these results seem arbitrary. The legal authorities betrayed a striking inability to reshape their own categories for people who did not fit. Of course, it is impossible to know what might have happened if some piece of history had been otherwise. Still, it is tempting to wonder: What if the California legal authorities had changed their racial scheme, rather than forcing the Chinese and Mexican applicants into it? The officials then might have noticed that nationality, not race, distinguished these groups. What if these officials and the justices in 1922 had tried to take the point of view of the people they were labeling? Perhaps, from this vantage point, the justices would have realized the need for reasons—beyond racial classification—

for granting or withholding legal rights and privileges.

. . . Trying to take seriously the point of view of people labeled *different* is a way to move beyond current difficulties in the treatment of differences in our society. This . . . statement . . . is addressed to people in positions of sufficient power to label others different and to make choices about how to treat difference. If you have such power, you may realize the dilemma of difference: by taking another person's difference into account in awarding goods or distributing burdens, you risk reiterating the significance of that difference and, potentially, its stigma and stereotyping consequences. But if you do not take another person's difference into account—in a world that has made that difference matter—you may also recreate and reestablish both the difference and its negative implications. If you draft or enforce laws, you may worry that the effects of the laws will not be neutral whether you take difference into account or you ignore it. If you employ people, judge guilt or innocence, or make other decisions affecting lives, you may want and need the discretion to make an individualized assessment, free from any focus on categorical differences. But if that discretion is exercised without constraint, difference may be taken into account in a way that does not treat that person as an individual—and in a way that disguises this fact from view.

These dilemmas . . . become less paralyzing if you try to break out of unstated assumptions and take the perspective of the person you have called *different.* Once you do that, you may glimpse that your patterns for organizing the world are both arbitrary and foreclose their own reconsideration. You may find that the categories you take for granted do not well serve features you had not focused upon in the past. You may see an injury that you had not noticed or take more seriously a harm that you had otherwise discounted. If you try to take the view of the other person, you will find that the "difference" you notice is part of the relationship or comparison you draw between that person and someone else, with reference to a norm, and you will then get the chance to examine the reference point you usually take for granted. Maybe you will conclude that the reference point itself should change. Employers do not have to treat pregnancy and parenthood as a disability, but instead as a part of the lives of valued workers. You may find that you had so much ignored the point of view of others that you did not realize that you were mistaking your point of view for reality. Perhaps you will find that the way things are is not the only way things could be—that changing the way you classify, evaluate, reward, and punish may make the differences you had noticed less significant, or even irrelevant, to the way you run your life. . . .

Impartiality and Partial Truths

It is a paradox. Only by admitting our partiality can we strive for impartiality. Impartiality is the guise partiality takes to seal bias against exposure. It looks neutral to apply a rule denying unemployment benefits to anyone who cannot fulfill the work schedule, but it is not neutral if the work schedule was devised with one religious Sabbath, and not another, in mind. The idea of impartiality implies human access to a view beyond human experience, a "God's eye" point of view.

Not only do humans lack this inhuman perspective, but humans who claim it are untruthful, trying to exercise power to cut off conversation and debate. Doris Lessing argues that a single absolute truth would mean the end of human discourse but that we are happily saved from that end because any truth, once uttered, becomes immediately one truth among many, subject to more discourse and dispute. If we treat other points of view as irritants in the way of our own vision, we are still hanging on to faulty certainty. Even if we admit the limits of our view, while treating those limits as gaps and leaving the rest in place, we preserve the pretense that our view is sufficiently rooted in reality to resist any real change prompted by another.

Acknowledging partiality may cure the pretense of impartiality. But unless we have less capacity to step outside our own skins than I think we do, we then have a choice of which partial view to advance or accept. Whose partial view should resolve conflicts over how to treat assertions of difference, whether assigned or claimed? Preferring the standpoint of an historically denigrated group can reveal truths obscured by the dominant view, but it can also reconfirm the underlying conceptual scheme of the dominant view by focusing on it. Similarly, the perspective of those who are labeled different may offer an important challenge to the view of those who imposed the label, but it is a corrective lens, another partial view, not absolute truth. We then fight over whether to prefer it. "Standpoint theories" may also deny the multiple experiences of members of the denigrated group and create a new claim of essentialism.

Instead of an impartial view, we should strive for the standpoint of some-

one who is committed to the moral relevance of contingent particulars. Put in personal terms, if I pretend to be impartial, I hide my partiality; however, if I embrace partiality, I risk ignoring you, your needs, and your alternative reality—or, conversely, embracing and appropriating your view into yet another rigid, partial view. I conclude that I must acknowledge and struggle against my partiality by making an effort to understand your reality and what it means for my own. I need to stop seeking certainty and acknowledge the complexity of our shared and colliding realities, as well as the tragic impossibility of all prevailing at once. It is this complexity that constitutes our reciprocal realities, and it is the conflict between our realities that constitutes us, whether we engage in it overtly or submerge it under a dominant view.

Moral action . . . takes place in a field of complexity, and we act ethically when we recognize what we give up as well as what we embrace. The solution is not to adopt and cling to some new standpoint but, instead, to strive to become and remain open to perspectives and claims that challenge our own. Justice, like philosophy, ought to trust rather to the multitude and variety of its arguments than to the conclusiveness of any one. . . .

The Problem of Deference

This call to be open, to canvas personal experience, applies to all legal controversies but it is especially important in the context of cases that present the dilemma of difference. Here the judicial mainstays of neutrality and distance prove most risky, for they blind judges to their own involvement in recreating the negative meanings of difference. Yet the dangers of making differences matter also argue against categorical solutions. By struggling to respond humanly to the dilemma in each particular context, the judge can supply the possibility of connection otherwise missing in the categorical treatments of difference.

Choosing Among Divergent Demands

Urging judges to allow themselves to be moved by the arguments may seem misguided. A judge who identifies with every perspective may simply feel indecisive and overburdened. Would feeling the tugs in all directions render us powerless to choose? It may be just this fear that explains our attachment to simplifying categories, stereotypes, and fixed ways of thought. Some of us may fear being overwhelmed by the world, others fear being too moved by it, others fear being powerless before it. Challenging familiar categories and styles of reasoning may threaten the search for order, decisiveness, and manageability that maintain the predictability in our lives. But there are other ways to hold things together than the methods we have used in the past.

Some may aspire to a jurisprudence of individualism, never treating any individual as a member of a group. Yet, resonant as it is with many American traditions, individualization is a myth: because our language is shared and our categories communally invented, any word I use to describe your uniqueness draws you into the classes of people sharing your traits. Even if ultimately I produce enough words so that the intersection of all classes you belong in contains only one member—you—we understand this

through a language of comparison with others. This language, however, seems to embroil us in the dilemma of difference.

What could we do instead? I believe we should welcome complexity and challenge complacency—and stop fearing that we will be unable to make judgments. We can and do make judgments all the time, in a way committed to making meaning, rather than recreating or ignoring difference. We make commitments when we make decisions; we reconfirm or remake current understandings by reflecting so deeply and particularly about a new situation that we challenge presumptive solutions. Instead of trying continually to fit people into categories, and to enforce or deny rights on that basis, we can and do make decisions by immersing in particulars to renew commitments to a fair world.

Thus, one reason we can still decide, amid powerfully competing claims, is that immersion in particulars does not require the relinquishment of general commitments. The struggle is not over the validity of principles and generalizations—it is over which ones should prevail in a given context. The choice from among principles, in turn, implicates choices about which differences, and which similarities, should matter. These are moral choices, choices about which voices should persuade those who judge.

Even when we understand them, some voices will lose. The fundamentalist Christians who supported the Balanced Treatment Act in Louisiana deserve respect and understanding: their view of the world may well be threatened by the curriculum taught to their children in the public schools. However, this is what the fight is about. Whose view of reality should prevail in public institutions? This deep conundrum involves the conflicts between the worldview animating any rule for the entire society, and the worldviews of sub-groups who will never share the dominant views. I am tempted to propose a seem-ingly "neutral" rule, such as a rule that judges interpreting the commitment to re-spect difference should make the choice that allows difference to flourish without imposing it on others. If exclusion of their worldview from the biology curriculum creates an intolerable choice for the funda-mentalists, they do and they must have the choice to establish their own educational in-stitutions, and their own separate commu-nity. Yet this seemingly "neutral" position is a comfortable view for a nonfundamen-talist like myself, who cannot appreciate the full impact of the evolution science cur-riculum as experienced by at least some fundamentalists. Rather than pretending to secure a permanent solution through a "neutral" rule, I must acknowledge the tragedy of non-neutrality—and admit that our very commitment to tolerance yields intolerance toward some views. If the fun-damentalists lose in this case, they can con-tinue to struggle to challenge the meaning of the commitment to separate church and state, and they may convince the rest of us in the next round. Although it may be lit-tle solace for the minority group, its chal-lenge achieves something even when it loses, by reminding the nation of our com-mitment to diversity, and our inability, thus far, to achieve it fully.

Thus, choices from among compet-ing commitments do not end after the Court announces its judgment. Continu-ing skepticism about the reality endorsed by the Court—or any source of govern-mental power—is the only guard against tyranny.

The continuing process of debate over deeply held but conflicting com-mitments is both the mechanism and the promise of our governmental system. Within that system, the Supreme Court's power depends upon persuasion. As Hannah Arendt wrote: "The thinking process which is active in judging some-thing is not, like the thought process of pure reasoning, a dialogue between me and myself, but finds itself always and primarily, even if I am quite alone in making up my mind, in an anticipated communication with others with whom I know I must finally come to some agreement." The important question is, with whom must you come to agree-ment? In a society of diversity with lega-cies of discrimination, within a polity committed to self-governance, the judi-ciary becomes a critical arena for de-mands of inclusion. I see the judicial arena as a forum for contests over com-peting realities. The question remains, however, whose definitions of realities will govern in a given case and over time.

Court judgments endow some per-spectives, rather than others, with power. Judicial power is least accountable when judges leave unstated—and treat as a given—the perspective they select. Litiga-tion before the Supreme Court sometimes highlights individuals who otherwise sel-dom imprint their perspective on the polity. In eliciting these perspectives and accepting their challenge to the version of reality the justices otherwise would take for granted, the Court advances the fun-damental constitutional commitment to require reasons before exercises of power, whether public or private. Growing from our history, wrought from many strug-gles, is the tradition we have invented, and it is a tradition that declares that the status quo cannot be immune from de-mands for justification. Litigation over the meanings of difference represents de-mands for such accountability. By asking how power influences knowledge, the Court can address whether a "difference" has been assigned through past domination or as a remedy for past domination. In this way, the Court can solicit information about contrasting views of reality without casting off the moorings of historical experience, and in this inquiry, the Court can assess the risk of creating new patterns of domination while remedying inequalities of the past. As we compete for power to give reality to our visions, we confront tragic limits in our abilities to make meaning together. Yet we must continue to seek a language to speak across conflicting affiliations.

We need settings in which to engage in the clash of realities that breaks us out of settled and complacent meanings and creates opportunities for insight and growth. This is the special burden and opportunity for the Court: to enact and preside over the dialogue through which we remake the normative endowment that shapes current understandings.

When the Court performs these roles, it engenders justice. Justice is engendered when judges admit the limitations of their own viewpoints, when judges reach beyond those limits by trying to see from contrasting perspectives, and when people seek to exercise power to nurture differences, not to assign and control them. Rather than securing an illusory universality and objectivity, law is a medium through which particular people can engage in the continuous work of making justice.... Legal decisions engrave upon our culture the stories we tell to and about ourselves, the meanings that constitute the traditions we invent. Searching for words to describe realities too multiple and complex to be contained by their language, litigants and judges struggle over what will be revealed and what will be concealed in the inevitable partiality of human judgment. Through deliberate attention to our own partiality, we can begin to acknowledge the dangers of pretended impartiality. By taking difference into account, we can overcome our pretended indifference to difference, and people our worlds with those who can surprise and enrich one another. As we make audible, in official arenas, the struggles over which version of reality will secure power, we disrupt the silence of one perspective, imposed as if universal. Admitting the partiality of the perspective that temporarily gains official endorsement may embolden resistance to announced rules. But only by admitting that rules are resistible—and by justifying to the governed their calls for adherence—can justice be done in a democracy. It is only through the variety of relations constructed by the plurality of beings that truth can be known and community constructed. Then we can constitute ourselves as members of conflicting communities with enough reciprocal regard to talk across differences. We engender mutual regard for pain we know and pain we do not understand.

QUESTIONS

1. What is the role of "difference" in feminist legal thought?

2. Is there a "feminist point of view" when it comes to questions of law? Must one be a female to have such a view?

3. Evaluate Minow's feminist tools in her evaluation of the cases she discusses.

4. What is the role of "perspectivism" in feminist legal thought?

5. Ought law to be "sexist" in some regards? That is, should men and women be treated unequally in some respects? For example, ought the law to prohibit women of child-bearing years from working in conditions that would harm their reproductive capacities or a fetus? Ought the law to prohibit women from entering into "surrogate-mother" contracts? Should women but not men be legally entitled to work leave on the birth of a child?

Chapter 6

Practice Theory
Readings from Phillip Bobbitt and Dennis Patterson

Due appreciation of the strong arguments advanced by critical legal theorists has as its net effect a heightened awareness of legal indeterminacy and of the difficulty of defending the idea that law is an autonomous realm of thought and practice in which people are capable of "neutrality" and "objectivity" in judgment and decision-making. Having, for good reason, called into question these and other cherished assumptions and beliefs of contemporary legal thought, a sympathetic reader may wonder how to avoid sliding down the slippery slope of critical insight toward either legal cynicism or some even less attractive skeptical alternative.

We turn in this chapter to a type of legal theory that can be credited as a new attempt to reinstate cognitive jurisprudence—new, at least compared with the types of theory studied in previous chapters, and compared with theories with long and richly developed historical roots. The originality of practice theory is largely due to the later work of Wittgenstein, who developed a highly influential account of the nature of rule following, one that has found recent legal application and extension in the work of both Philip Bobbitt and Dennis Patterson. By way of introduction to the jurisprudential implications of Wittgenstein's ideas it is well to look at two important passages from his *Philosophical Investigations*.

> 201. ... There is a way of grasping a rule which is *not* an *interpretation*, but which is exhibited in what we call "obeying the rule" and "going against it" in actual cases. ... There is an inclination to say: every action according to the rule is an interpretation. But we ought to restrict the term "interpretation" to the substitution of one expression of the rule for another.
> 202. ... "Obeying a rule" is a practice. And to *think* one is obeying a rule is not to obey a rule.[1]

As we have seen in earlier readings, many authors take the view that the deepest understanding of law is achieved by taking the reasoning of judges

---

1. Ludwig Wittgenstein, *Philosophical Investigations*, ed. G. E. M. Anscombe and R. Raees, tr. G.E.M. Anscombe, 3rd ed. (New York: The Macmillan Company, 1971), pp. 201, 202.

and lawyers as theory formation or construction. The clearest example is Dworkin for whom an adequate conception of law must always be seen as the product of interpretation. Even in easy cases, he says, understanding a case is a matter of constructing an interpretation of it: the point of jurisprudence is to advance our knowledge of how to make an interpretation "the best it can be."

Dworkin's views in this regard are met with a direct challenge in Wittgenstein's passage cited above. The idea that all understanding is a matter of interpretation generates a philosophical puzzle, he says, for if all understanding requires interpretation, then why does not all interpretation require interpretation? Wittgenstein thinks the solution to this puzzle is to be found in the rejection of the very idea that all understanding is a matter of interpretation.

Assuming that all understanding is not interpretation, then what is it? Wittgenstein argued that understanding is best thought of not as an activity but as a capacity or ability. To use an example of Patterson's from *Law and Truth*,[2] if I ask you to pass the salt at the dinner table, your understanding of the request is exhibited by your action in passing the salt, and the understanding in question is not a reflection or interpretation of some kind. If we understand what is said we simply respond in the right way, given a certain context. This way of thinking about understanding casts a different light on the activity of interpretation: it is better understood as a reflective response after understanding breaks down. To keep with the example of the request to pass the salt, imagine the request is made not at a dinner party but at a wine tasting. In this context, if one participant in a wine tasting asks another to "pass the salt," what would count as understanding the request? On its face, at least, the request has no meaning. We might, of course, *construe or interpret* the request in different ways, and we might even come to accept one of these as the "meaning" of the request. Thus to respond to what is already understood exhibits an unreflective feature absent in interpretation. When we interpret something, we *construct and reflect upon* (possible) meanings; when we understand we *rely upon* meaning in "responding" or "going on." Put very simply, "understanding" is knowing how to "go on" in a practice of one kind or another.

Philip Bobbitt's work in constitutional theory can be understood as an adaptation for jurisprudential purposes of this account of "understanding." In a 1979 publication, he developed the idea that all the assertions in a well-formed judicial opinion can be translated into one of six modalities or forms of argument. Taken together, these are understood as constituting a system that functions as the grammar of constitutional argument. "Understanding" in constitutional law means knowing how to use these six modalities to make constitutional arguments. What is important about these modalities is that they are neither true nor false: they are the means by which propositions of constitutional law are shown to be true or false. They are what constitutional argument *depends upon*, what must be understood in order to engage in the

---

2. Dennis Patterson, *Law and Truth* (New York: Oxford University Press, 1996), p. 87.

practice. As Bobbitt puts it, "there is no constitutional argument outside these forms."

~

Reading 1

From Philip Bobbitt, *CONSTITUTIONAL INTERPRETATION*

The Modalities of Constitutional Argument

First, what is a *modality*? It is the way in which we characterize a form of expression as true. For instance, a logical modality may be attributed to a proposition, "p," by saying that it is logically necessary or contingent or logically impossible, that "p." This is to say that from a logical point of view, the dimension of possibility is critical to engage the inexorable force of inference while other dimensions of the proposition are from this point of view irrelevant. To say that it is known or unknown or known that it is not true that "p," is to employ an epistemic mode. That is to say that from an epistemological point of view, the role of knowledge engages the force of logic, while other features of "p," are irrelevant. And so on for other modalities. To say that it is obligatory, permissible or forbidden, that "p," is to mark a moral or deontic mode. To say that it is now or will be or was the case that "p," attributes a temporal modality. By contrast, simply to say "that p," or "it is de fide true that p," does not characterize the way in which "p," is true.

To see the difference among modalities, consider the following propositions with respect to a logical modality: it is necessarily the case that a professor's husband is a married man; it is possible that a professor could be a married man; it is impossible that a professor's wife could be a married man. The way in which these propositions are true, from a logical point of view, is determined by the relationship between the facts they assert and the possibility of those facts (principally the fact that "a husband is a married man" is necessarily true, i.e., it is impossible that it could be false). There are rules that will determine the truth or falsity of a proposition in this modality; these rules construe the facts stated by the proposition according to the standards of the modality, in this case, the logical possibility of the facts stated. Now consider instead the proposition: "all professors should be unmarried men." Whether this is true or not cannot be determined by our knowing the extent to which this state of affairs is possible. It might be true even if it were impossible; it might be false even if it were absolutely necessary (as once was the case at some universities). Thus we must apply the standards of a different modality—a moral or deontic mode—to determine the truth of the facts asserted.

To see the difference between a modal statement and an ordinary proposition, consider these two statements: (1) "One can never know whether another person is telling the truth"; and (2) "You are lying" or "I believe you are lying to me." To determine whether (1) is true requires an inquiry into the conditions of knowledge: what counts as knowing, what are grounds for doubt, and so on. But to determine the truth of (2) we need to find out something in the world (although it is not always clear precisely what, particularly in taking testimony from one whose word you doubt!). That is, (2) asserts the truth of a particular statement about the world while (1) asserts a truth about a statement, namely, that it cannot be known.

I will be speaking of constitutional modalities—the ways in which legal propositions are characterized as true from a constitutional point of view. In my earlier work I identified six such modalities. Of course, these might be divided or recategorized in different ways, but this particular array has been accepted, I think, by persons working in this area. These six modalities of constitutional argument are: the historical (relying on the intentions of the framers and ratifiers of the Constitution); textual (looking to the meaning of the words of the Constitution alone, as they would be interpreted by the average contemporary "man on the street"); structural (inferring rules from the relationships that the Constitution mandates among the structures it sets up); doctrinal (applying rules generated by precedent); ethical (deriving rules from those moral commitments of the American ethos that are reflected in the Constitution); and prudential (seeking to balance the costs and benefits of a particular rule). Now let us look at some examples, and a somewhat more formal statement of each form of argument.

Consider the question whether a state may validly enforce a law that makes it a crime to procure an abortion.

An historical modality may be attributed to constitutional arguments that claim that the framers and ratifiers of the Fourteenth Amendment intended, or did not intend, or that it cannot be ascertained whether it was their intention, to protect pregnant women from a state's coercion, through threats of fines and imprisonment, to bear children. Similarly, a historical modality might approach the abortion question as did the framers and ratifiers of the Fourteenth Amendment intend to countenance, or to overturn by means of the Amendment, or are their intentions unclear as to the effect of the Amendment regarding those state laws that existed at the time of ratification that prohibited abortions?

Oftentimes this modality is confused with textual argument since both can have reference to the specific text of the Constitution. Historical, or "originalist" approaches to construing the text, however, are distinctive in their reference back to what a particular provision is thought to have meant to its ratifiers. Thus, when Justice Taney in the *Dred Scott* case was called upon to construe the scope of the diversity jurisdiction in Article III, which provides for suits "between citizens of the several states," so that he might decide whether a slave could seek his freedom in a diversity suit before a federal court, he wrote:

> It becomes necessary to determine who were the citizens of the several states when the constitution was adopted. And in order to do this we must recur to the governments and institutions of the colonies. We must inquire who at the time were recognized as citizens of the states, whose rights and liberties outraged by the English government and who declared their independence and assumed the powers of govern-

ment to defend their rights of arms. We refer to these historical facts for the purpose of showing the fixed opinions concerning the Negro race upon which the statesmen of that day spoke and acted.

Now consider the same question—who are the "citizens" of the phrase that provides for suits in federal court "between citizens of different states" ("diversity" suits)—from another point of view. A textual modality may be attributed to arguments that the text of the Constitution would, to the average person, appear to declare, or deny, or be too vague to say whether, a suit between a black American citizen resident in a state and a white American citizen resident in another state, is a "controversy between citizens of different states." I would imagine that the contemporary meaning of these words is rather different than that which Taney found them to mean to the framers and ratifiers of 1789. One should not be tempted to conclude, however, that textual approaches are inevitably more progressive than originalist approaches. Sometimes the text can be a straitjacket, confining the judge to language that would have been different if its drafters had foreseen later events. Thus, consider whether wiretapping is prohibited by the Fourth Amendment, which guarantees "the right of the people to be secure in their persons, houses, papers and effects against unreasonable searches and seizures." Here is Chief Justice Taft in a case in which incriminating information was largely obtained by federal prohibition officers intercepting messages on the telephones of the conspirators:

> The amendment itself [he says] shows that the search is to be of material

things—the person, the house, his papers or his effects. The amendment does not forbid what was done here for there was no seizure. The evidence was secured by the sense of hearing and that only. There was not entry of the houses. The language of the amendment cannot be extended and expanded.

By contrast, a later court had no trouble finding that wiretapping came within the Amendment. It simply relied upon historical argument—the intentions that animated the adoption of the amendment—and concluded that:

> The purpose of the . . . Fourth Amendment [is] to keep the state out of constitutionally protected areas until it has reason to believe that a specific crime has been or is being committed.

Consider another constitutional question: can a court issue a subpoena (or should it enjoin some other subpoena) for the disclosure of the President's working notes and diaries? To say that the institutional relationships promulgated by the Constitution require or are incompatible with or tolerate a particular answer to this question is to use a structural mode of argument. There are many recent, celebrated examples of this form of argument to be found in the cases of the U.S. Supreme Court; indeed the 1980s were particularly notable for the Court's focus on structural issues. But structural argument is hardly a recent invention. *McCulloch v. Maryland*, the principal foundation case for constitutional analysis, relies almost wholly on structural approaches. In determining whether a Maryland tax on the Federal Bank of the United States could be enforced, Chief Justice Marshall studiedly refuses to specify the particular text that supports his argument, and explicitly rejects reliance on historical arguments, preferring instead to state the rationale on inferences from the structure of federalism. Such a structure could not be maintained, he concluded, if the states, whose officials are elected by a state's constituency, could tax the agencies of the federal government present in a state and thereby tax a nationwide constituency. The constitutional structure would not tolerate such a practice.

In the following passage, taken from an 1884 case, we may observe another typical example. In this case the defendant and others were convicted in a federal court for having conspired to intimidate a black person from voting for a member of Congress, in violation of federal statutes. The question was: does Congress have the power to punish violations of election laws under the Constitution since the text nowhere provides such a power? Justice Miller wrote for the Court:

> That a government whose essential character is republican ... has no power by appropriate laws to secure this election from the influence of violence, of corruption, and of fraud, is a proposition so startling as to arrest attention and demand the gravest consideration. ... The proposition that it has no such power is supported by the old argument often heard, often repeated, and in this court never assented to, that when a question of the power of Congress arises the advocate of the power must be able to place his finger on words which expressly grant it. ... It is not true, therefore, that electors for members of Congress owe their right to vote to the State law in any sense which makes the exercise of the right to depend exclusively on the law of the State. ... It is as essential to

the successful working of this government that the great organisms of its executive and legislative branches should be the free choice of the people as that the original form of it should be so ... In a republican government like ours ... the temptation to control these elections by violence and corruption is a constant source of danger.

Structural arguments are a little less intuitively obvious than arguments from the text or history of the Constitution, so perhaps it would be well to briefly outline their characteristic form. Usually, arguments in this modality are straightforward: first, an uncontroversial statement about a constitutional structure is introduced [for example, in the case above, the statement that the right to vote for a member of Congress is provided for in the Constitution]; second, a relationship is inferred from this structure [that this right, for example, gives rise to the federal power to protect it and is not dependent on state protection]; third, a factual assertion about the world is made [that, if unprotected, the structure of federal representation would be at the mercy of local violence]. Finally a conclusion is drawn that provides the rule in the case. . . .

Consider whether the state can require mandatory testing for the AIDS virus antibodies. To say that it is wise, or unwise, or simply unclear on the present facts whether or not it is wise to permit such testing is to propose an evaluation from a prudential point of view. In the first half of this century, this mode of constitutional argument was principally associated with doctrines that sought to protect the political position of the courts. But the dramatic national crises of depression and world war soon provided ample reason to introduce the practical effects of constitutional doctrine into the rationales underpinning doctrine. For example, one such case arose when, in the depths of the midwestern farm depression, the Minnesota legislature passed a statute providing that anyone who was unable to pay a mortgage could be granted a moratorium from foreclosure. On its face such a statute not only appeared to realize the fears of the framers that state legislatures would compromise the credit market by enacting debtor relief statutes, but also plainly to violate the Contracts Clause that was the textual outcome of such concerns. Moreover, the structure of national economic union strongly counseled against permitting states to protect their constituents by exploding a national recovery program that depended on restoring confidence to banking operations. Nevertheless the Supreme Court upheld the statute, observing that:

> An emergency existed in Minnesota which furnished a proper occasion for the exercise of the reserved power of the state to protect the vital interests of the community.

Very simply, the Court recognized the political expediency of the legislature's action and acquiesced in it. Another national crisis framed the background of the Bowles case, ten years later. Congress had passed the Emergency Price Control Act providing for administrative action to freeze or reduce rents for housing accommodations in areas adjacent to defense establishments. The district court held against the government and struck down the Act as unconstitutional, but the Supreme Court reversed the decision in language that is frankly prudential:

> We need not determine what constitutional limits there are to price-fixing legislation. Congress was dealing here with conditions created by activities resulting from a great war effort. A nation which can demand the lives of its men and women in waging of that war is under no constitutional necessity of providing a system of price control on the domestic front which will assure each landlord a "fair return" on his property. . . . Congress has done all that due process under the war emergency requires.

These cases provide examples of prudential argument, but this approach is by no means confined to the extremes a nation undergoes in emergencies. Of course in such circumstances prudential arguments are likeliest to be decisive. But, as one of prudentialism's most eloquent practitioners argued, such an approach has a place in every decision:

> The accomplished fact, affairs and interests that have formed around it, and perhaps popular acceptance of it— these are elements . . . that may properly enter into a decision . . . ; and they may also enter into the shaping of the judgment, the applicable principle itself.

Prudential argument is actuated by facts, as these play into political and economic policies as to which the Constitution is itself agnostic. The legal rule to be applied is derived from a calculus of costs and benefits, when the facts are taken into account. Accordingly, this often gives rise to a "balancing test" (the balance being a scales, not a tightrope.)

By contrast, when we say that a neutral, general principle derived from the caselaw construing the Constitution should apply, does not apply or may apply, we make an appeal in a doctrinal mode. (It should also be observed . . . that doctrinal arguments are not confined to arguments originating in caselaw; there are also precedents of other institutions, e.g., the practices of earlier Presidents as well as the various corollaries incident to fashioning rules on the basis of precedent.)

To familiarize oneself with this form of argument, let us take up this question: to what extent can a state constitutionally aid parochial schools? Suppose, for example, that parochial school students whose schools are not on the route of free public school buses are given a cash allowance by the state to provide for their transportation. Does this offend the Establishment Clause of the First Amendment because the state is bearing the burdens of costs that would otherwise be born by church members, in much the way that the government in Great Britain, a country that has an established church, provides funds to supplement the income of the Church of England? A judge confronting such a case would probably begin, not by reading the text of the First Amendment which states a rule in rather general terms, but by turning to precedent to find similar cases in which authoritative decisions would govern the present one. Not surprisingly, in the area of Establishment jurisprudence there is a great deal of constitutional doctrine, developed in many cases. The standards these cases develop and apply can be stated as legal rules; the case "on point"—that is, whose facts are similar in those aspects that are relevant to the legal question being posed—is probably *Everson v. Board of Education*, which sustained the power of local authorities to provide free transportation for children attending church schools. In *Everson* the Supreme Court treated the provision of transportation as a form of public welfare legislation, noting that it was being extended by the state "to all

its citizens without regard to their religious belief." The Court wrote:

> It is undoubtedly true that children are helped to get to church schools. There is even a possibility that some of the children might not be sent to the church schools if the parents were compelled to pay their children's bus fares out of their pockets when transportation to a public school would have been paid for by the State.

Transportation, however, benefited the child in the same way as did police protection at crossings, fire protection, connections for sewage disposal, public highways, and sidewalks. Based on this rationale, subsequent cases have developed a three-pronged test: does the state program have a secular purpose; is its principal effect neither to advance nor inhibit religion; does its administration excessively entangle the state in religious affairs?

Applying this test to the question above, the judge might write: "*Everson* must be distinguished from the instant case because the program in *Everson* provided transportation common to all students, whereas here only some students—the parochial ones—are given cash allowances. While we do not question that the legislature had a secular purpose in mind, we think the evidence indicated that the effect of these allowances was in fact to make the parochial schools more attractive to parents than their secular counterparts, and thereby advance the cause of religious institutions. Moreover, the oversight required of the state to ensure that the allowances are in fact spent on providing a system of parochial school transportation intrudes the administrative apparatus of the state into the affairs of the church schools. This can only lead to the interference with budgets and an insistence on allocations for transportation that will excessively entangle the state in the administration of church affairs. Accordingly the program must be held unconstitutional."

Or a judge might write: "*Everson*, which also involved public transportation to parochial school students, governs this case. Here as there, the state's program provides aid to students and their parents, and not—as in cases that have applied Everson and struck down state assistance in this area—direct assistance to church-related schools. Its secular purpose, to provide school transportation at greater efficiency and less cost to the state than expanding its own bus fleets, is apparent. Like school lunches, public health services, and secular textbooks, the transportation provided here confers a benefit on the parochial student that is at parity with what the secular student receives. Thus its effect is neither to advance nor inhibit religion, but rather to avoid exacting a penalty from the parochial student. Finally, whatever state management is required to administer the program will be limited to the oversight of transportation; such involvement as there may be need not, therefore, excessively entangle the state in those religious matters with regard to which it has no role."

In either case, the hypothetical judge has applied a rule derived from the relevant case law. The rule is neutral as to the parties; that is, it applies equally to Catholics and Jews and atheist claimants and does not vary depending on who is bringing or defending the suit. And the rule is general, that is, it applies to all cases in which the state is arguably giving assistance to religious institutions, and is not confined to the facts of the original case that gave birth to the rule. One more point, however, should be made about this modality: its operation is not confined to the application of stare decisis, that is, the strict adherence to previously decided cases. On the contrary, in the American system one of the principles of doctrinalism is that the Supreme Court may reverse the relevant precedent. This would appear to follow from the family of modalities—that provide alternative legal rules—and the supremacy of the Constitution to the acts of government (including, of course, the judicial branch). The Court is entitled, indeed obligated, to overrule itself when it is persuaded that a particular precedent was wrongly decided and should not be applied.

Finally, let us consider the modality of ethical argument. This form of argument denotes an appeal to those elements of the American cultural ethos that are reflected in the Constitution. The fundamental American constitutional ethos is the ideal of limited government, the presumption of which holds that all residual authority remains in the private sphere. Thus when we argue that a particular constitutional conclusion is obliged by, or permitted, or forbidden by the American ethos that has allocated certain decisions to the individual or to private institutions, we are arguing in an ethical mode.

Ethical arguments arise as a consequence of the fundamental constitutional arrangement by which rights in the American system can be defined as those choices beyond the power of government to compel. Thus structural and ethical arguments have some similarities, as each is essentially an inferred set of arguments. Like structural arguments, ethical arguments do not depend on the construction of any particular piece of text, but rather on the necessary relationships that can be inferred from the overall arrangement expressed in the text. Structural argument infers rules from the powers granted to governments; ethical argument, by contrast, infers rules from the powers denied to government. The principal error one can make regarding ethical argument is to assume that any statute or executive act is unconstitutional if it causes effects that are incompatible with the American cultural ethos. This equates ethical argument, a constitutional form, with moral argument generally.

Let us review a hypothetical example that shows the basic pattern of ethical argument. Note that while the American cultural ethos may encompass cheeseburgers, rock and roll, and a passion for Japanese electronics, the American constitutional ethos is largely confined to the reservation of powers not delegated to a limited government.

It was recently reported that a state judge in South Carolina had given the choice of thirty-year prison sentences or castration to three convicted sex offenders. Suppose a convicted man accepted the bargain and was released on probation terms that incorporated this pledge (as by drug-induced impotence). Then suppose that he ceased taking the prescribed drug. If his probation were revoked, a constitutional challenge to the terms of his probation might take this form:

1. The reservation to the individual of the decision to have children is deeply rooted in the American notion of autonomy; there is no express constitutional power to implement a program of eugenics.

2. Moreover, such programs are not a conventionally appropriate means to any express power.
3. Those means denied the federal government are also denied the states.
4. The South Carolina sentence amounted to ordering a man to comply with a eugenics scheme that deemed him ineligible to procreate.

The element of the American ethos at stake is the reservation to individuals and families of the freedom to make certain kinds of decisions. Similar sorts of arguments are to be found in cases in which a state attempted to bar schools from teaching foreign languages; in which a state passed a compulsory education act requiring every school-age child to attend public school (that is, implicitly outlawing private schools); in which a local zoning ordinance was applied to prohibit a grandmother from living with her grandchildren; in which a hospital sought authority to amputate a gangrenous limb from an elderly man who refused his consent; in which a man allegedly suffering from delusions (but concededly harmless) was confined to a mental hospital for almost twenty-five years without treatment. One may test one's mastery of this form of argument by taking each of these examples and stating an ethical argument to resolve it, e.g., (1) There is no express constitutional power to monopolize education; (2) moreover, a statute outlawing private education is not an appropriate means to any express power (such as regulating commerce or providing for armed forces); (3) the decision to educate one's children privately or parochially or publicly is reserved to the family; (4) a statute compelling attendance exclusively at public schools amounts to a scheme to coerce families into a particular educational choice and destroy private educational options.

These then are the six modalities of constitutional argument in the United States. I have argued elsewhere that each of these forms of argument can be used to construct an ideology, a set of political and practical commitments whose values are internally consistent and can be distinguished, externally, from competing ideologies. . . . For the moment, however, I am merely concerned that the reader should not conclude that, because of this relationship—because, for example, some persons may believe that one particular modality represents the only legitimate means of interpreting the Constitution (e.g., historical argument) since it is verifiable by a result to materials (e.g., the intentions of the ratifiers) that

are mandated according to a particular political theory of interpretation (e.g. "originalism")—the modalities of argument are no more than instrumental, rhetorical devices to be deployed in behalf of various political ideologies. The modalities of constitutional argument are the ways in which law statements in constitutional matters are assessed; standing alone they assert nothing about the world. But they need only stand alone to provide the means for making constitutional argument.

There is no constitutional legal argument outside these modalities. Outside these forms, a proposition about the U.S. constitution can be a fact, or be elegant, or be amusing or even poetic, and although such assessments exist as legal statements in some possible legal world, they are not actualized in our legal world.

After publication of *Constitutional Fate*[2] in which the idea of a "grammar" of constitutional argument was developed, Bobbitt's work was subjected to the kind of scrutiny normal for recognition of a major contribution to jurisprudence. As a result of this scrutiny he acknowledged a serious shortcoming in the original work: failure to address the problem of conflict between and among the modalities. In *Constitutional Interpretation*, published ten years after the original work, he concludes not only that such conflict is inevitable but that modal arguments are not commensurable, that is, that conflicting outcomes derived from them cannot be brought into harmony and/or assessed by any single measure or method of evaluation.

> How do we justify the result of a constitutional decision in a particular case? It would appear that the incommensurate nature of the various modalities of argument that enable legitimation makes such an assessment impossible. For if these modes lead to different outcomes, we have no rule that enables us to choose among them. . . . This is the "contradiction" so beloved of law professors generally, and especially the theorists of the Critical Legal Studies group.[3]

---

2. Philip Bobbitt, *Constitutional Fate* (New York: Oxford University Press, 1982).

3. Bobbitt, *Constitutional Interpretation*, p. 164.

Bobbitt concludes that so far as the "grammar" of constitutional argument is concerned, at least in some cases it will be impossible to say that one outcome is legally better than another. Legal argument, in other words, is modular in nature: each mode of argument develops in accordance with its own internal logic, without regard to concern about whether its conclusion will be compatible with the outcome of other modes of argument. Where divergence of outcome is extreme, a case cannot be resolved apart from reliance on exercise of individual conscience.

> A judge who never felt the constraints of the various modalities, who felt that any decision could be satisfactorily defended, would be very foolish and very unimaginative. Only a law student or a law professor could say that "everything can be defended" or that "it will always be possible to find" convincing ways to make a set of distinctions look credible. . . . And yet, in difficult cases, these constraints are not determinative. The case must be *decided*.
>
> What justifies the sensibility that makes such a decision, if, as I have claimed, it is not made according to a rule? There are no grounds independent of the sensibility that is judging those grounds. We can say only: these are the sensibilities we have.[4]

What is important about this development in Bobbitt's thought is that in so-called "hard" cases resolution of the problem of modal conflict must occur *outside* the orbit established by use of the forms of argument—by appeal to conscience and individual decision.

> This system [the system of constitutional adjudication] . . . requires individual decision precisely because the modalities conflict. The result is not any less law because the outcome is not the same for all deciders; indeed it could not really be law, it could not follow the forms of argument and recognize their character as modalities, if it were any other way. The space for moral reflection on our ideologies is created by the conflict among modalities, just as garden walls can create a space for a garden. (Brackets mine.)[5]

Recursion to conscience is a kind of rational end-point in Bobbitt's jurisprudence. It would be a mistake, however, to present such reversion as entailed by the conception of law as a practice. At least one advocate of practice theory argues that Wittgenstein's understanding of practice rules out reversion to conscience as a rational end-point. The primary reason is that whereas conscience is inherently private, meaning—including legal meaning—is inherently public. Dennis Patterson argues that for this reason when modes of legal argument conflict, one must have recourse to something *publicly* accessible—something susceptible to *intersubjective* confirmation.

---

4. Ibid., p. 167.
5. Ibid., p. 177.

A brief comment on the claim that informs Patterson's argument in the following passage may be helpful. Most people would agree that a person's intention to make a phone call immediately after reading this page is private in the sense that the person is the only authority for knowledge of that intention—we are our own authority for the truth of first-person avowals of intention, and of feeling, including moral feeling or conscience. *Descriptions* of personal experiences, however, involve subsumption of the experience under a concept, for example the experience of "an intention", or of "excitement" or of "moral outrage." The key Wittgensteinian point that all concepts must have criteria and that those criteria must be matters of intersubjective agreement, even when the *experience* described by a concept is essentially personal and private, finds new emphasis and is central to Patterson's argument for the public nature of criteria for application of legal concepts.

~

Reading 2

From Dennis Patterson,
LAW AND TRUTH

For recursion to conscience to succeed as a solution to the problem of modal conflict, it must be possible to wed to the exercise of individual conscience an account of constitutional argument that relies ... heavily on a public, intersubjective practice of legal argument. It is far from clear that this is even possible.

Consider any proposition of constitutional law. To the question of how one settles the truth or falsity of a proposition of constitutional law, Bobbitt answers that one employs the modalities. The use of the modalities is a practice—they (and the ways they are used) are public, cultural property. This means that the truth of a constitutional proposition is not a function of what anyone thinks or believes about the proposition; rather, one uses the modalities of argument to show the truth of the proposition. Because the modalities of constitutional argument are public coin, no private meanings are possible.

Recursion to the private realm of conscience is necessary only in the event of modal conflict. Because modal conflict is resolved by conscience, individuals—most importantly judges—must make moral choices. Thus, it is individual conscience that decides the truth and falsity of controversial propositions of constitutional law. The process of decision in easy constitutional cases (cases in which the modes do not conflict) will be public, but in "hard cases" (those of modal conflict), individual conscience is the only analytical apparatus at work.

Were Bobbitt true to the force of his own argument, he would have to admit that the inevitable conflicts among the modalities can only be settled in the public sphere. Conflicts among the modalities are resolved not by what individuals decide, but by what they ultimately accept as an adequate resolution of modal conflict. No particular resolution of

modal conflict springs forth from conscience as a fully formed resolution, as
persuasion—not conscience—ultimately
drives choice. In a passage we considered
earlier, in ... discussion of Ronald
Dworkin's jurisprudence, Charles Taylor
put the matter this way:

> What if someone does not "see" the ad-
> equacy of our interpretation, does not
> accept our reading? We try to show
> him how it makes sense of the original
> nonsense or partial sense [or, in Bob-
> bitt's terms, modal conflict]. But for
> him to follow us he must read the orig-
> inal language as we do, he must rec-
> ognize these expressions as puzzling
> in a certain way, and hence be looking
> for a solution to our problem. If he
> does not, what can we do? The answer,
> it would seem, can only be more of the
> same. We have to show him through
> the reading of other expressions why
> this expression must be read in the
> way we propose. But success here re-
> quires that he follow us in these other
> readings, and so on, it would seem, po-
> tentially forever. We cannot escape an

ultimate appeal to a common understanding of the expressions, of the
"language" involved.*

What is missing in Bobbitt's otherwise compelling account of the practice of
constitutional law is some description of
the practice of persuasion that is so much
a part of constitutional law and law generally. How is it that lawyers convince one
another of a particular reading of the law
when the meaning of law is put in question? Why is one rendering of a modal
conflict followed by some courts or judges
and not others? It is an obvious and important feature of law that the merits of a
single judicial decision play no role in the
wider discourse of law unless and until
another judge or court finds the reasoning persuasive.[†] The cultural methods
and resources for persuasion simply cannot be ignored. By leaving the resolution
of modal conflict to the uncharted realm
of conscience, Bobbitt leaves for another
day further discussion of a central aspect
of the practice of constitutional law that
he has otherwise described so well.

Patterson's rejection of recourse to conscience raises the natural question: If
one does not appeal to conscience when faced with modal conflict, what is
the next step in the process of adjudication? We have seen that his answer
to this question involves the development of what he calls the "practice of
persuasion" in law. But in what does this consist? His answer is that "persuasion" consists of showing someone that a proposition of law is true. But
what do we mean when we say that a proposition of law is true? Here his
answer is best explained in the final chapters of *Law and Truth*, where Patterson aligns his view of legal truth with the "holistic" conception of truth
in science developed by W. V. O. Quine.

---

*Charles Taylor, "Interpretation and the Sciences of Man," in 2 *Philosophy and the Human Sciences
(Philosophical Papers)* 17 (1985).

[†]See generally Richard Bronaugh, "Persuasive Precedent," in *Precedent in Law* 217, 47 (Lawrence
Goldstein, ed., 1987) (providing a philosophical account of persuasion in appeal to precedent.)

Reading 3

From Dennis Patterson,
LAW AND TRUTH

In Quine's view the whole idea of knowledge as a process of building from the simple to the complex, and the concomitant notion that knowledge is a matter of correspondence between word (concept) and world, had to be scrapped. In its place, Quine substituted holism, the view that the truth of any one statement or proposition is a function not of its relationship to the world but of the degree to which it "hangs together" with everything else we take to be true. Quine stated his view this way:

> The totality of our so-called knowledge or beliefs, from the most casual matters of geography and history to the profound laws of atomic physics or even of pure mathematics and logic, is a manmade fabric which impinges on experience only along the edges. Or, to change the figure, total science is like a field of force whose boundary conditions are experience. A conflict with experience at the periphery occasions readjustments in the interior of the field. Truth values have to be redistributed over some of our statements. Reevaluation of some statements entails reevaluation of others, because of their logical interconnections—the logical laws being in turn simply certain further statements of the system, certain further elements of the field. Having reevaluated one statement we must reevaluate some others, which may be statements logically connected with the first or may be

the statements of logical connections themselves. But the total field is so underdetermined by its boundary conditions, experience, that there is much latitude of choice as to what statements to reevaluate in the light of any single contrary experience. No particular experiences are linked with any particular statements in the interior of the field, except indirectly, through considerations of equilibrium affecting the field as a whole.

If this view is right, it is misleading to speak of the empirical content of an individual statement—especially if it is a statement at all remote from the experiential periphery of the field. Furthermore it becomes folly to seek a boundary between synthetic statements, which hold contingently on experience, and analytic statements, which hold come what may. Any statement can be held true come what may, if we make drastic enough adjustments elsewhere in the system.*

Quine's picture of knowledge of the external world changed the way people thought about the construction of knowledge. The breakthrough was to see knowledge not as a matter of foundations—building up from bedrock—but a function of one's being able to move about within a holistic web (be it a web of theory or intersubjective practice). . . .

How, in law, do we move from contradiction to truth? . . . Quine's metaphor

---

*W. V. O. Quine, "Two Dogmas of Empiricism," in *From A Logical Point of View* (Cambridge, Mass.: Harvard University Press, 1961), p. 43.

of science as a "total field of force" is the best way to think of legal interpretation. . . . In law, it is misleading to speak of the truth of a proposition of law in isolation from other propositions within the legal "web of belief."

In choosing between different interpretations, we favor those that clash least with everything else we take to be true. . . . In law, we choose the proposition that best hangs together with everything else we take to be true.

In the passages above two points are worthy of particular notice. First, Patterson affirms Bobbitt's incommensurability claim about modal argument: he speaks of moving from "contradiction," not merely from conflict among the forms of argument, and he cites with approval the idea that constitutional law has a "commensurability problem." Second, he introduces a new element into the conception of legal argument: namely, a distinct form of argumentative practice designed to determine choice among conflicting outcomes produced by use of the forms of argument. Two features of the practice are significant: (1) It consists of interpretation directed toward the resolution of conflict and (2) it is not governed by the forms of legal argument but by a measure described as "fit with what is not in question."

In the following passages he describes the activity of "moving beyond contradiction," that is, of resolving modal incommensurability, but his concern is not with incommensurability per se but with resolution of any serious conflict between and/or among the modes of legal argument. In this regard he attempts to develop a legal-specific version of Quinian holism. One form of conflict receives particular attention: conflict between various *conceptions* of a form of argument. Two examples are discussed, in each of which the applicability of an established form of argument is persuasively *called into question*, that is, is challenged. Patterson explains how, in his view, the challenge is successful in each case, not in virtue of "conscience" or private conviction of any sort, but in virtue of its "fit with everything not legally in question."

Reading 4

From Dennis Patterson,
LAW AND TRUTH

We have identified . . . forms of argument as central to law. These forms of argument serve as backing for [legal decision-making]. . . . But backings may themselves be called into question. Consider the most common occasion of the

historical form of argument, that of statutory interpretation. The nerve of statutory interpretation is appeal to historical facts as backing for the move from history to decision (historical argument). . . . However, if historical argument is to have any validity, beliefs about legislative history must themselves be true, for if they are false, then the move from history to judgment cannot be sustained.

Richard Posner has challenged conventional beliefs about the status of facts of legislative history. On several occasions, . . . [he] has argued that the canons of statutory interpretation are an improper guide to the meaning of statutes because they are based on false assumptions regarding the nature of the legislative process. The basic assumption Posner calls into question is an imputation of omniscience to Congress:

> Most of the canons of statutory construction go wrong not because they misconceive the nature of judicial interpretation of the legislative or political process but because they impute omniscience to Congress. Omniscience is always an unrealistic assumption, and particularly so when one is dealing with the legislative process. The basic reason why statutes are so frequently ambiguous in application is not that they are poorly drafted—though many are—and not that the legislators failed to agree on just what they wanted the statute to accomplish in the statute—though often they do fail—but that a statute necessarily is drafted in advance of, and with imperfect application for the problems that will be encountered in, its application.*

As an example of a canon founded on the assumption of legislative omniscience, consider that of expressio unius est exclusio alterius (the expression of one thing is the exclusion of another). Posner's point, one that is well taken, is

that the canon would only make sense if all omissions in legislative drafting were deliberate. As an example, Posner raises the Supreme Court's decision in *Touche Ross Co. v. Redington*,[†] where the Court used the canon as the basis for refusing to create private remedies for certain statutory violations. Posner objects:

> Whether the result in the private-action cases is right or wrong, the use of expressio unius is not helpful. If a statute fails to include effective remedies because the opponents were strong enough to prevent their inclusion, the courts should honor the legislative compromise. But if the omission was an oversight, or if Congress thought that the courts would provide appropriate remedies for statutory violations as a matter of course, the judges should create the remedies necessary to carry out the legislature's objectives.[‡]

By calling into question certain of the assumptions of the historical form of argument, Posner turns what is normally backing (historical argument) into something that itself requires backing. . . .

What Posner calls into question are certain of the beliefs and assumptions of the historical form of argument. Posner is not rejecting legal argument per se, nor is he putting in question any other aspect of legal reasoning. His is a quite specific and localized complaint. In fact, much of the strength of his criticism is drawn from the fact that he is able to make his points about unrealistic historical assumptions without upsetting any other part of the system of beliefs.

---

*Richard A. Posner, "Statutory Interpretation: In the Classroom and in the Courtroom", 811 *University of Chicago Law Review* (1983).
[†]442 U.S. 560 (1979).
[‡]Posner, "Statutory Interpretation," p. 813.

Patterson discusses, in addition to Posner's challenge to the efficacy of one form of historical argument, an interpretation of one of the cases in Part II of this book, *United Steelworkers of America v. Weber*. In the first passages below he presents the problem of conflict among forms of argument, not as experienced by someone outside the judicial process, but by dissenting judges in the case. Worthy of note in this discussion is Patterson's view that neither the majority nor dissenting opinion was able to develop a persuasive resolution of the modal conflict in question. The reason has to do with the inadequacy of conceptual resources employed by authors of both majority and dissenting opinions. One of the opinions—by Justice Blackmun—appears better than the others, that is, more persuasive in Patterson's sense. But so far as the written opinions in the case are concerned, the constitutional issue raised by the case remains unresolved.

In the final selection here Patterson discusses what he takes to be a persuasive—or at least a more persuasive—analysis of the case by William Eskridge. In Patterson's view, what makes Eskridge's analysis convincing is exactly what makes Posner's analysis convincing: he traces the legal problem in question to an inadequate understanding of the *nature* of historical argument, more specifically to inadequate criteria governing historical confirmation for legal argument. Suggesting more appropriate criteria—what Eskridge calls "evolutive" criteria for historical argument—he is able to provide more "persuasive" argument for the outcome of that case favored by the majority of the court. What is important for Patterson is the *method* employed to resolve conflict in connection with use of the historical mode of argument: "fit with everything else that is not in question."

~

Reading 5

From Dennis Patterson, *LAW AND TRUTH*

Consider [again] a direct challenge to the efficacy of a form of argument. Let us stay with historical argument. Together with textual and doctrinal argument, historical argument is among the most common of the forms of argument. In American jurisprudence, lawyers often ask what motivated a legislature to draft the law as it did. The focus is often on a prob-lem, issue, or set of historical circumstances to which the legislature or Congress was responding when the legislation in question was drafted. In short, appeal to history as a guide to purpose and intent is a cardinal move in the lawyer's argumentative framework. . . .

In *United Steel Workers of America* v. *Weber** Brian Weber, an employee of

*443 U.S. 193 (1979).

Kaiser Aluminum and Chemical Corporation sued his employer under Title VII of the Civil Rights Act, alleging that he had been the victim of unlawful discrimination. In an effort to adjust racial imbalances in its skilled worker population, Kaiser, a private employer, voluntarily adopted an affirmative action plan that provided craft training to blacks with less seniority than white workers. Because the plan involved employment and training, Weber alleged that it violated two key provisions of Title VII. The essence of these two provisions was to prohibit "discrimination" on the basis of, among other things, race.

Section 703(d) of the act prohibits discrimination "against any individual because of his race, color, religion, sex, or national origin in admission to, or employment in, any program established to provide apprenticeship or other training." Unfortunately, the key word in the statute—"discriminate"—is not defined in the act. By Weber's lights, the language of Section 703(d) prevented any and all forms of discrimination. But the majority of the Supreme Court of the United States disagreed with Weber, and for plausible reasons. The statutory history of the act, and these sections in particular, were at variance with the "literalist" reading urged by Weber.

Both the majority and dissenting opinions review the historical circumstances surrounding promulgation, debate, and passage of the act. The majority's argument is reflected in paragraphs like the following:

> Congress' primary concern in enacting the prohibition against racial discrimination in Title VII was with the plight of the Negro in our economy, and the prohibition against racial discrimination in employment was primarily addressed to the problem of opening opportunities for Negroes in occupations which have been traditionally closed to them. In view of the legislative history, the very statutory words intended as a spur or catalyst to cause "employers and unions to self-examine and to self-evaluate their employment practices and to endeavor to eliminate, so far as possible, the last vestiges of an unfortunate and ignominious page in this country's history," *Albemarle Paper Co.* v. *Moody*, 422 U.S. 405, 418, cannot be interpreted as an absolute prohibition against all private, voluntary, race-conscious affirmative action efforts to hasten the elimination of such vestiges.

From the majority's analysis of the history of the act, it is clear that Congress had at least two expectations. First, that blacks would obtain jobs "which have a future" in numbers sufficient to eradicate their economic deprivation. Second, that no employer would be forced to adopt an affirmative action plan. Voluntary affirmative action of the type employed by Kaiser would be permitted to correct racial imbalances. The natural inference is that "Congress chose not to forbid all voluntary race-conscious affirmative action." With the statutory language duly massaged by history, the majority of the Court held "that Title VII's prohibition in § 703(a) and (d) against racial discrimination does not condemn all private, voluntary, race conscious affirmative action programs."

Clear statutory language precludes the need to resort to history, for history—like parol evidence—is something one resorts to only when the text under consideration is ambiguous or otherwise unclear. At least that is how Justice Rehnquist saw the matter. But Justice Rehnquist was not afraid to match fact for fact with the majority. . . . His dissent is correctly regarded as besting the majority at its own game, that of marshaling historical facts. Yet, despite the overwhelming evidence that Congress's intent was to avoid government-mandated affirmative action programs, that was not the question raised by the *Weber* case. The Kaiser plan was a voluntary plan by a private corporation. Thus, the historical evidence did not cut quite as deeply as either the majority or the dissent would like. Nevertheless, this left the dissent with its best argument, a textual one: the language of the statute prohibits discrimination. There being no compelling argument that the historical evidence points in a direction different from the language of the provisions under consideration, the dissent has the better of the argument.

Owing perhaps to the realization that its opinion founders on the history to which it had resort, the majority buoyed their position with what might be called a "modified intentionalist" stance.* It is clear from legislative history that Congress had two purposes in effecting the act. The first was to obtain more jobs for blacks. The second was achieving a "color-blind" society. Obviously, these two purposes were in conflict, and the majority offered no analysis of how it came to prefer one over the other.

Some scholars believe the weaknesses in the majority's opinion are avoided in the concurring opinion of Justice Blackmun. Eschewing the grounds of text and history, Justice Blackmun rested his affirmation of the Kaiser plan on the grounds of doctrine and prudence. In a

passage worth quoting at length, Justice Blackmun argues that Weber's reading of the statute

> places voluntary compliance with Title VII in profound jeopardy. The only way for the employer and the union to keep their footing on the "tightrope" it creates would be to eschew all forms of voluntary affirmative action. Even a whisper of emphasis on minority recruiting would be forbidden. Because Congress intended to encourage private efforts to come into compliance with Title VII, see *Alexander v. Gardner Denver Co.*, 415 U.S. 336,44, 94 S.Ct. 1011, 1017, 39 L.Ed.2d 147 (1974), Judge Wisdom [who wrote the court of appeals opinion] concluded that employers and unions who had committed "arguable violations" of Title VII should be free to make reasonable responses without fear of liability to whites. 563 F.2d, at 230. Preferential hiring along the lines of the Kaiser program is a reasonable response for the employer, whether or not a court, on these facts, could order the same step as a remedy. The company is able to avoid identifying victims of past discrimination, and so avoids claims for back pay that would inevitably follow a response limited to such victims. If past victims should be benefited by the program, however, the company mitigates its liability to those persons. Also, to the extent that Title VII liability is predicated on the "disparate effect" of an employer's past hiring practices, the program makes it less likely that such an effect can be demonstrated. Cf. *County of Los Angeles v. Davis*, 440 U.S. 625,633–634, 99 S.Ct. 1379, 1384, 59 L.Ed.2d 642 (1979) (hiring could moot a past Title VII claim). And the Court has recently held that

---

*The phrase is William Eskridge's. See William N. Eskridge Jr., "Dynamic Statutory Interpretation," 135 *University of Pennsylvania Law Review* 1479, 1491 (1987).

work-force statistics resulting from private affirmative action were probative of benign intent in a "disparate treatment" case. *Furnco Construction Corp. v. Waters*, 438 U.S. 567, 579–580, 98 S.Ct. 2943, 2950–951, 57 L.Ed.2d 957 (1958).

Certain forms of legal argument dominate the majority and dissenting opinions in *Weber*. Each opinion begins at the level of textual argument. The nub of textual argument is the meaning a legal text has to the common, professional reader. Historical argument proceeds by appeal to the then-present legislative context. What was Congress trying to do with this statute? What was its point or purpose? . . . In *Weber* neither the textual nor the historical forms of argument yielded a compelling conclusion. Yes, the text of the statute does preclude "discrimination." But that term of art is not defined. When one looks to history for elucidation, one finds competing—if not conflicting—congressional purposes and aspirations. At the level of text and history, no clear direction is indicated.

Justice Blackmun's concurring opinion employs two different forms of legal argument: prudential and doctrinal. A prudential argument is one that measures the consequences of a decision. It asks after the effects of deciding a case one way rather than another. In his concurring opinion, Justice Blackmun argues that the effect of reading Title VII in the manner urged by the respondent, Weber, would be deleterious in the extreme, and he offers reasons for his conclusion that it is on the whole better to side with the majority. The measure of good and bad effects employed by Black-

mun comes not from a utilitarian calculus, but from precedent. Blackmun cleverly weaves prudential judgment with doctrinal argument to break the deadlock between text and history played out in the majority and dissenting opinions. To decide the case as Weber urges means departing from precedents sanctioning private affirmative actions plans. Additionally, reversing the lower court's decision would have negative effects in related matters such as "disparate effect" and "disparate treatment." By fitting his prudential arguments within the fold of precedent, Blackmun breaks free of the intractable differences between the majority and the dissent, thereby enabling him to write an opinion that is far more persuasive than its competitors. . . .

[In light of this] discussion . . . I want to consider William Eskridge's challenge to the conventional understanding of the historical form of argument. . . . Eskridge describes two perspectives that are usually brought to bear in the interpretation of statutes: (1) textual perspective: the statutory text, which is the formal focus of interpretation and a constraint on the range of interpretive options available, and (2) historical perspective:* the original legislative expectations surrounding the statute's creation, including compromises reached. To these two perspectives, which we recognize as the textual and historical forms of argument, Eskridge adds a third, the "evolutive perspective," which he describes as "the subsequent evolution of the statute and its present context, especially the ways in which the societal and legal environment of the statute has materially changed over time."†

---

*Ibid., p. 1483.
†Ibid.

In an effort to make his argument against the background of conventional understanding of legal argument, Eskridge notes that "[w]hen the statutory text clearly answers the interpretive question . . . it normally will be the most important consideration."* Of course, the ordinary meaning of the text is not always dispositive, as was the case in *Weber*. When text is not dispositive, the door opens for dynamic statutory interpretation.

Why is *Weber* a good candidate for dynamic statutory interpretation? Eskridge regards the question in *Weber* as one particularly amenable to dynamic analysis because it recognizes not only that the very nature of the problem had changed since 1964, but also that the legal and societal context of Title VII had changed. In 1964, the legal culture, legislators, judges, administrators, and commentators focused on how to root out discrimination inspired by racial animus. People thought that rooting out actual prejudice would create a color-blind society. The intellectual focus changed over the next fifteen years, as the legal community came to realize that discrimination could be just as invidious even when it could not be established that prejudice was at its root. The concept of the continuing effects of historical patterns of discrimination suggested that current institutions might perpetuate discrimination even though no one in those institutions remained personally prejudiced. This insight was not a historical concern of the 1964 Act, but it evolved into a current concern and was recognized in subsequent statues, judicial decisions, and commentary.†

While Eskridge labels his argument "evolutive," the argument is clearly historical in nature. The point of the argument is to put in question the conventional limits on historical argument, which preclude asking anything about history other than from the then-present perspective. Eskridge puts the historical form of argument in question by making the case for the legal significance of failed legislative aspirations. Where the text of a statute is unclear, as he argues it was in *Weber*, and history demonstrates a clear historical aspiration on the part of Congress, subsequent history (both social and legal) should play a justificatory role.

How are we to assess Eskridge's argument for a dynamic reading of statutes? This question is one about our current practices: do the means exist for adjudicating between rival conceptions of the historical form of argument? Notice how Eskridge's argument dovetails with historical argument, conventionally understood. He is not asking that our long-standing approach to historical evidence be abandoned or even altered. In fact, the strength of this new conception of the importance of history actually builds off of historical argument, traditionally understood.

In what can only be characterized as a pragmatic argument, Eskridge claims that his dynamic conception of history is consistent with rule of law virtues, raises no countermajoritarian difficulties, enhances the legitimacy of government, and assigns to judges no tasks not already within their competence. In short, dynamic statutory interpretation is appealing "because it rests upon a realistic

---

*Ibid.
†Ibid., p. 1493.

vision of the legislative and interpretive processes and because it promotes more candid decisionmaking in statutory interpretation cases."*

Eskridge's model of dynamic statutory interpretation enables us to pull together the three distinct but related threads . . . of a [practice-based] jurisprudence. He begins by employing the forms of argument to frame the issues at stake in the Weber case. Textual and historical arguments point in no clear direction. Something labeled "Dynamic Statutory Interpretation" is introduced, which, at first glance, appears to be something new and different. Indeed, it is different but in a distinct way. Our conventional understanding of historical argument is put in question and a proposal made for improving how we use history to show the truth of propositions of law. Of course, there are criteria for what is to count as an adequate historical argument, and Eskridge deftly employs those criteria to make the case that his proposed recasting of historical argument fits well with everything else we take to be true about statutory interpretation. Here we have the employment of conventional criteria of truth evaluation (the forms of argument), the reflective practice of putting a form of argument in question (recasting historical argument in dynamic terms), and appeal to conventional interpretive criteria (consistency with rule of law virtues, etc.), all in an effort to demonstrate the superiority of his enhanced understanding of the historical form of argument. . . .

To describe only the forms of argument is to present an incomplete account of the nature of law. In addition to the problem of conflict among the forms of argument, the forms themselves are contested in a number of different ways. . . . The truth of legal propositions does not consist solely in the text of the law being produced "in the right way." The forms of argument are the legal grammar of meaning-making. We use the forms of argument to show what the legislatively produced text means. . . .

The discussion . . . of Posner's criticisms of the canons of statutory construction provided one example of the interpretive activity of calling into question beliefs about history which are basic to the historical form of argument. . . . Posner uses the unchallenged portion of the field of legal argument to make his point that the falsity of beliefs about the legislative process has deleterious and measurable consequences for the integrity of legal judgment. In this way, his argument confirms an essential element of . . . jurisprudence; that legal argument is "horizontal" in nature. When a problem in some aspect of the argumentative field arises, solutions are measured not against a practice-transcendent ideal but by the degree to which the proposed solution fits with everything not then in question.

A more wide-ranging challenge to the forms of argument is illustrated by William Eskridge's proposal for a rethinking of the nature of historical argument. . . . Eskridge takes our conventional approach to resort to history as an element in the justificatory matrix of law and forces us to see history from a dynamic and not a static perspective. Again, just as in the case of Posner, Eskridge uses the elements of law not then

---

*Ibid., p. 1538.

in question to persuade us that his is truly a legal argument, not an import from another discipline. As with Posner, it is the form of the argument that is of interest. . . .

In my view, normativity in law arises from linguistic practices. . . . I do not believe that communal agreement can explain normativity. The relation goes the other way: normativity—intersubjective linguistic practice—makes agreement possible. In this chapter, I attempted to go beyond existing accounts of law as a linguistic practice to put the debate in a wider context and to develop the position in a new way. Agreement and disagreement are distinct yet related argumentative legal phenomena. Without some description of their role in legal argument, no complete jurisprudence is possible.

QUESTIONS

1. What is Bobbitt's theory of the modalities?

2. What is the role of conflict among the modalities in Bobbitt's theory?

3. What role does justice play in Bobbitt's theory?

4. Is Bobbitt's constitutional theory a version of legal positivism?

5. How does Bobbitt's approach to constitutional questions differ from Dworkin's? Can their views be reconciled?

6. What is Patterson's criticism of Bobbitt on the question of legal interpretation?

7. What is Patterson's account of interpetation in law?

8. What does Patterson say about challenges to forms of argument?

9. What is Patterson's point in using Quine in formulating his theory?

10. What are the key differences in approach between Bobbitt and Patterson?

Chapter 7

New Natural Law Theory
Readings from John Finnis

To complete the study of contemporary jurisprudential types we come full circle to natural law theory and to its most well-known representative. Cast firmly in that tradition, John Finnis takes significant steps away from its classical expression, thus the label generally applied to his work: "new natural law theory." Equally important for our purposes, however, is his departure from main-line jurisprudential thought wherein a primary focus of attention is on methods for establishing correct legal decisions (recall the pedigree test in positivism, reflective equilibrium in constructivism, and Pareto superiority in consequentialism, for example). In a series of interesting arguments, Finnis changes the terms in which the correctness of legal decision-making is discussed, taking exception to all such methods so far developed. The most we can do, he says, is to identify *unreasonable* decisions in law. To appreciate the effect of this shift of focus in legal inquiry it may be helpful to recall the Neo-Platonic doctrine of *via negativa*, "the negative way." According to this doctrine the limitations of human cognitive capacities prevent apprehension of the nature of divine being but do allow knowledge of a negative sort; we can know, for example, that predicates like "drunkenness" or "fury" do not apply to divine being. The analogy with Finnis' thought is remote, of course, but it may serve to highlight an attractive aspect of his legal philosophy. Whereas in theology the negative way is intended to preserve the transcendence of divine being while at the same time avoiding complete skepticism, in the theory of legal decision-making it has the effect of preserving the indeterminacy of law acknowledged by legal philosophers from Aristotle to Unger, but without reversion to either skepticism or subjectivism. Slide toward either of these undesirable alternatives is blocked by a set of constraints that operate, or at least should operate, *in a negative way*; that is, their effect is to show that some legal decision or other is *unreasonable* in some way.

To appreciate Finnis' understanding of the role of negation in legal decision-making, we must briefly touch on three additional ideas that form the core of his jurisprudence. First, the starting point for thinking about law is the precept of "basic human goods," that is, goods which are the basis for moral and personal development—life (and health), knowledge, play, and sociability (friendship), for example. Knowledge of these is "self-evident," and he is careful to explain what that means. Closely connected to this account of human goods is the idea that freedom of choice makes possible *different combinations* of goods. These combinations exhibit no hierarchical order, that is, no person's chosen combination of goods is better than another person's combination because *each* of the *basic* human goods is intrinsically valuable. Thus, whereas classical natural law theorists viewed human life as directed toward a single natural end or purpose, Finnis sees the possibility of *multiple forms* of human happiness. A final salient feature of new natural law theory is emphasis on the requirements of practical reasonableness, that is, reasonableness about how to advance the realization of basic human goods. Finnis shares with natural law theorists, generally, belief that correct legal judgments derive from understanding the moral principles upon which law is founded, but he follows the Aristotelian wing of this tradition in assigning a special role to practical reason in the achievement of correctness.

Reading 1 explores the process of practical reasoning in some detail. If, as Finnis claims, positive law is somehow dependent upon, or grounded in, principles and rules that are a matter of objective reasonableness, how should we understand this dependence or grounding? Following Aristotle and Aquinas, Finnis asserts that law is universal only in part; it consists of rules deducible directly from first order principles, but not entirely. Law also consists of "versions" or "crystallizations" of principles that are conventional in nature. In discussing "rules of the road," for example, he says that it is of no moral consequence whether the law of a country prescribes driving on the right or the left side of the road. It is of moral consequence, however, that people respect their own and other person's safety. Rules of the road are derived from general moral considerations having to do with duties to ourselves and others, but the specific form they take is derived from what Finnis calls "subordinate theorems" of these general moral considerations. The nation-specific rule that one must drive on the left-hand side of the road is a version or determination of general principles characterized not by moral necessity but by the kind of variability and flexibility associated with human choice and creativity.

~

Reading 1

From John Finnis,
NATURAL LAW AND NATURAL RIGHTS

Derivation of "Positive" From "Natural" Law

"In every law positive well made is somewhat of the law of reason. . . ; and to discern . . . the law of reason from the law positive is very hard. And though it be hard, yet it is much necessary in every moral doctrine, and in all laws made for the commonwealth." These words of the sixteenth-century lawyer Christopher St. German express the fundamental concern of any sound "natural law theory" of law: to understand the relationship(s) between the particular laws of particular societies and the permanently relevant principles of practical reasonableness. . . .

In Aquinas's view, the law consists in part of rules which are "derived from natural law like conclusions deduced from general principles" and for the rest of rules which are "derived from natural laws like implementations [*determinationes*] of general directives." This notion of *determinatio* he explains on the analogy of architecture (or any other practical art), in which a general idea or form (say, "house", "door", "door-knob") is to be made determinate as this particular house, door, door-knob, with specifications which are certainly derived from and shaped by the general idea but which could have been more or less different in many (even in every) particular dimension and aspect, and which therefore require of the artificer a multitude of choices. The (making of the) artefact is controlled but not fully determined by the basic idea (say, the client's order), and until it is fully determinate the artefact is nonexistent or incomplete. To count as a door in a human habitation, an object must be more than half a metre high and need not be more than 2–5 metres, but no door will be built at all if the artificer cannot make up his mind on a particular height. Stressing, as it were, the artificer's virtually complete freedom in reason to choose say 2.2 rather than 2.1 or 2.3 metres, Aquinas says that laws of this second sort have their force 'wholly in human law', and Hooker names his second category "merely human laws".

These last formulae, so strongly emphasizing the legislator's rational freedom of choice in such cases, can be mis-leading unless one bears in mind that they enunciate only a subordinate theorem within a general theory. The general theory is that, in Aquinas's words, "every law laid down by men has the character of law just in so far as it is derived from the natural law," or in St. German's words, already quoted, "in every law positive well made is somewhat of the law of reason." The compatibility between this theory and the subordinate theorem can be best understood by reference to one or two concrete examples.

A first example is hackneyed, but simple and clear. Consider the rule of the road. There is a sense in which (as the subordinate theorem implies) the rule of the road gets "all its force" from the authoritative custom, enactment, or other determination which laid it down. For until the stipulation "drive on the left, and at less than 70 miles per hour" was posited by one of these means, there was no legal rule of the road; moreover, there was no need for the legislator to have a reason for choosing "left" rather than "right" or "70" rather than "65." But there is also a sense in which (as the general theory claims) the rule of the road gets "all its normative force" ultimately from the permanent principles of practical reason (which require us to respect our own and others' physical safety) in combination with non-posited facts such as that traffic is dangerous and can be made safer by orderly traffic flows and limitation of speed, that braking distances and human reaction times are such-and-such etc.

A second example is richer. If material goods are to be used efficiently for human well-being . . . there must normally be a regime of private property. . . . This regime will be constituted by rules assigning property rights in such goods, or many of them, to individuals or small groups. But precisely what rules should be laid down in order to constitute such a regime is not settled ("determined") by this general requirement of justice. Reasonable choice of such rules is to some extent guided by the circumstances of a particular society, and to some extent "arbitrary." The rules adopted will thus for the most part be "determinations" of the general requirement, derived from it but not entailed by it, even in conjunction with a description of those particular circumstances. . . .

Moreover, in the vast area where the legislator is constructing "determinations" rather than applying or ratifying determinate principles or rules of reason, there are relatively few points at which his choice can reasonably be regarded as "unfettered" or "arbitrary" (in the sense that it reasonably can be when one confronts two or more feasible alternatives which are in all respects equally satisfactory, or equally unsatisfactory, or incommensurably satisfactory/unsatisfactory). The basic legal norms of a law-abiding citizen are "Do not commit offences," "abstain from torts," "perform contracts," "pay debts," "discharge liabilities," "fulfil obligations," etc.; and, taking these norms for granted without stating them, the lawmaker defines offences (from murder to road-traffic offences), torts, the formation, incidents, and discharge of contracts, etc., etc. But this task of definition (and re-definition in the changing conditions of society) has its own principles, which are not the citizen's. The reasonable legislator's principles include the desiderata of the Rule of Law. . . . But they also include a multitude of other substantive principles related, some very closely, others more remotely, some invariably and others

contingently, to the basic principles and methodological requirements of practical reason.

What are these basic norms for the legislator? Normally they are not the subject of direct and systematic enquiry by lawyers. But it should be recalled that the "legislator" here, for convenience (and at the expense of some significant differentiations), includes any judiciary that, like the judge at common law, enjoys a creative role. Now the principles that should guide the judge in his interpretation and application of both statutory and common or customary law to particular issues are the subject of scientific discussion by lawyers. These principles are almost all "second-order," in that they concern the interpretation and application of other rules or principles whose existence they presuppose. They therefore are not directly the concern of legislators who have authority not merely to interpret and supplement but also to change and abolish existing rules and to introduce novel rules. Nevertheless, the second-order principles are themselves mostly crystallizations or versions (adapted to their second-order role) of "first-order" principles which ought to guide even a "sovereign legislature" in its acts of enactment. Moreover, a legislator who ignores a relevant first-order principle in his legislation is likely to find that his enactments are controlled, in their application by citizens, courts, and officials, by that principle in its second-order form, so that in the upshot the law on the particular subject will tend to turn out to be a *"determinatio"* of that principle (amongst others).

Many of the second-order principles or maxims employed by lawyers express the desirability of stability and predictability in the relations between one person and another, and between persons and things. Such maxims are obviously connected very closely not only with the formal features of law . . . and the desiderata of the Rule of Law . . . but also with the willingness of lawyers and indeed of men in society in every age to attribute authoritative force to usage, practice, custom. . . . And there is a corresponding first-order principle or set of principles to which any legislator ought to give considerable weight—that those human goods which are the fragile and cumulative achievements of past effort, investment, discipline, etc. are not to be treated lightly in the pursuit of future goods. More prosaically, the tangible expenses and waste of dislocative change are to be taken literally into account—the legislative choice between 'drive on the left' and 'drive on the right' is a matter of indifference in the abstract, but not in a society where by informal convention people already tend to drive on the left, and have adjusted their habits, their vehicle construction, road design, and street furniture accordingly.

Starting with these second-order maxims favouring continuity in human affairs—i.e. favouring the good of diachronic order, as distinct from the good of a future end-state, we can trace a series of related second-order principles which include the principle of stability but more and more go beyond it to incorporate new principles or values. In each case these are available in first-order form to guide a legislator. Prose-form requires a linear exposition here which oversimplifies and disguises their interrelations: (i) compulsory acquisition of property rights to be compensated, in respect of *"damnum emergens"* (actual losses) if not of *"itterum cessans"* (loss of expected profits); (ii) no liability for un-

intentional injury without fault; (iii) no criminal liability without *"mens rea"*; (iv) estoppel (*nemo contra factum proprium venire potest* [no man can contravene or contradict his own particular deed] [brackets mine]); (v) no judicial aid to one who pleads his own wrong (he who seeks equity must do equity); (vi) no aid to abuse of rights; (vii) fraud unravels everything; (viii) profits received without justification and at the expense of another must be restored; (ix) "pacta sunt servanda" (contracts are to be performed); (x) relative freedom to change existing patterns of legal relationships by agreement; (xi) in assessments of the legal effects of purported acts-in-the-law, the weak to be protected against their weaknesses; (xii) disputes not to be resolved without giving both sides an opportunity to be heard; (xiii) no one to be allowed to judge his own cause.

These "general principles of law" are indeed principles. That is to say, they justify, rather than require, particular rules and determinations, and are qualified in their application to particular circumstances by other like principles. Moreover, any of them may on occasion be outweighed and overridden (which is not the same as violated, amended, or repealed) by other important components of the common good, other principles of justice. Nor is it to be forgotten that there are norms of justice that may never be overridden or outweighed, corresponding to the absolute rights of man. . . . Still, the general principles of law which have been recited here do operate, over vast ranges of legislative *"determinationes,"* to modify the pursuit of particular social goods. And this modification need not be simply a matter of abstaining from certain courses of conduct: the principles which require compensation, or ascertainment of *"mens rea,"* or "natural justice" . . . can be adequately met only by the positive creation of complex administrative and judicial structures.

In sum: the derivation of law from the basic principles of practical reasoning has indeed the two principal modes identified and named by Aquinas; but these are not two streams flowing in separate channels. The central principle of the law of murder, of theft, of marriage, of contract . . . may be a straightforward application of universally valid requirements of reasonableness, but the effort to integrate these subject matters into the Rule of Law will require of judge and legislator countless elaborations which in most instances partake of the second mode of derivation. This second mode, the sheer *"determinatio"* by more or less free authoritative choice, is itself not only linked with the basic principles by intelligible relationship to goals (such as traffic safety . . .) which are directly related to basic human goods, but also is controlled by wide-ranging formal and other structuring principles (in both first- and second-order form) which themselves are derived from the basic principles by the first mode of derivation. . . .

I said that a principal source of the need for authority is the luxuriant variety of appropriate but competing choices of "means" to "end." Now we can see how this range of choices is both increased and controlled by the complex of interacting "principles of law." True, the reasoning of those in authority frequently ends without identifying any uniquely reasonable decision; so the rulers must choose, and their choice (*determinatio*) determines what thereafter is uniquely just for those subject to their authority. But, having stressed that it is thus authority, not simply reasoning,

that settles most practical questions in the life of a community, I now must stress the necessary rider. To be, itself, authoritative in the eyes of a reasonable man, a *"determinatio"* must be consistent with the basic requirements of practical reasonableness, though it need not necessarily or even usually be the *"determinatio"* he would himself have made had he had the opportunity; it need not even be one he would regard as "sensible." Our jurisprudence therefore needs to be completed by a closer analysis of this authoritativeness or "binding force" of positive law. . . , and by some consideration of the significance of wrongful exercises of authority. . . .

It may, however, be helpful to conclude the present discussion by reverting to the textbook categories, "[positive] law," "sources of law," "morality." The tradition of "natural law" theorizing is not characterized by any particular answer to questions: "Is every 'settled' legal rule and legal solution set by appeal exclusively to 'positive' sources such as statute, precedent, and custom? Or is the 'correctness' of some judicial decisions determinable only by appeal to some 'moral' ('extra-legal') norm? And are the boundaries between settled and the unsettled law, or between the correct, the eligible, and the incorrect judicial decision determinable by reference only to positive sources or legal rules?" The tradition of natural law theorizing is not concerned to minimize the range and determinacy of positive law or the general sufficiency of positive sources as solvents of legal problems.

Rather, the concern of the tradition . . . has been to show that the act of "positing" law (whether judicial or legislatively or otherwise) is an act which can and should be guided by "moral" principles and rules; that those moral norms are a matter of objective reasonableness, not of whim, or convention, or mere "decision"; and that those same moral norms justify (a) the very institution of positive law, (b) the main institutions, techniques, and modalities within tradition (e.g. separation of powers), and (c) the main institutions regulated and sustained by law (e.g. government, contract, property, marriage, and criminal liability). What characterizes the tradition is that it is not content merely to observe the historical or sociological fact that "morality" thus affects "law," but instead seeks to determine what the requirements of practical reasonableness really are, so as to afford a rational basis for the activities of legislators, judges, and citizens.

In Reading 2 Finnis expands his account of the derivation of positive law. In the previous reading he approached legal determination "from the bottom up," as it were: the primary concern was with the conventional or purely human element in law—what he called "subordinate theorems." He also makes clear, however, that the normative force of positive law resides in "permanent principles of practical reason." Finnis is aware that any account of natural law that posits a necessary connection between positive law and knowable moral principles must give an adequate account of how that knowledge is funded and this is the focus of the next reading.

Natural law principles for Finnis derive from what he calls "integral human fulfillment," a particular kind of fulfillment connected with basic as distinct from nonbasic human goods. In the first part of the section to follow he defines and delineates what is meant by "basic human goods." Closely connected with the idea of basic human goods is a companion concept Finnis calls the "first principle of natural morality": the principle that one ought to choose and to will those and only those possibilities whose willing is compatible with integral human fulfillment—understood now as basic human goods in either individual life, social life, or both. This is, as he remarks, a very abstract principle, one open to the question whether it can do any real work in explaining concrete legal decision-making. By way of answering this concern he concedes that *by itself* the "first principle of morality" is inadequate to account for the "derivation" of positive law from natural law. However, he argues that in the actual exercise of moral and legal reasoning, this abstract principle is given content through what he calls "intermediate principles," or "modes of responsibility." He discusses three of these in particular: (1) the Golden Rule, (2) the principle that one should not answer injury with injury, even when one could do so fairly, and (3) the principle that one should not do evil that good may come, but he says that additional modes of moral responsibility have been identified that might be added to the list, for example, moral reflection having to do with "detachment," "creative fidelity," and "purity of heart." Intermediate principles are discovered in moral reflection, and in Finnis's view they do not strike us as isolated insights; rather they seem interconnected, parts of a larger framework of moral thought and action. For Finnis, the impression of unity between and among moral principles is best explained by saying that the various modes of responsibility are expressions of the single, abstract, principle referred to earlier as the "first principle of morality."

~

Reading 2

From John Finnis,
NUCLEAR DETERRENCE, MORALITY AND REALISM

The Idea of Basic Human Goods

"Good," in the widest sense in which it is applied to human actions and their principles, refers to anything a person can in any way desire. "Good is any object of any interest." But people desire many things—e.g. pleasure, wealth, and power—which when made principles of action seem to empty a person and to divide persons from one another.

There are, however, other goods—e.g. knowledge of truth, and living in friendship—pursuit of which seems of itself to promote persons and bring them together. Goods like these are intrinsic aspects—that is, real parts—of the integral fulfillment of persons. We call these intrinsic aspects of personal full-being "basic human goods": basic not to survival but to human full-being.

Some goods are definite objectives, desired states of affairs—e.g. getting an enemy to surrender unconditionally, fulfilling the goals of the current five-year plan, or successfully completing a research project. But the basic human goods, in themselves, are not definite objectives. Interest in peace and justice, for example, goes beyond any particular ob-

jective sought for their sake, for they transcend any particular state of affairs which can instantiate them. People dedicated to such goods never finish doing what can be done to serve them. Peace and justice are more than things one wants, or goals one hopes to reach. Acting alone and in various forms of community with other persons, one can contribute to the realization of such goods and share in them, but can never lay hold of them, appropriate them, exhaust them.

But if the basic human goods are thus not definite objectives, not goals to be achieved, how do they guide action? By providing the reasons to consider some possibilities as choice worthy opportunities. Thus the enemy's unconditional surrender becomes an objective to be pursued in the belief that it will contribute to lasting peace; the fulfillment of the five-year plan's goals is sought as a step toward a dreamed-of just world order; particular projects of theoretical research are carried on in the hope that their results will add to knowledge. These reasons for choosing and acting, provided by basic human goods, require no prior reasons. The prospects of human fulfillment held out by peace, justice, knowledge, and so on, naturally arouse corresponding interests in human persons as potential agents.

Thus, human practical reflection and deliberation begins from the basic human goods. To identify them is to identify expanding fields of possibility which underlie all the reasons one has for choosing and carrying out one's choices. Considered in this way, the basic human goods explain both human life's constant and universal features, and its diversity and open-endedness.

And because the basic human goods are at once principles of practical reason and aspects of the full-being of persons, there is no necessary opposition between pursuit of these goods and absolute respect for persons. Indeed, the grounding of ethics in these goods is the first step towards providing both a defence of the absolute dignity of each person, and the reason for every person to be moral.

Which Are the Basic Human Goods?

Many goods, though important, are not basic, because not intrinsic to the fulfillment of persons. External goods—anything human persons make, or have, considered as distinct from persons—cannot be basic. It is always for ulterior reasons, reasons which culminate within persons, that individuals and communities are concerned with such goods. Even goods of a more personal and interpersonal character are not yet basic if they can be desired only as instrumental to some further good. Political liberty, for example, is a great good; but it is not itself basic, for by itself it does not fulfill persons but only enables them to pursue various forms of fulfillment. People want liberty

in order to pursue the truth, to worship as they think right, to participate in the responsible play of political decision making, to live in friendship, and so on.

"Enjoyment" refers to a variety of states of consciousness, which have in common only that they are preferred to many other states of consciousness. A preferred state of consciousness is at best part of a person's sharing in some good, part of the instantiation of a good in a certain state of affairs. Thus enjoyment is not a basic good. Still, in so far as "enjoy" refers to conscious participation in one or more of the basic goods, one needs no ulterior reason to enjoy oneself.

There are several basic human goods. This is clear from reflection on one's own deliberation, and from observation of the ways people organize their lives. Truth and friendship, for example, mark out fields of concern which plainly are distinct; neither is reducible to the other or to any more fundamental interest. This diversity of basic human goods is neither a mere contingent fact about human psychology nor an accident of history. Rather, being aspects of the integral fulfillment of human persons, these goods correspond to the inherent complexity of human nature, as it is found both in individuals and in various forms of association.

As animate, human persons are living organic substances. Life itself—its maintenance and transmission—health, and safety are one form of basic human good. Health professions are directed to this good; and to it most people devote a substantial part of their activities.

As rational, human beings can know reality and appreciate beauty and whatever intensely engages their capacities to know and feel, and to integrate the two. Knowledge and aesthetic experience are another category of basic good.

As simultaneously rational and animal, human persons can transform the natural world by using realities, beginning with their own bodily selves, to express meanings and/or serve purposes within human cultures. Such bestowing of meaning and value can be realized in diverse degrees; its fullness is another category of basic good: excellence in work and play.

All these are goods in which everyone to some extent shares prior to any deliberate pursuit of them. Life, knowledge, and the various skills are first received as gifts of nature, and as parts of a cultural heritage. But children quickly come to see these goods as fields in which they can care for, expand, and improve upon what they have received. Life, knowledge, and excellence in performance are basic human goods and principles of practical reasoning in so far as they can be understood and, being understood, can be cherished, enhanced, and handed on to others.

But there is another dimension of human persons. As agents through deliberation and choice, they can strive to avoid or overcome various forms of conflict and alienation, and can seek after various forms of harmony, integration, and community (fellowship). Choices themselves are essential constituents of this relational dimension of persons. The already given ("natural") aspects of personal unity and interpersonal relationship provide grounds for this dimension, yet it goes beyond what is naturally given.

Most obvious among the basic human goods of this relational dimension are various forms of harmony between and among persons and groups of persons: friendship, peace, fraternity, and so on. Within individuals and their personal lives, similar goods can be realized: inner peace, self-integration (above all, the integration of feelings with one's practical intelligence and judgment), and authenticity. And beyond merely human relationships, there can be harmony between humans and the wider reaches of reality, especially reality's sources, principles and ground(s). Concern for this last good underlies such diverse activities as a believer's worship and an environmentalist's work to save an endangered species.

The relational goods are instantiated in appropriate syntheses of many elements—feelings, experiences, beliefs, choices, performances, persons, and groups of persons, and wider realities. Ideally, the harmonies achieved in these syntheses enhance their diverse elements, but in fact conflict is seldom overcome without some loss to the elements synthesized. Defective forms of harmony often are built on a significant level of conflict. Established working relationships between exploiters and exploited, for example, are a sort of peace, though radically defective. Such defective harmonies, as harmonies, are intelligible goods; they can serve as principles of practical reasoning and action. But they are mutilated forms of basic human goods.

The First Moral Principle

To understand right and wrong, one must bear two things in mind. First, the possibilities of fulfillment are always unfolding, for there are several basic human goods, and endless ways of serving and sharing in them. Second, human beings, even when they work together, can only do so much. No one can undertake every project, or serve in every possible way. Nor can any community. Choices must be made.

Irresistibly compulsive behavior, bad luck, ineptitude, and the unwelcome results of honest human error are not wrongs. Only by choosing badly can individuals and groups go wrong morally. On any ethical theory, moral norms are standards for choosing well.

But how can there be bad choosing, if human goods are as we have said? Without reasons for choosing grounded in basic human goods, there could be no options; yet, we have also said, the choice of an option is never rationally necessary—otherwise there would not be two or more real options. Every choice is grounded in some intelligible good, and to that extent is rational, yet no choice has a monopoly on rationality. Moreover, virtually every choice has some negative impact on some good or other; no possibility can be chosen without setting aside at least some reason against choosing it.

Partly in response to this complexity, the consequentialist tries to distinguish good from bad choices by their effectiveness in maximizing good or minimizing evil. But consequentialism cannot serve as a coherent method of moral judgment. For, although one may in various ways and for various purposes commensurate the measurable value and disvalue promised by different instantiations of goods, one cannot commensurate the goods and bads which make diverse possibilities choice worthy opportunities: such goods and bads go beyond what is definite at any moment of choice.

But if consequentialism is unworkable, how can basic human goods mark the moral distinction between choosing well and choosing badly? The basic principle of the distinction between right and wrong is not easy to discern reflectively and articulate. Before attempting to formulate it, we shall sketch, but only sketch, the outline of morality's foundation, as we see it.

All moral theorists, including consequentialists, recognize that the foundation of morality is broader and deeper than the prospective results of the options between which one must choose. Common morality suggested an ultimate foundation in "the blessings of the covenant," "the Kingdom," "beatitude," "the order of charity," and so forth. Secular moral theories pointed towards realities such as "the kingdom of ends," "the realm of freedom," "the greatest good of the greatest number," and so forth.

Like consequentialists, we think it clear that morality's foundation is to be located in the goods of human persons, as individuals and in community. Unlike consequentialists, we believe that an adequate description of morality's foundation will take into account aspects of these goods irreducible to even the widest and most long-run prospective consequences of eligible options. Among the important aspects of human goods are possibilities still unknown, for example the answers to questions no one today is in a position to ask, and forms of human community to which present aspirations for a better world do not even reach out. Other aspects of human goods, of the first importance for morality, come to be in the personalities and communities of those who cherish and serve them, and so act rightly in respect of their instantiations. For example, authenticity, neighborliness, and just social order come to be in good persons and communities, in and through their morally right choices, yet are not among the premoral values and disvalues upon which the consequentialist tries to ground moral judgment.

Plainly, the basic human goods, conceived so inclusively, cannot ground morality by differentiating possible choices with respect to the potential effectiveness of those choices in realizing instances of the goods. Rather, the moral foundation determines the rightness and wrongness of choices by differentiating attitudes toward basic goods. Underlying the willingness to make one choice or another, there can be entirely different dispositions of the moral agent toward the basic human goods.

Right choices are those which can be made by moral agents whose attitude toward the moral foundation is one for which there is no single adequate word. Certainly, it involves respect for all of the basic human goods in all their aspects, yet "respect" has too passive a connotation. The right attitude is one of concern and interest, but all connotations of partiality must be excluded from these words. The right attitude is perhaps best called "appreciation," provided that this word is used with its connotation of readiness to serve and to cherish what one appreciates. Morally right choices are those choices which can be made by one whose will is disposed toward the entire moral foundation with this attitude of appreciation.

Having completed a sketch of the outline of morality's foundation, we shall now articulate as best we can the moral truths which are at and very near the beginning of the process of moral judgment. First, we propose a formulation of the first principle of morality, and then, in the next section, we unfold some of its most immediate specifications. The very abstract language in which the first principle has to be articulated renders it, we realize, quite opaque; but the somewhat less abstract language in which its specifications will be discussed will help make the first principle itself more understandable.

The first principle of morality can, perhaps, best be formulated: In voluntarily acting for human goods and avoiding what is opposed to them, one ought to choose and otherwise will those and only those possibilities whose willing is compatible with integral human fulfillment.

This formulation can be misunderstood. "Integral human fulfillment" does not refer to individualistic self-fulfillment, but to the good of all persons and communities. All the goods in which any person can share can also fulfill others, and individuals can share in goods such as friendship only with others.

Nor is integral human fulfillment some gigantic synthesis of all the instantiations of goods in a vast state of affairs, such as might be projected as the goal of a world-wide billion-year plan. Ethics cannot be an architectonic art in that way; there can be no plan to bring about integral human fulfillment. It is a guiding ideal rather than a realizable idea, for the basic goods are open ended.

And integral human fulfillment is not a supreme human good, beyond basic human goods such as truth and friendship. It does not provide reasons for acting as the basic goods do. It only moderates the interplay of such reasons, so that deliberation will be thoroughly reasonable.

Specifications of the First Moral Principle

But this principle may at first seem too abstruse to be of service. How can any specific moral norms be derived from it?

No specific moral norm can be derived immediately from the first principle. But it does imply intermediate principles from which specific norms can be deduced. Among these intermediate principles is the Golden Rule, or the related principle of universalizability—for a will marked by egoism or partiality cannot be open to integral human fulfillment. And this intermediate principle in turn leads to some specific moral judgments—e.g. Jane who wants her husband Jack to be faithful plainly violates it by sleeping with Sam. Thus there is a route from the first principle to specific moral norms. By reflection on the case we have just identified, we try in the next four paragraphs to clarify the intuitively obvious relationship between the first principle and the Golden Rule, and between the Golden Rule and specific norms of fairness.

Human choices are limited in many ways; some limits are inevitable but others are not. Among inevitable limits are those on people's insight into the basic goods, ideas of how to serve them, and available resources. In so far as such limits are outside one's control, morality cannot demand that they be transcended.

Some limits on choice, however, are avoidable. For one can voluntarily narrow the range of people and goods one cares about. Sometimes this voluntary narrowing has an intelligible basis, as when a person of many gifts chooses a profession and allows other talents to lie fallow. But sometimes avoidable limitations are voluntarily set or accepted without any such reason.

Sources or limitations of this last kind thus meet two conditions: (i) they are effective only by one's own choices; and (ii) they are non-rational motives, not grounded in intelligible require-

ments of the basic goods. Normally, the acting person either can allow these non-rational limiting factors to operate, or can transcend them. For they are one's own feelings and emotions, in so far as these are not integrated with the rational appeal of the basic goods and of the communal fulfillment in those goods. Such non-integrated feelings offer motives for behaviour, yet are not in themselves reasons for action. (However, one who gives in to them, whether through malice or weakness of will, always can find some reason for choosing in line with them.)

The first and master principle of morality rationally prescribes that non-integrated feelings be transcended. The Golden Rule requires one not to narrow one's interests and concerns by a certain set of such feelings—one's preference for oneself and those who are near and dear. It does not forbid one to treat different persons differently, when that is required by inevitable limits, or by intelligible requirements of shared goods themselves.

The first principle has other specifications, besides the Golden Rule, because non-rational preferences among persons are not the only feelings which incline one to prefer limited to integral human fulfillment. Hostile feelings such as anger and hatred towards oneself or others lead intelligent, sane, adult persons to actions which are often called "stupid," "irrational," and "childish." Self-destructive and spiteful actions destroy, damage, or block some instantiations of basic human goods; willing such actions is plainly not in line with a will to integral human fulfillment. Yet behaviour motivated by hostility need not violate the Golden Rule. People sometimes act self-destructively without being unfair to others. Moreover, revenge can be fair: an eye for an eye. But fairness does not eliminate the unreasonableness of acting on hostile feelings in ways that intelligibly benefit no one. Thus the Golden Rule is not the only intermediate principle which specifies the first principle of morality and generates specific moral norms.

So an ethics of the Kantian type is mistaken if it claims that universalizability is the only principle of morality. Respect for persons—treating them always as ends in themselves, and never as mere means—must mean more than treating others fairly. The dignity of persons, as bearers of and sharers in human goods, sets at least one other moral demand: Do not answer injury with injury, even when one can do so fairly.

Not only feelings of hostility, but positive feelings can motivate one to do evil—i.e. to destroy, damage, or impede an instantiation of some basic human good. One can choose to bring about evil as a means. One does evil to avoid some other evil, or to attain some ulterior good.

In such cases, the choice can seem entirely rational, and consequentialists might commend it. But, as we have said, the appearance of rationality is based on a false assumption: that human goods do not matter except in so far as they are instantiated and can be commensurated. . . . This way of trying to deal with human goods cannot be rational; the preceding sections of the present chapter indicate part of the reason why. What is morally important includes possible instantiations of goods diverse in kind from one another, and also includes not only those instantiations one now considers but the field of possibility opened up by the basic human goods. The indeterminacy of this aspect of the good utterly defies measurement.

Thus, it is unreasonable to choose to destroy, damage, or impede some instance of a basic good for the sake of an ulterior end. In doing this, one does not have the reason of maximizing good or minimizing evil—there is no such reason, for the goods at stake in choosable options are not rationally commensurable. Rather one is motivated by different feelings towards different instances of good involved. In this sort of case, one willy-nilly plays favourites among instantiations of goods, just as in violating the Golden Rule one plays favourites among persons.

And so, in addition to the Golden Rule and the principle which excludes acting on hostile feelings, there is another intermediate principle: Do not do evil that good may come. Because this principle generates moral absolutes, it is often considered a threat to people's vital concrete interests. But while it may be a threat to some interests, the moral absolutes it generates also protect real human goods which are parts of the fulfillment of actual persons, and it is reasonable to sacrifice important concrete interests to the integral fulfillment of persons.

Why? Because otherwise one plays favourites among the goods. Why not play favourites? Because doing so is incompatible with a will towards integral human fulfillment. Why worry about integral human fulfillment? That is like asking why man is man. Integral human fulfillment is not something alien to the moral agent, but is what the moral agent as a person is, and is together with others, and is most abundantly, and is still to be. And is, not only as moral in distinction from other human concerns, but as moral including most perfectly and harmoniously every truly human concern.

The Golden Rule and the other two principles enunciated in this section shape the rational prescription of the first principle of morality into definite responsibilities. Hence, we here call such intermediate principles 'modes of responsibility'. Besides the three modes we have discussed, there are others which moral reflection in the great cultures has uncovered: detachment, creative fidelity, purity of heart, and so on. Although we will not treat them here, the theory of moral principles we propose has a place for such fruits of previous moral reflection.

Notice that the conception of "basic human goods" developed in Reading 2 plays no *direct* role in the exercise of moral and legal reasoning. That is because moral considerations enter the reflective landscape only when freedom of choice is exercised. For Finnis, moral choice is always choice between and among basic human goods. The central question in dealing with choice among basic goods is not what the standard of choice *should be*; that is an unanswerable question because basic human goods are intrinsic values and as such incommensurable. The comparative worth of a basic good like friendship is not measurable by any general standard of value, and no basic good can be said to have priority over it. In dealing with the exercise of moral and legal reasoning, therefore, Finnis is concerned primarily with whether any choice among basic goods can be shown to be *unreasonable*. He clearly thinks that some choices are unreasonable and that as such they are morally wrong. For Finnis, the only way to know that a choice is morally wrong is to know that it is destructive of some basic human good. But how can this be determined? Here Finnis has recourse to the "modes of responsibility" discussed in Reading 2. If, for example, it is clear that a choice violates the Golden Rule or the principle that one should not answer injury with injury, even when one can do so fairly, then we can be sure that it is destructive of a basic human good. Finnis's discussion in Reading 3 of "Human Action" and "Specific Moral Norms" spells out this line of thought in some detail.

Reading 3

From John Finnis,
NUCLEAR DETERRENCE, MORALITY AND REALISM

Human Action

Specific moral norms are deduced from the intermediate principles of morality. But one cannot explain this process without first saying something about human action. Many people, including philosophers too, unreflectively assume a rather simple model of human action, with three elements: (i) a possible state of affairs which a potential agent wants to realize; (ii) a plan to realize it by causal factors in the agent's power; and (iii) the carrying out of the more or less complex set of performances to bring about the desired result.

This model of action is inadequate. . . . From a moral point of view, actions are significant primarily as the acting person's voluntary synthesis with, or participation in, human goods. There are at least three ways in which one's actions have this moral significance. These constitute three senses of "doing"; from the moral point of view, these are irreducibly diverse and must be carefully distinguished if acts are to be described adequately for moral evaluation.

First, one acts when one chooses something for its intrinsic value, intending it as an end, as something by which one immediately participates in a good. For example, when one gives a gift as an act of friendship, one chooses to realize a certain state of affairs—giving the gift—as a way of serving the good of friendship, the very fulfillment of self and other in this form of harmony, which is instantiated by giving and receiving the gift.

Secondly, one acts in a different way, when one chooses something not for itself but as a means to some ulterior end. What is chosen is not willed as an instantiation of a basic good, but as something through which one expects to bring about an instantiation of a good. For example, one consults a physician for the sake of health; one fights a war for the sake of peace; many people work only to get their pay, which they then use to pursue what they consider intrinsically good. The chosen means need not be such that it would never be chosen for its intrinsic value: for business purposes one

sometimes makes a trip one might take as a vacation. The first two sorts of doing can be present together, as when one mixes business with pleasure.

Thirdly, one acts in a still different way in so far as one voluntarily accepts side-effects caused incidentally to acting in either of the two prior ways. Here one is aware that executing one's choice will affect, for good or ill, instances of goods other than the instances on which one's interest directly bears. Although one does not choose this impact on other goods, one foresees and accepts it— sometimes gladly (e.g. when one accepts the bonus of making new friends when one decides to go on a course of training), sometimes reluctantly (e.g. when one accepts the loss of a diseased organ to save one's life, or the leading of some listeners or readers into errors or confusions, when one tries to communicate something complicated). . . .

Because willing something as an end, as a means, and as a side-effect relate acting persons to goods in different ways, the meanings of 'doing' which they ground are quite distinct, as we already noticed. A professional's playing a game only to make money is not playing the game in the same sense—it is not the same doing—as the amateur's playing of the game for the sake of the excellent performance itself. One who unwillingly benefits another by incidental effects of some action is not doing the other a favour.

The significance of these differences is clearest in negative cases. One may reveal shameful truths about another out of spite, or to arouse shame and provide an occasion for repentance, or as a side-effect of preventing the conviction of an innocent person. In all three cases, one can be said to "destroy a reputation." But these are very different acts; only in very different senses do they destroy reputation. And corresponding to the ambiguity of "action" (and action-words) are diverse meanings of other words important in moral evaluation: "responsible," "deliberate," "intentional," and so on.

In formulating moral norms, it is especially important to distinguish the meanings of "intentional." One intends in a different sense what one tries to bring about as an instantiation of a good and what one chooses as a means to something ulterior. . . . [Sometimes] one does not intend what one accepts as a side-effect. But while, in common idiom, foreseen, accepted (and thus voluntarily caused) side-effects are often called unintended if the question is whether they were part of the agent's plan, they often are said to be intended if the question is whether they were caused inadvertently or "accidentally."

Specific Moral Norms

The derivation of specific moral norms from modes of responsibility can now be explained. Its heart is a deduction which can be formulated in a categorical syllogism. In the simplest case, the normative premiss is a mode of responsibility, which excludes a certain way of willing in respect to the relevant goods. The other premiss is a description of a type of action, which is sufficient to make it clear that an action of this kind cannot be willed except in the excluded way. The conclusion is that doing an act of that kind is morally wrong.

Actions not excluded by any mode are morally permissible; those whose common omission would violate some mode are morally required. Many ways

of describing actions, especially when interest is centered on their consequences, do not reveal what is necessary to derive a moral norm. For example, if killing is defined as "any behaviour or a person which causes the death of a person," the description is insufficient for moral evaluation. Descriptions of actions adequate for moral evaluation must say or imply how the agent's will bears on relevant goods.

Not all the modes of responsibility apply to all the three sorts of doing, identified in the preceding section. Universalizability does. Parents who show affection for a favourite child but are cold toward another violate the Golden Rule in a doing which immediately instantiates the good of familial friendship. Superiors who assign harder jobs to subordinates they dislike, and easier to subordinates they like, violate universalizability in choosing means. Commanders who tried to avoid killing non-combatants when liberating allied territory, but made no similar effort to avoid such incidental killing in their operations in the enemy homeland, acted unfairly in accepting side-effects.

Thus, accepting bad side-effects of one's choices can be wrong if one does it unfairly. Similarly, even without unfairness to anyone, those excessively attached to some good can go wrong in accepting grave side-effects—for example, the aging champion boxer who ruins his health in trying to retain his title.

Still, one cannot act at all without accepting some bad side-effects. In any choice, one at least devotes part of one's limited time and other resources to the pursuit of a particular good, and leaves unserved other goods for which one might have acted. So there could not be a general moral principle entirely excluding the willing of every negative impact on a basic human good. One sometimes can accept bad side-effects as inevitable concomitants of a fully reasonable response to the intelligible requirements of goods.

Thus, the principle that evil may not be done that good may come applies only to the choice of a means to an ulterior end, not to the acceptance of side-effects. Whenever one chooses to destroy, damage, or impede one instantiation of a basic good for the sake of some other instantiation of that or another basic good, the second instantiation is preferred to the first. Since the goods immanent in possibilities available for choice cannot be commensurated, this preference must be arbitrary. Such a choice is at odds with openness to integral human fulfillment. But to accept a similar state of affairs as an unwanted side-effect need not be. For it is not necessarily excluded by any mode of responsibility, and so it need not be at odds with integral human fulfillment. For example, the choice to kill a suffering person by a purposeful omission of treatment is morally excluded, as a case of doing evil that good may come. But a choice not to treat, when made to avoid the burdens of treating and with death accepted as a side-effect, need not be wrong.

If an action's description, however limited, makes plain that such an action involves a choice to destroy, damage, or impede some instance of a basic human good, the wrongness of any action which meets the description is settled. Additional factors may affect the degree of wrongness, but further description of the act cannot reverse its basic moral quality. So, moral norms derived from this mode of responsibility can be called "moral absolutes." The norm, for instance, which forbids hanging one innocent person to satisfy a mob and protect any number of others is an absolute; no further information could make doing that right, though circumstances could mitigate its wickedness.

Different modes of responsibility work differently, so not all specific norms are absolute. Universalizability can exclude as unfair an action proposed under a limited description, yet allow as fair an action which includes all the elements of that description together with some other morally relevant features. For example: fairness demands keeping a promise, whenever there is no motive to break it except the sorts of motive whose operation promises are meant to exclude. But if one has another reason to break a promise—e.g. that keeping it would have such grave consequences that even those to whom it was made would agree it should be broken—one may break the promise without violating the Golden Rule.

In general, specific norms derived from the universalizability principle are not absolute. Ordinary language obscures this fact, by often building the moral specification into the act-description—e.g. by limiting "stealing" to the wrongful taking of another's property. However, instances of justified taking can include all the elements which are present in unjustifiable taking; the addition rather than the subtraction of relevant features makes the taking justifiable.

Since universalizability usually does not yield moral absolutes, one who considers it the first principle of morality will not admit them, at least not in the sense of those absolute norms which are generated by the principle that evil may not be done that good may come. . . . But such an ethics is inadequate in many ways. It can condemn some things, but can justify nothing, inasmuch as it offers only a necessary and not a sufficient condition for moral rightness.

The theory we have outlined in this chapter subordinates morality to human persons and their fulfillment, both as individuals and in communion. Yet the dignity of human persons is protected by moral absolutes. Among those absolutes, we believe, is one which forbids choices to destroy human lives. Killing people is not a permissible means to promote other goods or prevent other evils. yet accepting death(s) as a side-effect of one's chosen action is not the same thing as a choice to kill. . . .

The primary claim of natural law theorists throughout jurisprudential history has been that morality is a necessary condition of law. One interesting feature of Finnis's new natural law theory is his defense of the converse of this claim: the proposition that law is a necessary condition of morality. In Reading 4 Finnis argues that this must be the case in virtue of certain undesirable features of human existence. The core of his argument is that there are some basic human goods which require the co-ordination of many people. Goods of this kind cannot exist without law because law is required for resolution of certain difficulties which he calls "co-ordination problems." Resolution of these problems is *necessary* for the realization of some basic human goods, and in that sense law is a necessary condition for the emergence, preservation, and development of morality. The fulcrum of his defense of this thesis is Finnis's conception of a "complete community."

Reading 4

From John Finnis,
NATURAL LAW AND NATURAL RIGHTS

Complete Community

Family is a very thoroughgoing form of association, controlling or influencing every corner of the lives of its members for a considerable proportion of their lifetime. But it is incomplete and inadequate. Indeed, it cannot even properly provide for the unimpaired transmission of its own genetic basis; a family that breeds within itself is headed for physical self-destruction. And its weakness as an economic unit, capable of supporting the health and culture of its members, has already been mentioned and needs no elaboration here. Economic, cultural, and sporting associations, in turn, are more or less explicitly specialized in their concerns. And as for friendship in its full rise, if the friendship of husband and wife is an incomplete basis for ample well-being, so is any other. So there emerges the desirability of a "complete community," an all-round association in which would be co-ordinated the initiatives and activities of individuals, of families, and of the vast network of intermediate associations. The point of this all-round association would be to secure the whole ensemble of material and other conditions, including forms of collaboration, that tend to favour, facilitate, and foster the realization by each individual of his or her personal development. (Remember: this personal development includes, as an integral element and not merely as a means or pre-condition, both individual self-direction and community with others in family, friendship, work, and play.)

Such an ensemble of conditions includes some co-ordination (at least the negative co-ordination of establishing restraints against interferences) of any and every individual life-plan and any and every form of association. So there is no aspect of human affairs that as such is outside the range of such a complete community. Now Aristotle, by a premature generalization from incomplete empirical data, declared that the Greek polis was the paradigmatic form of complete and self-sufficient community for securing the all-round good of its members. So the form of community that today claims to be complete and self-sufficient, the territorial state, retains the label "political community" or "body politic"; for though it does not fit Aristotle's descriptions of paradigmatic forms of polis, it claims the all-embracing function which Aristotle (after Plato) ascribed to the polis. There can be "parish pump politics," "College politics," and so on; but "politics" without qualification signifies the field of action and discourse to do with the affairs of complete communities.

Nor is "politics" the only term whose focal meaning concerns complete community. "Law" is another such term. We can certainly speak intelligibly and usefully of the law of some lesser group, even of a gang. But, as the common understanding of the unqualified expressions "law" and "the law" indicates, the central case of law and legal system is the law and legal system of a complete community. That is why it is characteristic of legal systems that (i) they claim authority to regulate all forms of human behaviour (a claim which in the hands of the lawyer becomes the artificial postulate that legal systems are gapless); (ii) they therefore claim to be the supreme authority for their respective community, and to regulate the conditions under which the members of that community can participate in any other normative system or association; (iii) they characteristically purport to "adopt" rules and normative arrangements (e.g. contracts) from other associations within and without the complete community, thereby giving them legal force for that community; they thus maintain the notion of completeness and supremacy without pretending to be either the only association to which their members may reasonably belong or the only complete community with whom their members may have dealings, and without striving to foresee and provide substantively for every activity and arrangement in which their members may wish to engage.

All these defining features, devices, and postulates of law have their foundation, from the viewpoint of practical reasonableness, in the requirement that the activities of individuals, families, and specialized associations be co-ordinated. This requirement itself derives partly from the requirements of impartiality as between persons, and of impartiality as between the basic values and openness to all of them, given certain facts about the ensemble of empirical conditions under which basic goods such as health, education, science, and art can be realized and realized in the lives of each person according to the measure of his own inclinations and capacities. . . .

QUESTIONS

1. What exactly is Finnis's argument against the positivist claim that law is dependent upon moral perception and moral judgment?

2. What are some "basic human goods"? How are these goods different from other, non-basic goods? Can you think of an example of a basic good *not* mentioned by Finnis?

3. Finnis says that only by choosing badly can individuals and groups go wrong morally and that to do so is to choose a possibility for action which is not "compatible with integral human fulfillment." How do we determine this incompatibility, according to Finnis? Give an example not discussed by Finnis.

4. Explain Finnis's conception of a "complete community." Why is it important for an understanding of law?

5. Finnis argues that positive law is derived from natural law. What exactly does "derived" mean here? Finnis gives two examples: a "rule of the road" and a rule of property law. Give two additional examples.

6. For Finnis and Bobbitt, the concept of incommensurability plays an important role in their understanding of law. Explain for each why this concept is important.

7. Explain the difference between Finnis's account of the derivation of positive law from natural law and Dworkin's account of "constructive interpretation."

8. State succinctly Finnis's objection to consequentialism.

9. Both Finnis and Unger agree that both what the law is and what the law should be are indeterminate in certain ways. Explain how Finnis's understanding of this indeterminacy differs from Unger's.

10. Explain the connection and the difference between Martha Minow's treatment of the problem of "difference" and Finnis's treatment of the "principles of practical reason" and "modes of responsibility."

Part II

Cases in Statutory Interpretation, Contract Law, Tort Law, and Public Law

Note on the Editing of the Cases

The cases that follow have been edited by the authors. In law school casebooks, portions of cases that have been omitted are shown through the use of ellipses. Additionally, editors usually remain faithful to the original in matters of paragraph indentation, italicization, signals, and case citations.

In the present format, we have edited the text of opinions without the use of ellipses. Additionally, in a very few places we have altered paragraph indentation. The order of the analysis in every opinion is faithful to the original. After due experimentation with many readers, we have taken these modest liberties in an effort to improve readability and comprehension.

Chapter 8

Statutory Interpretation

As every student learns in the first days of law school, in American law there are two categorically distinct sources of law: decisions by judges (the common law) and statutes (promulgated by federal and state legislatures). Discerning the meaning of statutory provisions is the business of statutory interpretation. More and more, judicial time and energy are taken up with the reading and interpretation of statutes.

The cases that follow present some of the most time-honored questions in the context of statutory interpetation. This is an ancient subject. In the fifth book of his *Nichomachean Ethics*, Aristotle recommended his own theory of statutory interpretation. He thought that when the meaning of a statute was in doubt, the best thing for judges to do was to ask how the legislature would answer the question in dispute. As you read through these cases, you will see that this approach is still favored by many judges.

PHILO RIGGS, as Guardian ad litem et al., Appellants,
v. ELMER E. PALMER et al., Respondents
Court of Appeals of New York
22 N.E. 188 (1889)

OPINION: EARL, J.

On the 13th day of August 1880, Francis B. Palmer made his last will and testament, in which he gave small legacies to his two daughters, Mrs. Riggs and Mrs. Preston, the plaintiffs in this action, and the remainder of his estate to his grandson, the defendant, Elmer E. Palmer, subject to the support of Susan Palmer, his mother, with a gift over to the two daughters, subject to the support of Mrs. Palmer, in case Elmer should survive him and die under age, unmarried and without any issue. The testator at the date of his will owned a farm and considerable personal property. He was a widower, and thereafter, in March 1882, he was married to Mrs. Bresee, with whom before his marriage he entered into an ante-nuptial contract in which it was agreed that, in lieu of dower and all other claims upon his estate in case she survived him, she should have her support upon his farm during her life, and such support was expressly charged upon the farm. At the date of the will, and, subsequently, to the death of the testator, Elmer lived with him as a member of his family, and at his death was sixteen years old. He knew of the provisions made in his favor in the will, and, that he might prevent his grandfather from revoking such provisions, which he had manifested some intention to do, and to obtain the speedy enjoyment and immediate possession of his property, he willfully murdered him by poisoning him. He now claims the property, and the sole question for our determination is, can he have it? The defendants say that the testator is dead; that his will was made in due form and has been admitted to probate, and that, therefore, it must have effect according to the letter of the law.

It is quite true that statutes regulating the making, proof and effect of wills, and the devolution of property, if literally construed, and if their force and effect can in no way and under no circumstances be controlled or modified, give this property to the murderer.

The purpose of those statutes was to enable testators to dispose of their estates to the objects of their bounty at death, and to carry into effect their final wishes legally expressed; and in considering and giving effect to them this purpose must be kept in view. It was the intention of the law-makers that the donees in a will should have the property given to them. But it never could have been their intention that a donee who murdered the testator to make the will operative should have any benefit under it.

If such a case had been present to their minds, and it had been supposed necessary to make some provision of law to meet it, it cannot be doubted that they would have provided for it. It is a familiar canon of construction that a thing which is within the intention of the makers of a statute is as much within the statute as if it were within the letter; and

a thing which is within the letter of the statute is not within the statute, unless it be within the intention of the makers. The writers of laws do not always express their intention perfectly, but either exceed it or fall short of it, so that judges are to collect it from probable or rational conjectures only, and this is called rational interpretation; and Rutherforth, in his Institutes (p. 407), says: "When we make use of rational interpretation, sometimes we restrain the meaning of the writer so as to take in less, and sometimes we extend or enlarge his meaning so as to take in more than his words express."

Such a construction ought to be put upon a statute as will best answer the intention which the makers had in view, for *qui haeret in litera, haeret in cortice* (He who considers but the letter of an instrument goes but skin deep). In Bacon's Abridgment (Statutes I, 5); Puffendorf (book 5, chapter 12), Rutherforth (pp. 422, 427), and in Smith's Commentaries (814), many cases are mentioned where it was held that matters embraced in the general words of statutes, nevertheless, were not within the statutes, because it could not have been the intention of the law-makers that they should be included. They were taken out of the statutes by an equitable construction, and it is said in Bacon: "By an equitable construction, a case not within the letter of the statute is sometimes holden to be within the meaning, because it is within the mischief for which a remedy is provided. The reason for such construction is that the law-makers could not set down every case in express terms. In order to form a right judgment whether a case be within the equity of a statute, it is a good way to suppose the law-maker present, and that you have asked him this question, did you intend to comprehend this case? Then you must give yourself such answer as you imagine he, being an upright and reasonable man, would have given. If this be that he did mean to comprehend it, you may safely hold the case to be within the equity of the statute; for while you do no more than he would have done, you do not act contrary to the statute, but in conformity thereto." In some cases the letter of a legislative act is restrained by an equitable construction; in others it is enlarged; in others the construction is contrary to the letter. The equitable construction which restrains the letter of a statute is defined by Aristotle, as frequently quoted, in this manner: *Aequitas est correctio legis generaliter latae qua parti deficit.* (Equity is the correction of that within the law whereof it is deficient by reason of its generality.) If the law-makers could, as to this case, be consulted, would they say that they intended by their general language that the property of a testator or of an ancestor should pass to one who had taken his life for the express purpose of getting his property? In 1 Blackstone's Commentaries (91) the learned author, speaking of the construction of statutes, says: "If there arise out of them any absurd consequences manifestly contradictory to common reason, they are, with regard to those collateral consequences, void. When some collateral matter arises out of the general words, and happen to be unreasonable, then the judges are in decency to conclude that the consequence was not foreseen by the parliament, and, therefore, they are at liberty to expound the statute by equity and only quoad hoc disregard it"; and he gives as an illustration, if an act of parliament gives a man power to try all causes that arise within his manor of Dale, yet, if a cause

should arise in which he himself is party, the act is construed not to extend to that because it is unreasonable that any man should determine his own quarrel. There was a statute in Bologna that whoever drew blood in the streets should be severely punished, and yet it was held not to apply to the case of a barber who opened a vein in the street. It is commanded in the Decalogue that no work shall be done upon the Sabbath, and yet, giving the command a rational interpretation founded upon its design, the Infallible Judge held that it did not prohibit works of necessity, charity or benevolence on that day. What could be more unreasonable than to suppose that it was the legislative intention in the general laws passed for the orderly, peaceable and just devolution of property, that they should have operation in favor of one who murdered his ancestor that he might speedily come into the possession of his estate? Such an intention is inconceivable. We need not, therefore, be much troubled by the general language contained in the laws.

Besides, all laws as well as all contracts may be controlled in their operation and effect by general, fundamental maxims of the common law. No one shall be permitted to profit by his own fraud, or to take advantage of his own wrong, or to found any claim upon his own iniquity, or to acquire property by his own crime. These maxims are dictated by public policy, have their foundation in universal law administered in all civilized countries, and have nowhere been superseded by statutes. They were applied in the decision of the case of the New York Mutual Life Insurance Company v. Armstrong (117 U.S. 591). There it was held that the person who procured a policy upon the life of another, payable at his death, and then murdered the assured to make the policy payable, could not recover thereon. Mr. Justice FIELD, writing the opinion, said: "Independently of any proof of the motives of Hunter in obtaining the policy, and even assuming that they were just and proper, he forfeited all rights under it when, to secure its immediate payment, he murdered the assured. It would be a reproach to the jurisprudence of the country if one could recover insurance money payable on the death of a party whose life he had feloniously taken. As well might he recover insurance money upon a building that he had willfully fired."

These maxims, without any statute giving them force or operation, frequently control the effect and nullify the language of wills. A will procured by fraud and deception, like any other instrument, may be decreed void and set aside, and so a particular portion of a will may be excluded from probate or held inoperative if induced by the fraud or undue influence of the person in whose favor it is. (Allen v. M'Pherson, 1 H.L. Cas. 191; Harrison's Appeal, 48 Conn. 202.) So a will may contain provisions which are immoral, irreligious or against public policy, and they will be held void.

Here there was no certainty that this murderer would survive the testator, or that the testator would not change his will, and there was no certainty that he would get this property if nature was allowed to take its course. He, therefore, murdered the testator expressly to vest himself with an estate. Under such circumstances, what law, human or divine, will allow him to take the estate and enjoy the fruits of his crime? The will spoke and became operative at the death of the testator. He caused that death, and thus by his crime made it speak and have op-

eration. Shall it speak and operate in his favor? If he had met the testator and taken his property by force, he would have had no title to it. Shall he acquire title by murdering him? If he had gone to the testator's house and by force compelled him, or by fraud or undue influence had induced him to will him his property, the law would not allow him to hold it. But can he give effect and operation to a will by murder, and yet take the property? To answer these questions in the affirmative, it seems to me, would be a reproach to the jurisprudence of our state, and an offense against public policy.

Under the civil law evolved from the general principles of natural law and justice by many generations of jurisconsults, philosophers and statesmen, one cannot take property by inheritance or will from an ancestor or benefactor whom he has murdered. (Domat, part 2, book 1, tit. 1, § 3; Code Napoleon, § 727; Mackeldy's Roman Law, 530, 550.) In the Civil Code of Lower Canada the provisions on the subject in the Code Napoleon have been substantially copied. But, so far as I can find, in no country where the common law prevails has it been deemed important to enact a law to provide for such a case. Our revisers and law-makers were familiar with the civil law, and they did not deem it important to incorporate into our statutes its provisions upon this subject. This is not a casus omissus. It was evidently supposed that the maxims of the common law were sufficient to regulate such a case and that a specific enactment for that purpose was not needed.

For the same reasons the defendant Palmer cannot take any of this property as heir. Just before the murder he was not an heir, and it was not certain that he ever would be. He might have died before his grandfather, or might have been disinherited by him. He made himself an heir by the murder, and he seeks to take property as the fruit of his crime. What has before been said as to him as legatee applies to him with equal force as an heir. He cannot vest himself with title by crime.

My view of this case does not inflict upon Elmer any greater or other punishment for his crime than the law specifies. It takes from him no property, but simply holds that he shall not acquire property by his crime, and thus be rewarded for its commission.

Our attention is called to Owens v. Owens (100 N.C. 240), as a case quite like this. There a wife had been convicted of being an accessory before the fact to the murder of her husband, and it was held that she was, nevertheless, entitled to dower. I am unwilling to assent to the doctrine of that case. The statutes provide dower for a wife who has the misfortune to survive her husband and thus lose his support and protection. It is clear beyond their purpose to make provision for a wife who by her own crime makes herself a widow and willfully and intentionally deprives herself of the support and protection of her husband. As she might have died before him, and thus never have been his widow, she cannot by her crime vest herself with an estate. The principle which lies at the bottom of the maxim, *volenti non fit injuria* (A person who consents cannot receive an injury), should be applied to such a case, and a widow should not, for the purpose of acquiring, as such, property rights, be permitted to allege a widowhood which she has wickedly and intentionally created.

The facts found entitled the plaintiffs to the relief they seek. The error of the referee was in his conclusion of law. Instead of granting a new trial, therefore, I think the proper judgment upon the facts found should be ordered here. The facts have been passed upon twice with the same result, first upon the trial of Palmer for murder, and then by the referee in this action. We are, therefore, of opinion that the ends of justice do not require that they should again come in question.

The judgment of the General Term and that entered upon the report of the referee should, therefore, be reversed and judgment should be entered as follows: That Elmer E. Palmer and the administrator be enjoined from using any of the personalty or real estate left by the testator for Elmer's benefit; that the devise and bequest in the will to Elmer be declared ineffective to pass the title to him; that by reason of the crime of murder committed upon the grandfather he is deprived of any interest in the estate left by him; that the plaintiffs are the true owners of the real and personal estate left by the testator, subject to the charge in favor of Elmer's mother and the widow of the testator, under the ante-nuptial agreement, and that the plaintiffs have costs in all the courts against Elmer.

All concur with EARL, J., except GRAY, J., who reads dissenting opinion.

DISSENT: GRAY, J. (dissenting).

This appeal presents an extraordinary state of facts, and the case, in respect of them, I believe, is without precedent in this state.

The respondent, a lad of sixteen years of age, being aware of the provisions in his grandfather's will, which constituted him the residuary legatee of the testator's estate, caused his death by poison in 1882. For this crime he was tried and was convicted of murder in the second degree, and at the time of the commencement of this action he was serving out his sentence in the state reformatory. This action was brought by two of the children of the testator for the purpose of having those provisions of the will in the respondent's favor canceled and annulled.

The appellants' argument for a reversal of the judgment, which dismissed their complaint, is that the respondent unlawfully prevented a revocation of the existing will, or a new will from being made, by his crime, and that he terminated the enjoyment by the testator of his property and effected his own succession to it by the same crime. They say that to permit the respondent to take the property willed to him would be to permit him to take advantage of his own wrong.

To sustain their position the appellants' counsel has submitted an able and elaborate brief, and, if I believed that the decision of the question could be affected by considerations of an equitable nature, I should not hesitate to assent to views which commend themselves to the conscience. But the matter does not lie within the domain of conscience. We are bound by the rigid rules of law, which have been established by the legislature, and within the limits of which the determination of this question is confined. The question we are dealing with is, whether a testamentary disposition can be altered, or a will revoked, after the testator's death, through an appeal to the courts, when the legislature has, by its enactments, prescribed exactly when and how wills may be made, altered and revoked, and, apparently, as it seems to me, when they have been fully complied with, has left no room for the exercise of an equitable jurisdiction by courts over

such matters. Modern jurisprudence, in recognizing the right of the individual, under more or less restrictions, to dispose of his property after his death, subjects it to legislative control, both as to extent and as to mode of exercise. Complete freedom of testamentary disposition of one's property has not been and is not the universal rule; as we see from the provisions of the Napoleonic Code, from those systems of jurisprudence in other countries which are modeled upon the Roman law, and from the statutes of many of our states. To the statutory restraints, which are imposed upon the disposition of one's property by will, are added strict and systematic statutory rules for the execution, alteration and revocation of the will; which must be, at least, substantially, if not exactly, followed to insure validity and performance. The reason for the establishment of such rules, we may naturally assume, consists in the purpose to create those safeguards about these grave and important acts, which experience has demonstrated to be the wisest and surest. That freedom, which is permitted to be exercised in the testamentary disposition of one's estate by the laws of the state, is subject to its being exercised in conformity with the regulations of the statutes. The capacity and the power of the individual to dispose of his property after death, and the mode by which that power can be exercised, are matters of which the legislature has assumed the entire control, and has undertaken to regulate with comprehensive particularity.

The appellants' argument is not helped by reference to those rules of the civil law, or to those laws of other governments, by which the heir or legatee is excluded from benefit under the testament, if he has been convicted of killing, or attempting to kill, the testator. In the absence of such legislation here, the courts are not empowered to institute such a system of remedial justice. The deprivation of the heir of his testamentary succession by the Roman law, when guilty of such a crime, plainly, was intended to be in the nature of a punishment imposed upon him. The succession, in such a case of guilt, escheated to the exchequer. (See Domat's Civil Law, pt. 2, book 1, tit. 1, § 3.)

I concede that rules of law, which annul testamentary provision made for the benefit of those who have become unworthy of them, may be based on principles of equity and of natural justice. It is quite reasonable to suppose that a testator would revoke or alter his will, where his mind has been so angered and changed as to make him unwilling to have his will executed as it stood. But these principles only suggest sufficient reasons for the enactment of laws to meet such cases.

The statutes of this state have prescribed various ways in which a will may be altered or revoked; but the very provision, defining the modes of alteration and revocation, implies a prohibition of alteration or revocation in any other way. The words of the section of the statute are: "No will in writing, except in the cases hereinafter mentioned, nor any part thereof, shall be revoked or altered otherwise," etc. Where, therefore, none of the cases mentioned are met by the facts, and the revocation is not in the way described in the section, the will of the testator is unalterable. I think that a valid will must continue as a will always, unless revoked in the manner provided by the statutes. Mere intention to revoke a will does not have the effect of revocation. The intention to revoke is necessary to constitute the effective revocation of a will; but it must be demonstrated by one of the acts contemplated by the statute. As WOODWORTH, J., said in Dan v. Brown (4 Cow. 490): "Revocation is an act of the mind, which must be demonstrated by some outward and visible sign of revocation." The same learned judge said in that case: "The rule is that if the testator lets the will stand until he dies, it is his will; if he does not suffer it to do so, it is not his will." (Goodright v. Glasier, 4 Burr. 2512, 2514; Pemberton v. Pemberton, 13 Ves. 290.)

The finding of fact of the referee, that, presumably, the testator would have altered his will, had he known of his grandson's murderous intent, cannot affect the question. We may concede it to the fullest extent; but still the cardinal objection is undisposed of, that the making and the revocation of a will are purely matters of statutory regulation, by which the court is bound in the determination of questions relating to these acts. Two cases in this state and in Kentucky, at an early day, seem to me to be much in point. Gains v. Gains (2 Marshall, 190), was decided by the Kentucky Court of Appeals in 1820. It was there urged that the testator intended to have destroyed his will, and that he was forcibly prevented from doing so by the defendant in error or devisee, and it was insisted that the will, though not expressly, was thereby virtually revoked. The court held, as the act concerning wills prescribed the manner in which a will might be revoked, that as none of the acts evidencing revocation were done, the intention could not be substituted for the act. In that case the will was snatched away and forcibly retained. In 1854, Surrogate BRADFORD, whose opinions are entitled to the highest consideration, decided the case of Leaycraft v. Simmons (3 Bradf. 35). In that case the testator, a man of eighty-nine years of age, desired to make a codicil to his will, in order to enlarge the provisions for his daughter. His son having the custody of the instrument, and the one to be prejudiced by the change, refused to produce the will, at testator's request, for the purpose of alteration. The learned surrogate refers to the provisions of the civil law for such and other cases of unworthy conduct in the heir or legatee, and says, "our statute has undertaken to prescribe the mode in which wills can be revoked (citing the statutory provision). This is the law by which I am governed in passing upon questions touching the revocation of wills. The whole of this subject is now regulated by statute, and a mere intention to revoke, however well authenticated, or however defeated, is not sufficient." And he held that the will must be admitted to probate. I may refer also to a case in the Pennsylvania courts. In that state the statute prescribed the mode for repealing or altering a will, and in Clingan v. Mitcheltree (31 Pa. State Rep. 25) the Supreme Court of the state held, where a will was kept from destruction by the fraud and misrepresentation of the devisee, that to declare it canceled as against the fraudulent party would be to enlarge the statute

I cannot find any support for the argument that the respondent's succession to the property should be avoided because of his criminal act, when the laws are silent. Public policy does not demand it, for the demands of public policy are satisfied by the proper execution of the laws and the punishment of the crime. There has been no convention between the testator and his legatee, nor is there any such contractual element in such a disposition of property by a testator, as to impose or imply conditions in the legatee. The appellants' argument practically amounts to this: That as the legatee has been guilty of a crime, by the commission of which he is placed in a position to sooner receive the benefits of the testamentary provision, his rights to the property should be forfeited and he should be divested of his estate. To allow their argument to prevail would involve the diversion by the court of the testator's estate into the hands of persons, whom, possibly enough, for all we know, the testator might not have chosen or desired as its recipients. Practically the court is asked to make another will for the testator. The laws do not warrant this judicial action, and mere presumption would not be strong enough to sustain it.

But more than this, to concede appellants' views would involve the imposition of an additional punishment or penalty upon the respondent. What power or warrant have the courts to add to the respondent's penalties by depriving him of property? The law has punished him for his crime, and we may not say that it was an insufficient punishment. In the trial and punishment of the respondent the law has vindicated itself for the outrage which he committed, and further judicial utterance upon the subject of punishment or deprivation of rights is barred. We may not, in the language of the court in People v. Thornton (25 Hun, 456), "enhance the pains, penalties and forfeitures provided by law for the punishment of crime."

The judgment should be affirmed, with costs.

QUESTIONS AND DISCUSSION POINTS

1. What are some of the legal and moral issues raised by this case?

2. State what you think are the one or two legal questions posed by the case.

3. What language in the statute is essential to the decision in this case?

4. What are the sources for the meaning of the statute?

5. What is the relationship between the question of the meaning of the statute and the question of the justice of giving Elmer his inheritance?

6. Do the Majority and Dissent have different ways or theories for reading statutes?

CHURCH OF THE HOLY TRINITY
v. UNITED STATES
Supreme Court of the United States
143 U.S. 457 (1892)

MR. JUSTICE BREWER delivered the opinion of the court.

Plaintiff in error is a corporation, duly organized and incorporated as a religious society under the laws of the State of New York. E. Walpole Warren was, prior to September, 1887, an alien residing in England. In that month the plaintiff in error made a contract with him, by which he was to remove to the city of New York and enter into its service as rector and pastor; and in pursuance of such contract, Warren did so remove and enter upon such service. It is claimed by the United States that this contract on the part of the plaintiff in error was forbidden by the act of February 26, 1885, 23 Stat. 332, c. 164, and an action was commenced to recover the penalty prescribed by that act. The Circuit Court held that the contract was within the prohibition of the statute, and rendered judgment accordingly, (36 Fed. Rep. 303;) and the single question presented for our determination is whether it erred in that conclusion.

The first section describes the act forbidden, and is in these words:

Be it enacted by the Senate and House of Representatives of the United States of America in Congress assembled, That from and after the passage of this act it shall be unlawful for any person, company, partnership, or corporation, in any manner whatsoever, to prepay the transportation, or in any way assist or encourage the importation or migration of any alien or aliens, any foreigner or foreigners, into the United States, its Territories, or the District of Columbia, under contract or agreement, parol or special, express or implied, made previous to the importation or migration of such alien or aliens, foreigner or foreigners, to perform labor or service of any kind in the United States, its Territories, or the District of Columbia.

It must be conceded that the act of the corporation is within the letter of this section, for the relation of rector to his church is one of service, and implies labor on the one side with compensation on the other. Not only are the general words labor and service both used, but also, as it were to guard against any narrow interpretation and emphasize a breadth of meaning, to them is added "of any kind"; and, further, as noticed by the Circuit Judge in his opinion, the fifth section, which makes specific exceptions, among them professional actors, artists, lecturers, singers and domestic servants, strengthens the idea that every other kind of labor and service was intended to be reached by the first section. While there is great force to this reasoning, we cannot think Congress intended to denounce with penalties a transaction like that in the present case. It is a familiar rule, that a thing may be within the letter of the statute and yet not within the statute, because not within its spirit, nor within the intention of its makers. This has been often asserted, and the reports are full of cases illustrating its application. This is not the substitution of the will of the judge for that of the legislator, for frequently words of general meaning are used in a statute, words broad enough to include an act in question, and yet a consideration of the whole legislation, or of the circumstances surrounding its enactment, or of the absurd results which follow from giving such broad meaning to the words, makes it unreasonable to believe that the legislator intended to include the particular act. . . .

Among other things which may be considered in determining the intent of the legislature is the title of the act. We do not mean that it may be used to add to or take from the body of the statute, Hadden v. The Collector, 5 Wall. 107, but it may help to interpret its meaning. In the case of United States v. Fisher, 2 Cranch, 358, 386, Chief Justice Marshall said: "On the influence which the title ought to have in construing the enacting clauses much has been said; and yet it is not easy to discern the point of difference between the opposing counsel in this respect. Neither party contends that the title of an act can control plain words in the body of the statute; and neither denies that, taken with other parts, it may assist in removing ambiguities. Where the intent is plain, nothing is left to construction. Where the mind labors to discover the design of the legislature, it seizes everything from which aid can be derived; and in such case the title claims of degree of notice, and will have its due share of consideration." . . .

It will be seen that words as general as those used in the first section of this act were by that decision limited, and the intent of Congress with respect to the act was gathered partially, at least, from its title. Now, the title of this act is, "An act to prohibit the importation and migration of foreigners and aliens under contract or agreement to perform labor in the United States, its Territories and the District of Columbia." Obviously the thought expressed in this reaches only to the work of the manual laborer, as distinguished from that of the professional man. No one reading such a title would suppose that Congress had in its mind any purpose of staying the coming into this country of ministers of the gospel, or, indeed, of any class whose toil is that of the brain. The common understanding of the terms labor and laborers does not include preaching and preachers; and it is to be assumed that words and phrases are used in their ordinary meaning. So whatever of light is thrown upon the statute by the language of the title indicates an exclusion from its penal provisions of all contracts for the employment of ministers, rectors and pastors.

Again, another guide to the meaning of a statute is found in the evil which it is designed to remedy; and for this the court properly looks at contemporaneous events, the situation as it existed, and as it was pressed upon the attention of the legislative body. United States v. Union Pacific Railroad, 91 U.S. 72, 79. The situation which called for this statute was briefly but fully stated by Mr. Justice Brown when, as District Judge, he decided the case of United States v. Craig, 28 Fed. Rep. 795, 798: "The motives and history of the act are matters of common knowledge. It had become the practice for large capitalists in this country to contract with their agents abroad for the shipment of great numbers of an ignorant and servile class of foreign laborers, under contracts, by which the employer agreed, upon the one hand, to prepay their passage, while, upon the other hand, the laborers agreed to work after their arrival for a certain time at a low rate of wages. The effect of this was to break down the labor market, and to reduce other laborers engaged in like occupations to the level of the assisted immigrant. The evil finally became so flagrant that an appeal was made to Congress for relief by the passage of the act in question, the design of which was to raise the standard of foreign immigrants, and to discountenance the migration of those who had not sufficient means in their own hands, or those of their friends, to pay their passage."

It appears, also, from the petitions, and in the testimony presented before the committees of Congress, that it was this cheap unskilled labor which was making the trouble, and the influx of which Congress sought to prevent. It was never suggested that we had in this country a surplus of brain toilers, and, least of all, that the market for the services of Christian ministers was depressed by foreign competition. Those were matters to which the attention of Congress, or of the people, was not directed. So far, then, as the evil which was sought to be remedied interprets the statute, it also guides to an exclusion of this contract from the penalties of the act.

A singular circumstance, throwing light upon the intent of Congress, is found in this extract from the report of the Senate Committee on Education and Labor, recommending the passage of the bill: "The general facts and considerations which induce the committee to recommend the passage of this bill are set forth in the Report of the Committee of the House. The committee report the bill back without amendment, although there are certain features thereof which might well be changed or modified, in the hope that the bill may not fail of passage during the present session. Especially would the committee have otherwise recommended amendments, substituting for the expression 'labor and service,' whenever it occurs in the body of the bill, the words 'manual labor' or 'manual service,' as sufficiently broad to accomplish the purposes of the bill, and that such amendments would remove objections which a sharp and perhaps unfriendly criticism may urge to the proposed legislation. The committee, however, believing that the bill in its present form will be construed as including only those whose labor or service is manual in character, and being very desirous that the bill become a law before the adjournment, have reported the bill without change." 6059, Congressional Record, 48th Congress. And, referring back to the report of the Committee of the House, there appears this language: "It seeks to restrain and prohibit the immigration or importation of laborers who would have never seen our shores but for the inducements and allurements of men whose only object is to obtain labor at the lowest possible rate, regardless of the social and material well-being of our own citizens and regardless of the evil consequences which result to American laborers from such immigration. This class of immigrants care nothing about our institutions, and in many instances never even heard of them; they are men whose passage is paid by the importers; they come here under contract to labor for a certain number of years; they are ignorant of our social condition, and that they may remain so they are isolated and prevented from coming into contact with Americans. They are generally from the lowest social stratum, and live upon the coarsest food and in hovels of a character before unknown to American workmen. They, as a rule, do not become citizens, and are certainly not a desirable acquisition to the body politic. The inevitable tendency of their presence among us is to degrade American labor, and to reduce it to the level of the imported pauper labor." Page 5359, Congressional Record, 48th Congress.

We find, therefore, that the title of the act, the evil which was intended to be remedied, the circumstances surrounding the appeal to Congress, the reports of the committee of each house, all concur in affirming that the intent of Congress was simply to stay the influx of this cheap unskilled labor. . . .

Suppose in the Congress that passed this act some member had offered a bill which in terms declared that, if any Roman Catholic church in this country should contract with Cardinal Manning to come to this country and enter into its service as pastor and priest; or any Episcopal church should enter into a like contract with Canon Farrar; or any Baptist church should make similar arrangements with Rev. Mr. Spurgeon; or any Jewish synagogue with some eminent Rabbi, such contract should be adjudged unlawful and void, and the church making it be subject to prosecution and punishment, can it be believed that it would have received a minute of approving thought or a single vote? Yet it is contended that such was in effect the meaning of this statute. The construction invoked cannot be accepted as correct. It is a case where there was presented a definite evil, in view of which the legislature used general terms with the purpose of reaching all phases of that evil, and thereafter, unexpectedly, it is developed that the general language thus employed is broad enough to reach cases and acts which the whole history and life of the country affirm could not have been intentionally legislated against. It is the duty of the courts, under those circumstances, to say that, however broad the language of the statute may be, the act, although within the letter, is not within the intention of the legislature, and therefore cannot be within the statute.

The judgment will be reversed, and the case remanded for further proceedings in accordance with this opinion.

QUESTIONS AND DISCUSSION POINTS

1. With respect to interpretive matters, what are the major differences between this case and *Riggs* v. *Palmer*?

2. What role, if any, should Congress's objectives in writing the statute play in the interpretation of the words of the statute?

3. Does it matter that Reverend Warren did not deprive anyone else of a position with the *Church of the Holy Trinity*?

4. Should the plain meaning of the statute be the controlling factor?

5. How do you justify your position on how the statute ought to be read? As part of the exercise of justification, how do you defend your reading of other statutes against the readings of others? By what criteria do you decide that one interpretation of the statute is better than another?

〜

UNITED STEELWORKERS OF AMERICA, AFL-CIO-CLC
v. WEBER et al.
Supreme Court of the United States
443 U.S. 193 (1979)

MR. JUSTICE BRENNAN delivered the opinion of the Court.

Challenged here is the legality of an affirmative action plan—collectively bargained by an employer and a union—that reserves for black employees 50% of the openings in an in-plant craft-training program until the percentage of black craftworkers in the plant is commensurate with the percentage of blacks in the local labor force. The question for decision is whether Congress, in Title VII of the Civil Rights Act of 1964, 78 Stat. 253, as amended, 42 U.S.C. § 2000 et seq., left employers and unions in the private sector free to take such race-conscious steps to eliminate manifest racial imbalances in traditionally segregated job categories. We hold that Title VII does not prohibit such race-conscious affirmative action plans.

I.

In 1974, petitioner United Steelworkers of America (USWA) and petitioner Kaiser Aluminum & Chemical Corp. (Kaiser) entered into a master collective-bargaining agreement covering terms and conditions of employment at 15 Kaiser plants. The agreement contained, inter alia, an affirmative action plan designed to eliminate conspicuous racial imbalances in Kaiser's then almost exclusively white craftwork forces. Black craft-hiring goals were set for each Kaiser plant equal to the percentage of blacks in the respective local labor forces. To enable plants to meet these goals, on-the-job training programs were established to teach unskilled production workers—black and white—the skills necessary to become craft workers. The plan reserved for black employees 50% of the openings in these newly created in-plant training programs.

This case arose from the operation of the plan at Kaiser's plant in Gramercy, La. Until 1974, Kaiser hired as craft workers for that plant only persons who had had prior craft experience. Because blacks had long been excluded from craft unions,[1] few were able to present such credentials. As a consequence, prior to 1974 only 1.83% (5 out of 273) of the skilled craftworkers at the Gramercy plant were black, even though the work force in the Gramercy area was approximately 39% black.

Pursuant to the national agreement Kaiser altered its craft-hiring practice in the Gramercy plant. Rather than hiring already trained outsiders, Kaiser established a training program to train its production workers to fill craft openings. Selection of craft trainees was made on the basis of seniority, with the proviso that at least 50% of the new trainees were to be black until the percentage of black skilled craftworkers in the Gramercy plant approximated the percentage of blacks in the local labor force. See 415 F.Supp. 761, 764.

During 1974, the first year of the operation of the Kaiser-USWA affirmative action plan, 13 craft trainees were selected from Gramercy's production work force. Of these, seven were black and six white. The most senior black selected into the program had less seniority than seven white production workers whose bids for admission were rejected. Thereafter one of those white production workers, respondent Brian Weber (hereafter respondent), instituted this class action in the United States District Court for the Eastern District of Louisiana.

The complaint alleged that the filling of craft trainee positions at the Gramercy plant pursuant to the affirmative action program had resulted in junior black employees' receiving training in preference to senior white employees, thus discriminating against respondent and other similarly situated white employees in violation of §§ 703(a)[2] and (d)[3] of Title VII.

---

1. Judicial findings of exclusion from crafts on racial grounds are so numerous as to make such exclusion a proper subject for judicial notice. See, e.g., United States v. Elevator Constructors, 538 F.2d 1012 (CA3 1976); Associated General Contractors of Massachusetts v. Altschuler, 490 F.2d 9 (CA1 1973); Southern Illinois Builders Assn. v. Ogilvie, 471 F.2d 680 (CA7 1972); Contractors Assn. of Eastern Pennsylvania v. Secretary of Labor, 442 F.2d 159 (CA3 1971); Insulators & Asbestos Workers v. Vogler, 407 F.2d 1047 (CA5 1969); Buckner v. Goodyear Tire & Rubber Co., 339 F.Supp. 1108 (ND Ala. 1972), aff'd without opinion, 476 F.2d 1287 (CA5 1973).

2. Section 703(a), 78 Stat. 255, as amended, 86 Stat. 109, 42 U.S.C. @ 2000e–2(a), provides:

(a) . . . It shall be an unlawful employment practice for an employer—

1. to fail or refuse to hire or to discharge any individual, or otherwise to discriminate against any individual with respect to his compensation, terms, conditions, or privileges of employment, because of such individual's race, color, religion, sex, or national origin; or
2. to limit, segregate, or classify his employees or applicants for employment in any way which would deprive or tend to deprive any individual of employment opportunities or otherwise adversely affect his status as an employee, because of such individual's race, color, religion, sex, or national origin.

3. Section 703(d), 78 Stat. 256, 42 U.S.C. @ 2000e–2(d), provides:

"It shall be an unlawful employment practice for any employer, labor organization, or joint labor-management committee controlling apprenticeship or other training or retraining, including on-the-job training programs to discriminate against any individual because of his race, color, religion, sex, or national origin in admission to, or employment in, any program established to provide apprenticeship or other training."

The District Court held that the plan violated Title VII, entered a judgment in favor of the plaintiff class, and granted a permanent injunction prohibiting Kaiser and the USWA "from denying plaintiffs, Brian F. Weber and all other members of the class, access to on-the-job training programs on the basis of race." App. 171. A divided panel of the Court of Appeals for the Fifth Circuit affirmed, holding that all employment preferences based upon race, including those preferences incidental to bona fide affirmative action plans, violated Title VII's prohibition against racial discrimination in employment. 563 F.2d 216 (1977). We granted certiorari. 439 U.S. 1045 (1978). We reverse.

II.

We emphasize at the outset the narrowness of our inquiry. Since the Kaiser-USWA plan does not involve state action, this case does not present an alleged violation of the Equal Protection Clause of the Fourteenth Amendment. Further, since the Kaiser-USWA plan was adopted voluntarily, we are not concerned with what Title VII requires or with what a court might order to remedy a past proved violation of the Act. The only question before us is the narrow statutory issue of whether Title VII forbids private employers and unions from voluntarily agreeing upon bona fide affirmative action plans that accord racial preferences in the manner and for the purpose provided in the Kaiser-USWA plan.

Respondent argues that Congress intended in Title VII to prohibit all race-conscious affirmative action plans. Respondent's argument rests upon a literal interpretation of §§ 703(a) and (d) of the Act. Those sections make it unlawful to "discriminate . . . because of . . . race" in

hiring and in the selection of apprentices for training programs. Since, the argument runs, McDonald v. Santa Fe Trail Transp. Co., 427 U.S. 273 (1976), settled that Title VII forbids discrimination against whites as well as blacks, and since the Kaiser-USWA affirmative action plan operates to discriminate against white employees solely because they are white, it follows that the Kaiser-USWA plan violates Title VII.

Respondent's argument is not without force. But it overlooks the significance of the fact that the Kaiser-USWA plan is an affirmative action plan voluntarily adopted by private parties to eliminate traditional patterns of racial segregation. In this context respondent's reliance upon a literal construction of §§ 703(a) and (d) and upon McDonald is misplaced. It is a "familiar rule, that a thing may be within the letter of the statute and yet not within the statute, because not within its spirit, nor within the intention of its markets." Holy Trinity Church v. United States, 143 U.S. 457, 459 (1892). The prohibition against racial discrimination in §§ 703(a) and (d) of Title VII must therefore be read against the background of the legislative history of Title VII and the historical context from which the Act arose. See Train v. Colorado Public Interest Research Group, 426 U.S. 1, 10 (1976); National Woodwork Mfrs. Assn. v. NLRB, 386 U.S. 612, 620 (1967); United States v. American Trucking Assns., 310 U.S. 534, 543–544 (1940). Examination of those sources makes clear that an interpretation of the sections that forbade all race-conscious affirmative action would "bring about an end completely at variance with the purpose of the statute" and must be rejected.

Congress' primary concern in enacting the prohibition against racial discrimination in Title VII of the Civil Rights Act of 1964 was with "the plight of the Negro in our economy." 110 Cong. Rec. 6548 (1964) (remarks of Sen. Humphrey). Before 1964, blacks were largely relegated to "unskilled and semi-skilled jobs." Ibid. (remarks of Sen. Humphrey); id., at 7204 (remarks of Sen. Clark); d., at 7379–7380 (remarks of Sen. Kennedy). Because of automation the number of such jobs was rapidly decreasing. See id., at 6548 (remarks of Sen. Humphrey); id., at 7204 (remarks of Sen. Clark). As a consequence, "the relative position of the Negro worker [was] steadily worsening. In 1947 the nonwhite unemployment rate was only 64 percent higher than the white rate; in 1962 it was 124 percent higher." Id., at 6547 (remarks of Sen. Humphrey). See also id., at 7204 (remarks of Sen. Clark). Congress considered this a serious social problem. As Senator Clark told the Senate:

> The rate of Negro unemployment has gone up consistently as compared with white unemployment for the past 15 years. This is a social malaise and a social situation which we should not tolerate. That is one of the principal reasons why the bill should pass. Id., at 7220.I

Congress feared that the goals of the Civil Rights Act—the integration of blacks into the mainstream of American society—could not be achieved unless this trend were reversed. And Congress recognized that that would not be possible unless blacks were able to secure jobs "which have a future." Id., at 7204 (remarks of Sen. Clark). See also id., at 7379–7380 (remarks of Sen. Kennedy). As Senator Humphrey explained to the Senate: "What good does it do a Negro to be able to eat in a fine restaurant if he can-

not afford to pay the bill? What good does it do him to be accepted in a hotel that is too expensive for his modest income? How can a Negro child be motivated to take full advantage of integrated educational facilities if he has no hope of getting a job where he can use that education?" Id., at 6547. . . .

Given this legislative history, we cannot agree with respondent that Congress intended to prohibit the private sector from taking effective steps to accomplish the goal that Congress designed Title VII to achieve. The very statutory words intended as a spur or catalyst to cause "employers and unions to self-examine and to self-evaluate their employment practices and to endeavor to eliminate, so far as possible, the last vestiges of an unfortunate and ignominious page in this country's history," Albemarle Paper Co. v. Moody, 422 U.S. 405, 418 (1975), cannot be interpreted as an absolute prohibition against all private, voluntary, race-conscious affirmative action efforts to hasten the elimination of such vestiges.[4] It would be ironic indeed if a law triggered by a Nation's concern over centuries of racial injustice and intended to improve the lot of those who had "been excluded from the American dream for so long," 110 Cong. Rec. 6552 (1964) (remarks of Sen. Humphrey), constituted the first legislative prohibition of all voluntary, private, race-conscious efforts to abolish traditional patterns of racial segregation and hierarchy.

---

4. The problem that Congress addressed in 1964 remains with us. In 1962, the nonwhite unemployment rate was 124% higher than the white rate. See 110 Cong. Rec. 6547 (1964) (remarks of Sen. Humphrey). In 1978, the black unemployment rate was 129% higher. See Monthly Labor Review, U.S. Department of Labor, Bureau of Labor Statistics 78 (Mar. 1979).

Our conclusion is further reinforced by examination of the language and legislative history of § 703(j) of Title VII.[5] Opponents of Title VII raised two related arguments against the bill. First, they argued that the Act would be interpreted to require employers with racially imbalanced work forces to grant preferential treatment to racial minorities in order to integrate. Second, they argued that employers with racially imbalanced work forces would grant preferential treatment to racial minorities, even if not required to do so by the Act. See 110 Cong. Rec. 8618–8619 (1964) (remarks of

---

5. Section 703(j) of Title VII, 78 Stat. 257, 42 U.S.C. @ 2000e–2(j), provides:

Nothing contained in this title shall be interpreted to require any employer, employment agency, labor organization, or joint labor-management committee subject to this title to grant preferential treatment to any individual or to any group because of the race, color, religion, sex, or national origin of such individual or group on account of an imbalance which may exist with respect to the total number or percentage of persons of any race, color, religion, sex, or national origin employed by any employer, referred or classified for employment by any employment agency or labor organization, admitted to membership or classified by any labor organization, or admitted to, or employed in, any apprenticeship or other training program, in comparison with the total number or percentage of persons of such race, color, religion, sex, or national origin in any community, State, section, or other area, or in the available work force in any community, State, section, or other area.

Section 703(j) speaks to substantive liability under Title VII, but it does not preclude courts from considering racial imbalance as evidence of a Title VII violation. See Teamsters v. United States, 431 U.S. 324, 339–340, n. 20 (1977). Remedies for substantive violations are governed by @ 706(g), 42 U.S.C. @ 2000e–5(g).

Sen. Sparkman). Had Congress meant to prohibit all race-conscious affirmative action, as respondent urges, it easily could have answered both objections by providing that Title VII would not require or permit racially preferential integration efforts. But Congress did not choose such a course. Rather, Congress added § 703(j) which addresses only the first objection. The section provides that nothing contained in Title VII "shall be interpreted to require any employer . . . to grant preferential treatment . . . to any group because of the race . . . of such . . . group on account of" a de facto racial imbalance in the employer's work force. The section does not state that "nothing in Title VII shall be interpreted to permit" voluntary affirmative efforts to correct racial imbalances. The natural inference is that Congress chose not to forbid all voluntary race-conscious affirmative action.

We therefore hold that Title VII's prohibition in §§ 703(a) and (d) against racial discrimination does not condemn all private, voluntary, race-conscious affirmative action plans.

At the same time, the plan does not unnecessarily trammel the interests of the white employees. The plan does not require the discharge of white workers and their replacement with new black hirees. Cf. McDonald v. Santa Fe Trail Transp. Co., 427 U.S. 273 (1976). Nor does the plan create an absolute bar to the advancement of white employees; half of those trained in the program will be white. Moreover, the plan is a temporary measure; it is not intended to maintain racial balance, but simply to eliminate a manifest racial imbalance. Preferential selection of craft trainees at the Gramercy plant will end as soon as the percentage of black skilled craftworkers in the

Gramercy plant approximates the percentage of blacks in the local labor force. See 415 F.Supp., at 763.

We conclude, therefore, that the adoption of the Kaiser-USWA plan for the Gramercy plant falls within the area of discretion left by Title VII to the private sector voluntarily to adopt affirmative action plans designed to eliminate conspicuous racial imbalance in traditionally segregated job categories.[6] Accordingly, the judgment of the Court of Appeals for the Fifth Circuit is Reversed. MR. JUSTICE POWELL and MR. JUSTICE STEVENS took no part in the consideration or decision of these cases.

MR. JUSTICE REHNQUIST, with whom THE CHIEF JUSTICE joins, dissenting.

In a very real sense, the Court's opinion is ahead of its time: it could more appropriately have been handed down five years from now, in 1984, a year coinciding with the title of a book from which the Court's opinion borrows, perhaps subconsciously, at least one idea. Orwell describes in his book a governmental official of Oceania, one of the three great world powers, denouncing the current enemy, Eurasia, to an assembled crowd:

> It was almost impossible to listen to him without being first convinced and then maddened. . . . The speech had been proceeding for perhaps twenty minutes when a messenger hurried onto the platform and a scrap of paper

was slipped into the speaker's hand. He unrolled and read it without pausing in his speech. Nothing altered in his voice or manner, or in the content of what he was saying, but suddenly the names were different. Without words said, a wave of understanding rippled through the crowd. Oceania was at war with Eastasia! . . . The banners and posters with which the square was decorated were all wrong! . . .

> [T]he speaker had switched from one line to the other actually in midsentence, not only without a pause, but without even breaking the syntax.

> —G. Orwell, *1984* 181–182 (1949).

I.

Today's decision represents an equally dramatic and equally unremarked switch in this Court's interpretation of Title VII.

The operative sections of Title VII prohibit racial discrimination in employment simpliciter. Taken in its normal meaning, and as understood by all Members of Congress who spoke to the issue during the legislative debates, see infra, at 231–251, this language prohibits a covered employer from considering race when making an employment decision, whether the race be black or white. Several years ago, however, a United States District Court held that "the dismissal of white employees charged with misappropriating company property while not dismissing a similarly charged Negro employee does not raise a claim upon which Title VII relief may be granted." McDonald v. Santa Fe Trail Transp. Co., 427 U.S. 273, 278 (1976). This Court unanimously reversed, concluding from the "uncontradicted legislative history" that "Title VII prohibits racial discrimination against the white petitioners in this case

---

6. Our disposition makes unnecessary consideration of petitioners' argument that their plan was justified because they feared that black employees would bring suit under Title VII if they did not adopt an affirmative action plan. Nor need we consider petitioners' contention that their affirmative action plan represented an attempt to comply with Exec. Order No. 11246, 3 CFR 339 (1964–1965 Comp.).

upon the same standards as would be applicable were they Negroes. . . ." Id., at 280.

We have never wavered in our understanding that Title VII "prohibits all racial discrimination in employment, without exception for any group of particular employees." Id., at 283 (emphasis in original). In Griggs v. Duke Power Co., 401 U.S. 424, 431 (1971), our first occasion to interpret Title VII, a unanimous Court observed that "[di]scriminatory preference, for any group, minority or majority, is precisely and only what Congress has proscribed." And in our most recent discussion of the issue, we uttered words seemingly dispositive of this case: "It is clear beyond cavil that the obligation imposed by Title VII is to provide an equal opportunity for each applicant regardless of race, without regard to whether members of the applicant's race are already proportionately represented in the work force." Furnco Construction Corp. v. Waters, 438 U.S. 567, 579 (1978) (emphasis in original).

Today, however, the Court behaves much like the Orwellian speaker earlier described, as if it had been handed a note indicating that Title VII would lead to a result unacceptable to the Court if interpreted here as it was in our prior decisions. Accordingly, without even a break in syntax, the Court rejects "a literal construction of § 703(a)" in favor of newly discovered "legislative history," which leads it to a conclusion directly contrary to that compelled by the "uncontradicted legislative history" unearthed in Mc-Donald and our other prior decisions. Now we are told that the legislative history of Title VII shows that employers are free to discriminate on the basis of race: an employer may, in the Court's words, "trammel the interests of the white em-

ployees" in favor of black employees in order to eliminate "racial imbalance." Ante, at 208. Our earlier interpretations of Title VII, like the banners and posters decorating the square in Oceania, were all wrong.

As if this were not enough to make a reasonable observer question this Court's adherence to the oft-stated principle that our duty is to construe rather than rewrite legislation, United States v. Rutherford, 442 U.S. 544, 555 (1979), the Court also seizes upon § 703(j) of Title VII as an independent, or at least partially independent, basis for its holding. Totally ignoring the wording of that section, which is obviously addressed to those charged with the responsibility of interpreting the law rather than those who are subject to its proscriptions, and totally ignoring the months of legislative debates preceding the section's introduction and passage, which demonstrate clearly that it was enacted to prevent precisely what occurred in this case, the Court infers from § 703(j) that "Congress chose not to forbid all voluntary race-conscious affirmative action." Ante, at 206.

Thus, by a tour de force reminiscent not of jurists such as Hale, Holmes, and Hughes, but of escape artists such as Houdini, the Court eludes clear statutory language, "uncontradicted" legislative history, and uniform precedent in concluding that employers are, after all, permitted to consider race in making employment decisions. It may be that one or more of the principal sponsors of Title VII would have preferred to see a provision allowing preferential treatment of minorities written into the bill. Such a provision, however, would have to have been expressly or impliedly excepted from Title VII's explicit prohibition on all racial discrimination in employment. There is no such exception in the Act. And a reading of the legislative debates concerning Title VII, in which proponents and opponents alike uniformly denounced discrimination in favor of, as well as discrimination against, Negroes, demonstrates clearly that any legislator harboring an unspoken desire for such a provision could not possibly have succeeded in enacting it into law.

II.

Were Congress to act today specifically to prohibit the type of racial discrimination suffered by Weber, it would be hard pressed to draft language better tailored to the task than that found in § 703(d) of Title VII:

> It shall be an unlawful employment practice for any employer, labor organization, or joint labor-management committee controlling apprenticeship or other training or retraining, including on-the-job training programs to discriminate against any individual because of his race, color, religion, sex, or national origin in admission to, or employment in, any program established to provide apprenticeship or other training.
> —78 Stat. 256, 42 U.S.C. § 2000e–2(d).

---

7. Section 703(a)(1) provides the third express prohibition in Title VII of Kaiser's discriminatory admission quota:

"It shall be an unlawful employment practice for an employer—

"**1.** to fail or refuse to hire or to discharge any individual, or otherwise to discriminate against any individual with respect to his compensation, terms, conditions, or privileges of employment, because of such individual's race, color, religion, sex, or national origin. . . ." 78 Stat. 255, 42 U.S.C. @ 2000e–2(a)(1).

Equally suited to the task would be § 703(a)(2), which makes it unlawful for an employer to classify his employees "in any way which would deprive or tend to deprive any individual of employment opportunities or otherwise adversely affect his status as an employee, because of such individual's race, color, religion, sex, or national origin." 78 Stat. 255, 42 U.S.C. § 2000e–2(a)(2).[7] Entirely consistent with these two express prohibitions is the language of § 703(j) of Title VII, which provides that the Act is not to be interpreted "to require any employer . . . to grant preferential treatment to any individual or to any group because of the race . . . of such individual or group" to correct a racial imbalance in the employer's work force. 42 U.S.C. § 2000e–2(j).[8] Seizing on the word "require," the Court infers that Congress must have intended to "per-

---

8. The full text of @ 703(j), 78 Stat. 257, 42 U.S.C. @ 2000e–2(j), provides as follows:

"Nothing contained in this title shall be interpreted to require any employer, employment agency, labor organization, or joint labor-management committee subject to this title to grant preferential treatment to any individual or to any group because of the race, color, religion, sex, or national origin of such individual or group on account of an imbalance which may exist with respect to the total number or percentage of persons of any race, color, religion, sex, or national origin employed by any employer, referred or classified for employment by any employment agency or labor organization, admitted to membership or classified by any labor organization, or admitted to, or employed in, any apprenticeship or other training program, in comparison with the total number or percentage of persons of such race, color, religion, sex, or national origin in any community, State, section, or other area, or in the available work force in any community, State, section, or other area."

mit" this type of racial discrimination. Not only is this reading of § 703(j) outlandish in the light of the flat prohibitions of §§ 703(a) and (d), but also, as explained in Part III, it is totally belied by the Act's legislative history. Quite simply, Kaiser's racially discriminatory admission quota is flatly prohibited by the plain language of Title VII. This normally dispositive fact,[9] n9 however, gives the Court only momentary pause. An "interpretation" of the statute upholding Weber's claim would, according to the Court, "'bring about an end completely at variance with the purpose of the statute.'" Ante, at 202, quoting United States v. Public Utilities Comm'n, 345 U.S. 295, 315 (1953). To support this conclusion, the Court calls upon the "spirit" of the Act, which it divines

from passages in Title VII's legislative history indicating that enactment of the statute was prompted by Congress' desire "'to open employment opportunities for Negroes in occupations which [had] been traditionally closed to them.'" Ante, at 203, quoting 110 Cong. Rec. 6548 (1964) (remarks of Sen. Humphrey).[10] But the legislative history invoked by the Court to avoid the plain language of §§ 703(a) and (d) simply misses the point. To be sure, the reality of employment discrimination against Negroes provided the primary impetus for passage of Title VII. But this fact by no means supports the proposition that Congress intended to leave employers free to discriminate against white persons.[11] In most cases, "[l]egislative history . . . is more vague than the statute we are called upon to interpret."

---

9. "If the words are plain, they give meaning to the act, and it is neither the duty nor the privilege of the courts to enter speculative fields in search of a different meaning.

". . . [W]hen words are free from doubt they must be taken as the final expression of the legislative intent, and are not to be added to or subtracted from by considerations drawn . . . from any extraneous source." Caminetti v. United States, 242 U.S. 470, 490 (1917).

10. In holding that Title VII cannot be interpreted to prohibit use of Kaiser's racially discriminatory admission quota, the Court reasons that it would be "ironic" if a law inspired by the history of racial discrimination in employment against blacks forbade employers from voluntarily discriminating against whites in favor of blacks. I see no irony in a law that prohibits all voluntary racial discrimination, even discrimination directed at whites in favor of blacks. The evil inherent in discrimination against Negroes is that it is based on an immutable characteristic, utterly irrelevant to employment decisions. The characteristic becomes no less immutable and irrelevant, and discrimination based thereon becomes no less evil, simply because the person excluded is a member of one race rather than another. Far from ironic, I find a prohibition on all preferential treatment based on race as elementary and fundamental as the principle that "two wrongs do not make a right."

11. The only shred of legislative history cited by the Court in support of the proposition that "Congress did not intend wholly to prohibit private and voluntary affirmative action efforts," ante, at 203, is the following excerpt from the Judiciary Committee Report accompanying the civil rights bill reported to the House:

No bill can or should lay claim to eliminating all of the causes and consequences of racial and other types of discrimination against minorities. There is reason to believe, however, that national leadership provided by the enactment of Federal legislation dealing with the most troublesome problems will create an atmosphere conducive to voluntary or local resolution of other forms of discrimination.

—H.R. Rep. No. 914, 88th Cong., 1st Sess., pt. 1, p. 18 (1963) (hereinafter H.R. Rep.), quoted ante, at 203–204

The Court seizes on the italicized language to support its conclusion that Congress did not intend to prohibit voluntary imposition of racially discriminatory employment quotas. The Court, however, stops too short in its reading of the House Report. The words immediately following the material excerpted by the Court are as follows:

United States v. Public Utilities Comm'n, supra, at 320 (Jackson, J., concurring). Here, however, the legislative history of Title VII is as clear as the language of §§ 703(a) and (d), and it irrefutably demonstrates that Congress meant precisely what it said in §§ 703(a) and (d)—that no racial discrimination in employment is permissible under Title VII, not even preferential treatment of minorities to correct racial imbalance.

III.

In undertaking to review the legislative history of Title VII, I am mindful that the topic hardly makes for light reading, but I am also fearful that nothing short of a thorough examination of the congressional debates will fully expose the magnitude of the Court's misinterpretation of Congress' intent.

"It is, however, possible and necessary for the Congress to enact legislation which prohibits and provides the means of terminating the most serious types of discrimination. This H.R. 7152, as amended, would achieve in a number of related areas. It would reduce discriminatory obstacles to the exercise of the right to vote and provide means of expediting the vindication of that right. It would make it possible to remove the daily affront and humiliation involved in discriminatory denials of access to facilities ostensibly open to the general public. It would guarantee that there will be no discrimination upon recipients of Federal financial assistance. It would prohibit discrimination in employment, and provide means to expedite termination of discrimination in public education. It would open additional avenues to deal with redress of denials of equal protection of the laws on account of race, color, religion, or national origin by State or local authorities.

—H.R. Rep., pt. 1, p. 18

When thus read in context, the meaning of the italicized language in the Court's excerpt of the House Report becomes clear. By dealing with "the most serious types of

A.

Introduced on the floor of the House of Representatives on June 20, 1963, the bill—H.R. 7152—that ultimately became the Civil Rights Act of 1964 contained no compulsory provisions directed at private discrimination in employment. The bill was promptly referred to the Committee on the Judiciary, where it was amended to include Title VII. With two exceptions, the bill reported by the House Judiciary Committee contained §§ 703(a) and (b) as they were ultimately enacted. Amendments subsequently adopted on the House floor added § 703's prohibition against sex discrimination and § 703(d)'s coverage of "on-the-job training."

After noting that "[t]he purpose of [Title VII] is to eliminate . . . discrimination in employment based on race, color, religion, or national origin," the Judiciary

---

discrimination," such as discrimination in voting, public accommodations, employment, etc., H.R. 7152 would hopefully inspire "voluntary or local resolution of other forms of discrimination," that is, forms other than discrimination in voting, public accommodations, employment, etc.

One can also infer from the House Report that the Judiciary Committee hoped that federal legislation would inspire voluntary elimination of discrimination against minority groups other than those protected under the bill, perhaps the aged and handicapped to name just two. In any event, the House Report does not support the Court's proposition that Congress, by banning racial discrimination in employment, intended to permit racial discrimination in employment.

Thus, examination of the House Judiciary Committee's report reveals that the Court's interpretation of Title VII, far from being compelled by the Act's legislative history, is utterly without support in that legislative history. Indeed, as demonstrated in Part III, infra, the Court's interpretation of Title VII is totally refuted by the Act's legislative history.

Committee's Report simply paraphrased the provisions of Title VII without elaboration. H.R. Rep., pt. 1, p. 26. In a separate Minority Report, however, opponents of the measure on the Committee advanced a line of attack which was reiterated throughout the debates in both the House and Senate and which ultimately led to passage of § 703(j). Noting that the word "discrimination" was nowhere defined in H.R. 7152, the Minority Report charged that the absence from Title VII of any reference to "racial imbalance" was a "public relations" ruse and that "the administration intends to rely upon its own construction of 'discrimination' as including the lack of racial balance. . .". H.R. Rep., pt. 1, pp. 67–68. To demonstrate how the bill would operate in practice, the Minority Report posited a number of hypothetical employment situations, concluding in each example that the employer "may be forced to hire according to race, to 'racially balance' those who work for him in every job classification or be in violation of Federal law." Id., at 69 (emphasis in original).[12]

When H.R. 7152 reached the House floor, the opening speech in support of its passage was delivered by Representative Celler, Chairman of the House Judiciary Committee and the Congressman responsible for introducing the legislation. A portion of that speech responded to criticism "seriously misrepresen[ting] what the bill would do and grossly distort[ing] its effects":

> [T]he charge has been made that the Equal Employment Opportunity Commission to be established by Title VII of the bill would have the power to prevent a business from employing and promoting the people it wished, and that a 'Federal Inspector' could

then order the hiring and promotion only of employees of certain races or religious groups. This description of the bill is entirely wrong. . . .

---

12. One example has particular relevance to the instant litigation:

> Under the power granted in this bill, if a carpenters' hiring hall, say, had 20 men awaiting call, the first 10 in seniority being white carpenters, the union could be forced to pass them over in favor of carpenters beneath them in seniority but of the stipulated race. And if the union roster did not contain the names of the carpenters of the race needed to 'racially balance' the job, the union agent must, then, go into the street and recruit members of the stipulated race in sufficient number to comply with Federal orders, else his local could be held in violation of Federal law.
>
> —H.R. Rep., pt. 1, p. 71.

From this and other examples, the Minority Report concluded: "That this is, in fact, a not too subtle system of racism-in-reverse cannot be successfully denied." Id., at 73.

Obviously responding to the Minority Report's charge that federal agencies, particularly the Equal Employment Opportunity Commission would equate "discrimination" with "racial imbalance," the Republican sponsors of the bill on the Judiciary Committee stated in a separate Report:

> It must also be stressed that the Commission must confine its activities to correcting abuse, not promoting equality with mathematical certainty. In this regard, nothing in the title permits a person to demand employment. . . . Internal affairs of employers and labor organizations must not be interfered with except to the limited extent that correction is required in discrimination practices. Its primary task is to make certain that the channels of employment are open to persons regardless of their race and that jobs in companies or membership in unions are strictly filled on the basis of qualification.
>
> —Id., pt. 2, p. 29.

The Republican supporters of the bill concluded their remarks on Title VII by declaring that "[a]ll vestiges of inequality based solely on race must be removed. . . ." Id., at 30.

Even [a] court could not order that any preference be given to any particular race, religion or other group, but would be limited to ordering an end of discrimination. The statement that a Federal inspector could order the employment and promotion only of members of a specific racial or religious group is therefore patently erroneous. . . . The Bill would do no more than prevent . . . employers from discriminating against or in favor of workers because of their race, religion, or national origin.

"It is likewise not true that the Equal Employment Opportunity Commission would have power to rectify existing 'racial or religious imbalance' in employment by requiring the hiring of certain people without regard to their qualifications simply because they are of a given race or religion. Only actual discrimination could be stopped.

—110 Cong. Rec. 1518 (1964)

Representative Celler's construction of Title VII was repeated by several other supporters during the House debate.[13]

Thus, the battle lines were drawn early in the legislative struggle over Title VII, with opponents of the measure charging that agencies of the Federal Government such as the Equal Employment Opportunity Commission (EEOC), by interpreting the word "discrimination" to mean the existence of "racial imbalance," would "require" employers to grant preferential treatment to minorities, and supporters responding that the EEOC would be granted no such power and that, indeed, Title VII prohibits discrimination "in favor of workers because of their race." Supporters of H.R. 7152 in the House ultimately prevailed by a vote of 290 to 130,[14] and the measure was sent to the Senate to begin what became the longest debate in that body's history.

---

13. Representative Lindsay had this to say:

This legislation . . . does not, as has been suggested heretofore both on and off the floor, force acceptance of people in . . . jobs . . . because they are Negro. It does not impose quotas or any special privileges of seniority or acceptance. There is nothing whatever in this bill about racial balance as appears so frequently in the minority report of the Committee.

"What the bill does do is prohibit discrimination because of race. . . .
—110 Cong. Rec. 1540 (1964)

Representative Minish added: "Under title VII, employment will be on the basis of merit, not of race. This means that no quota system will be set up, no one will be forced to hire incompetent help because of race or religion, and no one will be given a vested right to demand employment for a certain job." Id., at 1600. Representative Goodell, answering the charge that Title VII would be interpreted "to requir[e] a racial

balance," id., at 2557, responded: "There is nothing here as a matter of legislative history that would require racial balancing. . . . We are not talking about a union having to balance its membership or an employer having to balance the number of employees. There is no quota involved. It is a matter of an individual's rights having been violated, charges having been brought, investigation carried out and conciliation having been attempted and then proof in court that there was discrimination and denial of rights on the basis of race or color." Id., at 2558. After H.R. 7152 had been passed and sent to the Senate, Republican supporters of the bill in the House prepared an interpretative memorandum making clear that "title VII does not permit the ordering of racial quotas in businesses or unions and does not permit interferences with seniority rights of employees or union members." Id., at 6566.

14. Eleven members did not vote.

B.

The Senate debate was broken into three phases: the debate on sending the bill to Committee, the general debate on the bill prior to invocation of cloture, and the debate following cloture. . . .

[W]ith virtual clairvoyance the Senate's leading supporters of Title VII anticipated precisely the circumstances of this case and advised their colleagues that the type of minority preference employed by Kaiser would violate Title VII's ban on racial discrimination. To further accentuate the point, Senator Clark introduced another memorandum dealing with common criticisms of the bill, including the charge that racial quotas would be imposed under Title VII. The answer was simple and to the point: "Quotas are themselves discriminatory." Id., at 7218.

Despite these clear statements from the bill's leading and most knowledgeable proponents, the fears of the opponents were not put to rest. Senator Robertson reiterated the view that "discrimination" could be interpreted by a federal "bureaucrat" to require hiring quotas. Id., at 7418–7420.[15] Senators Smathers and Sparkman, while conceding that Title VII does not in so many words require the use of hiring quotas, repeated the opposition's view that employers would be coerced to grant preferential hiring treatment to minorities by

agencies of the Federal Government.[16] Senator Williams was quick to respond:

"Those opposed to H.R. 7152 should realize that to hire a Negro solely because he is a Negro is racial discrimination, just as much as a 'white only' employment policy. Both forms of discrimination are prohibited by Title VII of this bill. The language of that title simply states that race is not a qualification for employment. . . . Some people charge that H.R. 7152 favors the Negro, at the expense of the white majority. But how can the language of equality favor one race or one religion over another? Equality can have only one meaning, and that meaning is self-evident to reasonable men. Those who say that equality means favoritism do violence to common sense." Id., at 8921. Senator Williams concluded his remarks by noting that Title VII's only purpose is "the elimination of racial and religious discrimination in employment." Ibid.[17] On May 25, Senator Humphrey again took the floor to defend the bill against "the well-financed drive by cer-

---

15. Senator Robertson's observations prompted Senator Humphrey to make the following offer: "If the Senator can find in Title VII . . . any language which provides that an employer will have to hire on the basis of percentage or quota related to color . . . I will start eating the pages one after another, because it is not in there." 110 Cong. Rec. 7420 (1964).

16. Referring to the EEOC, Senator Smathers argued that Title VII "would make possible the creation of a Federal bureaucracy which would, in the final analysis, cause a man to hire someone whom he did not want to hire, not on the basis of ability, but on the basis of religion, color, or creed. . . ." Id., at 8500. Senator Sparkman's comments were to the same effect. See n. 23, infra. Several other opponents of Title VII expressed similar views. See 110 Cong. Rec. 9034–9035 (1964) (remarks of Sens. Stennis and Tower); id., at 9943–994 (remarks of Sens. Long and Talmadge); id., at 10513 (remarks of Sen. Robertson).

17. Several other proponents of H.R. 7152 commented briefly on Title VII, observing that it did not authorize the imposition of quotas to correct racial imbalance. See id., at 9113 (remarks of Sen. Keating); id., at 9881–9882 (remarks of Sen. Allott); id., at 10520 (remarks of Sen. Carlson); id., at 11768 (remarks of Sen. McGovern).

tain opponents to confuse and mislead the American people." Id., at 11846. Turning once again to the issue of preferential treatment, Senator Humphrey remained faithful to the view that he had repeatedly expressed:

"The title does not provide that any preferential treatment in employment shall be given to Negroes or to any other persons or groups. It does not provide that any quota systems may be established to maintain racial balance in employment. In fact, the title would prohibit preferential treatment for any particular group, and any person, whether or not a member of any minority group, would be permitted to file a complaint of discriminatory employment practices." Id., at 11848 (emphasis added).

While the debate in the Senate raged, a bipartisan coalition under the leadership of Senators Dirksen, Mansfield, Humphrey, and Kuchel was working with House leaders and representatives of the Johnson administration on a number of amendments to H.R. 7152 designed to enhance its prospects of passage. The so-called "Dirksen-Mansfield" amendment was introduced on May 26 by Senator Dirksen as a substitute for the entire House-passed bill. The substitute bill, which ultimately became law, left unchanged the basic prohibitory language of §§ 703(a) and (d), as well as the remedial provisions in § 706(g). It added, however, several provisions defining and clarifying the scope of Title VII's substantive prohibitions. One of those clarifying amendments, § 703(j), was specifically directed at the opposition's concerns regarding racial balancing and preferential treatment of minorities, providing in pertinent part: "Nothing contained in [Title VII] shall be interpreted to require any employer . . . to grant pref-

erential treatment to any individual or to any group because of the race . . . of such individual or group on account of" a racial imbalance in the employer's work force. 42 U.S.C. § 2000e–2(j); quoted in full in n. 8, supra.

The Court draws from the language of § 703(j) primary support for its conclusion that Title VII's blanket prohibition on racial discrimination in employment does not prohibit preferential treatment of blacks to correct racial imbalance. Alleging that opponents of Title VII had argued (1) that the Act would be interpreted to require employers with racially imbalanced work forces to grant preferential treatment to minorities and (2) that "employers with racially imbalanced work forces would grant preferential treatment to racial minorities, even if not required to do so by the Act," ante, at 205, the Court concludes that § 703(j) is responsive only to the opponents' first objection and that Congress therefore must have intended to permit voluntary, private discrimination against whites in order to correct racial imbalance.

Contrary to the Court's analysis, the language of § 703(j) is precisely tailored to the objection voiced time and again by Title VII's opponents. Not once during the 83 days of debate in the Senate did a speaker, proponent or opponent, suggest that the bill would allow employers voluntarily to prefer racial minorities over white persons.[18] In light of Title VII's flat prohibition

---

18. The Court cites the remarks of Senator Sparkman in support of its suggestion that opponents had argued that employers would take it upon themselves to balance their work forces by granting preferential treatment to racial minorities. In fact, Senator Sparkman's comments accurately reflected the opposition's "party line." He argued that while the language of Title VII does not expressly require imposition of racial quotas (no one,

on discrimination "against any individual . . . because of such individual's race," § 703(a), 42 U.S.C. § 2000e–2(a), such a contention would have been, in any event, too preposterous to warrant response. Indeed, speakers on both sides of the issue, as the legislative history makes clear, recognized that Title VII would tolerate no voluntary racial preference, whether in favor of blacks or whites. The complaint consistently voiced by the opponents was that Title VII, particularly the word "discrimination," would be interpreted by federal agencies such as the EEOC to require the correction of racial imbalance through the granting of preferential treatment to minorities. Verbal assurances that Title VII would not require—indeed, would not permit—preferential treatment of blacks having failed, supporters of H.R. 7152 responded by proposing an amendment carefully worded to meet, and put to rest, the opposition's charge. Indeed, unlike §§ 703(a) and (d), which are by their terms directed at entities—e.g., employers, labor unions—whose actions are restricted by Title VII's prohibitions, the language of § 703(j) is specifically directed at entities—

federal agencies and courts—charged with the responsibility of interpreting Title VII's provisions.[19]

In light of the background and purpose of § 703(j), the irony of invoking the section to justify the result in this case is obvious. The Court's frequent references to the "voluntary" nature of Kaiser's racially discriminatory admission quota bear no relationship to the facts of this case. Kaiser and the Steelworkers acted under pressure from an agency of the Federal Government, the Office of Federal Contract Compliance, which found that minorities were being "under utilized" at Kaiser's plants. See n. 2, supra. That is, Kaiser's work force was racially imbalanced. Bowing to that pressure, Kaiser instituted an admissions quota preferring blacks over whites, thus confirming that the fears of Title VII's opponents were

---

of course, had ever argued to the contrary), the law would be applied by federal agencies in such a way that "some kind of quota system will be used." Id., at 8619. Senator Sparkman's view is reflected in the following exchange with Senator Stennis:

"Mr. Sparkman. At any rate, when the Government agent came to interview an employer who had 100 persons in his employ, the first question would be, 'How many Negroes are you employing?' Suppose the population of that area was 20 percent Negro. Immediately the agent would say, 'You should have at least 20 Negroes in your employ, and they should be distributed among your supervisory personnel and in all the other categories'; and the agent would insist that that be done immediately.

"Mr. Stennis. . . .

"The Senator from Alabama has made very clear his point about employment on the quota

basis. Would not the same basis be applied to promotions?

"Mr. Sparkman. Certainly it would. As I have said, when the Federal agents came to check on the situation in a small business which had 100 employees, and when the agents said to the employer, 'You must hire 20 Negroes, and some of them must be employed in supervisory capacities,' and so forth, and so on, the agent would also say, 'And you must promote the Negroes, too, in order to distribute them evenly among the various ranks of your employees.'" Id., at 8618 (emphasis added).

Later in his remarks, Senator Sparkman stated: "Certainly the suggestion will be made to a small business that may have a small Government contract . . . that if it does not carry out the suggestion that has been made to the company by an inspector, its Government contract will not be renewed." Ibid. Except for the size of the business, Senator Sparkman has seen his prophecy fulfilled in this case.

19. Compare @ 703(a), 42 U.S.C. @ 2000e–2(a) ("It shall be an unlawful employment practice for an employer . . ."), with @ 703(j), 42 U.S.C. @ 2000e–2(j) ("Nothing contained in this subchapter shall be interpreted . . .").

well founded. Today, § 703(j), adopted to allay those fears, is invoked by the Court to uphold imposition of a racial quota under the very circumstances that the section was intended to prevent.[20] . . .

V.

Our task in this case, like any other case involving the construction of a statute, is to give effect to the intent of Congress. To divine that intent, we traditionally look first to the words of the statute and, if they are unclear, then to the statute's legislative history. Finding the desired result hopelessly foreclosed by these conventional sources, the Court turns to a third source—the "spirit" of the Act. But close examination of what the Court proffers as the spirit of the Act reveals it as the spirit animating the present majority, not the 88th Congress. For if the spirit of the Act eludes the cold words of the statute itself, it rings out with unmistakable clarity in the words of the elected representatives who made the Act law. It is equality. Senator Dirksen, I think, captured that spirit in a speech delivered on the floor of the Senate just moments before the bill was passed:

> . . . [T]oday we come to grips finally with a bill that advances the enjoyment of living; but, more than that, it advances the equality of opportunity.
>
> "I do not emphasize the word 'equality' standing by itself. It means equality of opportunity in the field of education. It means equality of opportunity in the field of employment. It means equality of opportunity in the field of participation in the affairs of government. . . .
>
> "That is it.
>
> "Equality of opportunity, if we are going to talk about conscience, is the mass conscience of mankind that

speaks in every generation, and it will continue to speak long after we are dead and gone.

—110 Cong. Rec. 14510 (1964).

There is perhaps no device more destructive to the notion of equality than the *numerus clausus*—the quota. Whether described as "benign discrimination" or "affirmative action," the racial quota is nonetheless a creator of castes, a two-

---

20. In support of its reading of @ 703(j), the Court argues that "a prohibition against all voluntary, race-conscious, affirmative action efforts would disserve" the important policy, expressed in the House Report on H.R. 7152, that Title VII leave "management prerogatives, and union freedoms . . . undisturbed to the greatest extent possible." H.R. Rep., pt. 2, p. 29, quoted ante, at 206. The Court thus concludes that "Congress did not intend to limit traditional business freedom to such a degree as to prohibit all voluntary, race-conscious affirmative action." Ante, at 207.

The sentences in the House Report immediately following the statement quoted by the Court, however, belie the Court's conclusion:

> Internal affairs of employers and labor organizations must not be interfered with except to the limited extent that correction is required in discrimination practices. Its primary task is to make certain that the channels of employment are open to persons regardless of their race and that jobs in companies or membership in unions are strictly filled on the basis of qualification.
>
> —H.R. Rep., pt. 2, p. 29

Thus, the House Report invoked by the Court is perfectly consistent with the countless observations elsewhere in Title VII's voluminous legislative history that employers are free to make employment decisions without governmental interference, so long as those decisions are made without regard to race. The whole purpose of Title VII was to deprive employers of their "traditional business freedom" to discriminate on the basis of race. In this case, the "channels of employment" at Kaiser were hardly "open" to Brian Weber.

edged sword that must demean one in order to prefer another. In passing Title VII, Congress outlawed all racial discrimination, recognizing that no discrimination based on race is benign, that no action disadvantaging a person because of his color is affirmative. With today's holding, the Court introduces into Title VII a tolerance for the very evil that the law was intended to eradicate, without offering even a clue as to what the limits on that tolerance may be. We are told simply that Kaiser's racially discriminatory admission quota "falls on the permissible side of the line." Ante, at 208. By going not merely beyond, but directly against Title VII's language and legislative history, the Court has sown the wind. Later courts will face the impossible task of reaping the whirlwind.

QUESTIONS AND DISCUSSION POINTS

1. What constitutional questions does this case raise?

2. Can you separate the historical from the legal questions?

3. What weight, if any, do you accord the Congressional debates in reaching a decision about what the statute means in this case?

4. Does the fact that the defendant (U.S. Steel) is a private company make any difference to you?

5. Assume that Congress chose a "color-blind" conception of equality because the members believed that would lead to greater Black representation in the work force. If that assumption did not come to pass, what role should that fact play in the Court's decision in this case?

6. Do the Majority and the Dissent have different "theories" of statutory interpretation? What are some of those differences and how do those differences make a difference in the outcome of the case?

~

MANUEL LUJAN, JR., Secretary of the Interior, Petitioner,
v. DEFENDERS OF WILDLIFE, et al.
Supreme Court of the United States
504 U.S. 555 (1992)

SCALIA, J., announced the judgment of the Court and delivered the opinion of the Court with respect to Parts I, II, III-A, and IV, in which REHNQUIST, C.J., and WHITE, KENNEDY, SOUTER, and THOMAS, JJ., joined, and an opinion with respect to Part III-B, in which REHNQUIST, C.J., and WHITE and THOMAS, JJ., joined. KENNEDY, J., filed an opinion concurring in part and concurring in the judgment, in which SOUTER, J., joined, post, p. 2146. STEVENS, J., filed an opinion concurring in the judgment, post, p. 2147. BLACKMUN, J., filed a dissenting opinion, in which O'CONNOR, J., joined, post, p. 2151.

Justice SCALIA delivered the opinion of the Court with respect to Parts I,

II, III-A, and IV, and an opinion with respect to Part III-B, in which THE CHIEF JUSTICE, Justice WHITE, and Justice THOMAS join.

This case involves a challenge to a rule promulgated by the Secretary of the Interior interpreting s 7 of the Endangered Species Act of 1973 (ESA), 87 Stat. 884, 892, as amended, 16 U.S.C. s 1536, in such fashion as to render it applicable only to actions within the United States or on the high seas. The preliminary issue, and the only one we reach, is whether respondents here, plaintiffs below, have standing to seek judicial review of the rule.

I.

The ESA, 87 Stat. 884, as amended, 16 U.S.C. s 1531 et seq., seeks to protect species of animals against threats to their continuing existence caused by man. See generally TVA v. Hill, 437 U.S. 153, 98 S.Ct. 2279, 57 L.Ed.2d 117 (1978). The ESA instructs the Secretary of the Interior to promulgate by regulation a list of those species which are either endangered or threatened under enumerated criteria, and to define the critical habitat of these species. 16 U.S.C. ss 1533, 1536. Section 7(a)(2) of the Act then provides, in pertinent part:

> Each Federal agency shall, in consultation with and with the assistance of the Secretary [of the Interior], insure that any action authorized, funded, or carried out by such agency . . . is not likely to jeopardize the continued existence of any endangered species or threatened species or result in the destruction or adverse modification of habitat of such species which is determined by the Secretary, after consultation as appropriate with affected States, to be critical.
>
> —16 U.S.C. § 1536(a)(2).

In 1978, the Fish and Wildlife Service (FWS) and the National Marine Fisheries Service (NMFS), on behalf of the Secretary of the Interior and the Secretary of Commerce respectively, promulgated a joint regulation stating that the obligations imposed by § 7(a)(2) extend to actions taken in foreign nations. 43 Fed.Reg. 874 (1978). The next year, however, the Interior Department began to reexamine its position. A revised joint regulation, reinterpreting s 7(a)(2) to require consultation only for actions taken in the United States or on the high seas, was proposed in 1983, 48 Fed.Reg. 29990, and promulgated in 1986, 51 Fed.Reg. 19926; 50 CFR 402.01 (1991).

Shortly thereafter, respondents, organizations dedicated to wildlife conservation and other environmental causes, filed this action against the Secretary of the Interior, seeking a declaratory judgment that the new regulation is in error as to the geographic scope of § 7(a)(2) and an injunction requiring the Secretary to promulgate a new regulation restoring the initial interpretation. The District Court granted the Secretary's motion to dismiss for lack of standing. Defenders of Wildlife v. Hodel, 658 F.Supp. 43, 47–48 (Minn.1987). The Court of Appeals for the Eighth Circuit reversed by a divided vote. Defenders of Wildlife v. Hodel, 851 F.2d 1035 (1988). On remand, the Secretary moved for summary judgment on the standing issue, and respondents moved for summary judgment on the merits. The District Court denied the Secretary's motion, on the ground that the Eighth Circuit had already determined the standing question in this case; it granted respondents' merits motion, and ordered the Secretary to publish a revised regulation. Defenders of Wildlife v. Hodel, 707 F.Supp. 1082 (Minn.1989).

The Eighth Circuit affirmed. 911 F.2d 117 (1990). We granted certiorari, 500 U.S. 915, 111 S.Ct. 2008, 114 L.Ed.2d 97 (1991).

II.

While the Constitution of the United States divides all power conferred upon the Federal Government into "legislative Powers," Art. I, s 1, "[t]he executive Power," Art. II, § 1, and "[t]he judicial Power," Art. III, § 1, it does not attempt to define those terms. To be sure, it limits the jurisdiction of federal courts to "Cases" and "Controversies," but an executive inquiry can bear the name "case" (the Hoffa case) and a legislative dispute can bear the name "controversy" (the Smoot-Hawley controversy). Obviously, then, the Constitution's central mechanism of separation of powers depends largely upon common understanding of what activities are appropriate to legislatures, to executives, and to courts.

In The Federalist No. 48, Madison expressed the view that "[i]t is not infrequently a question of real nicety in legislative bodies whether the operation of a particular measure will, or will not, extend beyond the legislative sphere," whereas "the executive power [is] restrained within a narrower compass and . . . more simple in its nature," and "the judiciary [is] described by landmarks still less uncertain." The Federalist No. 48, p. 256 (Carey and McClellan eds. 1990). One of those landmarks, setting apart the "Cases" and "Controversies" that are of the justiciable sort referred to in Article III—"serv[ing] to identify those disputes which are appropriately resolved through the judicial process," Whitmore v. Arkansas, 495 U.S. 149, 155, 110 S.Ct. 1717, 1722, 109 L.Ed.2d 135 (1990)—is the doctrine of standing. Though some of its elements express merely prudential considerations that are

part of judicial self-government, the core component of standing is an essential and unchanging part of the case-or-controversy requirement of Article III. See, e.g., Allen v. Wright, 468 U.S. 737, 751, 104 S.Ct. 3315, 3324, 82 L.Ed.2d 556 (1984).

Over the years, our cases have established that the irreducible constitutional minimum of standing contains three elements. First, the plaintiff must have suffered an "injury in fact"—an invasion of a legally protected interest which is (a) concrete and particularized, see id., at 756, 104 S.Ct., at 3327; Warth v. Seldin, 422 U.S. 490, 508, 95 S.Ct. 2197, 2210, 45 L.Ed.2d 343 (1975); Sierra Club v. Morton, 405 U.S. 727, 740–741, n. 16, 92 S.Ct. 1361, 1368–1369, n. 16, 31 L.Ed.2d 636 (1972)[1]; and (b) "actual or imminent, not 'conjectural' or 'hypothetical,' " Whitmore, supra, 495 U.S., at 155, 110 S.Ct., at 1723 (quoting Los Angeles v. Lyons, 461 U.S. 95, 102, 103 S.Ct. 1660, 1665, 75 L.Ed.2d 675 (1983)). Second, there must be a causal connection between the injury and the conduct complained of—the injury has to be "fairly . . . trace[able] to the challenged action of the defendant, and not . . . th[e] result [of] the independent action of some third party not before the court." Simon v. Eastern Ky. Welfare Rights Organization, 426 U.S. 26, 41–42, 96 S.Ct. 1917, 1926, 48 L.Ed.2d 450 (1976). Third, it must be "likely," as opposed to merely "speculative," that the injury will be "redressed by a favorable decision." Id., at 38, 43, 96 S.Ct., at 1924, 1926.

The party invoking federal jurisdiction bears the burden of establishing these elements. See FW/PBS, Inc. v. Dal-

---

1. By particularized, we mean that the injury must affect the plaintiff in a personal and individual way.

las, 493 U.S. 215, 231, 110 S.Ct. 596, 608, 107 L.Ed.2d 603 (1990); Warth, supra, 422 U.S., at 508, 95 S.Ct., at 2210. Since they are not mere pleading requirements but rather an indispensable part of the plaintiff's case, each element must be supported in the same way as any other matter on which the plaintiff bears the burden of proof, i.e., with the manner and degree of evidence required at the successive stages of the litigation. See Lujan v. National Wildlife Federation, 497 U.S. 871, 883–889, 110 S.Ct. 3177, 3185–3189, 111 L.Ed.2d 695 (1990); Gladstone, Realtors v. Village of Bellwood, 441 U.S. 91, 114–115, and n. 31, 99 S.Ct. 1601, 1614–1615, and n. 31, 60 L.Ed.2d 66 (1979); Simon, supra, 426 U.S., at 45, n. 25, 96 S.Ct., at 1927, and n. 25; Warth, supra, 422 U.S., at 527, and n. 6, 95 S.Ct., at 2219, and n. 6 (Brennan, J., dissenting). At the pleading stage, general factual allegations of injury resulting from the defendant's conduct may suffice, for on a motion to dismiss we "presum[e] that general allegations embrace those specific facts that are necessary to support the claim." National Wildlife Federation, supra, 497 U.S., at 889, 110 S.Ct., at 3189. In response to a summary judgment motion, however, the plaintiff can no longer rest on such "mere allegations," but must "set forth" by affidavit or other evidence "specific facts," Fed.Rule Civ.Proc. 56(e), which for purposes of the summary judgment motion will be taken to be true. And at the final stage, those facts (if controverted) must be "supported adequately by the evidence adduced at trial." Gladstone, supra, 441 U.S., at 115, n. 31, 99 S.Ct., at 1616, n. 31. When the suit is one challenging the legality of government action or inaction, the nature and extent of facts that must be averred (at the summary judgment stage) or proved (at the trial stage) in order to establish standing depends considerably upon whether the plaintiff is himself an object of the action (or forgone action) at issue. If he is, there is ordinarily little question that the action or inaction has caused him injury, and that a judgment preventing or requiring the action will redress it. When, however, as in this case, a plaintiff's asserted injury arises from the government's allegedly unlawful regulation (or lack of regulation) of someone else, much more is needed. In that circumstance, causation and redressability ordinarily hinge on the response of the regulated (or regulable) third party to the government action or inaction—and perhaps on the response of others as well. The existence of one or more of the essential elements of standing "depends on the unfettered choices made by independent actors not before the courts and whose exercise of broad and legitimate discretion the courts cannot presume either to control or to predict," ASARCO Inc. v. Kadish, 490 U.S. 605, 615, 109 S.Ct. 2037, 2044, 104 L.Ed.2d 696 (1989) (opinion of KENNEDY, J.); see also Simon, supra, 426 U.S., at 41–42, 96 S.Ct., at 1925, 1926; and it becomes the burden of the plaintiff to adduce facts showing that those choices have been or will be made in such manner as to produce causation and permit redressability of injury. E.g., Warth, supra, 422 U.S., at 505, 95 S.Ct., at 2208. Thus, when the plaintiff is not himself the object of the government action or inaction he challenges, standing is not precluded, but it is ordinarily "substantially more difficult" to establish. Allen, supra, 468 U.S., at 758, 104 S.Ct., at 3328; Simon, supra, 426 U.S., at 44–45, 96 S.Ct., at 1927; Warth, supra, 422 U.S., at 505, 95 S.Ct., at 2208.

III.

We think the Court of Appeals failed to apply the foregoing principles in denying the Secretary's motion for summary judgment. Respondents had not made the requisite demonstration of (at least) injury and redressability.

A.

Respondents' claim to injury is that the lack of consultation with respect to certain funded activities abroad "increas[es] the rate of extinction of endangered and threatened species." Complaint P 5, App. 13. Of course, the desire to use or observe an animal species, even for purely esthetic purposes, is undeniably a cognizable interest for purpose of standing. See, e.g., Sierra Club v. Morton, 405 U.S., at 734, 92 S.Ct., at 1366. "But the 'injury in fact' test requires more than an injury to a cognizable interest. It requires that the party seeking review be himself among the injured." Id., at 734–735, 92 S.Ct., at 1366. To survive the Secretary's summary judgment motion, respondents had to submit affidavits or other evidence showing, through specific facts, not only that listed species were in fact being threatened by funded activities abroad, but also that one or more of respondents' members would thereby be "directly" affected apart from their " 'special interest' in th[e] subject." Id., at 735, 739, 92 S.Ct., at 1366, 1368. See generally Hunt v. Washington State Apple Advertising Comm'n, 432 U.S. 333, 343, 97 S.Ct. 2434, 2441, 53 L.Ed.2d 383 (1977).

With respect to this aspect of the case, the Court of Appeals focused on the affidavits of two Defenders' members— Joyce Kelly and Amy Skilbred. Ms. Kelly stated that she traveled to Egypt in 1986 and "observed the traditional habitat of

the endangered nile crocodile there and intend[s] to do so again, and hope[s] to observe the crocodile directly," and that she "will suffer harm in fact as the result of [the] American . . . role . . . in overseeing the rehabilitation of the Aswan High Dam on the Nile . . . and [in] develop [ing] . . . Egypt's . . . Master Water Plan." App. 101. Ms. Skilbred averred that she traveled to Sri Lanka in 1981 and "observed th[e] habitat" of "endangered species such as the Asian elephant and the leopard" at what is now the site of the Mahaweli project funded by the Agency for International Development (AID), although she "was unable to see any of the endangered species"; "this development project," she continued, "will seriously reduce endangered, threatened, and endemic species habitat including areas that I visited . . . [, which] may severely shorten the future of these species"; that threat, she concluded, harmed her because she "intend[s] to return to Sri Lanka in the future and hope[s] to be more fortunate in spotting at least the endangered elephant and leopard." Id., at 145–146. When Ms. Skilbred was asked at a subsequent deposition if and when she had any plans to return to Sri Lanka, she reiterated that "I intend to go back to Sri Lanka," but confessed that she had no current plans: "I don't know [when]. There is a civil war going on right now. I don't know. Not next year, I will say. In the future." Id., at 318.

We shall assume for the sake of argument that these affidavits contain facts showing that certain agency-funded projects threaten listed species—though that is questionable. They plainly contain no facts, however, showing how damage to the species will produce "imminent" injury to Mses. Kelly and Skilbred. That the women "had visited" the areas of the projects before the projects commenced proves nothing. As we have said in a related context, " 'Past exposure to illegal conduct does not in itself show a present case or controversy regarding injunctive relief . . . if unaccompanied by any continuing, present adverse effects.' " Lyons, 461 U.S., at 102, 103 S.Ct., at 1665 (quoting O'Shea v. Littleton, 414 U.S. 488, 495–496, 94 S.Ct. 669, 676, 38 L.Ed.2d 674 (1974)). And the affiants' profession of an "inten[t]" to return to the places they had visited before—where they will presumably, this time, be deprived of the opportunity to observe animals of the endangered species—is simply not enough. Such "some day" intentions—without any description of concrete plans, or indeed even any specification of when the some day will be—do not support a finding of the "actual or imminent" injury that our cases require. See supra, at 2136.

Besides relying upon the Kelly and Skilbred affidavits, respondents propose a series of novel standing theories. The first, inelegantly styled "ecosystem nexus," proposes that any person who uses any part of a "contiguous ecosystem" adversely affected by a funded activity has standing even if the activity is located a great distance away. This approach, as the Court of Appeals correctly observed, is inconsistent with our opinion in National Wildlife Federation, which held that a plaintiff claiming injury from environmental damage must use the area affected by the challenged activity and not an area roughly "in the vicinity" of it. 497 U.S., at 887–889, 110 S.Ct., at 3188–3189; see also Sierra Club, 405 U.S., at 735, 92 S.Ct., at 1366. It makes no difference that the general-purpose section of the ESA states that the Act was intended in part "to provide a means whereby the ecosystems upon which endangered species and threatened species depend may be conserved," 16 U.S.C. § 1531(b). To say that the Act protects ecosystems is not to say that the Act creates (if it were possible) rights of action in persons who have not been injured in fact, that is, persons who use portions of an ecosystem not perceptibly affected by the unlawful action in question.

Respondents' other theories are called, alas, the "animal nexus" approach, whereby anyone who has an interest in studying or seeing the endangered animals anywhere on the globe has standing; and the "vocational nexus" approach, under which anyone with a professional interest in such animals can sue. Under these theories, anyone who goes to see Asian elephants in the Bronx Zoo, and anyone who is a keeper of Asian elephants in the Bronx Zoo, has standing to sue because the Director of the Agency for International Development (AID) did not consult with the Secretary regarding the AID-funded project in Sri Lanka. This is beyond all reason. Standing is not "an ingenious academic exercise in the conceivable," United States v. Students Challenging Regulatory Agency Procedures (SCRAP), 412 U.S. 669, 688, 93 S.Ct. 2405, 2416, 37 L.Ed.2d 254 (1973), but as we have said requires, at the summary judgment stage, a factual showing of perceptible harm. It is clear that the person who observes or works with a particular animal threatened by a federal decision is facing perceptible harm, since the very subject of his interest will no longer exist. It is even plausible—though it goes to the outermost limit of plausibility—to think that a person who observes or works with animals of a particular species in the very area of the world where that species is threatened by a federal decision is facing such harm, since some animals that might have been the subject of his interest will no longer exist, see Japan Whaling Assn. v. American Cetacean Society, 478 U.S. 221, 231, n. 4, 106 S.Ct. 2860, 2866, n. 4, 92 L.Ed.2d 166 (1986). It goes beyond the limit, however, and into pure speculation and fantasy, to say that anyone who observes or works with an endangered species, anywhere in the world, is appreciably harmed by a single project affecting some portion of that species with which he has no more specific connection.[2]

---

2. The dissent embraces each of respondents' "nexus" theories, rejecting this portion of our analysis because it is "unable to see how the distant location of the destruction necessarily (for purposes of ruling at summary judgment) mitigates the harm" to the plaintiff. Post, at 2154. But summary judgment must be entered "against a party who fails to make a showing sufficient to establish the existence of an element essential to that party's case, and on which that party will bear the burden of proof at trial." Celotex Corp. v. Catrett, 477 U.S. 317, 322, 106 S.Ct. 2548, 2552, 91 L.Ed.2d 265 (1986). Respondents had to adduce facts, therefore, on the basis of which it could reasonably be found that concrete injury to their members was, as our cases require, "certainly impending." The dissent may be correct that the geographic remoteness of those members (here in the United States) from Sri Lanka and Aswan does not "necessarily" prevent such a finding—but it assuredly does so when no further facts have been brought forward (and respondents have produced none) showing that the impact upon animals in those distant places will in some fashion be reflected here. The dissent's position to the contrary reduces to the notion that distance never prevents harm, a proposition we categorically reject. It cannot be that a person with an interest in an animal automatically has standing to enjoin federal threats to that species of animal, anywhere in the world. Were that the case, the plaintiff in Sierra Club, for example, could have avoided the necessity of establishing anyone's use of Mineral King by merely identifying one of its members interested in an endangered species of flora or fauna at that location. Justice BLACKMAN's accusation that a special rule is being crafted for "environmental claims," post, at 2154, is correct, but he is the craftsman.

Besides failing to show injury, respondents failed to demonstrate redressability. Instead of attacking the separate decisions to fund particular projects allegedly causing them harm, respondents chose to challenge a more generalized level of Government action (rules regarding consultation), the invalidation of which would affect all overseas projects. This programmatic approach has obvious practical advantages, but also obvious difficulties insofar as proof of causation or redressability is concerned. As we have said in another context, "suits challenging, not specifically identifiable Government violations of law, but the particular programs agencies establish to carry out their legal obligations . . . [are], even when premised on allegations of several instances of violations of law, . . . rarely if ever appropriate for federal-court adjudication." Allen, 468 U.S., at 759–760, 104 S.Ct., at 3329.

The most obvious problem in the present case is redressability. Since the agencies funding the projects were not parties to the case, the District Court could accord relief only against the Secretary: He could be ordered to revise his regulation to require consultation for foreign projects. But this would not remedy respondents' alleged injury unless the funding agencies were bound by the Secretary's regulation, which is very much an open question. Whereas in other contexts the ESA is quite explicit as to the Secretary's controlling authority, see, e.g., 16 U.S.C. § 1533(a)(1) ("The Secretary shall" promulgate regulations determining endangered species); § 1535(d)(1) ("The Secretary is authorized to provide financial assistance to any State"), with respect to consultation the initiative, and hence arguably the initial responsibility for determining statutory necessity, lies with the agencies, see § 1536(a)(2) ("Each Federal agency shall, in consultation with and with the assistance of the Secretary, insure that any" funded action is not likely to jeopardize endangered or threatened species) (emphasis added). When the Secretary promulgated the regulation at issue here, he thought it was binding on the agencies, see 51 Fed.Reg. 19928 (1986). The Solicitor General, however, has repudiated that position here, and the agencies themselves apparently deny the Secretary's authority. (During the period when the Secretary took the view that § 7(a)(2) did apply abroad, AID and FWS engaged in a running controversy over whether consultation was required with respect to the Mahaweli project, AID insisting that consultation applied only to domestic actions.)

Respondents assert that this legal uncertainty did not affect redressability (and hence standing) because the District Court itself could resolve the issue of the Secretary's authority as a necessary part of its standing inquiry. Assuming that it is appropriate to resolve an issue of law such as this in connection with a threshold standing inquiry, resolution by the District Court would not have remedied respondents' alleged injury anyway, because it would not have been binding upon the agencies. They were not parties to the suit, and there is no reason they should be obliged to honor an incidental legal determination the suit produced. The Court of Appeals tried to finesse this problem by simply proclaiming that "[w]e are satisfied that an injunction requiring the Secretary to publish [respondents' desired] regulatio[n] . . . would result in consultation." Defenders of Wildlife, 851 F.2d, at 1042, 1043–1044. We do not know what would justify that confidence, particularly when the Justice De-

partment (presumably after consultation with the agencies) has taken the position that the regulation is not binding. The short of the matter is that redress of the only injury in fact respondents complain of requires action (termination of funding until consultation) by the individual funding agencies; and any relief the District Court could have provided in this suit against the Secretary was not likely to produce that action.

A further impediment to redressability is the fact that the agencies generally supply only a fraction of the funding for a foreign project. AID, for example, has provided less than 10% of the funding for the Mahaweli project. Respondents have produced nothing to indicate that the projects they have named will either be suspended, or do less harm to listed species, if that fraction is eliminated. As in Simon, 426 U.S., at 43–44, 96 S.Ct., at 1926–1927, it is entirely conjectural whether the nonagency activity that affects respondents will be altered or affected by the agency activity they seek to achieve. There is no standing.

IV.

The Court of Appeals found that respondents had standing for an additional reason: because they had suffered a "procedural injury." The so-called "citizen-suit" provision of the ESA provides, in pertinent part, that "any person may commence a civil suit on his own behalf (A) to enjoin any person, including the United States and any other governmental instrumentality or agency . . . who is alleged to be in violation of any provision of this chapter." 16 U.S.C. § 1540(g). The court held that, because § 7(a)(2) requires interagency consultation, the citizen-suit provision creates a "procedural righ[t]" to consultation in all "persons"—so that anyone can file suit in federal court to challenge the Secretary's (or presumably any other official's) failure to follow the assertedly correct consultative procedure, notwithstanding his or her inability to allege any discrete injury flowing from that failure. 911 F.2d, at 121–122. To understand the remarkable nature of this holding one must be clear about what it does not rest upon: This is not a case where plaintiffs are seeking to enforce a procedural requirement the disregard of which could impair a separate concrete interest of theirs (e.g., the procedural requirement for a hearing prior to denial of their license application, or the procedural requirement for an environmental impact statement before a federal facility is constructed next door to them). Nor is it simply a case where concrete injury has been suffered by many persons, as in mass fraud or mass tort situations. Nor, finally, is it the unusual case in which Congress has created a concrete private interest in the outcome of a suit against a private party for the government's benefit, by providing a cash bounty for the victorious plaintiff. Rather, the court held that the injury-in-fact requirement had been satisfied by congressional conferral upon all persons of an abstract, self-contained, noninstrumental "right" to have the Executive observe the procedures required by law. We reject this view.

We have consistently held that a plaintiff raising only a generally available grievance about government— claiming only harm to his and every citizen's interest in proper application of the Constitution and laws, and seeking relief that no more directly and tangibly benefits him than it does the public at large—does not state an Article III case or controversy. For example, in Fairchild

v. Hughes, 258 U.S. 126, 129–130, 42 S.Ct. 274, 275, 66 L.Ed. 499 (1922), we dismissed a suit challenging the propriety of the process by which the Nineteenth Amendment was ratified. Justice Brandeis wrote for the Court:

> "[This is] not a case within the meaning of . . . Article III. . . . Plaintiff has [asserted] only the right, possessed by every citizen, to require that the Government be administered according to law and that the public moneys be not wasted. Obviously this general right does not entitle a private citizen to institute in the federal courts a suit. . . ." Ibid.

In Massachusetts v. Mellon, 262 U.S. 447, 43 S.Ct. 597, 67 L.Ed. 1078 (1923), we dismissed for lack of Article III standing a taxpayer suit challenging the propriety of certain federal expenditures. We said:

> The party who invokes the power [of judicial review] must be able to show not only that the statute is invalid but that he has sustained or is immediately in danger of sustaining some direct injury as the result of its enforcement, and not merely that he suffers in some indefinite way in common with people generally. . . . Here the parties plaintiff have no such case. . . . [T]heir complaint . . . is merely that officials of the executive department of the government are executing and will execute an act of Congress asserted to be unconstitutional; and this we are asked to prevent. To do so would be not to decide a judicial controversy, but to assume a position of authority over the governmental acts of another and co-equal department, an authority which plainly we do not possess.
> —Id., at 488–489, 43 S.Ct., at 601

In Ex parte Levitt, 302 U.S. 633, 58 S.Ct. 1, 82 L.Ed. 493 (1937), we dismissed a suit contending that Justice Black's appointment to this Court violated the Ineligibility Clause, Art. I, § 6, cl. 2. "It is an established principle," we said, "that to entitle a private individual to invoke the judicial power to determine the validity of executive or legislative action he must show that he has sustained or is immediately in danger of sustaining a direct injury as the result of that action and it is not sufficient that he has merely a general interest common to all members of the public." 302 U.S., at 634, 58 S.Ct., at 1. See also Doremus v. Board of Ed. of Hawthorne, 342 U.S. 429, 433–434, 72 S.Ct. 394, 396–397, 96 L.Ed. 475 (1952) (dismissing taxpayer action on the basis of Mellon).

We hold that respondents lack standing to bring this action and that the Court of Appeals erred in denying the summary judgment motion filed by the United States. The opinion of the Court of Appeals is hereby reversed, and the cause is remanded for proceedings consistent with this opinion. It is so ordered.

Justice KENNEDY, with whom Justice SOUTER joins, concurring in part and concurring in the judgment.

Although I agree with the essential parts of the Court's analysis, I write separately to make several observations. I agree with the Court's conclusion in Part III-A that, on the record before us, respondents have failed to demonstrate that they themselves are "among the injured." Sierra Club v. Morton, 405 U.S. 727, 735, 92 S.Ct. 1361, 1366, 31 L.Ed.2d 636 (1972). This component of the standing inquiry is not satisfied unless

> [p]laintiffs . . . demonstrate a "personal stake in the outcome." . . . Abstract injury is not enough. The plaintiff must

show that he "has sustained or is immediately in danger of sustaining some direct injury" as the result of the challenged official conduct and the injury or threat of injury must be both "real and immediate," not "conjectural" or "hypothetical."
> —Los Angeles v. Lyons, 461 U.S. 95, 101–102, 103 S.Ct. 1660, 1665, 75 L.Ed.2d 675 (1983) (citations omitted)

While it may seem trivial to require that Mses. Kelly and Skilbred acquire airline tickets to the project sites or announce a date certain upon which they will return, see ante, at 2138, this is not a case where it is reasonable to assume that the affiants will be using the sites on a regular basis, see Sierra Club v. Morton, supra, 405 U.S., at 735, n. 8, 92 S.Ct., at 1366, n. 8, nor do the affiants claim to have visited the sites since the projects commenced. With respect to the Court's discussion of respondents' "ecosystem nexus," "animal nexus," and "vocational nexus" theories, ante, at 2139–2140, I agree that on this record respondents' showing is insufficient to establish standing on any of these bases. I am not willing to foreclose the possibility, however, that in different circumstances a nexus theory similar to those proffered here might support a claim to standing. See Japan Whaling Assn. v. American Cetacean Society, 478 U.S. 221, 231, n. 4, 106 S.Ct. 2860, 2866, n. 4, 92 L.Ed.2d 166 (1986) ("[R]espondents . . . undoubtedly have alleged a sufficient 'injury in fact' in that the whale watching and studying of their members will be adversely affected by continued whale harvesting").

In light of the conclusion that respondents have not demonstrated a concrete injury here sufficient to support standing under our precedents, I would not reach the issue of redressability that is discussed by the plurality in Part III-B.

I also join Part IV of the Court's opinion with the following observations. As Government programs and policies become more complex and farreaching, we must be sensitive to the articulation of new rights of action that do not have clear analogs in our common-law tradition. Modern litigation has progressed far from the paradigm of Marbury suing Madison to get his commission, Marbury v. Madison, 5 U.S. (1 Cranch) 137, 2 L.Ed. 60 (1803), or Ogden seeking an injunction to halt Gibbons' steamboat operations, Gibbons v. Ogden, 22 U.S. (9 Wheat.) 1, 6 L.Ed. 23 (1824). In my view, Congress has the power to define injuries and articulate chains of causation that will give rise to a case or controversy where none existed before, and I do not read the Court's opinion to suggest a contrary view. See Warth v. Seldin, 422 U.S. 490, 500, 95 S.Ct. 2197, 2205, 45 L.Ed.2d 343 (1975); ante, at 2145–2146. In exercising this power, however, Congress must at the very least identify the injury it seeks to vindicate and relate the injury to the class of persons entitled to bring suit. The citizen-suit provision of the Endangered Species Act does not meet these minimal requirements, because while the statute purports to confer a right on "any person . . . to enjoin . . . the United States and any other governmental instrumentality or agency . . . who is alleged to be in violation of any provision of this chapter," it does not of its own force establish that there is an injury in "any person" by virtue of any "violation." 16 U.S.C. § 1540(g)(1)(A).

The Court's holding that there is an outer limit to the power of Congress to confer rights of action is a direct and necessary consequence of the case and controversy limitations found in Article III. I agree that it would exceed those limitations if, at the behest of Congress and in the absence of any showing of concrete injury, we were to entertain citizen suits to vindicate the public's nonconcrete interest in the proper administration of the laws. While it does not matter how many persons have been injured by the challenged action, the party bringing suit must show that the action injures him in a concrete and personal way. This requirement is not just an empty formality. It preserves the vitality of the adversarial process by assuring both that the parties before the court have an actual, as opposed to professed, stake in the outcome, and that "the legal questions presented . . . will be resolved, not in the rarified atmosphere of a debating society, but in a concrete factual context conducive to a realistic appreciation of the consequences of judicial action." Valley Forge Christian College v. Americans United for Separation of Church and State, Inc., 454 U.S. 464, 472, 102 S.Ct. 752, 758, 70 L.Ed.2d 700 (1982). In addition, the requirement of concrete injury confines the Judicial Branch to its proper, limited role in the constitutional framework of Government.

An independent judiciary is held to account through its open proceedings and its reasoned judgments. In this process it is essential for the public to know what persons or groups are invoking the judicial power, the reasons that they have brought suit, and whether their claims are vindicated or denied. The concrete injury requirement helps assure that there can be an answer to these questions; and, as the Court's opinion is careful to show, that is part of the constitutional design.

With these observations, I concur in Parts I, II, III-A, and IV of the Court's opinion and in the judgment of the Court.

Justice STEVENS, concurring in the judgment.

Because I am not persuaded that Congress intended the consultation requirement in § 7(a)(2) of the Endangered Species Act of 1973 (ESA), 16 U.S.C. § 1536(a)(2), to apply to activities in foreign countries, I concur in the judgment of reversal. I do not, however, agree with the Court's conclusion that respondents lack standing because the threatened injury to their interest in protecting the environment and studying endangered species is not "imminent." Nor do I agree with the plurality's additional conclusion that respondents' injury is not "redressable" in this litigation.

I.

In my opinion a person who has visited the critical habitat of an endangered species has a professional interest in preserving the species and its habitat, and intends to revisit them in the future has standing to challenge agency action that threatens their destruction. Congress has found that a wide variety of endangered species of fish, wildlife, and plants are of "aesthetic, ecological, educational, historical, recreational, and scientific value to the Nation and its people." 16 U.S.C. § 1531(a)(3). Given that finding, we have no license to demean the importance of the interest that particular individuals may have in observing any species or its habitat, whether those individuals are motivated by esthetic enjoyment, an interest in professional research, or an economic interest in preservation of the species. Indeed, this Court has often held that injuries to such interests are sufficient to confer standing, and the Court reiterates that holding today. See ante, at 2137. The Court nevertheless concludes that respondents have not suffered "in-

jury in fact" because they have not shown that the harm to the endangered species will produce "imminent" injury to them. I disagree. An injury to an individual's interest in studying or enjoying a species and its natural habitat occurs when someone (whether it be the Government or a private party) takes action that harms that species and habitat. In my judgment, therefore, the "imminence" of such an injury should be measured by the timing and likelihood of the threatened environmental harm, rather than—as the Court seems to suggest, ante, at 2138–2139, and n. 2—by the time that might elapse between the present and the time when the individuals would visit the area if no such injury should occur.

To understand why this approach is correct and consistent with our precedent, it is necessary to consider the purpose of the standing doctrine. Concerned about "the proper—and properly limited—role of the courts in a democratic society," we have long held that "Art. III judicial power exists only to redress or otherwise to protect against injury to the complaining party." Warth v. Seldin, 422 U.S. 490, 498–499, 95 S.Ct. 2197, 2205, 45 L.Ed.2d 343 (1975). The plaintiff must have a "personal stake in the outcome" sufficient to "assure that concrete adverseness which sharpens the presentation of issues upon which the court so largely depends for illumination of difficult . . . questions." Baker v. Carr, 369 U.S. 186, 204, 82 S.Ct. 691, 703, 7 L.Ed.2d 663 (1962). For that reason, "[a]bstract injury is not enough. It must be alleged that the plaintiff 'has sustained or is immediately in danger of sustaining some direct injury' as the result of the challenged statute or official conduct. . . . The injury or threat of injury must be both 'real and immediate,' not 'conjectural,' or 'hypothetical.' " O'Shea v. Littleton, 414 U.S. 488, 494, 94 S.Ct. 669, 675, 38 L.Ed.2d 674 (1974) (quoting Golden v. Zwickler, 394 U.S. 103, 109–110, 89 S.Ct. 956, 960, 22 L.Ed.2d 113 (1969)).

Consequently, we have denied standing to plaintiffs whose likelihood of suffering any concrete adverse effect from the challenged action was speculative. See, e.g., Whitmore v. Arkansas, 495 U.S. 149, 158–159, 110 S.Ct. 1717, 1724–1725, 109 L.Ed.2d 135 (1990); Los Angeles v. Lyons, 461 U.S. 95, 105, 103 S.Ct. 1660, 1665, 75 L.Ed.2d 675 (1983); O'Shea, 414 U.S., at 497, 94 S.Ct., at 676. In this case, however, the likelihood that respondents will be injured by the destruction of the endangered species is not speculative. If respondents are genuinely interested in the preservation of the endangered species and intend to study or observe these animals in the future, their injury will occur as soon as the animals are destroyed. Thus the only potential source of "speculation" in this case is whether respondents' intent to study or observe the animals is genuine. In my view, Joyce Kelly and Amy Skilbred have introduced sufficient evidence to negate petitioner's contention that their claims of injury are "speculative" or "conjectural." As Justice BLACKMUN explains, post, at 2152–2153, a reasonable finder of fact could conclude, from their past visits, their professional backgrounds, and their affidavits and deposition testimony, that Ms. Kelly and Ms. Skilbred will return to the project sites and, consequently, will be injured by the destruction of the endangered species and critical habitat.

The plurality also concludes that respondents' injuries are not redressable in this litigation for two reasons. First, respondents have sought only a declaratory judgment that the Secretary of the Interior's regulation interpreting § 7(a)(2) to require consultation only for agency actions in the United States or on the high seas is invalid and an injunction requiring him to promulgate a new regulation requiring consultation for agency actions abroad as well. But, the plurality opines, even if respondents succeed and a new regulation is promulgated, there is no guarantee that federal agencies that are not parties to this case will actually consult with the Secretary. Furthermore, the plurality continues, respondents have not demonstrated that federal agencies can influence the behavior of the foreign governments where the affected projects are located. Thus, even if the agencies consult with the Secretary and terminate funding for foreign projects, the foreign governments might nonetheless pursue the projects and jeopardize the endangered species. See ante, at 2142. Neither of these reasons is persuasive.

We must presume that if this Court holds that § 7(a)(2) requires consultation, all affected agencies would abide by that interpretation and engage in the requisite consultations. Certainly the Executive Branch cannot be heard to argue that an authoritative construction of the governing statute by this Court may simply be ignored by any agency head. Moreover, if Congress has required consultation between agencies, we must presume that such consultation will have a serious purpose that is likely to produce tangible results. As Justice BLACKMUN explains, it is not mere speculation to think that foreign governments, when faced with the threatened withdrawal of United States assistance, will modify their projects to mitigate the harm to endangered species.

II.

Although I believe that respondents have standing, I nevertheless concur in the judgment of reversal because I am persuaded that the Government is correct in its submission that § 7(a)(2) does not apply to activities in foreign countries. As with all questions of statutory construction, the question whether a statute applies extraterritorially is one of congressional intent. Foley Bros., Inc. v. Filardo, 336 U.S. 281, 284–285, 69 S.Ct. 575, 577, 93 L.Ed. 680 (1949). We normally assume that "Congress is primarily concerned with domestic conditions," id., at 285, 69 S.Ct., at 577, and therefore presume that " 'legislation of Congress, unless a contrary intent appears, is meant to apply only within the territorial jurisdiction of the United States,' " EEOC v. Arabian American Oil Co., 499 U.S. 244, 248, 111 S.Ct. 1227,1230, 113 L.Ed.2d 274 (1991) (quoting Foley Bros., 336 U.S., at 285, 69 S.Ct., at 577). Section 7(a)(2) provides, in relevant part:

> Each Federal agency shall, in consultation with and with the assistance of the Secretary [of the Interior or Commerce, as appropriate], insure that any action authorized, funded, or carried out by such agency (hereinafter in this section referred to as an 'agency action') is not likely to jeopardize the continued existence of any endangered species or threatened species or result in the destruction or adverse modification of habitat of such species which is determined by the Secretary, after consultation as appropriate with affected States, to be critical, unless such agency has been granted an exemption for such action by the Committee pursuant to subsection (h) of this section. . . .
> —16 U.S.C. § 1536(a)(2)

Nothing in this text indicates that the section applies in foreign countries. Indeed,

the only geographic reference in the section is in the "critical habitat" clause, which mentions "affected States." The Secretary of the Interior and the Secretary of Commerce have consistently taken the position that they need not designate critical habitat in foreign countries. See 42 Fed.Reg. 4869 (1977) (initial regulations of the Fish and Wildlife Service and the National Marine Fisheries Service on behalf of the Secretary of the Interior and the Secretary of Commerce). Consequently, neither Secretary interprets § 7(a)(2) to require federal agencies to engage in consultations to ensure that their actions in foreign countries will not adversely affect the critical habitat of endangered or threatened species.

That interpretation is sound, and, in fact, the Court of Appeals did not question it. There is, moreover, no indication that Congress intended to give a different geographic scope to the two clauses in s 7(a)(2). To the contrary, Congress recognized that one of the "major causes" of extinction of endangered species is the "destruction of natural habitat." S.Rep. No. 93-307, p. 2 (1973); see also H.Rep. No. 93-412, p. 2 (1973), U.S.Code Cong. & Admin.News 1973, pp. 2989, 2990; TVA v. Hill, 437 U.S. 153, 179, 98 S.Ct. 2279, 2294, 57 L.Ed.2d 117 (1978). It would thus be illogical to conclude that Congress required federal agencies to avoid jeopardy to endangered species abroad, but not destruction of critical habitat abroad.

The lack of an express indication that the consultation requirement applies extraterritorially is particularly significant because other sections of the ESA expressly deal with the problem of protecting endangered species abroad. Section 8, for example, authorizes the President to provide assistance to "any foreign country (with its consent) . . . in the development and management of programs in that country which [are] . . . necessary or useful for the conservation of any endangered species or threatened species listed by the Secretary pursuant to section 1533 of this title." 16 U.S.C. § 1537(a). It also directs the Secretary of the Interior, "through the Secretary of State," to "encourage" foreign countries to conserve fish and wildlife and to enter into bilateral or multilateral agreements. Section 9 makes it unlawful to import endangered species into (or export them from) the United States or to otherwise traffic in endangered species "in interstate or foreign commerce." §§ 1538(a)(1)(A), (E), (F). Congress thus obviously thought about endangered species abroad and devised specific sections of the ESA to protect them. In this context, the absence of any explicit statement that the consultation requirement is applicable to agency actions in foreign countries suggests that Congress did not intend that § 7(a)(2) apply extraterritorially.

Finally, the general purpose of the ESA does not evince a congressional intent that the consultation requirement be applicable to federal agency actions abroad. The congressional findings explaining the need for the ESA emphasize that "various species of fish, wildlife, and plants in the United States have been rendered extinct as a consequence of economic growth and development untempered by adequate concern and conservation," and that these species "are of aesthetic, ecological, educational, historical, recreational, and scientific value to the Nation and its people." §§ 1531(1), (3) (emphasis added). The lack of similar findings about the harm caused by development in other countries suggests that Congress was primarily concerned with balancing development and conservation

goals in this country. In short, a reading of the entire statute persuades me that Congress did not intend the consultation requirement in § 7(a)(2) to apply to activities in foreign countries. Accordingly, notwithstanding my disagreement with the Court's disposition of the standing question, I concur in its judgment.

Justice BLACKMUN, with whom Justice O'CONNOR joins, dissenting.

I part company with the Court in this case in two respects. First, I believe that respondents have raised genuine issues of fact—sufficient to survive summary judgment—both as to injury and as to redressability. Second, I question the Court's breadth of language in rejecting standing for "procedural" injuries. I fear the Court seeks to impose fresh limitations on the constitutional authority of Congress to allow citizen suits in the federal courts for injuries deemed "procedural" in nature. I dissent.

I.

Article III of the Constitution confines the federal courts to adjudication of actual "Cases" and "Controversies." To ensure the presence of a "case" or "controversy," this Court has held that Article III requires, as an irreducible minimum, that a plaintiff allege (1) an injury that is (2) "fairly traceable to the defendant's allegedly unlawful conduct" and that is (3) "likely to be redressed by the requested relief." Allen v. Wright, 468 U.S. 737, 751, 104 S.Ct. 3315, 3324, 82 L.Ed.2d 556 (1984).

A.

To survive petitioner's motion for summary judgment on standing, respondents need not prove that they are actually or imminently harmed. They need show only a "genuine issue" of material fact as to standing. Fed.Rule Civ.Proc. 56(c). This is not a heavy burden. A "genuine issue" exists so long as "the evidence is such that a reasonable jury could return a verdict for the nonmoving party [respondents]." Anderson v. Liberty Lobby, Inc., 477 U.S. 242, 248, 106 S.Ct. 2505, 2510, 91 L.Ed.2d 202 (1986). This Court's "function is not [it] self to weigh the evidence and determine the truth of the matter but to determine whether there is a genuine issue for trial." Id., at 249, 106 S.Ct., at 2511.

The Court never mentions the "genuine issue" standard. Rather, the Court refers to the type of evidence it feels respondents failed to produce, namely, "affidavits or other evidence showing, through specific facts" the existence of injury. The Court thereby confuses respondents' evidentiary burden (i.e., affidavits asserting "specific facts") in withstanding a summary judgment motion under Rule 56(e) with the standard of proof (i.e., the existence of a "genuine issue" of "material fact") under Rule 56(c).

Were the Court to apply the proper standard for summary judgment, I believe it would conclude that the sworn affidavits and deposition testimony of Joyce Kelly and Amy Skilbred advance sufficient facts to create a genuine issue for trial concerning whether one or both would be imminently harmed by the Aswan and Mahaweli projects. In the first instance, as the Court itself concedes, the affidavits contained facts making it at least "questionable" (and therefore within the province of the factfinder) that certain agency-funded projects threaten listed species.[3] The only remaining issue, then, is whether Kelly and Skilbred have shown that they personally would suffer imminent harm.

I think a reasonable finder of fact could conclude from the information in the affidavits and deposition testimony that either Kelly or Skilbred will soon return to the project sites, thereby satisfying the "actual or imminent" injury standard. The Court dismisses Kelly's and Skilbred's general statements that they intended to revisit the project sites as "simply not enough." Ibid. But those statements did not stand alone. A reasonable finder of fact could conclude, based not only upon their statements of intent to return, but upon their past visits to the project sites, as well as their professional backgrounds, that it was likely that Kelly and Skilbred would make a return trip to the project areas. Contrary to the Court's contention that Kelly's and Skilbred's past visits "prov[e] nothing,"

---

3. The record is replete with genuine issues of fact about the harm to endangered species from the Aswan and Mahaweli projects. For example, according to an internal memorandum of the Fish and Wildlife Service, no fewer than eight listed species are found in the Mahaweli project area (Indian elephant, leopard, purple-faced langur, toque macaque, red face malkoha, Bengal monitor, mugger crocodile, and python). App. 78. The memorandum recounts that the Sri Lankan Government has specifically requested assistance from the Agency for International Development (AID) in "mitigating the negative impacts to the wildlife involved." Ibid. In addition, a letter from the Director of the Fish and Wildlife Service to AID warns: "The magnitude of the Accelerated Mahaweli Development Program could have massive environmental impacts on such an insular ecosystem as the Mahaweli River system." Id., at 215. It adds: "The Sri Lankan government lacks the necessary finances to undertake any long-term management programs to avoid the negative impacts to the wildlife." Id., at 216. Finally, in an affidavit submitted by petitioner for purposes of this litigation, an AID official states that an AID environmental assessment "showed that the [Mahaweli] project could affect several endangered species." Id., at 159.

ibid., the fact of their past visits could demonstrate to a reasonable factfinder that Kelly and Skilbred have the requisite resources and personal interest in the preservation of the species endangered by the Aswan and Mahaweli projects to make good on their intention to return again. Cf. Los Angeles v. Lyons, 461 U.S. 95, 102, 103 S.Ct. 1660, 1665, 75 L.Ed.2d 675 (1983) ("Past wrongs were evidence bearing on whether there is a real and immediate threat of repeated injury") (internal quotation marks omitted). Similarly, Kelly's and Skilbred's professional backgrounds in wildlife preservation, also make it likely—at least far more likely than for the average citizen—that they would choose to visit these areas of the world where species are vanishing.

By requiring a "description of concrete plans" or "specification of when the some day [for a return visit] will be," the Court, in my view, demands what is likely an empty formality. No substantial barriers prevent Kelly or Skilbred from simply purchasing plane tickets to return to the Aswan and Mahaweli projects. This case differs from other cases in which the imminence of harm turned largely on the affirmative actions of third parties beyond a plaintiff's control. See Whitmore v. Arkansas, 495 U.S. 149, 155–156, 110 S.Ct. 1717, 1723, 109 L.Ed.2d 135 (1990) (harm to plaintiff death-row inmate from fellow inmate's execution depended on the court's one day reversing plaintiff's conviction or sentence and considering comparable sentences at resentencing); Los Angeles v. Lyons, 461 U.S., at 105, 103 S.Ct., at 1667 (harm dependent on police's arresting plaintiff again and subjecting him to chokehold); Rizzo v. Goode, 423 U.S. 362, 372, 96 S.Ct. 598, 605, 46 L.Ed.2d 561 (1976) (harm rested upon "what one of a small, un-named minority of policemen might do to them in the future because of that unknown policeman's perception of departmental disciplinary procedures"); O'Shea v. Littleton, 414 U.S. 488, 495–498, 94 S.Ct. 669, 675–677, 38 L.Ed.2d 674 (1974) (harm from discriminatory conduct of county magistrate and judge dependent on plaintiffs' being arrested, tried, convicted, and sentenced); Golden v. Zwickler, 394 U.S. 103, 109, 89 S.Ct. 956, 960, 22 L.Ed.2d 113 (1969) (harm to plaintiff dependent on a former Congressman's (then serving a 14-year term as a judge) running again for Congress). To be sure, a plaintiff's unilateral control over his or her exposure to harm does not necessarily render the harm nonspeculative. Nevertheless, it suggests that a finder of fact would be far more likely to conclude the harm is actual or imminent, especially if given an opportunity to hear testimony and determine credibility.

I fear the Court's demand for detailed descriptions of future conduct will do little to weed out those who are genuinely harmed from those who are not. More likely, it will resurrect a code-pleading formalism in federal court summary judgment practice, as federal courts, newly doubting their jurisdiction, will demand more and more particularized showings of future harm. Just to survive summary judgment, for example, a property owner claiming a decline in the value of his property from governmental action might have to specify the exact date he intends to sell his property and show that there is a market for the property, lest it be surmised he might not sell again. A nurse turned down for a job on grounds of her race had better be prepared to show on what date she was prepared to start work, that she had arranged daycare for her child, and that she would not have accepted work at another hospital instead. And a Federal Tort Claims Act plaintiff alleging loss of consortium should make sure to furnish this Court with a "description of concrete plans" for her nightly schedule of attempted activities.

The Court also concludes that injury is lacking, because respondents' allegations of "ecosystem nexus" failed to demonstrate sufficient proximity to the site of the environmental harm. To support that conclusion, the Court mischaracterizes our decision in Lujan v. National Wildlife Federation, 497 U.S. 871, 110 S.Ct. 3177, 111 L.Ed.2d 695 (1990), as establishing a general rule that "a plaintiff claiming injury from environmental damage must use the area affected by the challenged activity." In National Wildlife Federation, the Court required specific geographical proximity because of the particular type of harm alleged in that case: harm to the plaintiff's visual enjoyment of nature from mining activities. 497 U.S., at 888, 110 S.Ct., at 3188. One cannot suffer from the sight of a ruined landscape without being close enough to see the sites actually being mined. Many environmental injuries, however, cause harm distant from the area immediately affected by the challenged action. Environmental destruction may affect animals traveling over vast geographical ranges, see, e.g., Japan Whaling Assn. v. American Cetacean Society, 478 U.S. 221, 106 S.Ct. 2860, 92 L.Ed.2d 166 (1986) (harm to American whale watchers from Japanese whaling activities), or rivers running long geographical courses, see, e.g., Arkansas v. Oklahoma, 503 U.S. 91, 112 S.Ct. 1046, 117 L.Ed.2d 239 (1992) (harm to Oklahoma residents from wastewater treatment plant 39 miles from border). It cannot seriously be con-

tended that a litigant's failure to use the precise or exact site where animals are slaughtered or where toxic waste is dumped into a river means he or she cannot show injury. The Court also rejects respondents' claim of vocational or professional injury. The Court says that it is "beyond all reason" that a zoo "keeper" of Asian elephants would have standing to contest his Government's participation in the eradication of all the Asian elephants in another part of the world. I am unable to see how the distant location of the destruction necessarily (for purposes of ruling at summary judgment) mitigates the harm to the elephant keeper. If there is no more access to a future supply of the animal that sustains a keeper's livelihood, surely there is harm.

I have difficulty imagining this Court applying its rigid principles of geographic formalism anywhere outside the context of environmental claims. As I understand it, environmental plaintiffs are under no special constitutional standing disabilities. Like other plaintiffs, they need show only that the action they challenge has injured them, without necessarily showing they happened to be physically near the location of the alleged wrong. The Court's decision today should not be interpreted "to foreclose the possibility . . . that in different circumstances a nexus theory similar to those proffered here might support a claim to standing."

(KENNEDY, J., concurring in part and concurring in judgment).

B.

A plurality of the Court suggests that respondents have not demonstrated redressability: a likelihood that a court ruling in their favor would remedy their injury. Duke Power Co. v. Carolina Environmental Study Group, Inc., 438 U.S. 59, 74–75, and n. 20, 98 S.Ct. 2620, 2630–2631, and n. 20, 57 L.Ed.2d 595 (1978) (plaintiff must show "substantial likelihood" that relief requested will redress the injury). The plurality identifies two obstacles. The first is that the "action agencies" (e.g., AID) cannot be required to undertake consultation with petitioner Secretary, because they are not directly bound as parties to the suit and are otherwise not indirectly bound by being subject to petitioner Secretary's regulation. Petitioner, however, officially and publicly has taken the position that his regulations regarding consultation under § 7 of the Act are binding on action agencies. 50 CFR § 402.14(a) (1991). And he has previously taken the same position in this very litigation, having stated in his answer to the complaint that petitioner "admits the Fish and Wildlife Service (FWS) was designated the lead agency for the formulation of regulations concerning section 7 of the [Endangered Species Act]." I cannot agree with the plurality that the Secretary (or the Solicitor General) is now free, for the convenience of this appeal, to disavow his prior public and litigation positions. More generally, I cannot agree that the Government is free to play "Three-Card Monte" with its description of agencies' authority to defeat standing against the agency given the lead in administering a statutory scheme.

Emphasizing that none of the action agencies are parties to this suit (and having rejected the possibility of their being indirectly bound by petitioner's regulation), the plurality concludes that "there is no reason they should be obliged to honor an incidental legal determination the suit produced." I am not as willing as the plurality is to assume that agencies at least will not try to follow the law.

Respondents have raised at least a genuine issue of fact that the projects harm endangered species and that the actions of AID and other United States agencies can mitigate that harm. The plurality overlooks an Interior Department memorandum listing eight endangered or threatened species in the Mahaweli project area and recounting that "[t]he Sri Lankan government has requested the assistance of AID in mitigating the negative impacts to the wildlife involved." Further, a letter from the Director of the Fish and Wildlife Service to AID states:

> The Sri Lankan government lacks the necessary finances to undertake any long-term management programs to avoid the negative impacts to the wildlife. The donor nations and agencies that are financing the [Mahaweli project] will be the key as to how successfully the wildlife is preserved. If wildlife problems receive the same level of attention as the engineering project, then the negative impacts to the environment can be alleviated. This means that there has to be long-term funding in sufficient amounts to stem the negative impacts of this project.

I do not share the plurality's astonishing confidence that, on the record here, a factfinder could only conclude that AID was powerless to ensure the protection of listed species at the Mahaweli project. As for the Aswan project, the record again rebuts the plurality's assumption that donor agencies are without any authority to protect listed species. Kelly asserted in her affidavit—and it has not been disputed—that the Bureau of Reclamation was "overseeing" the rehabilitation of the Aswan project. I find myself unable to agree with the plurality's analysis of redressability, based as it is on its invitation of executive lawlessness, ignorance of principles of collateral estoppel, unfounded assumptions about causation, and erroneous conclusions about what the record does not say. In my view, respondents have satisfactorily shown a genuine issue of fact as to whether their injury would likely be redressed by a decision in their favor.

II.

The Court concludes that any "procedural injury" suffered by respondents is insufficient to confer standing. It rejects the view that the "injury-in-fact requirement [is] satisfied by congressional conferral upon all persons of an abstract, self-contained, noninstrumental 'right' to have the Executive observe the procedures required by law." Whatever the Court might mean with that very broad language, it cannot be saying that "procedural injuries" as a class are necessarily insufficient for purposes of Article III standing.

Most governmental conduct can be classified as "procedural." Many injuries caused by governmental conduct, therefore, are categorizable at some level of generality as "procedural" injuries. Yet, these injuries are not categorically beyond the pale of redress by the federal courts. When the Government, for example, "procedurally" issues a pollution permit, those affected by the permittee's pollutants are not without standing to sue. Only later cases will tell just what the Court means by its intimation that "procedural" injuries are not constitutionally cognizable injuries. In the meantime, I have the greatest of sympathy for the courts across the country that will struggle to understand the Court's stan-dardless exposition of this concept today.

The Court expresses concern that allowing judicial enforcement of "agencies' observance of a particular, statutorily prescribed procedure" would "transfer from the President to the courts the Chief Executive's most important constitutional duty, to 'take Care that the Laws be faithfully executed,' Art. II, § 3." In fact, the principal effect of foreclosing judicial enforcement of such procedures is to transfer power into the hands of the Executive at the expense—not of the courts—but of Congress, from which that power originates and emanates.

Under the Court's anachronistically formal view of the separation of powers, Congress legislates pure, substantive mandates and has no business structuring the procedural manner in which the Executive implements these mandates. To be sure, in the ordinary course, Congress does legislate in black-and-white terms of affirmative commands or negative prohibitions on the conduct of officers of the Executive Branch. In complex regulatory areas, however, Congress often legislates, as it were, in procedural shades of gray. That is, it sets forth substantive policy goals and provides for their attainment by requiring Executive Branch officials to follow certain procedures, for example, in the form of reporting, consultation, and certification requirements. The Court recently has considered two such procedurally oriented statutes. In Japan Whaling Assn. v. American Cetacean Society, 478 U.S. 221, 106 S.Ct. 2860, 92 L.Ed.2d 166 (1986), the Court examined a statute requiring the Secretary of Commerce to certify to the President that foreign nations were not conducting fishing operations or trading which "dimi nis[h] the effectiveness" of an international whaling convention. Id., at 226, 106 S.Ct., at 2864. The Court expressly found standing to sue. Id., at 230–231, n. 4, 106 S.Ct., at 2865–2866, n. 4. In Robertson v. Methow Valley Citizens Council, 490 U.S. 332, 348, 109 S.Ct. 1835, 1844, 104 L.Ed.2d 351 (1989), this Court considered injury from violation of the "action-forcing" procedures of the National Environmental Policy Act (NEPA), in particular the requirements for issuance of environmental impact statements.

The consultation requirement of § 7 of the Endangered Species Act is a similar, action-forcing statute. Consultation is designed as an integral check on federal agency action, ensuring that such action does not go forward without full consideration of its effects on listed species. Once consultation is initiated, the Secretary is under a duty to provide to the action agency "a written statement setting forth the Secretary's opinion, and a summary of the information on which the opinion is based, detailing how the agency action affects the species or its critical habitat." 16 U.S.C. § 1536(b)(3)(A). The Secretary is also obligated to suggest "reasonable and prudent alternatives" to prevent jeopardy to listed species. Ibid. The action agency must undertake as well its own "biological assessment for the purpose of identifying any endangered species or threatened species" likely to be affected by agency action. § 1536(c)(1). After the initiation of consultation, the action agency "shall not make any irreversible or irretrievable commitment of resources" which would foreclose the "formulation or implementation of any reasonable and prudent alternative measures" to avoid jeopardizing listed species. § 1536(d). These action-forcing procedures are "designed to protect some threatened concrete interest," of persons who observe and work with en-

dangered or threatened species. That is why I am mystified by the Court's unsupported conclusion that "[t]his is not a case where plaintiffs *604 are seeking to enforce a procedural requirement the disregard of which could impair a separate concrete interest of theirs."

Congress legislates in procedural shades of gray not to aggrandize its own power but to allow maximum Executive discretion in the attainment of Congress' legislative goals. Congress could simply impose a substantive prohibition on Executive conduct; it could say that no agency action shall result in the loss of more than 5% of any listed species. Instead, Congress sets forth substantive guidelines and allows the Executive, within certain procedural constraints, to decide how best to effectuate the ultimate goal. See American Power & Light Co. v. SEC, 329 U.S. 90, 105, 67 S.Ct. 133, 142, 91 L.Ed. 103 (1946). The Court never has questioned Congress' authority to impose such procedural constraints on Executive power. Just as Congress does not violate separation of powers by structuring the procedural manner in which the Executive shall carry out the laws, surely the federal courts do not violate separation of powers when, at the very instruction and command of Congress, they enforce these procedures.

To prevent Congress from conferring standing for "procedural injuries" is another way of saying that Congress may not delegate to the courts authority deemed "executive" in nature. (Congress may not "transfer from the President to the courts the Chief Executive's most important constitutional duty, to 'take Care that the Laws be faithfully executed,' Art. II, § 3"). Here Congress seeks not to delegate "executive" power but only to strengthen the procedures it has legislatively mandated. "We have long recognized that the nondelegation doctrine does not prevent Congress from seeking assistance, within proper limits, from its coordinate Branches." Touby v. United States, 500 U.S. 160, 165, 111 S.Ct. 1752, 1756, 114 L.Ed.2d 219 (1991). "Congress does not violate the Constitution merely because it legislates in broad terms, leaving a certain degree of discretion to executive or judicial actors."

Ironically, this Court has previously justified a relaxed review of congressional delegation to the Executive on grounds that Congress, in turn, has subjected the exercise of that power to judicial review. INS v. Chadha, 462 U.S. 919, 953–954, n. 16, 103 S.Ct. 2764, 2785–2786, n. 16, 77 L.Ed.2d 317 (1983); American Power & Light Co. v. SEC, 329 U.S., at 105–106, 67 S.Ct. at 142–143. The Court's intimation today that procedural injuries are not constitutionally cognizable threatens this understanding upon which Congress has undoubtedly relied. In no sense is the Court's suggestion compelled by our "common understanding of what activities are appropriate to legislatures, to executives, and to courts." In my view, it reflects an unseemly solicitude for an expansion of power of the Executive Branch. It is to be hoped that over time the Court will acknowledge that some classes of procedural duties are so enmeshed with the prevention of a substantive, concrete harm that an individual plaintiff may be able to demonstrate a sufficient likelihood of injury just through the breach of that procedural duty. For example, in the context of the NEPA requirement of environmental-impact statements, this Court has acknowledged "it is now well settled that NEPA itself does not mandate particular results [and] simply pre-

scribes the necessary process," but "these procedures are almost certain to affect the agency's substantive decision." Robertson v. Methow Valley Citizens Council, 490 U.S., at 350, 109 S.Ct., at 1846 (emphasis added). See also Andrus v. Sierra Club, 442 U.S. 347, 350–351, 99 S.Ct. 2335, 2337, 60 L.Ed.2d 943 (1979) ("If environmental concerns are not interwoven into the fabric of agency planning, the 'action-forcing' characteristics of [the environmental-impact statement requirement] would be lost"). This acknowledgment of an inextricable link between procedural and substantive harm does not reflect improper appellate factfinding. It reflects nothing more than the proper deference owed to the judgment of a coordinate branch—Congress—that certain procedures are directly tied to protection against a substantive harm.

In short, determining "injury" for Article III standing purposes is a fact-specific inquiry. "Typically . . . the standing inquiry requires careful judicial examination of a complaint's allegations to ascertain whether the particular plaintiff is entitled to an adjudication of the particular claims asserted." Allen v. Wright, 468 U.S., at 752, 104 S.Ct., at 3325. There may be factual circumstances in which a congressionally imposed procedural requirement is so insubstantially connected to the prevention of a substantive harm that it cannot be said to work any conceivable injury to an individual litigant. But, as a general matter, the courts owe substantial deference to Congress' substantive purpose in imposing a certain procedural requirement. In all events, "[o]ur separation-of-powers analysis does not turn on the labeling of an activity as 'substantive' as opposed to 'procedural.' " Mistretta v. United States, 488 U.S. 361, 393, 109 S.Ct. 647, 665, 102

L.Ed.2d 714 (1989). There is no room for a per se rule or presumption excluding injuries labeled "procedural" in nature.

III.

In conclusion, I cannot join the Court on what amounts to a slash-and-burn expe- dition through the law of environmental standing. In my view, "[t]he very essence of civil liberty certainly consists in the right of every individual to claim the protection of the laws, whenever he receives an injury." Marbury v. Madison, 1 Cranch 137, 163, 2 L.Ed. 60 (1803). I dissent.

QUESTIONS AND DISCUSSION POINTS

1. The basic issue in this case concerns "standing." Can you tell what this means and, moreover, why it is of such importance?

2. If a question about the meaning of the Constitution is an important one, what difference should it make who brings the case asking the question?

3. Articulate the competing positions regarding the question of "nexus" and state each position in the form of premises and conclusions.

4. Once you have completed question 3, can you tell how the nexus question connects with the constitutional text?

Chapter 9

Contract Law

Contract law is one of the most basic areas of private law. Private law concerns the obligations individuals owe to one another (in contrast to public law, which considers the obligations of citizens to their government, and vice versa). Contract law considers the role of private agreement in creating obligations. One way to think about contract law is to think of it as a way for individuals to impose obligations on themselves. There is no obligation to enter into contracts: no one is forced to enter into an agreement without his or her consent. However, once we decide to make a contract, the law enforces the obligations we have imposed on ourselves.

Of course, whether we have imposed obligations on ourselves, either by contract or otherwise, is itself a legal question. In contract law, the parties reach agreement through a formation process that characteristically begins with an offer by the party known at law as the "offeror." The offeror creates in his or her counterpart, the "offeree," what is know as "the power of acceptance." By making an offer, the offeror creates the possibility that the offeree will accept the offer, thereby binding the offeror to the offer as made. If the offeree alters the offeror's offer, the common law considers this a counteroffer. Now the original offeror becomes the offeree, with the power of acceptance.

For a promise to be enforceable at law, the common law requires that the promise be supported by consideration or some substitute therefor. For example, if someone offers to buy your house, that person will offer to buy it at a price. The price offered is itself a promise, albeit a conditional one: "If you accept my offer to purchase, I will pay you $100,000 in cash." At one time, the law required that all contracts be supported by consideration. Over time, this requirement has been relaxed. In addition to consideration, the law enforces promises where the offeree relies on a promise made by the offeror (assuming the reliance was reasonable). For example, if I promise to make you a car salesperson if you leave your current employment, the mere act of leaving your current employment may be sufficient to keep me to my promise.

Once it is clear that the parties have an enforceable agreement (a contract), we must identify the terms of the agreement. Sometimes the parties use the same words but mean different things by them. At other times the parties think they have an agreement when, in fact, they have vastly different assumptions about their agreement (for example, if the parties use a generic term like "chicken," and there is a variety of types of chicken, it is unclear whether the parties have indeed reached agreement).

As you read these opinions, try and summarize the arguments for each position. Do you see strengths and weaknesses in each opinion? Above all, try to identify the presuppositions of each opinion, those points of departure that form the intellectual center of each point of view.

~

LOUISE W. HAMER
v. FRANKLIN SIDWAY
Court of Appeals of New York, Second Division
27 N.E. 256 (1891)

Appeal from an order of the general term of the supreme court in the fourth judicial department, reversing a judgment entered on the decision of the court at special term in the county clerk's office of Chemung county on the 1st day of October, 1889. The plaintiff presented a claim to the executor of William E. Story, Sr., for $5,000 and interest from the 6th day of February, 1875. She acquired it through several mesne assignments from William E. Story, 2d. The claim being rejected by the executor, this action was brought.

It appears that William E. Story, Sr. was the uncle of William E. Story 2d., and that at the celebration of the golden wedding of Samuel Story and wife, father and mother of William E. Story, Sr., on the 20th day of March, 1869, in the presence of the family and invited guests, he promised his nephew that if he would refrain from drinking, using tobacco, swearing, and playing cards or billiards for money until he became 21 years of age, he would pay him the sum of $5,000. The nephew assented thereto, and fully performed the conditions inducing the promise. When the nephew arrived at the age of 21 years, and on the 31st day of January, 1875, he wrote to his uncle, informing him that he had performed his part of the agreement, and had thereby become entitled to the sum of $5,000. The uncle received the letter, and a few days later, and on the 6th day of February, he wrote and mailed to his nephew the following letter:

'Buffalo, Feb. 6, 1875. W. E. Story, Jr.— Dear Nephew: Your letter of the 31st ult. came to hand all right, saying that you had lived up to the promise made to me several years ago. I have no doubt but you have, for which you shall have five thousand dollars, as I promised you. I had the money in the bank the day you was twenty-one years old that I intend for you, and you shall have the money certain. Now, Willie, I do not intend to interfere with this money in any was till I think you are capable of taking care of it, and the sooner that time comes the better it will please me. I would hate very much to have you start out in some adventure that you thought all right and lose this money in one year. The first five thousand dollars that I got together cost me a heap of hard work. You would hardly believe me when I tell you that to obtain this I shoved a jack-plane many a day, butchered three or four years, then came to this city, and, after three months' perseverance, I obtained a situation in a grocery store. I opened this store early, closed late, slept in the fourth story of the building in a room 30 by 40 feet, and not a human being in the building but myself. All this I done to live as cheap as I could to save something. I don't want you to take up with this kind of fare. I was here in the cholera season of '49 and '52, and the deaths averaged 80 to 125 I was working for, told me, if I left them, to go home, but Mr. Fisk, the gentleman i was working for, told me, if I left them, after it got healthy he probably would not want me. I stayed. All the money I have saved I know just how I got it. It did not come to me in any mysterious way, and the reason I speak of this is that money got in this way stops longer with a fellow that gets it with hard knocks than it does when he finds it. Willie, you are twenty-one, and you have many a thing to learn yet. This money you have earned much easier than I did, besides acquiring good habits at the same time, and you are quite welcome to the money. Hope you will make good use of it. I was ten long years getting this together after I was your age. Now, hoping this will be satisfactory, I stop. One thing more. Twenty-one years ago I bought you 15 sheep. These sheep were put out to double every four years. I kept track of them the first eight years. I have not heard much about them since. Your father and grandfather promised me that they would look after them till you were of age. Have they done so? I hope they have. By this time you have between five and six hundred sheep, worth a nice little income this spring. Willie, I have said much more than I expected to. Hope you can make out what I have written. To-day is the seventeenth day that I have not been out of my room, and have had the doctor as many days. Am a little better to day. Think I will get out next week. You need not mention to father, as he al-

ways worries about small matters. Truly yours,

W. E. STORY

P. S. You can consider this money on interest.

The nephew received the letter, and thereafter consented that the money should remain with his uncle in accordance with the terms and conditions of the letter. The uncle died on the 29th day of January, 1887, without having paid over to his nephew any portion of the said $5,000 and interest.

PARKER, J., (after stating the facts as above). The question which provoked the most discussion by counsel on this appeal, and which lies at the foundation of plaintiff's asserted right of recovery, is whether by virtue of a contract defendant's testator, William E. Story, became indebted to his nephew, William E. Story, 2d, on his twenty-first birthday in the sum of $5,000. The trial court found as a fact that 'on the 20th day of March, 1869, William E. Story agreed to and with William E. Story, 2d, that if he would refrain from drinking liquor, using tobacco, swearing, and playing cards or billiards for money until should become twenty-one years of age, then he, the said William E. Story, would at that time pay him, the said William E. Story, 2d, the sum of $5,000 for such refraining, to which the said William E. Story, 2d, agreed,' and that he 'in all things fully performed his part of said agreement.' The defendant contends that the contract was without consideration to support it, and therefore invalid. He asserts that the promisee, by refraining from the use of liquor and tobacco, was not harmed, but benefited; that that which he did was best for him to do, independently of his uncle's promise,—and insists that it follows that, unless the promisor was benefited, the contract was without consideration,—a contention which, if well founded, would seem to leave open for controversy in many cases whether that which the promisee did or omitted to do was in fact of such benefit to him as to leave no consideration to support the enforcement of the promisor's agreement. Such a rule could not be tolerated, and is without foundation in the law. The exchequer chamber in 1875 defined 'consideration' as follows: 'A valuable consideration, in the sense of the law, may consist either in some right, interest, profit, or benefit accruing to the one party, or some forbearance, detriment, loss, or responsibility given, suffered, or undertaken by the other.' Courts 'will not ask whether the thing which forms the consideration does in fact benefit the promisee or a third party, or is of any substantial value to any one. It is enough that something is promised, done, forborne, or suffered by the party to whom the promise is made as consideration for the promise made to him.' Anson, Cont. 63. 'In general a waiver of any legal right at the request of another party is a sufficient consideration for a promise.' Pars. Cont. *444. 'Any damage, or suspension, or forbearance of a right will be sufficient to sustain a promise.' 2 Kent, Comm. (12th Ed.). Pollock in his work on Contracts, (page 166,) after citing the definition given by the exchequer chamber, already quoted, says: 'The second branch of this judicial description is really the most important one. 'Consideration' means not so much that one party is profiting as that the other abandons some legal right in the present, or limits his legal freedom of action in the future, as an inducement for the promise of the first.'

Now, applying this rule to the facts before us, the promisee used tobacco, occasionally drank liquor, and he had a legal right to do so. That right he abandoned for a period of years upon the strength of the promise of the testator that for such forbearance he would give him $5,000. We need not speculate on the effort which may have been required to give up the use of those stimulants. It is sufficient that he restricted his lawful freedom of action within certain prescribed limits upon the faith of his uncle's agreement, and now, having fully performed the conditions imposed, it is of no moment whether such performance actually proved a benefit to the promisor, and the court will not inquire into it; but, were it a proper subject of inquiry, we see nothing in this record that would permit a determination that the uncle was not benefited in a legal sense.

Few cases have been found which may be said to be precisely in point, but such as have been, support the position we have taken. In Shadwell v. Shadwell, 9 C. B. (N. S.) 159, an uncle wrote to his nephew as follows:

> My dear Lancey: I am so glad to hear of your intended marriage with Ellen Nicholl, and, as I promised to assist you at starting, I am happy to tell you that I will pay you 150 pounds yearly during my life and until your annual income derived from your profession of a chancery barrister shall amount to 600 guineas, of which your own admission will be the only evidence that I shall receive or require. Your affectionate uncle,
>
> CHARLES SHADWELL

It was held that the promise was binding, and made upon good consideration. In Lakota v. Newton, (an unreported case in the superior court of Worcester,

Mass.,) the complaint averred defendant's promise that 'if you [meaning the plaintiff] will leave off drinking for a year I will give you $100,' plaintiff's assent thereto, performance of the condition by him, and demanded judgment therefor. Defendant demurred, on the ground, among others, that the plaintiff's declaration did not allege a valid and sufficient consideration for the agreement of the defendant. The demurrer was overruled.

In Talbott v. Stemmons, 12 S. W. Rep. 297, (a Kentucky case, not yet officially reported,) the step-grandmother of the plaintiff made with him the following agreement: 'I do promise and bind myself to give my grandson Albert R. Talbott $500 at my death if he will never take another chew of tobacco or smoke another cigar during my life, from this date up to my death; and if he breaks this pledge he is to refund double the amount to his mother.' The executor of Mrs. Stemmons demurred to the complaint on the ground that the agreement was not based on a sufficient consideration. The demurrer was sustained, and an appeal taken therefrom to the court of appeals, where the decision of the court below was reversed. In the opinion of the court it is said that 'the right to use and enjoy the use of tobacco was a right that belonged to the plaintiff, and not forbidden by law. The abandonment of its use may have saved him money, or contributed to his health; nevertheless, the surrender of that right caused the promise, and, having the right to contract with reference to the subjectmatter, the abandonment of the use was a sufficient consideration to uphold the promise.' Abstinence from the use of intoxicating liquors was held to furnish a good consideration for a promissory note in Lindell v. Rokes, 60 Mo. 249. . . .

In further consideration of the questions presented, then, it must be deemed established for the purposes of this appeal that on the 31st day of January, 1875, defendant's testator was indebted to William E. Story, 2d, in the sum of $5,000; and, if this action were founded on that contract, it would be barred by the statute of limitations, which has been pleaded, but on that date the nephew wrote to his uncle as follows:

> Dear Uncle: I am 21 years old to-day, and I am now my own boss; and I believe, according to agreement, that there is due me $5,000. I have lived up to the contract to the letter in every sense of the word.

A few days later, and on February 6th, the uncle replied, and, so far as it is material to this controversy, the reply is as follows:

> Dear Nephew: Your letter of the 31st ult. came to hand all right, saying that you had lived up to the promise made to me several years ago. I have no doubt but you have, for which you shall have $5,000, as I promised you. I had the money in the bank the day you was 21 years old that I intend for you, and you shall have the money certain. Now, Willie, I don't intend to interfere with this money in any way until I think you are capable of taking care of it, and the sooner that time comes the better it will please me. I would hate very much to have you start out in some adventure that you thought all right, and lose this money in one year. . . . This money you have earned much easier than I did, besides acquiring good habits at the same time; and you are quite welcome to the money. Hope you will make good use of it.
>
> W. E. STORY.
>
> P. S. You can consider this money on interest.

The trial court found as a fact that 'said letter was received by said William E. Story, 2d, who thereafter consented that said money should remain with the said William E. Story in accordance with the terms and conditions of said letter.' And further, 'that afterwards, on the 1st day of March, 1877, with the knowledge and consent of his said uncle, he duly sold, transferred, and assigned all his right, title, and interest in and to said sum of $5,000 to his wife, Libbie H. Story, who thereafter duly sold, transferred, and assigned the same to the plaintiff in this action.' We must now consider the effect of the letter and the nephew's assent thereto. Were the relations of the parties thereafter that of debtor and creditor simply, or that of trustee and cestui que trust? If the former, then this action is not maintainable, because barred by lapse of time. If the latter, the result must be otherwise. No particular expressions are necessary to create a trust. Any language clearly showing the settler's intention is sufficient if the property and disposition of it are definitely stated.

A person in the legal possession of money or property acknowledging a trust with the assent of the cestui que trust becomes from that time a trustee if the acknowledgment be founded on a valuable consideration. His antecedent relation to the subject, whatever it may have been, no longer controls. 2 Story, Eq. Jur., s 972. If before a declaration of trust a party be a mere debtor, a subsequent agreement recognizing the fund as already in his hands, and stipulating for its investment on the creditor's account, will have the effect to create a trust. Day v. Roth, 18 N. Y. 448. It is essential that the letter, interpreted in the light of surrounding circumstances, must show an intention on the part of the uncle to become a trustee before he will be held to have become such; but in an effort to ascertain the construction which should be given to it we are also to observe the rule that the language of the promisor is to be interpreted in the sense in which he had reason to suppose it was understood by the promisee. White v. Hoyt, 73 N. Y. 505, 511. At the time the uncle wrote the letter he was indebted to his nephew in the sum of $5,000, and payment had been requested. The uncle, recognizing the indebtedness, wrote the nephew that he would keep the money until he deemed him capable of taking care of it. He did not say, 'I will pay you at some other time,' or use language that would indicate that the relation of debtor and creditor would continue. On the contrary, his language indicated that he had set apart the money the nephew had 'earned,' for him, so that when he should be capable of taking care of it he should receive it with interest. He said: 'I had the money in the bank the day you were 21 years old that I intend for you, and you shall have the money certain.' That he had set apart the money is further evidenced by the next sentence: 'Now, Willie, I don't intend to interfere with this money in any way until I think you are capable of taking care of it.' Certainly the uncle must have intended that his nephew should understand that the promise not 'to interfere with this money' referred to the money in the bank, which he declared was not only there when the nephew became 21 years old, but was intended for him. True, he did not use the word 'trust,' or state that the money was deposited in the name of William E. Story, 2d, or in his own name in trust for him, but the language used must have been intended to assure the nephew that his money had been set apart for him, to be kept without interference until he should be capable of taking care of it, for the uncle said in substance and in effect: 'This money you have earned much easier than I did. . . . You are quite welcome to the money. I had it in the bank the day you were 21 years old, and don't intend to interfere with it in any way until I think you are capable of taking care of it; and the sooner that time comes the better it will please me.' In this declaration there is not lacking a single element necessary for the creation of a valid trust, and to that declaration the nephew as-sented. The learned judge who wrote the opinion of the general term seems to have taken the view that the trust was executed during the life-time of defendant's testator by payment to the nephew, but, as it does not appear from the order that the judgment was reversed on the facts, we must assume the facts to be as found by the trial court, and those facts support its judgment. The order appealed from should be reversed, and the judgment of the special term affirmed, with costs payable out of the estate. All concur.

QUESTIONS AND DISCUSSION POINTS

1. This case considers the meaning of "consideration." The Court clearly indicates that consideration is necessary to form a binding contract. Does the Court indicate *why* the law imposes a requirement of consideration?

2. One question raised by the facts of this case is the nature of the "agreement" between uncle and nephew. What sort of "agreement" or "understanding" was it? Does the nature of the "arrangement" matter? If so, how?

3. What is the relationship of the concepts of consideration and bargain? If there is a bargain between the parties, does that mean that there is necessarily consideration present? Or, is it the case that consideration is a requirement independent of bargain?

4. Does it matter to the Court that the nephew would have benefited from the "arrangement" whether he received the promised $5,000 or not? Additionally, to what extent does it matter that the uncle never received any benefit from the agreement? Or did he?

5. Try expressing the consideration requirement in one or two sentences, and see if it is possible. After doing that, try to think again of the justification(s) for the consideration requirement. Does your formulation of the consideration requirement embody that (those) justification(s), and if so, how well?

6. Can you think of promises the law should not enforce? If there are promises the law should not enforce, how do you distinguish between enforceable and unenforceable promises?

C & J FERTILIZER, INC., Appellant,
v. ALLIED MUTUAL INSURANCE COMPANY, Appellee
Supreme Court of Iowa
227 N.W.2d 169 (1975)

OPINION: This action to recover for burglary loss under two separate insurance policies was tried to the court, resulting in a finding plaintiff had failed to establish a burglary within the policy definitions. Plaintiff appeals from judgment entered for defendant. We reverse and remand. Trial court made certain findings of fact in support of its conclusion reached. Plaintiff operated a fertilizer plant in Olds, Iowa. At time of loss, plaintiff was insured under policies issued by defendant and titled "Broad Form Storekeepers Policy" and "Mercantile Burglary and Robbery Policy." Each policy defined "burglary" as meaning:

> ... the felonious abstraction of insured property (1) from within the premises by a person making felonious entry therein by actual force and violence, of which force and violence there are visible marks made by tools, explosives, electricity or chemicals upon, or physical damage to, the exterior of the premises at the place of such entry. . . .

On Saturday, April 18, 1970, all exterior doors to the building were locked when plaintiff's employees left the premises at the end of the business day. The following day, Sunday, April 19, 1970, one of plaintiff's employees was at the plant and found all doors locked and secure. On Monday, April 20, 1970, when the employees reported for work, the exterior doors were locked, but the front office door was unlocked. There were truck tire tread marks visible in the mud in the driveway leading to and from the plexiglas door entrance to the warehouse. It

was demonstrated this door could be forced open without leaving visible marks or physical damage. There were no visible marks on the exterior of the building made by tools, explosives, electricity or chemicals, and there was no physical damage to the exterior of the building to evidence felonious entry into the building by force and violence. Chemicals had been stored in an interior room of the warehouse. The door to this room, which had been locked, was physically damaged and carried visible marks made by tools. Chemicals had been taken at a net loss to plaintiff in the sum of $9,582. Office and shop equipment valued at $400.30 was also taken from the building. Trial court held the policy definition of "burglary" was unambiguous, there was nothing in the record "upon which to base a finding that the door to plaintiff's place of business was entered feloniously, by actual force and violence," and, applying the policy language, found for defendant. Certain other facts in the record were apparently deemed irrelevant by trial court because of its view the applicable law required it to enforce the policy provision. Because we conclude different rules of law apply, we also consider those facts. The "Broad Form Storekeepers Policy" was issued April 14, 1969; the "Mercantile Burglary and Robbery Policy" on April 14, 1970. Those policies are in evidence. Prior policies apparently were first purchased in 1968. The agent, who had power to bind insurance coverage for defendant, was told plaintiff would be handling farm chemicals. After inspecting the building then used by plaintiff for storage he made certain suggestions regarding security. There ensued a conversation in which he pointed out there had to be visible evidence of burglary. There was no testimony by anyone that plaintiff was then or thereafter informed the policy to be delivered would define burglary to require "visible marks made by tools, explosives, electricity or chemicals upon, or physical damage to, the exterior of the premises at the place of . . . entry." The import of this conversation with defendant's agent when the coverage was sold is best confirmed by the agent's complete and vocally-expressed surprise when defendant denied coverage. From what the agent saw (tire tracks and marks on the interior of the building) and his contacts with the investigating officers ". . . the thought didn't enter my mind that it wasn't covered. . . ." From the trial testimony it was obvious the only understanding was that there should be some hard evidence of a third-party burglary vis-a-vis an "inside job." The latter was in this instance effectively ruled out when the thief was required to break an interior door lock to gain access to the chemicals.

The agent testified the insurance was purchased and "the policy was sent out afterwards." The president of plaintiff corporation, a 37-year-old farmer with a high school education, looked at that portion of the policy setting out coverages, including coverage for burglary loss, the amounts of insurance, and the "location and description." He could not recall reading the fine print defining "burglary" on page three of the policy.

Trial court's "findings" must be examined in light of our applicable rules. Ordinarily in a law action tried to the court its findings of fact having adequate evidentiary support shall not be set aside unless induced by an erroneous view of the law. It follows, the rule does not preclude inquiry into the question whether, conceding the truth of a finding of fact, the trial court applied erroneous rules of law which materially affected the decision. Beneficial Finance Company of Waterloo v. Lamos, 179 N.W.2d 573, 578 (Iowa 1970) and citations.

Extrinsic evidence that throws light on the situation of the parties, the antecedent negotiations, the attendant circumstances and the objects they were thereby striving to attain is necessarily to be regarded as relevant to ascertain the actual significance and proper legal meaning of the agreement. The question of interpretation, i.e., the meaning to be given contractual words, is one to be determined by the court unless the interpretation depends on extrinsic evidence or on a choice among reasonable inferences to be drawn from extrinsic evidence. Construction of a contract means determination of its legal operation—its effect upon the action of the courts. "[Construction] [of a contract] is always a matter of law for the court." 3 Corbin on Contracts § 544, p. 227. "[Courts] in construing and applying a standardized contract seek to effectuate the reasonable expectations of the average member of the public who accepts it." Restatement (Second) of Contracts, supra, § 237, comment e , p. 540.

Trial court in the case *sub judice* [this is a reference to the trial court below], concentrating on the policy "definition" of burglary, limited its consideration of the facts to the issue whether there was evidence which satisfied that provision. Thus we find the language "There was no physical damage to the exterior of the building to evidence felonious entry to the building by force and violence"; "There is nothing in the record upon which to base a finding that the door to plaintiff's place of business was entered feloniously, by actual force and violence"; "The evidence in this case is just as consistent with a theory that an employee entered the building with a key as it is to a theory that the building was entered by force and violence." (Emphasis supplied.). Trial court never made a finding there was or was not a burglary. We have noted its examination of the evidence was tailored to fit the policy "definition" of burglary: " 'Burglary' means the felonious abstraction of insured property (1) from within the premises by a person making felonious entry therein by actual force and violence, of which force and violence there are visible marks. . . ." (Emphasis supplied.). Nor did trial court consider the evidence in light of the layman's concept of burglary (who might well consider a stealing intruder in his home or business premises as a burglar, whether or not the door was entered by force and violence) or the legal definition of burglary, hereinafter referred to. Trial court made no determination regarding burglary in those contexts.

Insofar as trial court was construing the policy—that being a matter of law for the court—we are not bound by its conclusions. Neither are we bound by trial court's rule this case is controlled by the fine-print "definition" of burglary, if that rule was erroneously applied below.

Trial court did find "[There] does not appear to have been a discussion of the policy provisions between the parties at the time the policy was secured." That finding is well supported: there is no evidence plaintiff knew of the definition of burglary contained in the policy until after the event. But both parties agree there

was conversation concerning the type of insurance and the property to be insured. While plaintiff's president's testimony is ambivalent as to whether it occurred before or after the predecessor policies were issued, the defendant's agent was clear the conversation occurred before any policies were delivered.

There is nothing about trial court's factual findings which precludes this court from construing said contract to arrive at a proper determination of its legal operation as between these parties, or from considering whether the decision appealed from resulted from the application of an erroneous rule of law. And if the definition of "burglary" in defendant's policy is not enforceable here, then trial court's finding there was no evidence of forcible entry through an outside door is not controlling in the disposition of this case. Plaintiff's theories of recovery based on "reasonable expectations," implied warranty and unconscionability must be viewed in light of accelerating change in the field of contracts.

I. Revolution in Formation of Contractual Relationships

Many of our principles for resolving conflicts relating to written contracts were formulated at an early time when parties of equal strength negotiated in the historical sequence of offer, acceptance, and reduction to writing. The concept that both parties assented to the resulting document had solid footing in fact. Only recently has the sweeping change in the inception of the document received widespread recognition:

> Standard form contracts probably account for more than ninety-nine percent of all contracts now made. Most

persons have difficulty remembering the last time they contracted other than by standard form; except for casual oral agreements, they probably never have. But if they are active, they contract by standard form several times a day. Parking lot and theater tickets, package receipts, department store charge slips, and gas station credit card purchase slips are all standard form contracts. . . . The contracting still imagined by courts and law teachers as typical, in which both parties participate in choosing the language of their entire agreement, is no longer of much more than historical importance.

> —W. Slawson, *Standard Form Contracts and Democratic Control of Lawmaking Power*, 84 Harv. L. Rev. 529 (1971)

With respect to those interested in buying insurance, it has been observed that:

> His chances of successfully negotiating with the company for any substantial change in the proposed contract are just about zero. The insurance company tenders the insurance upon a 'take it or leave it' basis.

Few persons solicited to take policies understand the subject of insurance or the rules of law governing the negotiations, and they have no voice in dictating the terms of what is called the contract. They are clear upon two or three points which the agent promises to protect, and for everything else they must sign ready-made applications and accept ready-made policies carefully concocted to conserve the interests of the company.

The subject, therefore, is *sui generis*, and the rules of a legal system devised to govern the formation of ordinary contracts between man and man cannot be mechanically applied to it. The concept that persons must obey public laws enacted by their own representatives does not offend a fundamental sense of justice: an inherent element of assent pervades the process.

But the inevitable result of enforcing all provisions of the adhesion contract, frequently, as here, delivered subsequent to the transaction and containing provisions never assented to, would be an abdication of judicial responsibility in face of basic unfairness and a recognition that persons' rights shall be controlled by private lawmakers without the consent, express or implied, of those affected. A question is also raised whether a court may constitutionally allow that power to exist in private hands except where appropriate safeguards are present, including a right to meaningful judicial review.

The statutory requirement that the form of policies be approved by the commissioner of insurance, § 515.109, The Code, neither resolves the issue whether the fine-print provisions nullify the insurance bargained for in a given case nor ousts the court from necessary jurisdiction. In this connection it has been pertinently stated:

> Insurance contracts continue to be contracts of adhesion, under which the insured is left little choice beyond electing among standardized provisions offered to him, even when the standard forms are prescribed by public officials rather than insurers. Moreover, although statutory and administrative regulations have made increasing inroads on the insurer's autonomy by prescribing some kinds of provisions and proscribing others, most insurance policy provisions are still drafted by insurers. Regulation is relatively weak in most instances, and even the provisions prescribed or approved by legislative or administrative action ordinarily are in essence adoptions,

outright or slightly modified, of proposals made by insurers' draftsmen. Under such circumstances as these, judicial regulation of contracts of adhesion, whether concerning insurance or some other kind of transaction, remains appropriate. *See also* 3 Corbin on Contracts § 559, p. 267.

The mass-produced boiler-plate "contracts," necessitated and spawned by the explosive growth of complex business transactions in a burgeoning population left courts frequently frustrated in attempting to arrive at just results by applying many of the traditional contract-construing stratagems. As long as fifteen years ago Professor Llewellyn, reflecting on this situation in his book "The Common Law Tradition—Deciding Appeals," pp. 362–71 wrote,

> What the story shows thus far is first, scholars persistently off-base while judges grope over well-nigh a century in irregular but dogged fashion for escape from a recurring discomfort of imbalance that rests on what is in fact substantial non agreement despite perfect semblance of agreement. (pp. 367–368). The answer, I suggest, is this: Instead of thinking about 'assent' to boiler-plate clauses, we can recognize that so far as concerns the specific, there is no assent at all. What has in fact been assented to, specifically, are the few dickered terms, and the broad type of transaction, and but one thing more. That one thing more is a blanket assent (not a specific assent) to any not unreasonable or indecent terms the seller may have on his form, which do not alter or eviscerate the reasonable meaning of the dickered terms. The fine print which has not been read has no business to cut under the reasonable meaning of those dickered terms which constitute the dominant and

> only real expression of agreement, but much of it commonly belongs in. (p. 370)

In fairness to the often-discerned ability of the common law to develop solutions for changing demands, it should be noted appellate courts take cases as they come, constrained by issues the litigants formulated in trial court—a point not infrequently overlooked by academicians. Nor can a lawyer in the ordinary case be faulted for not risking a client's cause on an uncharted course when there is a reasonable prospect of reaching a fair result through familiar channels of long-accepted legal principles, for example, those grounded on ambiguity in language, the duty to define limitations or exclusions in clear and explicit terms, and interpretation of language from the viewpoint of an ordinary person, not a specialist or expert.

Plaintiff's claim it should be granted relief under the legal doctrines of reasonable expectations, implied warranty and unconscionability should be viewed against the above backdrop.

II. Reasonable Expectations

This court adopted the doctrine of reasonable expectations in Rodman v. State Farm Mutual Ins. Co., 208 N.W.2d 903, 905–908 (Iowa 1973). The Rodman court approved the following articulation of that concept:

> The objectively reasonable expectations of applicants and intended beneficiaries regarding the terms of insurance contracts will be honored even though painstaking study of the policy provisions would have negated those expectations. 208 N.W.2d at 906. Restatement (Second) of Contracts, supra, § 237, comments e and f , pp. 540–41; 1 Corbin on

Contracts § 1, p. 2 ("That portion of the field of law that is classified and described as the law of contracts attempts the realization of reasonable expectations that have been induced by the making of a promise"); 7 Williston on Contracts § 900, pp. 33–34 ("Some courts, recognizing that very few insureds even try to read and understand the policy or application, have declared that the insured is justified in assuming that the policy which is delivered to him has been faithfully prepared by the company to provide the protection against the risk which he had asked for. . . . Obviously this judicial attitude is a far cry from the old motto 'caveat emptor.' ").

At comment f to § 237 of Restatement (Second) of Contracts, supra pp. 540–41, we find the following analysis of the reasonable expectations doctrine:

Although customers typically adhere to standardized agreements and are bound by them without even appearing to know the standard terms in detail, they are not bound to unknown terms which are beyond the range of reasonable expectation. A debtor who delivers a check to his creditor with the amount blank does not authorize the insertion of an infinite figure. Similarly, a party who adheres to the other party's standard terms does not assent to a term if the other party has reason to believe that the adhering party would not have accepted the agreement if he had known that the agreement contained the particular term. Such a belief or assumption may be shown by the prior negotiations or inferred from the circumstances. Reason to believe may be inferred from the fact that the term is bizarre or oppressive, from the fact that it eviscerates the non-standard terms explicitly agreed to, or from the fact that it eliminates the dominant purpose of the transaction.

The inference is reinforced if the adhering party never had an opportunity to read the term, or if it is illegible or otherwise hidden from view. This rule is closely related to the policy against unconscionable terms and the rule of interpretation against the draftsman.

Nor can it be asserted the above doctrine does not apply here because plaintiff knew the policy contained the provision now complained of and cannot be heard to say it reasonably expected what it knew was not there. A search of the record discloses no such knowledge.

The evidence does show, as above noted, a "dicker" for burglary insurance coverage on chemicals and equipment. The negotiation was for what was actually expressed in the policies' "Insuring Agreements" the insurer's promise "To pay for loss by burglary or by robbery of a watchman, while the premises are not open for business, of merchandise, furniture, fixtures and equipment within the premises. . . ."

In addition, the conversation included statements from which the plaintiff should have understood defendant's obligation to pay would not arise where the burglary was an "inside job." Thus the following exclusion should have been reasonably anticipated:

Exclusions. This policy does not apply: (b) to loss due to any fraudulent, dishonest or criminal act by any Insured, a partner therein, or an officer, employee, director, trustee or authorized representative thereof.

But there was nothing relating to the negotiations with defendant's agent which would have led plaintiff to reasonably anticipate defendant would bury within the definition of "burglary" another exclusion denying coverage when, no matter how extensive the proof of a third-party burglary, no marks were left on the exterior of the premises. This escape clause, here triggered by the burglar's talent (an investigating law officer, apparently acquainted with the current modus operandi, gained access to the steel building without leaving any marks by leaning on the overhead plexiglas door while simultaneously turning the locked handle), was never read to or by plaintiff's personnel, nor was the substance explained by defendant's agent.

Moreover, the burglary "definition" which crept into this policy comports neither with the concept a layman might have of that crime, nor with a legal interpretation. See State v. Murray, 222 Iowa 925, 931, 270 N.W. 355, 358 (1936) ("We have held that even though the door was partially open, by opening it farther, in order to enter the building, this is a sufficient breaking to comply with the demands of the statute"); State v. Ferguson, 149 Iowa 476, 478–479, 128 N.W. 840, 841–842 (1910) ("It need not appear that this office was an independent building, for it is well known that it is burglary for one to break and enter an inner door or window, although the culprit entered through an open outer door. . . ."); see State v. Hougland, 197 N.W.2d 364, 365 (Iowa 1972).

The most plaintiff might have reasonably anticipated was a policy requirement of visual evidence (abundant here) indicating the burglary was an "outside" not an "inside" job. The exclusion in issue, masking as a definition, makes insurer's obligation to pay turn on the skill of the burglar, not on the event the parties bargained for: a bona-fide third party burglary resulting in loss of plaintiff's chemicals and equipment.

The "reasonable expectations" attention to the basic agreement, to the concept of substance over form, was appropriately applied by this court for the insurer's benefit in Central Bearings Co. v. Wolverine Insurance Company, 179 N.W.2d 443 (Iowa 1970), a case antedating Rodman. We there reversed a judgment for the insured which trial court apparently grounded on a claimed ambiguity in the policy. In denying coverage on what was essentially a products liability claim where the insured purchased only a "Premises-Operations" policy (without any misrepresentation, misunderstanding or overreaching) we said at page 449 of 179 N.W.2d:

> In summation we think the insured as a reasonable person would understand the policy coverage purchased meant the insured was not covered for loss if the 'accident' with concomitant damage to a victim occurred away from the premises and after the operation or sale was complete.

The same rationale of reasonable expectations should be applied when it would operate to the advantage of the insured. Appropriately applied to this case, the doctrine demands reversal and judgment for plaintiff.

We reverse and remand for judgment in conformance herewith.
REVERSED AND REMANDED.

DISSENT BY: LeGrand, J.

I dissent from the result reached by the majority because it ignores virtually every rule by which we have heretofore adjudicated such cases and affords plaintiff ex post facto insurance coverage which it not only did not buy but which it knew it did not buy.

The majority revokes, at least for this case, the principle that in law cases tried to the court the findings are binding on us if supported by substantial evidence and that we view the evidence in its most favorable light to sustain rather than defeat those findings.

While it may be very well to talk in grand terms about "mass advertising" by insurance companies and "incessant" assurances as to coverage which mislead the "unwary," particularly about "fine-print" provisions, such discussion should somehow be related to the case under review. Our primary duty, after all, is to resolve this dispute for these litigants under this record.

There is total silence in this case concerning any of the practices the majority finds offensive; nor is there any claim plaintiff was beguiled by such conduct into believing it had more protection than it actually did. Like all other appeals, this one should be decided on what the record discloses—a fact which the majority concedes but promptly disregards.

Crucial to a correct determination of this appeal is the disputed provision of each policy defining burglary as "the felonious abstraction of insured property by a person making felonious entry by actual force and violence, of which force and violence there are visible marks made by tools, explosives, electricity or chemicals upon, or physical damage to, the exterior of the premises at the place of such entry." The starting point of any consideration of that definition is a determination whether it is ambiguous. Yet the majority does not even mention ambiguity.

The purpose of such a provision, of course, is to omit from coverage "inside jobs" or those resulting from fraud or complicity by the assured. The overwhelming weight of authority upholds such provisions as legitimate in purpose and unambiguous in application. Once this indisputable fact is recognized, plaintiff's arguments virtually collapse. We may not—at least we should not—by any accepted standard of construction meddle with contracts which clearly and plainly state their meaning simply because we dislike that meaning, even in the case of insurance policies.

Nor can the doctrine of reasonable expectations be applied here. We adopted that rule in Rodman v. State Farm Mutual Automobile Insurance Company, 208 N.W.2d 903, 906, 907 (Iowa 1973). We refused, however, to apply it in that case, where we said:

The real question here is whether the principle of reasonable expectations should be extended to cases where an ordinary layman would not misunderstand his coverage from a reading of the policy and where there are no circumstances attributable to the insurer which foster coverage expectations. Plaintiff does not contend he misunderstood the policy. He did not read it. He now asserts in retrospect that if he had read it he would not have understood it. He does not say he was misled by conduct or representations of the insurer. He simply asked trial court to require the policy to cover his loss because if he had purchased his automobile insurance from another company the loss would have been covered, he did not know it was not covered, and if he had known it was not covered he would have purchased a different policy. Trial court declined to do so. We believe trial court correctly refused in these circumstances to extend the principle of reasonable expectations to impose liability.

Yet here the majority would extend the doctrine far beyond the point of refusal in Rodman. Here we have affirmative and unequivocal testimony from an officer and director of the plaintiff corporation that he knew the disputed provision was in the policies because "it was just like the insurance policy I have on my farm."

I cannot agree plaintiff may now assert it reasonably expected from these policies something it knew was not there.

For these several reasons—the principal one being that the findings of the trial court have substantial evidentiary support—I would affirm the judgment. Moore, C.J., Rees and Uhlenhopp, JJ. join this dissent.

QUESTIONS AND DISCUSSION POINTS

1. In comparing the Majority and Dissenting opinions, it is important to identify the precise points of disagreement between them. Do you think the Majority and Dissent agree on the meaning of "contract"? Can you identify the ways in which they differ? And if you decide that the Majority and Dissent have different conceptions of contract, how do you decide between them?

2. Does it matter that the plaintiff in this case probably never read the contract? Should that fact be held against him?

3. Would it matter if the plaintiff both needed insurance and could not get a better definition of "burglary" from another insurance company? What if the bank required insurance on the property because the property was mortgaged—would that fact make a difference?

4. Do you believe the plaintiff's building was burglarized? Do you think the Majority thought so?

5. What if you knew that the only reason the definition of "burglary" was so written was to prevent "inside jobs"? Would that make a difference to you in deciding this case?

6. What are the precise objections of the Dissent to the Majority opinion?

7. The Majority opinion suggests that the bargaining power of the parties is an important consideration in establishing the rights and obligations of the parties. What are the court's arguments for this proposition? Do you find them persuasive?

8. The opinion makes reference to the work of Karl Llewellyn, whom we know as one of the leading figures of American legal realism. Should Llewellyn's views play a role in deciding this case? What authority do his views have? If they have authority, why is this so?

ORA LEE WILLIAMS, Appellant,
v. WALKER-THOMAS FURNITURE COMPANY, Appellee
United States Court of Appeals, District of Columbia Circuit
350 F.2d 445 (1965)

J. SKELLY WRIGHT, Circuit Judge:

Appellee, Walker-Thomas Furniture Company, operates a retail furniture store in the District of Columbia. During the period from 1957 to 1962 each appellant in these cases purchased a number of household items from Walker-Thomas, for which payment was to be made in installments. The terms of each purchase were contained in a printed form contract which set forth the value of the purchased item and purported to lease the item to appellant for a stipulated monthly rent payment. The contract then provided, in substance, that title would remain in Walker-Thomas until the total of all the monthly payments made equaled the stated value of the item, at which time appellants could take title. In the event of a default in the payment of any monthly installment, Walker-Thomas could repossess the item.

The contract further provided that 'the amount of each periodical installment payment to be made by (purchaser) to the Company under this present lease shall be inclusive of and not in addition to the amount of each installment payment to be made by (purchaser) under such prior leases, bills or accounts; and all payments now and hereafter made by (purchaser) shall be credited pro rata on all outstanding leases, bills and accounts due the Company by (purchaser) at the time each such payment is made.' The effect of this rather obscure provision was to keep a balance due on every item purchased until the balance due on all items, whenever purchased, was liquidated. As a result, the debt incurred at the time of purchase of each item was secured by the right to repossess all the items previously purchased by the same purchaser, and each new item purchased automatically became subject to a security interest[1] arising out of the previous dealings.

On May 12, 1962, appellant Thorne purchased an item described as a Daveno, three tables, and two lamps, having total stated value of $391.10. Shortly thereafter, he defaulted on his monthly payments and appellee sought to replevy [take back (ed.)] all the items purchased since the first transaction in 1958. Similarly, on April 17, 1962, appellant Williams bought a stereo set of stated value of $514.95.[2] She too defaulted shortly thereafter, and appellee sought to replevy all the items purchased since December, 1957. The Court of General Sessions granted judgment for appellee. The District of Columbia Court of Appeals affirmed, and we granted appellants' motion for leave to appeal to this court.

Appellants' principal contention, rejected by both the trial and the appellate courts below, is that these contracts, or at least some of them, are unconscionable and, hence, not enforceable. In its opinion in Williams v. Walker-Thomas Fur-

---

1. A security interest is a lien on personal property. If payment of the underlying debt is not made in accordance with the terms of the contract, the lien holder may seize the liened property, and sell it, in order to satisfy the amount owed.

2. At the time of this purchase her account showed a balance of $164 still owing from her prior purchases. The total of all the purchases made over the years in question came to $1,800. The total payments amounted to $1,400.

niture Company, 198 A.2d 914, 916 (1964), the District of Columbia Court of Appeals explained its rejection of this contention as follows:

> Appellant's second argument presents a more serious question. The record reveals that prior to the last purchase appellant had reduced the balance in her account to $164. The last purchase, a stereo set, raised the balance due to $678. Significantly, at the time of this and the preceding purchases, appellee was aware of appellant's financial position. The reverse side of the stereo contract listed the name of appellant's social worker and her $218 monthly stipend from the government. Nevertheless, with full knowledge that appellant had to feed, clothe and support both herself and seven children on this amount, appellee sold her a $514 stereo set. 'We cannot condemn too strongly appellee's conduct. It raises serious questions of sharp practice and irresponsible business dealings. A review of the legislation in the District of Columbia affecting retail sales and the pertinent decisions of the highest court in this jurisdiction disclose, however, no ground upon which this court can declare the contracts in question contrary to public policy. We note that were the Maryland Retail Installment Sales Act, Art. 83 ss 128–153, or its equivalent, in force in the District of Columbia, we could grant appellant appropriate relief. We think Congress should consider corrective legislation to protect the public from such exploitive contracts as were utilized in the case at bar.

We do not agree that the court lacked the power to refuse enforcement to contracts found to be unconscionable. In other jurisdictions, it has been held as a matter of common law that unconscionable contracts are not enforceable.

While no decision of this court so holding has been found, the notion that an unconscionable bargain should not be given full enforcement is by no means novel. In Scott v. United States, 79 U.S. (12 Wall.) 443, 445, 20 L.Ed. 438 (1870), the Supreme Court stated:

> If a contract be unreasonable and unconscionable, but not void for fraud, a court of law will give to the party who sues for its breach damages, not according to its letter, but only such as he is equitably entitled to.

Since we have never adopted or rejected such a rule, the question here presented is actually one of first impression.

Congress has recently enacted the Uniform Commercial Code, which specifically provides that the court may refuse to enforce a contract which it finds to be unconscionable at the time it was made. 28 D.C.CODE § 2–302 (Supp. IV 1965). The enactment of this section, which occurred subsequent to the contracts here in suit, does not mean that the common law of the District of Columbia was otherwise at the time of enactment, nor does it preclude the court from adopting a similar rule in the exercise of its powers to develop the common law for the District of Columbia. In fact, in view of the absence of prior authority on the point, we consider the congressional adoption of s 2–302 persuasive authority for following the rationale of the cases from which the section is explicitly derived.[3] Accord-

---

3. See Comment, § 2–302, Uniform Commercial Code (1962). Compare Note, 45 VA.L.REV. 583, 590 (1959), where it is predicted that the rule of § 2–302 will be followed by analogy in cases which involve contracts not specifically covered by the section. Cf. 1 STATE OF NEW YORK LAW REVISION COMMISSION, REPORT AND RECORD OF HEARINGS ON THE UNIFORM COMMERCIAL CODE 108–110 (1954) (remarks of Professor Llewellyn).

ingly, we hold that where the element of unconscionability is present at the time a contract is made, the contract should not be enforced.

Unconscionability has generally been recognized to include an absence of meaningful choice on the part of one of the parties together with contract terms which are unreasonably favorable to the other party. Whether a meaningful choice is present in a particular case can only be determined by consideration of all the circumstances surrounding the transaction. In many cases the meaningfulness of the choice is negated by a gross inequality of bargaining power.[4] The manner in which the contract was entered is also relevant to this consideration. Did each party to the contract, considering his obvious education or lack of it, have a reasonable opportunity to understand the terms of the contract, or were the important terms hidden in a maze of fine print and minimized by deceptive sales practices? Ordinarily, one who signs an agreement without full knowledge of its terms might be held to assume the risk that he has entered a one-sided bargain.[5] But when a party of little bargaining power, and hence little real choice, signs a commercially unreasonable contract with little or no knowledge of its terms, it is hardly likely that his consent, or even an objective manifestation of his consent, was ever given to all the terms. In such a case the usual rule that the terms of the agreement are not to be questioned[6] should be abandoned and the court should consider whether the terms of the contract are so unfair that

---

4. See Henningsen v. Bloomfield Motors, Inc., 32 N.J. 358, 161 A.2d 69 (1960). A.2d at 86, and authorities there cited. Inquiry into the relative bargaining power of the two parties is not an inquiry wholly divorced from the general question of unconscionability, since a one-sided bargain is itself evidence of the inequality of the bargaining parties. This fact was vaguely recognized in the common law doctrine of intrinsic fraud, that is, fraud which can be presumed from the grossly unfair nature of the terms of the contract. See the oft-quoted statement of Lord Hardwicke in Earl of Chesterfield v. Janssen, 28 Eng. Rep. 82, 100 (1751):

> ... (Fraud) may be apparent from the intrinsic nature and subject of the bargain itself; such as no man in his senses and not under delusion would make. . . .

And cf. Hume v. United States, supra Note 3, 132 U.S. at 413, 10 S.Ct. at 137, where the Court characterized the English cases as "cases in which one party took advantage of the other's ignorance of arithmetic to impose upon him, and the fraud was apparent from the face of the contracts." See also Greer v. Tweed, supra Note 3.

5. FN8. See RESTATEMENT, CONTRACTS s 70 (1932); Note, 63 HARV.L.REV. 494 (1950). See also Daley v. People's Building, Loan & Savings Ass'n, 178 Mass. 13, 59 N.E. 452, 453 (1901), in which Mr. Justice Holmes, while sitting on the Supreme Judicial Court of Massachusetts, made this observation:

> ... Courts are less and less disposed to interfere with parties making such contracts as they choose, so long as they interfere with no one's welfare but their own. . . . It will be understood that we are speaking of parties standing in an equal position where neither has any oppressive advantage or power. . . .

6. This rule has never been without exception. In cases involving merely the transfer of unequal amounts of the same commodity, the courts have held the bargain unenforceable for the reason that "in such a case, it is clear, that the law cannot indulge in the presumption of equivalence between the consideration and the promise." 1 WILLISTON, CONTRACTS s 115 (3d ed. 1957).

enforcement should be withheld.[7]

In determining reasonableness or fairness, the primary concern must be with the terms of the contract considered in light of the circumstances existing when the contract was made. The test is not simple, nor can it be mechanically applied. The terms are to be considered "in the light of the general commercial background and the commercial needs of the particular trade or case." Corbin suggests the test as being whether the terms are "so extreme as to appear unconscionable according to the mores and business practices of the time and place." 1 CORBIN, op. cit. We think this formulation correctly states the test to be applied in those cases where no meaningful choice was exercised upon entering the contract.

Because the trial court and the appellate court did not feel that enforcement could be refused, no findings were made on the possible unconscionability of the contracts in these cases. Since the record is not sufficient for our deciding the issue as a matter of law, the cases must be remanded to the trial court for further proceedings. So ordered.

DANAHER, Circuit Judge (dissenting):

The District of Columbia Court of Appeals obviously was as unhappy about the situation here presented as any of us can possibly be. Its opinion in the Williams case, quoted in the majority text, concludes: "We think Congress should consider corrective legislation to protect the public from such exploitive contracts as were utilized in the case at bar." My view is thus summed up by an able court which made no finding that there had actually been sharp practice. Rather the appellant seems to have known precisely where she stood.

There are many aspects of public policy here involved. What is a luxury to some may seem an outright necessity to others. Is public oversight to be required of the expenditures of relief funds? A washing machine, e.g., in the hands of a relief client might become a fruitful source of income. Many relief clients may well need credit, and certain business establishments will take long chances on the sale of items, expecting their pricing policies will afford a degree of protection commensurate with the risk. Perhaps a remedy when necessary will be found within the provisions of the "Loan Shark" law, D.C.CODE §§ 26–601 et seq. (1961).

I mention such matters only to emphasize the desirability of a cautious approach to any such problem, particularly since the law for so long has allowed parties such great latitude in making their own contracts. I dare say there must annually be thousands upon thousands of installment credit transactions in this jurisdiction, and one can only speculate as to the effect the decision in these cases will have.

I join the District of Columbia Court of Appeals in its disposition of the issues.

---

7. See the general discussion of "Boiler-Plate Agreements" in LEWELLYN, THE COMMON LAW TRADITION 362–371 (1960).

QUESTIONS AND DISCUSSION POINTS

1. The plaintiff is a merchant of furniture and home furnishings (including stereo equipment). To guarantee payment for purchases made on credit, which the merchant advanced, the Walker-Thomas company required

that not only the immediate item purchased, but all property ever purchased by a customer be pledged as security for the unpaid purchase price of any item purchased. Do you think such an arrangement is fair to the purchaser? Can you think of arguments in defense of such a practice?

2. The majority opinion makes reference to the Uniform Commercial Code (UCC), specifically Article 2, the sales article. This statute contains a section, number 2–302, which prohibits enforcement of "unconscionable" contracts. Can you tell what it is about the contracts in this case that the court found to be unconscionable? Was it the substance of the agreements—their terms—or was it the conditions under which the agreements were entered into?

3. What grounds does the court use to support its decision that the contract is unenforceable? Is there a common law answer to the question posed by the case? If not, what is the source of law in the case? Is this source an appropriate one for resolution of the question posed by the case?

4. Critics of this decision often say that decisions of this sort increase the costs of goods and credits, thereby raising prices for everyone. Are you persuaded that this claim is true? Even if it is true, does it matter?

5. What do you think of the Dissent's argument that Mrs. Walker seemed to understand perfectly well what she was agreeing to? If she did understand the agreement, do you think the decision undermines her autonomy?

~

In the Matter of BABY M, a pseudonym for an actual person
Supreme Court of New Jersey
537 A.2D 1227 (1988)

WILENTZ, C.J.

In this matter the Court is asked to determine the validity of a contract that purports to provide a new way of bringing children into a family. For a fee of $10,000, a woman agrees to be artificially inseminated with the semen of another woman's husband; she is to conceive a child, carry it to term, and after its birth surrender it to the natural father and his wife. The intent of the contract is that the child's natural mother will thereafter be forever separated from her child. The wife is to adopt the child, and she and the natural father are to be *411 regarded as

its parents for all purposes. The contract providing for this is called a "surrogacy contract," the natural mother inappropriately called the "surrogate mother."

We invalidate the surrogacy contract because it conflicts with the law and public policy of this State. While we recognize the depth of the yearning of infertile couples to have their own children, we find the payment of money to a "surrogate" mother illegal, perhaps criminal, and potentially degrading to women. Although in this case we grant custody to the natural father, the evidence having clearly proved such custody to be in the best interests of the infant, we void both the termination of the surrogate mother's parental rights 109 N.J. 396, 537 A.2D 1227, and the adoption of the child by the wife/stepparent. We thus restore the "surrogate" as the mother of the child. We remand the issue of the natural mother's visitation rights to the trial court, since that issue was not reached below and the record before us is not sufficient to permit us to decide it de novo.

We find no offense to our present laws where a woman voluntarily and without payment agrees to act as a "surrogate" mother, provided that she is not subject to a binding agreement to surrender her child. Moreover, our holding today does not preclude the Legislature from altering the current statutory scheme, within constitutional limits, so as to permit surrogacy contracts. Under current law, however, the surrogacy agreement before us is illegal and invalid.

I. Facts

In February 1985, William Stern and Mary Beth Whitehead entered into a surrogacy contract. It recited that Stern's wife, Elizabeth, was infertile, that they wanted a child, and that Mrs. Whitehead was willing to provide that child as the mother with Mr. Stern as the father.

The contract provided that through artificial insemination using Mr. Stern's sperm, Mrs. Whitehead would become pregnant, carry the child to term, bear it, deliver it to the Sterns, and thereafter do whatever was necessary to terminate her maternal rights so that Mrs. Stern could thereafter adopt the child. Mrs. Whitehead's husband, Richard, was also a party to the contract; Mrs. Stern was not. Mr. Whitehead promised to do all acts necessary to rebut the presumption of paternity under the Parentage Act. N.J.S.A. 9:17–43a(1),-44a. Although Mrs. Stern was not a party to the surrogacy agreement, the contract gave her sole custody of the child in the event of Mr. Stern's death. Mrs. Stern's status as a nonparty to the surrogate parenting agreement presumably was to avoid the application of the baby-selling statute to this arrangement. N.J.S.A. 9:3–54.

Mr. Stern, on his part, agreed to attempt the artificial insemination and to pay Mrs. Whitehead $10,000 after the child's birth, on its delivery to him. In a separate contract, Mr. Stern agreed to pay $7,500 to the Infertility Center of New York ("ICNY"). The Center's advertising campaigns solicit surrogate mothers and encourage infertile couples to consider surrogacy. ICNY arranged for the surrogacy contract by bringing the parties together, explaining the process to them, furnishing the contractual form, and providing legal counsel.

The history of the parties' involvement in this arrangement suggests their good faith. William and Elizabeth Stern were married in July 1974, having met at the University of Michigan, where both were Ph.D. candidates. Due to financial considerations and Mrs. Stern's pursuit of a medical degree and residency, they decided to defer starting a family until 1981. Before then, however, Mrs. Stern learned that she might have multiple sclerosis and that the disease in some cases renders pregnancy a serious health risk. Her anxiety appears to have exceeded the actual risk, which current medical authorities assess as minimal. Nonetheless that anxiety was evidently quite real, Mrs. Stern fearing that pregnancy might precipitate blindness, paraplegia, or other forms of debilitation. Based on the perceived risk, the Sterns decided to forego having their own children. The decision had special significance for Mr. Stern. Most of his family had been destroyed in the Holocaust. As the family's only survivor, he very much wanted to continue his bloodline.

Initially the Sterns considered adoption, but were discouraged by the substantial delay apparently involved and by the potential problem they saw arising from their age and their differing religious backgrounds. They were most eager for some other means to start a family. The paths of Mrs. Whitehead and the Sterns to surrogacy were similar. Both responded to advertising by ICNY. The Sterns' response, following their inquiries into adoption, was the result of their long-standing decision to have a child. Mrs. Whitehead's response apparently resulted from her sympathy with family members and others who could have no children (she stated that she wanted to give another couple the "gift of life"); she also wanted the $10,000 to help her family.

Both parties, undoubtedly because of their own self-interest, were less sensitive to the implications of the transaction than they might otherwise have been. Mrs. Whitehead, for instance, appears not to have been concerned about whether the Sterns would make good parents for her child; the Sterns, on their part, while conscious of the obvious possibility that surrendering the child might cause grief to Mrs. Whitehead, overcame their qualms because of their desire for a child. At any rate, both the Sterns and Mrs. Whitehead were committed to the arrangement; both thought it right and constructive.

Mrs. Whitehead had reached her decision concerning surrogacy before the Sterns, and had actually been involved as a potential surrogate mother with an-

other couple. After numerous unsuccessful artificial inseminations, that effort was abandoned. Thereafter, the Sterns learned of the Infertility Center, the possibilities of surrogacy, and of Mary Beth Whitehead. The two couples met to discuss the surrogacy arrangement and decided to go forward. On February 6, 1985, Mr. Stern and Mr. and Mrs. Whitehead executed the surrogate parenting agreement. After several artificial inseminations over a period of months, Mrs. Whitehead became pregnant. The pregnancy was uneventful and on March 27, 1986, Baby M was born.

Not wishing anyone at the hospital to be aware of the surrogacy arrangement, Mr. and Mrs. Whitehead appeared to all as the proud parents of a healthy female child. Her birth certificate indicated her name to be Sara Elizabeth Whitehead and her father to be Richard Whitehead. In accordance with Mrs. Whitehead's request, the Sterns visited the hospital unobtrusively to see the newborn child.

Mrs. Whitehead realized, almost from the moment of birth, that she could not part with this child. She had felt a bond with it even during pregnancy. Some indication of the attachment was conveyed to the Sterns at the hospital when they told Mrs. Whitehead what they were going to name the baby. She apparently broke into tears and indicated that she did not know if she could give up the child. She talked about how the baby looked like her other daughter, and made it clear that she was experiencing great difficulty with the decision. Nonetheless, Mrs. Whitehead was, for the moment, true to her word. Despite powerful inclinations to the contrary, she turned her child over to the Sterns on March 30 at the Whiteheads' home.

The Sterns were thrilled with their new child. They had planned extensively for its arrival, far beyond the practical furnishing of a room for her. It was a time of joyful celebration—not just for them but for their friends as well.

The Sterns looked forward to raising their daughter, whom they named Melissa. While aware by then that Mrs. Whitehead was undergoing an emotional crisis, they were as yet not cognizant of the depth of that crisis and its implications for their newly-enlarged family.

Later in the evening of March 30, Mrs. Whitehead became deeply disturbed, disconsolate, stricken with unbearable sadness. She had to have her child. She could not eat, sleep, or concentrate on anything other than her need for her baby. The next day she went to the Sterns' home and told them how much she was suffering.

The depth of Mrs. Whitehead's despair surprised and frightened the Sterns. She told them that she could not live without her baby, that she must have her, even if only for one week, that thereafter she would surrender her child. The Sterns, concerned that Mrs. Whitehead might indeed commit suicide, not wanting under any circumstances to risk that, and in any event believing that Mrs. Whitehead would keep her word, turned the child over to her. It was not until four months later, after a series of attempts to regain possession of the child, that Melissa was returned to the Sterns, having been forcibly removed from the home where she was then living with Mr. and Mrs. Whitehead, the home in Florida owned by Mary Beth Whitehead's parents.

The struggle over Baby M began when it became apparent that Mrs. Whitehead could not return the child to Mr. Stern. Due to Mrs. Whitehead's refusal to relinquish the baby, Mr. Stern filed a complaint seeking enforcement of the surrogacy contract. He alleged, accurately, that Mrs. Whitehead had not only refused to comply with the surrogacy contract but had threatened to flee from New Jersey with the child in order to avoid even the possibility of his obtaining custody. The court papers asserted that if Mrs. Whitehead were to be given notice of the application for an order requiring her to relinquish custody, she would, prior to the hearing, leave the state with the baby. And that is precisely what she did. After the order was entered, ex parte, the process server, aided by the police, in the presence of the Sterns, entered Mrs. Whitehead's home to execute the order. Mr. Whitehead fled with the child, who had been handed to him through a window while those who came to enforce the order were thrown off balance by a dispute over the child's current name.

The Whiteheads immediately fled to Florida with Baby M. They stayed initially with Mrs. Whitehead's parents, where one of Mrs. Whitehead's children had been living. For the next three months, the Whiteheads and Melissa lived at roughly twenty different hotels, motels, and homes in order to avoid apprehension. From time to time Mrs. Whitehead would call Mr. Stern to discuss the matter; the conversations, recorded by Mr. Stern on advice of counsel, show an escalating dispute about rights, morality, and power, accompanied by threats of Mrs. Whitehead to kill herself, to kill the child, and falsely to accuse Mr. Stern of sexually molesting Mrs. Whitehead's other daughter. Eventually the Sterns discovered where the Whiteheads were staying, commenced supplementary proceedings in Florida, and obtained an order requiring the Whiteheads to turn over the child. Police in Florida enforced the order, forcibly removing the child from her grandparents' home. She was soon thereafter brought to New Jersey and turned over to the Sterns. The prior order of the court, issued ex parte, awarding custody of the child to the Sterns pendente lite, was reaffirmed by the trial court after consideration of the certified representations of the parties (both represented by counsel) concerning the unusual sequence of events that had unfolded. Pending final judgment, Mrs. Whitehead was awarded limited visitation with Baby M. The Sterns' complaint, in addition to seeking possession and ultimately custody of the child, sought enforcement of the surrogacy contract. Pursuant to the contract, it asked that the child be permanently placed in their custody, that Mrs. Whitehead's parental rights be terminated, and that Mrs. Stern be allowed to adopt the child, i.e., that, for all purposes, Melissa become the Sterns' child. The trial took thirty-two days over a period of more than two months. . . .

Soon after the conclusion of the trial, the trial court announced its opinion from the bench. 217 N.J.Super. 313, 525 A.2d 1128 (1987). It held that the surrogacy contract was valid; ordered that Mrs. Whitehead's parental rights be terminated and that sole custody of the child be granted to Mr. Stern; and, after hearing brief testimony from Mrs. Stern, immediately entered an order allowing the adoption of Melissa by Mrs. Stern, all in accordance with the surrogacy contract. Pending the outcome of the appeal, we granted a continuation of visitation to Mrs. Whitehead, although slightly more limited than the visitation allowed during the trial.

Although clearly expressing its view that the surrogacy contract was valid, the trial court devoted the major portion of its opinion to the question of the baby's best interests. The inconsistency is apparent. The surrogacy contract calls for the surrender of the child to the Sterns, permanent and sole custody in the Sterns, and termination of Mrs. Whitehead's parental rights, all without qualification, all regardless of any evaluation of the best interests of the child. As a matter of fact the contract recites (even before the child was conceived) that it is in the best interests of the child to be placed with Mr. Stern. In effect, the trial court awarded custody to Mr. Stern, the natural father, based on the same kind of evidence and analysis as might be expected had no surrogacy contract existed. Its rationalization, however, was that while the surrogacy contract was valid, specific performance would not be granted unless that remedy was in the best interests of the child. The factual issues confronted and decided by the trial court were the same as if Mr. Stern and Mrs. Whitehead had had the child out of wedlock, intended or unintended, and then disagreed about custody. The trial court's awareness of the irrelevance of the contract in the court's determination of custody is suggested by its remark that beyond the question of the child's best interests, "[a]ll other concerns raised by counsel constitute commentary." 217 N.J.Super. at 323, 525 A.2d 1128.

Mrs. Whitehead contends that the surrogacy contract, for a variety of reasons, is invalid. She contends that it conflicts with public policy since it guarantees that the child will not have the nurturing of both natural parents—presumably New Jersey's goal for families. She further argues that it deprives the mother of her constitutional right to the companionship of her child, and that it conflicts with statutes concerning termination of parental rights and adoption. With the contract thus void, Mrs. Whitehead claims primary custody (with visitation rights in Mr. Stern) both on a best interests basis (stressing the "tender years" doctrine) as well as on the policy basis of discouraging surrogacy contracts. She maintains that even if custody would ordinarily go to Mr. Stern, here it should be awarded to Mrs. Whitehead to deter future surrogacy arrangements.

In a brief filed after oral argument, counsel for Mrs. Whitehead suggests that the standard for determining best interests where the infant resulted from a surrogacy contract is that the child should be placed with the mother absent a showing of unfitness.

The Sterns claim that the surrogacy contract is valid and should be enforced, largely for the reasons given by the trial court. They claim a constitutional right of privacy, which includes the right of procreation, and the right of consenting adults to deal with matters of reproduction as they see fit. As for the child's best interests, their position is factual: given all of the circumstances, the child is better off in their custody with no residual parental rights reserved for Mrs. Whitehead.

II. Invalidity and Unenforceability of Surrogacy Contract

We have concluded that this surrogacy contract is invalid. Our conclusion has two bases: direct conflict with existing statutes and conflict with the public policies of this State, as expressed in its statutory and decisional law.

One of the surrogacy contract's basic purposes, to achieve the adoption of a child through private placement, though permitted in New Jersey "is very much disfavored." Sees v. Baber, 74 N.J. 201, 217, 377 A.2d 628 (1977). Its use of money for this purpose—and we have no doubt whatsoever that the money is being paid to obtain an adoption and not, as the Sterns argue, for the personal services of Mary Beth Whitehead—is illegal and perhaps criminal. N.J.S.A. 9:3–54. In addition to the inducement of money, there is the coercion of contract: the natural mother's irrevocable agreement, prior to birth, even prior to conception, to surrender the child to the adoptive couple. Such an agreement is totally unenforceable in private placement adoption. Sees, 74 N.J. at 212–14, 377 A.2d 628. Even where the adoption is through an approved agency, the formal agreement to surrender occurs only after birth (as we read N.J.S.A. 9:2–16 and –17, and similar statutes), and then, by regulation, only after the birth mother has been offered counseling. N.J.A.C. 10:121A-5.4(c). Integral to these invalid provisions of the surrogacy contract is the related agreement, equally invalid, on the part of the natural mother to cooperate with, and not to contest, proceedings to terminate her parental rights, as well as her contractual concession, in aid of the adoption, that the child's best interests would be served by awarding custody to the natural father and his wife—all of this before she has even conceived, and, in some cases, before she has the slightest idea of what the natural father and adoptive mother are like.

The foregoing provisions not only directly conflict with New Jersey statutes, but also offend long-established State policies. These critical terms, which are at the heart of the contract, are invalid and unenforceable; the conclusion therefore follows, without more, that the entire contract is unenforceable.

A. Conflict with Statutory Provisions

The surrogacy contract conflicts with: (1) laws prohibiting the use of money in connection with adoptions; (2) laws requiring proof of parental unfitness or abandonment before termination of parental rights is ordered or an adoption is granted; and (3) laws that make surrender of custody and consent to adoption revocable in private placement adoptions.

1. Our law prohibits paying or accepting money in connection with any placement of a child for adoption. N.J.S.A. 9:3–54a. Violation is a high misdemeanor. N.J.S.A. 9:3–54c. Excepted are fees of an approved agency (which must be a non-profit entity, N.J.S.A. 9:3–38a) and certain expenses in connection with childbirth. N.J.S.A. 9:3–54b.[1]

Considerable care was taken in this case to structure the surrogacy arrangement so as not to violate this prohibition. The arrangement was structured as follows: the adopting parent, Mrs. Stern, was not a party to the surrogacy contract; the money paid to Mrs. Whitehead was stated to be for her services—not for the adoption; the sole purpose of the contract was stated as being that "of giving a child to William Stern, its natural and biological father"; the money was purported to be "compensation for services and expenses and in no way . . . a fee for termination of parental rights or a payment in exchange for consent to surrender a child for adoption"; the fee to the Infertility Center ($7,500) was stated to be for legal representation, advice, administra-

tive work, and other "services." Nevertheless, it seems clear that the money was paid and accepted in connection with an adoption.

The Infertility Center's major role was first as a "finder" of the surrogate mother whose child was to be adopted, and second as the arranger of all proceedings that led to the adoption. Its role as adoption finder is demonstrated by the provision requiring Mr. Stern to pay another $7,500 if he uses Mary Beth Whitehead again as a surrogate, and by ICNY's agreement to "coordinate arrangements for the adoption of the child by the wife." The surrogacy agreement requires Mrs. Whitehead to surrender Baby M for the purposes of adoption. The agreement notes that Mr. and Mrs. Stern wanted to have a child, and provides that the child be "placed" with Mrs. Stern in the event Mr. Stern dies be-

---

1. N.J.S.A. 9:3–54 reads as follows:

   a. No person, firm, partnership, corporation, association or agency shall make, offer to make or assist or participate in any placement for adoption and in connection therewith

      1. Pay, give or agree to give any money or any valuable consideration, or assume or discharge any financial obligation; or
      2. Take, receive, accept or agree to accept any money or any valuable consideration.

   b. The prohibition of subsection a. shall not apply to the fees or services of any approved agency in connection with a placement for adoption, nor shall such prohibition apply to the payment or reimbursement of medical, hospital or other similar expenses incurred in connection with the birth or any illness of the child, or to the acceptance of such reimbursement by a parent of the child.

   c. Any person, firm, partnership, corporation, association or agency violating this section shall be guilty of a high misdemeanor.

fore the child is born. The payment of the $10,000 occurs only on surrender of custody of the child and "completion of the duties and obligations" of Mrs. Whitehead, including termination of her parental rights to facilitate adoption by Mrs. Stern. As for the contention that the Sterns are paying only for services and not for an adoption, we need note only that they would pay nothing in the event the child died before the fourth month of pregnancy, and only $1,000 if the child were stillborn, even though the "services" had been fully rendered. Additionally, one of Mrs. Whitehead's estimated costs, to be assumed by Mr. Stern, was an "Adoption Fee," presumably for Mrs. Whitehead's incidental costs in connection with the adoption.

Mr. Stern knew he was paying for the adoption of a child; Mrs. Whitehead knew she was accepting money so that a child might be adopted; the Infertility Center knew that it was being paid for assisting in the adoption of a child. The actions of all three worked to frustrate the goals of the statute. It strains credulity to claim that these arrangements, touted by those in the surrogacy business as an attractive alternative to the usual route leading to an adoption, really amount to something other than a private placement adoption for money.

The prohibition of our statute is strong. Violation constitutes a high misdemeanor, N.J.S.A. 9:3–54c, a third-degree crime, N.J.S.A. 2C:43–1b, carrying a penalty of three to five years imprisonment. N.J.S.A. 2C:43–6a(3). The evils inherent in baby-bartering are loathsome for a myriad of reasons. The child is sold without regard for whether the purchasers will be suitable parents. N. Baker, Baby Selling: The Scandal of Black Market Adoption 7 (1978). The natural mother does not receive the benefit of counseling and guidance to assist her in making a decision that may affect her for a lifetime. In fact, the monetary incentive to sell her child may, depending on her financial circumstances, make her decision less voluntary. Id. at 44. Furthermore, the adoptive parents may not be fully informed of the natural parents' medical history.

Baby-selling potentially results in the exploitation of all parties involved. Ibid. Conversely, adoption statutes seek to further humanitarian goals, foremost among them the best interests of the child. H. Witmer, E. Herzog, E. Weinstein, & M. Sullivan, Independent Adoptions: A Follow-Up Study 32 (1967). The negative consequences of baby-buying are potentially present in the surrogacy context, especially the potential for placing and adopting a child without regard to the interest of the child or the natural mother.

2. The termination of Mrs. Whitehead's parental rights, called for by the surrogacy contract and actually ordered by the court, 217 N.J.Super. at 399–400, 525 A.2d 1128, fails to comply with the stringent requirements of New Jersey law. Our law, recognizing the finality of any termination of parental rights, provides for such termination only where there has been a voluntary surrender of a child to an approved agency or to the Division of Youth and Family Services ("DYFS"), accompanied by a formal document acknowledging termination of parental rights, N.J.S.A. 9:2–16, –17; N.J.S.A. 9:3–41; N.J.S.A. 30:4C–23, or where there has been a showing of parental abandonment or unfitness. A termination may ordinarily take one of three forms: an action by an approved agency, an action by DYFS, or an action in connection with a private placement adoption. The three are governed by separate statutes, but the standards for termination are substantially the same, except that whereas a written surrender is effective when made to an approved agency or to DYFS, there is no provision for it in the private placement context. See N.J.S.A. 9:2–14; N.J.S.A. 30:4C–23. N.J.S.A. 9:2–18 to 20 governs an action by an approved agency to terminate parental rights. Such an action, whether or not in conjunction with a pending adoption, may proceed on proof of written surrender, N.J.S.A. 9:2–16, –17, "forsaken parental obligation," or other specific grounds such as death or insanity, N.J.S.A. 9:2–19. Where the parent has not executed a formal consent, termination requires a showing of "forsaken parental obligation," i.e., "willful and continuous neglect or failure to perform the natural and regular obligations of care and support of a child." N.J.S.A. 9:2–13(d). See also N.J.S.A. 9:3–46a,47c.

Where DYFS is the agency seeking termination, the requirements are similarly stringent, although at first glance they do not appear to be so. DYFS can, as can any approved agency, accept a formal voluntary surrender or writing having the effect of termination and giving DYFS the right to place the child for adoption. N.J.S.A. 30:4C-23. Absent such formal written surrender and consent, similar to that given to approved agencies, DYFS can terminate parental rights in an action for guardianship by proving that "the best interests of such child require that he be placed under proper guardianship." N.J.S.A. 30:4C-20. Despite this "best interests" language, however, this Court has recently held in New Jersey Div. of Youth & Family Servs. v.

A.W., 103 N.J. 591, 512 A.2d 438 (1986), that in order for DYFS to terminate parental rights it must prove, by clear and convincing evidence, that "[t]he child's health and development have been or will be seriously impaired by the parental relationship," id. at 604, 512 A.2d 438, that "[t]he parents are unable or unwilling to eliminate the harm and delaying permanent placement will add to the harm," id. at 605, 512 A.2d 438, that "[t]he court has considered alternatives to termination," id. at 608, 512 A.2d 438, and that "[t]he termination of parental rights will not do more harm than good," id. at 610, 512 A.2d 438. This interpretation of the statutory language requires a most substantial showing of harm to the child if the parental relationship were to continue, far exceeding anything that a "best interests" test connotes.

In order to terminate parental rights under the private placement adoption statute, there must be a finding of "intentional abandonment or a very substantial neglect of parental duties without a reasonable expectation of a reversal of that conduct in the future." N.J.S.A. 9:3–48c(1). This requirement is similar to that of the prior law (i.e., "forsaken parental obligations," L.1953, c. 264, s 2(d) (codified at N.J.S.A. 9:3–18(d) (repealed))), and to that of the law providing for termination through actions by approved agencies, N.J.S.A. 9:2–13(d). See also In re Adoption by J.J.P., 175 N.J.Super. 420, 427, 419 A.2d 1135 (App.Div.1980) (noting that the language of the termination provision in the present statute, N.J.S.A. 9:3–48c(1), derives from this Court's construction of the prior statute in In re Adoption of Children by D., 61 N.J. 89, 94–95, 293 A.2d 171 (1972)).

In Sees v. Baber, 74 N.J. 201, 377 A.2d 628 (1977) we distinguished the requirements for terminating parental rights in a private placement adoption from those required in an approved agency adoption. We stated that in an unregulated private placement, "neither consent nor voluntary surrender is singled out as a statutory factor in terminating parental rights." Id. at 213, 377 A.2d 628. Sees established that without proof that parental obligations had been forsaken, there would be no termination in a private placement setting.

As the trial court recognized, without a valid termination there can be no adoption. In re Adoption of Children by D., supra, 61 N.J. at 95, 293 A.2d 171. This requirement applies to all adoptions, whether they be private placements, ibid., or agency adoptions, N.J.S.A. 9:3–46a, –47c.

Our statutes, and the cases interpreting them, leave no doubt that where there has been no written surrender to an approved agency or to DYFS, termination of parental rights will not be granted in this state absent a very strong showing of abandonment or neglect. That showing is required in every context in which termination of parental rights is sought, be it an action by an approved agency, an action by DYFS, or a private placement adoption proceeding, even where the petitioning adoptive parent is, as here, a stepparent. While the statutes make certain procedural allowances when stepparents are involved, the substantive requirement for terminating the natural parents' rights is not relaxed one iota. It is clear that a "best interests" determination is never sufficient to terminate parental rights; the statutory criteria must be proved.

In this case a termination of parental rights was obtained not by proving the statutory prerequisites but by claiming the benefit of contractual provisions. From all that has been stated above, it is clear that a contractual agreement to abandon one's parental rights, or not to contest a termination action, will not be enforced in our courts. The Legislature would not have so carefully, so consistently, and so substantially restricted termination of parental rights if it had intended to allow termination to be achieved by one short sentence in a contract. Since the termination was invalid, it follows, as noted above, that adoption of Melissa by Mrs. Stern could not properly be granted.

3. The provision in the surrogacy contract stating that Mary Beth Whitehead agrees to "surrender custody . . . and terminate all parental rights" contains no clause giving her a right to rescind. It is intended to be an irrevocable consent to surrender the child for adoption—in other words, an irrevocable commitment by Mrs. Whitehead to turn Baby M over to the Sterns and thereafter to allow termination of her parental rights. The trial court required a "best interests" showing as a condition to granting specific performance of the surrogacy contract.

Having decided the "best interests" issue in favor of the Sterns, that court's order included, among other things, specific performance of this agreement to surrender custody and terminate all parental rights. Mrs. Whitehead, shortly after the child's birth, had attempted to revoke her consent and surrender by refusing, after the Sterns had allowed her to have the child "just for one week," to return Baby M to them. The trial court's award of specific performance therefore reflects its view that the consent to surrender the child was irrevocable. We accept the trial court's construction of the contract; indeed it appears quite clear that this was the parties' intent. Such a provision, however, making irrevocable the natural mother's consent to surrender custody of her child in a private placement adoption, clearly conflicts with New Jersey law.

Our analysis commences with the statute providing for surrender of custody to an approved agency and termination of parental rights on the suit of that agency. The two basic provisions of the statute are N.J.S.A. 9:2–14 and 9:2–16. The former provides explicitly that [e]xcept as otherwise provided by law or by order or judgment of a court of competent jurisdiction or by testamentary disposition, no surrender of the custody of a child shall be valid in this state unless made to an approved agency pursuant to the provisions of this act. . . . There is no exception "provided by law," and it is not clear that there could be any "order or judgment of a court of competent jurisdiction" validating a surrender of custody as a basis for adoption when that surrender was not in conformance with the statute. Requirements for a voluntary surrender to an approved agency are set forth in N.J.S.A. 9:2–16. This section allows an approved agency to take a voluntary surrender of custody from the parent of a child but provides stringent requirements as a condition to its validity. The surrender must be in writing, must be in such form as is required for the recording of a deed, and, pursuant to N.J.S.A. 9:2–17, must be such as to declare that the person executing the same desires to relinquish the custody of the child, acknowledge the termination of parental rights as to such custody in favor of the approved agency, and acknowledge full understanding of the effect of such surrender as provided by this act.

If the foregoing requirements are met, the consent, the voluntary surrender of custody shall be valid whether or not the person giving same is a minor and shall be irrevocable except at the discretion of the approved agency taking such surrender or upon order or judgment of a court of competent jurisdiction, setting aside such surrender upon proof of fraud, duress, or misrepresentation. [N.J.S.A. 9:2–16.]

The importance of that irrevocability is that the surrender itself gives the agency the power to obtain termination of parental rights—in other words, permanent separation of the parent from the child, leading in the ordinary case to an adoption. N.J.S.A. 9:2–18 to 20.

This statutory pattern, providing for a surrender in writing and for termination of parental rights by an approved agency, is generally followed in connection with adoption proceedings and proceedings by DYFS to obtain permanent custody of a child. Our adoption statute repeats the requirements necessary to accomplish an irrevocable surrender to an approved agency in both form and substance. N.J.S.A. 9:3–41a. It provides that the surrender "shall be valid and binding without regard to the age of the person executing the surrender," ibid.; and although the word "irrevocable" is not used, that seems clearly to be the intent of the provision. The statute speaks of such surrender as constituting "relinquishment of such person's parental rights in or guardianship or custody of the child named therein and consent by such person to adoption of the child." Ibid. (emphasis supplied). We emphasize "named therein," for we construe the statute to allow a surrender only after the birth of the child. The formal consent to surrender enables the approved agency to terminate parental rights.

Similarly, DYFS is empowered to "take voluntary surrenders and releases of custody and consents to adoption[s]" from parents, which surrenders, releases, or consents "when properly acknowledged . . . shall be valid and binding irrespective of the age of the person giving the same, and shall be irrevocable except at the discretion of the Bureau of Childrens Services [currently DYFS] or upon order of a court of competent jurisdiction." N.J.S.A. 30:4C-23. Such consent to surrender of the custody of the child would presumably lead to an adoption placement by DYFS.

It is clear that the Legislature so carefully circumscribed all aspects of a consent to surrender custody—its form and substance, its manner of execution, and the agency or agencies to which it may be made—in order to provide the basis for irrevocability. It seems most unlikely that the Legislature intended that a consent not complying with these requirements would also be irrevocable, especially where, as here, that consent falls radically short of compliance. Not only do the form and substance of the consent in the surrogacy contract fail to meet statutory requirements, but the surrender of custody is made to a private party. It is not made, as the statute requires, either to an approved agency or to DYFS.

These strict prerequisites to irrevocability constitute a recognition of the most serious consequences that flow from such consents: termination of parental rights, the permanent separation of parent from child, and the ultimate adoption of the child. Because of those consequences, the Legislature severely limited the circumstances under which such consent would be irrevocable. The legislative goal is furthered by regulations requiring approved agencies, prior to accepting irrevocable consents, to provide advice and counseling to women, making it more likely that they fully understand and appreciate the consequences of their acts. N.J.A.C. 10:121A-5.4(c).

Contractual surrender of parental rights is not provided for in our statutes as now written. Indeed, in the Parentage Act, N.J.S.A. 9:17–38 to –59, there is a specific provision invalidating any agreement "between an alleged or presumed father and the mother of the child" to bar an action brought for the purpose of determining paternity "[r]egardless of [the contract's] terms." N.J.S.A. 9:17–45. Even a settlement agreement concerning parentage reached in a judicially-mandated consent conference is not valid unless the proposed settlement is approved beforehand by the court. There is no doubt that a contractual provision purporting to constitute an irrevocable agreement to surrender custody of a child for adoption is invalid.

In Sees v. Baber, supra, 74 N.J. 201, 377 A.2d 628, we noted that a natural mother's consent to surrender her child and to its subsequent adoption was no longer required by the statute in private placement adoptions. After tracing the statutory history from the time when such a consent had been an essential prerequisite to adoption, we concluded that such a consent was now neither necessary nor sufficient for the purpose of terminating parental rights. Id. at 213, 377 A.2d 628. The consent to surrender custody in that case was in writing, had been executed prior to physical surrender of the infant, and had been explained to the mother by an attorney. The trial court found that the consent to surrender of custody in that private placement adoption was knowing, voluntary, and deliberate. Id. at 216, 377 A.2d 628. The physical surrender of the child took place four days after its birth. Two days thereafter the natural mother changed her mind, and asked that the adoptive couple give her baby back to her. We held that she was entitled to the baby's return. The effect of our holding in that case necessarily encompassed our conclusion that "in an unsupervised private placement, since there is no statutory obligation to consent, there can be no legal barrier to its retraction." Id. at 215, 377 A.2d 628. The only possible relevance of consent in these matters, we noted, was that it might bear on whether there had been an abandonment of the child, or a forsaking of parental obligations. Otherwise, consent in a private placement adoption is not only revocable but, when revoked early enough, irrelevant.

The provision in the surrogacy contract whereby the mother irrevocably agrees to surrender custody of her child and to terminate her parental rights conflicts with the settled interpretation of New Jersey statutory law. There is only one irrevocable consent, and that is the one explicitly provided for by statute: a consent to surrender of custody and a placement with an approved agency or with DYFS. The provision in the surrogacy contract, agreed to before conception, requiring the natural mother to surrender custody of the child without any right of revocation is one more indication of the essential nature of this transaction: the creation of a contractual system of termination and adoption designed to circumvent our statutes.

B. Public Policy Considerations

The surrogacy contract's invalidity, resulting from its direct conflict with the above statutory provisions, is further un-

derlined when its goals and means are measured against New Jersey's public policy. The contract's basic premise, that the natural parents can decide in advance of birth which one is to have custody of the child, bears no relationship to the settled law that the child's best interests shall determine custody. See Fantony v. Fantony, 21 N.J. 525, 536–37, 122 A.2d 593 (1956); see also Sheehan v. Sheehan, 38 N.J.Super. 120, 125, 118 A.2d 89 (App.Div.1955) ("WHATEVER THE AGREEMENT OF THE PARENTS, The Ultimate determination of custody lies with the court in the exercise of its supervisory jurisdiction as parens patriae."). The fact that the trial court remedied that aspect of the contract through the "best interests" phase does not make the contractual provision any less offensive to the public policy of this State.

The surrogacy contract guarantees permanent separation of the child from one of its natural parents. Our policy, however, has long been that to the extent possible, children should remain with and be brought up by both of their natural parents. That was the first stated purpose of the previous adoption act, L.1953, c. 264, s 1, codified at N.J.S.A. 9:3–17 (repealed): "it is necessary and desirable (a) to protect the child from unnecessary separation from his natural parents. . . ." While not so stated in the present adoption law, this purpose remains part of the public policy of this State. See, e.g., Wilke v. Culp, 196 N.J.Super. 487, 496, 483 A.2d 420 (App.Div.1984), certif. den., 99 N.J. 243, 491 A.2d 728 (1985); In re Adoption by J.J.P., supra, 175 N.J.Super. at 426, 419 A.2d 1135. This is not simply some theoretical ideal that in practice has no meaning. The impact of failure to follow that policy is nowhere better shown than in the results of this surrogacy contract. A child, instead of starting off its life with as much peace and security as possible, finds itself immediately in a tug-of-war between contending mother and father.

The surrogacy contract violates the policy of this State that the rights of natural parents are equal concerning their child, the father's right no greater than the mother's. "The parent and child relationship extends equally to every child and to every parent, regardless of the marital status of the parents." N.J.S.A. 9:17–40. As the Assembly Judiciary Committee noted in its statement to the bill, this section establishes "the principle that regardless of the marital status of the parents, all children and all parents have equal rights with respect to each other." Statement to Senate No. 888, Assembly Judiciary, Law, Public Safety and Defense Committee (1983) (emphasis supplied). The whole purpose and effect of the surrogacy contract was to give the father the exclusive right to the child by destroying the rights of the mother.

The policies expressed in our comprehensive laws governing consent to the surrender of a child stand in stark contrast to the surrogacy contract and what it implies. Here there is no counseling, independent or otherwise, of the natural mother, no evaluation, no warning.

The only legal advice Mary Beth Whitehead received regarding the surrogacy contract was provided in connection with the contract that she previously entered into with another couple. Mrs. Whitehead's lawyer was referred to her by the Infertility Center, with which he had an agreement to act as counsel for surrogate candidates. His services consisted of spending one hour going through the contract with the Whiteheads, section by section, and answering their questions. Mrs. Whitehead received

no further legal advice prior to signing the contract with the Sterns.

Mrs. Whitehead was examined and psychologically evaluated, but if it was for her benefit, the record does not disclose that fact. The Sterns regarded the evaluation as important, particularly in connection with the question of whether she would change her mind. Yet they never asked to see it, and were content with the assumption that the Infertility Center had made an evaluation and had concluded that there was no danger that the surrogate mother would change her mind. From Mrs. Whitehead's point of view, all that she learned from the evaluation was that "she had passed." It is apparent that the profit motive got the better of the Infertility Center. Although the evaluation was made, it was not put to any use, and understandably so, for the psychologist warned that Mrs. Whitehead demonstrated certain traits that might make surrender of the child difficult and that there should be further inquiry into this issue in connection with her surrogacy. To inquire further, however, might have jeopardized the Infertility Center's fee. The record indicates that neither Mrs. Whitehead nor the Sterns were ever told of this fact, a fact that might have ended their surrogacy arrangement.

Under the contract, the natural mother is irrevocably committed before she knows the strength of her bond with her child. She never makes a totally voluntary, informed decision, for quite clearly any decision prior to the baby's birth is, in the most important sense, uninformed, and any decision after that, compelled by a pre-existing contractual commitment, the threat of a lawsuit, and the inducement of a $10,000 payment, is less than totally voluntary. Her interests are of little concern to those who controlled this transaction.

Although the interest of the natural father and adoptive mother is certainly the predominant interest, realistically the only interest served, even they are left with less than what public policy requires. They know little about the natural mother, her genetic makeup, and her psychological and medical history. Moreover, not even a superficial attempt is made to determine their awareness of their responsibilities as parents.

Worst of all, however, is the contract's total disregard of the best interests of the child. There is not the slightest suggestion that any inquiry will be made at any time to determine the fitness of the Sterns as custodial parents, of Mrs. Stern as an adoptive parent, their superiority to Mrs. Whitehead, or the effect on the child of not living with her natural mother.

This is the sale of a child, or, at the very least, the sale of a mother's right to her child, the only mitigating factor being that one of the purchasers is the father. Almost every evil that prompted the prohibition on the payment of money in connection with adoptions exists here.

The differences between an adoption and a surrogacy contract should be noted, since it is asserted that the use of money in connection with surrogacy does not pose the risks found where money buys an adoption. Katz, "Surrogate Motherhood and the Baby-Selling Laws," 20 Colum.J.L. & Soc.Probs. 1 (1986).

First, and perhaps most important, all parties concede that it is unlikely that surrogacy will survive without money. Despite the alleged selfless motivation of surrogate mothers, if there is no payment, there will be no surrogates, or very few. That conclusion contrasts with adoption; for obvious reasons, there remains a steady supply, albeit insufficient, despite the prohibitions against payment. The adoption itself, relieving the natural mother of the financial burden of supporting an infant, is in some sense the equivalent of payment.

Second, the use of money in adoptions does not produce the problem—conception occurs, and usually the birth itself, before illicit funds are offered. With surrogacy, the "problem," if one views it as such, consisting of the purchase of a woman's procreative capacity, at the risk of her life, is caused by and originates with the offer of money.

Third, with the law prohibiting the use of money in connection with adoptions, the built-in financial pressure of the unwanted pregnancy and the consequent support obligation do not lead the mother to the highest paying, ill-suited, adoptive parents. She is just as well-off surrendering the child to an approved agency. In surrogacy, the highest bidders will presumably become the adoptive parents regardless of suitability, so long as payment of money is permitted.

Fourth, the mother's consent to surrender her child in adoptions is revocable, even after surrender of the child, unless it be to an approved agency, where by regulation there are protections against an ill-advised surrender. In surrogacy, consent occurs so early that no amount of advice would satisfy the potential mother's need, yet the consent is irrevocable. The main difference, that the unwanted pregnancy is unintended while the situation of the surrogate mother is voluntary and intended, is really not significant. Initially, it produces stronger reactions of sympathy for the mother whose pregnancy was unwanted than for the surrogate mother, who "went into this with her eyes wide open." On reflection, however, it appears that the essential evil is the same, taking advantage of a woman's circumstances (the unwanted pregnancy or the need for money) in order to take away her child, the difference being one of degree.

In the scheme contemplated by the surrogacy contract in this case, a middle man, propelled by profit, promotes the sale. Whatever idealism may have motivated any of the participants, the profit motive predominates, permeates, and ultimately governs the transaction. The demand for children is great and the supply small. The availability of contraception, abortion, and the greater willingness of single mothers to bring up their children has led to a shortage of babies offered for adoption. See N. Baker, Baby Selling: The Scandal of Black Market Adoption, supra; Adoption and Foster Care, 1975: Hearings on Baby Selling Before the Subcomm. On Children and Youth of the Senate Comm. on Labor and Public Welfare, 94th Cong.1st Sess. 6 (1975) (Statement of Joseph H. Reid, Executive Director, Child Welfare League of America, Inc.). The situation is ripe for the entry of the middleman who will bring some equilibrium into the market by increasing the supply through the use of money. Intimated, but disputed, is the assertion that surrogacy will be used for the benefit of the rich at the expense of the poor. See, e.g., Radin, "Market Inalienability," 100 Harv.L.Rev. 1849, 1930 (1987). In response it is noted that the Sterns are not rich and the Whiteheads not poor. Nevertheless, it is clear to us that it is unlikely that surrogate mothers will be as proportionately numerous among those women in the top twenty percent income bracket as among those in the bottom twenty percent. Ibid. Put differently, we doubt that infertile cou-ples in the low-income bracket will find upper income surrogates.

In any event, even in this case one should not pretend that disparate wealth does not play a part simply because the contrast is not the dramatic "rich versus poor." At the time of trial, the Whiteheads' net assets were probably negative—Mrs. Whitehead's own sister was foreclosing on a second mortgage. Their income derived from Mr. Whitehead's labors. Mrs. Whitehead is a homemaker, having previously held part-time jobs. The Sterns are both professionals, she a medical doctor, he a biochemist. Their combined income when both were working was about $89,500 a year and their assets sufficient to pay for the surrogacy contract arrangements.

The point is made that Mrs. Whitehead agreed to the surrogacy arrangement, supposedly fully understanding the consequences. Putting aside the issue of how compelling her need for money may have been, and how significant her understanding of the consequences, we suggest that her consent is irrelevant. There are, in a civilized society, some things that money cannot buy. In America, we decided long ago that merely because conduct purchased by money was "voluntary" did not mean that it was good or beyond regulation and prohibition. West Coast Hotel Co. v. Parrish, 300 U.S. 379, 57 S.Ct. 578, 81 L.Ed. 703 (1937). Employers can no longer buy labor at the lowest price they can bargain for, even though that labor is "voluntary," 29 U.S.C. § 206 (1982), or buy women's labor for less money than paid to men for the same job, 29 U.S.C. § 206(d), or purchase the agreement of children to perform oppressive labor, 29 U.S.C. § 212, or purchase the agreement of workers to subject themselves to unsafe or unhealthful working conditions, 29 U.S.C. §§ 651 to 678. (Occupational Safety and Health Act of 1970).

There are, in short, values that society deems more important than granting to wealth whatever it can buy, be it labor, love, or life. Whether this principle recommends prohibition of surrogacy, which presumably sometimes results in great satisfaction to all of the parties, is not for us to say. We note here only that, under existing law, the fact that Mrs. Whitehead "agreed" to the arrangement is not dispositive.

The long-term effects of surrogacy contracts are not known, but feared—the impact on the child who learns her life was bought, that she is the offspring of someone who gave birth to her only to obtain money; the impact on the natural mother as the full weight of her isolation is felt along with the full reality of the sale of her body and her child; the impact on the natural father and adoptive mother once they realize the consequences of their conduct. Literature in related areas suggests these are substantial considerations, although, given the newness of surrogacy, there is little information. See N. Baker, Baby Selling: The Scandal of Black Market Adoption, supra; Adoption and Foster Care, 1975: Hearings on Baby Selling Before the Subcomm. on Children and Youth of the Senate Comm. on Labor and Public Welfare, 94th Cong. 1st Sess. (1975).

The surrogacy contract is based on, principles that are directly contrary to the objectives of our laws. It guarantees the separation of a child from its mother; it looks to adoption regardless of suitability; it totally ignores the child; it takes the child from the mother regardless of her wishes and her maternal fitness; and it does all of this, it accomplishes all of its goals, through the use of money.

Beyond that is the potential degradation of some women that may result from this arrangement. In many cases, of course, surrogacy may bring satisfaction, not only to the infertile couple, but to the surrogate mother herself. The fact, however, that many women may not perceive surrogacy negatively but rather see it as an opportunity does not diminish its potential for devastation to other women.

In sum, the harmful consequences of this surrogacy arrangement appear to us all too palpable. In New Jersey the surrogate mother's agreement to sell her child is void. Its irrevocability infects the entire contract, as does the money that purports to buy it.

For affirmance in part, reversal in part and remandment—Chief Justice WILENTZ and Justices CLIFFORD, HANDLER, POLLOCK, O'HERN, GARIBALDI and STEIN—7.

Opposed—None.

QUESTIONS AND DISCUSSION POINTS

1. Among the many issues raised by this case, the paramount issue is the question of freedom of contract. The Court finds the contract between the parties to be unenforceable. How many different arguments does the court make in support of its conclusion that the contract is unenforceable?

2. Consider the Court's first argument, to the effect that the contract is unenforceable because it conflicts with the law of New Jersey, specifically the statute that prohibits using money in connection with an adoption.

The Court seems to dismiss the parties's efforts to avoid this statute. Is there any way the contract might have been redrafted to avoid the reach of the statute?

3. The Court takes an overall negative view of using contract as a way of adopting children. The Court's concerns all center around the best interests of the child. Is the Legislative and Court animosity to payment for private adoption based on anything more than faith that the State and not private corporations is in the best position to assess what is in the best interests of the child? If it were possible to "privatize" the adoption process (i.e., to have private agencies perform all the tasks now done by the State), would the objections to private adoptions be met?

4. The Court makes a "public policy" argument against the surrogacy contract. The general claim is that the long-term effects of the surrogacy arrangement cannot be appreciated. But do any or all of these criticisms also apply to adoption which, of course, is permitted by law?

5. The Court concludes that Mrs. Whitehead failed to understand the surrogacy contract. Are you persuaded that this is the case? If her consent to the surrogacy arrangement is superfluous to the Court's decision, why is this issue discussed at all?

Chapter 10

Tort Law

Tort law governs the obligations we owe to others simply by virtue of their status as persons. Much of tort law concerns compensation for personal injuries which one person inflicts, intentionally or otherwise, on another. Tort law is a form of corrective justice: its principal function is to compensate victims for injuries inflicted by tortfeasors who, by virtue of their conduct, have breached a duty owed to the injured party, which breach of duty has in fact caused injury.

We have just mentioned the four basic concepts of tort law: duty, breach of duty, causation, and injury. In general, we each owe a duty to all others not to injure them and to refrain from interfering with their rights to be in the world free from interference by us. We breach that duty when we create an unreasonable risk to the safety of another. The law imposes liability upon us when a risk we create causes injury to another. When this occurs, we must pay damages in an amount that makes the injured party whole again.

~

HELEN PALSGRAF, Respondent,
v. THE LONG ISLAND RAILROAD COMPANY, Appellant
Court of Appeals of New York
162 N.E. 99 (1928)

CARDOZO, Ch. J.

Plaintiff was standing on a platform of defendant's railroad after buying a ticket to go to Rockaway Beach. A train stopped at the station, bound for another place. Two men ran forward to catch it. One of the men reached the platform of the car without mishap, though the train was already moving. The other man, carrying a package, jumped aboard the car, but seemed unsteady as if about to fall. A guard on the car, who had held the door open, reached forward to help him in, and another guard on the platform pushed him from behind. In this act, the package was dislodged, and fell upon the rails. It was a package of small size, about fifteen inches long, and was covered by a newspaper. In fact it contained fireworks, but there was nothing in its appearance to give notice of its contents. The fireworks when they fell exploded. The shock of the explosion threw down some scales at the other end of the platform, many feet away. The scales struck the plaintiff, causing injuries for which she sues.

The conduct of the defendant's guard, if a wrong in its relation to the holder of the package, was not a wrong in its relation to the plaintiff, standing far away. Relatively to her it was not negligence at all. Nothing in the situation gave notice that the falling package had in it the potency of peril to persons thus removed. Negligence is not actionable unless it involves the invasion of a legally protected interest, the violation of a right. "Proof of negligence in the air, so to speak, will not do" (Pollock, Torts [11th ed.], p. 455; Martin v. Herzog, 228 N.Y. 164, 170; cf. Salmond, Torts [6th ed.], p. 24). "Negligence is the absence of care, according to the circumstances" (WILLES, J., in Vaughan v. Taff Vale Ry. Co., 5 H. & N. 679, 688; 1 Beven, Negligence [4th ed.], 7; Paul v. Consol. Fireworks Co., 212 N.Y. 117; Adams v. Bullock, 227 N.Y. 208, 211; Parrott v. Wells-Fargo Co., 15 Wall. [U.S.] 524). The plaintiff as she stood upon the platform of the station might claim to be protected against intentional invasion of her bodily security. Such invasion is not charged. She might claim to be protected against unintentional invasion by conduct involving in the thought of reasonable men an unreasonable hazard that such invasion would ensue. These, from the point of view of the law, were the bounds of her immunity, with perhaps some rare exceptions, survivals for the most part of ancient forms of liability, where conduct is held to be at the peril of the actor (Sullivan v. Dunham, 161 N.Y. 290). If no hazard was apparent to the eye of ordinary vigilance, an act innocent and harmless, at least to outward seeming, with reference to her, did not take to itself the quality of a tort because it happened to be a wrong, though apparently not one involving the risk of bodily insecurity, with reference to some

one else. "In every instance, before negligence can be predicated of a given act, back of the act must be sought and found a duty to the individual complaining, the observance of which would have averted or avoided the injury" (MCSHERRY, C.J., in W. Va. Central R. Co. v. State, 96 Md. 652, 666; cf. Norfolk & Western Ry. Co. v. Wood, 99 Va. 156, 158, 159; Hughes v. Boston & Maine R.R. Co., 71 N.H. 279, 284; U.S. Express Co. v. Everest, 72 Kan. 517; Emry v. Roanoke Nav. Co., 111 N.C. 94, 95; Vaughan v. Transit Dev. Co., 222 N.Y. 79; Losee v. Clute, 51 N.Y. 494; DiCaprio v. N.Y.C.R.R. Co., 231 N.Y. 94; 1 Shearman & Redfield on Negligence, § 8, and cases cited; Cooley on Torts [3d ed.], p. 1411; Jaggard on Torts, vol. 2, p. 826; Wharton, Negligence, § 24; Bohlen, Studies in the Law of Torts, p. 601). "The ideas of negligence and duty are strictly correlative" (BOWEN, L. J., in Thomas v. Quartermaine, 18 Q.B.D. 685, 694). The plaintiff sues in her own right for a wrong personal to her, and not as the vicarious beneficiary of a breach of duty to another.

A different conclusion will involve us, and swiftly too, in a maze of contradictions. A guard stumbles over a package which has been left upon a platform. It seems to be a bundle of newspapers. It turns out to be a can of dynamite. To the eye of ordinary vigilance, the bundle is abandoned waste, which may be kicked or trod on with impunity. Is a passenger at the other end of the platform protected by the law against the unsuspected hazard concealed beneath the waste? If not, is the result to be any different, so far as the distant passenger is concerned, when the guard stumbles over a valise which a truckman or a porter has left upon the walk? The passenger far away, if the victim of a wrong at all, has a cause of action, not derivative, but original and primary. His claim to be protected against invasion of his bodily security is neither greater nor less because the act resulting in the invasion is a wrong to another far removed.

In this case, the rights that are said to have been violated, the interests said to have been invaded, are not even of the same order. The man was not injured in his person nor even put in danger. The purpose of the act, as well as its effect, was to make his person safe. If there was a wrong to him at all, which may very well be doubted, it was a wrong to a property interest only, the safety of his package. Out of this wrong to property, which threatened injury to nothing else, there has passed, we are told, to the plaintiff by derivation or succession a right of action for the invasion of an interest of another order, the right to bodily security. The diversity of interests emphasizes the futility of the effort to build the plaintiff's right upon the basis of a wrong to some one else. The gain is one of emphasis, for a like result would follow if the interests were the same. Even then, the orbit of the danger as disclosed to the eye of reasonable vigilance would be the orbit of the duty. One who jostles one's neighbor in a crowd does not invade the rights of others standing at the outer fringe when the unintended contact casts a bomb upon the ground. The wrongdoer as to them is the man who carries the bomb, not the one who explodes it without suspicion of the danger. Life will have to be made over, and human nature transformed, before prevision so extravagant can be accepted as the norm of conduct, the customary standard to which behavior must conform.

The argument for the plaintiff is built upon the shifting meanings of such words as "wrong" and "wrongful," and shares their instability. What the plaintiff must show is "a wrong" to herself, i.e., a violation of her own right, and not merely a wrong to some one else, nor conduct "wrongful" because unsocial, but not "a wrong" to any one. We are told that one who drives at reckless speed through a crowded city street is guilty of a negligent act and, therefore, of a wrongful one irrespective of the consequences.

Negligent the act is, and wrongful in the sense that it is unsocial, but wrongful and unsocial in relation to other travelers, only because the eye of vigilance perceives the risk of damage. If the same act were to be committed on a speedway or a race course, it would lose its wrongful quality.

The risk reasonably to be perceived defines the duty to be obeyed, and risk imports relation; it is risk to another or to others within the range of apprehension (Seavey, Negligence, Subjective or Objective, 41 H.L. Rev. 6; Boronkay v. Robinson & Carpenter, 247 N.Y. 365). This does not mean, of course, that one who launches a destructive force is always relieved of liability if the force, though known to be destructive, pursues an unexpected path. "It was not necessary that the defendant should have had notice of the particular method in which an accident would occur, if the possibility of an accident was clear to the ordinarily prudent eye" (Munsey v. Webb, 231 U.S. 150, 156; Condran v. Park & Tilford, 213 N.Y. 341, 345; Robert v. U.S.E.F. Corp., 240 N.Y. 474, 477).

Some acts, such as shooting, are so imminently dangerous to any one who may come within reach of the missile, however unexpectedly, as to impose a duty of prevision not far from that of an insurer. Even today, and much oftener in earlier stages of the law, one acts sometimes at one's peril (Jeremiah Smith, Tort and Absolute Liability, 30 H.L. Rv. 328; Street, Foundations of Legal Liability, vol. 1, pp. 77, 78). Under this head, it may be, fall certain cases of what is known as transferred intent, an act willfully dangerous to A resulting by misadventure in injury to B (Talmage v. Smith, 101 Mich. 370, 374) These cases aside, wrong is defined in terms of the natural or probable, at least when unintentional (Parrot v. Wells-Fargo Co. [The Nitro-Glycerine Case], 15 Wall. [U.S.] 524). The range of reasonable apprehension is at times a question for the court, and at times, if varying inferences are possible, a question for the jury. Here, by concession, there was nothing in the situation to suggest to the most cautious mind that the parcel wrapped in newspaper would spread wreckage through the station. If the guard had thrown it down knowingly and willfully, he would not have threatened the plaintiff's safety, so far as appearances could warn him. His conduct would not have involved, even then, an unreasonable probability of invasion of her bodily security. Liability can be no greater where the act is inadvertent.

Negligence, like risk, is thus a term of relation. Negligence in the abstract, apart from things related, is surely not a tort, if indeed it is understandable at all (BOWEN, L.J., in Thomas v. Quartermaine, 18 Q.B.D. 685, 694). Negligence is not a tort unless it results in the commission of a wrong, and the commission of a wrong imports the violation of a right, in this case, we are told, the right to be protected against interference with one's bodily security. But bodily security is protected, not against all forms of interference or aggression, but only against some. One who seeks redress at law does not make out a cause of action by showing without more that there has been damage to his person. If the harm was not willful, he must show that the act as to him had possibilities of danger so many and apparent as to entitle him to be protected against the doing of it though the harm was unintended. Affront to personality is still the keynote of the wrong. Confirmation of this view will be found in the history and development of the action on the case. Negligence as a basis of civil liability was unknown to mediaeval law (8 Holdsworth, History of English Law, p. 449; Street, Foundations of Legal Liability, vol. 1, pp. 189, 190). For damage to the person, the sole remedy was trespass, and trespass did not lie in the absence of aggression, and that direct and personal (Holdsworth, op. cit. p. 453; Street, op. cit. vol. 3, pp. 258, 260, vol. 1, pp. 71, 74.) Liability for other damage, as where a servant without orders from the master does or omits something to the damage of another, is a plant of later growth (Holdsworth, op. cit. 450, 457; Wigmore, Responsibility for Tortious Acts, vol. 3, Essays in Anglo-American Legal History, 520, 523, 526, 533). When it emerged out of the legal soil, it was thought of as a variant of trespass, an offshoot of the parent stock. This appears in the form of action, which was known as trespass on the case (Holdsworth, op. cit. p. 449; cf. Scott v. Shepard, 2 Wm. Black. 892; Green, Rationale of Proximate Cause, p. 19). The victim does not sue derivatively, or by right of subrogation, to vindicate an interest invaded in the person of another. Thus to view his cause of action is to ignore the fundamental difference between tort and crime (Holland, Jurisprudence [12th ed.], p. 328). He sues for breach of a duty owing to himself.

The law of causation, remote or proximate, is thus foreign to the case before us. The question of liability is always anterior to the question of the measure of the consequences that go with liability. If there is no tort to be redressed, there is no occasion to consider what damage might be recovered if there were a finding of a tort. We may assume, without deciding, that negligence, not at large or in the abstract, but in relation to the plaintiff, would entail liability for any and all consequences, however novel or extraordinary (Bird v. St. Paul F. & M. Ins. Co., 224 N.Y. 47, 54; Ehrgott v. Mayor, etc., of N.Y., 96 N.Y. 264; Smith v. London & S.W. Ry. Co., L.R. 6 C.P. 14; 1 Beven, Negligence, 106; Street, op. cit. vol. 1, p. 90; Green, Rationale of Proximate Cause, pp. 88, 118; cf. Matter of Polemis, L.R. 1921, 3 K.B. 560; 44 Law Quarterly Review, 142). There is room for argument that a distinction is to be drawn according to the diversity of interests invaded by the act, as where conduct negligent in that it threatens an insignificant invasion of an interest in property results in an unforseeable invasion of an interest of another order, as, e.g., one of bodily security. Perhaps other distinctions may be necessary. We do not go into the question now. The consequences to be followed must first be rooted in a wrong.

The judgment of the Appellate Division and that of the Trial Term should be reversed, and the complaint dismissed, with costs in all courts.

POUND, LEHMAN and KELLOGG, JJ., concur with CARDOZO, Ch. J.; ANDREWS, J., dissents in opinion in which CRANE and O'BRIEN, JJ., concur.

Judgment reversed, etc.

ANDREWS, J. (dissenting).

Assisting a passenger to board a train, the defendant's servant negligently knocked a package from his arms. It fell between the platform and the cars. Of its contents the servant knew and could know nothing. A violent explosion followed. The concussion broke some scales standing a considerable distance away. In falling they injured the plaintiff, an intending passenger.

Upon these facts may she recover the damages she has suffered in an action brought against the master? The result we shall reach depends upon our theory as to the nature of negligence. Is it a relative concept—the breach of some duty owing to a particular person or to particular persons? Or where there is an act which unreasonably threatens the safety of others, is the doer liable for all its proximate consequences, even where they result in injury to one who would generally be thought to be outside the radius of danger? This is not a mere dispute as to words. We might not believe that to the average mind the dropping of the bundle would seem to involve the probability of harm to the plaintiff standing many feet away whatever might be the case as to the owner or to one so near as to be likely to be struck by its fall. If, however, we adopt the second hypothesis we have to inquire only as to the relation between cause and effect. We deal in terms of proximate cause, not of negligence.

Negligence may be defined roughly as an act or omission which unreasonably does or may affect the rights of others, or which unreasonably fails to protect oneself from the dangers resulting from such acts. Here I confine myself to the first branch of the definition. Nor do I comment on the word "unreasonable." For present purposes it sufficiently describes that average of conduct that society requires of its members.

There must be both the act or the omission, and the right. It is the act itself, not the intent of the actor, that is important. (Hover v. Barkhoof, 44 N.Y. 113; Mertz v. Connecticut Co., 217 N.Y. 475.) In criminal law both the intent and the result are to be considered. Intent again is material in tort actions, where punitive damages are sought, dependent on actual malice—not on merely reckless conduct. But here neither insanity nor infancy lessens responsibility. (Williams v. Hays, 143 N.Y. 442.)

As has been said, except in cases of contributory negligence, there must be rights which are or may be affected. Often though injury has occurred, no rights of him who suffers have been touched. A licensee or trespasser upon my land has no claim to affirmative care on my part that the land be made safe. (Meiers v. Koch Brewery, 229 N.Y. 10.) Where a railroad is required to fence its tracks against cattle, no man's rights are injured should he wander upon the road because such fence is absent. (Di Caprio v. N.Y.C.R.R., 231 N.Y. 94.) An unborn child may not demand immunity from personal harm. (Drobner v. Peters, 232 N.Y. 220.)

But we are told that "there is no negligence unless there is in the particular case a legal duty to take care, and this duty must be one which is owed to the plaintiff himself and not merely to others." (Salmond, Torts [6th ed.], 24.) This, I think too narrow a conception. Where there is the unreasonable act, and some right that may be affected there is negligence whether damage does or does not result. That is immaterial. Should we drive down Broadway at a reckless speed, we are negligent whether we strike an approaching car or miss it by an inch. The act itself is wrongful. It is a wrong not only to those who happen to be within the radius of danger but to all who might have been there—a wrong to the public at large. Such is the language of the street. Such the language of the courts when speaking of contributory negligence. Such again and again their language in speaking of the duty of some defendant and discussing proximate cause in cases where such a discussion is wholly irrelevant on any other theory. (Perry v. Rochester Line Co., 219 N.Y. 60.) As was said by Mr. Justice HOLMES many years ago, "the measure of the defendant's duty in determining whether a wrong has been committed is one thing, the measure of liability when a wrong has been committed is another." (Spade v. Lynn & Boston R.R. Co., 172 Mass. 488.) Due care is a duty imposed on each one of us to protect society from unnecessary danger, not to protect A, B or C alone.

It may well be that there is no such thing as negligence in the abstract. "Proof of negligence in the air, so to speak, will not do." In an empty world negligence would not exist. It does involve a relationship between man and his fellows. But not merely a relationship between man and those whom he might reasonably expect his act would injure. Rather, a relationship between him and those whom he does in fact injure. If his act has a tendency to harm some one, it harms him a mile away as surely as it does those on the scene. We now permit children to recover for the negligent killing of the father. It was never prevented on the theory that no duty was owing to them. A husband may be compensated for the loss of his wife's services. To say that the wrongdoer was negligent as to the husband as well as to the wife is merely an attempt to fit facts to theory. An insurance company paying a fire loss recovers its payment of the negligent incendiary. We speak of subrogation—of suing in the right of the insured. Behind the cloud of words is the fact they hide, that the act, wrongful as to the insured, has also injured the company. Even if it be true that the fault of father, wife or insured will prevent recovery, it is because we consider the original negligence not the proximate cause of the injury. (Pollock, Torts [12th ed.], 463.)

In the well-known Polemis Case (1921, 3 K.B. 560), SCRUTTON, L. J., said that the dropping of a plank was negligent for it might injure "workman or cargo or ship." Because of either possibility the owner of the vessel was to be made good for his loss. The act being wrongful the doer was liable for its proximate results. Criticized and explained as this statement may have been, I think it states the law as it should be and as it is. (Smith v. London & Southwestern Ry. Co., [1870–71] 6 C.P. 14; Anthony v. Slaid, 52 Mass. 290; Wood v. Penn, R.R. Co., 177 Penn. St. 306; Trashansky v. Hershkovitz, 239 N.Y. 452.)

The proposition is this. Every one owes to the world at large the duty of refraining from those acts that may unreasonably threaten the safety of others. Such an act occurs. Not only is he wronged to whom harm might reasonably be expected to result, but he also who is in fact injured, even if he be outside what would generally be thought the danger zone. There needs be duty due the one complaining but this is not a duty to a particular individual because as to him harm might be expected. Harm to some one being the natural result of the act, not only that one alone, but all those in fact injured may complain. We have never, I think, held otherwise. Indeed in the Di Caprio case we said that a breach of a general ordinance defining the degree of care to be exercised in one's calling is evidence of negligence as to every one. We did not limit this statement to those who might be expected to be exposed to danger. Unreasonable risk being taken, its consequences are not confined to those who might probably be hurt.

If this be so, we do not have a plaintiff suing by "derivation or succession." Her action is original and primary. Her claim is for a breach of duty to herself—not that she is subrogated to any right of action of the owner of the parcel or of a passenger standing at the scene of the explosion.

The right to recover damages rests on additional considerations. The plaintiff's rights must be injured, and this injury must be caused by the negligence. We build a dam, but are negligent as to its foundations. Breaking, it injures property down stream. We are not liable if all this happened because of some reason other than the insecure foundation. But when injuries do result from our unlawful act we are liable for the consequences. It does not matter that they are unusual, unexpected, unforeseen and unforseeable. But there is one limitation. The damages must be so connected with the negligence that the latter may be said to be the proximate cause of the former.

These two words have never been given an inclusive definition. What is a cause in a legal sense, still more what is a proximate cause, depend in each case upon many considerations, as does the existence of negligence itself. Any philosophical doctrine of causation does not help us. A boy throws a stone into a pond. The ripples spread. The water level rises. The history of that pond is altered to all eternity. It will be altered by other causes also. Yet it will be forever the resultant of all causes combined. Each one will have an influence. How great only omniscience can say. You may speak of a chain, or if you please, a net. An analogy is of little aid. Each cause brings about future events. Without each the future would not be the same. Each is proximate in the sense it is essential. But that is not what we mean by the word. Nor on the other hand do we mean sole cause. There is no such thing.

Should analogy be thought helpful, however, I prefer that of a stream. The spring, starting on its journey, is joined by tributary after tributary. The river, reaching the ocean, comes from a hundred sources. No man may say whence any drop of water is derived. Yet for a time distinction may be possible. Into the clear creek, brown swamp water flows from the left. Later, from the right comes water stained by its clay bed. The three may remain for a space, sharply divided. But at last, inevitably no trace of separation remains. They are so commingled that all distinction is lost.

As we have said, we cannot trace the effect of an act to the end, if end there is. Again, however, we may trace it part of the way. A murder at Sarajevo may be the necessary antecedent to an assassination in London twenty years hence. An overturned lantern may burn all Chicago. We may follow the fire from the shed to the last building. We rightly say the fire started by the lantern caused its destruction.

A cause, but not the proximate cause. What we do mean by the word "proximate" is, that because of convenience, of public policy, of a rough sense of justice, the law arbitrarily declines to trace a series of events beyond a certain point. This is not logic. It is practical politics. Take our rule as to fires. Sparks from my burning haystack set on fire my house and my neighbor's. I may recover from a negligent railroad. He may not. Yet the wrongful act as directly harmed the one as the other. We may regret that the line was drawn just where it was, but drawn somewhere it had to be. We said the act of the railroad was not the proximate cause of our neighbor's fire. Cause it surely was. The words we used were simply indicative of our notions of public policy. Other courts think differently. But somewhere they reach the point where they cannot say the stream comes from any one source.

Take the illustration given in an unpublished manuscript by a distinguished and helpful writer on the law of torts. A chauffeur negligently collides with another car which is filled with dynamite, although he could not know it. An explosion follows. A, walking on the sidewalk nearby, is killed. B, sitting in a window of a building opposite, is cut by flying glass. C, likewise sitting in a window a block away, is similarly injured. And a further illustration. A nursemaid, ten blocks away, startled by the noise, involuntarily drops a baby from her arms to the walk. We are told that C may not recover while A may. As to B it is a question for court or jury. We will all agree that the baby might not. Because, we are again told, the chauffeur had no reason to believe his conduct involved any risk of injuring either C or the baby. As to them he was not negligent.

But the chauffeur, being negligent in risking the collision, his belief that the scope of the harm he might do would be limited is immaterial. His act unreasonably jeopardized the safety of any one who might be affected by it. C's injury and that of the baby were directly traceable to the collision. Without that, the injury would not have happened. C had the right to sit in his office, secure from such dangers. The baby was entitled to use the sidewalk with reasonable safety.

The true theory is, it seems to me, that the injury to C, if in truth he is to be denied recovery, and the injury to the baby is that their several injuries were not the proximate result of the negligence. And here not what the chauffeur had reason to believe would be the result of his conduct, but what the prudent would foresee, may have a bearing. May have some bearing, for the problem of proximate cause is not to be solved by any one consideration.

It is all a question of expediency. There are no fixed rules to govern our judgment. There are simply matters of which we may take account. We have in a somewhat different connection spoken of "the stream of events." We have asked whether that stream was deflected— whether it was forced into new and unexpected channels. (Donnelly v. Piercy Contracting Co., 222 N.Y. 210). This is rather rhetoric than law. There is in truth little to guide us other than common sense.

There are some hints that may help us. The proximate cause, involved as it may be with many other causes, must be, at the least, something without which the event would not happen. The court must ask itself whether there was a natural and continuous sequence between cause and effect. Was the one a substantial factor in producing the other? Was there a direct connection between them, without too many intervening causes? Is the effect of cause on result not too attentuated? Is the cause likely, in the usual judgment of mankind, to produce the result? Or by the exercise of prudent foresight could the result be foreseen? Is the

result too remote from the cause, and here we consider remoteness in time and space. (Bird v. St. Paul F. & M. Ins. Co., 224 N.Y. 47, where we passed upon the construction of a contract—but something was also said on this subject.) Clearly we must so consider, for the greater the distance either in time or space, the more surely do other causes intervene to affect the result. When a lantern is overturned the firing of a shed is a fairly direct consequence. Many things contribute to the spread of the conflagration—the force of the wind, the direction and width of streets, the character of intervening structures, other factors. We draw an uncertain and wavering line, but draw it we must as best we can.

Once again, it is all a question of fair judgment, always keeping in mind the fact that we endeavor to make a rule in each case that will be practical and in keeping with the general understanding of mankind.

Here another question must be answered. In the case supposed it is said, and said correctly, that the chauffeur is liable for the direct effect of the explosion although he had no reason to suppose it would follow a collision. "The fact that the injury occurred in a different manner than that which might have been expected does not prevent the chauffeur's negligence from being in law the cause of the injury." But the natural results of a negligent act—the results which a prudent man would or should foresee—do have a bearing upon the decision as to proximate cause. We have said so repeatedly. What should be foreseen? No human foresight would suggest that a collision itself might injure one a block away. On the contrary, given an explosion, such a possibility might be reasonably expected. I think the direct connection, the foresight of which the courts speak, assumes prevision of the explosion, for the immediate results of which, at least, the chauffeur is responsible.

It may be said this is unjust. Why? In fairness he should make good every injury flowing from his negligence. Not because of tenderness toward him we say he need not answer for all that follows his wrong. We look back to the catastrophe, the fire kindled by the spark, or the explosion. We trace the consequences—not indefinitely, but to a certain point. And to aid us in fixing that point we ask what might ordinarily be expected to follow the fire or the explosion.

This last suggestion is the factor which must determine the case before us. The act upon which defendant's liability rests is knocking an apparently harmless package onto the platform. The act was negligent. For its proximate consequences the defendant is liable. If its contents were broken, to the owner; if it fell upon and crushed a passenger's foot, then to him. If it exploded and injured one in the immediate vicinity, to him also as to A in the illustration. Mrs. Palsgraf was standing some distance away. How far cannot be told from the record—apparently twenty-five or thirty feet. Perhaps less. Except for the explosion, she would not have been injured. We are told by the appellant in his brief "it cannot be denied that the explosion was the direct cause of the plaintiff's injuries." So it was a substantial factor in producing the result—there was here a natural and continuous sequence—direct connection. The only intervening cause was that instead of blowing her to the ground the concussion smashed the weighing machine which in turn fell upon her. There was no remoteness in time, little in space. And surely, given such an explosion as here it needed no great foresight to predict that the natural result would be to injure one on the platform at no greater distance from its scene than was the plaintiff. Just how no one might be able to predict. Whether by flying fragments, by broken glass, by wreckage of machines or structures no one could say. But injury in some form was most probable.

Under these circumstances I cannot say as a matter of law that the plaintiff's injuries were not the proximate result of the negligence. That is all we have before us. The court refused to so charge. No request was made to submit the matter to the jury as a question of fact, even would that have been proper upon the record before us.

The judgment appealed from should be affirmed, with costs.

QUESTIONS AND DISCUSSION POINTS

1. This case—one of the most important in the development of tort law—concerns the scope of the "duty" requirement in tort. How does Judge Cardozo frame the duty requirement? And how does his formulation differ from that of Judge Andrews in the Dissent?

2. One of the important ways lawyers reason to conclusions is analogy. What analogies does Judge Cardozo use to make his case for limiting the scope of the duty requirement?

3. How does the concept of "bodily security" figure in Judge Cardozo's formulation of his argument?

4. Look carefully at Judge Andrews's formulation of the duty question. Does he ask the same question as Judge Cardozo, or does he pose the question differently? What are the implications of this, if any?

5. As you can see, much of the disagreement between judges Cardozo and Andrews concerns the meaning of "unreasonable." Does each judge use legal and/or nonlegal sources for the meaning of "unreasonable"? Is it possible to give meaning to this concept without, at some point, going "outside" the law?

MARGERY M. DILLON et al., Plaintiffs and Appellants,
v. DAVID LUTHER LEGG, Defendant and Respondent
Supreme Court of California
441 P.2d 912 (1968)

Action to recover for damages suffered by mother for emotional trauma and physical injury from witnessing the infliction of death or injury to her child due to the negligence of tort-feasor. Judgment for defendant reversed.

OPINION: TOBRINER, J.

That the courts should allow recovery to a mother who suffers emotional trauma and physical injury from witnessing the infliction of death or injury to her child for which the tort-feasor is liable in negligence would appear to be a compelling proposition. As Prosser points out:

> All ordinary human feelings are in favor of her [the mother's] action against the negligent defendant. If a duty to her requires that she herself be in some recognizable danger, then it has properly been said that when a child is endangered, it is not beyond contemplation that its mother will be somewhere in the vicinity, and will suffer serious shock. (Prosser, Law of Torts (3d ed. 1964) p. 353.)

Nevertheless, past American decisions have barred the mother's recovery. Refusing the mother the right to take her case to the jury, these courts ground their position on an alleged absence of a required "duty" of due care of the tort-feasor to the mother. Duty, in turn, they state, must express public policy; the imposition of duty here would work disaster because it would invite fraudulent claims and it would involve the courts in the hopeless task of defining the extent of the tort-feasor's liability. In substance, they say, definition of liability being impossible, denial of liability is the only realistic alternative.

We have concluded that neither of the feared dangers excuses the frustration of the natural justice upon which the mother's claim rests. We shall point out that in the past we have rejected the argument that we should deny recovery upon a legitimate claim because other fraudulent ones may be urged. We shall further explain that the alleged inability to fix definitions for recovery on the different facts of future cases does not justify the denial of recovery on the specific facts of the instant case; in any event, proper guidelines can indicate the extent of liability for such future cases.

In the instant case plaintiff's first cause of action alleged that on or about September 27, 1964, defendant drove his automobile in a southerly direction on Bluegrass Road near its intersection with Clover Lane in the County of Sacramento, and at that time plaintiff's infant daughter, Erin Lee Dillon, lawfully crossed Buegrass Road. The complaint further alleged that defendant's negligent operation of his vehicle caused it to "collide with the deceased Erin Lee Dillon resulting in injuries to decedent which proximately resulted in her death." Plaintiff, as the mother of the decedent, brought an action for compensation for the loss.

Plaintiff's second cause of action alleged that she, Margery M. Dillon, "was in close proximity to the . . . collision and personally witnessed said collision." She further alleged that "because of the negligence of defendants . . . and as a proximate cause [sic] thereof plaintiff . . . sustained great emotional disturbance and shock and injury to her nervous system" which caused her great physical and mental pain and suffering.

Plaintiff's third cause of action alleged that Cheryl Dillon, another infant daughter, was "in close proximity to the . . . collision and personally witnessed said collision." Because of the negligence, Cheryl Dillon "sustained great emotional disturbance and shock and injury to her nervous system" which caused her great physical and mental pain and suffering.

On December 22, 1965, defendant, after he had filed his answer, moved for judgment on the pleadings, contending that:

No cause of action is stated in that allegation that plaintiff sustained emotional distress, fright or shock induced by apprehension of negligently caused danger or injury or the witnessing of negligently caused injury to a third person. Amaya v. Home Ice, Fuel & Supply Co., 59 Cal.2d 295 [29 Cal.Rptr. 33, 379 P.2d 513] (1963). Even where a child, sister or spouse is the object of the plaintiff's apprehension no cause of action is stated, supra, p. 303, unless the complaint alleges that the plaintiff suffered emotional distress, fright or shock as a result of fear for his own safety. Reed v. Moore, 156 Cal.App.2d 43 (1957) at page 45 [319 P.2d 80].

The court granted a judgment on the pleadings against the mother's count, the second cause of action, and denied it as to the sister's count, the third cause of action. The court, further, dismissed the second cause of action. Margery M. Dillon, the mother, appealed from that judgment.

Thereafter, on January 26, further proceedings took place as to the third cause of action, Cheryl Dillon's claim for emotional trauma from witnessing her sister's death while "watching her sister lawfully cross Bluegrass Road."

Defendant moved for summary judgment on this count. In opposition plaintiff contended that the declaration of one McKinley disclosed that Mrs. Dillon testified at her deposition that when she saw the car rolling over Erin she noted that Cheryl was on the curb, but that the deposition of Cheryl Dillon contradicts such statements. Plaintiff therefore submitted that "Since the declarations filed by defendant are contradictory and the testimony contained in the testimony of Mrs. Dillon does not establish as a matter of law that Cheryl Dillon was not in the zone of danger or had fear for her own safety, plaintiff respectfully submits that the motion must be denied."

The court denied the motion for summary judgment on the third cause as to Cheryl on the ground that the pretrial order precluded it. The trial court apparently sustained the motion for judgment on the pleadings on the second cause as to the mother because she was not within the zone of danger and denied that motion as to the third cause involving Cheryl because of the possibility that she was within such zone of danger or feared for her own safety. Thus we have before us a case that dramatically illustrates the difference in result flowing from the alleged requirement that a plaintiff cannot recover for emotional trauma in witnessing the death of a child or sister unless she also feared for her own safety because she was actually within the zone of physical impact.

The posture of this case differs from that of Amaya v. Home Ice, Fuel & Supply Co. (1963) 59 Cal.2d 295, 298 [29 Cal.Rptr. 33, 379 P.2d 513], which involved "fright or nervous shock (with consequent bodily illness) induced solely by . . . apprehension of negligently caused danger or injury to a third person" because the complaint here presents the claim of the emotionally traumatized mother, who admittedly was not within the zone of danger, as contrasted with that of the sister, who may have been within it. The case thus illustrates the fallacy of the rule that would deny recovery in the one situation and grant it in the other. In the first place, we can hardly justify relief to the sister for trauma which she suffered upon apprehension of the child's death and yet deny it to the mother merely because of a happenstance that the sister was some few yards closer to the accident.

The instant case exposes the hopeless artificiality of the zone-of-danger rule. In the second place, to rest upon the zone-of-danger rule when we have rejected the impact rule becomes even less defensible.

We have, indeed, held that impact is not necessary for recovery (Cook v. Maier (1939) 33 Cal.App.2d 581, 584 [92 P.2d 434]). The zone-of-danger concept must, then, inevitably collapse because the only reason for the requirement of presence in that zone lies in the fact that one within it will fear the danger of impact. At the threshold, then, we point to the incongruity of the rules upon which any rejection of plaintiff's recovery must rest.

We turn then to an analysis of the concept of duty, which, as we have stated, has furnished the ground for the rejection of such claims as the instant one. Normally the simple facts of plaintiff's complaint would establish a cause of action: the complaint alleges that defendant drove his car (1) negligently, as a (2) proximate result of which plaintiff suffered (3) physical injury. Proof of these facts to a jury leads to recovery in damages; indeed, such a showing represents a classic example of the type of accident with which the law of negligence has been designed to deal.

The assertion that liability must nevertheless be denied because defendant bears no "duty" to plaintiff:

> begs the essential question—whether the plaintiff's interests are entitled to legal protection against the defendant's conduct. . . . It [duty] is a shorthand statement of a conclusion, rather than an aid to analysis in itself. . . . But it should be recognized that "duty" is not sacrosanct in itself, but only an expression of the sum total of those con-

siderations of policy which lead the law to say that the particular plaintiff is entitled to protection."
—(Prosser, Law of Torts, supra, at pp. 332–333.)

The history of the concept of duty in itself discloses that it is not an old and deep-rooted doctrine but a legal device of the latter half of the nineteenth century designed to curtail the feared propensities of juries toward liberal awards.

It must not be forgotten that "duty" got into our law for the very purpose of combatting what was then feared to be a dangerous delusion (perhaps especially prevalent among juries imbued with popular notions of fairness untempered by paramount judicial policy), viz., that the law might countenance legal redress for all foreseeable harm.
—(Fleming, An Introduction to the Law of Torts (1967) p. 47)

Indeed, the idea of court-imposed restrictions on recovery by means of the concept of "duty" contrasted dramatically with the preceding legal system of feudal society. In the enclosed feudal society, the actor bore responsibility for any damage he inflicted without regard to whether he was at fault or owed a "duty" to the injured person. Thus, at that time, the defendant owed a duty to all the world to conduct himself without causing injury to his fellows. It may well be that the physical contraction of the feudal society imposed an imperative for maximum procurable safety and a corresponding absolute responsibility upon its members.

The Industrial Revolution, which cracked the solidity of the feudal society and opened up wide and new areas of expansion, changed the legal concepts. Just as the new competitiveness in the economic sphere figuratively broke out of the walls of the feudal community, so it broke through the rule of strict liability. In the place of strict liability it introduced the theory that an action for negligence would lie only if the defendant breached a duty which he owed to plaintiff. As Lord Esher said in Le Lievre v. Gould (1893) 1 Q.B. 491, 497: "A man is entitled to be as negligent as he pleases towards the whole world if he owes no duty to them."

We have pointed out that this late 19th century concept of duty, as applied to the instant situation, has led the courts to deny liability. We have noted that this negation of duty emanates from the twin fears that courts will be flooded with an onslaught of (1) fraudulent and (2) indefinable claims. We shall point out why we think neither fear justified.

1. This court in the past has rejected the argument that we must deny recovery upon a legitimate claim because other fraudulent ones may be urged. The denial of "duty" in the instant situation rests upon the prime hypothesis that allowance of such an action would lead to successful assertion of fraudulent claims. (See, e.g., Waube v. Warrington (1935) 216 Wis. 603, 613 [258 N.W. 497].) The rationale apparently assumes that juries, confronted by irreconcilable expert medical testimony, will be unable to distinguish the deceitful from the bona fide. The argument concludes that only a per se rule denying the entire class of claims that potentially raises this administrative problem can avoid this danger.

In the first instance, the argument proceeds from a doubtful factual assumption. Whatever the possibilities of fraudulent claims of physical injury by disinterested spectators of an accident, a question not in issue in this case, we certainly cannot doubt that a mother who sees her child killed will suffer physical injury from shock. "It seems sufficiently obvious that the shock of a mother at danger or harm to her child may be both a real and a serious injury." (Prosser, Law of Torts, *supra*, at p. 353.)

Over a half-century ago this court recognized the likelihood that such fright and fear would cause physical injury. In Sloane v. Southern California Ry. Co. (1896) 111 Cal. 668, 680 [44 P. 320, 32 L.R.A. 193], we affirmed a judgment for damages for a plaintiff who alleged physical injury resulting from mental suffering, saying:

> It is a matter of general knowledge that an attack of sudden fright or an exposure to imminent peril has produced in individuals a complete change in their nervous system, and rendered one who was physically strong and vigorous weak and timid.

Since no one can seriously question that fear or grief for one's child is as likely to cause physical injury as concern over one's own well-being, rejection of the fraudulent claims contention in Sloane clearly applies here.

2. The alleged inability to fix definitions for recovery on the different facts of future cases does not justify the denial of recovery on the specific facts of the instant case; in any event, proper guidelines can indicate the extent of liability for such future cases.

In order to limit the otherwise potentially infinite liability which would follow every negligent act, the law of torts holds defendant amenable only for injuries to others which to defendant at the time were reasonably foreseeable.

In the absence of "overriding policy considerations . . . foreseeability of risk [is] of . . . primary importance in establishing the element of duty." (Grafton v. Mollica (1965) 231 Cal.App.2d 860, 865 [42 Cal.Rptr. 306]. See also McEvoy v. American Pool Corp. (1948) 32 Cal.2d 295 [195 P.2d 783]; Hergenrether v. East (1964) 61 Cal.2d 440 [39 Cal.Rptr. 4, 393 P.2d 164].) As a classic opinion states: "The risk reasonably to be perceived defines the duty to be obeyed." (Palsgraf v. Long Island R.R. Co. (1928) 248 N.Y. 339, 344 [162 N.E. 99, 59 A.L.R. 253].) Defendant owes a duty, in the sense of a potential liability for damages, only with respect to those risks or hazards whose likelihood made the conduct unreasonably dangerous, and hence negligent, in the first instance. (See Keeton, Legal Cause in the Law of Torts (1963) 18–20; Seavey, Mr. Justice Cardozo and the Law of Torts (1939) 52 Harv.L.Rev. 372; Seavey, Principles of Torts (1942) 56 Harv.L.Rev. 72.) Harper and James state the prevailing view. The obligation turns on whether:

> . . . the offending conduct foreseeably involved unreasonably great risk of harm to the interests of someone other than the actor. . . . [The] obligation to refrain from . . . particular conduct is owed only to those who are foreseeably endangered by the conduct and only with respect to those risks or hazards whose likelihood made the conduct unreasonably dangerous. Duty, in other words, is measured by the scope of the risk which negligent conduct foreseeably entails.
> —(2 Harper & James, The Law of Torts, *supra*, at p. 1018; fns. omitted)

This foreseeable risk may be of two types. The first class involves actual physical impact. A second type of risk applies to the instant situation.

> In other cases, however, plaintiff is outside the zone of physical risk (or there is no risk of physical impact at all), but bodily injury or sickness is brought on by emotional disturbance which in turn is caused by defendant's conduct. Under general principles recovery should be had in such a case if defendant should foresee fright or shock severe enough to cause substantial injury in a person normally constituted. Plaintiff would then be within the zone of risk in very much the same way as are plaintiffs to whom danger is extended by acts of third persons, or forces of nature, or their own responses (where these things are foreseeable).
>
> —(2 Harper & James, The Law of Torts, supra, at pp. 1035–1036; fns. omitted)

Since the chief element in determining whether defendant owes a duty or an obligation to plaintiff is the foreseeability of the risk, that factor will be of prime concern in every case. Because it is inherently intertwined with foreseeability such duty or obligation must necessarily be adjudicated only upon a case-by-case basis. We cannot now predetermine defendant's obligation in every situation by a fixed category; no immutable rule can establish the extent of that obligation for every circumstance of the future. We can, however, define guidelines which will aid in the resolution of such an issue as the instant one.

We note, first, that we deal here with a case in which plaintiff suffered a shock which resulted in physical injury and we confine our ruling to that case. In deter-

mining, in such a case, whether defendant should reasonably foresee the injury to plaintiff, or, in other terminology, whether defendant owes plaintiff a duty of due care, the courts will take into account such factors as the following: (1) Whether plaintiff was located near the scene of the accident as contrasted with one who was a distance away from it. (2) Whether the shock resulted from a direct emotional impact upon plaintiff from the sensory and contemporaneous observance of the accident, as contrasted with learning of the accident from others after its occurrence. (3) Whether plaintiff and the victim were closely related, as contrasted with an absence of any relationship or the presence of only a distant relationship.

The evaluation of these factors will indicate the degree of the defendant's foreseeability: obviously defendant is more likely to foresee that a mother who observes an accident affecting her child will suffer harm than to foretell that a stranger witness will do so. Similarly, the degree of foreseeability of the third person's injury is far greater in the case of his contemporaneous observance of the accident than that in which he subsequently learns of it. The defendant is more likely to foresee that shock to the nearby, witnessing mother will cause physical harm than to anticipate that someone distant from the accident will suffer more than a temporary emotional reaction. All these elements, of course, shade into each other; the fixing of obligation, intimately tied into the facts, depends upon each case.

In light of these factors the court will determine whether the accident and harm was reasonably foreseeable. Such reasonable foreseeability does not turn on whether the particular plaintiff as an individual would have in actuality fore-seen the exact accident and loss; it con-templates that courts, on a case-to-case basis, analyzing all the circumstances, will decide what the ordinary man un-der such circumstances should reason-ably have foreseen. The courts thus mark out the areas of liability, excluding the remote and unexpected.

In the instant case, the presence of all the above factors indicates that plaintiff has alleged a sufficient prima facie case. Surely the negligent driver who causes the death of a young child may reason-ably expect that the mother will not be far distant and will upon witnessing the ac-cident suffer emotional trauma. As Dean Prosser has stated: "when a child is en-dangered, it is not beyond contemplation that its mother will be somewhere in the vicinity, and will suffer serious shock." (Prosser, The Law of Torts, supra, at p. 353. See also 2 Harper & James, The Law of Torts, supra, at p. 1039.)

We are not now called upon to de-cide whether, in the absence or reduced weight of some of the above factors, we would conclude that the accident and in-jury were not reasonably foreseeable and that therefore defendant owed no duty of due care to plaintiff. In future cases the courts will draw lines of demarcation upon facts more subtle than the com-pelling ones alleged in the complaint be-fore us.

The courts have in the past, in anal-ogous situations, drawn the limits of lia-bility, applying general guidelines such as those above set forth to the specific facts of the cases. As examples of that process of definition we set forth the his-tory of the "open car" cases, the rulings on recovery by persons not in privity of contract for defendant's negligence in drafting instruments, the decisions on

the intentional infliction of emotional in-jury, the modern English cases, and some illustrative opinions that adjudicate the specific issue before us.

The ability of courts to limit liability predicated on tests largely based upon foreseeability is well illustrated by the "open car" cases. The prototype case is the suit against the owner of a vehicle for damage caused plaintiff by a third party who can commandeer the vehicle be-cause of the owner's carelessness in leav-ing the keys inside. In Richardson v. Ham (1955) 44 Cal.2d 772 [285 P.2d 269], we posited liability on the owner of a bulldozer because of a "foreseeable risk of intermeddling" (p. 776), noting espe-cially the great danger the bulldozer cre-ated and the special temptation it pre-sented to third parties. Similarly, in Hergenrether v. East, supra, 61 Cal.2d 440, we upheld such liability of a truck owner on the basis of "greater potential-ity of foreseeable risk" (p. 444) because of the possible danger of the vehicle, the time for which it was unattended, and the type of persons who frequent the neighborhood in which it was left.

These decisions have not led to un-trammeled liability. Rather, applying the foreseeability test, the courts have held that the mere act of leaving a key in an au-tomobile, although it may possibly raise a foreseeable risk that the car will be stolen, does not increase the risk of injury to other property and hence does not warrant lia-bility: [even] if she could have foreseen the theft, she had no reason to believe that the thief would be an incompetent driver." (Richards v. Stanley (1954) 43 Cal.2d 60, 66 [271 P.2d 23].) In short:

Each case must be considered on its own facts to determine whether the [situation] in toto justifies the conclusion that the foreseeable risk of harm imposed is unreasonable, and that the defendant owner or one in charge of a vehicle has a duty to third persons in the class of the plaintiffs to refrain from subjecting them to such risk.

—(Hergenrether v. East, supra, 61 Cal.2d 440, 445; see also England v. Mapes Produce Co. (1965) 238 Cal.App.2d 120 [47 Cal.Rptr. 506]; Murray v. Wright (1958) 166 Cal.App.2d 589 [333 P.2d 111].)

In another category of cases, those involving the liability of a tort-feasor to a third person with whom he was not in privity of contract for negligent draftsmanship of a legal document, we have recognized the right of the injured party to compensation and set out guidelines for the determination of future cases. In Lucas v. Hamm (1961) 56 Cal.2d 583, 588 [15 Cal.Rptr. 821, 364 P.2d 685], we applied this rule to an attorney who drew a defective will, thereby causing damage to the intended third-party beneficiary. (See also Biakanja v. Irving (1958) 49 Cal.2d 647, 650 [320 P.2d 16, 65 A.L.R.2d 1358].)

In sanctioning recovery for injury caused by intentional infliction of mental distress, this court did not defer to the argument that liability should not be imposed because of the possible future difficulty in delimiting the area of liability. Defendants urged that if recovery were to be allowed for intentional infliction of emotional distress, actions would soon be forthcoming based upon every minor personal insult or indignity. We said:

That administrative difficulties do not justify the denial of relief for serious invasions of mental and emotional tranquility is demonstrated by the cases recognizing the right of privacy.

—(State Rubbish Collectors Assn. v. Siliznoff, supra, 38 Cal.2d 330, 338.)

We rejected the contention "that to allow recovery in the absence of physical injury will open the door to unfounded claims and a flood of litigation, and that the requirement that there be physical injury is necessary to insure that serious mental suffering actually occurred" (State Rubbish Collectors Assn. v. Siliznoff, supra, 38 Cal.2d 330, 338).

Indeed, the argument that "there is no point at which such actions would stop" is no more plausible today than when it was advanced in Winterbottom v. Wright (1842) 10 M. & W. 109, 111. History has exposed the fallacy of the claim that abolition of privity in enterprise liability cases would lead to "the most absurd and outrageous consequences, to which I can see no limit" (p. 114). In taking another giant step forward, in imposing product liability in tort, we were not halted by the spectre of an inability to pre-judge every future case. The setting of boundaries upon that doctrine makes the problem of fixing lines of limitation here appear, by comparison, almost minuscule. The widening of the area of liability and the possibility of the encouragement of unfounded and undefinable claims in the products liability field was sweeping; here we deal with a comparatively isolated and unusual situation. We do not believe that the fear that we cannot successfully adjudicate future cases of this sort, pursuant to the suggested guidelines, should bar recovery in an otherwise meritorious cause.

[T]he history of the cases does not show the development of a logical rule but rather a series of changes and abandonments. Upon the argument in each situation that the courts draw a Maginot Line to withstand an onslaught of false claims, the cases have assumed a variety of postures. At first they insisted that there be no recovery for emotional trauma at all. (Amaya v. Home Ice, Fuel & Supply Co., supra, 59 Cal.2d 295, dissenting opinion by Peters, J., p. 328 fn. 9.) Retreating from this position, they gave relief for such trauma only if physical impact occurred. (Id. at p. 325 fn. 4.) They then abandoned the requirement for physical impact but insisted that the victim fear for her own safety (Amaya v. Home Ice, Fuel & Supply Co., supra, 59 Cal.2d 295), holding that a mother could recover for fear for her children's safety if she simultaneously entertained a personal fear for herself. (Lindley v. Knowlton, supra, 179 Cal. 298.) They stated that the mother need only be in the "zone of danger" (Reed v. Moore (1957) 156 Cal.App.2d 43, 47 [319 P.2d 80]). The final anomaly would be the instant case in which the sister, who observed the accident, would be granted recovery because she was in the "zone of danger," but the mother, not far distant, would be barred from recovery.

The successive abandonment of these positions exposes the weakness of artificial abstractions which bar recovery contrary to the general rules. As the commentators have suggested, the problem should be solved by the application of the principles of tort, not by the creation of exceptions to them. Legal history shows that artificial islands of exceptions, created from the fear that the legal process will not work, usually do not withstand the waves of reality and, in time, descend into oblivion.

We have explained that recovery here will not expose the courts to false claims or a flood of litigation. The test that we have set forth will aid in the proper resolution of future cases. Indeed, the general principles of tort law are acknowledged to work successfully in all other cases of emotional trauma.

Yet for some artificial reason this delimitation of liability is alleged to be unworkable in the most egregious case of them all: the mother's emotional trauma at the witnessed death of her child. If we stop at this point, however, we must necessarily question and reject not merely recovery here, but the viability of the judicial process for ascertaining liability for tortious conduct itself. To the extent that it is inconsistent with our ruling here, we therefore overrule Amaya v. Home Ice Fuel & Supply Co., supra, 59 Cal.2d 295.

To deny recovery would be to chain this state to an outmoded rule of the 19th century which can claim no current credence. No good reason compels our captivity to an indefensible orthodoxy.

QUESTIONS AND DISCUSSION POINTS

1. Like the *Palsgraf* case, this case discusses the scope of the concept of "duty." In *Palsgraf*, the question was the reach of the sphere of duty. In *Dillon*, the question is again one of scope, but this time the scope question concerns the scope of injuries compensable at law.

   The Court begins by rejecting an argument, that being the problem of "fraudulent cases." What sort of argument is this? For this argument to be successful, what sort of evidence would have to be marshalled in support of it? Are you persuaded that the court deals adequately with the argument?

2. As mentioned, this case involves the concept of "duty." How does the Court define the scope of persons to whom a duty is owed? Is the limit set by the court principled, or is it based on factors other than principle?

3. Would it be better if tort law made injurers liable for all the effects of their acts? What arguments support doing anything less?

4. Can you think of an argument that would support limiting liability in cases such as *Dillon* to physical injury alone? Does the Court consider such an argument?

5. When the Court makes reference to "public policy," to what do you think the Court refers? Are public policy considerations legal arguments by another name?

～

MARIA E. THING, Plaintiff and Appellant,
v. JAMES V. LaCHUSA et al., Defendants and Respondents
Supreme Court of California
771 P.2d 814 (1989)

OPINION BY: EAGLESON

The narrow issue presented by the parties in this case is whether the Court of Appeal correctly held that a mother who did not witness an accident in which an automobile struck and injured her child may recover damages from the negligent driver for the emotional distress she suffered when she arrived at the accident scene. The more important question this issue poses for the court, however, is whether the "guidelines" enunciated by this court in Dillon v. Legg (1968) are adequate, or if they should be refined to create greater certainty in this area of the law.

Although terms of convenience identify the cause of action here as one for negligent infliction of emotional distress (NIED) and the plaintiff as a "bystander" rather than a "direct victim," the common law tort giving rise to plaintiff's claim is negligence.

It is in that context that we consider the appropriate application of the concept of "duty" in an area that has long divided this court—recognition of the right of persons, whose only injury is emotional distress, to recover damages when that distress is caused by knowledge of the injury to a third person caused by the defendant's negligence. Although we again find ourselves divided, we shall resolve some of the uncertainty over the parameters of the NIED action, uncertainty that has troubled lower courts, litigants, and, of course, insurers.

As our subsequent discussion will explain, the right to recover for NIED suffered as a result of observing the pain and suffering accompanying an injury to another, has been extended to plaintiffs who are neither "bystanders" present at the scene of the injury causing incident nor percipient witnesses "who view the defendant's negligent conduct."

Upon doing so, we shall conclude that the societal benefits of certainty in the law, as well as traditional concepts of tort law, dictate limitation of bystander recovery of damages for emotional distress.

In the absence of physical injury or impact to the plaintiff himself, damages for emotional distress should be recoverable only if the plaintiff: (1) is closely related to the injury victim, (2) is present at the scene of the injury-producing event at the time it occurs and is then aware that it is causing injury to the victim and, (3) as a result suffers emotional distress beyond that which would be anticipated in a disinterested witness.

On December 8, 1980, John Thing, a minor, was injured when struck by an automobile operated by defendant James V. La Chusa. His mother, plaintiff Maria Thing, was nearby, but neither saw nor heard the accident. She became aware of the injury to her son when told by a daughter that John had been struck by a car. She rushed to the scene where she saw her bloody and unconscious child, who she believed was dead, lying in the roadway. Maria sued defendants, alleging that she suffered great emotional disturbance, shock, and injury to her nervous system as a result of these events, and that the injury to John and emotional distress she suffered were proximately caused by defendants' negligence.

The trial court granted defendants' motion for summary judgment, ruling that, as a matter of law, Maria could not establish a claim for negligent infliction of emotional distress because she did not contemporaneously and sensorily perceive the accident. Although prior decisions applying the guidelines suggested by this court in Dillon v. Legg, compelled the ruling of the trial court, the Court of Appeal reversed the judgment dismissing Maria's claim after considering the decision of this court in Ochoa v. Superior Court (1985).

The Court of Appeal reasoned that while Maria's argument, premised on Molien v. Kaiser Foundation Hospitals (1980), that she was a direct victim of La Chusa's negligence, did not afford a basis for recovery, contemporaneous awareness of a sudden occurrence causing injury to her child was not a prerequisite to recovery under Dillon.

We granted review to consider whether Ochoa supports the holding of the Court of Appeal. We here also further define and circumscribe the circumstances in which the right to such recovery exists. To do so it is once again necessary to return to basic principles of tort law.

Emotional Distress as a Compensable Item of Damage in Intentional Torts

Although the theory of recovery in issue here is the tort of "negligence," recognition of emotional distress as a distinct item of damage for which recovery may be had even absent physical injury or impact is not limited to negligence actions. Indeed, recovery for intentional conduct that invades the individual's right to peace of mind was recognized long before such recovery was permitted in negligence actions. It is useful, therefore, to place emotional distress as a basis for a negligence action in perspective by briefly reviewing the development of common law recognition of a protectible interest in individual peace of mind—i.e., the right to be free from socially unacceptable conduct that seriously affects another's peace of mind.

The range of mental or emotional injury subsumed within the rubric "emotional distress" and for which damages are presently recoverable "includes fright, nervousness, grief, anxiety, worry, mortification, shock, humiliation and indignity, as well as physical pain."

Express or implicit recognition that peace of mind warrants legal protection is found in recovery for emotional distress as an aggravation of damages sought under intentional tort theories. Initially, emotional distress was recognized simply as an item of damages in those actions. With few exceptions, causing mental distress did not itself create a right of action, and where mental distress alone exists the common law rarely permitted recovery of damages.

Possibly the first exception to that limitation existed in recovery for assault. Assault is a tort which today recognizes the right of the individual to peace of mind, to live without fear of personal harm. "A civil action for assault is based upon an invasion of the right of a person to live without being put in fear of personal harm."

It has been noted, however, that actions based on intentional conduct were originally authorized not in recognition of or to redress a right to mental tranquility, but to afford an alternate dispute resolution mechanism. Legal action was preferable to redress on the field of honor.

Emotional distress is also an accepted item of damage that may be recovered in actions for abuse of process. Here, too, recovery has not been limited to circumstances in which the mental distress is an aggravation of a physical injury or impact.

Recognition of emotional distress as a compensable injury when caused by an intentional tort carried with it a judgment that the defendant's conduct was sufficiently outrageous or unacceptable that an award of damages was justified to punish the tort feasor and deter such conduct by others. This development led in turn to a focus on the nature of the defendant's conduct, rather than on identifying a traditional tort to justify recovery for infliction of emotional distress, and culminated in recognition of the tort now known as intentional infliction of emotional distress.

As one treatise summarizes the shift: "In many instances where the only substantial harm was emotional, recovery was allowed by finding some traditional legal peg on which to hang it. Thus if the court could find a battery or trespass, however technical, it was much less reluctant to uphold plaintiff's claim for mental suffering. Gradually, however, the understanding grew that resort to such devices obscured the principle that best explained the holdings of the courts. A more general willingness to provide for liability, where the harm was intentionally or even recklessly inflicted, emerged. The character of the defendant's behavior became of prime importance."

Prosser and Keaton on Torts explains:

The early cases refused all remedy for mental injury, unless it could be brought within the scope of some already recognized tort. Thus it was held that mere words, however violent, threatening or insulting, did not constitute an assault, and hence afforded no ground for redress. It might well be inquired why the trespass action for assault, which was a remedy designed to keep the peace, never was extended to words which were more insulting, unendurable, and generally provocative than blows. Perhaps it was the proximity of the criminal law, with its fixed notion that assault must always be something in the nature of an attempted battery. In any event, the result was a rule which permitted recovery for a gesture that might frighten the plaintiff for a moment, and denied it for menacing words which kept the plaintiff in terror for a month. But if some independent tort, such as assault, battery, false imprisonment, or seduction could be made out, the cause of action served as a peg upon which to hang the mental damages, and recovery was freely permitted. Such "parasitic" damages were the entering wedge.

It has gradually become recognized that there is no magic inherent in the name given to a tort, or in any arbitrary classification, and that the infliction of mental injury may be a cause of action in itself.

With recognition of intentional infliction of emotional distress as a discrete tort cause of action, this court accepted both freedom from emotional distress as an interest worthy of protection in its own right, and the proposition that it is possible to quantify and compensate for the invasion of that interest through an award of monetary damages even when the severity of the emotional distress is not manifested in physical symptoms. If a cause of action is otherwise established, it is settled that damages may be given for mental suffering naturally ensuing from the acts complained of [citations], and in the case of many torts, such as assault, battery, false imprisonment, and defamation, mental suffering will frequently constitute the principal element of damages. In cases where mental suffering constitutes a major element of damages it is anomalous to deny recovery because the defendant's intentional misconduct fell short of producing some physical injury.

In Siliznoff, the court rejected arguments that permitting recovery for emotional distress without proof of physical injury would invite fraudulent claims and create difficulties in proof that serious mental distress resulted from the tortious conduct. The court reasoned that the defendant's conduct often afforded greater proof of a serious invasion of the victim's mental tranquility than did the presence or absence of resulting physical symptoms.

Limitations in Negligence Actions

A parallel line of negligence cases permitting recovery of damages for emotional distress had developed in California at the time Siliznoff, was decided. Initially, however, in negligence cases the right to recover for emotional distress had been limited to circumstances in which the victim was himself injured and emotional distress was a "parasitic" item of damages, or if a plaintiff who had been in the "zone of danger" did not suffer injury from impact, but did suffer physical injury as a result of the emotional trauma.

Where the conduct was negligent, emotional distress caused solely by fear for a third person's safety or apprehension of injury to the third person, was first recognized as an injury for which damages could be sought in Dillon v. Legg.

But shortly before Dillon, in Amaya v. Home Ice, Fuel & Supply Co., the court had declined the opportunity to broaden the right to recover for emotional distress. Amaya, after confirming that the "impact rule" making a contemporaneous physical impact a prerequisite to recovery for negligently induced fright or shock was not applicable in California, held damages could not be recovered by persons outside the zone of danger created by the defendant's negligence even when that shock was reflected in physiological symptoms. The court quoted with approval the statement of the general rule of non liability for nervous shock induced by fear for a third party applied by the Court of Appeal in Reed v. Moore (1957): "As a general rule, no recovery is permitted for a mental or emotional disturbance, or for a bodily injury or illness resulting there from, in the absence of a contemporaneous bodily contact or independent cause of action, or an element of wilfulness, wantonness, or maliciousness, in cases in which there is no injury other than one to a third person, even though recovery would have been permitted had the wrong been directed against the plaintiff. The rule is frequently applied to mental or emotional disturbances caused by another's danger, or sympathy for another's suffering. It has been regarded as applicable to a mental or emotional disturbance resulting from an injury not only to a stranger, but also to a relative of the plaintiff, such as a child, sister, father, or spouse."

The court explained the restriction on the right to recover damages for emotional distress in negligence actions on the ground that the defendant had not breached a legal duty to the plaintiff. The court concluded that existence of a duty could not be defined, or left to the jury to find, on the basis of whether the injury was foreseeable. Rather the existence and scope of the defendant's duty in this context was one for the court.

Several factors led to that conclusion. First was the observation that there are circumstances in which although a foreseeable risk exists, there is no duty to avoid creation of that risk. Another was the then prevalent view of other courts and commentators that the type of harm—fright or nervous shock with consequent bodily illness induced solely by apprehension of danger to another person—was not reasonably foreseeable. Ultimately, however, the court weighed the interest of the plaintiff in freedom from invasion of mental tranquility against the costs involved in recognizing a duty and concluded that factors militating against recognition of a legal duty to the third party plaintiff predominated.

First among these policy considerations was efficient administration of justice. The court's concern here was the possibility of fraud and the difficulty in resolving disputes among witnesses over the extent and severity of the injury where negligent conduct rather than intentional conduct allegedly produced the emotional distress. A second important administrative factor was concern that it would be impossible to limit the circumstances in which liability would exist for emotional distress caused by apprehension of danger or injury not to the plaintiff but to a third person. The court concluded, also, that socioeconomic and moral factors mandate that there be some limit to the liability of the negligent actor.

> The concept of relative fault weighed equally with the administrative concerns. As long as our system of compensation is based on the concept of fault, we must also weigh "the moral blame attached to the defendant's conduct." Here is felt the difference between the social importance of conduct that negligently causes harm and conduct that is intended to do so. It is often said that in the latter case the defendant will be held liable for a broader range of consequences because, as the consequences are intended, they are the more "foreseeable." But in many intentional tort cases the defendant has been held liable under this reasoning for consequences far beyond those which he actually intended. It follows that, once more, "foreseeability" is not the real answer. Rather, the increased liability imposed on an intentional wrong doer appears to reflect the psychological fact that solicitude for the interests of the actor weighs less in the balance as his moral guilt increases and the social utility of his conduct diminishes.

The Amaya view was short lived, however. Only five years later, the decision was overruled in Dillon v. Legg. In the ensuing 20 years, like the pebble cast into the pond, Dillon's progeny have created ever widening circles of liability. Post-Dillon decisions have now permitted plaintiffs who suffer emotional distress, but no resultant physical injury, and who were not at the scene of and thus did not witness the event that injured another, to recover damages on grounds that a duty was owed to them solely because it was foreseeable that they would suffer that distress on learning of injury to a close relative.

In Dillon itself, the issue was limited. The mother and sister of a deceased infant each sought damages for "great emotional disturbance and shock and injury to her nervous system" which had caused them great mental pain and suffering. Allegedly these injuries were caused by witnessing the defendant's negligently operated vehicle collide with and roll over the infant as she lawfully crossed a street. The mother was not herself endangered by the defendant's conduct. The sister may have been. The trial court had therefore granted the defendant's motion for judgment on the pleadings as to the mother, but had denied it with respect to the sister of the decedent. Faced with the incongruous result demanded by the "zone of danger" rule which denied recovery for emotional distress and consequent physical injury unless the plaintiff himself had been threatened with injury, the court overruled Amaya.

Reexamining the concept of "duty" as applicable to the Dillon facts, the court now rejected the argument that the possibility of fraudulent claims justified denial of recovery, at least insofar as a mother who sees her child killed is concerned, as "no one can seriously question that fear or grief for one's child is as likely to cause physical injury as concern over one's own well-being."

The court held instead that the right to recover should be determined by application of "the neutral principles of foreseeability, proximate cause and consequential injury that generally govern tort law."

The difficulty in defining the limits on recovery anticipated by the Amaya court was rejected as a basis for denying recovery, but the court did recognize that "to limit the otherwise potentially infinite liability which would follow every negligent act, the law of torts holds defendant amenable only for injuries to others which to defendant at the time were reasonably foreseeable."

Thus, while the court indicated that foreseeability of the injury was to be the primary consideration in finding duty, it simultaneously recognized that policy considerations mandated that infinite liability be avoided by restrictions that would somehow narrow the class of potential plaintiffs. But the test limiting liability was itself amorphous.

Because a general duty exists to avoid causing foreseeable injury to another, the concept of "foreseeability" enters into both the willingness of the court to recognize the existence of a duty, the breach of which permits an action for damages, and into the determination by a trier of fact whether the specific injury in issue was foreseeable. The court explained the distinction in whether a particular plaintiff's injury was reasonably foreseeable in light of a particular defendant's conduct, but rather to evaluate more generally whether the category of negligent conduct at issue is sufficiently likely to result in the kind of harm experienced that liability may appropriately be imposed on the negligent party.

"The jury, by contrast, considers 'foreseeability' in two more focused, fact-specific settings. First, the jury may consider the likelihood or foreseeability of injury in determining whether, in fact, the particular defendant's conduct was negligent in the first place. Second, foreseeability may be relevant to the jury's determination of whether the defendant's negligence was a proximate or legal cause of the plaintiff's injury."

In the present context, however, we are concerned not with whether an injury is "foreseeable" as a result of the negligent conduct. As the court recognized in Dillon, it is no less "foreseeable" that a person outside the "zone of danger" will suffer emotional distress on observing the injury of a close relative than it is that this person would suffer such distress if he or she were also threatened with injury. Thus, the court's role in deciding whether a "duty" to these persons should be recognized does not depend solely on the "foreseeability" of the emotional distress, but on these policy considerations.

In adopting foreseeability of the injury as the basis of a negligent actor's duty, the Dillon court identified the risks that could give rise to that duty as both physical impact and emotional disturbance brought on by the conduct. Having done so, the Dillon court conceded: "We cannot now predetermine defendant's obligation in every situation by a fixed category; no immutable rule can establish the extent of that obligation for every circumstance of the future."

In an effort to give some initial definition to this newly approved expansion of the cause of action for NIED the court

enunciated "guidelines" that suggested a limitation on the action to circumstances like those in the case before it.

"We note, first, that we deal here with a case in which plaintiff suffered a shock which resulted in physical injury and we confine our ruling to that case. In determining, in such a case, whether defendant should reasonably foresee the injury to plaintiff [mother], or in other terminology, whether defendant owes plaintiff a duty of due care, the courts will take into account such factors as the following:

1. Whether plaintiff was located near the scene of the accident as contrasted with one who was a distance away from
2. Whether the shock resulted from a direct emotional impact upon plaintiff from the sensory and contemporaneous observance of the accident, as contrasted with learning of the accident from others after its occurrence.
3. Whether plaintiff and the victim were closely related, as contrasted with an absence of any relationship or the presence of only a distant relationship.

The evaluation of these factors will indicate the degree of the defendant's foreseeability; obviously defendant is more likely to foresee that a mother who observes an accident affecting her child will suffer harm than to foretell that a stranger witness will do so. Similarly, the degree of foreseeability of the third person's injury is far greater in the case of his contemporaneous observance of the accident than that in which he subsequently learns of it. The defendant is more likely to foresee that shock to the nearby, witnessing mother will cause physical harm than to anticipate that someone distant from the accident will suffer more than a temporary emotional reaction. All of these elements, of course, shade into each other; the fixing of the obligation, intimately tied into the facts, depends upon each case.

In light of these factors the court will determine whether the accident and harm was reasonably foreseeable. Such reasonable foreseeability does not turn on whether the particular [defendant] as an individual would have in actuality foreseen the exact accident and loss; it contemplates that courts, on a case-to-case basis, analyzing all the circumstances, will decide what the ordinary man under such circumstances should reasonably have foreseen. The courts thus mark out the areas of liability, excluding the remote and unexpected.

The Dillon court anticipated and accepted uncertainty in the short term in application of its holding, but was confident that the boundaries of this NIED action could be drawn in future cases. In sum, as former Justice Potter Stewart once suggested with reference to that undefinable category of materials that are obscene, the Dillon court was satisfied that trial and appellate courts would be able to determine the existence of a duty because the court would know it when it saw it. Underscoring the questionable validity of that assumption, however, was the obvious and unaddressed problem that the injured party, the negligent tort feasor, their insurers, and their attorneys had no means short of suit by which to determine if a duty such as to impose liability for damages would be found in cases other than those that were "on all fours" with Dillon. Thus, the only thing that was foreseeable from the Dillon decision was the uncertainty that

continues to this time as to the parameters of the third party NIED action.

Post-Dillon Extension

The expectation of the Dillon majority that the parameters of the tort would be further defined in future cases has not been fulfilled. Instead, subsequent decisions of the Courts of Appeal and this court, have created more uncertainty. And, just as the "zone of danger" limitation was abandoned in Dillon as an arbitrary restriction on recovery, the Dillon guidelines have been relaxed on grounds that they, too, created arbitrary limitations on recovery. Little consideration has been given in post-Dillon decisions to the importance of avoiding the limitless exposure to liability that the pure foreseeability test of "duty" would create and towards which these decisions have moved.

Several post-Dillon decisions of this court are particularly noteworthy in this expansive progression. In the first, Krouse v. Graham (1977), this court held that the NIED plaintiff need not "visually" perceive the third party injury to satisfy the Dillon guideline suggesting that the plaintiff suffer shock from " 'the sensory and contemporaneous observance of the accident, ...' " It was sufficient that the plaintiff knew the position of his wife just outside the automobile in which he was seated the instant before she was struck by defendant's automobile which he had seen and realized was going to strike her. He was, therefore, a "percipient witness to the impact causing [her] injuries."

We also find in Krouse, the roots of the uncertainty reflected by the instant case over whether the plaintiff must perceive the injury causing incident at all or may recover for emotional distress suffered on viewing its "immediate consequences" even though not present at the scene when it occurred. Krouse created uncertainty as to the meaning and importance of the plaintiff's status as a "percipient witness" by approving the conclusion of the Court of Appeal in Archibald v. Braverman (1969), that visual perception of the accident was not required without commenting on the context in which the Archibald court made its ruling. That decision had allowed recovery by a mother who "did not actually witness the tort but viewed the child's injuries within moments after the occurrence of the injury-producing event."

Thus, it appeared that this court agreed that persons who were not present at the accident scene could recover damages for the emotional distress they later suffered when told by others of the injury to their loved one or when they later came to the scene.

Krouse was followed by Justus v. Atchison (1977), in which the court identified the issue as whether the plaintiff fathers' causes of action for the emotional impact of observing the stillborn birth of their children satisfied the Dillon guideline of shock resulting from a direct emotional impact from the sensory and contemporaneous observance of an "accident." The court did not decide this question, ruling instead that the plaintiffs could not recover because neither had learned of the death of the fetus until informed by a doctor. Thus the "disabling shock" occurred only upon being informed by another of the injury. By implication, however, it seemed that the injury producing event need not be a sudden occurrence or accident.

However, the court in Hoyem v. Manhattan Beach City Sch. Dist. (1978), reaffirmed the requirement that the shock or emotional distress necessary to a cause of action for NIED under Dillon must "result from a 'direct emotional impact' on the plaintiff caused by 'sensory and contemporaneous observance of the accident.' "

But in Nazaroff v. Superior Court (1978), after considering this court's post-Dillon decisions and those of the Courts of Appeal, including Archibald v. Braverman, the concept of contemporaneous observance was broadened. The court held that a mother who, while searching for her missing three-year-old child, heard a neighbor scream his name, realized the child must have fallen into the neighbor's pool, and saw the child being pulled from the pool and given cardiopulmonary resuscitation as she ran up, could state a cause of action under Dillon. The court reasoned that it was not necessary that the plaintiff perceive the accident if she suffered physical harm that resulted from "the direct emotional impact from the contemporaneous observation of the immediate consequences of the defendants' negligent act, which was the proximate cause of the injury and death of her son."

The court explained that the plaintiff may have mentally reconstructed the accident and the child might still have been experiencing the injuries caused by the defendants' negligence when his mother first observed him.

With the Nazaroff decision, therefore, the Dillon guideline of sensory perception of an accident or injury was no longer considered a prerequisite to recovery. It was still necessary, however, that the plaintiff who had witnessed the immediate consequences of an injury producing incident suffer emotional distress sufficient to result in physical injury.

Both the physical harm and accident or sudden occurrence elements were eliminated, however, in Molien v. Kaiser Foundation Hospitals, at least as to those plaintiffs who could claim to be "direct victims" of the defendant's negligence. The court held in Molien that a defendant hospital and doctor owed a duty directly to the husband of a patient who had been diagnosed erroneously as having syphilis, and had been told to so advise the husband in order that he could receive testing and, if necessary, treatment.

In finding the existence of a duty to the husband of the patient, the court reasoned that the risk of harm to the husband was reasonably foreseeable, and that the tortious conduct was directed to him as well as the patient.

The status of the plaintiff mother in Dillon was distinguished as she suffered her injury solely as a "percipient witness" to the infliction of injury on another. She was therefore a "bystander" rather than a "direct victim."

The court did not further explain this distinction, or its relevance to whether the plaintiff should be allowed to recover damages for emotional distress. Both decisions had looked to the relationships of the parties to find foreseeability of the injury and thus a "duty to the plaintiff." The basis for finding a duty to the mother in Dillon was the foreseeability of her emotional distress to "the negligent driver who causes the death of a young child [and] may reasonably expect that the mother will not be far distant and will upon witnessing the accident suffer emotional trauma."

In Molien:

[The] risk of harm to plaintiff was reasonably foreseeable to defendants. It is easily predictable that an erroneous diagnosis of syphilis and its probable source would produce marital discord and resultant emotional distress to a married patient's spouse; [the physician's] advice to Mrs. Molien to have her husband examined for the disease confirms that plaintiff [husband] was a foreseeable victim of the negligent diagnosis. We thus agree with plaintiff that the alleged tortious conduct of defendant was directed to him as well as to his wife.

Because the risk of harm to him was reasonably foreseeable we hold that under these circumstances defendants owed plaintiff a duty to exercise due care in diagnosing the physical condition of his wife.

Molien neither established criteria for characterizing a plaintiff as a "direct" victim, nor explained the justification for permitting "direct" victims to recover when "bystander" plaintiffs could not.

The immediate effect of the decision, however, was to permit some persons who had no prior relationship with the defendant that gave rise to a duty, who did not suffer physical injury as a result of emotional distress, who did not observe the negligent conduct, and who had not been at or near the scene of the negligent act to recover for emotional distress on a pure foreseeability-of-the-injury basis. The limitations on recovery for emotional distress that had been suggested in the Dillon "guidelines" were not applicable to "direct" victims of a defendant's negligence.

The subtleties in the distinction between the right to recover as a "bystander" and as a "direct victim" created what one Court of Appeal has described as an "amorphous nether realm." In Andalon v. Superior Court, the court found that a physician's duty arose out of contract, after it had abandoned the effort to resolve the "direct" or "bystander" dilemma:

> The problem which arises from this cryptic explanation is: how are we to distinguish between "direct victim" cases and "bystander" cases? An impression is given that the foreseeability of the particular injury to the husband alone explains the result. The inference suggested is that a "direct victim" is a person whose emotional distress is a reasonably foreseeable consequence of the conduct of the defendant. This does not provide criteria which delimit what counts as reasonable foreseeability. It leads into the quagmire of novel claims which the Supreme Court foresaw as an unacceptable consequence of a "pure" foreseeability analysis.
>
> [Foreseeability], the court noted later in Newton v. Kaiser Foundations Hospitals, "is endless because foreseeability, like light, travels indefinitely in a vacuum."

Molien, thus, left to future cases the "unenviable tasks of distinguishing bystander from direct victim cases and establishing limits for the latter with a 'foreseeable' diversity of results."

The Dillon-Molien waters, described by the Court of Appeal in this case as "murky," were further muddied when the right to recover in the negligence action was expanded to include "bystander" plaintiffs who suffered emotional distress, but no contemporaneous or consequential physical injury. We had reasoned in Molien that the requirement of physical injury was no more necessary

to ensure that a claim of serious emotional distress is genuine in NIED actions than it was in actions for intentional infliction of emotional distress. Rather the question was one of proof to be left to the jury.

Cases subsequent to Molien assumed that the reasoning which led the court to abandon the physical-injury requirement extended to "bystander" NIED actions. Physical manifestation of the serious nature of the mental distress suffered by the plaintiff was no longer an element of the cause of action.

Ochoa v. Superior Court, partially explained and limited "direct victim" recovery under Molien, to situations in which the defendant's negligence is "by its very nature directed at" the plaintiff. However, Ochoa also indicated that the dimensions of the NIED tort might be expanded further for "bystander" plaintiffs. Ochoa confirmed that recovery was permitted even though the injury producing event was not sudden or accidental, and even though its negligent cause was not immediately apparent. The court observed that the factors set forth in Dillon had been offered only as guidelines, and suggested that none was essential to recovery for NIED. Foreseeability that the injury would cause emotional distress was the proper inquiry.

That dictum in Ochoa was broader than the issue presented in Ochoa, however. The plaintiff mother had observed the effects of the defendants' negligent failure to diagnose and properly treat the illness of her teenage son. Her observation of his pain and suffering, and his deteriorating condition, as the defendants failed to either properly care for him or accede to her entreaty that she be permitted to obtain care for him, was the cause of the emotional distress for which she sought to recover. The allegations of the complaint satisfied only two of the Dillon factors—she was at the scene of the negligent injury producing conduct and was closely related to the person whose physical injury caused her distress. Defendants' negligence in failing to give proper medical treatment, however, was not a sudden accidental occurrence and thus the second Dillon factor was not met: "Whether the shock resulted from a direct emotional impact upon plaintiff from the sensory and contemporaneous observance of the accident."

This court, after reviewing several decisions of the Courts of Appeal which had limited recovery for NIED to percipient witnesses of a "sudden occurrence," held that this requirement was an unwarranted restriction on the cause of action authorized in Dillon. "Such a restriction arbitrarily limits liability when there is a high degree of foreseeability of shock to the plaintiff and the shock flows from an abnormal event, and, as such, unduly frustrates the goal of compensation—the very purpose which the cause of action was meant to further."

Ochoa also held that the NIED plaintiff need not be aware that the conduct was "tortious." Reasoning that such a requirement leads to anomalous results, the court held that "when there is observation of the defendant's conduct and the child's injury and contemporaneous awareness the defendant's conduct or lack thereof is causing harm to the child, recovery is permitted."

Thus, the plaintiff in that case did not have to know that the defendants had negligently misdiagnosed her son. It was enough that she knew that they were refusing or neglecting to give him additional treatment and this was the cause of the additional injury he was suffering.

In sum, however, as to "bystander" NIED actions, Ochoa held only that recovery would be permitted if the plaintiff observes both the defendant's conduct and the resultant injury, and is aware at that time that the conduct is causing the injury. The Court of Appeal erred in concluding that Ochoa, held that these NIED plaintiffs need not witness the defendant's conduct.

Under criteria that permit recovery by close relatives who suffer shock and trauma from their sensory perception of the defendant's conduct and their relative's injury, if the traumatized reaction was foreseeable, Ochoa upheld not only a cause of action by the mother of the deceased child, but also the father whose complaint alleged that he had visited the child only once and "was extremely distressed by what he saw."

His recovery was limited, however, to the distress suffered on the one occasion on which he witnessed the apparent neglect of his son by the defendants. He was not permitted to recover for distress suffered when he learned from his wife after her subsequent visits to the child of the continuing neglect of and suffering experienced by the child.

Clarification of the Right to Recover for NIED

Not surprisingly, this "case-to-case" or ad hoc approach to development of the law that misled the Court of Appeal in this case has not only produced inconsistent rulings in the lower courts, but has provoked considerable critical comment by scholars who attempt to reconcile the cases.

Proposals to eliminate the arbitrary results of the proliferating, inconsistent and often conflicting Dillon progeny include the suggestion that recovery be allowed in any case in which recovery for physical injury is permitted.

Another would limit recovery to the close-relatives class contemplated by Dillon, but allow recovery whenever mental distress to the plaintiff was foreseeable.

At the other extreme, respondent here and amicus curiae Association for California Tort Reform argue, in essence, that the Dillon "guidelines" should be recognized as substantive limitations or elements of the tort.

In his thoughtful article documenting the conflicting and sometimes arbitrary results of attempts by lower courts to apply Dillon and Molien, Professor Diamond analyzes the "flaws" in the Dillon analysis which he believes have contributed to the problem. He concludes that the Dillon-based cause of action identifies a "duty" on the basis of the purely fortuitous circumstances in which an injury occurs. As a result, when recovery for emotional distress alone is permitted under the Dillon guidelines, "foreseeability" is not a realistic indicator of potential liability and does not afford a rational limitation on recovery. Nor, Diamond suggests, do the Dillon guidelines, particularly under the expanded right to recovery created by Molien (and, we note, Ochoa), provide such limitation.

In his view, only one of the Dillon guidelines is even relevant to foreseeability—the relationship of the plaintiff to the person suffering physical injury—because it is foreseeable that the emotional distress suffered by a close relative on witnessing that injury will be greater than that of a stranger.

Diamond argues that the fact that it is foreseeable that a close relative will suffer psychological trauma at witnessing the injury does not adequately limit liability for damages for such intangible losses. When recovery for emotional distress was permitted only as an item of "parasitic" damage suffered by a plaintiff who had been physically injured, the defendant's exposure was limited by more predictable factors. Foreseeability that various activities may cause physical injury limits the potential universe of persons who may be harmed. This, in turn, by limiting the negligent actor's exposure makes it possible to protect potential victims and the defendant through insurance or other risk-spreading mechanisms whose cost is more closely related to the risk, and ensures that this exposure bears a more rational relationship to the defendant's culpability.

Another scholar suggests that any foreseeable plaintiff be permitted to recover for NIED and loss of filial consortium, but only for economic loss, thereby reconciling the divergent paths and limitations on recovery for noneconomic damages in these related torts with that permitted in actions for wrongful life.

Diamond agrees that this solution would permit recovery by all foreseeable plaintiffs in "intangible" tort cases, while restricting recovery to "economically acceptable" limits.

In the NIED context, however, permitting recovery of economic damages by all foreseeable plaintiffs would expose defendants to risks no less arbitrary and unacceptable than those presently existing. While the recovery by individual victims might be less, the number of potential plaintiffs traumatized by reason of defendant's negligent conduct toward another, would turn on fortuitous circumstances wholly unrelated to the culpability of the defendant.

Our own prior decisions identify factors that will appropriately circumscribe the right to damages, but do not deny recovery to plaintiffs whose emotional injury is real even if not accompanied by out-of-pocket expense. Notwithstanding the broad language in some of those decisions, it is clear that foreseeability of the injury alone is not a useful "guideline" or a meaningful restriction on the scope of the NIED action. The Dillon experience confirms, as one commentator observed, that "[foreseeability] proves too much. Although it may set tolerable limits for most types of physical harm, it provides virtually no limit on liability for non physical harm."

It is apparent that reliance on foreseeability of injury alone in finding a duty, and thus a right to recover, is not adequate when the damages sought are for an intangible injury. In order to avoid limitless liability out of all proportion to the degree of a defendant's negligence, and against which it is impossible to insure without imposing unacceptable costs on those among whom the risk is spread, the right to recover for negligently caused emotional distress must be limited.

We acknowledged and addressed one aspect of this problem in Elden v. Sheldon (1988), holding that cohabitation, without formal marriage, did not constitute the close relationship contemplated by the Dillon guidelines and that foreseeability of injury alone does not justify imposition of liability for negligently caused emotional distress. In so doing, we again recognized that policy considerations justify restrictions on recovery for emotional distress not withstanding the sometimes arbitrary result, and that the court has an obligation to establish those restrictions.

Elden confirmed that those policy considerations include both the burden on the courts in applying vaguely defined criteria and the importance of limiting the scope of liability for negligence.

If the consequences of a negligent act are not limited an intolerable burden is placed on society. A "bright line in this area of the law is essential."

The issue resolved in Elden was too narrow to create that "bright line" for all NIED actions. This case, however, presents a broader question and thus affords the court a better opportunity to meet its obligation to create a clear rule under which liability may be determined. In so doing we balance the impact of arbitrary lines which deny recovery to some victims whose injury is very real against that of imposing liability out of proportion to culpability for negligent acts. We also weigh in the balance the importance to the administration of justice of clear guidelines under which litigants and trial courts may resolve disputes. Thus, as we did in Elden, we turn to the concerns which prompted the Amaya court, to deny recovery for negligent infliction of emotional distress.

Among the concerns of the Amaya court was the social cost of imposing liability on a negligent tort feasor for all foreseeable emotional distress suffered by relatives who witnessed the injury. The court again faced this problem in Borer v. American Airlines, Inc. (1977), in which the court was asked to recognize a child's right to recover for the loss of a parent's consortium, an action that, like NIED, seeks monetary damages for mental or emotional loss. Refusing to permit such "filial" consortium actions, the court concluded that the cause of action for loss of consortium must be narrowly circumscribed.

Loss of consortium is an intangible injury for which money damages do not afford an accurate measure or suitable recompense; recognition of a right to recover for such losses may substantially increase the number of claims asserted in ordinary accident cases, the expense of settling or resolving such claims, and the ultimate liability of the defendants.

The decision, we explained, was one of policy. We reasoned that we could not "ignore the social burden of providing damages merely because the money to pay such awards comes initially from the 'negligent' defendant or his insurer. Realistically the burden must be borne by the public generally in increased insurance premiums or, otherwise, in the enhanced danger that accrues from the greater number of people who may choose to go without any insurance. We must also take into account the cost of administration of a system to determine and pay [the] awards. . . ."

While we emphasized in Borer, that our refusal to extend the right to recover damages in consortium cases did not signal a refusal to allow damages for intangible losses in other contexts, the policy bases for the decision are relevant to defining the NIED cause of action. Crucial to the Borer decision were the intangible nature of the loss, the inadequacy of monetary damages to make whole the loss, the difficulty in measuring the damage, and the societal cost of attempting to compensate the plaintiff. Multiplication of the defendant's liability was an additional concern.

The number of family members who might seek damages on the basis of a single incident could unreasonably enlarge the defendant's burden. We rejected a suggestion that principles enunciated in Dillon mandated recognition of the children's cause of action, noting what was

then the Dillon limitation—that the Dillon plaintiff have suffered physical injury—which limited the class of potential plaintiffs.

Similar concerns led the court to reject a parent's cause of action for loss of a child's consortium in a companion case.

Our opinion in Borer v. American Airlines, explains the policy considerations which impelled us to conclude that a child should not have a cause of action for loss of parental consortium. Those reasons for the most part apply fully to the present issue of a parental claim for loss of filial consortium. The intangible character of the loss, which can never really be compensated by money damages; the difficulty of measuring damages; the dangers of double recovery or multiple claims and of extensive liability—all these considerations apply similarly to both cases.

The court again recognized the need to limit recovery of monetary damages for intangible loss in Turpin v. Sortini (1982). There, in an action for "wrongful life," the court limited damages to economic loss and observed that "a monetary award of general damages cannot in any meaningful sense compensate the plaintiff."

Ochoa v. Superior Court, footnote 6, offers additional guidance, justifying what we acknowledge must be arbitrary lines to similarly limit the class of potential plaintiffs if emotional injury absent physical harm is to continue to be a recoverable item of damages in a negligence action.

The impact of personally observing the injury-producing event in most, although concededly not all, cases distinguishes the plaintiff's resultant emotional distress from the emotion felt when one learns of the injury or death of a loved one from another, or observes pain and suffering but not the traumatic cause of the injury. Greater certainty and a more reasonable limit on the exposure to liability for negligent conduct is possible by limiting the right to recover for negligently caused emotional distress to plaintiffs who personally and contemporaneously perceive the injury-producing event and its traumatic consequences.

A distinction between distress caused by personal observation of the injury and by hearing of the tragedy from another is justified because compensation should be limited to abnormal life experiences which cause emotional distress. While receiving news that a loved one has been injured or has died may cause emotional distress, it is the type of experience for which in a general way one is prepared, an experience which is common. By contrast few persons are forced to witness the death or injury of a loved one or to suddenly come upon the scene without warning in situations where tortious conduct is involved. In the present case, for example, while it is common to visit a loved one in a hospital and to be distressed by the loved one's pain and suffering, it is highly uncommon to witness the apparent neglect of the patient's immediate medical needs by medical personnel.

Similar reasoning justifies limiting recovery to persons closely related by blood or marriage since, in common experience, it is more likely that they will suffer a greater degree of emotional distress than a disinterested witness to negligently caused pain and suffering or death. Such limitations are indisputably arbitrary since it is foreseeable that in some cases unrelated persons have a relationship to the victim or are so affected by the traumatic event that they suffer equivalent emotional distress. As we have observed, however, drawing arbitrary lines is unavoidable if we are to limit liability and establish meaningful rules for application by litigants and lower courts.

No policy supports extension of the right to recover for NIED to a larger class of plaintiffs. Emotional distress is an intangible condition experienced by most persons, even absent negligence, at some time during their lives. Close relatives suffer serious, even debilitating, emotional reactions to the injury, death, serious illness, and evident suffering of loved ones. These reactions occur regardless of the cause of the loved one's illness, injury, or death. That relatives will have severe emotional distress is an unavoidable aspect of the "human condition." The emotional distress for which monetary damages may be recovered, however, ought not to be that form of acute emotional distress or the transient emotional reaction to the occasional gruesome or horrible incident to which every person may potentially be exposed in an industrial and sometimes violent society. Regardless of the depth of feeling or the resultant physical or mental illness that results from witnessing violent events, persons unrelated to those injured or killed may not now recover for such emotional upheaval even if negligently caused. Close relatives who witness the accidental injury or death of a loved one and suffer emotional trauma may not recover when the loved one's conduct was the cause of that emotional trauma. The overwhelming majority of "emotional distress" which we endure, therefore, is not compensable.

Unlike an award of damages for intentionally caused emotional distress which is punitive, the award for NIED simply reflects society's belief that a negligent actor bears some responsibility for the effect of his conduct on persons other than those who suffer physical injury. In identifying those persons and the circumstances in which the defendant will be held to redress the injury, it is appropriate to restrict recovery to those persons who will suffer an emotional impact beyond the impact that can be anticipated whenever one learns that a relative is injured, or dies, or the emotion felt by a "disinterested" witness. The class of potential plaintiffs should be limited to those who because of their relationship suffer the greatest emotional distress. When the right to recover is limited in this manner, the liability bears a reasonable relationship to the culpability of the negligent defendant.

The elements which justify and simultaneously limit an award of damages for emotional distress caused by awareness of the negligent infliction of injury to a close relative are those noted in Ochoa—the traumatic emotional effect on the plaintiff who contemporaneously observes both the event or conduct that causes serious injury to a close relative and the injury itself. Even if it is "foreseeable" that persons other than closely related percipient witnesses may suffer emotional distress, this fact does not justify the imposition of what threatens to become unlimited liability for emotional distress on a defendant whose conduct is simply negligent. Nor does such abstract "foreseeability" warrant continued reliance on the assumption that the limits of liability will become any clearer if lower courts are permitted to continue approaching the issue on a "case-to-case" basis some 20 years after Dillon.

We conclude, therefore, that a plaintiff may recover damages for emotional distress caused by observing the negligently inflicted injury of a third person if, but only if, said plaintiff: (1) is closely related to the injury victim; (2) is present at the scene of the injury-producing event at the time it occurs and is then aware that it is causing injury to the victim; (3) as a result suffers serious emotional distress—a reaction beyond that which would be anticipated in a disinterested witness and which is not an abnormal response to the circumstances. These factors were present in Ochoa and each of this court's prior decisions upholding recovery for NIED.

In most cases no justification exists for permitting recovery for NIED by persons who are only distantly related to the injury victim. Absent exceptional circumstances, recovery should be limited to relatives residing in the same household, or parents, siblings, children, and grandparents of the victim.

Once the rhetoric of the dissent has been pierced, it is clear that the dissent, too, recognizes that foreseeability of injury cannot be the sole test of liability, and that the court must ultimately define the limits of liability. While not forth rightly acknowledging the inescapable necessity of limits that will in some cases seem arbitrary, the dissent itself suggests a different, but no less arbitrary, limit—that the plaintiff may recover if he or she witnesses the "immediate" consequences of the third party injury (Why stop there? Is that a less arbitrary line?).

It is obvious, moreover, that the difficulty in defining the parameters of the line espoused by the dissent has been the cause of further arbitrariness in the irreconcilable rulings of trial courts and the conflicting appellate rulings on cases in which the factual differences offer little or no meaningful distinctions.

The dissent's suggestion that Rowland v. Christian (1968), should extend to actions for negligent infliction of emotional distress lacks support in our decisions. Neither Rowland v. Christian nor the other cases cited by the dissent are cases in which damages for negligently inflicted emotional distress were in issue. Recovery for this type of damage, when no other injury is present, has never been subject only to the general principles of foreseeability applied in Rowland v. Christian that the dissent would have us adopt here as the basis of liability.

As explained by the Hawaii Supreme Court, "serious mental distress may be found where a reasonable [person] normally constituted, would be unable to adequately cope with the mental distress engendered by the circumstances of the case."

The dictum in Ochoa suggesting that the factors noted in the Dillon guidelines are not essential in determining whether a plaintiff is a foreseeable victim of defendant's negligence should not be relied on. The merely negligent actor does not owe a duty the law will recognize to make monetary amends to all persons who may have suffered emotional distress on viewing or learning about the injurious consequences of his conduct. To the extent they are inconsistent with this conclusion, are disapproved.

Experience has shown that, contrary to the expectation of the Dillon majority, and with apology to Bernard Witkin, there are clear judicial days on which a court can foresee forever and thus determine liability but none on which that foresight alone provides a socially and judicially acceptable limit on recovery of damages for that injury.

The undisputed facts establish that plaintiff was not present at the scene of the accident in which her son was injured. She did not observe defendant's conduct and was not aware that her son was being injured. She could not, therefore, establish a right to recover for the emotional distress she suffered when she subsequently learned of the accident and observed its consequences. The order granting summary judgment was proper. The judgment of the Court of Appeal is reversed. Each party shall bear its own costs on appeal.

CONCUR BY: KAUFMAN, J.

Concurring. We granted review in this case because of the obvious and continuing difficulties that have plagued trial courts and litigants in the area of negligent infliction of emotional distress. Of course, any meaningful review of the issue necessarily entails reappraising, in the light of 20 years of experience, our landmark holding in Dillon v. Legg (1968), that a plaintiff may recover for the emotional distress induced by the apprehension of negligently caused injury to a third person. Two such "reappraisals" have now been suggested.

The majority opinion by Justice Eagleson proposes to convert Dillon's flexible "guidelines" for determining whether the risk of emotional injury was foreseeable or within the defendant's duty of care, into strict "elements" necessary to recovery. While conceding that such a doctrinaire approach will necessarily lead to "arbitrary" results, Justice Eagleson nevertheless concludes that "certainty and a more reasonable limit on the exposure to liability for negligent conduct" require strict limitations.

Dillon set forth three factors which the courts should "take into account" in determining whether the injury was "foreseeable": (1) whether the plaintiff was "located near the scene of the accident," (2) whether the emotional distress resulted "from the sensory and contemporaneous observance of the accident," and (3) whether the plaintiff and the victim "were closely related.

Justice Broussard, in dissent, opposes the effort to rigidify the Dillon guidelines. He urges, instead, that the court remain faithful to the guidelines as originally conceived as specific but "flexible" limitations on liability and adhere to Dillon's original reliance on "foreseeability as a general limit on tort liability."

Justice Broussard denies that Dillon has failed to afford adequate guidance to the lower courts or to confine liability within reasonable limits. On the contrary, the Dillon approach, in the dissent's view, has provided and continues to provide a workable and "principled basis for determining liability.

Although Justice Mosk has penned a separate dissent, he expresses "general agreement" with Justice Broussard's views and adds nothing to the Dillon analysis apart from an interesting side light on the short but eventful life of Amaya v. Home Ice, Fuel & Supply Co. (1963). Accordingly, I have confined my critique to the majority opinion and the Broussard dissent.

With all due respect, I do not believe that either the majority opinion or the dissent has articulated a genuinely "principled" rule of law. On the one hand, experience has shown that rigid doctrinal limitations on bystander liability, such as that suggested by Justice Eagleson, result inevitably in indisparate treatment of plaintiffs in substantially the same position. To be sure, the majority freely one might say almost cheerfully acknowledges that its position is arbitrary; yet nowhere does it consider the cost of such

institutionalized caprice, not only to the individuals involved, but to the integrity of the judiciary as a whole.

On the other hand, two decades of adjudication under the inexact guidelines created by Dillon and touted by the dissent, has, if anything, created a body of case law marked by even greater confusion and inconsistency of result.

The situation, therefore, calls for a wholesale reappraisal of the wisdom of permitting recovery for emotional distress resulting from injury to others.

The history of negligent infliction of emotional distress is a chronicle of "false starts." Initially, the courts were reluctant to allow any recovery for intangible harms such as fright or emotional distress resulting from negligent conduct. Later, plaintiffs were permitted to recover for the emotional distress occasioned by the fear for their own safety, but only when accompanied by physical impact.

The "impact" rule was soon recognized as inherently arbitrary, however, because of the obvious discontinuity between the rule's scope and its underlying purpose. As one commentator wryly observed, "[A] near miss may be as frightening as a direct hit."

Thus, the "impact" rule was eventually replaced by a rule allowing recovery for the emotional distress resulting from threats to the plaintiff's safety, regardless of physical impact, if the plaintiff was within the "zone of physical impact or danger."

Note, Limiting Liability for the Negligent Infliction of Emotional Distress: The "Bystander Recovery" Cases (1981).

> The seminal California decision rejecting the impact test in favor of the zone-of-danger rule is Amaya v. Home, Ice, Fuel & Supply Co.

In reaffirming the zone-of-danger rule, the Amaya court rejected the argument that liability should be extended in favor of one who claims injury through fright or shock induced by negligent conduct directed not to oneself but to a third person. While acknowledging that emotional trauma induced by the apprehension of danger to a loved one was eminently "foreseeable," the Amaya court nevertheless refused to recognize that freedom from such distress constituted a legally protected interest. A number of policy reasons were cited by the Amaya court in support of its decision, including: the risk of fraudulent claims based upon such intangible "psychic" injuries; the threat of unlimited liability and the attendant economic strain on the insurance system; the disproportionality between the culpability of the negligent tort feasor and the liability imposed; and the impossibility of formulating a "sensible or just stopping point."

Only five years later, however, in Dillon v. Legg, the court reversed field, rejecting Amaya's zone-of-danger test as "hopelessly artificial" and recognizing for the first time in American jurisprudence the concept of "bystander" liability. In Dillon, the plaintiff's daughter was struck and killed by a car negligently driven by the defendant. Plaintiff, who observed the accident from an unspecified location, sought damages for the emotional distress resulting from the incident; plaintiff's other daughter, who was standing on the curb, also claimed emotional distress. The trial court sustained a motion for summary judgment as to the plaintiff, the decedent's mother, on the ground that the pleadings failed to establish that she was within the zone of danger and feared for her own safety, but denied a similar motion as to the daughter because of the possibility that she was within such zone and feared for her own safety.

The Dillon court reversed, explaining its reasoning as follows: "[We] can hardly justify relief to the sister for trauma which she suffered upon apprehension of the child's death and yet deny it to the mother merely because of a happen stance that the sister was some few yards closer to the accident. The instant case exposes the hopeless artificiality of the zone-of-danger rule.

And so the Dillon court recognized the mother's right to recover for emotional distress caused by the apprehension of danger to her daughter; delineated its now-famous guidelines for determining foreseeability; and left to "future cases" the task of delimiting "bystander" liability "upon facts more subtle than the compelling ones alleged in the complaint before us."

Of course, it was immediately apparent that the Dillon court's holding was not really based on any inherent flaw or "artificiality" in the zone-of-danger rule. As the Dillon dissent pointed out, that rule was designed to compensate for the emotional distress occasioned by the fear of physical impact solely "to oneself." A rule which permitted such recovery to one within the zone of physical impact or danger was not arbitrary at all. It became arbitrary only after the court recognized fear for the safety of others as a legally protected interest.

Indeed, as discussed below, the zone-of-danger rule remains a viable measure of emotional distress in many states where the bystander-recovery rule has been rejected as inherently arbitrary.

Dillon Rejected as Hopelessly Arbitrary

In light of the foregoing, it is perhaps not surprising to find that during the last 20 years Dillon has played to decidedly mixed reviews among our sister states. While many have adopted the Dillon approach or some variation there on, many others have explicitly rejected "bystander" recovery and adopted in its place the "zone-of-danger" rule articulated in the very decision which Dillon overruled, Amaya v. Home Ice Fuel & Supply Co.

Indeed, despite the wide range of opinion on the subject of negligent infliction of emotional distress, several recent decisions have noted that the majority of jurisdictions where the question has been considered have rejected the Dillon approach in favor of the zone-of-danger rule.

While the courts rejecting bystander liability have cited a number of reasons, one argument in particular has been considered dispositive: Dillon's confident prediction that future courts would be able to fix just and sensible boundaries on bystander liability has been found to be wholly illusory, both in theory and in practice.

["No arguments have been presented that persuade us that the problems we see in limiting liability once it is extended beyond the zone of danger of physical impact can be justly overcome."]; (T)here appears to be no rational way to restrict the scope of liability even as attempted by Dillon's three limiting standards."]; [" 'Assuming that there are cogent reasons for extending liability in favor of victims of shock resulting from injury to others, there appears to be no rational way to limit the scope of liability.' "].)

Other factors frequently cited but not considered dispositive in light of the in surmountable problem of formulating just and sensible limitations on liability include the fear of a proliferation of claims, the potential for fraudulent claims, the disproportionality between fault and liability, and the undue burden on the insurance system.

As the New York Court of Appeals, writing one year after Dillon, presciently observed: "Every parent who loses a child or whose child suffers an injury is likely to sustain grievous psychological trauma. Any rule based on eye witnessing the accident could stand only until the first case comes along in which the parent is in the immediate vicinity but did not see the accident." Of course, that case "came along" in California only one short year after Dillon. In Archibald v.Braverman (1969), the court allowed recovery by a mother who "did not actually witness the tort but viewed the child's injuries within moments after the occurrence of the injury-producing event."

Similar cases have followed. In Nazaroff v. Superior Court (1978), for example, the court reversed the entry of summary judgment in favor of the defendant, holding that a mother who had witnessed her infant son being pulled from a pool minutes after drowning could state a claim for negligent infliction of emotional distress. In the very case now under review, the Court of Appeal reversed the entry of summary judgment in favor of defendants, the owners and driver of a car which struck the child of the plaintiff, Maria Thing, where the evidence showed that Maria did not see the impact but rushed to the scene in time to see her son lying in the street, bleeding, and rode in the ambulance that took him to the hospital for treatment of severe injuries.

Of course, not all interpretations of Dillon have been so liberal. In Arauz v.

Gerhardt (1977), for example, the court denied recovery to a mother who arrived at the scene of a car accident involving her child within five minutes of the event; the court noted that the plaintiff was "not at the scene of the accident at the time of the impact and [was] not near enough to the scene to have any sensory perception of the impact."

In Hathaway v. Superior Court (1980), the court denied recovery to the parents of a child who was electrocuted while playing in a relative's yard as the parents relaxed inside. Though the plaintiffs arrived less than one minute after the accident and saw the child lying in a puddle, gagging and spitting up, the court held that Dillon precluded recovery because the infant "was no longer gripping the water cooler and receiving the electrical charge."

Twenty-five years ago, this court posed a series of rhetorical questions concerning the guidelines later adopted in Dillon: "[How] soon is 'fairly contemporaneous?' What is the magic in the plaintiff's being 'present'? Is the shock any less immediate if the mother does not know of the accident until the injured child is brought home? And what if the plaintiff is present at the scene but is nevertheless unaware of the danger or injury to the third person until shortly after the accident has occurred . . . ?"

As the foregoing sampling of Dillon's progeny vividly demonstrates, we are no closer to answers today than we were then. The questions, however, are no longer hypothetical, they are real: Is there any rational basis to infer that Mrs. Arauz was any less traumatized than Mrs. Dillon because she saw her bloody infant five minutes after it was struck by defendant's car? Was the Hathaways' suffering mitigated by the fact that they witnessed their child literally in death's throes, but failed to witness the precipitating event? Could it be argued that the emotional distress is even more traumatic, more foreseeable, for parents such as the Hathaways who fail to witness the accident and later blame themselves for allowing it to occur?

Clearly, to apply the Dillon guidelines strictly and deny recovery for emotional distress because the plaintiff was not a contemporaneous eyewitness of the accident but viewed the immediate consequences, ill serves the policy of compensating foreseeable victims of emotional trauma. Yet once it is admitted that temporal and spatial limitations bear no rational relationship to the likelihood of psychic injury, it becomes impossible to define, as the Amaya court well understood, any "sensible or just stopping point."

By what humane and principled standard might a court decide, as a matter of law, that witnessing the bloody and chaotic aftermath of an accident involving a loved one is compensable if viewed within 1 minute of impact but noncompensable after 15? or 30? Is the shock of standing by while others undertake frantic efforts to save the life of one's child any less real or foreseeable when it occurs in an ambulance or emergency room rather than at the "scene"?

Obviously, a "flexible" construction of the Dillon guidelines cannot, ultimately, avoid drawing arbitrary and irrational distinctions any more than a strict construction. Justice Burke was right when he observed of the Dillon guidelines, "Upon analysis, their seeming certainty evaporates into arbitrariness, and inexplicable distinctions appear."

Of course, it could be argued that recovery, not rationality is the essential thing; that ultimately justice is better served by arbitrarily denying recovery to some, than by absolutely denying recovery to all. I find this argument to be unpersuasive, however, for two reasons. First, the cost of the institutionalized caprice which Dillon has wrought should not be underestimated. The foremost duty of the courts in a free society is the principled declaration of public norms.

The legitimacy, prestige and effectiveness of the judiciary—the "least dangerous branch"—ultimately depend on public confidence in our unwavering commitment to this ideal. Any breakdown in principled decision making, any rule for which no principled basis can be found and clearly articulated, subverts and discredits the institution as a whole.

It is not always easy, of course, to accommodate the desire for individual justice with the need for reasoned, well-grounded, general principles. We sacrifice the latter for the sake of the former, however, only at our peril. For the "power-base" of the courts, as noted above, is rather fragile; it consists of the perception of our role in the structure of American government as the voice of reason, and the faith that the laws we make today, we ourselves will be bound by tomorrow. Any "rule" such as Dillon's which permits and even encourages judgments based not on universal standards but individual expediency, erodes the public trust which we serve, and on which we ultimately depend.

There is a second reason, apart from the inherently corrosive effect of arbitrary rules, that points to the conclusion that "bystander" liability should not be retained. The interest in freedom from emotional distress caused by negligent injury to a third party is simply not, in my view, an interest which the law can or should protect. It is not that the interest is less than compelling. The suffering of a parent from the death or injury of a child is terribly poignant, and has always been so. It is the very universality of such injury, however, which renders it inherently unsuitable to legal protection. The observation of the New York Court of Appeals in this regard is particularly pertinent: "While it may seem that there should be a remedy for every wrong, this is an ideal limited perforce by the realities of this world. The risks of indirect harm from the loss or injury of loved ones is pervasive and inevitably realized at one time or another. Only a very small part of that risk is brought about by the culpable acts of others. This is the risk of living and bearing children. It is enough that the law establishes liability in favor of those directly or intentionally harmed."

A final argument against overruling Dillon is, of course, the simple fact that it has been the law for 20 years. Stare decisis should not be lightly dismissed in any thoughtful reconsideration of the law. History and experience, however, are the final judge of whether a decision was right or wrong, whether it should be retained, modified or abandoned. In this case, history and experience have shown, as the Amaya court accurately predicted, that the quest for sensible and just limits on bystander liability is "an inherently fruitless one."

Adherence to precedent cannot justify the perpetuation of a policy ill-conceived in theory and unfair in practice. As Justice Harlan aptly observed: "[A] judicious reconsideration of precedent cannot be as threatening to public faith in the judiciary as continued adherence to a rule unjustified in reason, which produces different results for breaches of duty in situations that cannot be differentiated in policy. . . ."

For the foregoing reasons, therefore, I would overrule Dillon v. Legg, and reinstate Amaya v. Home Ice, Fuel & Supply Co., as the law of this state. Since the plaintiff was indisputably not within the zone of danger and could not assert a claim for emotional distress as the result of fear for her own safety, she could not establish a right to recover.

Accordingly, I concur in the majority's conclusion that the order granting summary judgment in this case was proper.
DISSENT BY: MOSK; BROUSSARD

DISSENT: MOSK, J. (Omitted)

BROUSSARD, J. I dissent.

"[The] problem [of negligent infliction of emotional distress] should be solved by the application of the principles of tort, not by the creation of exceptions to them. Legal history shows that artificial islands of exceptions, created from the fear that the legal process will not work, usually do not withstand the waves of reality and, in time, descend into oblivion." (Dillon v. Legg (1968)).

The majority grope for a "bright line" rule for negligent infliction of emotional distress actions, only to grasp an admittedly arbitrary line which will deny recovery to victims whose injuries from the negligent acts of others are very real. In so doing, the majority reveal a myopic reading of Dillon v. Legg. They impose a strict requirement that plaintiff be present at the scene of the injury-producing event at the time it occurs and is aware that it is causing injury to the victim. This strict requirement rigidifies what Dillon forcefully told us should be a flexible rule, and will lead to arbitrary results. I would follow the mandate of

Dillon and maintain that foreseeability and duty determine liability, with a view toward a policy favoring reasonable limitations on liability. There is no reason why these general rules of tort law should not apply to negligent infliction of emotional distress actions.

We held in Dillon that a mother who witnesses the negligent infliction of death or injury on her child may recover for the resulting emotional distress even though the mother does not fear imminent physical harm. We recognized that the primary consideration in finding liability was foreseeability and rejected the "hopeless artificiality" of the zone-of-danger rule.

The majority themselves note that "foreseeability of the injury [is] the basis of a negligent actor's duty," and quote from Dillon that this issue must necessarily be adjudicated only upon "a case-by-case basis."

" 'We cannot now predetermine defendant's obligation in every situation by a fixed category; no immutable rule can establish the extent of that obligation for every circumstance of the future.' "

Though Dillon made foreseeability its lode star, it provided three factors for courts to consider in determining whether a negligent infliction of emotional distress cause of action was stated in a particular case: "(1) Whether plaintiff was located near the scene of the accident as contrasted with one who was a distance away from it. (2) Whether the shock resulted from a direct emotional impact upon plaintiff from the sensory and contemporaneous observance of the accident, as contrasted with learning of the accident from others after its occurrence. (3) Whether plaintiff and the victim were closely related, as contrasted with an absence of any relationship or the presence of only a distant relationship."

Dillon denounced "artificial abstractions which bar recovery contrary to the general rules" of tort law, and emphasized that "mechanical rules of thumb which are at variance with these principles do more harm than good.' However, some courts have rigidly and mechanically applied the Dillon guidelines— many times at the cost of injustice to a victim of a tort feasor's negligent act. Professor Diamond, although quoted extensively by the majority, warned against a strict application of the Dillon guidelines: "[Courts] have applied the Dillon guidelines mechanically, viewing them as strict preconditions to recovery. This mechanical application has led to the erection of arbitrary limitations on recovery bearing little relation to the principles of foreseeability espoused so forcefully in Dillon. While in some instances mental distress is compensated, other equally foreseeable mental injuries are not. The result is feast or famine for the plaintiff depending on the fortuities of time, location, or characterization of the plaintiff as 'direct' or 'indirect.' "

The majority ignore the fundamental mandate of Dillon to consider foreseeability and duty in finding liability. Their only justification for this and a strict rule that will limit liability at the cost of arbitrary results is an amorphous "policy" one. They ironically use the term "amorphous" to describe the concepts of foreseeability and duty and state that

> [i]N the present context, however, we are concerned not with whether an injury is 'foreseeable' as a result of the negligent conduct. [T]he court's role in deciding whether a 'duty' to these persons should be recognized does not depend solely on the 'foreseeability' of

the emotional distress, but on these policy considerations.

> [I]t is clear that foreseeability of the injury alone is *not* a useful 'guideline' or a meaningful restriction on the scope of the NIED action. . . . Policy considerations justify restrictions on recovery for emotional distress notwithstanding the sometimes arbitrary result, and that the court has an obligation to establish those restrictions." The majority admit their "policy" reasons are only a balance of "arbitrary lines which deny recovery to some victims whose injury is very real against that of imposing liability out of proportion to culpability for negligent acts," with a view to the "administration of justice of clear guidelines."

For these reasons, the majority impose the strict requirement that plaintiff be present at the scene of the injury producing event at the time it occurs and is then aware that it is causing injury to the victim. They freely admit to "drawing arbitrary lines" but complain that it is "unavoidable if we are to limit liability and establish meaningful rules for application by litigants and lower courts." Thus what in Dillon were guidelines to assist courts in assessing liability become a tripartite test, which includes the above-mentioned strict and arbitrary requirement, and displaces the consideration of foreseeability.

The majority declare "that a plaintiff may recover damages for emotional distress caused by observing the negligently inflicted injury of a third person if, but only if, said plaintiff: (1) is closely related to the injury victim; (2) is present at the scene of the injury producing event at the time it occurs and is then aware that it is causing injury to the victim; and (3) as a result suffers serious emotional distress, a reaction beyond that which would be anticipated in a disinterested witness and which is not an abnormal response to the circumstances."

Under the majority's strict requirement, a mother who arrives moments after an accident caused by another's negligence will not be permitted recovery. No matter that the mother would see her six-year-old son immediately after he was electrocuted, lying in a puddle of water in a dying state, gagging and choking in his own vomit, as in Hathaway v. Superior Court (1980).

No matter that the mother would be following her daughters' car and would come upon the wreckage of the car "before the dust had settled" to find the mangled bodies of her daughters, who were dead or dying, as in Parsons v. Superior Court (1978). The answer to the question of how this court should limit liability does not lie in the majority's rigid application of Dillon and the toleration of arbitrary results that will flow there from. As the Wyoming Supreme Court suggested, in Gates v. Richardson, the nature of the shock to be compensated requires a realistic approach to the contemporaneous-perception factor: "It is more than the shock one suffers when he learns of the death or injury of a child, sibling or parent over the phone, from a witness, or at the hospital. It is more than bad news. The kind of shock the tort requires is the result of the immediate aftermath of an accident. It may be the crushed body, the bleeding, the cries of pain, and in some cases, the dying words which are really a continuation of the event. The immediate aftermath may be more shocking than the actual impact. . . ."

The court there held that a close relative generally should be permitted recovery if she "observed the serious bodily harm or death shortly after its occurrence but without material change in the condition and location of the victim." Portee v. Jaffee (1980), [recovery allowed to mother who arrived minutes after her son became wedged in an elevator shaft and was present and listened to his moans and cries during the futile four-and-one-half-hour struggle to free him before he died].)

The majority's strict requirement does not simply comprise a "bright line" rule that rationally limits liability. It is arbitrary and will lead to unjust results. Dillon condemned the "hopeless artificiality" that the majority propounds, and described the "artificial abstractions which bar recovery contrary to the general rules" of tort law. The requirement is exactly the "mechanical rules of thumb" that Dillon explicitly admonished us not to create. We should follow Dillon and its progeny and maintain the rational and traditional rule that reasonable foreseeability is the basis for determining liability.

> In order to limit the otherwise potentially infinite liability which would follow every negligent act, the law of torts holds defendant amenable only for injuries to others which to defendant at the time were reasonably foreseeable.

As Dillon instructed, there is "no good reason why the general rules of tort law, including the concepts of negligence, proximate cause, and foreseeability, long applied to all other types of injury, should not govern the case now before us."

Dillon's test of reasonable foreseeability "facilitates rational risk spreading and correlates liability with the risks that the defendant should expect."

Of course I share the majority's policy concern that tortfeasors not face unlimited liability for their negligent acts. As stated above, the Dillon court recognized foreseeability as a general limit on tort liability. The court stated that the purpose of the three guidelines was actually to limit a defendant's liability to "injuries to others which to defendant at the time were reasonably foreseeable."

Although I disagree with the majority's method of placing undue and what appears to be almost total reliance on a policy rationale, the Dillon guidelines also attempt to implement public policy in favor of reasonable limitations on liability.

The Dillon court did not intend the guidelines to be exclusive, and it specifically reserved the question of "whether, in the absence or reduced weight of some of the [three listed] factors, we would conclude that the accident and injury were not reasonably foreseeable and that therefore defendant owed no duty of care to plaintiff."

To determine whether defendants owed plaintiff a duty of care in this case, I think it is fruitful to reexamine the second Dillon guideline in light of Rowland v. Christian (1968), our leading case defining a defendant's duty of care. In Rowland, decided just two months after Dillon, we held that in the absence of a statutory exception to the legislative mandate that all persons are liable for injuries caused by failure to exercise due care:

> No such exception should be made unless clearly supported by public policy. A departure from this fundamental principle involves the balancing of a number of considerations; the major ones are the foreseeability of harm to the plaintiff, the degree of certainty that the plaintiff suffered injury, the closeness of the connection between

the defendant's conduct and the injury suffered, the moral blame attached to the defendant's conduct, the policy of preventing future harm, the extent of the burden to the defendant and consequences to the community of imposing a duty to exercise care with resulting liability for breach, and the availability, cost, and prevalence of insurance for the risk involved.

While our cases defining a bystander's cause of action for negligent infliction of emotional distress consistently emphasize the first of the Rowland factors, foreseeability of harm to plaintiff, discussion of the others has been limited. The second, fourth, and fifth factors may be disposed of quickly: certainty of injury is usually a jury question, particularly since we no longer require physical manifestations of mental distress; moral blame almost always militates in favor of recovery; and the policy of preventing future harm favors the plaintiff, but only slightly since, in most cases, any Dillon claim is simply added to the primary victim's complaint. The third, sixth and seventh factors, however, merit more discussion.

This court has emphasized the importance of the third Rowland factor nexus between defendant's conduct and the risk of injury in establishing limitations on recovery. In J'Aire Corp. v. Gregory (1979), we stated that case law "[places] a limit on recovery by focusing judicial attention on the foreseeability of the injury and the nexus between the defendant's conduct and the plaintiff's injury." There, we limited recovery for the tort of negligent interference with economic advantage "to instances where the risk of harm is foreseeable and is closely connected with the defendant's conduct, where damages are not wholly speculative and the injury is not part of the plaintiff's ordinary business risk."

The sixth and seventh Rowland factors—the burden on the defendant and the community, and the cost and availability of insurance—also merit further evaluation. Amici curiae contend that recovery in this case would mark an unwarranted expansion of Dillon, resulting in a new category of plaintiffs, fewer settlements, higher administrative costs and premiums, delays in payment, increased litigation, and higher awards. Amici insist that Dillon's second guideline should be applied strictly, as a prerequisite for recovery. Apparently they have convinced the majority since the majority approvingly quote the reasoning in Borer v. American Airlines, Inc. (1977): "We reasoned that we could not 'ignore the social burden of providing damages merely because the money to pay such awards comes initially from the "negligent" defendant or his insurer. Realistically the burden must be borne by the public generally in increased insurance premiums or, otherwise, in the enhanced danger that accrues from the greater number of people who may choose to go without any insurance. We must also take into account the cost of administration of a system to determine and pay [the] awards.

Their brief was submitted by the National Association of Independent Insurers, the Association of California Insurance Companies, and the American Insurance Association.

The authorities upon which amici rely do not persuade me that Dillon has significantly contributed to any substantial increase in litigation and insurance premiums. Nor do I find any indication that other jurisdictions are retreating from Dillon. As the Dillon court responded to the contention that otherwise meritorious claims should be barred out of fear of increases in the number of suits and of fraudulent claims:

> [We] should be sorry to adopt a rule which would bar all such claims on grounds of policy alone, and in order to prevent the possible success of unrighteous or groundless actions. Such a course involves the denial of redress in meritorious cases, and it necessarily implies a certain degree of distrust, which [we] do not share, in the capacity of legal tribunals to get at the truth in this class of claim.

I also do not believe courts lack the means to prevent unmeritorious cases from going to trial. As the case at bar demonstrates, trial courts are well aware of their duty to determine before trial whether the defendant could have owed the plaintiff a duty of care under the facts.

As for the instant case, I agree with Justice Benke of the Court of Appeal who in her concurring opinion indicated that the plaintiff mother's claim should be permitted because "[under] current law, it cannot be said [plaintiff] is to be denied recovery because she did not see, hear or otherwise perceive the actual accident or injury. Case law permits the cause of action if she witnessed the immediate consequences of the event itself. It is a question of fact whether she did, and hence I would reverse the judgment below." Justice Benke declined to take a more liberal standard that "would extend liability far beyond existing limitations." Her view is consistent both with Rowland, and with the balance struck in Dillon, between compensating legitimate claims and limiting liability.

I would conclude that the competing considerations cited in Rowland, as applied to this particular Dillon cause of action by the mother who sensorily perceived the immediate consequences of an accident involving her son, does not justify a departure from this state's fundamental principle that a person is liable for injuries caused by his failure to exercise reasonable care under the circumstances. The majority's strict requirement that plaintiff be present at the scene of the injury-producing event at the time it occurs and is then aware that it is causing injury to the victim will only bring about arbitrary results that will frustrate justice for victims of the negligent acts of others. We should apply the concepts of forseeability and duty to negligent infliction of emotional distress actions, with a view toward a policy favoring reasonable restrictions on liability. This is a principled basis for determining liability and would also conform this area with other areas of negligence law.

The majority charge that, as former Supreme Court Justice Potter Stewart once said about obscenity, the Dillon guidelines mistakenly assumed that a court would know "duty" when it saw it. But more appropriate to the majority's opinion and the arbitrary and unjust results it will soon engender is what Potter Stewart said, very simply, upon being appointed to the United States Supreme Court: "Fairness is what justice really is."

QUESTIONS AND DISCUSSION POINTS

1. Summarize the Majority's approach to the duty question. After you have done this, consider the three best arguments against the Majority's approach to the duty question. Finally, ask yourself why it took so long for the arguments made by the Majority to be successful.

2. What are the arguments against treating emotional distress differently from physical injury? How strong or weak are these arguments?

3. The Majority speak in their opinion about a "societal benefit" from their approach to duty. What does this mean?

4. Use Dworkin's approach to law to construct justifications for both the majority, concurring, and the dissenting opinions.

5. In his dissent, Justice Broussard seems to reject all limitations on the scope of duty. Is this a fair comment?

~

HYMOWITZ
v. ELI LILLY and COMPANY et al.
Court of Appeals of New York
539 N.E.2d 1069 (1989)

Plaintiffs in these appeals allege that they were injured by the drug diethylstilbestrol (DES) ingested by their mothers during pregnancy. They seek relief against defendant DES manufacturers. While not class actions, these cases are representative of nearly 500 similar actions pending in the courts in this State; the rules articulated by the court here, therefore, must do justice and be administratively feasible in the context of this mass litigation. With this in mind, we now resolve the issue twice expressly left open by this court, and adopt a market share theory, using a national market, for determining liability and apportioning damages in DES cases in which identification of the manufacturer of the drug that injured the plaintiff is impossible (*see, Kaufman v Lilly & Co.*, 65 NY2d 449, 456; *Bichler v Lilly & Co.*, 55 NY2d 571, 580). We also hold that the Legislature's revival for one year of actions for injuries caused by DES that were previously barred by the Statute of Limitations is constitutional under the State and Federal Constitutions.

I.

The history of the development of DES and its marketing in this country has been repeatedly chronicled (*see*, e.g., *Bichler v Lilly & Co.*, supra; *Martin v Abbott Labs.*, 102 Wash 2d 581, 689 P2d 368; *Sindell v Abbott Labs.*, 26 Cal 3d 588, 607 P2d 924, cert denied 449 U.S. 912; Sheiner, DES and a Proposed Theory of Enterprise Liability, 46 Fordham L Rev 963). Briefly, DES is a synthetic substance that mimics the effect of estrogen, the naturally formed female hormone. It was invented in 1937 by British researchers, but never patented.

In 1941, the Food and Drug Administration (FDA) approved the new drug applications (NDA) of 12 manufacturers to market DES for the treatment of various maladies, not directly involving pregnancy. In 1947, the FDA began approving the NDAs of manufacturers to market DES for the purpose of prevent-

ing human miscarriages; by 1951, the FDA had concluded that DES was generally safe for pregnancy use, and stopped requiring the filing of NDAs when new manufacturers sought to produce the drug for this purpose. In 1971, however, the FDA banned the use of DES as a miscarriage preventative, when studies established the harmful latent effects of DES upon the offspring of mothers who took the drug. Specifically, tests indicated that DES caused vaginal adenocarcinoma, a form of cancer, and adenosis, a precancerous vaginal or cervical growth.

Although strong evidence links prenatal DES exposure to later development of serious medical problems, plaintiffs seeking relief in court for their injuries faced two formidable and fundamental barriers to recovery in this State; not only is identification of the manufacturer of the DES ingested in a particular case generally impossible, but, due to the latent nature of DES injuries, many claims were barred by the Statute of Limitations before the injury was discovered.

The identification problem has many causes. All DES was of identical chemical composition. Druggists usually filled prescriptions from whatever was on hand. Approximately 300 manufacturers produced the drug entering and leaving the market continuously during the 24 years that DES was sold for pregnancy use. The long latency period of a DES injury compounds the identification problem; memories fade, records are lost or destroyed, and witnesses die. Thus the pregnant women who took DES generally never knew who produced the drug they took, and there was no reason to attempt to discover this fact until many years after ingestion, at which time the information is not available.

We recognized this predicament in *Bichler v Lilly & Co.* (*supra*, at 579), where the court stated that in DES cases it is a "practical impossibility for most victims [to] pinpoint . . . the manufacturer directly responsible for their particular injury". We allowed plaintiff's recovery in that case, however, notwithstanding the failure of the plaintiff to identify the manufacturer of the injurious DES, on the limited basis that "the evidence was legally sufficient to support the jury verdict for the plaintiff" on the law as charged to the jury, and unobjected to by the defendant (*see, Kaufman v Lilly & Co.*, 65 NY2d 449, 456, *supra*). The question, therefore, of whether nonidentification of the manufacturer precludes plaintiffs from recovering for DES caused injuries, remained unresolved after *Bichler v Lilly & Co.* (*supra*).

The present appeals are before the court in the context of summary judgment motions. In all of the appeals defendants moved for summary judgment dismissing the complaints because plaintiffs could not identify the manufacturer of the drug that allegedly injured them. In three of the appeals defendants also moved on Statute of Limitations grounds, arguing that the revival of the actions was unconstitutional under the State and Federal Constitutions, and that the complaints, therefore, are time barred and should be dismissed. The trial court denied all of these motions. On the Statute of Limitations issue, the trial court also granted plaintiffs' cross motions, dismissing defendants' affirmative defenses that the actions were time barred. The Appellate Division affirmed in all respects and certified to this court the questions of whether the orders of the trial court were properly made. We answer these questions in the affirmative.

II.

In a products liability action, identification of the exact defendant whose product injured the plaintiff is, of course, generally required (*see, e.g., Morrissey v Conservative Gas Corp.*, 285 App Div 825, affd 1 NY2d 741; Prosser and Keeton, Torts § 103, at 713 [5th ed]). In DES cases in which such identification is possible, actions may proceed under established principles of products liability (*Bichler v Lilly & Co., supra*, at 579). The record now before us, however, presents the question of whether a DES plaintiff may recover against a DES manufacturer when identification of the producer of the specific drug that caused the injury is impossible.

A.

As we noted in *Bichler v Lilly & Co.* (*supra*, at 580, n 5), the accepted tort doctrines of alternative liability and concerted action are available in some personal injury cases to permit recovery where the precise identification of a wrongdoer is impossible. However, we agree with the near unanimous views of the high State courts that have considered the matter that these doctrines in their unaltered common-law forms do not permit recovery in DES cases (*see, e.g., Sindell v Abbott Labs., supra; Collins v Lilly & Co.*, 116 Wis 2d 166, 342 NW2d 37; *Martin v Abbott Labs., supra; but see, Abel v Lilly & Co.*, 418 Mich 311, 343 NW2d 164 [held that there was a question of fact presented as to alternative liability and concerted action]).

The paradigm of alternative liability is found in the case of *Summers v Tice* (33 Cal 2d 80, 199 P2d 1). In *Summers* (*supra*), plaintiff and the two defendants were hunting, and defendants carried identical shotguns and ammunition. During the hunt, defendants shot simultaneously at the same bird, and plaintiff was struck by bird shot from one of the defendants' guns. The court held that where two defendants breach a duty to the plaintiff, but there is uncertainty regarding which one caused the injury, "the burden is upon each such actor to prove that he has not caused the harm" (Restatement [Second] of Torts § 433B [3]; *Bichler v Lilly & Co., supra*, at 580, n 5; *cf., Ravo v Rogatnick*, 70 NY2d 305 [successive tort-feasors may be held jointly and severally liable for an indivisible injury to the plaintiff]). The central rationale for shifting the burden of proof in such a situation is that without this device both defendants will be silent, and plaintiff will not recover; with alternative liability, however, defendants will be forced to speak, and reveal the culpable party, or else be held jointly and severally liable themselves. Consequently, use of the alternative liability doctrine generally requires that the defendants have better access to information than does the plaintiff, and that all possible tort-feasors be before the court (*see, Summers v Tice, supra, at 86*; Restatement [Second] of Torts § 433B, comment h). It is also recognized that alternative liability rests on the notion that where there is a small number of possible wrongdoers, all of whom breached a duty to the plaintiff, the likelihood that any one of them injured the plaintiff is relatively high, so that forcing them to exonerate themselves, or be held liable, is not unfair (*see, Sindell v Abbott Labs., supra*, at 603).

In DES cases, however, there is a great number of possible wrongdoers, who entered and left the market at different times, and some of whom no longer exist. Additionally, in DES cases many years elapse between the ingestion of the drug and injury. Consequently, DES defendants are not in any better position than are plaintiffs to identify the manufacturer of the DES ingested in any given case, nor is there any real prospect of having all the possible producers before the court. Finally, while it may be fair to employ alternative liability in cases involving only a small number of potential wrongdoers, that fairness disappears with the decreasing probability that any one of the defendants actually caused the injury. This is particularly true when applied to DES where the chance that a particular producer caused the injury is often very remote (*Sindell v Abbott Labs., supra*, at 603; *Collins v Lilly & Co., supra*, at 184). Alternative liability, therefore, provides DES plaintiffs no relief.

Nor does the theory of concerted action, in its pure form, supply a basis for recovery. This doctrine, seen in drag racing cases, provides for joint and several liability on the part of all defendants having an understanding, express or tacit, to participate in "a common plan or design to commit a tortious act" (Prosser and Keeton, Torts § 46, at 323 [5th ed]; *see, Bichler v Lilly & Co., supra*, at 580–581; *De Carvalho v Brunner*, 223 NY 284). As we noted in *Bichler v Lilly & Co.*, and as the present record reflects, drug companies were engaged in extensive parallel conduct in developing and marketing DES (*see, id .*, at 585). There is nothing in the record, however, beyond this similar conduct to show any agreement, tacit or otherwise, to market DES for pregnancy use without taking proper steps to ensure the drug's safety. Parallel activity, without more, is insufficient to establish the agreement element necessary to maintain a concerted action claim (*Sindell v Abbott Labs., supra*, at 605; *Collins v Lilly & Co., supra*, at 185; *Martin v Abbott Labs., supra*, at 599). Thus this theory also fails in supporting an action by DES plaintiffs.

In short, extant common-law doctrines, unmodified, provide no relief for the DES plaintiff unable to identify the manufacturer of the drug that injured her. This is not a novel conclusion; in the last decade a number of courts in other jurisdictions also have concluded that present theories do not support a cause of action in DES cases. Some courts, upon reaching this conclusion, have declined to find any judicial remedy for the DES plaintiffs who cannot identify the particular manufacturer of the DES ingested by their mothers (see, Zafft v Lilly & Co., 676 SW2d 241 [Mo] [en banc]; Mulcahy v Lilly & Co., 386 NW2d 67 [Iowa] [stating that any change in the law to allow for recovery in nonidentification DES cases should come from the Legislature]). Other courts, however, have found that some modification of existing doctrine is appropriate to allow for relief for those injured by DES of unknown manufacture (e.g., Sindell v Abbott Labs., supra; Collins v Lilly & Co., supra; Martin v Abbott Labs., supra).

We conclude that the present circumstances call for recognition of a realistic avenue of relief for plaintiffs injured by DES. These appeals present many of the same considerations that have prompted this court in the past to modify the rules of personal injury liability, in order "to achieve the ends of justice in a more modern context" (see, People v Hobson, 39 NY2d 479, 489; Codling v Paglia, 32 NY2d 330, 341), and we perceive that here judicial action is again required to overcome the " 'inordinately difficult problems of proof' " caused by contemporary products and marketing techniques (see, Bichler v Lilly & Co., supra, at 579–580 [quoting Caprara v Chrysler Corp., 52 NY2d 114, 123]).

Indeed, it would be inconsistent with the reasonable expectations of a modern society to say to these plaintiffs that because of the insidious nature of an injury that long remains dormant, and because so many manufacturers, each behind a curtain, contributed to the devastation, the cost of injury should be borne by the innocent and not the wrongdoers. This is particularly so where the Legislature consciously created these expectations by reviving hundreds of DES cases. Consequently, the ever-evolving dictates of justice and fairness, which are the heart of our common-law system, require formation of a remedy for injuries caused by DES (see, Woods v Lancet, 303 NY 349, 355; see, also, Kaye, The Human Dimension in Appellate Judging: A Brief Reflection on a Timeless Concern, 73 Cornell L Rev 1004).

We stress, however, that the DES situation is a singular case, with manufacturers acting in a parallel manner to produce an identical, generically marketed product, which causes injury many years later, and which has evoked a legislative response reviving previously barred actions. Given this unusual scenario, it is more appropriate that the loss be borne by those that produced the drug for use during pregnancy, rather than by those who were injured by the use, even where the precise manufacturer of the drug cannot be identified in a particular action. We turn then to the question of how to fairly and equitably apportion the loss occasioned by DES, in a case where the exact manufacturer of the drug that caused the injury is unknown.

B.

The past decade of DES litigation has produced a number of alternative approaches to resolve this question. Thus, in a sense, we are now in an enviable position; the efforts of other courts provided examples for contending with this difficult issue, and enough time has passed so that the actual administration and real effects of these solutions now can be observed. With these useful guides in hand, a path may be struck for our own conclusion.

First, this court's opinion in *Bichler v Lilly & Co. (supra)* must be considered. There the jury was instructed on a modified version of concerted action, which, in effect, substituted the fact of conscious parallel activity by manufacturers for the usual common-law requirement that there be proof of an actual agreement between actors to jointly act tortiously (*id.,* at 584). The defendant in *Bichler* did not object to this instruction, and the modified concerted action theory became the law applicable to that particular case (*id.,* at 583–584).

Now given the opportunity to assess the merits of this theory, we decline to adopt it as the law of this State. Parallel behavior, the major justification for visiting liability caused by the product of one manufacturer upon the head of another under this analysis, is a common occurrence in industry generally. We believe, therefore, that inferring agreement from the fact of parallel activity alone improperly expands the concept of concerted action beyond a rational or fair limit; among other things, it potentially renders small manufacturers, in the case of DES and in countless other industries, jointly liable for all damages stemming from the defective products of an entire industry (accord, *Sindell v Abbott Labs., supra,* at 605).

A narrower basis for liability, tailored more closely to the varying culpableness of individual DES producers, is the market share concept. First judicially articulated by the California Supreme

Court in *Sindell v Abbott Labs. (supra)*, variations upon this theme have been adopted by other courts (*see, Collins v Lilly & Co., supra; Martin v Abbott Labs., supra*). In *Sindell v Abbott Labs (supra)*, the court synthesized the market share concept by modifying the *Summers v Tice (supra)* alternative liability rationale in two ways. It first loosened the requirement that all possible wrongdoers be before the court, and instead made a "substantial share" sufficient. The court then held that each defendant who could not prove that it did not actually injure plaintiff would be liable according to that manufacturer's market share. The court's central justification for adopting this approach was its belief that limiting a defendant's liability to its market share will result, over the run of cases, in liability on the part of a defendant roughly equal to the injuries the defendant actually caused (*id.,* at 612).

In the recent case of *Brown v Superior Ct.* (44 Cal 3d 1049, 751 P2d 470), the California Supreme Court resolved some apparent ambiguity in *Sindell v Abbott Labs.,* and held that a manufacturer's liability is several only, and, in cases in which all manufacturers in the market are not joined for any reason, liability will still be limited to market share, resulting in a less than 100% recovery for a plaintiff. Finally, it is noteworthy that determining market shares under *Sindell v Abbott Labs.* proved difficult and engendered years of litigation. After attempts at using smaller geographical units, it was eventually determined that the national market provided the most feasible and fair solution, and this national market information was compiled (*see, In re Complex DES Litig.,* No. 830/109, Cal Super Ct).

Four years after *Sindell v Abbott Labs.,* the Wisconsin Supreme Court followed with *Collins v Lilly & Co.* (116 Wis 2d 166, 342 NW2d 37, *supra*). Deciding the identification issue without the benefit of the extensive California litigation over market shares, the Wisconsin court held that it was prevented from following *Sindell* due to "the practical difficulty of defining and proving market share" (*id.*, at 189, 342 NW2d, at 48). Instead of focusing on tying liability closely to the odds of actual causation, as the *Sindell* court attempted, the Collins court took a broader perspective, and held that each defendant is liable in proportion to the amount of risk it created that the plaintiff would be injured by DES. Under the Collins structure, the "risk" each defendant is liable for is a question of fact in each case, with market shares being relevant to this determination (*id.*, at 191, 200). Defendants are allowed, however, to exculpate themselves by showing that their product could not have caused the injury to the particular plaintiff (*id.*, at 198).

The Washington Supreme Court, writing soon after *Collins v Lilly & Co.*, took yet another approach (*see, Martin v Abbott Labs.*, 102 Wash 2d 581, 689 P2d 368, *supra*). The Martin court first rejected the *Sindell* market share theory due to the belief (which later proved to be erroneous in *Brown v Superior Ct.* [*supra*]) that California's approach distorted liability by inflating market shares to ensure plaintiffs of full recovery (*id.*, at 601). The Martin court instead adopted what it termed "market share alternative liability," justified, it concluded, because "[each] defendant contributed to the risk of injury to the public, and, consequently, the risk of injury to individual plaintiffs" (*id.*, at 604, 689 P2d, at 382).

Under the Washington scheme, defendants are first allowed to exculpate themselves by proving by the prepon-derance of the evidence that they were not the manufacturer of the DES that injured plaintiff. Unexculpated defendants are presumed to have equal market shares, totaling 100%. Each defendant then has the opportunity to rebut this presumption by showing that its actual market share was less than presumed. If any defendants succeed in rebutting this presumption, the liability shares of the remaining defendants who could not prove their actual market share are inflated, so that the plaintiff received a 100% recovery (*id.*, at 605–606). The market shares of defendants is a question of fact in each case, and the relevant market can be a particular pharmacy, or county, or State, or even the country, depending upon the circumstances the case presents (*George v Parke-Davis*, 107 Wash 2d 584, 733 P2d 507).

Turning to the structure to be adopted in New York, we heed both the lessons learned through experience in other jurisdictions and the realities of the mass litigation of DES claims in this State. Balancing these considerations, we are led to the conclusion that a market share theory, based upon a national market, provides the best solution. As California discovered, the reliable determination of any market smaller than the national one likely is not practicable. Moreover, even if it were possible, of the hundreds of cases in the New York courts, without a doubt there are many in which the DES that allegedly caused injury was ingested in another State. Among the thorny issues this could present, perhaps the most daunting is the spectre that the particular case could require the establishment of a separate market share matrix. We feel that this is an unfair, and perhaps impossible burden to routinely place upon the litigants in individual cases.

Nor do we believe that the Wisconsin approach of assessing the "risk" each defendant caused a particular plaintiff, to be litigated anew as a question of fact in each case, is the best solution for this State. Applied on a limited scale this theory may be feasible, and certainly is the most refined approach by allowing a more thorough consideration of how each defendant's actions threatened the plaintiff. We are wary, however, of setting loose, for application in the hundreds of cases pending in this State, a theory which requires the fact finder's individualized and open-ended assessment of the relative liabilities of scores of defendants in every case. Instead, it is our perception that the injustices arising from delayed recoveries and inconsistent results which this theory may produce in this State outweigh arguments calling for its adoption.

Consequently, for essentially practical reasons, we adopt a market share theory using a national market. We are aware that the adoption of a national market will likely result in a disproportion between the liability of individual manufacturers and the actual injuries each manufacturer caused in this State. Thus our market share theory cannot be founded upon the belief that, over the run of cases, liability will approximate causation in this State (see, Sindell v Abbott Labs., supra, at 612). Nor does the use of a national market provide a reasonable link between liability and the risk created by a defendant to a particular plaintiff (see, Collins v Lilly & Co., supra; Martin v Abbott Labs., supra). Instead, we choose to apportion liability so as to correspond to the over-all culpability of each defendant, measured by the amount of risk of injury each defendant created to the pub-

lic-at-large. Use of a national market is a fair method, we believe, of apportioning defendants' liabilities according to their total culpability in marketing DES for use during pregnancy. Under the circumstances, this is an equitable way to provide plaintiffs with the relief they deserve, while also rationally distributing the responsibility for plaintiffs' injuries among defendants.

To be sure, a defendant cannot be held liable if it did not participate in the marketing of DES for pregnancy use; if a DES producer satisfies its burden of proof of showing that it was not a member of the market of DES sold for pregnancy use, disallowing exculpation would be unfair and unjust. Nevertheless, because liability here is based on the over-all risk produced, and not causation in a single case, there should be no exculpation of a defendant who, although a member of the market producing DES for pregnancy use, appears not to have caused a particular plaintiff's injury. It is merely a windfall for a producer to escape liability solely because it manufactured a more identifiable pill, or sold only to certain drugstores. These fortuities in no way diminish the culpability of a defendant for marketing the product, which is the basis of liability here.

Finally, we hold that the liability of DES producers is several only, and should not be inflated when all participants in the market are not before the court in a particular case. We understand that, as a practical matter, this will prevent some plaintiffs from recovering 100% of their damages. However, we eschewed exculpation to prevent the fortuitous avoidance of liability, and thus, equitably, we decline to unleash the same forces to increase a defendant's liability beyond its fair share of responsi-bility.[1]

Disposition: Accordingly, in each case the order of the Appellate Division should be affirmed, with costs, and the certified question answered in the affir-mative.

---

1. The dissenter misapprehends the basis for li-ability here. We have not by the backdoor adopted a theory of concerted action. We avoided extending this theory, because its con-comitant requirement of joint and several liabil-ity expands the burden on small manufacturers beyond a rational or fair limit. This result is reached by the dissent, not by the majority, so that criticism on this front is misplaced.

We are confronted here with an unprece-dented identification problem, and have pro-vided a solution that rationally apportions lia-bility. We have heeded the practical lessons learned by other jurisdictions, resulting in our adoption of a national market theory with full knowledge that it concedes the lack of a logical link between liability and causation in a single case. The dissent ignores these lessons, and, en-deavoring to articulate a theory it perceives to be closer to traditional law, sets out a construct in which liability is based upon chance, not upon the fair assessment of the acts of defendants. Under the dissent's theory, a manufacturer with a large market share may avoid liability in many cases just because it manufactured a memorably shaped pill. Conversely, a small manufacturer can be held jointly liable for the full amount of every DES injury in this State simply because the shape of its product was not remarkable, even though the odds, realistically, are exceed-ingly long that the small manufacturer caused the injury in any one particular case.

Therefore, although the dissent's theory based upon a "shifting the burden of proof" and joint and several liability is facially reminiscent of prior law, in the case of DES it is nothing more than advocating that bare fortuity be the test for liability. When faced with the novel identifica-tion problem posed by DES cases, it is prefer-able to adopt a new theory that apportions fault rationally, rather than to contort extant doc-trines beyond the point at which they provide a sound premise for determining liability.

DISSENT: Mollen, J.

The emergence of the market share concept of liability in the field of prod-ucts liability reflects a recognition by several jurisdictions throughout the United States that due to the incidence of mass production and marketing of various drugs and fungible goods, con-sumers are many times harmed by a product which is not easily traceable to a specific manufacturer, particularly in those situations where the harm oc-curred many years prior to the discov-ery of the injuries and the cause thereof. Such is the situation in the DES cases now before us. Under traditional com-mon-law tort principles, a plaintiff is re-quired to establish the existence of a causal relationship between the act or omission of the defendant or defendants and the injury sustained (see, *Morrissey v Conservative Gas Corp.*, 1 NY2d 741; Prosser and Keeton, Torts § 41, at 263 [5th ed]). However, given the reality of the situation in DES cases, including the lengthy passage of time, the generic form of most DES pills and the unavail-ability of pharmaceutical and physician records, it is, as a practical matter, im-possible for most DES plaintiffs to bear the burden of proof of establishing the traditional tort element of causation.

Moreover, as noted by the majority, the tort doctrines of alternative liability and concerted action, both of which pro-vide for recovery in situations where a plaintiff, through no fault of his or her own, cannot identify the actual wrong-doer, do not provide appropriate relief to these DES plaintiffs. Unlike the scenario present in the DES cases, the principle of alternative liability presupposes that the number of possible wrongdoers are few in number, that one of the joined defendants had to have actually caused the plaintiff's injury and that the defendants are in a much better position than the plaintiff to identify the actual wrongdoer and, therefore, the burden is shifted to the defendants to prove who was the actual wrongdoer and who among them are to be exculpated (*see, Summers v Tice*, 33 Cal 2d 80, 199 P2d 1; Restatement [Second] of Torts § 433B [3]). However, in view of the difference in the factual circumstances, the theory of alternative liability does not provide a workable solution for DES plaintiffs.

The concept of concerted action liability requires, inter alia, that the plaintiff prove that all of the joined defendants had an understanding, expressed or implied, to participate in a common plan or design to commit a tortious act or to lend assistance to the wrongdoer (*see*, Prosser and Keeton, Torts, § 46, at 323 [5th ed]). Typically, DES plaintiffs allege that the concerted action of the DES manufacturers consisted of using one another's marketing techniques, relying upon each other's testing and encouraging one another to market DES without performing adequate testing or warnings. The courts, with few exceptions (see, e.g., *Abel v Lilly & Co.*, 418 Mich 311, 343 NW2d 164), have rejected the applicability of concerted action liability to DES cases because the plaintiffs cannot establish the existence of an express or tacit agreement among DES manufacturers to market or produce DES without proper testing or warnings (*see, e.g., Sindell v Abbott Labs.*, 26 Cal 3d 588, 607 P2d 924, *cert denied* 449 *U.S. 921*; *Martin v Abbott Labs.*, 102 Wash 2d 581, 689 P2d 368; *Collins v Lilly & Co.*, 116 Wis 2d 166, 342 NW2d 37). The parallel or imitative conduct of DES manufacturers in producing and/or marketing DES, as the majority expressly notes, is insufficient, in and of itself, to establish concerted action liability (majority opn, at 506).

The principle of market share liability in DES litigation was first espoused by the California Supreme Court in *Sindell v Abbott Labs. (supra)*, as a valid theory of manufacturer's liability based upon each manufacturer's share of the market. This approach provides DES plaintiffs with a means by which to recover damages for their injuries without the plaintiffs being held to the traditional tort requirement of identifying the actual wrongdoer. The public policy underpinnings of the Sindell rationale is that, from a perspective of fairness and equity, the DES manufacturers are in a better position than the innocent plaintiffs who have sustained grievous injuries to bear the cost of such injuries. Thus, the Sindell court held that once a plaintiff has joined a "substantial share" of the DES manufacturers of the relevant market in the action and has established that the sustained injuries were caused by the ingestion of DES by the plaintiff's mother during pregnancy, the burden of proof shifts to each defendant to demonstrate, by a preponderance of the evidence, that it did not produce or market the pill ingested by the plaintiff's mother. Those DES defendants who could not exculpate themselves, would then be liable for the proportion of the judgment which represented its share of the market. The intended result of the Sindell approach is that, "each manufacturer's liability for an [particular DES] injury would be approximately equivalent to the damage caused by the DES it manufactured" (*supra*, at 613, 607 P2d, at 938).

The Wisconsin and Washington Supreme Courts subsequently adopted collective liability theories in DES cases based upon similar policy considerations; namely, as between the injured plaintiffs and the negligent defendants, the latter should bear the cost of injury (*Collins v Lilly & Co.*, 116 Wis 2d 166, 342 NW2d 37, *supra*; *Martin v Abbott Labs.*, 102 Wash 2d 581, 689 P2d 368, *supra*). Both the *Collins* and *Martin* courts reasoned that since all of the DES manufacturers and distributors contributed to the risk of injury to the public and, consequently, the risk of injury to individual plaintiffs, each defendant shared, in some measure, a degree of culpability in producing or marketing DES. In *Collins*, the Wisconsin Supreme Court adopted a "risk contribution" theory of liability, and, in *Martin*, the Washington Supreme Court adopted what it termed a "market share alternative liability" theory. These two approaches differ from the *Sindell* theory primarily in the manner in which the damages are apportioned. Significantly, both the Supreme Courts of Wisconsin and Washington in the *Collins* and *Martin* cases, as did the Supreme Court of California in *Sindell*, provided that the joined or impleaded defendants may exculpate themselves from liability if they can establish, by a preponderance of the evidence, that they did not produce or market the particular DES pill taken by the plaintiff's mother. Notably, in *Collins*, the Wisconsin Supreme Court explained that it would not adopt a risk contribution theory which would have imposed liability solely upon the DES defendants' participation in the creation of the risk of injury even though some of the defendants could establish that they could not have actually caused the plaintiff's injury. The *Collin's* court noted, "[we] still require it be shown that the defendant drug company reasonably could have contributed in some way to the actual injury" (*supra*, at 191, n 10, 342

NW2d, at 49, n 10). In fact, none of the jurisdictions which have adopted varying theories of collective liability in DES cases, has refused to permit exculpation of those defendants which have been able to prove that they could not have produced or marketed the pill which caused the particular plaintiff's injuries, thereby recognizing that to preclude exculpation would directly and unnecessarily contravene the established common-law tort principles of causation (*see, Sindell v Abbott Labs., supra; Collins v Lilly & Co., supra; Martin v Abbott Labs., supra; Abel v Lilly & Co., supra; McCormack v Abbott Labs.*, 617 F Supp 1521; *see also, Burnside v Abbott Labs.*, 351 Pa Super 264, 505 A2d 973).

Clearly, the development and underlying purpose of the various concepts of liability in DES cases has been to provide a means whereby the plaintiffs, who cannot identify the actual manufacturer of the pill ingested by their mother, are alleviated of the traditional burden of proof of causation and to shift that burden to the defendants. The various theories of collective liability which have been adopted in the several jurisdictions in an effort to provide plaintiffs with a means to recovery for their injuries, were not intended to, and did not, provide DES plaintiffs with an unprecedented strict liability cause of action. However, the majority herein, by precluding exculpation of those defendants in DES cases who produced DES for pregnancy purposes but who can establish, by a preponderance of the evidence, that they did not and could not have produced or marketed the pill which caused the plaintiff's injuries, has created such a radical concept and purports to limit it to DES claims. In the majority's view, the defendant's liability in DES cases is premised upon the overall risk of injury which they created to the public-at-large in producing and marketing DES for pregnancy purpose and, therefore, exculpation of those defendants who can establish that the plaintiff's mother did not ingest their pill, would be inconsistent with the overall risk theory of liability. By taking this view, however, the majority, while stating that it is adopting a market share theory of liability, is, in essence, despite its disclaimer of doing so, adopting a concerted action theory of liability, but has eliminated therefrom the requirement that the plaintiffs establish that the defendants tacitly agreed to produce and market DES for pregnancy use without proper testing and without adequate warnings of the potential dangers involved. Such a result, represents a radical departure from fundamental tenets of tort law and is unnecessarily unfair and inequitable to the defendants who have proven, or can prove, that they did not produce the pill which caused the injury. Moreover, this result is directly contrary to the majority's own statement that it is rejecting the "conscious parallelism" theory utilized in *Bichler v Lilly & Co.* (79 AD2d 317, affd 55 NY2d 571), because, as stated by the majority herein, "[parallel] behavior, the major justification for visiting liability caused by the product of one manufacturer upon the head of another under this analysis, is a common occurrence in industry generally. We believe, therefore, that inferring agreement from the fact of parallel activity alone improperly expands the concept of concerted action beyond a rational or fair limit; among other things, it potentially renders small manufacturers, in the case of DES and in countless other industries, jointly liable for all damages stemming from the defective products of an entire industry" (majority opn, at 508–509).

I fully concur with the above-stated position of the majority and thus, I cannot agree that the imposition of liability on drug companies, in this case DES manufacturers, solely upon their contribution, in some measure, to the risk of injury by producing and marketing a defective drug, without any consideration given to whether the defendant drug companies actually caused the plaintiff's injuries, is appropriate or warranted. Rather, I would adopt a market share theory of liability, based upon a national market, which would provide for the shifting of the burden of proof on the issue of causation to the defendants and would impose liability upon all of the defendants who produced and marketed DES for pregnancy purposes, except those who were able to prove that their product could not have caused the injury. Under this approach, DES plaintiffs, who are unable to identify the actual manufacturer of the pill ingested by their mother, would only be required to establish, (1) that the plaintiff's mother ingested DES during pregnancy; (2) that the plaintiff's injuries were caused by DES; and (3) that the defendant or defendants produced and marketed DES for pregnancy purposes. Thereafter, the burden of proof would shift to the defendants to exculpate themselves by establishing, by a preponderance of the evidence, that the plaintiff's mother could not have ingested their particular pill. Of those defendants who are unable to exculpate themselves from liability, their respective share of the plaintiff's damages would be measured by their share of the national market of DES produced and marketed for pregnancy purposes during the period in question.

I would further note that while, on the one hand, the majority would not permit defendants who produced DES for pregnancy purposes to exculpate themselves, the majority at the same time deprives the plaintiffs of the opportunity to recover fully for their injuries by limiting the defendants' liability for the plaintiff's damages to several liability. In my view, the liability for the plaintiff's damages of those defendants who are unable to exculpate themselves should be joint and several thereby ensuring that the plaintiffs will receive full recovery of their damages. In addition to being fair to the DES plaintiffs, the imposition of joint and several liability is consistent with that portion of the revival statute which specifically exempted DES claims from those provisions which provide, with certain exceptions, for several liability of joint tort-feasors (*see*, L 1986, ch 682, § 12; CPLR 1600 et seq.). Moreover, in order to ease the financial burden on the specific defendants named in the lawsuit, the defendants would have the option of seeking contribution from their fellow defendants for damages in excess of each defendant's particular market share, and a defendant should be permitted leave to implead those DES manufacturers who the plaintiff has not joined, in order to ensure, where possible, full contribution (*see, e.g., Dole v Dow Chem. Co.*, 30 NY2d 143). Admittedly, adherence to joint and several liability could result in a disproportion between a defendant's potential liability for the damages suffered by the plaintiff and defendant's actual national market share; however, the opportunity to present exculpatory evidence reduces the risk of imposing liability on innocent defendants.

The application of the aforesaid principles, although somewhat innovative and a modification of traditional tort law, (i.e., the burden of proof is on the plaintiff to prove proximate causation) would, in view of the exigent circumstances, be in furtherance of a valid public policy of imposing the burden of bearing the cost of severe injuries upon those who are responsible for placing into the stream of commerce the causative instrumentality of such injuries. Adherence to this principle would not be too dissimilar from the accepted doctrine of res ipsa loquitur which provides, in essence, that where an instrumentality which caused the plaintiff's injuries was in the exclusive control of the defendant and the accident which occurred is one which would not ordinarily happen without negligence, these facts are sufficient to justify an inference of negligence and to shift the burden upon the defendant of coming forward with an explanation (*see, e.g., Galbraith v Busch*, 267 NY 230, 234; Richardson, Evidence § 93, at 68 [Prince 10th ed]). Thus, this approach, unlike that taken by the majority, does not represent an unnecessary and radical departure from basic principles of tort law. By characterizing this approach as "nothing more than advocating that bare fortuity be the test for liability" (majority opn, at 513, n 3) the majority fails to perceive that this is no more and no less than a basic principle of tort law; i.e., a plaintiff may not recover for his or her injuries from a defendant who could not have caused those injuries. When the majority eliminates this fundamental causative factor as a basis for recovery, it effectively indulges in the act of judicial legislating. I would further note that if the Legislature had intended to adopt this radical approach which is at total variance with traditional tort law, it could readily have done so when it enacted the revival statute for, among others, DES plaintiffs. Its refusal to do so can certainly not be deemed to be an invitation to this court to assume the legislative role.

QUESTIONS AND DISCUSSION POINTS

1. As stated in the introduction to the torts cases, duty is one of the central elements in tort law. What role does the concept of duty play in the Majority's analyses of liability? Does the fact that this case is a products liability action [an action for damages arising from the sale of a dangerous product] change the nature of the duty requirement?

2. Obviously, one of the most difficult issues in this case is the question of causation. Normally, a successful tort action requires more than a showing that the defendant engaged in dangerous conduct. Does the court show that the defendant drug company did more than manufacture a dangerous drug? If not, can you explain how the court could find the company liable for conduct that was "merely dangerous"?

3. The most interesting aspect of this case may be the twin facts of the defendant having produced a dangerous and harmful drug and the plaintiffs being unable to prove that the specific defendant's conduct was, in fact, injurious to them. The court handles this, in part, with its discussion of *Summers v. Tice*. Are the facts of this case sufficiently close to those of *Summers* such that the cases should be treated the same?

4. If we accept the Majority's use of *Summers v. Tice*, does not logic require that, like the defendants in *Summers*, all manufacturers of DES be jointly and severally liable?

5. The Dissent complains that the Majority's decision is at odds with the common law of torts. What are the Dissent's arguments for this claim? Are they persuasive?

∽

VINCENT et al.
v. LAKE ERIE TRANSPORTATION COMPANY
Supreme Court of Minnesota
124 N.W. 221 (1910)

Where, under stress of weather, a master, for the purpose of preserving his vessel, maintains her moorings to a dock after the full discharge of the vessel's cargo, and the dock is damaged by the striking and pounding of the vessel, the dock owner may recover from the shipowner for the injury sustained, although prudent seamanship required the master to follow the course pursued. O'BRIEN, J.

The steamship Reynolds, owned by the defendant, was for the purpose of discharging her cargo on November 27, 1905, moored to plaintiff's dock in Duluth. While the unloading of the boat was taking place a storm from the northeast developed, which at about 10 o'clock p. m., when the unloading was completed, had so grown in violence that the wind was then moving at 50 miles per hour and continued to increase during the night. There is some evidence that one, and perhaps two, boats were able to enter the harbor that night, but it is plain that navigation was practically suspended from the hour mentioned until the morning of the 29th, when the storm abated, and during that time no master would have been justified in attempting to navigate his vessel, if he could avoid do ing so. After the discharge of the cargo the Reynolds signaled for a tug to tow her from the dock, but none could be obtained because of the severity of the storm. If the lines holding the ship to the dock had been cast off, she would doubtless have drifted away; but, instead, the lines were kept fast, and as soon as one parted or chafed it was replaced, sometimes with a larger one. The vessel lay upon the outside of the dock, her bow to the east, the wind and waves striking her starboard quarter with such force that she was constantly being lifted and thrown against the dock, resulting in its damage, as found by the jury, to the amount of $500.

We are satisfied that the character of the storm was such that it would have been highly imprudent for the master of the Reynolds to have attempted to leave the dock or to have permitted his vessel to drift a way from it. One witness testified upon the trial that the vessel could have been warped into a slip, and that, if the attempt to bring the ship into the slip had failed, the worst that could have happened would be that the vessel would have been blown ashore upon a soft and muddy bank. The witness was not present in Duluth at the time of the storm, and, while he may have been right in his conclusions, those in charge of the dock and the vessel at the time of the storm were not required to use the highest human intelligence, nor were they required to resort to every possible experiment which could be suggested for the preservation of their property. Nothing

more was demanded of them than ordinary prudence and care, and the record in this case fully sustains the contention of the appellant that, in holding the vessel fast to the dock, those in charge of her exercised good judgment and prudent seamanship.

It is claimed by the respondent that it was negligence to moor the boat at an exposed part of the wharf, and to continue in that position after it became apparent that the storm was to be more than usually severe. We do not agree with this position. The part of the wharf where the vessel was moored appears to have been commonly used for that purpose. It was situated within the harbor at Duluth, and must, we think, be considered a proper and safe place, and would undoubtedly have been such during what would be considered a very severe storm. The storm which made it unsafe was one which surpassed in violence any which might have reasonably been anticipated.

The appellant contends by ample assignments of error that, because its conduct during the storm was rendered necessary by prudence and good seamanship under conditions over which it had no control, it cannot be held liable for any injury resulting to the property of others, and claims that the jury should have been so instructed. An analysis of the charge given by the trial court is not necessary, as in our opinion the only question for the jury was the amount of damages which the plaintiffs were entitled to recover, and no complaint is made upon that score.

The situation was one in which the ordinary rules regulating properly rights were suspended by forces beyond human control, and if, without the direct intervention of some act by the one sought to be held liable, the property of another was injured, such injury must be attributed to the act of God, and not to the wrongful act of the person sought to be charged. If during the storm the Reynolds had entered the harbor, and while there had become disabled and been thrown against the plaintiffs' dock, the plaintiffs could not have recovered. Again, if while attempting to hold fast to the dock the lines had parted, without any negligence, and the vessel carried against some other boat or dock in the harbor, there would be no liability upon her owner. But here those in charge of the vessel deliberately and by their direct efforts held her in such a position that the damage to the dock resulted, and, having thus preserved the ship at the expense of the dock, it seems to us that her owners are responsible to the dock owners to the extent of the injury inflicted.

In Depue v. Flatau, 100 Minn. 299, 111 N. W. 1, 8 L. R. A. (N. S.) 485, this court held that where the plaintiff, while lawfully in the defendants' house, became so ill that he was incapable of traveling with safety, the defendants were responsible to him in damages for compelling him to leave the premises. If, however, the owner of the premises had furnished the traveler with proper accommodations and medical attendance, would he have been able to defeat an action brought against him for their reasonable worth?

In Ploof v. Putnam, 71 Atl. 188, 20 L. R. A. (N. S.) 152, the Supreme Court of Vermont held that where, under stress of weather, a vessel was without permission moored to a private dock at an island in Lake Champlain owned by the defendant, the plaintiff was not guilty of trespass, and that the defendant was responsible in damages because his representative upon the island unmoored the vessel, permitting it to drift upon the shore, with resultant injuries to it. If, in that case, the vessel had been permitted to remain, and the dock had suffered an injury, we believe the shipowner would have been held liable for the injury done.

Theologians hold that a starving man may, without moral guilt, take what is necessary to sustain life; but it could hardly be said that the obligation would not be upon such person to pay the value of the property so taken when he became able to do so. And so public necessity, in times of war or peace, may require the taking of private property for public purposes; but under our system of jurisprudence compensation must be made. Let us imagine in this case that for the better mooring of the vessel those in charge of her had appropriated a valuable cable lying upon the dock. No matter how justifiable such appropriation might have been, it would not be claimed that, because of the overwhelming necessity of the situation, the owner of the cable could not recover its value.

This is not a case where life or property was menaced by any object or thing belonging to the plaintiff, the destruction of which became necessary to prevent the threatened disaster. Nor is it a case where, because of the act of God, or unavoidable accident, the infliction of the injury was beyond the control of the defendant, but is one where the defendant prudently and advisedly availed itself of the plaintiffs' property for the purpose of preserving its own more valuable property, and the plaintiffs are entitled to compensation for the injury done. Order affirmed.

LEWIS, J.

I dissent. It was assumed on the trial before the lower court that appellant's liability depended on whether the master of the ship might, in the exercise of reasonable care, have sought a place of safety before the storm made it impossible to leave the dock. The majority opinion assumes that the evidence is conclusive that appellant moored its boat at respondent's dock pursuant to contract, and that the vessel was lawfully in position at the time the additional cables were fastened to the dock, and the reasoning of the opinion is that, because appellant made use of the stronger cables to hold the boat in position, it became liable under the rule that it had voluntarily made use of the property of another for the purpose of saving its own. In my judgment, if the boat was lawfully in position at the time the storm broke, and the master could not, in the exercise of due care, have left that position without subjecting his vessel to the hazards of the storm, then the damage to the dock, caused by the pounding of the boat, was the result of an inevitable accident. If the master was in the exercise of due care, he was not at fault. The reasoning of the opinion admits that if the ropes, or cables, first attached to the dock had not parted, or if, in the first instance, the master had used the stronger cables, there would be no liability. If the master could not, in the exercise of reasonable care, have anticipated the severity of the storm and sought a place of safety before it became impossible, why should he be required to anticipate the severity of the storm, and, in the first instance, use the stronger cables? I am of the opinion that one who constructs a dock to the navigable line of waters, and enters into contractual relations with the owner of a vessel to moor at the same, takes the risk of damage to his dock by a boat caught there by a storm, which event could not have been avoided in the exercise of due care, and further, that the legal status of the parties in such a case is not changed by renewal of cables to keep the boat from being cast adrift at the mercy of the tempest.

JAGGARD, J., concurs herein.

QUESTIONS AND DISCUSSION POINTS

1. This case poses a very basic question: "What sort of case is this?" Is it a property case or a torts case? What are arguments for seeing it as one, the other, or both?

2. The Majority seems to see the case as a torts case. Remember, this is an appeal, and it is pretty clear the case was tried below as a negligence action. If it is a negligence action, how can the shipowner be held liable for damages when the court concludes he exercised ordinary prudence?

3. What is wrong with understanding the case as an exception to the general rules of property? That is, can we best make sense of the decision as a "private" version of government "takings" law? (That is, a case where private land is taken by the government for public benefit but compensation is paid.)

4. What sort of argument is made by the Dissent? Does the Dissent see the case as a contracts case?

5. If the boat were properly moored to the dock pursuant to contract, should the dock owner absorb the loss as the normal consequence of running a mooring? If the risk of occasional storm were expected by both parties, would it not be fair to put the risk of loss on the dock owner?

Chapter 11

Public Law

The simplest way to characterize public law is by contrast with private law. Whereas private law concerns the obligations we owe to one another by virtue of our status as persons, public law concerns the obligations of our government to us. Put another way, public law concerns the limits upon government in the intervention and regulation of our private lives.

Of course, much of the subject of public law concerns the role of the federal Constitution in the creation, regulation, and enhancement of personal rights. Not surprisingly, all four of the cases in this section involve interpretation of the Constitution. As you read each case, try to identify the manner in which each opinion builds a position out of various consitutional materials and forms of argument. And as you compare opinions on a given question, try to identify what it is about the arguments you find strong and weak, and how you might defend your position against the criticisms and questions of those who may not share your point of view.

Finally, ask yourself if there really is something that might be called a "constitutional point of view"? Are the consitutional arguments placeholders for arguments made from, say, political or moral theory? Or is it in fact the case that constitutional argument is, in some sense, autonomous?

~

TEXAS, Petitioner,
v. Gregory Lee JOHNSON
Supreme Court of the United States
491 U.S. 397 (1989)

Justice BRENNAN delivered the opinion of the Court.

After publicly burning an American flag as a means of political protest, Gregory Lee Johnson was convicted of desecrating a flag in violation of Texas law. This case presents the question whether his conviction is consistent with the First Amendment. We hold that it is not.

I.

While the Republican National Convention was taking place in Dallas in 1984, respondent Johnson participated in a political demonstration dubbed the "Republican War Chest Tour." As explained in literature distributed by the demonstrators and in speeches made by them, the purpose of this event was to protest the policies of the Reagan administration and of certain Dallas-based corporations.

The demonstrators marched through the Dallas streets, chanting political slogans and stopping at several corporate locations to stage "die-ins" intended to dramatize the consequences of nuclear war. On several occasions they spray-painted the walls of buildings and over-turned potted plants, but Johnson him-self took no part in such activities. He did, however, accept an American flag handed to him by a fellow protestor who had taken it from a flagpole outside one of the targeted buildings. The demon-stration ended in front of Dallas City Hall, where Johnson unfurled the Amer-ican flag, doused it with kerosene, and set it on fire. While the flag burned, the protestors chanted: "America, the red, white, and blue, we spit on you." After the demonstrators dispersed, a witness to the flag burning collected the flag's re-mains and buried them in his backyard. No one was physically injured or threat-ened with injury, though several wit-nesses testified that they had been seri-ously offended by the flag burning. Of the approximately 100 demonstrators, Johnson alone was charged with a crime. The only criminal offense with which he was charged was the desecration of a venerated object in violation of Tex. Pe-nal Code Ann. §42.09(a)(3) (1989).[1] After a trial, he was convicted, sentenced to one year in prison, and fined $2,000. The Court of Appeals for the Fifth District of Texas at Dallas affirmed Johnson's con-viction, but the Texas Court of Criminal Appeals reversed, holding that the State could not, consistent with the First Amendment, punish Johnson for burn-ing the flag in these circumstances.

The Court of Criminal Appeals began by recognizing that Johnson's conduct was symbolic speech protected by the First Amendment: "Given the context of an organized demonstration, speeches, slogans, and the distribution of literature, anyone who observed appellant's act would have understood the message that appellant intended to convey. The act for which appellant was convicted was clearly 'speech' contemplated by the First Amendment." Id., at 95. To justify John-son's conviction for engaging in symbolic speech, the State asserted two interests: preserving the flag as a symbol of na-tional unity and preventing breaches of the peace. The Court of Criminal Appeals held that neither interest supported his conviction.

Acknowledging that this Court had not yet decided whether the Government may criminally sanction flag desecration in order to preserve the flag's symbolic value, the Texas court nevertheless con-cluded that our decision in West Virginia Board of Education v. Barnette, 319 U.S. 624, 63 S.Ct. 1178, 87 L.Ed. 1628 (1943), suggested that furthering this interest by curtailing speech was impermissible. "Recognizing that the right to differ is the centerpiece of our First Amendment free-

---

1. Texas Penal Code Ann. s 42.09 (1989) pro-vides in full: "§ 42.09. Desecration of Venerated Object

"a. A person commits an offense if he inten-tionally or knowingly desecrates:

"1. a public monument;

"2. a place of worship or burial; or

"3. a state or national flag.

"b. For purposes of this section, 'desecrate' means deface, damage, or otherwise physically mistreat in a way that the ac-tor knows will seriously offend one or more persons likely to observe or dis-cover his action.

"c. An offense under this section is a Class A misdemeanor."

doms," the court explained, "a government cannot mandate by fiat a feeling of unity in its citizens. Therefore, that very same government cannot carve out a symbol of unity and prescribe a set of approved messages to be associated with that symbol when it cannot mandate the status or feeling the symbol purports to represent." 755 S.W.2d, at 97. Noting that the State had not shown that the flag was in "grave and immediate danger," Barnette, supra, at 639, 63 S.Ct., at 1186, of being stripped of its symbolic value, the Texas court also decided that the flag's special status was not endangered by Johnson's conduct. 755 S.W.2d, at 97.

As to the State's goal of preventing breaches of the peace, the court concluded that the flag-desecration statute was not drawn narrowly enough to encompass only those flag burnings that were likely to result in a serious disturbance of the peace. And in fact, the court emphasized, the flag burning in this particular case did not threaten such a reaction. "'Serious offense' occurred," the court admitted, "but there was no breach of peace nor does the record reflect that the situation was potentially explosive. One cannot equate 'serious offense' with incitement to breach the peace." Id., at 96. The court also stressed that another Texas statute, Tex. Penal Code Ann. § 42.01 (1989), prohibited breaches of the peace. Citing Boos v. Barry, 485 U.S. 312, 108 S.Ct. 1157, 99 L.Ed.2d 333 (1988), the court decided that s 42.01 demonstrated Texas' ability to prevent disturbances of the peace without punishing this flag desecration. 755 S.W.2d, at 96.

Because it reversed Johnson's conviction on the ground that § 42.09 was unconstitutional as applied to him, the state court did not address Johnson's argument that the statute was, on its face,

unconstitutionally vague and overbroad. We granted certiorari, and now affirm.

II.

Johnson was convicted of flag desecration for burning the flag rather than for uttering insulting words. This fact somewhat complicates our consideration of his conviction under the First Amendment. We must first determine whether Johnson's burning of the flag constituted expressive conduct, permitting him to invoke the First Amendment in challenging his conviction. If his conduct was expressive, we next decide whether the State's regulation is related to the suppression of free expression. If the State's regulation is not related to expression, then the less stringent standard we announced in United States v. O'Brien (391 U.S. 367, 377, 88 S.Ct. 1673, 1679, 20 L.Ed.2d 672 (1968)) for regulations of noncommunicative conduct controls. If it is, then we are outside of O'Brien's test, and we must ask whether this interest justifies Johnson's conviction under a more demanding standard. A third possibility is that the State's asserted interest is simply not implicated on these facts, and in that event the interest drops out of the picture.

The First Amendment literally forbids the abridgment only of "speech," but we have long recognized that its protection does not end at the spoken or written word. While we have rejected "the view that an apparently limitless variety of conduct can be labeled 'speech' whenever the person engaging in the conduct intends thereby to express an idea," United States v. O'Brien, supra, 88 S.Ct., at 1678, we have acknowledged that conduct may be "sufficiently imbued with elements of communication to fall within the scope of the First and Fourteenth Amendments," Spence v. Washington, 418 U.S. 405, 94 S.Ct. 2727, 41 L.Ed.2d 842 (1974). In deciding whether particular conduct possesses sufficient communicative elements to bring the First Amendment into play, we have asked whether "[a]n intent to convey a particularized message was present, and [whether] the likelihood was great that the message would be understood by those who viewed it." Hence, we have recognized the expressive nature of students' wearing of black armbands to protest American military involvement in Vietnam, Tinker v. Des Moines Independent Community School Dist., 393 U.S. 503, 505, 89 S.Ct. 733, 735, 21 L.Ed.2d 731 (1969); of a sit-in by blacks in a "whites only" area to protest segregation, Brown v. Louisiana, 383 U.S. 131, 141–142, 86 S.Ct. 719, 723–24, 15 L.Ed.2d 637 (1966); of the wearing of American military uniforms in a dramatic presentation criticizing American involvement in Vietnam, Schacht v. United States, 398 U.S. 58, 90 S.Ct. 1555, 26 L.Ed.2d 44 (1970); and of picketing about a wide variety of causes, see, e.g., Food Employees v. Logan Valley Plaza, Inc., 391 U.S. 308, 313–314, 88 S.Ct. 1601, 1605–06, 20 L.Ed.2d 603 (1968).

Especially pertinent to this case are our decisions recognizing the communicative nature of conduct relating to flags. Attaching a peace sign to the flag; refusing to salute the flag; and displaying a red flag, we have held, all may find shelter under the First Amendment. That we have had little difficulty identifying an expressive element in conduct relating to flags should not be surprising. The very purpose of a national flag is to serve as a symbol of our country; it is, one might say, "the one visible manifestation of two hundred years of nationhood." Thus, we have observed:

[T]he flag salute is a form of utterance. Symbolism is a primitive but effective way of communicating ideas. The use of an emblem or flag to symbolize some system, idea, institution, or personality,

is a short cut from mind to mind. Causes and nations, political parties, lodges and ecclesiastical groups seek to knit the loyalty of their followings to a flag or banner, a color or design.

We have not automatically concluded, however, that any action taken with respect to our flag is expressive. Instead, in characterizing such action for First Amendment purposes, we have considered the context in which it occurred. In Spence, for example, we emphasized that Spence's taping of a peace sign to his flag was "roughly simultaneous with and concededly triggered by the Cambodian incursion and the Kent State tragedy." 94 S.Ct., at 2730. The State of Washington had conceded, in fact, that Spence's conduct was a form of communication, and we stated that "the State's concession is inevitable on this record." Id., at 2730.

The State of Texas conceded for purposes of its oral argument in this case that Johnson's conduct was expressive conduct, Tr. of Oral Arg. 4, and this concession seems to us as prudent as was Washington's in Spence. Johnson burned an American flag as part—indeed, as the culmination—of a political demonstration that coincided with the convening of the Republican Party and its renomination of Ronald Reagan for President. The expressive, overtly political nature of this conduct was both intentional and overwhelmingly apparent. At his trial, Johnson explained his reasons for burning the flag as follows: "The American Flag was burned as Ronald Reagan was being renominated as President. And a more powerful statement of symbolic speech, whether you agree with it or not, couldn't have been made at that time. It's quite a just position [juxtaposition]. We had new patriotism and no patriotism." 5 Record 656. In these circumstances, Johnson's burning of the flag was conduct "sufficiently imbued with elements of communication," Spence, 418 U.S., at 409, 94 S.Ct., at 2730, to implicate the First Amendment.

III.

The government generally has a freer hand in restricting expressive conduct than it has in restricting the written or spoken word. It may not, however, proscribe particular conduct because it has expressive elements. "[W]hat might be termed the more generalized guarantee of freedom of expression makes the communicative nature of conduct an inadequate basis for singling out that conduct for proscription. A law directed at the communicative nature of conduct must, like a law directed at speech itself, be justified by the substantial showing of need that the First Amendment requires." Community for Creative Non-Violence v. Watt, 227 U.S.App.D.C. 19, 55–56, 703 F.2d 586, 622–623 (1983) (Scalia, J., dissenting) (emphasis in original), rev'd sub nom. Clark v. Community for Creative Non-Violence, supra. It is, in short, not simply the verbal or nonverbal nature of the expression, but the governmental interest at stake, that helps to determine whether a restriction on that expression is valid.

Thus, although we have recognized that where "'speech' and 'nonspeech' elements are combined in the same course of conduct, a sufficiently important governmental interest in regulating the nonspeech element can justify incidental limitations on First Amendment freedoms," O'Brien, supra, at 376, 88 S.Ct., at 1678, we have limited the applicability of O'Brien's relatively lenient standard to those cases in which "the governmental interest is unrelated to the suppression of free expression." Id., at 377, 88 S.Ct., at 1679. In stating, moreover, that O'Brien's test "in the last analysis is little, if any, different from the standard applied to

time, place, or manner restrictions," we have highlighted the requirement that the governmental interest in question be unconnected to expression in order to come under O'Brien's less demanding rule.

In order to decide whether O'Brien's test applies here, therefore, we must decide whether Texas has asserted an interest in support of Johnson's conviction that is unrelated to the suppression of expression. If we find that an interest asserted by the State is simply not implicated on the facts before us, we need not ask whether O'Brien's test applies.

The State offers two separate interests to justify this conviction: preventing breaches of the peace and preserving the flag as a symbol of nationhood and national unity. We hold that the first interest is not implicated on this record and that the second is related to the suppression of expression.

A.

Texas claims that its interest in preventing breaches of the peace justifies Johnson's conviction for flag desecration.[2]

---

2. Relying on our decision in Boos v. Barry, 485 U.S. 312, 108 S.Ct. 1157, 99 L.Ed.2d 333 (1988), Johnson argues that this state interest is related to the suppression of free expression within the meaning of United States v. O'Brien, 391 U.S. 367, 88 S.Ct. 1673, 20 L.Ed.2d 672 (1968). He reasons that the violent reaction to flag burnings feared by Texas would be the result of the message conveyed by them, and that this fact connects the State's interest to the suppression of expression. Brief for Respondent 12, n. 11. This view has found some favor in the lower courts. See Monroe v. State Court of Fulton County, 739 F.2d 568, 574–575 (CA11 1984). Johnson's theory may overread Boos insofar as it suggests that a desire to prevent a violent audience reaction is "related to expression" in the same way that a desire to prevent an audience from being offended is "related to expression." Because we find that the State's interest in preventing breaches of the peace is not implicated on these facts, however, we need not venture further into this area.

However, no disturbance of the peace actually occurred or threatened to occur because of Johnson's burning of the flag. Although the State stresses the disruptive behavior of the protestors during their march toward City Hall, it admits that "no actual breach of the peace occurred at the time of the flagburning or in response to the flagburning."

The State's position, therefore, amounts to a claim that an audience that takes serious offense at particular expression is necessarily likely to disturb the peace and that the expression may be prohibited on this basis.

Our precedents do not countenance such a presumption. On the contrary, they recognize that a principal "function of free speech under our system of government is to invite dispute. It may indeed best serve its high purpose when it induces a condition of unrest, creates dissatisfaction with conditions as they are, or even stirs people to anger." Terminiello v. Chicago, 337 U.S. 1, 4, 69 S.Ct. 894, 896, 93 L.Ed. 1131 (1949).

It would be odd indeed to conclude both that "if it is the speaker's opinion that gives offense, that consequence is a reason for according it constitutional protection," FCC v. Pacifica Foundation, 438 U.S. 726, 745, 98 S.Ct. 3026, 3038, 57 L.Ed.2d 1073 (1978) (opinion of STEVENS, J.), and that the government may ban the expression of certain disagreeable ideas on the unsupported presumption that their very disagreeableness will provoke violence.

Thus, we have not permitted the government to assume that every expression of a provocative idea will incite a riot, but have instead required careful consideration of the actual circumstances surrounding such expression, asking whether the expression "is directed to in-

citing or producing imminent lawless action and is likely to incite or produce such action." Brandenburg v. Ohio, 395 U.S. 444, 447, 89 S.Ct. 1827, 1829, 23 L.Ed.2d 430 (1969) (reviewing circumstances surrounding rally and speeches by Ku Klux Klan). To accept Texas' arguments that it need only demonstrate "the potential for a breach of the peace," and that every flag burning necessarily possesses that potential, would be to eviscerate our holding in Brandenburg. This we decline to do.

Nor does Johnson's expressive conduct fall within that small class of "fighting words" that are "likely to provoke the average person to retaliation, and thereby cause a breach of the peace." Chaplinsky v. New Hampshire, 315 U.S. 568, 574, 62 S.Ct. 766, 770, 86 L.Ed. 1031 (1942). No reasonable onlooker would have regarded Johnson's generalized expression of dissatisfaction with the policies of the Federal Government as a direct personal insult or an invitation to exchange fisticuffs.

We thus conclude that the State's interest in maintaining order is not implicated on these facts. The State need not worry that our holding will disable it from preserving the peace. We do not suggest that the First Amendment forbids a State to prevent "imminent lawless action." Brandenburg, supra, at 447, 89 S.Ct., at 1829.

B.

The State also asserts an interest in preserving the flag as a symbol of nationhood and national unity. In Spence, we acknowledged that the government's interest in preserving the flag's special symbolic value "is directly related to expression in the context of activity" such as affixing a peace symbol to a flag.

We are equally persuaded that this interest is related to expression in the case of Johnson's burning of the flag. The State, apparently, is concerned that such conduct will lead people to believe either that the flag does not stand for nationhood and national unity, but instead reflects other, less positive concepts, or that the concepts reflected in the flag do not in fact exist, that is, that we do not enjoy unity as a Nation. These concerns blossom only when a person's treatment of the flag communicates some message, and thus are related "to the suppression of free expression" within the meaning of O'Brien. We are thus outside of O'Brien's test altogether.

IV.

It remains to consider whether the State's interest in preserving the flag as a symbol of nationhood and national unity justifies Johnson's conviction. As in Spence, "[w]e are confronted with a case of prosecution for the expression of an idea through activity," and "[a]ccordingly, we must examine with particular care the interests advanced by [petitioner] to support its prosecution." 94 S.Ct., at 2730. Johnson was not, we add, prosecuted for the expression of just any idea; he was prosecuted for his expression of dissatisfaction with the policies of this country, expression situated at the core of our First Amendment values.

Moreover, Johnson was prosecuted because he knew that his politically charged expression would cause "serious offense." If he had burned the flag as a means of disposing of it because it was dirty or torn, he would not have been convicted of flag desecration under this Texas law: federal law designates burning as the preferred means of disposing of a flag "when it is in such condition that

it is no longer a fitting emblem for display," 36 U.S.C. s 176(k), and Texas has no quarrel with this means of disposal. The Texas law is thus not aimed at protecting the physical integrity of the flag in all circumstances, but is designed instead to protect it only against impairments that would cause serious offense to others.

Whether Johnson's treatment of the flag violated Texas law thus depended on the likely communicative impact of his expressive conduct. Our decision in Boos v. Barry, tells us that this restriction on Johnson's expression is content based. In Boos, we considered the constitutionality of a law prohibiting "the display of any sign within 500 feet of a foreign embassy if that sign tends to bring that foreign government into 'public odium' or 'public disrepute.'" Rejecting the argument that the law was content neutral because it was justified by "our international law obligation to shield diplomats from speech that offends their dignity," we held that "[t]he emotive impact of speech on its audience is not a 'secondary effect'" unrelated to the content of the expression itself.

According to the principles announced in Boos, Johnson's political expression was restricted because of the content of the message he conveyed. We must therefore subject the State's asserted interest in preserving the special symbolic character of the flag to "the most exacting scrutiny." Boos v. Barry, supra, 485 U.S., at 321, 108 S.Ct., at 1164.

Texas argues that its interest in preserving the flag as a symbol of nationhood and national unity survives this close analysis. Quoting extensively from the writings of this Court chronicling the flag's historic and symbolic role in our society, the State emphasizes the "'special place' " reserved for the flag in our Nation. The State's argument is not that it has an interest simply in maintaining the flag as a symbol of something, no matter what it symbolizes; indeed, if that were the State's position, it would be difficult to see how that interest is endangered by highly symbolic conduct such as Johnson's. Rather, the State's claim is that it has an interest in preserving the flag as a symbol of nationhood and national unity, a symbol with a determinate range of meanings.

According to Texas, if one physically treats the flag in a way that would tend to cast doubt on either the idea that nationhood and national unity are the flag's referents or that national unity actually exists, the message conveyed thereby is a harmful one and therefore may be prohibited. If there is a bedrock principle underlying the First Amendment, it is that the government may not prohibit the expression of an idea simply because society finds the idea itself offensive or disagreeable. We have not recognized an exception to this principle even where our flag has been involved.

If we were to hold that a State may forbid flag burning wherever it is likely to endanger the flag's symbolic role, but allow it wherever burning a flag promotes that role—as where, for example, a person ceremoniously burns a dirty flag—we would be saying that when it comes to impairing the flag's physical integrity, the flag itself may be used as a symbol—as a substitute for the written or spoken word or a "short cut from mind to mind"—only in one direction. We would be permitting a State to "prescribe what shall be orthodox" by saying that one may burn the flag to convey one's attitude toward it and its referents only if one does not endanger the flag's

representation of nationhood and national unity.

We never before have held that the Government may ensure that a symbol be used to express only one view of that symbol or its referents. Indeed, in Schacht v. United States, we invalidated a federal statute permitting an actor portraying a member of one of our Armed Forces to "'wear the uniform of that armed force if the portrayal does not tend to discredit that armed force.' " This proviso, we held, "which leaves Americans free to praise the war in Vietnam but can send persons like Schacht to prison for opposing it, cannot survive in a country which has the First Amendment."

We perceive no basis on which to hold that the principle underlying our decision in Schacht does not apply to this case. To conclude that the government may permit designated symbols to be used to communicate only a limited set of messages would be to enter territory having no discernible or defensible boundaries. Could the government, on this theory, prohibit the burning of state flags? Of copies of the Presidential seal? Of the Constitution? In evaluating these choices under the First Amendment, how would we decide which symbols were sufficiently special to warrant this unique status? To do so, we would be forced to consult our own political preferences, and impose them on the citizenry, in the very way that the First Amendment forbids us to do.

There is, moreover, no indication—either in the text of the Constitution or in our cases interpreting it—that a separate juridical category exists for the American flag alone. Indeed, we would not be surprised to learn that the persons who framed our Constitution and wrote the Amendment that we now construe were not known for their reverence for the Union Jack. The First Amendment does not guarantee that other concepts virtually sacred to our Nation as a whole—such as the principle that discrimination on the basis of race is odious and destructive—will go unquestioned in the marketplace of ideas. See Brandenburg v. Ohio, 395 U.S. 444, 89 S.Ct. 1827, 23 L.Ed.2d 430 (1969). We decline, therefore, to create for the flag an exception to the joust of principles protected by the First Amendment. It is not the State's ends, but its means, to which we object. It cannot be gainsaid that there is a special place reserved for the flag in this Nation, and thus we do not doubt that the government has a legitimate interest in making efforts to "preserv[e] the national flag as an unalloyed symbol of our country." Spence, 418 U.S., at 412, 94 S.Ct., at 2731. We reject the suggestion, urged at oral argument by counsel for Johnson, that the government lacks "any state interest whatsoever" in regulating the manner in which the flag may be displayed. Congress has, for example, enacted precatory regulations describing the proper treatment of the flag, and we cast no doubt on the legitimacy of its interest in making such recommendations. To say that the government has an interest in encouraging proper treatment of the flag, however, is not to say that it may criminally punish a person for burning a flag as a means of political protest. "National unity as an end which officials may foster by persuasion and example is not in question. The problem is whether under our Constitution compulsion as here employed is a permissible means for its achievement." Barnette, 319 U.S., at 640, 63 S.Ct., at 1186.

We are fortified in today's conclusion by our conviction that forbidding criminal punishment for conduct such as Johnson's will not endanger the special role played by our flag or the feelings it inspires. To paraphrase Justice Holmes, we submit that nobody can suppose that this one gesture of an unknown man will change our Nation's attitude towards its flag. See Abrams v. United States, 250 U.S. 616, 628, 40 S.Ct. 17, 21, 63 L.Ed. 1173 (1919) (Holmes, J., dissenting). Indeed, Texas' argument that the burning of an American flag "'is an act having a high likelihood to cause a breach of the peace,'" and its statute's implicit assumption that physical mistreatment of the flag will lead to "serious offense," tend to confirm that the flag's special role is not in danger; if it were, no one would riot or take offense because a flag had been burned.

We are tempted to say, in fact, that the flag's deservedly cherished place in our community will be strengthened, not weakened, by our holding today. Our decision is a reaffirmation of the principles of freedom and inclusiveness that the flag best reflects, and of the conviction that our toleration of criticism such as Johnson's is a sign and source of our strength. Indeed, one of the proudest images of our flag, the one immortalized in our own national anthem, is of the bombardment it survived at Fort McHenry. It is the Nation's resilience, not its rigidity, that Texas sees reflected in the flag—and it is that resilience that we reassert today. The way to preserve the flag's special role is not to punish those who feel differently about these matters. It is to persuade them that they are wrong. "To courageous, self-reliant men, with confidence in the power of free and fearless reasoning applied through the processes of popular government, no danger flowing from speech can be deemed clear and present, unless the incidence of the evil apprehended is so imminent that it may befall before there is opportunity for full discussion. If there be time to expose through discussion the falsehood and fallacies, to avert the evil by the processes of education, the remedy to be applied is more speech, not enforced silence." Whitney v. California, 274 U.S. 357, 377, 47 S.Ct. 641, 649, 71 L.Ed. 1095 (1927) (Brandeis, J., concurring). And, precisely because it is our flag that is involved, one's response to the flag burner may exploit the uniquely persuasive power of the flag itself. We can imagine no more appropriate response to burning a flag than waving one's own, no better way to counter a flag burner's message than by saluting the flag that burns, no surer means of preserving the dignity even of the flag that burned than by—as one witness here did—according its remains a respectful burial. We do not consecrate the flag by punishing its desecration, for in doing so we dilute the freedom that this cherished emblem represents.

V.

Johnson was convicted for engaging in expressive conduct. The State's interest in preventing breaches of the peace does not support his conviction because Johnson's conduct did not threaten to disturb the peace. Nor does the State's interest in preserving the flag as a symbol of nationhood and national unity justify his criminal conviction for engaging in political expression. The judgment of the Texas Court of Criminal Appeals is therefore Affirmed.

Chief Justice REHNQUIST, with whom Justice WHITE and Justice O'CONNOR join, dissenting.

In holding this Texas statute unconstitutional, the Court ignores Justice Holmes' familiar aphorism that "a page of history is worth a volume of logic." New York Trust Co. v. Eisner, 256 U.S. 345, 349, 41 S.Ct. 506, 507, 65 L.Ed. 963 (1921). For more than 200 years, the American flag has occupied a unique position as the symbol of our Nation, a uniqueness that justifies a governmental prohibition against flag burning in the way respondent Johnson did here. At the time of the American Revolution, the flag served to unify the Thirteen Colonies at home, while obtaining recognition of national sovereignty abroad.

During that time, there were many colonial and regimental flags, adorned with such symbols as pine trees, beavers, anchors, and rattlesnakes, bearing slogans such as "Liberty or Death," "Hope," "An Appeal to Heaven," and "Don't Tread on Me." The first distinctive flag of the Colonies was the "Grand Union Flag"—with 13 stripes and a British flag in the left corner—which was flown for the first time on January 2, 1776, by troops of the Continental Army around Boston. By June 14, 1777, after we declared our independence from England, the Continental Congress resolved:

> That the flag of the thirteen United States be thirteen stripes, alternate red and white: that the union be thirteen stars, white in a blue field, representing a new constellation.
> —8 Journal of the Continental Congress 1774–1789, p. 464 (W. Ford ed. 1907).

One immediate result of the flag's adoption was that American vessels harassing British shipping sailed under an authorized national flag. Without such a flag, the British could treat captured seamen as pirates and hang them summarily; with a national flag, such seamen were treated as prisoners of war.

During the War of 1812, British naval forces sailed up Chesapeake Bay and marched overland to sack and burn the city of Washington. They then sailed up the Patapsco River to invest the city of Baltimore, but to do so it was first necessary to reduce Fort McHenry in Baltimore Harbor. Francis Scott Key, a Washington lawyer, had been granted permission by the British to board one of their warships to negotiate the release of an American who had been taken prisoner. That night, waiting anxiously on the British ship, Key watched the British fleet firing on Fort McHenry. Finally, at daybreak, he saw the fort's American flag still flying; the British attack had failed. Intensely moved, he began to scribble on the back of an envelope the poem that became our national anthem:

> O say can you see by the dawn's early light, What so proudly we hail'd at the twilight's last gleaming, Whose broad stripes & bright stars, thro' the perilous fight O'er the ramparts we watch'd were so gallantly streaming? And the rocket's red glare, the bomb bursting in air, Gave proof through the night that our flag was still there, O say does that star-spangled banner yet wave O'er the land of the free & the home of the brave?

The American flag played a central role in our Nation's most tragic conflict, when the North fought against the South. The lowering of the American flag at Fort Sumter was viewed as the start of the war. G. Preble, History of the Flag of the United States of America 453 (1880). The Southern States, to formalize their separation from the Union, adopted the "Stars and Bars" of the Confederacy. The Union troops marched to the sound of "Yes We'll Rally Round The Flag Boys, We'll Rally Once Again." President Abraham

Lincoln refused proposals to remove from the American flag the stars representing the rebel States, because he considered the conflict not a war between two nations but an attack by 11 States against the National Government. Id., at 411. By war's end, the American flag again flew over "an indestructible union, composed of indestructible states." Texas v. White, 74 U.S. (7 Wall.) 700, 725, 19 L.Ed. 227 (1869).

In the First and Second World Wars, thousands of our countrymen died on foreign soil fighting for the American cause. At Iwo Jima in the Second World War, United States Marines fought hand to hand against thousands of Japanese. By the time the Marines reached the top of Mount Suribachi, they raised a piece of pipe upright and from one end fluttered a flag. That ascent had cost nearly 6,000 American lives. The Iwo Jima Memorial in Arlington National Cemetery memorializes that event. President Franklin Roosevelt authorized the use of the flag on labels, packages, cartons, and containers intended for export as lend-lease aid, in order to inform people in other countries of the United States' assistance. Presidential Proclamation No. 2605, 58 Stat. 1126.

During the Korean war, the successful amphibious landing of American troops at Inchon was marked by the raising of an American flag within an hour of the event. Impetus for the enactment of the Federal Flag Desecration Statute in 1967 came from the impact of flag burnings in the United States on troop morale in Vietnam. Representative L. Mendel Rivers, then Chairman of the House Armed Services Committee, testified that "[t]he burning of the flag . . . has caused my mail to increase 100 percent from the boys in Vietnam, writing me and asking me what is going on in America." Desecration of the Flag, Hearings on H.R. 271 before Subcommittee No. 4 of the House Committee on the Judiciary, 90th Cong., 1st Sess., 189 (1967). Representative Charles Wiggins stated: "The public act of desecration of our flag tends to undermine the morale of American troops. That this finding is true can be attested by many Members who have received correspondence from servicemen expressing their shock and disgust of such conduct." 113 Cong.Rec. 16459 (1967).

The flag symbolizes the Nation in peace as well as in war. It signifies our national presence on battleships, airplanes, military installations, and public buildings from the United States Capitol to the thousands of county courthouses and city halls throughout the country. Two flags are prominently placed in our courtroom. Countless flags are placed by the graves of loved ones each year on what was first called Decoration Day, and is now called Memorial Day. The flag is traditionally placed on the casket of deceased members of the Armed Forces, and it is later given to the deceased's family. 10 U.S.C. §§ 1481, 1482. Congress has provided that the flag be flown at half-staff upon the death of the President, Vice President, and other government officials "as a mark of respect to their memory." 36 U.S.C. § 175(m). The flag identifies United States merchant ships, 22 U.S.C. § 454, and "[t]he laws of the Union protect our commerce wherever the flag of the country may float." United States v. Guthrie, 58 U.S. (17 How.) 284, 309, 15 L.Ed. 102 (1855). No other American symbol has been as universally honored as the flag. In 1931, Congress declared "The Star-Spangled Banner" to be our national anthem. 36 U.S.C. § 170. In 1949, Congress declared

June 14th to be Flag Day. s 157. In 1987, John Philip Sousa's "The Stars and Stripes Forever" was designated as the national march. Pub.L. 101–186, 101 Stat. 1286. Congress has also established "The Pledge of Allegiance to the Flag" and the manner of its deliverance. 36 U.S.C. § 172. The flag has appeared as the principal symbol on approximately 33 United States postal stamps and in the design of at least 43 more, more times than any other symbol. United States Postal Service, Definitive Mint Set 15 (1988).

Both Congress and the States have enacted numerous laws regulating misuse of the American flag. Until 1967, Congress left the regulation of misuse of the flag up to the States. Now, however, 18 U.S.C. § 700(a) provides that:

> Whoever knowingly casts contempt upon any flag of the United States by publicly mutilating, defacing, defiling, burning, or trampling upon it shall be fined not more than $1,000 or imprisoned for not more than one year, or both.

Congress has also prescribed, inter alia, detailed rules for the design of the flag, 4 U.S.C. § 1, the time and occasion of flag's display, 36 U.S.C. § 174, the position and manner of its display, § 175, respect for the flag, § 176, and conduct during hoisting, lowering, and passing of the flag, § 177. With the exception of Alaska and Wyoming, all of the States now have statutes prohibiting the burning of the flag. Most of the state statutes are patterned after the Uniform Flag Act of 1917, which in § 3 provides: "No person shall publicly mutilate, deface, defile, defy, trample upon, or by word or act cast contempt upon any such flag, standard, color, ensign or shield." Proceedings of National Conference of Commissioners on Uniform State Laws 323–324 (1917). Most were passed by the States at about the time of World War I. Rosenblatt, Flag Desecration Statutes: History and Analysis, 1972 Wash.U.L.Q. 193, 197.

The American flag, then, throughout more than 200 years of our history, has come to be the visible symbol embodying our Nation. It does not represent the views of any particular political party, and it does not represent any particular political philosophy. The flag is not simply another "idea" or "point of view" competing for recognition in the marketplace of ideas. Millions and millions of Americans regard it with an almost mystical reverence regardless of what sort of social, political, or philosophical beliefs they may have. I cannot agree that the First Amendment invalidates the Act of Congress, and the laws of 48 of the 50 States, which make criminal the public burning of the flag.

More than 80 years ago in Halter v. Nebraska, 205 U.S. 34, 27 S.Ct. 419, 51 L.Ed. 696 (1907), this Court upheld the constitutionality of a Nebraska statute that forbade the use of representations of the American flag for advertising purposes upon articles of merchandise. The Court there said: "For that flag every true American has not simply an appreciation but a deep affection. . . . Hence, it has often occurred that insults to a flag have been the cause of war, and indignities put upon it, in the presence of those who revere it, have often been resented and sometimes punished on the spot." Id., at 41, 27 S.Ct., at 421.

Only two Terms ago, in San Francisco Arts & Athletics, Inc. v. United States Olympic Committee, 483 U.S. 522, 107 S.Ct. 2971, 97 L.Ed.2d 427 (1987), the Court held that Congress could grant exclusive use of the word "Olympic" to the United States Olympic Committee. The Court thought that this "restrictio[n] on expressive speech properly [was] characterized as incidental to the primary congressional purpose of encouraging and rewarding the USOC's activities." Id., at 536, 107 S.Ct., at 2981. As the Court stated, "when a word [or symbol] acquires value 'as the result of organization and the expenditure of labor, skill, and money' by an entity, that entity constitutionally may obtain a limited property right in the word [or symbol]." Id., at 532, 107 S.Ct., at 2974, quoting International News Service v. Associated Press, 248 U.S. 215, 239, 39 S.Ct. 68, 72, 63 L.Ed. 211 (1918). Surely Congress or the States may recognize a similar interest in the flag.

But the Court insists that the Texas statute prohibiting the public burning of the American flag infringes on respondent Johnson's freedom of expression. Such freedom, of course, is not absolute. See Schenck v. United States, 249 U.S. 47, 39 S.Ct. 247, 63 L.Ed. 470 (1919). In Chaplinsky v. New Hampshire, 315 U.S. 568, 62 S.Ct. 766, 86 L.Ed. 1031 (1942), a unanimous Court said: "Allowing the broadest scope to the language and purpose of the Fourteenth Amendment, it is well understood that the right of free speech is not absolute at all times and under all circumstances. There are certain well-defined and narrowly limited classes of speech, the prevention and punishment of which have never been thought to raise any Constitutional problem. These include the lewd and obscene, the profane, the libelous, and the insulting or 'fighting' words—those which by their very utterance inflict injury or tend to incite an immediate breach of the peace. It has been well observed that such utterances are no essential part of any exposition of ideas, and are of such slight social value as a step to truth that any benefit that may be derived from them is clearly outweighed by the social interest in order and morality." Id., at 571–572, 62 S.Ct., at 769 (footnotes omitted).

The Court upheld Chaplinsky's conviction under a state statute that made it unlawful to "address any offensive, derisive or annoying word to any person who is lawfully in any street or other public place." Id., at 569, 62 S.Ct., at 768. Chaplinsky had told a local marshal, "You are a God damned racketeer" and a "damned Fascist and the whole government of Rochester are Fascists or agents of Fascists." Ibid.

Here it may equally well be said that the public burning of the American flag by Johnson was no essential part of any exposition of ideas, and at the same time it had a tendency to incite a breach of the peace. Johnson was free to make any verbal denunciation of the flag that he wished; indeed, he was free to burn the flag in private. He could publicly burn other symbols of the Government or effigies of political leaders. He did lead a march through the streets of Dallas, and conducted a rally in front of the Dallas City Hall. He engaged in a "die-in" to protest nuclear weapons. He shouted out various slogans during the march, including: "Reagan, Mondale which will it be? Either one means World War III"; "Ronald Reagan, killer of the hour, Perfect example of U.S. power"; and "red, white and blue, we spit on you, you stand for plunder, you will go under." Brief for Respondent 3. For none of these acts was he arrested or prosecuted; it was only when he proceeded to burn publicly an American flag stolen from its rightful owner that he violated the Texas statute.

The Court could not, and did not, say that Chaplinsky's utterances were not ex-

pressive phrases—they clearly and succinctly conveyed an extremely low opinion of the addressee. The same may be said of Johnson's public burning of the flag in this case; it obviously did convey Johnson's bitter dislike of his country. But his act, like Chaplinsky's provocative words, conveyed nothing that could not have been conveyed and was not conveyed just as forcefully in a dozen different ways. As with "fighting words," so with flag burning, for purposes of the First Amendment: It is "no essential part of any exposition of ideas, and [is] of such slight social value as a step to truth that any benefit that may be derived from [it] is clearly outweighed" by the public interest in avoiding a probable breach of the peace. The highest courts of several States have upheld state statutes prohibiting the public burning of the flag on the grounds that it is so inherently inflammatory that it may cause a breach of public order. See, e.g., State v. Royal, 113 N.H. 224, 229, 305 A.2d 676, 680 (1973); State v. Waterman, 190 N.W.2d 809, 811–812 (Iowa 1971); see also State v. Mitchell, 32 Ohio App.2d 16, 30, 288 N.E.2d 216, 226 (1972).

The result of the Texas statute is obviously to deny one in Johnson's frame of mind one of many means of "symbolic speech." Far from being a case of "one picture being worth a thousand words," flag burning is the equivalent of an inarticulate grunt or roar that, it seems fair to say, is most likely to be indulged in not to express any particular idea, but to antagonize others. Only five years ago we said in City Council of Los Angeles v. Taxpayers for Vincent, 466 U.S. 789, 812, 104 S.Ct. 2118, 2132, 80 L.Ed.2d 772 (1984), that "the First Amendment does not guarantee the right to employ every conceivable method of communication at all times and in all places." The Texas statute deprived Johnson of only one rather inarticulate symbolic form of protest—a form of protest that was profoundly offensive to many—and left him with a full panoply of other symbols and every conceivable form of verbal expression to express his deep disapproval of national policy. Thus, in no way can it be said that Texas is punishing him because his hearers—or any other group of people—were profoundly opposed to the message that he sought to convey. Such opposition is no proper basis for restricting speech or expression under the First Amendment. It was Johnson's use of this particular symbol, and not the idea that he sought to convey by it or by his many other expressions, for which he was punished.

Our prior cases dealing with flag desecration statutes have left open the question that the Court resolves today. In Street v. New York, 394 U.S. 576, 579, 89 S.Ct. 1354, 1359, 22 L.Ed.2d 572 (1969), the defendant burned a flag in the street, shouting "We don't need no damned flag" and "[i]f they let that happen to Meredith we don't need an American flag." The Court ruled that since the defendant might have been convicted solely on the basis of his words, the conviction could not stand, but it expressly reserved the question whether a defendant could constitutionally be convicted for burning the flag. Id., at 581, 89 S.Ct., at 1360.

Chief Justice Warren, in dissent, stated: "I believe that the States and Federal Government do have the power to protect the flag from acts of desecration and disgrace. . . . [I]t is difficult for me to imagine that, had the Court faced this issue, it would have concluded otherwise." Id., at 605, 89 S.Ct., at 1372. Justices Black

and Fortas also expressed their personal view that a prohibition on flag burning did not violate the Constitution. See id., at 610, 89 S.Ct., at 1374 (Black, J., dissenting) ("It passes my belief that anything in the Federal Constitution bars a State from making the deliberate burning of the American Flag an offense"); id., at 615–617, 89 S.Ct., at 1377–1378 (Fortas, J., dissenting) ("[T]he States and the Federal Government have the power to protect the flag from acts of desecration committed in public. . . . [T]he flag is a special kind of personality. Its use is traditionally and universally subject to special rules and regulation. . . . A person may 'own' a flag, but ownership is subject to special burdens and responsibilities. A flag may be property, in a sense; but it is property burdened with peculiar obligations and restrictions. Certainly . . . these special conditions are not per se arbitrary or beyond governmental power under our Constitution"). In Spence v. Washington, 418 U.S. 405, 94 S.Ct. 2727, 41 L.Ed.2d 842 (1974), the Court reversed the conviction of a college student who displayed the flag with a peace symbol affixed to it by means of removable black tape from the window of his apartment. Unlike the instant case, there was no risk of a breach of the peace, no one other than the arresting officers saw the flag, and the defendant owned the flag in question. The Court concluded that the student's conduct was protected under the First Amendment, because "no interest the State may have in preserving the physical integrity of a privately owned flag was significantly impaired on these facts." Id., at 415, 94 S.Ct., at 2732–2733. The Court was careful to note, however, that the defendant "was not charged under the desecration statute, nor did he permanently disfigure the flag or destroy it." Ibid.

In another related case, Smith v. Goguen, 415 U.S. 566, 94 S.Ct. 1242, 39

L.Ed.2d 605 (1974), the appellee, who wore a small flag on the seat of his trousers, was convicted under a Massachusetts flag-misuse statute that subjected to criminal liability anyone who "publicly . . . treats contemptuously the flag of the United States." Id., at 568–569, 94 S.Ct., at 1244–1245. The Court affirmed the lower court's reversal of appellee's conviction, because the phrase "treats contemptuously" was unconstitutionally broad and vague. Id., at 576, 94 S.Ct., at 1248. The Court was again careful to point out that "[c]ertainly nothing prevents a legislature from defining with substantial specificity what constitutes forbidden treatment of United States flags." Id., at 581–582, 94 S.Ct., at 1251. See also id., at 587, 94 S.Ct., at 1254 (WHITE, J., concurring in judgment) ("The flag is a national property, and the Nation may regulate those who would make, imitate, sell, possess, or use it. I would not question those statutes which proscribe mutilation, defacement, or burning of the flag or which otherwise protect its physical integrity, without regard to whether such conduct might provoke violence. . . . There would seem to be little question about the power of Congress to forbid the mutilation of the Lincoln Memorial. . . . The flag is itself a monument, subject to similar protection"); id., at 591, 94 S.Ct., at 1256 (BLACKMUN, J., dissenting) ("Goguen's punishment was constitutionally permissible for harming the physical integrity of the flag by wearing it affixed to the seat of his pants").

But the Court today will have none of this. The uniquely deep awe and respect for our flag felt by virtually all of us are bundled off under the rubric of "designated symbols," that the First Amendment prohibits the government from "establishing." But the government has not "established" this feeling; 200 years of history have done that. The government is simply recognizing as a fact the profound regard for the American flag created by that history when it enacts statutes prohibiting the disrespectful public burning of the flag.

The Court concludes its opinion with a regrettably patronizing civics lecture, presumably addressed to the Members of both Houses of Congress, the members of the 48 state legislatures that enacted prohibitions against flag burning, and the troops fighting under that flag in Vietnam who objected to its being burned: "The way to preserve the flag's special role is not to punish those who feel differently about these matters. It is to persuade them that they are wrong." The Court's role as the final expositor of the Constitution is well established, but its role as a Platonic guardian admonishing those responsible to public opinion as if they were truant school-children has no similar place in our system of government. The cry of "no taxation without representation" animated those who revolted against the English Crown to found our Nation—the idea that those who submitted to government should have some say as to what kind of laws would be passed. Surely one of the high purposes of a democratic society is to legislate against conduct that is regarded as evil and profoundly offensive to the majority of people—whether it be murder, embezzlement, pollution, or flag burning.

Our Constitution wisely places limits on powers of legislative majorities to act, but the declaration of such limits by this Court "is, at all times, a question of much delicacy, which ought seldom, if ever, to be decided in the affirmative, in a doubtful case." Fletcher v. Peck, 10 U.S. (6 Cranch) 87, 128, 3 L.Ed. 162 (1810) (Marshall, C.J.). Uncritical extension of constitutional protection to the burning of the flag risks the frustration of the very purpose for which organized governments are instituted. The Court decides that the American flag is just another symbol, about which not only must opinions pro and con be tolerated, but for which the most minimal public respect may not be enjoined. The government may conscript men into the Armed Forces where they must fight and perhaps die for the flag, but the government may not prohibit the public burning of the banner under which they fight. I would uphold the Texas statute as applied in this case.

QUESTIONS AND DISCUSSION POINTS

1. The Majority's analysis starts with the question whether Johnson's action constitutes "speech" and then proceeds to the question whether this "speech" is protected. What is/are the test(s) for whether or not speech is protected? Is/are this (these) tests the correct ones?

2. Do you think that Justice Rehnquist in dissent accepts the question at issue as the Majority formulates it? If not, in what ways does his analysis proceed?

3. The Dissent seems to view the flag as "special"—the secular equivalent of a religious artifact. Does the Dissent hold the view that the flag may under no circumstances be desecrated? Are there difficulties with such an argument?

4. How many different forms of argument are found in the Majority and Dissenting opinions? Do the two opinions connect with one another, or do they simply talk past each other?

5. Does it ever make sense to regulate the destruction of important cultural symbols on the basis of the quality of the speech involved? If so, is it not possible that what Johnson had to say simply did not justify the destruction of so important a cultural symbol? Is this, in effect, what the Dissent says?

~

HOME BUILDING & LOAN ASS'N
v. BLAISDELL et ux.
Supreme Court of the United States
290 U.S. 398 (1934)

Mr. Chief Justice HUGHES
delivered the opinion of the Court.

Appellant contests the validity of chapter 339 of the Laws of Minnesota of 1933, p. 514, approved April 18, 1933, called the Minnesota Mortgage Moratorium Law, as being repugnant to the contract clause (article 1, 10) and the due process and equal protection clauses of the Fourteenth Amendment of the Federal Constitution. The statute was sustained by the Supreme Court of Minnesota, and the case comes here on appeal.

The act provides that, during the emergency declared to exist, relief may be had through authorized judicial proceedings with respect to foreclosures of mortgages, and execution sales, of real estate; that sales may be postponed and periods of redemption may be extended. The act does not apply to mortgages subsequently made nor to those made previously which shall be extended for a period ending more than a year after the passage of the act. There are separate provisions in part 2 relating to homesteads, but these are to apply "only to cases not entitled to relief under some valid provision of Part One." The act is to remain in effect "only during the continuance of the emergency and in no event beyond May 1, 1935." No extension of the period for redemption and no postponement of sale is to be allowed

which would have the effect of extending the period of redemption beyond that date.

The act declares that the various provisions for relief are severable; that each is to stand on its own footing with respect to validity. We are here concerned with the provisions of part 1, 4, authorizing the district court of the county to extend the period of redemption from foreclosure sales "for such additional time as the court may deem just and equitable," subject to the above-described limitation. The extension is to be made upon application to the court, on notice, for an order determining the reasonable value of the income on the property involved in the sale, or, if it has no income, then the reasonable rental value of the property, and directing the mortgagor "to pay all or a reasonable part of such income or rental value, in or toward the payment of taxes, insurance, interest, mortgage indebtedness at such times and in such manner" as shall be determined by the court.[1] The section also provides that the time for redemption from fore-

---

1. That section is as follows: Sec. 4. Period of Redemption May be Extended.—Where any mortgage upon real property has been foreclosed and the period of redemption has not yet expired, or where a sale is hereafter had, in the case of real estate mortgage foreclosure proceedings, now pending, or which may hereafter be instituted prior to the expiration of two years from and after the passage of this Act, or upon the sale of any real property under any judgment or execution where the period of redemption has not yet expired, or where such sale is made hereafter within two years from and after the passage of this Act, the period of redemption may be extended for such additional time as the court may deem just and equitable but in no event beyond May 1st, 1935; provided that the mortgagor, or the owner in possession of said property, in the case of mortgage foreclosure proceedings, or the judgment debtor, in case of sale under judgment, or execution, shall prior to

the expiration of the period of redemption, apply to the district court having jurisdiction of the matter, on not less than 10 days' written notice to the mortgagee or judgment creditor, or the attorney of either, as the case may be, for an order determining the reasonable value of the income on said property, or, if the property has no income, then the reasonable rental value of the property involved in such sale, and directing and requiring such mortgagor or judgment debtor, to pay all or a reasonable part of such income or rental value, in or toward the payment of taxes, insurance, interest, mortgage or judgment indebtedness at such times and in such manner as shall be fixed and determined and ordered by the court; and the court shall thereupon hear said application and after such hearing shall make and file its order directing the payment by such mortgagor, or judgment debtor, of such an amount at such times and in such manner as to the court shall, under all the closure sales theretofore made, which otherwise would expire less than thirty days after the approval of the act, shall be extended to a date thirty days after its approval, and application may be made to the court within that time for a further extension as provided in the section. By another provision of the act, no action, prior to May 1, 1935, may be maintained for a deficiency judgment until the period of redemption as allowed by existing law or as extended under the provisions of the act has expired. Prior to the expiration of the extended period of redemption, the court may revise or alter the terms of the extension as changed circumstances may require.

Invoking the relevant provision of the statute, appellees applied to the district court of Hennepin County for an order extending the period of redemption from a foreclosure sale. Their petition stated that they owned a lot in Minneapolis which they had mortgaged to appellant; that the mortgage contained a valid power of sale by advertisement, and that by reason of their default the mortgage had been foreclosed and sold to appellant on May 2, 1932, for $3,700.98; that appellant was the holder of the sheriff's certificate of sale; that, because of the economic depression, appellees had been unable to obtain a new loan or to redeem, and that, unless the period of redemption were extended, the property would be irretrievably lost; and that the reasonable value of the property greatly exceeded the amount due on the mortgage, including all liens, costs, and expenses.

On the hearing, appellant objected to the introduction of evidence upon the ground that the statute was invalid under the federal and state Constitutions, and moved that the petition be dismissed. The motion was granted, and a motion for a new trial was denied. On appeal, the Supreme Court of the state reversed the decision of the district court. Evidence was then taken in the trial court, and appellant renewed its constitutional objections without avail. The court made findings of fact setting forth the mortgage made by the appellees on August 1, 1928, the power of

---

circumstances, appear just and equitable. Provided that upon the service of the notice or demand aforesaid that the running of the period of redemption shall be tolled until the court shall make its order upon such application. Provided, further, however, that if such mortgagor or judgment debtor, or personal representative, shall default in the payments, or any of them, in such order required, on his part to be done, or commits waste, his right to redeem from said sale shall terminate 30 days after such default and holders of subsequent liens may redeem in the order and manner now provided by law beginning 30 days after the filing of notice of such default with the clerk of such District Court, and his right to possession shall cease and the party acquiring title to any such real estate shall then be entitled to the immediate possession of said premises. If default is claimed by allowance of waste, such 30 day period shall not begin to run until the filing of an order of the court finding such waste. Provided, further, that the time of redemption from any real estate mortgage foreclosure or judgment or execution sale heretofore made, which otherwise would expire less than 30 days after the passage and approval of this Act, shall be and the same hereby is extended to a date 30 days after the passage and approval of this Act, and in such case, the mortgagor, or judgment debtor, or the assigns or personal representative of either, as the case may be, or the owner in the possession of the property, may, prior to said date, apply to said court for and the court may thereupon grant the relief as hereinbefore and in this section provided. Provided, further, that prior to May 1, 1935, no action shall be maintained in this state for a deficiency judgment until the period of redemption as allowed by existing law or as extended under the provisions of this Act, has expired.'

sale contained in the mortgage, the default and foreclosure by advertisement, and the sale to appellant on May 2, 1932, for $3,700.98. The court found that the time to redeem would expire on May 2, 1933, under the laws of the state as they were in effect when the mortgage was made and when it was foreclosed; that the reasonable value of the income on the property, and the reasonable rental value, was $40 a month; that the bid made by appellant on the foreclosure sale, and the purchase price, were the full amount of the mortgage indebtedness, and that there was no deficiency after the sale; that the reasonable present market value of the premises was $6,000; and that the total amount of the purchase price, with taxes and insurance premiums subsequently paid by appellant, but exclusive of interest from the date of sale, was $4,056.39. The court also found that the property was situated in the closely built-up portions of Minneapolis; that it had been improved by a two-car garage, together with a building two stories in height which was divided into fourteen rooms; that the appellees, husband and wife, occupied the premises as their homestead, occupying three rooms and offering the remaining rooms for rental to others.

The court entered its judgment extending the period of redemption of May 1, 1935, subject to the condition that the appellees should pay to the appellant $40 a month through the extended period from May 2, 1933; that is, that in each of the months of August, September, and October, 1933, the payments should be $80, in two installments, and thereafter $40 a month, all these amounts to go to the payment of taxes, insurance, interest, and mortgage indebtedness. It is this judgment, sustained by the Supreme Court of the state on the authority of its former opinion, which is here under review. The state court upheld the statute as an emergency measure. Although conceding that the obligations of the mortgage contract were impaired, the court decided that what it thus described as an impairment was, notwithstanding the contract cause of the Federal Constitution, within the police power of the state as that power was called into exercise by the public economic emergency which the Legislature had found to exist. Attention is thus directed to the preamble and first section of the statute which described the existing emergency in terms that were deemed to justify the temporary relief which the statute affords.[2]

---

2. The preamble and the first section of the act are as follows:

"Whereas, the severe financial and economic depression existing for several years past has resulted in extremely low prices for the products of the farms and the factories, a great amount of unemployment, an almost complete lack of credit for farmers, business men and property owners and a general and extreme stagnation of business, agriculture and industry, and

"Whereas, many owners of real property, by reason of said conditions, are unable, and it is believed, will for some time be unable to meet all payments as they come due of taxes, interest and principal of mortgages on their properties

and are, therefore, threatened with loss of such properties through mortgage foreclosure and judicial sales thereof, and

"Whereas, many such properties have been and are being bid in at mortgage foreclosure and execution sales for prices much below what is believed to be their real values and often for much less than the mortgage or judgment indebtedness, thus entailing deficiency judgments against the mortgage and judgment debtors, and

"Whereas, it is believed, and the Legislature of Minnesota hereby declares its belief, that the conditions existing as hereinbefore set forth has created an emergency of such nature that justifies and validates legislation for the extension of the time of redemption from mortgage

The state court, declaring that it could not say that this legislative finding was without basis, supplemented that finding by its own statement of conditions of which it took judicial notice. The court said:

> The preamble and the first section of the act are as follows: "Whereas, the severe financial and economic depression existing for several years past has resulted in extremely low prices for the products of the farms and the factories, a great amount of unemployment, an almost complete lack of credit for farmers, business men and property owners and a general and extreme stagnation of business, agriculture and industry; and Whereas, many owners of real property, by reason of said conditions, are unable, and it is believed, will for some time be unable to meet all payments as they come due of taxes, interest and principal of mortgages on their properties and are, therefore, threatened with loss of such properties through mortgage foreclosure and judicial sales thereof; and Whereas, many such properties have been and are being bid in at mortgage foreclosure and execution sales for prices much below what is believed to be their real values and often for much less than the mortgage or judgment indebtedness, thus entailing deficiency judgments against the mortgage and judgment debtors; and Whereas, it is believed, and the Legislature of Minnesota hereby declares its belief, that the conditions existing as hereinbefore set forth has created an emergency of such nature that justifies and validates legislation for the extension of the time of redemption from mortgage foreclosure and execution sales and other relief of a like character; and Whereas, the State of Minnesota possesses the right under its police power to declare a state of emergency to exist, and Whereas, the inherent and fundamental purposes of our government is to safeguard the public and promote the general welfare of the people; and Whereas, under existing conditions the foreclosure of many real estate mortgages by advertisement would prevent fair, open and competitive bidding at the time of sale in the manner now contemplated by law; and Whereas, it is believed, and the Legislature of Minnesota hereby declares its belief, that the conditions existing as hereinbefore

---

> foreclosure and execution sales and other relief of a like character; and
>
> "Whereas, the State of Minnesota possesses the right under its police power to declare a state of emergency to exist, and
>
> "Whereas, the inherent and fundamental purposes of our government is to safeguard the public and promote the general welfare of the people; and
>
> "Whereas, under existing conditions the foreclosure of many real estate mortgages by advertisement would prevent fair, open and competitive bidding at the time of sale in the manner now contemplated by law, and
>
> "Whereas, it is believed, and the Legislature of Minnesota hereby declares its belief, that the conditions existing as hereinbefore set forth have created an emergency of such a nature that justifies and validates changes in legislation providing for the temporary manner, method, terms and conditions upon which mortgage foreclosure sales may be had or postponed and jurisdiction to administer equitable relief in connection therewith may be conferred upon the District Court, and
>
> "Whereas, Mason's Minnesota Statutes of 1927, Section 9608, which provides for the postponement of mortgage foreclosure sales, has remained for more than thirty years, a provision of the statutes in contemplation of which provisions for foreclosure by advertisement have been agreed upon. "Section 1. Emergency Declared to Exist.—In view of the situation hereinbefore set forth, the Legislature of the State of Minnesota hereby declares that a public economic emergency does exist in the State of Minnesota."

set forth have created an emergency of such a nature that justifies and validates changes in legislation providing for the temporary manner, method, terms and conditions upon which mortgage foreclosure sales may be had or postponed and jurisdiction to administer equitable relief in connection therewith may be conferred upon the District Court; and Whereas, Mason's Minnesota Statutes of 1927, Section 9608, which provides for the postponement of mortgage foreclosure sales, has remained for more than thirty years, a provision of the statutes in contemplation of which provisions for foreclosure by advertisement have been agreed upon. Section 1. Emergency Declared to Exist.—In view of the situation hereinbefore set forth, the Legislature of the State of Minnesota hereby declares that a public economic emergency does exist in the State of Minnesota."

In addition to the weight to be given the determination of the Legislature that an economic emergency exists which demands relief, the court must take notice of other considerations. The members of the Legislature come from every community of the state and from all the walks of life. They are familiar with conditions generally in every calling, occupation, profession, and business in the state. Not only they, but the courts must be guided by what is common knowledge. It is common knowledge that in the last few years land values have shrunk enormously. Loans made a few years ago upon the basis of the then going values cannot possibly be replaced on the basis of present values. We all know that when this law was enacted the large financial companies, which had made it their business to invest in mortgages, had ceased to do so. No bank would directly or in-

directly loan on real estate mortgages. Life insurance companies, large investors in such mortgages, had even declared a moratorium as to the loan provisions of their policy contracts. The President had closed banks temporarily. The Congress, in addition to many extraordinary measures looking to the relief of the economic emergency, had passed an act to supply funds whereby mortgagors may be able within a reasonable time to refinance their mortgages or redeem from sales where the redemption has not expired. With this knowledge the court cannot well hold that the Legislature had no basis in fact for the conclusion that an economic emergency existed which called for the exercise of the police power to grant relief. Justice Olsen of the state court, in a concurring opinion, added the following:

The present nation wide and world wide business and financial crisis has the same results as if it were caused by flood, earthquake, or disturbance in nature. It has deprived millions of persons in this nation of their employment and means of earning a living for themselves and their families; it has destroyed the value of and the income from all property on which thousands of people depended for a living; it actually has resulted in the loss of their homes by a number of our people, and threatens to result in the loss of their homes by many other people in this state; it has resulted in such widespread want and suffering among our people that private, state, and municipal agencies are unable to adequately relieve the want and suffering, and Congress has found it necessary to step in and attempt to remedy the situation by federal aid. Millions of the people's money were and are yet tied up in closed banks and in business enterprises.

We approach the questions thus presented upon the assumption made below, as required by the law of the state, that the mortgage contained a valid power of sale to be exercised in case of default; that this power was validly exercised; that under the law then applicable the period of redemption from the sale was one year, and that it has been extended by the judgment of the court over the opposition of the mortgagee-purchaser; and that, during the period thus extended, and unless the order for extension is modified, the mortgagee-purchaser will be unable to obtain possession, or to obtain or convey title in fee, as he would have been able to do had the statute not been enacted. The statute does not impair the integrity of the mortgage indebtedness. The obligation for interest remains. The statute does not affect the validity of the sale or the right of a mortgagee-purchaser to title in fee, or his right to obtain a deficiency judgment, if the mortgagor fails to redeem within the prescribed period. Aside from the extension of time, the other conditions of redemption are unaltered. While the mortgagor remains in possession, he must pay the rental value as that value has been determined, upon notice and hearing, by the court. The rental value so paid is devoted to the carrying of the property by the application of the required payments to taxes, insurance, and interest on the mortgage indebtedness. While the mortgagee-purchaser is debarred from actual possession, he has, so far as rental value is concerned, the equivalent of possession during the extended period.

In determining whether the provision for this temporary and conditional relief exceeds the power of the state by reason of the clause in the Federal Constitution prohibiting impairment of the obligations of contracts, we must consider the relation of emergency to constitutional power, the historical setting of the contract clause, the development of the jurisprudence of this Court in the construction of that clause, and the principles of construction which we may consider to be established.

Emergency does not create power. Emergency does not increase granted power or remove or diminish the restrictions imposed upon power granted or reserved. The Constitution was adopted in a period of grave emergency. Its grants of power to the federal government and its limitations of the power of the States were determined in the light of emergency, and they are not altered by emergency. What power was thus granted and what limitations were thus imposed are questions which have always been, and always will be, the subject of close examination under our constitutional system. While emergency does not create power, emergency may furnish the occasion for the exercise of power. "Although an emergency may not call into life a power which has never lived, nevertheless emergency may afford a reason for the exertion of a living power already enjoyed." Wilson v. New, 243 U.S. 332, 348, 37 S.Ct. 298, 302, 61 L.Ed. 755, L.R.A. 1917E, 938, Ann.Cas. 1918A, 1024.

The constitutional question presented in the light of an emergency is whether the power possessed embraces the particular exercise of it in response to particular conditions. Thus, the war power of the federal government is not created by the emergency of war, but it is a power given to meet that emergency. It is a power to wage war successfully, and thus it permits the harnessing of the entire energies of the people in a supreme co-operative effort to preserve the nation. But even the war power does not remove constitutional limitations safeguarding essential liberties. When the provisions of the Constitution, in grant or restriction, are specific, so particularized as not to admit of construction, no question is presented. Thus, emergency would not permit a state to have more than two Senators in the Congress, or permit the election of President by a general popular vote without regard to the number of electors to which the States are respectively entitled, or permit the States to "coin money" or to "make anything but gold and silver coin a tender in payment of debts." But, where constitutional grants and limitations of power are set forth in general clauses, which afford a broad outline, the process of construction is essential to fill in the details. That is true of the contract clause. The necessity of construction is not obviated by the fact that the contract clause is associated in the same section with other and more specific prohibitions. Even the grouping of subjects in the same clause may not require the same application to each of the subjects, regardless of differences in their nature. See Groves v. Slaughter, 15 Pet. 449, 505, 10 L.Ed. 800; Atlantic Cleaners & Dyers v. United States, 286 U.S. 427, 434, 52 S.Ct. 607, 76 L.Ed. 1204.

In the construction of the contract clause, the debates in the Constitutional Convention are of little aid. But the reasons which led to the adoption of that clause, and of the other prohibitions of section 10 of article 1, are not left in doubt, and have frequently been described with eloquent emphasis. The widespread distress following the revolutionary period and the plight of debtors had called forth in the States an ignoble array of legislative schemes for the defeat of creditors and the invasion of contractual obligations. Legislative interferences had been so numerous and extreme that the confidence essential to prosperous trade had been undermined and the utter destruction of credit was threatened. "The sober people of America" were convinced that some "thorough reform" was needed which would "inspire a general prudence and industry, and give a regular course to the business of society." The Federalist, No. 44. It was necessary to interpose the restraining power of a central authority in order to secure the foundations even of "private faith." The occasion and general purpose of the contract clause are summed up in the terse statement of Chief Justice Marshall in Ogden v. Saunders, 12 Wheat. 213, 354, 355, 6 L.Ed. 606: "The power of changing the relative situation of debtor and creditor, of interfering with contracts, a power which comes home to every man, touches the interest of all, and controls the conduct of every individual in those things which he supposes to be proper for his own exclusive management, had been used to such an excess by the state legislatures, as to break in upon the ordinary intercourse of society, and destroy all confidence between man and man. This mischief had become so great, so alarming, as not only to impair commercial intercourse, and threaten the existence of credit, but to sap the morals of the people, and destroy the sanctity of private faith. To guard against the continuance of the evil, was an object of deep interest with all the truly wise, as well as the virtuous, of this great community, and was one of the important benefits expected from a reform of the government."

But full recognition of the occasion and general purpose of the clause does not suffice to fix its precise scope. Nor does an examination of the details of prior legislation in the States yield criteria which can be considered controlling. To ascertain the scope of the constitutional prohibition, we examine the course of judicial decisions in its application. These put it beyond question that the prohibition is not an absolute and and is not to be read with literal exactness like a mathematical formula. Justice Johnson, in Ogden v. Saunders, supra, page 286 of 12 Wheat., 6 L.Ed. 606, adverted to such a misdirected effort in these words: "It appears to me, that a great part of the difficulties of the cause, arise from not giving sufficient weight to the general intent of this clause in the constitution, and subjecting it to a severe literal construction, which would be better adapted to special pleadings." And, after giving his view as to the purport of the clause, "that the states shall pass no law, attaching to the acts of individuals other effects or consequences than those attached to them by the laws existing at their date; and all contracts thus construed, shall be enforced according to their just and reasonable purport," Justice Johnson added: "But to assign to contracts, universally, a literal purport, and to exact from them a rigid literal fulfilment, could not have been the intent of the constitution. It is repelled by a hundred examples. Societies exercise a positive control as well over the inception, construction and fulfilment of contracts, as over the form and measure of the remedy to enforce them."

The inescapable problems of construction have been: What is a contract? What are the obligations of contracts? What constitutes impairment of these obligations? What residuum of power is there still in the States, in relation to the operation of contracts, to protect the vital interests of the community? Questions of this character, "of no small nicety and intricacy, have vexed the legislative halls, as well as the judicial tribunals, with an uncounted variety and frequency of litigation and speculation." Story on the Constitution, § 1375.

The obligation of a contract is the law which binds the parties to perform their agreement. Sturges v. Crowninshield, 4 Wheat. 122, 197, 4 L.Ed. 529; Story, op. cit., § 1378. This Court has said that "the laws which subsist at the time and place of the making of a contract, and where it is to be performed, enter into and form a part of it, as if they were expressly referred to or incorporated in its terms. This principle embraces alike those which affect its validity, construction, discharge, and enforcement. . . . Nothing can be more material to the obligation than the means of enforcement. . . . The ideas of validity and remedy are inseparable, and both are parts of the obligation, which is guaranteed by the Constitution against invasion." Von Hoffman v. City of Quincy, 4 Wall. 535, 550, 552, 18 L.Ed. 403. See also, Walker v. Whitehead, 16 Wall. 314, 317, 21 L.Ed. 357. But this broad language cannot be taken without qualification. Chief Justice Marshall pointed out the distinction between obligation and remedy. Sturges v. Crowninshield, supra, 4 Wheat. 200, 4 L.Ed. 529. Said he: "The distinction between the obligation of a contract, and the remedy given by the legislature to enforce that obligation, has been taken at the bar, and exists in the nature of things. Without impairing the obligation of the contract, the remedy may certainly be modified as the wisdom of the nation shall direct." And in Von Hoffman v. City of Quincy, supra, 4 Wall. 553, 554, 18 L.Ed. 403, the general statement above quoted was limited by the further observation that "it is competent for the States to change the form of the remedy, or to modify it otherwise, as they may see fit, provided no substantial right secured by the contract is thereby impaired. No attempt has been made to fix definitely the line between alterations of the remedy, which are to be deemed legitimate, and those which, under the form of modifying the remedy, impair substantial rights. Every case must be determined upon its own circumstances." And Chief Justice Waite, quoting this language in Antoni v. Greenhow, 107 U.S. 769, 775, 2 S.Ct. 91, 96, 27 L.Ed. 468, added: "In all such cases the question becomes, therefore, one of reasonableness, and of that the legislature is primarily the judge."

The obligations of a contract are impaired by a law which renders them invalid, or releases or extinguishes them (Sturges v. Crowninshield, supra, 4 Wheat. 197, 198, 4 L.Ed. 529) and impairment, as above noted, has been predicated of laws which without destroying contracts derogate from substantial contractual rights. In Sturges v. Crowninshield, supra, a state insolvent law, which discharged the debtor from liability, was held to be invalid as applied to contracts in existence when the law was passed. See Ogden v. Saunders, supra. In Green v. Biddle, 8 Wheat. 1, 5 L.Ed. 547, the legislative acts, which were successfully assailed, exempted the occupant of land from the payment of rents and profits to the rightful owner, and were "parts of a system the object of which was to compel the rightful owner to relinquish his lands or pay for all lasting improvements made upon them, without his consent or default." In Bronson v. Kinzie, 1 How. 311, 11 L.Ed. 143, state legislation, which had been enacted for the relief of debtors in view of the seriously depressed condition of business, following the panic of 1837, and which provided that the equitable estate of the mortgagor should not be extinguished for twelve months after sale on foreclosure, and further prevented any sale unless two-thirds of the appraised value of the property should be bid therefor, was held to violate the constitutional provision. It will be observed that in the Bronson Case, aside from the requirement as to the amount of the bid at the sale, the extension of the period of redemption was unconditional, and there was no provision, as in the instant case, to secure to the mortgagee the rental value of the property during the extended period. McCracken v. Hayward, 2 How. 608, 11 L.Ed. 397; Gantly's Lessee v. Ewing, 3 How. 707, 11 L.Ed. 794, and Howard v. Bugbee, 24 How. 461, 16 L.Ed. 753, followed the decision in Bronson v. Kinzie; that of McCracken, condemning a statute which provided that an execution sale should not be made of property unless it would bring two-thirds of its value according to the opinion of three householders; that of Gantly's Lessee, condemning a statute which required a sale for not less than one-half the appraised value; and that of Howard, making a similar ruling as to an unconditional extension of two years for redemption from foreclosure sale. In Planter's Bank v. Sharp, 6 How. 301, 12 L.Ed. 447, a state law was found to be invalid which prevented a bank from transferring notes and bills receivable which it had been duly authorized to acquire. In Von Hoffman v. City of Quincy, supra, a statute which restricted the power of taxation which had previously been given to provide for the payment of municipal bonds was set aside. Louisiana ex rel. Nelson v. Police Jury of St. Martin's Parish, 111 U.S. 716, 4 S.Ct. 648, 28 L.Ed. 574, and Seibert v. Lewis, 122 U.S. 284, 7 S.Ct. 1190, 30 L.Ed. 1161, are similar cases. In Walker v. Whitehead, 16 Wall. 314, 21 L.Ed. 357, the statute, which was held to be repugnant to the contract clause, was enacted in 1870, and provided that, in all suits pending on any debt or contract made before June 1, 1865, the plaintiff should not have a verdict unless it appeared that all taxes chargeable by law on the same had been duly paid for each year since the contract was made; and, further, that in all cases of indebtedness of the described class the defendant might offset any losses he had suffered in consequence of the late war either from destruction or depreciation of property. See Daniels v. Tearney, 102 U.S. 415, 419, 26 L.Ed. 187. In Gunn v. Barry, 15 Wall. 610, 21 L.Ed. 212, and Edwards v. Kearzey, 96 U.S. 595, 24 L.Ed. 793, statutes applicable to prior contracts were condemned because of increases in the amount of the property of judgment debtors which were exempted from levy and sale on execution.

But, in Penniman's Case, 103 U.S. 714, 720, 26 L.Ed. 602, the Court decided that a statute abolishing imprisonment for debt did not, within the meaning of the Constitution, impair the obligation of contracts previously made; and the Court said: "The general doctrine of this court on this subject may be thus stated: In modes of proceeding and forms to enforce the contract the legislature has the control, and may enlarge, limit, or alter them, provided it does not deny a remedy or so embarrass it with conditions or restrictions as seriously to impair the

value of the right." In Barnitz v. Beverly, 163 U.S. 118, 16 S.Ct. 1042, 41 L.Ed. 93, the Court held that a statute which authorized the redemption of property sold on foreclosure, where no right of redemption previously existed, or which extended the period of redemption beyond the time formerly allowed, could not constitutionally apply to a sale under a mortgage executed before its passage. This ruling was to the same effect as that in Bronson v. Kinzie, supra, and Howard v. Bugbee, supra.

But in the Barnitz Case, the statute contained a provision for the prevention of waste, and authorized the appointment of a receiver of the premises sold. Otherwise the extension of the period for redemption was unconditional, and, in case a receiver was appointed, the income during the period allowed for redemption, except what was necessary for repairs and to prevent waste, was still to go to the mortgagor.

None of these cases, and we have cited those upon which appellant chiefly relies, is directly applicable to the question now before us in view of the conditions with which the Minnesota statute seeks to safeguard the interests of the mortgagee-purchaser during the extended period. And broad expressions contained in some of these opinions went beyond the requirements of the decision, and are not controlling. Cohens v. Virginia, 6 Wheat. 264, 399, 5 L.Ed. 257.

Not only is the constitutional provision qualified by the measure of control which the state retains over remedial processes, but the state also continues to possess authority to safeguard the vital interests of its people. It does not matter that legislation appropriate to that end "has the result of modifying or abrogating contracts already in effect." Stephenson v. Binford, 287 U.S. 251, 276, 53 S.Ct. 181, 189, 77 L.Ed. 288. Not only are existing laws read into contracts in order to fix obligations as between the parties, but the reservation of essential attributes of sovereign power is also read into contracts as a postulate of the legal order. The policy of protecting contracts against impairment presupposes the maintenance of a government by virtue of which contractual relations are worth while,—a government which retains adequate authority to secure the peace and good order of society. This principle of harmonizing the constitutional prohibition with the necessary residuum of state power has had progressive recognition in the decisions of this Court.

While the charters of private corporations constitute contracts, a grant of exclusive privilege is not to be implied as against the state. Charles River Bridge v. Warren Bridge, 11 Pet. 420, 9 L.Ed. 773. And all contracts are subject to the right of eminent domain. West River Bridge v. Dix, 6 How. 507, 12 L.Ed. 535. The reservation of this necessary authority of the state is deemed to be a part of the contract. In the case last cited, the Court answered the forcible challenge of the state's power by the following statement of the controlling principle, a statement reiterated by this Court speaking through Mr. Justice Brewer, nearly fifty years later, in Long Island Water Supply Co. v. Brooklyn, 166 U.S. 685, 692, 17 S.Ct. 718, 721, 41 L.Ed. 1165: "But into all contracts, whether made between states and individuals or between individuals only, there enter conditions which arise, not out of the literal terms of the contract itself. They are superinduced by the pre-existing and higher authority of the laws of nature, of nations, or of the community to which the parties belong. They are

always presumed, and must be presumed, to be known and recognized by all, are binding upon all, and need never, therefore, be carried into express stipulation, for this could add nothing to their force. Every contract is made in subordination to them, and must yield to their control, as conditions inherent and paramount, wherever a necessity for their execution shall occur."

The Legislature cannot "bargain away the public health or the public morals." Thus the constitutional provision against the impairment of contracts was held not to be violated by an amendment of the state Constitution which put an end to a lottery theretofore authorized by the Legislature. Stone v. Mississippi, 101 U.S. 814, 819, 25 L.Ed. 1079. The lottery was a valid enterprise when established under express state authority, but the Legislature in the public interest could put a stop to it. A similar rule has been applied to the control by the state of the sale of intoxicating liquors. Boston Beer Company v. Massachusetts, 97 U.S. 25, 32, 33, 24 L.Ed. 989. See Mugler v. Kansas, 123 U.S. 623, 664, 665, 8 S.Ct. 273, 31 L.Ed. 205. The states retain adequate power to protect the public health against the maintenance of nuisances despite insistence upon existing contracts. Northwestern Fertilizing Company v. Hyde Park, 97 U.S. 659, 667, 24 L.Ed. 1036; Butchers' Union Company v. Crescent City Company, 111 U.S. 746, 750, 4 S.Ct. 652, 28 L.Ed. 585. Legislation to protect the public safety comes within the same category of reserved power. Chicago, B. & Q.R.R. Co. v. Nebraska, 170 U.S. 57, 70, 74, 18 S.Ct. 513, 42 L.Ed. 948. This principle has had recent and noteworthy application to the regulation of the use of public highways by common carriers and "contract carriers," where the assertion of interference with existing contract rights has been without avail. Sproles v. Binford, 286 U.S. 374, 390, 391, 52 S.Ct. 581, 76 L.Ed. 1167.

The economic interests of the state may justify the exercise of its continuing and dominant protective power notwithstanding interference with contracts. In Manigault v. Springs, 199 U.S. 473, 26 S.Ct. 127, 50 L.Ed. 274, riparian owners in South Carolina had made a contract for a clear passage through a creek by the removal of existing obstructions. Later, the Legislature of the state, by virtue of its broad authority to make public improvements, and in order to increase the taxable value of the lowlands which would be drained, authorized the construction of a dam across the creek. The Court sustained the statute upon the ground that the private interests were subservient to the public right. The Court said: "It is the settled law of this court that the interdiction of statutes impairing the obligation of contracts does not prevent the state from exercising such powers as are vested in it for the promotion of the common weal, or are necessary for the general good of the public, though contracts previously entered into between individuals may thereby be affected. This power, which, in its various ramifications, is known as the police power, is an exercise of the sovereign right of the government to protect the lives, health, morals, comfort, and general welfare of the people, and is paramount to any rights under contracts between individuals." A statute of New Jersey (P.L.N.J. 1905, p. 461 (4 Comp.St. 1910, p. 5794)) prohibiting the transportation of water of the state into any other state was sustained against the objection that the statute impaired the obligation of contracts which had been made for furnishing such water to persons without the state. Said the Court, by Mr. Justice Holmes (Hudson County Water Co. v. McCarter, 209 U.S. page 357, 28 S.Ct. 529, 531, 52 L.Ed. 828, 14 Ann.Cas. 560): "One whose rights, such as they are, are subject to state restriction, cannot remove them from the power of the state by making a contract about them. The contract will carry with it the infirmity of the subject-matter." The general authority of the Legislature to regulate, and thus to modify, the rates charged by public service corporations, affords another illustration. Stone v. Farmers' Loan & Trust Company, 116 U.S. 307, 325, 326, 6 S.Ct. 334, 388, 1191, 29 L.Ed. 636. The argument is pressed that in the cases we have cited the obligation of contracts was affected only incidentally. This argument proceeds upon a misconception. The question is not whether the legislative action affects contracts incidentally, or directly or indirectly, but whether the legislation is addressed to a legitimate end and the measures taken are reasonable and appropriate to that end. Another argument, which comes more closely to the point, is that the state power may be addressed directly to the prevention of the enforcement of contracts only when these are of a sort which the Legislature in its discretion may denounce as being in themselves hostile to public morals, or public health, safety, or welfare, or where the prohibition is merely of injurious practices; that interference with the enforcement of other and valid contracts according to appropriate legal procedure, although the interference is temporary and for a public purpose, is not permissible. This is but to contend that in the latter case the end is not legitimate in the view that it cannot be reconciled with a fair interpretation of the constitutional provision. Undoubtedly, whatever is reserved of state power must be consistent with the fair intent of the constitutional limitation of that power. The reserved power cannot be construed so as to destroy the limitation, nor is the limitation to be construed to destroy the reserved power in its essential aspects. They must be construed in harmony with each other. This principle precludes a construction which would permit the state to adopt as its policy the repudiation of debts or the destruction of contracts or the denial of means to enforce them. But it does not follow that conditions may not arise in which a temporary restraint of enforcement may be consistent with the spirit and purpose of the constitutional provision and thus be found to be within the range of the reserved power of the state to protect the vital interests of the community. It cannot be maintained that the constitutional prohibition should be so construed as to prevent limited and temporary interpositions with respect to the enforcement of contracts if made necessary by a great public calamity such as fire, flood, or earthquake. See American Land Co. v. Zeiss, 219 U.S. 47, 31 S.Ct. 200, 55 L.Ed. 82. The reservation of state power appropriate to such extraordinary conditions may be deemed to be as much a part of all contracts as is the reservation of state power to protect the public interest in the other situations to which we have referred. And, if state power exists to give temporary relief from the enforcement of contracts in the presence of disasters due to physical causes such as fire, flood, or earthquake, that power cannot be said to be nonexistent when the urgent public need demanding such relief is produced by other and economic causes. Whatever doubt there may have been that the protective power of the state, its police power, may be exercised—without violating the true intent of the

provision of the Federal Constitution—in directly preventing the immediate and literal enforcement of contractual obligations by a temporary and conditional restraint, where vital public interests would otherwise suffer, was removed by our decisions relating to the enforcement of provisions of leases during a period of scarcity of housing. Block v. Hirsh, 256 U.S. 135, 41 S.Ct. 458, 65 L.Ed. 865, 16 A.L.R. 165. The case of Block v. Hirsh arose in the District of Columbia and involved the due process clause of the Fifth Amendment. The cases of the Marcus Brown Company and the Levy Leasing Company arose under legislation of New York, and the constitutional provision against the impairment of the obligation of contracts was invoked. The statutes of New York, declaring that a public emergency existed, directly interfered with the enforcement of covenants for the surrender of the possession of premises on the expiration of leases. Within the city of New York and contiguous counties, the owners of dwellings, including apartment and tenement houses (but excepting buildings under construction in September, 1920, lodging houses for transients and the larger hotels), were wholly deprived until November 1, 1922, of all possessory remedies for the purpose of removing from their premises the tenants or occupants in possession when the laws took effect (save in certain specified instances) providing the tenants or occupants were ready, able, and willing to pay a reasonable rent or price for their use and occupation. People v. La Fetra, 230 N.Y. 429, 438, 130 N.E. 601, 16 A.L.R. 152; Levy Leasing Co. v. Siegel, 230 N.Y. 634, 130 N.E. 923. In the case of the Marcus Brown Company the facts were thus stated by the District Court (269 F. 306, 312): "The tenant defendants herein, by law older than the state of New York, became at the land-lord's option trespassers on October 1, 1920. Plaintiff had then found and made a contract with a tenant it liked better, and had done so before these statutes were en-acted. By them plaintiff is, after defen-dants elected to remain in possession, for-bidden to carry out his bargain with the tenant he chose, the obligation of the covenant for peaceable surrender by de-fendants is impaired, and for the next two years Feldman et al. may, if they like, re-main in plaintiff's apartment, provided they make good month by month the al-legation of their answer, i.e., pay what 'a court of competent jurisdiction' regards as fair and reasonable compensation for such enforced use and occupancy." An-swering the contention that the legislation as thus applied contravened the constitu-tional prohibition, this Court, after refer-ring to its opinion in Block v. Hirsh, supra, said: "In the present case more emphasis is laid upon the impairment of the oblig-ation of the contract of the lessees to sur-render possession and of the new lease which was to have gone into effect upon October 1, last year. But contracts are made subject to this exercise of the power of the State when otherwise justified, as we have held this to be." 256 U.S. page 198, 41 S.Ct. 465, 466, 65 L.Ed. 877. This decision was followed in the case of the Levy Leasing Company, supra.

In these cases of leases, it will be ob-served that the relief afforded was tem-porary and conditional; that it was sus-tained because of the emergency due to scarcity of housing; and that provision was made for reasonable compensation to the landlord during the period he was prevented from regaining possession. The Court also decided that, while the declaration by the Legislature as to the existence of the emergency was entitled

to great respect, it was not conclusive; and, further, that a law "depending upon the existence of an emergency or other certain state of facts to uphold it may cease to operate if the emergency ceases or the facts change even though valid when passed." It is always open to judi-cial inquiry whether the exigency still ex-ists upon which the continued operation of the law depends. Chastleton Corpora-tion v. Sinclair, 264 U.S. 543, 547, 548, 44 S.Ct. 405, 406, 68 L.Ed. 841.

It is manifest from this review of our decisions that there has been a growing appreciation of public needs and of the necessity of finding ground for a rational compromise between individual rights and public welfare. The settlement and consequent contraction of the public do-main, the pressure of a constantly in-creasing density of population, the inter-relation of the activities of our people and the complexity of our economic in-terests, have inevitably led to an in-creased use of the organization of soci-ety in order to protect the very bases of individual opportunity. Where, in earlier days, it was thought that only the con-cerns of individuals or of classes were in-volved, and that those of the state itself were touched only remotely, it has later been found that the fundamental inter-ests of the state are directly affected; and that the question is no longer merely that of one party to a contract as against an-other, but of the use of reasonable means to safeguard the economic structure upon which the good of all depends.

It is no answer to say that this pub-lic need was not apprehended a century ago, or to insist that what the provision of the Constitution meant to the vision of that day it must mean to the vision of our time. If by the statement that what the Constitution meant at the time of its adoption it means to-day, it is intended to say that the great clauses of the Constitution must be confined to the interpretation which the framers, with the conditions and outlook of their time, would have placed upon them, the statement carries its own refutation. It was to guard against such a narrow conception that Chief Justice Marshall uttered the memorable warning: "We must never forget, that it is a constitution we are expounding" (McCulloch v. Maryland, 4 Wheat. 316, 407, 4 L.Ed. 579); "a constitution intended to endure for ages to come, and, consequently, to be adapted to the various crises of human affairs." Id. page 415 of 4 Wheat. When we are dealing with the words of the Constitution, said this Court in Missouri v. Holland, 252 U.S. 416, 433, 40 S.Ct. 382, 383, 64 L.Ed. 641, 11 A.L.R. 984, "we must realize that they have called into life a being the development of which could not have been foreseen completely by the most gifted of its begetters. . . . The case before us must be considered in the light of our whole experience and not merely in that of what was said a hundred years ago."

Nor is it helpful to attempt to draw a fine distinction between the intended meaning of the words of the Constitution and their intended application. When we consider the contract clause and the decisions which have expounded it in harmony with the essential reserved power of the states to protect the security of their peoples, we find no warrant for the conclusion that the clause has been warped by these decisions from its proper significance or that the founders of our government would have interpreted the clause differently had they had occasion to assume that responsibility in the conditions of the later day. The vast body of law which has been developed was unknown to the fathers, but it is believed to have preserved the essential content and the spirit of the Constitution. With a growing recognition of public needs and the relation of individual right to public security, the court has sought to prevent the perversion of the clause through its use as an instrument to throttle the capacity of the states to protect their fundamental interests. This development is a growth from the seeds which the fathers planted. It is a development forecast by the prophetic words of Justice Johnson in Ogden v. Saunders, already quoted. And the germs of the later decisions are found in the early cases of the Charles River Bridge and the West River Bridge, supra, which upheld the public right against strong insistence upon the contract clause. The principle of this development is, as we have seen, that the reservation of the reasonable exercise of the protective power of the state is read into all contracts, and there is no greater reason for refusing to apply this principle to Minnesota mortgages than to New York leases. Applying the criteria established by our decisions, we conclude:

1. An emergency existed in Minnesota which furnished a proper occasion for the exercise of the reserved power of the state to protect the vital interests of the community. The declarations of the existence of this emergency by the Legislature and by the Supreme Court of Minnesota cannot be regarded as a subterfuge or as lacking in adequate basis. Block v. Hirsh, supra. The finding of the Legislature and state court has support in the facts of which we take judicial notice. Atchison, T. & S.F. Rwy. Co. v. United States, 284 U.S. 248, 260, 52

S.Ct. 146, 76 L.Ed. 273. It is futile to attempt to make a comparative estimate of the seriousness of the emergency shown in the leasing cases from New York and of the emergency disclosed here. The particular facts differ, but that there were in Minnesota conditions urgently demanding relief, if power existed to give it, is beyond cavil. As the Supreme Court of Minnesota said (249 N.W. 334, 337), the economic emergency which threatened "the loss of homes and lands which furnish those in possession the necessary shelter and means of subsistence" was a "potent cause" for the enactment of the statute.

2. The legislation was addressed to a legitimate end; that is, the legislation was not for the mere advantage of particular individuals but for the protection of a basic interest of society.

3. In view of the nature of the contracts in question—mortgages of unquestionable validity—the relief afforded and justified by the emergency, in order not to contravene the constitutional provision, could only be of a character appropriate to that emergency, and could be granted only upon reasonable conditions.

4. The conditions upon which the period of redemption is extended do not appear to be unreasonable. The initial extension of the time of redemption for thirty days from the approval of the act was obviously to give a reasonable opportunity for the authorized application to the court. As already noted, the integrity of the mortgage indebtedness is not impaired; interest continues to run; the validity of the sale and the right of a mortgagee-purchaser to title or to obtain a deficiency judgment, if the mortgagor fails to redeem within the extended period, are maintained; and the conditions of redemption, if redemption there be, stand as they were under the prior law. The mortgagor during the extended period is not ousted from possession, but he must pay the rental value of the premises as ascertained in judicial proceedings and this amount is applied to the carrying of the property and to interest upon the indebtedness. The mortgagee-purchaser during the time that he cannot obtain possession thus is not left without compensation for the withholding of possession. Also important is the fact that mortgagees, as is shown by official reports of which we may take notice, are predominantly corporations, such as insurance companies, banks, and investment and mortgage companies. These, and such individual mortgagees as are small investors, are not seeking homes or the opportunity to engage in farming. Their chief concern is the reasonable protection of their investment security. It does not matter that there are, or may be, individual cases of another aspect. The Legislature was entitled to deal with the general or typical situation. The relief afforded by the statute has regard to the interest of mortgagees as well as to the interest of mortgagors. The legislation seeks to prevent the impending ruin of both by a considerate measure of relief.

In the absence of legislation, courts of equity have exercised jurisdiction in suits for the foreclosure of mortgages to fix the time and terms of sale and to refuse to confirm sales upon equitable grounds where they were found to be unfair or inadequacy of price was so gross as to shock the conscience. The "equity of redemption" is the creature of equity. While courts of equity could not alter the legal effect of the forfeiture of the estate at common law on breach of condition, they succeeded, operating on the conscience of the mortgagee, in maintaining that it was unreasonable that he should retain for his own benefit what was intended as a mere security, that the breach of condition was in the nature of a penalty, which ought to be relieved against, and that the mortgagor had an equity to redeem on payment of principal, interest and costs, notwithstanding the forfeiture at law. This principle of equity was victorious against the strong opposition of the common-law judges, who thought that by "the Growth of Equity on Equity the Heart of the Common Law is eaten out." The equitable principle became firmly established, and its application could not be frustrated even by the engagement of the debtor entered into at the time of the mortgage, the courts applying the equitable maxim "once a mortgage, always a mortgage, and nothing but a mortgage." Although the courts would have no authority to alter a statutory period of redemption, the legislation in question permits the courts to extend that period, within limits and upon equitable terms, thus providing a procedure and relief which are cognate to the historic exercise of the equitable jurisdiction. If it be determined, as it must be, that the contract clause is not an absolute and utterly unqualified restriction of the state's protective power, this legislation is clearly so reasonable as to be within the legislative competency. The legislation is temporary in operation. It is limited to the exigency which called it forth. While the postponement of the period of redemption from the foreclosure sale is to May 1, 1935, that period may be reduced by the order of the court under the statute, in case of a change in circumstances, and the operation of the statute

itself could not validly outlast the emergency or be so extended as virtually to destroy the contracts. We are of the opinion that the Minnesota statute as here applied does not violate the contract clause of the Federal Constitution. Whether the legislation is wise or unwise as a matter of policy is a question with which we are not concerned. What has been said on that point is also applicable to the contention presented under the due process clause. Block v. Hirsh, supra. Nor do we think that the statute denies to the appellant the equal protection of the laws. The classification which the statute makes cannot be said to be an arbitrary one.

The judgment of the Supreme Court of Minnesota is affirmed. Judgment affirmed.

Mr. Justice SUTHERLAND, dissenting.

Few questions of greater moment than that just decided have been submitted for judicial inquiry during this generation. He simply closes his eyes to the necessary implications of the decision who fails to see in it the potentiality of future gradual but ever-advancing encroachments upon the sanctity of private and public contracts. The effect of the Minnesota legislation, though serious enough in itself, is of trivial significance compared with the far more serious and dangerous inroads upon the limitations of the Constitution which are almost certain to ensue as a consequence naturally following any step beyond the boundaries fixed by that instrument. And those of us who are thus apprehensive of the effect of this decision would, in a matter so important, be neglectful of our duty should we fail to spread upon the permanent records of the court the reasons which move us to the opposite view.

A provision of the Constitution, it is hardly necessary to say, does not admit of two distinctly opposite interpretations. It does not mean one thing at one time and an entirely different thing at another time. If the contract impairment clause, when framed and adopted, meant that the terms of a contract for the payment of money could not be altered in invitum by a state statute enacted for the relief of hardly pressed debtors to the end and with the effect of postponing payment or enforcement during and because of an economic or financial emergency, it is but to state the obvious to say that it means the same now. This view, at once so rational in its application to the written word, and so necessary to the stability of constitutional principles, though from time to time challenged, has never, unless recently, been put within the realm of doubt by the decisions of this court. The true rule was forcefully declared in Ex parte Milligan, 4 Wall. 2, 120, 121, 18 L.Ed. 281, in the face of circumstances of national peril and public unrest and disturbance far greater than any that exist to-day. In that great case this court said that the provisions of the Constitution there under consideration had been expressed by our ancestors in such plain English words that it would seem the ingenuity of man could not evade them, but that after the lapse of more than seventy years they were sought to be avoided. "Those great and good men," the Court said, "foresaw that troublous times would arise, when rules and people would become restive under restraint, and seek by sharp and decisive measures to accomplish ends deemed just and proper; and that the principles of constitutional liberty would be in peril, unless established by irrepealable law. The history of the

world had taught them that what was done in the past might be attempted in the future." And then, in words the power and truth of which have become increasingly evident with the lapse of time, there was laid down the rule without which the Constitution would cease to be the "supreme law of the land," binding equally upon governments and governed at all times and under all circumstances, and become a mere collection of political maxims to be adhered to or disregarded according to the prevailing sentiment or the legislative and judicial opinion in respect of the supposed necessities of the hour:

> The Constitution of the United States is a law for rulers and people, equally in war and in peace, and covers with the shield of its protection all classes of men, at all times, and under all circumstances. No doctrine, involving more pernicious consequences, was ever invented by the wit of man than that any of its provisions can be suspended during any of the great exigencies of government. Such a doctrine leads directly to anarchy or despotism.

Chief Justice Taney, in Dred Scott v. Sandford, 19 How, 393, 426, 15 L.Ed. 691, said that, while the Constitution remains unaltered, it must be construed now as it was understood at the time of its adoption; that it is not only the same in words but the same in meaning, "and as long as it continues to exist in its present form, it speaks not only in the same words, but with the same meaning and intent with which it spoke when it came from the hands of its framers, and was voted on and adopted by the people of the United States. Any other rule of construction would abrogate the judicial character of this court, and make it the mere reflex of the popular opinion or passion of the day." And in South Carolina v. United States, 199 U.S. 437, 448, 449, 26 S.Ct. 110, 111, 59 L.Ed. 261, 4 Ann.Cas. 737, in an opinion by Mr. Justice Brewer, this court quoted these words with approval and said: "The Constitution is a written instrument. As such its meaning does not alter. That which it meant when adopted, it means now. Those things which are within its grants of power, as those grants were understood when made, are still within them; and those things not within them remain still excluded."

The words of Judge Campbell, speaking for the Supreme Court of Michigan in People ex rel. Twitchell v. Blodgett, 13 Mich. 127, 139, 140, are peculiarly apposite. "But it may easily happen," he said, "that specific provisions may, in unforeseen emergencies, turn out to have been inexpedient. This does not make these provisions any less binding. Constitutions can not be changed by events alone. They remain binding as the acts of the people in their sovereign capacity, as the framers of Government, until they are amended or abrogated by the action prescribed by the authority which created them. It is not competent for any department of the Government to change a constitution, or declare it changed, simply because it appears ill adapted to a new state of things. Restrictions have, it is true, been found more likely than grants to be unsuited to unforeseen circumstances. But, where evils arise from the application of such regulations, their force cannot be denied or evaded; and the remedy consists in repeal or amendment, and not in false constructions." The provisions of the Federal Constitution, undoubtedly, are pliable in the sense that in appropriate cases they have the capacity of bringing within their grasp every new condition which falls within their meaning. But, their meaning is changeless; it is only their application which is extensible. See South Carolina v. United States, supra, 199 U.S. pages 448, 449, 26 S.Ct. 110, 59 L.Ed. 261, 4 Ann.Cas. 737. Constitutional grants of power and restrictions upon the exercise of power are not flexible as the doctrines of the common law are flexible. These doctrines, upon the principles of the common law itself, modify or abrogate themselves whenever they are or whenever they become plainly unsuited to different or changed conditions. Funk v. United States, 290 U.S. 371, 54 S.Ct. 212, 78 L.Ed. 369, decided December 11, 1933. The distinction is clearly pointed out by Judge Cooley, 1 Constitutional Limitations (8th Ed.) 124:

A principal share of the benefit expected from written constitutions would be lost if the rules they established were so flexible as to bend to circumstances or be modified by public opinion. It is with special reference to the varying moods of public opinion, and with a view to putting the fundamentals of government beyond their control, that these instruments are framed; and there can be no such steady and imperceptible change in their rules as inheres in the principles of the common law. Those beneficent maxims of the common law which guard person and property have grown and expanded until they mean vastly more to us than they did to our ancestors, and are more minute, particular, and pervading in their protections; and we may confidently look forward in the future to still further modifications in the direction of improvement. Public sentiment and action effect such changes, and the courts recognize them; but a court or legislature which should allow a change in public sentiment to influence it in giving to a written constitution a construction not warranted by the intention of its founders, would be justly chargeable with reckless disregard of official oath and public duty; and if its course could become a precedent, these instruments would be of little avail. What a court is to do, therefore, is to declare the law as written, leaving it to the people themselves to make such changes as new circumstances may require. The meaning of the constitution is fixed when it is adopted, and it is not different at any subsequent time when a court has occasion to pass upon it.

The whole aim of construction, as applied to a provision of the Constitution, is to discover the meaning, to ascertain and give effect to the intent of its framers and the people who adopted it. Lake County v. Rollins, 130 U.S. 662, 670, 9 S.Ct. 651, 32 L.Ed. 1060. The necessities which gave rise to the provision, the controversies which preceded, as well as the conflicts of opinion which were settled by its adoption, are matters to be considered to enable us to arrive at a correct result. Knowlton v. Moore, 178 U.S. 41, 95, 20 S.Ct. 747, 44 L.Ed. 969. The history of the times, the state of things existing when the provision was framed and adopted should be looked to in order to ascertain the mischief and the remedy. Rhode Island v. Massachusetts, 12 Pet. 657, 723, 9 L.Ed. 1233; Craig v. Missouri, 4 Pet. 410, 431, 432, 7 L.Ed. 903. As nearly as possible we should place ourselves in the condition of those who framed and adopted it. In re Bain, 121 U.S. 1, 12, 7 S.Ct. 781, 30 L.Ed. 849. And, if the meaning be at all doubtful, the doubt should be resolved, wherever reasonably possible to do so, in a way to forward the ev-

ident purpose with which the provision was adopted. Maxwell v. Dow, 176 U.S. 581, 602, 20 S.Ct. 448, 494, 44 L.Ed. 597; Jarrolt v. Moberly, 103 U.S. 580, 586, 26 L.Ed. 492.

An application of these principles to the question under review removes any doubt, if otherwise there would be any, that the contract impairment clause denies to the several states the power to mitigate hard consequences resulting to debtors from financial or economic exigencies by an impairment of the obligation of contracts of indebtedness. A candid consideration of the history and circumstances which led up to and accompanied the framing and adoption of this clause will demonstrate conclusively that it was framed and adopted with the specific and studied purpose of preventing legislation designed to relieve debtors especially in time of financial distress. Indeed, it is not probable that any other purpose was definitely in the minds of those who composed the framers' convention or the ratifying state conventions which followed, although the restriction has been given a wider application upon principles clearly stated by Chief Justice Marshall in the Dartmouth College Case, 4 Wheat. 518, 644, 645, 4 L.Ed. 629.

Following the Revolution, and prior to the adoption of the Constitution, the American people found themselves in a greatly impoverished condition. Their commerce had been well-nigh annihilated. They were not only without luxuries, but in great degree were destitute of the ordinary comforts and necessities of life. In these circumstances they incurred indebtedness in the purchase of imported goods and otherwise far beyond their capacity to pay. From this situation there arose a divided sentiment. On the one hand, an exact observance of public and private engagements was insistently urged. A violation of the faith of the nation or the pledges of the private individual, it was insisted, was equally forbidden by the principles of moral justice and of sound policy. Individual distress, it was urged, should be alleviated only by industry and frugality, not by relaxation of law or by a sacrifice of the rights of others. Indiscretion or imprudence was not to be relieved by legislation, but restrained by the conviction that a full compliance with contracts would be exacted. On the other hand, it was insisted that the case of the debtor should be viewed with tenderness; and efforts were constantly directed toward relieving him from an exact compliance with his contract. As a result of the latter view, state laws were passed suspending the collection of debts, remitting or suspending the collection of taxes, providing for the emission of paper money, delaying legal proceedings, etc. There followed, as there must always follow from such a course, a long trail of ills; one of the direct consequences being a loss of confidence in the government and in the good faith of the people. Bonds of men whose ability to pay their debts was unquestionable could not be negotiated except at a discount of 30, 40, or 50 per cent. Real property could be sold only at a ruinous loss. Debtors, instead of seeking to meet their obligations by painful effort, by industry and economy, began to rest their hopes entirely upon legislative interference. The impossibility of payment of public or private debts was widely asserted, and in some instances threats were made of suspending the administration of justice by violence. The circulation of depreciated currency became common. Resentment against lawyers

and courts was freely manifested, and in many instances the course of the law was arrested and judges restrained from proceeding in the execution of their duty by popular and tumultuous assemblages. This state of things alarmed all thoughtful men, and led them to seek some effective remedy. Marshall, Life of Washington (1807), vol. 5, pp. 88–131.

That this brief outline of the situation is entirely accurate is borne out by all contemporaneous history, as well as by writers of distinction of a later period. Compare Edwards v. Kearzey, 96 U.S. 595, 604–607, 24 L.Ed. 793. The appended note might be extended for many pages by the addition of similar quotations from the same and other writers, but enough appears to establish beyond all question the extreme gravity of the emergency, the great difficulty and frequent impossibility which confronted debtors generally in any effort to discharge their obligations.

In an attempt to meet the situation, recourse was had to the Legislatures of the several states under the Confederation; and these bodies passed, among other acts, the following: Laws providing for the emission of bills of credit and making them legal tender for the payment of debts, and providing also for such payment by the delivery of specific property at a fixed valuation; installment laws, authorizing payment of overdue obligations at future intervals of time; stay laws and laws temporarily closing access to the courts; and laws discriminating against British creditors. I have selected, out of a vast number, a few historical comments upon the character and effect of these legislative devices.

In the midst of this confused, gloomy, and seriously exigent condition of affairs, the Constitutional Convention of 1787 met at Philadelphia. The defects of the Articles of Confederation were so great as to be beyond all hope of amendment, and the Convention, acting in technical excess of its authority, proceeded to frame for submission to the people of the several states an entirely new Constitution. Shortly prior to the meeting of the Convention, Madison had assailed a bill pending in the Virginia Assembly, proposing the payment of private debts in three annual installments, on the ground that "no legislative principle could vindicate such an interposition of the law in private contracts." The bill was lost by a single vote. Pelatiah Webster had likewise assailed similar laws as altering the value of contracts; and William Paterson, of New Jersey, had insisted that "the legislature should leave the parties to the law under which they contracted."

In the plan of government especially urged by Sherman and Ellsworth there was an article proposing that the Legislatures of the individual states ought not to possess a right to emit bills of credit, etc., "or in any manner to obstruct or impede the recovery of debts, whereby the interests of foreigners or the citizens of any other state may be affected." And on July 13, 1787, Congress in New York, acutely conscious of the evils engendered by state laws interfering with existing contracts, passed the Northwest Territory Ordinance, which contained the clause: "And, in the just preservation of rights and property, it is understood and declared, that no law ought ever to be made or have force in the said territory, that shall, in any manner whatever, interfere with or affect private contracts, or engagements, bona fide, and without fraud previously formed." It is not surprising, therefore, that, after the Con-

vention had adopted the clauses, no state shall "emit bills of credit," or "make any thing but gold and silver coin a tender in payment of debts," Mr. King moved to add a "prohibition on the states to interfere in private contracts." This was opposed by Governer Morris and Colonel Mason.

Colonel Mason thought that this would be carrying the restraint too far; that cases would happen that could not be foreseen where some kind of interference would be essential. This was on August 28. But Mason's view did not prevail, for, on September 14 following, the first clause of article 1, § 10, was altered so as to include the provision: "No state shall pass any law impairing the obligation of contracts," and in that form it was adopted.

Luther Martin, in an address to the Maryland House of Delegates, declared his reasons for voting against the provision. He said that he considered there might be times of such great public calamity and distress as should render it the duty of a government in some measure to interfere by passing laws totally or partially stopping courts of justice, or authorizing the debtor to pay by installments; that such regulations had been found necessary in most or all of the states "to prevent the wealthy creditor and the moneyed man from totally destroying the poor, though industrious debtor. Such times may again arrive." And he was apprehensive of any proposal which took from the respective states the power to give their debtor citizens "a moment's indulgence, however necessary it might be, and however desirous to grant them aid."

On the other hand, Sherman and Ellsworth defended the provision in a letter to the Governor of Connecticut. In the course of the Virginia debates, Randolph declared that the prohibition would be promotive of virtue and justice, and preventive of injustice and fraud; and he pointed out that the reputation of the people had suffered because of frequent interferences by the state Legislatures with private contracts. In the North Carolina debates, Mr. Davie declared that the prohibition against impairing the obligation of contracts and other restrictions ought to supersede the laws of particular states. He thought the constitutional provisions were founded on the strongest principles of justice. Pinckney, in the South Carolina debates, said that he considered the section including the clause in question as "the soul of the Constitution," teaching the states "to cultivate those principles of public honor and private honesty which are the sure road to national character and happiness."

The present exigency is nothing new. From the beginning of our existence as a nation, periods of depression, of industrial failure, of financial distress, of unpaid and unpayable indebtedness, have alternated with years of plenty. The vital lesson that expenditure beyond income begets poverty, that public or private extravagance, financed by promises to pay, either must end in complete or partial repudiation or the promises be fulfilled by self-denial and painful effort, though constantly taught by bitter experience, seems never to be learned; and the attempt by legislative devices to shift the misfortune of the debtor to the shoulders of the creditor without coming into conflict with the contract impairment clause has been persistent and oft-repeated.

The defense of the Minnesota law is made upon grounds which were discountenanced by the makers of the Constitution and have many times been rejected by this court. That defense should not now succeed, because it constitutes an effort to overthrow the constitutional provision by an appeal to facts and circumstances identical with those which brought it into existence. With due regard for the processes of logical thinking, it legitimately cannot be urged that conditions which produced the rule may now be invoked to destroy it.

The lower court, and counsel for the appellees in their argument here, frankly admitted that the statute does constitute a material impairment of the contract, but contended that such legislation is brought within the state power by the present emergency. If I understand the opinion just delivered, this court concedes that emergency does not create power, or increase granted power, or remove or diminish restrictions upon power granted or reserved. It then proceeds to say, however, that, while emergency does not create power, it may furnish the occasion for the exercise of power. I can only interpret what is said on that subject as meaning that, while an emergency does not diminish a restriction upon power, it furnishes an occasion for diminishing it; and this, as it seems to me, is merely to say the same thing by the use of another set of words, with the effect of affirming that which has just been denied.

It is quite true that an emergency may supply the occasion for the exercise of power, dependent upon the nature of the power and the intent of the Constitution with respect thereto. The emergency of war furnishes an occasion for the exercise of certain of the war powers. This the Constitution contemplates, since they cannot be exercised upon any other occasion. The existence of another kind of emergency authorizes the United States to protect each of the states of the Union against domestic violence. Const. art. 4, § 4. But we are here dealing, not with a power granted by the Federal Constitution, but with the state police power, which exists in its own right. Hence the question is, not whether an emergency furnishes the occasion for the exercise of that state power, but whether an emergency furnishes an occasion for the relaxation of the restrictions upon the power imposed by the contract impairment clause; and the difficulty is that the contract impairment clause forbids state action under any circumstances, if it have the effect of impairing the obligation of contracts. That clause restricts every state power in the particular specified, no matter what may be the occasion. It does not contemplate that an emergency shall furnish an occasion for softening the restriction or making it any the less a restriction upon state action in that contingency than it is under strictly normal conditions.

The Minnesota statute either impairs the obligation of contracts or it does not. If it does not, the occasion to which it relates becomes immaterial, since then the passage of the statute is the exercise of a normal, unrestricted, state power and requires no special occasion to render it effective. If it does, the emergency no more furnishes a proper occasion for its exercise than if the emergency were nonexistent. And so, while, in form, the suggested distinction seems to put us forward in a straight line, in reality it simply carries us back in a circle, like bewildered travelers lost in a wood, to the point where we parted company with the view of the state court.

If what has now been said is sound, as I think it is, we come to what really is the vital question in the case: Does the Minnesota statute constitute an impairment of the obligation of the contract now under review? In answering that question, we must first of all distinguish the present legislation from those statutes which, although interfering in some degree with the terms of contracts, or having the effect of entirely destroying them, have nevertheless been sustained as not impairing the obligation of contracts in the constitutional sense. Among these statutes are such as affect the remedy merely: "Whatever belongs merely to the remedy may be altered according to the will of the state, provided the alteration does not impair the obligation of the contract. But if that effect is produced, it is immaterial whether it is done by acting on the remedy or directly on the contract itself. In either case it is prohibited by the Constitution."

Another class of statutes is illustrated by those exempting from execution and sale certain classes of property, like the tools of an artisan. Chief Justice Taney, in Bronson v. Kinzie, supra, speaking obiter, said that a state might properly exempt necessary implements of agriculture, or the tool of a mechanic, or articles of necessity in household furniture. But this court, in Edwards v. Kearzey, supra, struck down a provision of the North Carolina Constitution which exempted every homestead, and the dwelling and buildings used therewith, not exceeding in value $1,000, on the ground of its unconstitutionality as applied to a contract already in existence. Referring to the opinion in Bronson v. Kinzie, the court said (page 604 of 96 U.S.) that the Chief Justice seems to have had in his mind the maxim "de minimis," etc. "Upon no other ground can any exemption be justified." It is quite true also that 'the reservation of essential attributes of sovereign power is also read into contracts'; and that the Legislature cannot 'bargain away the public health or the public morals.' General statutes to put an end to lotteries, the sale or manufacture of intoxicating liquors, the maintenance of nuisances, to protect the public safety, etc., although they have the indirect effect of absolutely destroying private contracts previously made in contemplation of a continuance of the state of affairs then in existence but subsequently prohibited, have been uniformly upheld as not violating the contract impairment clause. The distinction between legislation of that character and the Minnesota statute, however, is readily observable. It may be demonstrated by an example. A, engaged in the business of manufacturing intoxicating liquor within a state, makes a contract, we will suppose, with B to manufacture and deliver at a stipulated price and at some date in the future a quantity of whisky. Before the day arrives for the performance of the contract, the state passes a law prohibiting the manufacture and sale of intoxicating liquor. The contract immediately falls because its performance has ceased to be lawful. This is so because the contract is made upon the implied condition that a particular state of things shall continue to exist, "and when that state of things ceases to exist the bargain itself ceases to exist." Marshall v. Glanvill (1917) 2 K.B. 87, 91. In that case the plaintiff had been employed by the defendants upon a contract of service. While the contract was in force, the country became involved in the World War, and plaintiff was called into the military service. The court held that this rendered performance unlawful and that the contract was at an end.

The problem for our determination is whether the statute as construed and applied unreasonably infringes the liberty guaranteed to the plaintiff in error by the Fourteenth Amendment: "No state shall deprive any person of life, liberty or property without due process of law."

While this court has not attempted to define with exactness the liberty thus guaranteed, the term has received much consideration and some of the included things have been definitely stated. Without doubt, it denotes not merely freedom from bodily restraint but also the right of the individual to contract, to engage in any of the common occupations of life, to acquire useful knowledge, to marry, establish a home and bring up children, to worship God according to the dictates of his own conscience, and generally to enjoy those privileges long recognized at common law as essential to the orderly pursuit of happiness by free men.

The established doctrine is that this liberty may not be interfered with, under the guise of protecting the public interest, by legislative action which is arbitrary or without reasonable relation to some purpose within the competency of the state to effect. Determination by the Legislature of what constitutes proper exercise of police power is not final or conclusive but is subject to supervision by the courts. Lawton v. Steele, 152 U. S. 133, 137, 14 Sup. Ct. 499, 38 L. Ed. 385.

The present exigency is nothing new. From the beginning of our existence as a nation, periods of depression, of industrial failure, of financial distress, of unpaid and unpayable indebtedness, have alternated with years of plenty. The vital lesson that expenditure beyond income begets poverty, that public or private extravagance, financed by promises to pay, either must end in complete or partial repudiation or the promises be fulfilled by self-denial and painful effort, though constantly taught by bitter experience, seems never to be learned; and the attempt by legislative devices to shift the misfortune of the debtor to the shoulders of the creditor without coming into conflict with the contract impairment clause has been persistent and oft-repeated.

The defense of the Minnesota law is made upon grounds which were discountenanced by the makers of the Constitution and have many times been rejected by this Court. That defense should not now succeed because it constitutes an effort to overthrow the constitutional provision by an appeal to facts and circumstances identical with those which brought it into existence. With due regard for the processes of logical thinking, it legitimately cannot be urged that conditions which produced the rule may now be invoked to destroy it.

We come back, then, directly, to the question of impairment. As to that, the conclusion reached by the court here seems to be that the relief afforded by the statute does not contravene the constitutional provision because it is of a character appropriate to the emergency and allowed upon what are said to be reasonable conditions.

It is necessary, first of all, to describe the exact situation. Appellees obtained from appellant a loan of $3,800; and, to secure its payment, executed a mortgage upon real property consisting of land and a fourteen-room house and garage. The mortgage contained the conventional Minnesota provision for foreclosure by advertisement. The mortgagors agreed to pay the debt, together with interest and the taxes and insurance on the property. They defaulted; and, in strict accordance with the bargain, appellant foreclosed the mortgage by advertise-

ment and caused the premises to be sold. Appellant itself bought the property at the sale for a sum equal to the amount of the mortgage debt. The period of redemption from that sale was due to expire on May 2, 1933; and, assuming no redemption at the end of that day, under the law in force when the contract was made and when the property was sold and in accordance with the terms of the mortgage, appellant would at once have become the owner in fee and entitled to the immediate possession of the property. The statute here under attack was passed on April 18, 1933. It first recited and declared that an economic emergency existed. As applied to the present case, it arbitrarily extended the period of redemption expiring on May 2, 1933, to May 18, 1933—a period of sixteen days; and provided that the mortgagor might apply for a further extension to the district court of the county. That court was authorized to extend the period to a date not later than May 1, 1935, on the condition that the mortgagor should pay to the creditor all or a reasonable part of the income or rental value, as to the court might appear just and equitable, toward the payment of taxes, insurance, interest and principal mortgage indebtedness, and at such times and in such manner as should be fixed by the court. The court to whom the application in this case was made extended the time until May 1, 1935, upon the condition that payment by the mortgagor of the rental value, $40 per month, should be made.

It will be observed that, whether the statute operated directly upon the contract or indirectly by modifying the remedy, its effect was to extend the period of redemption absolutely for a period of sixteen days, and conditionally for a period of two years. That this brought about a substantial change in the terms of the contract reasonably cannot be denied. If the statute was meant to operate only upon the remedy, it nevertheless, as applied, had the effect of destroying for two years the right of the creditor to enjoy the ownership of the property, and consequently the correlative power, for that period, to occupy, sell, or otherwise dispose of it as might seem fit. This postponement, if it had been unconditional, undoubtedly would have constituted an unconstitutional impairment of the obligation. This Court so decided in Bronson v. Kinzie, supra, where the period of redemption was extended for a period of only twelve months after a sale under a decree; in Howard v. Bugbee, supra, where the extension was for two years; and in Barnitz v. Beverly, supra, where the period was extended for eighteen months. Those cases, we may assume, still embody the law, since they are not overruled.

The only substantial difference between those cases and the present one is that here the extension of the period of redemption and postponement of the creditor's ownership is accompanied by the condition that the rental value of the property shall, in the meantime, be paid. Assuming, for the moment, that a statute extending the period of redemption may be upheld if something of commensurate value be given the creditor by way of compensation, a conclusion that payment of the rental value during the two-year period of postponement is even the approximate equivalent of immediate ownership and possession is purely gratuitous.

How can such payment be regarded, in any sense, as compensation for the postponement of the contract right? The ownership of the property to which petitioner was entitled carried with it, not only the right to occupy or sell it, but,

ownership being retained, the right to the rental value as well. So that in the last analysis petitioner simply is allowed to retain a part of what is its own as compensation for surrendering the remainder. Moreover, it cannot be foreseen what will happen to the property during that long period of time. The buildings may deteriorate in quality; the value of the property may fall to a sum far below the purchase price; the financial needs of appellant may become so pressing as to render it urgently necessary that the property shall be sold for whatever it may bring.

However these or other supposable contingencies may be, the statute denies appellant for a period of two years the ownership and possession of the property—an asset which, in any event, is of substantial character, and which possibly may turn out to be of great value. The statute, therefore, is not merely a modification of the remedy; it effects a material and injurious change in the obligation. The legally enforceable right of the creditor when the statute was passed was, at once upon default of redemption, to become the fee-simple owner of the property. Extension of the time for redemption for two years, whatever compensation be given in its place, destroys that specific right and the correlative obligation, and does so none the less though it assume to create in invitum another and different right and obligation of equal value. Certainly, if A should contract with B to deliver a specified quantity of wheat on or before a given date, legislation, however much it might purport to act upon the remedy, which had the effect of permitting the contract to be discharged by the delivery of corn of equal value, would subvert the constitutional restriction.

A statute which materially delays enforcement of the mortgagee's contractual right of ownership and possession does not modify the remedy merely; it destroys, for the period of delay, all remedy so far as the enforcement of that right is concerned. The phrase "obligation of a contract" in the constitutional sense imports a legal duty to perform the specified obligation of that contract, not to substitute and perform, against the will of one of the parties, a different, albeit equally valuable, obligation. And a state, under the contract impairment clause, has no more power to accomplish such a substitution than has one of the parties to the contract against the will of the other. It cannot do so either by acting directly upon the contract or by bringing about the result under the guise of a statute in form acting only upon the remedy. If it could, the efficacy of the constitutional restriction would, in large measure, be made to disappear.

As this court has well said, whatever tends to postpone or retard the enforcement of a contract, to that extent weakens the obligation. According to one Latin proverb, "He who gives quickly, gives twice," and according to another, "He who pays too late, pays less." "Any authorization of the postponement of payment, or of means by which such postponement may be effected, is in conflict with the constitutional inhibition." Louisiana ex rel. Ranger v. New Orleans, 102 U.S. 203, 207, 26 L.Ed. 132. I am not able to see any real distinction between a statute which in substantive terms alters the obligation of a debtor-creditor contract so as to extend the time of its performance for a period of two years and a statute which, though in terms acting upon the remedy, is aimed at the obligation (as distinguished, for example, from the judicial procedure incident to the enforcement thereof), and which does in fact withhold from the creditor, for the same period of time, the stipulated fruits of his contract.

I quite agree with the opinion of the Court that whether the legislation under review is wise or unwise is a matter with which we have nothing to do. Whether it is likely to work well or work ill presents a question entirely irrelevant to the issue. The only legitimate inquiry we can make is whether it is constitutional. If it is not, its virtues, if it have any, cannot save it; if it is, its faults cannot be invoked to accomplish its destruction.

If the provisions of the Constitution be not upheld when they pinch as well as when they comfort, they may as well be abandoned. Being unable to reach any other conclusion than that the Minnesota statute infringes the constitutional restriction under review, I have no choice but to say so.

I am authorized to say that Mr. Justice VAN DEVANTER, Mr. Justice McREYNOLDS, and Mr. Justice BUTLER concur in this opinion.

QUESTIONS AND DISCUSSION POINTS

1. Can you identify the various argument forms employed by both the Majority and Dissenting opinions?

2. Identify the strongest and weakest argument for each side of the question posed by this case.

3. One way to characterize the majority's position is to say that they regard the Minnesota statute as a temporary, emergency measure. What arguments do the Majority advance in support of its conclusion that such measures are constitutionally permissible?

4. Does the Dissent's argument on the history of debtor-creditor relations undermine the Majority's position?

5. Even if you are convinced by the Majority's prudential arguments, are there any limits to this form of argument?

~

MEYER
v. STATE OF NEBRASKA
Supreme Court of the United States
262 U.S. 390 (1923)

Mr. Justice McREYNOLDS delivered the opinion of the Court.

Plaintiff in error was tried and convicted in the district court for Hamilton County, Nebraska, under an information which charged that on May 25, 1920, while an instructor in Zion Parochial School he unlawfully taught the subject of reading in the German language to Raymond Parpart, a child of 10 years, who had not attained and successfully passed the eighth grade. The information is based upon "An act relating to the teaching of foreign languages in the state of Nebraska," approved April 9, 1919 (Laws 1919, c. 249), which follows:

Section 1. No person, individually or as a teacher, shall, in any private, denominational, parochial or public school, teach any subject to any person in any language than the English language. Sec. 2. Languages, other than the English language, may be taught as languages only after a pupil shall have attained and successfully passed the eighth grade as evidenced by a certificate of graduation issued by the county superintendent of the county in which the child resides. Sec. 3. Any person who violates any of the pro-

visions of this act shall be deemed guilty of a misdemeanor and upon conviction, shall be subject to a fine of not less than twenty-five dollars ($25), nor more than one hundred dollars ($100), or be confined in the county jail for any period not exceeding thirty days for each offense. Sec. 4. Whereas, an emergency exists, this act shall be in force from and after its passage and approval.

The Supreme Court of the state affirmed the judgment of conviction. 107 Neb. 657, 187 N. W. 100. It declared the offense charged and established was "the direct and intentional teaching of the German language as a distinct subject to a child who had not passed the eighth grade," in the parochial school maintained by Zion Evangelical Lutheran Congregation, a collection of Biblical stories being used therefore. And it held that the statute forbidding this did not conflict with the Fourteenth Amendment, but was a valid exercise of the police power. The following excerpts from the opinion sufficiently indicate the reasons advanced to support the conclusion:

The salutary purpose of the statute is clear. The Legislature had seen the baneful effects of permitting foreigners, who had taken residence in this country, to rear and educate their children in the language of their native land. The result of that condition was found to be inimical to our own safety. To allow the children of foreigners, who had emigrated here, to be taught from early childhood the language of the country of their parents was to rear them with that language as their mother tongue. It was to educate them so that they must always think in that language, and, as a consequence, naturally inculcate in them the ideas and sentiments foreign to the best interests of this country.

The statute, therefore, was intended not only to require that the education of all children be conducted in the English language, but that, until they had grown into that language and until it had become a part of them, they should not in the schools be taught any other language. The obvious purpose of this statute was that the English language should be and become the mother tongue of all children reared in this state. The enactment of such a statute comes reasonably within the police power of the state. Pohl v. State, 132 N.E. (Ohio) 20; State v. Bartels, 181 N.W. (Ia.) 508.

It is suggested that the law is an unwarranted restriction, in that it applies to all citizens of the state and arbitrarily interferes with the rights of citizens who are not of foreign ancestry, and prevents them, without reason, from having their children taught foreign languages in school. That argument is not well taken, for it assumes that every citizen finds himself restrained by the statute. The hours which a child is able to devote to study in the confinement of school are limited. It must have ample time for exercise or play. Its daily capacity for learning is comparatively small. A selection of sub-

jects for its education, therefore, from among the many that might be taught, is obviously necessary. The legislature no doubt had in mind the practical operation of the law. The law affects few citizens, except those of foreign lineage. Other citizens, in their selection of studies, except perhaps in rare instances, have never deemed it of importance to teach their children foreign languages before such children have reached the eighth grade. In the legislative mind, the salutary effect of the statute no doubt outweighed the restriction upon the citizens generally, which, it appears, was a restriction of no real consequence.

The problem for our determination is whether the statute as construed and applied unreasonably infringes the liberty guaranteed to the plaintiff in error by the Fourteenth Amendment. "No State shall . . . deprive any person of life, liberty, or property, without due process of law."

While this Court has not attempted to define with exactness the liberty thus guaranteed, the term has received much consideration and some of the included things have been definitely stated. Without doubt, it denotes not merely freedom from bodily restraint but also the right of the individual to contract, to engage in any of the common occupations of life, to acquire useful knowledge, to marry, establish a home and bring up children, to worship God according to the dictates of his own conscience, and generally to enjoy those privileges long recognized at common law as essential to the orderly pursuit of happiness by free men. Slaughter-House Cases, 16 Wall. 36; Butchers' Union Co. v. Crescent City Co., 111 U.S. 746; Yick W v. Hopkins, 118 U.S. 356; Minnesota v. Barber, 136 U.S. 313; Allgeyer v. Louisiana, 165 U.S. 578; Lochner v. New York, 198 U.S. 45; Twining v. New Jersey, 211 U.S. 78; Chicago, Burlington & Quincy R.R. Co. v. McGuire, 219 U.S. 549; Truax v. Raich, 239 U.S. 33; Adams v. Tanner, 244 U.S. 590; New York Life Ins. Co. v. Dodge, 246 U.S. 357; Truax v. Corrigan, 257 U.S. 312; Adkins v. Children's Hospital, 216 U.S. 525; Wyeth v. Cambridge Board of Health, 200 Mass. 474. The established doctrine is that this liberty may not be interfered with, under the guise of protecting the public interest, by legislative action which is arbitrary or without reasonable relation to some purpose within the competency of the State to effect. Determination by the legislature of what constitutes proper exercise of police power is not final or conclusive but is subject to supervision by the courts. Lawton v. Steele, 152 U.S. 133, 137.

The American people have always regarded education and acquisition of knowledge as matters of supreme importance which should be diligently promoted. The Ordinance of 1787 declares, "Religion, morality, and knowledge being necessary to good government and the happiness of mankind, schools and the means of education shall forever be encouraged." Corresponding to the right of control, it is the natural duty of the parent to give his children education suitable to their station in life; and nearly all the States, including Nebraska, enforce this obligation by compulsory laws.

Practically, education of the young is only possible in schools conducted by especially qualified persons who devote themselves thereto. The calling always has been regarded as useful and honorable, essential, indeed, to the public welfare. Mere knowledge of the German language cannot reasonably be regarded as harmful. Heretofore it has been commonly looked upon as helpful and desirable.

Plaintiff in error taught this language in school as part of his occupation. His right thus to teach and the right of parents to engage him so to instruct their children, we think, are within the liberty of the Amendment.

The challenged statute forbids the teaching in school of any subject except in English; also the teaching of any other language until the pupil has attained and successfully passed the eighth grade, which is not usually accomplished before the age of twelve. The Supreme Court of the State has held that "the so-called ancient or dead languages" are not "within the spirit or the purpose of the act." Nebraska District of Evangelical Lutheran Synod v. McKelvie, 187 N.W. 927. Latin, Greek, Hebrew are not proscribed; but German, French, Spanish, Italian and every other alien speech are within the ban. Evidently the legislature has attempted materially to interfere with the calling of modern language teachers, with the opportunities of pupils to acquire knowledge, and with the power of parents to control the education of their own.

It is said the purpose of the legislation was to promote civic development by inhibiting training and education of the immature in foreign tongues and ideals before they could learn English and acquire American ideals; and "that the English language should be and become the mother tongue of all children reared in this State." It is also affirmed that the foreign born population is very large, that certain communities commonly use foreign words, follow foreign leaders, move in a foreign atmosphere, and that the children are thereby hindered from becoming citizens of the most useful type and the public safety is imperiled.

That the State may do much, go very far, indeed, in order to improve the quality of its citizens, physically, mentally and morally, is clear; but the individual has certain fundamental rights which must be respected. The protection of the Constitution extends to all, to those who speak other languages as well as to those born with English on the tongue. Perhaps it would be highly advantageous if all had ready understanding of our ordinary speech, but this cannot be coerced by methods which conflict with the Constitution—a desirable end cannot be promoted by prohibited means.

For the welfare of his Ideal Commonwealth, Plato suggested a law which should provide: "That the wives of our guardians are to be common, and their children are to be common, and no parent is to know his own child, nor any child his parent. . . . The proper officers will take the offspring of the good parents to the pen or fold, and there they will deposit them with certain nurses who dwell in a separate quarter; but the offspring of the inferior, or of the better when they chance to be deformed, will be put away in some mysterious, unknown place, as they should be." In order to submerge the individual and develop ideal citizens, Sparta assembled the males at seven into barracks and intrusted their subsequent education and training to official guardians. Although such measures have been deliberately approved by men of great genius, their ideas touching the relation between individual and State were wholly different from those upon which our institutions rest; and it hardly will be affirmed that any legislature could impose such restrictions upon the people of a State without doing violence to both letter and spirit of the Constitution.

The desire of the legislature to foster a homogeneous people with American ideals prepared readily to understand current discussions of civic matters is easy to appreciate. Unfortunate experiences during the late war and aversion toward every characteristic of truculent adversaries were certainly enough to quicken that aspiration. But the means adopted, we think, exceed the limitations upon the power of the State and conflict with rights assured to plaintiff in error. The interference is plain enough and no adequate reason therefor in time of peace and domestic tranquility has been shown.

The power of the State to compel attendance at some school and to make reasonable regulations for all schools, including a requirement that they shall give instructions in English, is not questioned. Nor has challenge been made of the State's power to prescribe a curriculum for institutions which it supports. Those matters are not within the present controversy. Our concern is with the prohibition approved by the Supreme Court. Adams v. Tanner, supra, p. 594, pointed out that mere abuse incident to an occupation ordinarily useful is not enough to justify its abolition, although regulation may be entirely proper. No emergency has arisen which renders knowledge by a child of some language other than English so clearly harmful as to justify its inhibition with the consequent infringement of rights long freely enjoyed. We are constrained to conclude that the statute as applied is arbitrary and without reasonable relation to any end within the competency of the State.

As the statute undertakes to interfere only with teaching which involves a modern language, leaving complete freedom as to other matters, there seems no adequate foundation for the suggestion that the purpose was to protect the child's health by limiting his mental activities. It is well known that proficiency in a foreign language seldom comes to one not instructed at an early age, and experience shows that this is not injurious to the health, morals or understanding of the ordinary child.

The judgment of the court below must be reversed and the cause remanded for further proceedings not inconsistent with this opinion.

Reversed.

QUESTIONS AND DISCUSSION POINTS

1. Can you identify the purpose of the statute the Court found unconstitutional? Is this purpose a legitimate purpose?

2. If you think there is a legitimate purpose to the statute in question, is the problem simply the means by which that purpose was effected, or was the statute struck down on other grounds?

3. The Court says that its inquiry concerns "liberty." What sort of liberty is this? Can you imagine other sorts of activities that might fall under this concept?

4. What is the State's argument regarding citizenship? Why does the Court reject it?

5. What if the children in question were instructed in German in all their subjects? How would the Court's analysis change, if at all?

∽

EVERSON
v. BOARD OF EDUCATION OF EWING TP. et al.
Supreme Court of the United States
330 U.S. 1 (1947)

Mr. Justice BLACK delivered the opinion of the Court.

A New Jersey statute authorizes its local school districts to make rules and contracts for the transportation of children to and from schools.[1] The appellee, a township board of education, acting pursuant to this statute authorized reimbursement to parents of money expended by them for the bus transportation of their children on regular busses operated by the public transportation system. Part

---

1. "Whenever in any district there are children living remote from any schoolhouse, the board of education of the district may make rules and contracts for the transportation of such children to and from school, including the transportation of school children to and from school other than a public school, except such school as is operated for profit in whole or in part.

"When any school district provides any transportation for public school children to and from school, transportation from any point in such established school route to any other point in such established school route shall be supplied to school children residing in such school district in going to and from school other than a public school, except such school as is operated for profit in whole or in part." New Jersey Laws 1941, c. 191, p. 581, N.J.Rev.Stat. 18:14–8, N.J.S.A.

of this money was for the payment of transportation of some children in the community to Catholic parochial schools. These church schools give their students, in addition to secular education, regular religious instruction conforming to the religious tenets and modes of worship of the Catholic Faith. The superintendent of these schools is a Catholic priest.

The appellant, in his capacity as a district taxpayer, filed suit in a State court challenging the right of the Board to reimburse parents of parochial school students. He contended that the statute and the resolution passed pursuant to it violated both the State and the Federal Constitutions. That court held that the legislature was without power to authorize such payment under the State constitution. 132 N.J.L. 98, 39 A.2d 75. The New Jersey Court of Errors and Appeals reversed, holding that neither the statute nor the resolution passed pursuant to it

was in conflict with the State constitution or the provisions of the Federal Constitution in issue. 133 N.J.L. 350, 44 A.2d 333. The case is here on appeal under 28 U.S.C. § 344(a), 28 U.S.C.A. § 344(a).

Since there has been no attack on the statute on the ground that a part of its language excludes children attending private schools operated for profit from enjoying state payment for their transportation, we need not consider this exclusionary language; it has no relevancy to any constitutional question here presented.[2] Furthermore, if the exclusion clause had been properly challenged, we do not know whether New Jersey's highest court would construe its statutes as precluding payment of the school transportation of any group of pupils, even those of a private school run for profit.[3]

Consequently, we put to one side the question as to the validity of the statute against the claim that it does not authorize payment for the transportation generally of school children in New Jersey.

The only contention here is that the State statute and the resolution, in so far as they authorized reimbursement to parents of children attending parochial schools, violate the Federal Constitution in

---

2. Appellant does not challenge the New Jersey statute or the resolution on the ground that either violates the equal protection clause of the Fourteenth Amendment by excluding payment for the transportation of any pupil who attends a "private school run for profit." Although the township resolution authorized reimbursement only for parents of public and Catholic school pupils, appellant does not allege, nor is there anything in the record which would offer the slightest support to an allegation, that there were any children in the township who attended or would have attended, but for want of transportation, any but public and Catholic schools. It will be appropriate to consider the exclusion of students of private schools operated for profit when and if it is proved to have occurred, is made the basis of a suit by one in a position to challenge it, and New Jersey's highest court has ruled adversely to the challenger. Striking down a state law is not a matter of such light moment that it should be done by a federal court ex mero motu on a postulate neither charged nor proved, but which rests on nothing but a possibility. Cf. Liverpool, New York & Philadelphia Steamship Co. v. Com'rs of Emigration, 113 U.S. 33, 39, 5 S.Ct. 352, 355, 28 L.Ed. 899.

---

3. It might hold the excepting clause to be invalid, and sustain the statute with that clause excised. Section 1:1–10 N.J.Rev.Stat., N.J.S.A., provides with regard to any statute that if "any provision thereof, shall be declared to be unconstitutional . . . in whole or in part, by a court of competent jurisdiction, such . . . article shall, to the extent that it is not unconstitutional, . . . be enforced . . . ." The opinion of the Court of Errors and Appeals in this very case suggests that state law now authorizes transportation of all pupils. Its opinion stated: "Since we hold that the legislature may appropriate general state funds or authorize the use of local funds for the transportation of pupils to any school, we conclude that such authorization of the use of local funds is likewise authorized by P.L.1941, Chapter 191, and R.S. 18:7–78." 133 N.J.L. 350, 354, 44 A.2d 333, 337.

these two respects, which to some extent, overlap. First. They authorize the State to take by taxation the private property of some and bestow it upon others, to be used for their own private purposes. This, it is alleged violates the due process clause of the Fourteenth Amendment. Second. The statute and the resolution forced inhabitants to pay taxes to help support and maintain schools which are dedicated to, and which regularly teach, the Catholic Faith. This is alleged to be a use of State power to support church schools contrary to the prohibition of the First Amendment which the Fourteenth Amendment made applicable to the states.

First. The due process argument that the State law taxes some people to help others carry out their private purposes is framed in two phases. The first phase is that a state cannot tax A to reimburse B for the cost of transporting his children to church schools. This is said to violate the due process clause because the children are sent to these church schools to satisfy the personal desires of their parents, rather than the public's interest in the general education of all children. This argument, if valid, would apply equally to prohibit state payment for the transportation of children to any non-public school, whether operated by a church, or any other nongovernment individual or group. But, the New Jersey legislature has decided that a public purpose will be served by using tax-raised funds to pay the bus fares of all school children, including those who attend parochial schools. The New Jersey Court of Errors and Appeals has reached the same conclusion. The fact that a state law, passed to satisfy a public need, coincides with the personal desires of the individuals most directly affected is certainly an inadequate reason for us to say that a legislature has erroneously appraised the public need.

It is true that this Court has, in rare instances, struck down state statutes on the ground that the purpose for which tax-raised funds were to be expended was not a public one. Citizens' Savings & Loan Association v. City of Topeka, 20 Wall. 655, 22 L.Ed. 455; City of Parkersburg v. Brown, 106 U.S. 487, 1 S.Ct. 442, 27 L.Ed. 238; Thompson v. Consolidated Gas Utilities Corp., 300 U.S. 55, 57 S.Ct. 364, 81 L.Ed. 510. But the Court has also pointed out that this far-reaching authority must be exercised with the most extreme caution. Green v. Frazier, 253 U.S. 233, 240, 40 S.Ct. 499, 501, 64 L.Ed. 878. Otherwise, a state's power to legislate for the public welfare might be seriously curtailed, a power which is a primary reason for the existence of states. Changing local conditions create new local problems which may lead a state's people and its local authorities to believe that laws authorizing new types of public services are necessary to promote the general well-being of the people. The Fourteenth Amendment did not strip the states of their power to meet problems previously left for individual solution. Davidson v. New Orleans, 96 U.S. 97, 103, 104, 24 L.Ed. 616; Barbier v. Connolly, 113 U.S. 27, 31, 32, 5 S.Ct. 357, 360, 28 L.Ed. 923; Fallbrook Irrigation District v. Bradley, 164 U.S. 112, 157, 158, 17 S.Ct. 56, 62, 63, 41 L.Ed. 369.

It is much too late to argue that legislation intended to facilitate the opportunity of children to get a secular education serves no public purpose. Cochran v. Louisiana State Board of Education, 281 U.S. 370, 50 S.Ct. 335, 74 L.Ed. 913; Holmes, J., in Interstate Consolidated Street Ry. Co. v. Commonwealth of Massachusetts, 207 U.S. 79, 87, 28 S.Ct. 26, 27, 52 L.Ed. 111, 12 Ann.Cas. 555. See opinion of Cooley, J., in Stuart v. School District No. 1 of Village of Kalamazoo, 1878, 30 Mich. 69. The same thing is no less true of legislation to reimburse needy parents, or all parents, for payment of the fares of their children so that they can ride in public busses to and from schools rather than run the risk of traffic and other hazards incident to walking or "hitchhiking." See Barbier v. Connolly, supra, 113 U.S. at page 31, 5 S.Ct. at page 359. See also cases collected 63 A.L.R. 413; 118 A.L.R. 806.

Nor does it follow that a law has a private rather than a public purpose because it provides that tax-raised funds will be paid to reimburse individuals on account of money spent by them in a way which furthers a public program. See Carmichael v. Southern Coal & Coke Co., 301 U.S. 495, 518, 57 S.Ct. 868, 876, 81 L.Ed. 1245, 109 A.L.R. 1327. Subsidies and loans to individuals such as farmers and home owners, and to privately owned transportation systems, as well as many other kinds of businesses, have been commonplace practices in our state and national history.

Insofar as the second phase of the due process argument may differ from the first, it is by suggesting that taxation for transportation of children to church schools constitutes support of a religion by the State. But if the law is invalid for this reason, it is because it violates the First Amendment's prohibition against the establishment of religion by law. This is the exact question raised by appellant's second contention, to consideration of which we now turn.

Second. The New Jersey statute is challenged as a "law respecting an establishment of religion." The First Amendment, as made applicable to the states by the Fourteenth, Murdock v. Commonwealth of Pennsylvania, 319 U.S. 105, 63 S.Ct. 870, 872, 87 L.Ed. 1292, 146 A.L.R. 81, commands that a state "shall make no law respecting an establishment of religion, or prohibiting the free exercise thereof." These words of the First Amendment reflected in the minds of early Americans a

vivid mental picture of conditions and practices which they fervently wished to stamp out in order to preserve liberty for themselves and for their posterity. Doubtless their goal has not been entirely reached; but so far has the Nation moved toward it that the expression "law respecting an establishment of religion," probably does not so vividly remind present-day Americans of the evils, fears, and political problems that caused that expression to be written into our Bill of Rights. Whether this New Jersey law is one respecting the "establishment of religion" requires an understanding of the meaning of that language, particularly with respect to the imposition of taxes. Once again,[4] there-

---

4. See Reynolds v. United States, 98 U.S. 145, 162, 25 L.Ed. 244; cf. Knowlton v. Moore, 178 U.S. 41, 89, 106, 20 S.Ct. 747, 766, 772, 44. A large proportion of the early settlers of this country came here from Europe to escape the bondage of laws which compelled them to support and attend government favored churches. The centuries immediately before and contemporaneous with the colonization of America had been filled with turmoil, civil strife, and persecutions, generated in large part by established sects determined to maintain their absolute political and religious supremacy. With the power of government supporting them, at various times and places, Catholics had persecuted Protestants, Protestants had persecuted Catholics, Protestant sects had persecuted other Protestant sects, Catholics of one shade of belief had persecuted Catholics of another shade of belief, and all of these had from time to time persecuted Jews. In efforts to force loyalty to whatever religious group happened to be on top and in league with the government of a particular time and place, men and women had been fined, cast in jail, cruelly tortured, and killed. Among the offenses for which these punishments had been inflicted were such things as speaking disrespectfully of the views of ministers of government-established churches, nonattendance at those churches, expressions of non-belief in their doctrines, and failure to pay taxes and tithes to support them.

fore, it is not inappropriate briefly to review the background and environment of the period in which that constitutional language was fashioned and adopted.

These practices of the old world were transplanted to and began to thrive in the soil of the new America. The very charters granted by the English Crown to the individuals and companies designated to make the laws which would control the destinies of the colonials authorized these individuals and companies to erect religious establishments which all, whether believers or non-believers, would be required to support and attend. An exercise of this authority was accompanied by a repetition of many of the old world practices and persecutions. Catholics found themselves hounded and proscribed because of their faith; Quakers who followed their conscience went to jail; Baptists were peculiarly obnoxious to certain dominant Protestant sects; men and women of varied faiths who happened to be in a minority in a particular locality were persecuted because they steadfastly persisted in worshipping God only as their own consciences dictated. And all of these dissenters were compelled to pay tithes and taxes to support government-sponsored churches whose ministers preached inflammatory sermons designed to strengthen and consolidate the established faith by generating a burning hatred against dissenters.

[P]arents might be reluctant to permit their children to attend schools which the state had cut off from such general government services as ordinary police and fire protection, connections for sewage disposal, public highways and sidewalks. Of course, cutting off church schools from these services, so separate and so indisputably marked off from the religious function, would make it far more difficult for the schools to operate. But such is obviously not the purpose of the First Amendment. That Amendment requires the state to be a neutral in its relations with groups of religious believers and non-believers; it does not require the state to be their adversary. State power is no more to be used so as to handicap religions, than it is to favor them. This Court has said that parents may, in the discharge of their duty under state compulsory education laws, send their children to a religious rather than a public school if the school meets the secular educational requirements which the state has power to impose. See Pierce v. Society of Sisters, 268 U.S. 510, 45 S.Ct. 571, 69 L.Ed. 1070, 39 A.L.R. 468. It appears that these parochial schools meet New Jersey's requirements. The State contributes no money to the schools. It does not support them. Its legislation, as applied, does no more than provide a general program to help parents get their children, regardless of their religion, safely and expeditiously to and from accredited schools.

The First Amendment has erected a wall between church and state. That wall must be kept high and impregnable. We could not approve the slightest breach. New Jersey has not breached it here. Affirmed.

Mr. Justice JACKSON, dissenting.

I find myself, contrary to first impressions, unable to join in this decision. I have a sympathy, though it is not ideological, with Catholic citizens who are compelled by law to pay taxes for public schools, and also feel constrained by conscience and discipline to support other schools for their own children. Such relief to them as this case involves is not in itself a serious burden to taxpayers and I had assumed it to be as little serious in principle. Study of this case convinces me otherwise. The Court's opinion marshals every argument in favor of state aid and puts the case in its most favorable light, but much of its reasoning confirms my conclusions that there are no good grounds upon which to support the present legislation. In fact, the undertones of the opinion, advocating complete and uncompromising separation of Church from State, seem utterly discordant with its conclusion yielding support to their commingling in educational matters. The case which irresistibly comes to mind as the most fitting precedent is that of Julia who, according to Byron's reports, "whispering 'I will ne'er consent,'—consented."

The Court sustains this legislation by assuming two deviations from the facts of this particular case; first, it assumes a state of facts the record does not support, and secondly, it refuses to consider facts which are inescapable on the record.

The Court concludes that this "legislation, as applied, does no more than provide a general program to help parents get their children, regardless of their religion, safely and expeditiously to and from accredited schools," and it draws a comparison between "state provisions intended to guarantee free transportation" for school children with services such as police and fire protection, and implies that we are here dealing with "laws authorizing new types of public services. . . ." This hypothesis permeates the opinion. The facts will not bear that construction.

The Township of Ewing is not furnishing transportation to the children in any form; it is not operating school busses itself or contracting for their operation; and it is not performing any public service of any kind with this tax-

payer's money. All school children are left to ride as ordinary paying passengers on the regular busses operated by the public transportation system. What the Township does, and what the taxpayer complains of, is at stated intervals to reimburse parents for the fares paid, provided the children attend either public schools or Catholic Church schools. This expenditure of tax funds has no possible effect on the child's safety or expedition in transit. As passengers on the public busses they travel as fast and no faster, and are as safe and no safer, since their parents are reimbursed as before. In addition to thus assuming a type of service that does not exist, the Court also insists that we must close our eyes to a discrimination which does exist.

The resolution which authorizes disbursement of this taxpayer's money limits reimbursement to those who attend public schools and Catholic schools. That is the way the Act is applied to this taxpayer.

The New Jersey Act in question makes the character of the school, not the needs of the children determine the eligibility of parents to reimbursement. The Act permits payment for transportation to parochial schools or public schools but prohibits it to private schools operated in whole or in part for profit. Children often are sent to private schools because their parents feel that they require more individual instruction than public schools can provide, or because they are backward or defective and need special attention. If all children of the state were objects of impartial solicitude, no reason is obvious for denying transportation reimbursement to students of this class, for these often are as needy and as worthy as those who go to public or parochial schools. Refusal to reimburse those who attend such schools is understandable only in the light of a purpose to aid the schools, because the state might well abstain from aiding a profit-making private enterprise. Thus, under the Act and resolution brought to us by this case children are classified according to the schools they attend and are to be aided if they attend the public schools or private Catholic schools, and they are not allowed to be aided if they attend private secular schools or private religious schools of other faiths.

Of course, this case is not one of a Baptist or a Jew or an Episcopalian or a pupil of a private school complaining of discrimination. It is one of a taxpayer urging that he is being taxed for an unconstitutional purpose. I think he is entitled to have us consider the Act just as it is written. The statement by the New Jersey court that it holds the Legislature may authorize use of local funds "for the transportation of pupils to any school," in view of the other constitutional views expressed, is not a holding that this Act authorizes transportation of *all* pupils to *all* schools. As applied to this taxpayer by the action he complains of, certainly the Act does not authorize reimbursement to those who choose any alternative to the public school except Catholic Church schools.

If we are to decide this case on the facts before us, our question is simply this: Is it constitutional to tax this complainant to pay the cost of carrying pupils to Church schools of one specified denomination?

Whether the taxpayer constitutionally can be made to contribute aid to parents of students because of their attendance at parochial schools depends upon the nature of those schools and their relation to the Church. The Constitution says nothing of education. It lays no obligation on the states to provide schools and does not undertake to regulate state systems of education if they see fit to maintain them. But they cannot, through school policy any more than through other means, invade rights secured to citizens by the Constitution of the United States. West Virginia State Board of Education v. Barnette, 319 U.S. 624. One of our basic rights is to be free of taxation to support a transgression of the constitutional command that the authorities "shall make no law respecting an establishment of religion, or prohibiting the free exercise thereof. . . ." U.S. Const., Amend. I; Cantwell v. Connecticut, 310 U.S. 296.

The function of the Church school is a subject on which this record is meager. It shows only that the schools are under superintendence of a priest and that "religion is taught as part of the curriculum." But we know that such schools are parochial only in name—they, in fact, represent a world-wide and age-old policy of the Roman Catholic Church. Under the rubric "Catholic Schools," the Canon Law of the Church, by which all Catholics are bound, provides:

> "1215. Catholic children are to be educated in schools where not only nothing contrary to Catholic faith and morals is taught, but rather in schools where religious and moral training occupy the first place. . . . (Canon 1372.)"

> "1216. In every elementary school the children must, according to their age, be instructed in Christian doctrine.

> "The young people who attend the higher schools are to receive a deeper religious knowledge, and the bishops shall appoint priests qualified for such work by their learning and piety. (Canon 1373.)"

> "1217. Catholic children shall not at-

tend non-Catholic, indifferent, schools that are mixed, that is to say, schools open to Catholics and non-Catholics alike. The bishop of the diocese only has the right, in harmony with the instructions of the Holy See, to decide under what circumstances, and with what safeguards to prevent loss of faith, it may be tolerated that Catholic children go to such schools. (Canon 1374.)"

"1224. The religious teaching of youth in any schools is subject to the authority and inspection of the Church.

"The local Ordinaries have the right and duty to watch that nothing is taught contrary to faith or good morals, in any of the schools of their territory.

"They, moreover, have the right to approve the books of Christian doctrine and the teachers of religion, and to demand, for the sake of safeguarding religion and morals, the removal of teachers and books. (Canon 1381.)" (Woywod, Rev. Stanislaus, The New Canon Law, under imprimatur of Most Rev. Francis J. Spellman, Archbishop of New York and others, 1940.)

It is no exaggeration to say that the whole historic conflict in temporal policy between the Catholic Church and non-Catholics comes to a focus in their respective school policies. The Roman Catholic Church, counseled by experience in many ages and many lands and with all sorts and conditions of men, takes what, from the viewpoint of its own progress and the success of its mission, is a wise estimate of the importance of education to religion. It does not leave the individual to pick up religion by chance. It relies on early and indelible indoctrination in the faith and order of the Church by the word and example of persons consecrated to the task.

Our public school, if not a product of Protestantism, at least is more consistent with it than with the Catholic culture and scheme of values. It is a relatively recent development dating from about 1840. It is organized on the premise that secular education can be isolated from all religious teaching so that the school can inculcate all needed temporal knowledge and also maintain a strict and lofty neutrality as to religion. The assumption is that after the individual has been instructed in worldly wisdom he will be better fitted to choose his religion. Whether such a disjunction is possible, and if possible whether it is wise, are questions I need not try to answer.

I should be surprised if any Catholic would deny that the parochial school is a vital, if not the most vital, part of the Romand Catholic Church. If put to the choice, that venerable institution, I should expect, would forego its whole service for mature persons before it would give up education of the young, and it would be a wise choice. Its growth and cohesion, discipline and loyalty, spring from its schools. Catholic education is the rock on which the whole structure rests, and to render tax aid to its Church school is indistinguishable to me from rendering the same aid to the Church itself.

It is of no importance in this situation whether the beneficiary of this expenditure of tax-raised funds is primarily the parochial school and incidentally the pupil, or whether the aid is directly bestowed on the pupil with indirect benefits to the school. The state cannot maintain a Church and it can no more tax its citizens to furnish free carriage to those who attend a Church. The prohibition against establishment of religion cannot be circumvented by a subsidy, bonus or reimbursement of expense to individuals for receiving religious instruction and indoctrination.

The Court, however, compares this to other subsidies and loans to individuals and says, "Nor does it follow that a law has a private rather than a public purpose because it provides that tax-raised funds will be paid to reimburse individuals on account of money spent by them in a way which furthers a public program. See Carmichael v. Southern Coal & Coke Co., 301 U.S. 495, 518." Of course, the state may pay out tax-raised funds to relieve pauperism, but it may not under our Constitution do so to induce or reward piety. It may spend funds to secure old age against want, but it may not spend funds to secure religion against skepticism. It may compensate individuals for loss of employment, but it cannot compensate them for adherence to a creed.

It seems to me that the basic fallacy in the Court's reasoning, which accounts for its failure to apply the principles it avows, is in ignoring the essentially religious test by which beneficiaries of this expenditure are selected. A policeman protects a Catholic, of course—but not because he is a Catholic; it is because he is a man and a member of our society. The fireman protects the Church school—but not because it is a Church school; it is because it is property, part of the assets of our society. Neither the fireman nor the policeman has to ask before he renders aid "Is this man or building identified with the Catholic Church?" But before these school authorities draw a check to reimburse for a student's fare they must ask just that question, and if the school is a Catholic one they may render aid because it is such, while if it is of any other faith or is run for profit, the help must be withheld. To consider the converse of the

Court's reasoning will best disclose its fallacy. That there is no parallel between police and fire protection and this plan of reimbursement is apparent from the incongruity of the limitation of this Act if applied to police and fire service. Could we sustain an Act that said the police shall protect pupils on the way to or from public schools and Catholic schools but not while going to and coming from other schools, and firemen shall extinguish a blaze in public or Catholic school buildings but shall not put out a blaze in Protestant Church schools or private schools operated for profit? That is the true analogy to the case we have before us and I should think it pretty plain that such a scheme would not be valid.

The Court's holding is that this taxpayer has no grievance because the state has decided to make the reimbursement a public purpose and therefore we are bound to regard it as such. I agree that this Court has left, and always should leave to each state, great latitude in deciding for itself, in the light of its own conditions, what shall be public purposes in its scheme of things. It may socialize utilities and economic enterprises and make taxpayers' business out of what conventionally had been private business. It may make public business of individual welfare, health, education, entertainment or security. But it cannot make public business of religious worship or instruction, or of attendance at religious institutions of any character. There is no answer to the proposition, that the effect of the religious freedom Amendment to our Constitution was to take every form of propagation of religion out of the realm of things which could directly or indirectly be made public business and thereby be supported in whole or in part at taxpayers' expense. That is a difference which the Constitution sets up between religion and almost every other subject matter of legislation, a difference which goes to the very root of religious freedom and which the Court is overlooking today. This freedom was first in the Bill of Rights because it was first in the forefathers' minds; it was set forth in absolute terms, and its strength is its rigidity. It was intended not only to keep the states' hands out of religion, but to keep religion's hands off the state, and, above all, to keep bitter religious controversy out of public life by denying to every denomination any advantage from getting control of public policy or the public purse. Those great ends I cannot but think are immeasurably compromised by today's decision.

This policy of our Federal Constitution has never been wholly pleasing to most religious groups. They all are quick to invoke its protections; they all are irked when they feel its restraints. This Court has gone a long way, if not an unreasonable way, to hold that public business of such paramount importance as maintenance of public order, protection of the privacy of the home, and taxation may not be pursued by a state in a way that even indirectly will interfere with religious proselyting. See dissent in Douglas v. Jeannette, 319 U.S. 157, 166; Murdock v. Pennsylvania, 319 U.S. 105; Martin v. Struthers, 319 U.S. 141; Jones v. Opelika, 316 U.S. 584, reversed on rehearing, 319 U.S. 103.

But we cannot have it both ways. Religious teaching cannot be a private affair when the state seeks to impose regulations which infringe on it indirectly, and a public affair when it comes to taxing citizens of one faith to aid another, or those of no faith to aid at all. If these principles seem harsh in prohibiting aid to Catholic education, it must not be forgotten that it is the same Constitution that alone assures Catholics the right to maintain these schools at all when predominant local sentiment would forbid them. Pierce v. Society of Sisters, 268 U.S. 510. Nor should I think that those who have done so well without this aid would want to see this separation between Church and State broken down. If the state may aid these religious schools, it may therefore regulate them. Many groups have sought aid from tax funds only to find that it carried political controls with it. Indeed this Court has declared that "It is hardly lack of due process for the Government to regulate that which it subsidizes." Wickard v. Filburn, 317 U.S. 111, 131.

But in any event, the great purposes of the Constitution do not depend on the approval or convenience of those they restrain. It cannot read the history of the struggle to separate political from ecclesiastical affairs, without a conviction that the Court today is unconsciously giving the clock's hands a backward turn.

QUESTIONS AND DISCUSSION POINTS

1. This case poses the question how best to read the First Amendment. What are the key words in the First Amendment, which require interpretation?

2. The clear struggle between the Majority and Dissent is over the question how far the State can go in "supporting" religion before there is a violation of the First Amendment. To get a sense of each side of the argument,

construct a continuum of actions deemed "supportive" of religious schools, and see if you can tell where the two sides diverge in their judgments about what constitutes "impermissible" support.

3. Can you imagine any activities in connection with "religious" schools the Dissent would deem appropriate?

4. For each opinion, try to construct a general philosophical justification for each position.

5. Which forms of argument are central to each opinion? Do one or more forms "work" better than others?

Glossary

Accessory before the fact. Someone who aids another in the commission of the crime who is not present at the commission of the crime.

Acquittal. The verdict in a criminal trial in which the defendant is found not guilty.

Actus reus. The "guilty act" or "deed of crime"; an act of wrongdoing that is forbidden by the law and that, when committed in conjunction with a specified state of mind (mens rea), constitutes a crime.

Adjudication. The legal process of resolving a dispute, including a court's act of hearing of the dispute and rendering a judgment.

Affiant. One who makes a written statement under oath. The statement is called an "affidavit" and the person signing under oath the "affiant".

Affidavit. A written statement made under oath.

Affirmative action plan. An employment program designed to remedy past discrimination in hiring minority employees.

Amicus curiae. "Friend of the court"; a person or group that files a brief with the court, supplying relevant information bearing on the case or urging a particular result. While not parties in a case, amici typically are third parties who will be indirectly affected by the court's decision.

Amid. See *amicus curiae.*

Answer. The legal document by which a defendant responds to the allegations contained in the complaint of the plaintiff.

Ante-nuptial contract. See *pre-nuptial agreement.*

Appeal. The resort to a superior or appellate court to review the decision of an inferior trial court.

Appellant. The party or person who appeals a decision (usually, but not always, the loser in the lower court).

Appellee. The party or person against whom an appeal is taken (usually, but not always, the winner in the lower court).

Brief. A written statement prepared by an attorney arguing a case in court; a summary of the facts of the case, relevant laws, and an argument of how the law applies to the facts in support of the attorney's position.

Burden of proof. The requirement that a party establish the facts of his or her case to the jury or trier of fact by the requisite standard established in the court. Normally in a civil proceeding the burden of proof is "preponderance of the evidence" (or 51 percent) and in a criminal proceeding the burden of proof is "beyond a reasonable doubt."

Casus omissus. A "case omitted"; a situation where no statute exists to govern the facts of a case and so the decision must be made according to common law.

Cause of action. A claim in law based on facts sufficient to bring the case to court; the grounds of an action against another (e.g., a suit in negligence).

Certiorari. A writ issued by a superior court to an inferior court requiring the latter court to produce the records of a particular case heard before it. Most often used with regard to the U.S. Supreme Court, which uses "cert." as a means of deciding which cases it wishes to hear.

Cestui que trust. (Pronounced: setty-key-trust). In a trust, there are at least three persons involved. The settlor is the person who uses his or her funds to establish or "set up" the trust. The trustee is the person who holds legal title to the trust, and is responsible for managing the trust. The beneficiary (the cestui que trust) is said to have equitable title to the trust and is the one for whose benefit the trust has been created.

Citation. A reference to an authority used (e.g., a prior case, a statute) to substantiate the validity of one's argument or position.

Class action. A suit where one or more members of a group (or class) sue on behalf of everyone similarly situated in the group. This type of civil suit requires that the "class" of persons be so large that it would be impractical for each of them to sue individually. The group must have a common interest and the representative must act on behalf of *all* members of the class.

Codicil. An addition to a will, which either amends or adds provisions to the will.

Collateral estoppel. The doctrine that prevents parties who have already received a valid judgment by a court from relitigating the same facts in front of another court in the future.

Collective bargaining. The process of negotiation between organized workers (such as unions) and their employer(s) in order to reach agreement on working conditions, wages and hours.

Common law. The origin of the Anglo-American legal systems; the system of law originally based on the customary and unwritten laws of England and developed by the doctrine of precedent as opposed to legislative enactments.

Complaint. The legal document (also called a petition) that informs a defendant of the grounds on which he or she is being sued.

Consideration. A basic element necessary to form a valid contract. The idea that one party gives something of value or a promise to another party in exchange for something of value or a promise.

Contributory negligence. A defense to an allegation by a plaintiff in a tort action that the defendant did not act in a legally responsible manner. The defendant can raise the defense claiming that the plaintiff acted with less care than a normal, reasonable person would do under the circumstances to protect himself and so is contributorily negligent in causing the harm.

Crime. A wrongful act against society as defined by law; a wrong that is prosecuted by a public official and punishable by fine, imprisonment, or death.

Damages. Monetary compensation awarded by a court for an injury caused by the act of another. Damages may be actual or compensatory (equal to the amount of loss proven) or exemplary or punitive (in excess of the actual damages given as a form of punishment to the wrongdoer).

De novo. "Anew"; "once again"; The standard of review usually used by appellate courts when deciding cases that have been appealed to them. If the court finds that the lower court did not abuse its discretion or make a clear error in giving the verdict, the appellate court will look at the law involved in the case de novo.

Decedent. One who has ceased to live; in criminal law, the victim of a homicide.

Defendant. The person against whom a lawsuit (cause of action) or criminal prosecution is brought.

Deficiency judgment. A judgment for a secured creditor for the remaining portion of the debt not secured by collateral.

Demurrer. A plea for the dismissal of a lawsuit on the grounds that even if the claims of the opposing party are true, they do not sustain the claim because they are legally insufficient or defective.

Dictum. A statement or remark, not necessary for the decision of a case, made by the judge in the judge's opinion; a statement not binding as precedent.

Discovery. That set of procedures through which the parties to a suit obtain information about matters relevant to the case.

Dissent. An opinion given by a judge in a case that differs from that given by the majority of the court. A dissent typically points out the deficiencies of the majority position and states reasons for arriving at a different conclusion.

Donee. The recipient of a gift.

Donor. The giver of a gift.

Dower. The part of a husband's property that his widow inherits for her lifetime.

Due process. The principle that guarantees parties that the law will be fairly applied to their cases through the administration of justice in the court system. The Fifth Amendment to the U.S. Constitution guarantees "substantive" due process, or protects persons and their property from unfair governmental interference or taking. The Fourteenth Amendment to the U.S. Constitution guarantees "procedural" due process, which guarantees them the fair administration of justice.

Duty. A legal obligation which requires a person to conform to a certain standard of performance or care.

Duty of Care. The idea that a person should act with the degree of responsibility so that if he or she does not act in this manner, he or she becomes liable to another party if the actions cause another's injury.

Equity. Justice administered according to fairness as opposed to the strictly formulated rules of the common law; a system of principles that originated in England as an alternative to the perceived harshness of rigidly applying the rules of the common law in every case.

Equity of redemption. The right of a party with mortgaged property (the mortgagor) to redeem the property from the holder of the mortgage after the mortgagor has defaulted on or breached the mortgage contract. The mortgagor can redeem the mortgage by paying the amount of the debt and interest in full.

Ex parte. Something done for the benefit of only one of the parties to a case. Normally, a ex parte hearing or an ex parte proceeding involves only one party in a case and can take place without notifying the other party.

Ex post facto. "After the fact"; a law that makes illegal an action which was done before the law was passed.

Such laws violate Article I, sections 9 and 10 of the U.S. Constitution.

Felony. Any group of "high" or "serious" crimes (as distinguished from minor offenses called misdemeanors) generally punishable either by imprisonment or death.

Felony-murder. An unlawful homicide occurring during the commission of (or attempt to commit) a felony and which (under this doctrine) is considered first-degree murder.

"Fighting words." Words that, given their nature and the context in which they are uttered, are very likely to provoke their hearer to an immediate breach of the peace. Such words have been held not protected by the First Amendment to the U.S. Constitution.

First impression. A case that presents a question of law never before considered by any court within the relevant jurisdiction and that is therefore not controlled by the doctrine of precedent.

Foreseeability. The idea that one party could expect a certain outcome or a harm to occur by the very nature of his or her actions. For example, if one drops a pencil from the top of the Empire State Building, it is foreseeable that the pencil could land in a crowded street and injure someone.

Guilty. The condition of having been found to have committed the crime charged.

Holding. A declaration of statement of the law as it applies to the facts of a specific case and given by the court in its opinion.

Homicide. Any killing of a human being by another human being. Homicide does not necessarily constitute a crime; to be a crime, homicide must be an unlawful killing (e.g., murder).

Ignoratia legis non excusat. "Ignorance of the law is no excuse"; the

fact that the defendant did not think her or his act was against the law does not prevent the law from punishing the prohibited act.

Implied warranty. A promise arising by operation of law that something (such as a good) is fit for the purpose which the seller knows it is intended.

Infancy. The state of being a minor; not yet having attained the age of maturity.

Injunction. A judge's order that a person do, or more commonly, refrain from doing a certain act. The court's power to issue an injunction is based in equity.

Instruction. Directions the judge gives to the jury, informing them of the law that they are to apply to the facts of the case in order to reach a verdict.

Issue. The biological descendants of a person; often the heirs of one's estate.

Joint and several liability. The notion that two people can both be responsible for an act (joint) or each of the individuals can be wholly responsible. The injured party can sue to recover from both parties or to recover entirely from one of the parties but he cannot sue each party twice for double recovery.

Judgment. The final decision of the court in a case, resolving the dispute and determining the rights and obligations of the parties involved.

Judicial Review. The power of the courts to review the decisions of lower courts or other areas of government.

Jurisdiction. The power of a court to make legally binding decisions over certain persons or property; the geographical area in which a court's decisions or a legislature's enactments are binding.

Legatee. One to whom an estate or property is granted in a will.

Liability. The condition of being responsible for damages resulting from an injurious act, for discharging an obligation or debt, or for paying a penalty for wrongdoing.

Licensee. A person who has the permission of the owner of property to enter the property but enters the property for his or her own purposes rather than for the purpose of the owner.

Malum in se. "That which is wrong in itself"; refers to an act that would be thought evil or wrong even without a specific criminal prohibition (e.g., murder).

Malum prohibitum. "That which is wrong because prohibited"; refers to an act that is wrong only because it is made so by a statute (e.g., failure to file for income tax).

Misceganation. "The mixing of the races"; older statutes (now invalid) typically defined miscegenation as marriage between a Caucasian (white) and a member of another race.

Misdemeanor. That class of criminal offenses less serious than felonies and punished with lesser severity.

Misfeasance. The doing of a wrongful or injurious act.

Moot case. A case that no longer presents an actual controversy, either because the issues involved have ceased to exist or they have been rendered "academic" by the circumstances.

Motion. A formal request made to a judge pertaining to any issue arising during a lawsuit.

Movant. The party who requests a motion.

Murder. The unlawful killing of a human being. Modern law distinguishes between several degrees of murder. First degree murder is a deliberate and premeditated homicide; second degree murder is a homicide committed with malice but without premeditation.

Napoleonic Code. The body of French civil law enacted under Napoleon in 1804; it has served as the model legal code for many countries.

Negligence. The failure to exercise due care for the safety and welfare of others; failure to exercise that degree of care which, under the circumstances, a reasonable person would take.

Nonfeasance. Nonperformance of an act that one has a duty to perform; neglect of a duty; failure to act so as to prevent harm.

Nuisance. An unreasonable or unwarranted use by a person of his or her own property that produces such annoyance, inconvenience, or discomfort as to interfere with the rights of others to use and enjoy their property.

Obiter dictum. See *dictum*.

On the merits. A decision of judgment based upon the essential facts of the case rather than upon a "technicality" such as improper jurisdiction.

Opinion. A statement of the reasons a certain decision or judgment was reached in a case. A majority opinion is usually written by one judge and represents the principles of law that a majority of the members of a court regard as central to the holding in a case. A concurring opinion agrees with the ultimate judgment of the majority but disagrees with the reasons leading to that result. A plurality opinion is agreed to by less than a majority so far as reasoning is concerned but is agreed to by a majority as stating the correct result. A per curiam opinion expressing the decision of the court but whose author is not identified. See also *dissent*.

Ordinance. The equivalent of a municipal statute passed by a city council and dealing with matters not already covered by federal or state law.

Overbreadth. A situation in which a law not only prohibits that which may constitutionally be prohibited but also prohibits conduct that is constitutionally protected (e.g., the freedom of speech under the First Amendment).

Overrule. To overturn or invalidate the holding of a prior case. A decision can be overruled only be the same court or by a higher court within the same jurisdiction.

Pendente lite. While a transaction is pending.

Petition. A formal, written application to a court requesting judicial action on a particular matter.

Petitioner. The person presenting a petition to a court; one who starts an equity proceeding; one who takes an appeal from a judgment.

Plaintiff. The person who brings a lawsuit or cause of action against another.

Plea. In the law of procedure, an answer or response to a complaint or an allegation of fact; in criminal procedure, the response of the defendant in answer to the charge made against him or her.

Pleadings. The complaint and the answer in a civil suit.

Precedent. The doctrine of Anglo-American law whereby once a court has formulated a principle of law as applied to a given set of facts, it will follow that principle and apply it in future cases where the facts are substantially similar. See also *stare decisis*.

Pre-nuptial agreement. A contract entered into before marriage that outlines the terms of the marriage and determines the property rights and the financial arrangements for each of the spouses during marriage and in the event of divorce.

Preponderance of the evidence. The general standard of proof in a civil case (i.e., one involving a lawsuit); to prevail, a party must show that the preponderance of the evidence (better than 50 percent) weighs in his or her favor.

Prima facie case. A case that, at first view or "on its face," is supported by enough evidence to entitle a party to have the case go to a jury.

Probation. A procedure whereby a defendant found guilty of a crime is released into society subject to conditions laid down by the court and under the supervision of a probation officer.

Proceeding. The form and manner of conducting legal business before a court or judicial officer; the series of events constituting the process through which judicial action takes place.

Promissory note. A written promise or contract to pay a specific amount of money to a specific person, or the bearer of the note, on a specific date.

Prosecution. The act of pursuing a lawsuit or criminal trial; the party initiating a criminal suit, i.e., the state.

Proximate cause. An event without which injury or damage would not have occurred and which is closely enough related to the occurrence of the injury to make it fair, reasonable, or just to hold the defendant liable for that injury.

Ration decidendi. The point in a case that determines the result or judgment; the basis or reason for the decision.

Reasonable doubt. The degree of certainty required of a juror before the juror may find a defendant guilty; innocence is to be presumed unless the guilt of the defendant is so clearly proven that the jury can see that no reasonable doubt remains as to the guilt or the defendant.

Reasonable person. A phrase used to refer to that hypothetical person who exercises those qualities of attention, knowledge, intelligence, and judgment that society requires of its members for the protection of their own interest and the interests of others.

Recidividt. A "habitual criminal," often subjected to extended terms of imprisonment under habitual offender status.

Relief. That assistance, redress, or benefit sought by a person filing a complaint before a court.

Remand. To send back for further proceedings, as when a higher court sends a case back to a lower court.

Remedy. That means by which a right is enforced or the violation of a right is redressed or compensated. The most common remedy at law consists of money damages.

Res ipsa loquitor. "The thing speaks for itself"; the idea in tort law where the negligence of the defendant can be inferred from the mere fact that the accident occurred because the defendant had full control of the thing that caused injury and when operated without negligence the thing causes no harm. For example, when an airplane crashes, the plaintiff can assert res ipsa loquitor saying that a plane does not fall from the sky when operated normally, therefore the crash must be caused by some negligence on the part of the airline.

Respondent. The party who contends against an appeal; the party who makes an answer to a complaint in an equity proceeding.

Reversal. The invalidating or setting aside of the contrary decision of a lower court.

Revocation. The cancellation or withdrawal of an offer to contract.

Scienter. The defendant's "guilty knowledge"; refers to the defendant's alleged previous knowledge of the cause that led to the injury complained of.

Sentence. The punishment a court orders to be inflicted upon a person convicted of a crime.

Sine qua non. "That without which there is not"; in tort law, the act of the defendant without which there would not have been a tortious injury to the plaintiff.

Specific performance. Where money damages are inadequate compensation for the breach of the contract, the specific performance remedy requires the breaching party to perform the contract under the exact terms agreed upon by the parties in the contract.

Standing. The legal requirement that a plaintiff be injured and so has a sufficient stake in the matter to initiate a lawsuit and seek a judicial conclusion.

Stare decisis. "Let the decision stand"; refers to the doctrine that courts should follow precedent, the authority of earlier, analogous cases.

Statute. An act of a legislature, consistent with constitutional authority and in such proper form that it becomes the law governing the conduct to which it refers.

Statute of limitations. Statutes that set forth the time periods during which an action can be brought or rights can be enforced. Once the time period in the statute of limitations has passed, no legal action can be brought against the defendant to recover for damages or enforce rights.

Statute of wills. Those statutory provisions of a particular jurisdiction stating the requirement for a valid will.

Strict liability. Liability without proof of fault. In civil law, one who engages in activity that carries an inherent risk of injury or is ultrahazardous (e.g., blasting) is often liable for all injuries proximately caused by that activity; in criminal law, strict liability offenses are those that do not require proof of mens rea (criminal intent).

Subpoena. A court order compelling a witness to appear and testify in a proceeding.

Suit. Any proceeding before a court in which a person pursues that remedy which the law affords as redress for the injury that person has suffered.

Summary judgment. A judgment in a civil suit, granted on the basis of the pleadings and prior to trial, holding that there is no genuine factual dispute between the parties regarding the legal issues involved and that the case need not therefore go before a jury.

Testator. One who is disposing of property by will.

Title in fee. Also called a "fee simple"; the right to the inheritance of real property (real estate) in full, without any restrictions or conditions to ownership.

Tort. A civil wrong, other than a breach of contract, for which a court will provide a remedy.

Tortfeasor. One who commits a tort.

Tortious. Used to describe conduct that subjects a person to tort liability.

Trial. A judicial examination and determination of issues between parties to action.

Ultra vires. An act beyond the scope of one's powers or authority, as, for example, by a corporation.

Unconscionability. A doctrine that allows a court to void a contract between parties because the terms of the contract are grossly unfair, oppressive, or in violation of other laws.

Verdict. The decision of a jury following the trial of a civil or criminal case.

Vest. To give someone a right to use something immediately or in the future.

Vicarious liability. The imputation of liability upon one person for the actions of another person.

Void. That which is entirely null, having no legal force.

Volenti non fit injuria. "To one who consents, no harm is done"; in tort, the doctrine that one generally cannot claim damages when one has consented to the activity that caused an injury.

Will. A document executed with specific legal formalities containing a person's instructions about the disposition of his or her property upon death.

Index

Abel v. Lilly & Co. 346, 352, 353
Abermarle Paper Co. v. Moody 178, 222
Abrahams v. United States 369
Abridgement (Bacon) 208
"accidental relations" 4
act of god 358
acts malum prohibitum et malum in se (crimes wrong because forbidden as distinct from wrong in themselves) 33
Adams v. Tanner 408, 409
Adkins v. Children's Hospital 408
"administration of justice" 7, 26
administrative law 136
affirmative action 219, 220, 221, 223, 224, 225, 234, 235
Agency for International Development 239, 240, 242, 250n. 3, 253
agreement 31
AID. *See* Agency for International Development
Airline case (Minow) 152
Alexander v. Gardner Denver Co. 179
Allen v. M'Pherson 210
Allen v. Wright 237, 238, 241, 249, 256
Allgeyer v. Louisiana 407
alternative liability doctrine 345, 346, 348, 351, 352, 353. *See also* concerted action
Altman, Andrew 119, 120, 121, 123, 124, 126, 131, 132
altruism
    and Altman, 132
    and Unger, 127
Amaya v. Home, Ice, Fuel & Supply Co. 307, 308, 314, 318, 320, 328, 333, 335, 338
American Evasion of Philosophy (West) 96n. 2
American Land Co. v. Zeiss 390
American Power & Light Co. v. SEC 255, 256
Andalon v. Superior Court 325
Anderson v. Liberty Lobby, Inc. 250
Andrus v. Sierra Club 256
Anglo-American law 61, 68, 102
Anglo-American legal system 99
Antoni v. Greenhow 386
Apuleian laws 15
Aquinas 3, 11, 16, 19, 130, 185, 186, 189
Archibald v. Braveman 323, 335
Arendt, Hannah 157
Aristotle 3, 4, 5, 6, 7, 8, 9, 10, 15, 17, 41, 101, 127, 184, 185, 203, 207, 209

Arnold, Thurman 125
Article I, "the legislative powers" 237, 244
Article II, "the executive power" 237, 255
Article III, "the judicial powers" 163, 237, 243, 245, 246, 254, 256
ASARCO Inc. v. Kadish 238
Associated General Contractors of Massachusetts v. Altshuler 220n. 1
"associative obligations." *See* "communal obligations"
Atchison, T & S.F. Rwy. Co. v. United States 392
Atlantic Cleaners & Dyers 384
Augustine 18, 19

Baby Selling (Baker) 285, 294
Bacon, Francis 208
Baker v. Carr 246
Barbier v. Connolly 413
"bare needs of human life" 7
Barnitz v. Beverly 387, 404
"basic human goods" 184, 190, 191, 192, 193, 194, 195, 196, 197, 198, 199, 201, 204
Beneficial Finance Company of Waterloo v. Lamos 266
benign discrimination. *See* affirmative action
Bentham, Jeremy 43, 82
Benthamite 115
"best interests of the child" test 279, 282, 283, 286, 287, 290, 292
Biakanja v. Irving 313
Bichler v. Eli Lilly 344, 345, 346, 347, 348, 354
Bill of Rights 112, 419
Bird v. St. Paul F. & M. Ins. Co. 300, 304
Black, Justice Hugo 244, 375, 410
Blackmun, Justice Harry 177, 179, 180, 235, 241n. 2, 247, 249, 376
Blackstone, William 3, 11, 26, 27, 36, 37, 43, 104, 209
Block v. Hirsch 390, 392
Bobbitt, Phillip 160, 161, 162, 170, 171, 172, 173, 175, 183
Bolognian law 35
Boorstin, Daniel 26
Boos v. Barry 363, 365n. 2, 367
Borer v. American Airlines 328, 343
Boronkay v. Robinson & Carpenter 298
Boston Beer Company v. Massachusetts 388
"Bowles" case 166

Brandeis, Justice Louis   243
Brandenberg v. Ohio   366, 369
breach of duty   296, 299
Breach of Duty (Holland)   299
Brennan, Justice   147, 149, 150, 219, 361
Bronaugh, Richard   173n.
Bronson v. Kinzie   386, 387, 401, 404
Brown v. Louisiana   364
Brown v. Superior Court   348, 349
Buckner v. Goodyear Tire & Rubber Co.   220n. 1
Burnside v. Abbott Labs   353
Butchers Union Company v. Crescent City Company   388, 407

C&J Fertilizer, Inc. v. Allied Mutual Insurance Company   265
Caesar   18
California Federal Savings & Loan Association v. Guerra   144
Caligula   32
Canon laws   34
Cantwell v. Connecticut   416
capitalism   113
Capitolinus   34
Caracalla   34
Cardozo, Justice Benjamin   296, 310
Carmichael v. Southern Coal and Coke, Co.   413, 418
Carneades   22, 23, 24, 25
Carvalho v. Brunner   346
Causation   296, 299
Celotex Corp. v. Catrett   241n. 2
Central Bearings Co. v. Wolverine Insurance Company   271
Chaplinsky v. New Hampshire   366, 373, 374
Charles River Bridge v. Warren Bridge   388
Charondas   15
Chastelton Corporation v. Sinclair   391
Chicago B. & Q.R.R. Co. v. Nebraska   388
Chicago Burlington & Quincy R.R. Co.   408
Chrysippus   23
Church of the Holy Trinity v. United States   215
Cicero   3, 11, 12, 13, 16, 19, 22, 24, 35, 43, 82
Citizens Savings and Loan Association v. City of Topeka   412
City Council of Los Angeles v. Taxpayers for Vincent   374
City of Parkersbure v. Brown   412
Civil Code of Lower Canada   210
civil conduct   32
civil government   34
civil law   31, 210, 214
Civil Rights Act of 1964 (Title VII)   144, 178, 179, 180, 181, 219–235
Clark v. Community for Creative Non-Violence   365
Clingan v. Mitcheltree   214
Cochran v. Louisiana State Board of Education   412
Cocles   14
Code Napoleon   210, 212
Codling v. Paglia   347
Cohen, Felix   125
Cohens v. Virginia   387

"collective bargaining"   219
collective liability   353
Collins v. Eli Lilly   345, 346, 347, 348, 349, 350, 352, 353
"commensurability problem" of constitutional law   175
Commentaries (Smith)   208
Commentaries on the Laws of England (Blackstone)   26, 27, 37, 209
Commodus   34
common good   20
common law   25, 26, 27, 35, 36, 99, 100, 103, 104, 108, 114, 115, 121, 124, 132, 207, 209
Common Law Tradition, The (Llewellyn)   269
"communal obligations" (Dworkin)   82, 83
community   19, 20
  bare (Dworkin)   84, 85
  true (Dworkin)   84, 85
Community for Creative non-Violence v. Watt   365
compact   31, 32
complete community (Finnis)   202, 293
Concept of Law (Hart)   44, 49, 51, 52, 53, 54, 56, 120, 121
"conceptions" (Dworkin)   75, 76
concerted action   345, 346, 348, 351, 352, 353. *See also* alternative liability doctrine
Condran v. Park & Tilford   298
Congress. *See* United States Congress
Consequentialism (Posner)   94
Consequentialism
  and Finnis   194, 197
  and Posner   94, 95, 96
"consideration"   258, 260, 261, 263, 264
Constitution. *See* United States Constitution
Constitutional Fate (Bobbitt)   170n. 3
Constitutional Interpretation (Bobbitt)   162, 170, 170n. 2
constitutional law   136
constructive interpretation (Dworkin)   86
constructivism   65, 78, 82, 184
constructivist model   78, 79, 80, 81, 82
constructivists   131
contract law   127, 132, 135, 136, 137, 138, 258
  individualist side of   137
  solidarity side of   137
Contractors Ass'n of Eastern Pennsylvania v. Secretary of Labor   220n. 1
Contracts Clause (of the U.S. constitution)   166, 387, 392
"contradiction"   175
conventionalism (Dworkin)   86, 87, 90
Cook v. Maier   308
Constitutional Limitations (Cooley)   396
Corbin on Contracts   266, 269, 270, 277
Corporation of the Presiding Bishop of the Church of Jesus Christ of Latter-Day Saints v. Amos   150
County of Los Angeles v. Davis   179
Craig v. Missouri   397
criminal law   136
Critical Legal Studies (CLS)   119, 121, 124, 125, 126, 131, 132, 133, 134, 135–139, 160, 170
critical legal theory   120, 140, 160

Cujus est solum ejus est usque as coelum (the owner of the soil owns the sky) 38
custom 19, 31, 44
customary Law 26
customary practices 99

Daley v. People's Building, Loan and Savings Ass'n 276n. 5
damnum absque iniuria (harm without legal injury) 39
Dan v. Brown 213
Daniels v. Tearney 387
Dartmouth College Case 397
Darwin, Charles 42
Davidson v. New Orleans 412
Day v. Roth 263
death penalty 149
Decalogue 209
decree 8, 10
Defenders of Wildlife v. Hodel 236, 242
De Jure Belli ac Pacis (Grotius) 21, 24
De Legibus (Cicero) 12, 13
Depue v. Flatau 358
DES 343–356
DES and a proposed theory of Enterprise Liability (Sheiner) 344
Desmosthenes 25
"development of human communities" 6
Dewey, John 113
DiCaprio v. New York Ry. Co. 297, 300, 302
"dilemma of difference" (Minow) 140, 141, 142, 143, 144, 146, 147, 150, 151, 152, 153, 154, 155, 156, 158
Dillon v. Legg 306, 315, 316, 318, 320–343
Dio Cassius 32
discretion 72–75, 76, 95
District of Evangelical Lutheran Synod v. McKelvie 408
divine law 28, 29, 30
divine reason 14
doctrinal argument 180
doctrinal incoherence (Altman) 135
"doctrine of intelligible essences" (Unger) 130, 131
"doctrine of reasonable expectations" (contracts) 269, 270, 271, 272, 273
Dole v. Dow Chemical 355
Domat's Civil Law 210, 213
Doremus v. Board of Ed of Hawthorne 244
Douglas, Justice William O. 153
Douglas v. Jeanette 419
Dred Scott v. Sanford 163, 395
due care 61
"due process." *See* Fifth Amendment; Fourteenth Amendment
Duke Power Co. v. Carolina Environmental Study Group, Inc. 253
duty 296, 297
Dworkin, Ronald 65, 66, 74, 75, 76, 77, 78, 82, 85, 86, 92, 95, 121, 123, 124, 125, 131, 132, 133, 134, 135, 136, 137, 138, 139, 161, 173
Dworkinian thought or jurisprudence 124, 125, 132, 133, 134, 135, 136, 138, 139

Dynamic Statutory Interpretation (Eskridge) 179n.
Dynamic statutory interpretation 181, 182

Earl of Chesterfield v. Janssen 276n. 4
"Earl of Lauderdale's fallacy" (Posner) 100
economic analysis of law 97, 101, 103, 104
Edwards v. Aguillard, 146, 147
Edwards v. Kearzey 387, 398
EEOC. *See* Equal Employment Opportunity Commission
EEOC v. Arabian American Oil Co. 248
"efficacy of laws" 50, 51, 52, 53
"efficient cause" 4
Ehrgott v. Mayor 300
Elden v. Sheldon 328
Emergency Price Controls Act 166
Emry v. Roanoake Transit Dev. Co. 297
Endangered Species Act 87, 236, 240, 241, 242, 245, 246, 247, 248, 249, 253, 255
England v. Mapes Produce Co. 313
English law 26, 27, 36, 38, 39, 63
"*epieikeia.*" *See* Equity
Equal Employment Opportunity Commission 229, 229, 230, 231, 233
equitable construction 208, 209
equity 9, 10
"equity of redemption" 393, 394
ESA. *See* Endangered Species Act
Eskridge, William 177, 179n., 180, 181, 182
"established law" 43
Establishment Clause (First Amendment of U.S. Constitution) 167
ethics 29, 33
Euphemus 22
Everson v. Board of Education, 167, 168, 410
"evolutive criteria for historical argument" (Eskridge) 177
"evolutive perspective" (Eskridge) 180
Executive Order No. 11246 224n. 6. *See also* affirmative action
Ex Parte Levitt 243
Ex Parte Milligan 395
"external attitude" 49
"external point of view" 50

Fairchild v. Hughes 243
Fallbrook Irrigation District v. Bradley 412
falsifiability (Posner) 105, 106
family 7
Fantony v. Fantony 290
FCC v. Pacifica 366
Federal Bank of the United States 164
Federalist Papers, The 237
Federal Tort Claims Act 252
feminist jurisprudence 140
Fifth Amendment 390
"fighting words" 373, 374
"final cause" 4, 5, 41, 42, 126
Finnis, John 184, 185, 190, 191, 198, 202, 204
First Amendment 146, 167, 361–369, 374–376, 412, 413, 414

"first order principles" (Finnis)   185, 186   *See also* "second order principles"

"first principle of natural morality" (Finnis)   190, 195, 196, 197, 198

Flag Desecration Statutes (Rosenblatt)   373

Fletcher v. Peck   377

Foley Bros., Inc. v. Filardo   248

Food Employees v. Logan Valley Plaza   364

"formal cause"   4

Forms and Limits of Adjudication   65n. 1

forseeablity   310, 311, 312, 319, 320, 321, 322, 324, 327, 328, 330, 331, 332, 333, 334, 338, 339, 340, 341

Fortas, Justice Abe   375

Foundations of Legal Liability (Street)   299

"four causes"   4

Fourteenth Amendment   163, 373, 378, 402, 406, 407, 412, 413

Fourth Amendment   164, 363

"freedom of choice" (Finnis)   185. *See also* "basic human goods"

freedom of speech   71

free market   113

free will   28, 42, 111

Fried, Charles   125

Fuller, Lon   65, 82, 95

Funk v. United States   396

Furnco Construction Corp. v. Waters   180, 225

FW/PBS, Inc. v. Dallas   237–238

Gains v. Gains   213

Galbraith v. Busch   355

Galileo   42

Gallic War of the Germans, The (Caesar)   18

Gantly's Lessee v. Ewing   386

Gates v. Richardson   340

George v. Parke-Davis   349

Gibbons v. Ogden   245

Giffen goods   105

Gladstone, Realtors v. Village of Bellwood   238

God   14, 17, 21, 23, 29, 30, 32, 42

Golden Rule (Finnis)   196, 197, 198, 200, 201

Golden v. Zwickler   247, 251

Goodright v. Glasier   213

"goods of human life"   7

Grafton v. Mollica   310

grammar of constitutional argument (Bob-bitt)   161, 170, 171, 182

Great Britain   167

Green v. Biddle   386

Green v. Frazier   412

Greer v. Tweed   276n. 4

Griggs v. Duke Power Co.   225

Grotius   3, 11, 21, 24, 36, 82

Groves v. Slaughter   384

Gunn v. Barry   387

Habermas, Jurgen   113

Hadden v. The Collector   216

Hale, Sir Matthew   225

Halter v. Nebrasks   373

Hamer v. Sidway   259

Hand, Learned   101

Hand's negligence formula   101

Harlan, Justice   153, 337

Hart, H.L.A.   41, 43, 44, 49, 50, 51, 52, 53, 54, 55, 56, 65, 66, 67, 95, 120, 121, 122, 123, 124, 125, 127, 131, 139

Harvard Law School   126

Hathaway v. Superior Court   336, 340

heavenly law   14

Henningsen v. Bloomfield Motors   68, 70, 72, 276n. 4

Hercules   125

Hergenrether v. East   310, 312

"historical perspective" (Eskridge)   180

History of the Flag of the United States of America (Preble)   371

Hobbes, Thomas   24

Hobbie v. Unemployment Appeals Commission   147, 148

Hoffa case   237

Holdsworth's History of English Law   299

holism (Quinian holism)   174, 175

Holmes, Oliver Wendell   52, 113, 225, 276n. 5, 301, 369, 370, 389, 412

Holy Trinity Church v. United States   221

Home Building & Loan Ass'n v. Blaisdell   377

Homer   7

Hook, Sidney   113

Hooker, Richard   186

Howard v. Bugbee   386, 387, 404

Hoyem v. Manhattan Beach City Sch. Dist.   323

Hudson County Water Co. v. McCarter   389

Hughes, Chief Justice Charles   225, 377

Hughes v. Boston & Maine Ry. Co.   297

human action (Finnis)   198, 199

Human Dimension in Appellate Judging, The (Kaye)   347

human law   7, 18, 19, 20, 27, 29, 33, 34

Hume v. United States   276n. 4

Hunt v. Washington State Apple Advertising Comm'n   239

Hymowitz v. Eli Lilly   343

Ideal Commonwealth (Plato)   409

Independent Adoptions (Herzog et al.)   285

Indeterminacy, realist analysis of (Altman)   120, 121, 122, 123, 124, 125, 126, 127, 128, 131, 132, 184

individual   7

individual conscience (Patterson)   172, 173

individualism   157

"individualistic" legal doctrine   127, 132

"Ineligibility Clause." *See* Article I

injury   296

"injury-in-fact"   237, 239, 243, 244, 254, 256

In re Adoption by J.J.P.   286, 290

In re Adoption of Children by D.   286, 287

In re Bain   397

Institutes (Rutherforth)   208

Insulators & Abestos Workers v. Vogler   220n. 1

INS v. Chadha   256

integral human fulfillment (Finnis)   190, 195

intermediale principles. *See* "Modes of responsibility"
"Internal attitude" 49
"internal inconsistency," Unger's view of 140
"internal point of view" 50
"internal statements" 52, 53, 54
international law 21
International News Service v. Associated Press 373
"Interpretation and the Sciences of Man" (Taylor) 173n.
Interstate Consolidated Ry. Co. v. Commonwealth of Massachusetts 412
"intersubjective agreement" 171
"intersubjective confirmation" (Patterson) 171
In the Matter of Baby M 278
Introduction to the Law of Torts, An (Fleming) 309
"intuitionism" 133
"is-ought objection" 42

Jackson, Justice Robert H. 228, 414
Jaggard on Torts, vol. 2 297
J'Aire Corp. v. Gregory 341
Japan Whaling Assn. V. American Crustacean Society 241, 244, 252, 254
Jarrolt v. Moberly 397
Johnson, Justice William 392
joint and several liability 346
Jones v. Opelika 419
Jupiter 14, 23
jurisprudence 10, 212
"just and unjust" 7
justice 7, 8, 9, 11, 12, 13, 22, 76, 210
"Justice Engendered" (Minow) 140, 141, 144, 151n. 1, 152
Justinian 29, 34
Justus v. Atchison 323

Kantian individualism 115
Kaufman v. Eli Lilly 344, 345
Kennedy, Duncan 132, 133, 135, 137, 138
Kennedy, Justice Anthony 235, 238, 244, 252
Kepler, Johannes 42
Knowledge and Politics (Unger) 126, 126n. 3, 128, 128n. 4, 129
Knowlton v. Moore 397, 413n. 4
Krouse v. Graham 322, 323

labor law 136
Lake County v. Rollins 397
Lakota v. Newton 261
Langdell, Christopher Columbus 104
Law and economics. *See* "Economic analysis of law"
Law and Truth (Patterson) 161, 172, 173, 174, 175, 177
"law as a patchwork quilt of irrenconcilable ideologies" (Altman) 134, 136, 137, 138
law as integrity (Dworkin) 86, 87, 88, 90, 91
law of a community (Hart) 66, 73
"law of demand" 105
law of nations 31
law of nature. *See* natural law

law of nuisance 36, 37, 38, 39
Law of Torts, The (Harper and James) 310, 311, 312
Law of War and Peace (Grotius) 21
Law's Empire (Dworkin) 65, 82, 86
"Laws of motion" 27
Lawton v. Steele 402, 408
legal argument
doctrinal 180
prudential 180
Legal Cause in the Law of Torts (Keeton) 310
legal indeterminacy. *See* realist analysis of legal indeterminacy
"legal objectivity" (Unger) 128
legal obligation (Dworkin) 66
legal positivism 3, 184
legal positivist 43, 124
legal process 82 (Fuller and Dworkin) 95
legal validity (Dworkin) 74
legislation 26, 74, 90, 95
legislative intent 10
legislator 32, 34, 98–99
legislature 34, 54, 98, 102
Le Lievre v. Gould 309
Lessing, Doris 155
Levy Leasing Co. v. Siegel 390
lex non exacte definit, sed arbitrio boni viri permittit (the law does not define exactly, but leaves something to the discretion of a just and wise judge) 36
Life and letters of Charles Darwin 42
Life of Washington (Marshall) 398
Lindell v. Rokes 262
Lindley v. Knowlton 314
Liverpool, New York & Philadelphia Steamship Co. v. Com'rs of Emmigration 411n. 2
Livian laws 15
Llewellyn, Karl 269, 275, 277n. 7
Lochner v. New York 407
Long Island Water Supply Co. v. Brooklyn 388
Los Angeles v. Lyons 237, 240, 244, 247, 251
Losee v. Clute 297
loss of consortium 328, 329
Louisiana ex rel. Nelson v. Police Jury of St. Martin's Parish 387
Louisiana ex rel. Ranger v. New Orleans 405
Lucas v. Hamm 313
Lucretia 14
Lujan v. Defenders of Wildlife 235, 238, 240, 252

MacIntyre, Alasdair 135
Mackeldy's Roman Law 210
Macrinus 34
Madison, James 237, 245
man 6, 28
Manigault v. Springs 389
Marbury v. Madison 237, 245, 257
Market Inalienability (Radin) 293
market share liability 349, 350, 351, 352, 353, 354, 355
Marshall, Chief Justice John 144, 164, 377, 384, 392, 397, 398

Marshall v. Glanville   402

Martin v. Abbott Labs   344, 345, 346, 347, 348, 350, 352, 353

Martin v. Herzog   297

Martin v. Struthers   419

Marxism   107

Massachusetts v. Mellon   243

"material cause"   4

Matter of Polemis   300, 302

Maxwell v. Dow   397

McClesky v. Kemp   149, 150, 152

McColluch v. Maryland   164, 392

McCormack v. Abbott Labs   353

McCracken v. Hayward   386

McDonald v. Santa Fe Trail Trans. Co.   221, 223, 224

McEvoy v. American Pool Corp.   310

"method of reflective equilibrium" (Rawls)   76, 78

Meyer v. State of Nebraska   406

Mill, John Stuart   113

Miller, Justice Samuel   165

Minnesota v. Barber   407

Minow, Martha   119, 140, 141, 143, 144, 151n. 1, 152

Missouri v. Holland   392

Mistretta v. United States   256

modal argument (Patterson)   171, 175

modal conflict (Patterson)   170, 171,172, 173, 177

modal incommensurability (Patterson)   175

"modalities" (Patterson)   161, 162, 163, 164, 165, 168, 170, 171

"modes of responsibility" (Finnis)   190, 197, 198, 200, 201

"modified intentionalist"   179

Molien v. Kaiser foundation Hospitals   324, 325, 327

Monroe v. State Court of Fulton County   365n. 2

Moore, G. E.   42

morality   4, 23

moral realism (Dworkin)   78

Morrissey v. Conservative Gas Corp.   345, 351

"moving beyond contradiction" (Patterson)   175

Mr. Justice Cardoza and the Law of Torts (Seavey)   310

Mugler v. Kansas   388

Mulcahy v. Lilly & Co.   347

municipal law   21, 24, 25, 27, 31, 32, 33, 34

Munsey v. Webb   298

Murdock v. Commonwealth of Pennsylvania   413

Murray v. Wright   313

Mysterious Science of the Law (Boorstin)   26

Napoleonic Code   210, 212

National Environmental Policy Act (NEPA)   255, 256

nationalism   110

National Woodwork Mfrs. Assn. V. NRLB   221

natural justice   213

Natural Law and Natural Rights (Finnis)   185, 202

natural law model   78, 79, 80, 81, 82

natural law theorists   185, 186, 189, 190, 202, 203, 210

natural law theory   3, 4, 7, 8, 10, 11, 12, 13, 16, 17, 18, 19, 20, 21, 22, 23, 24, 25, 26, 27, 28, 29, 30, 31, 32, 36, 37, 41, 42, 43, 78
  classical   104, 129
  of Aquinas   130

natural right   24, 27

nature   5, 6, 7, 8, 12, 13, 15, 29, 30, 41

Nazaroff v. Superior Court   323, 335

"necessary relations"   4

negligence   61, 101, 299

Negligence, Subjective or Objective (Seavey)   298

Negligent Infliction of Emotional Distress   315–343

NEID. *See* Negligent infliction of emotional distress

Neo-Platonism, doctrine of *via negativa*   184

NEPA. *See* National Environmental Policy Act

neutrality (Minow)   140
  and practice theory   160

New Academy   22

New Canon Law, The (Woywood)   417

New Jersey Div. Of Youth and Family Servs v. A.W.   286

New natural law theory (John Finnis)   184 , 202

Newton, Isaac   42

Newtonian physics   107

Newton v. Kaiser Foundation Hospitals   325

New York Life Insurance Co. v. Dodge   408

New York Mutual Life Insurance Company v. Armstrong   209

New York Trust Company v. Eisner   370

Nichomachean Ethics (Aristotle)   7, 8, 9, 10, 207

Nineteen Eighty-Four (Orwell)   224

Nineteenth Amendment   243

Norfolk & Western Ry. Co. v. Wood   297

normative theory (Posner)   108, 109, 114

Northwestern Fertilizer Company v. Hyde Park   388

Nozick, Robert M.   135

Nuclear Deterrence, Morality and Realism (Finnis)   191, 198

nuisance. *See* law of nuisance

"objective" nature of truth   4, 10

objectivity (Minow)   140, 160

Occupational Safety and Health Act   294

Ochoa v. Superior Court   316, 325, 326, 327, 329, 331, 332

O'Connor, Justice Sandra Day   150, 235, 249, 370

Ogden v. Saunders   384, 385, 386, 392

On Free Choice (Augustine)   18, 19

On Liberty (Mill)   113

"open texture of the law" (Hart)   55, 56, 63, 127

Orwell, George   224

O'Shea v. Littleton   240, 247, 251

Owens v. Owens   211

pacta sunt servanda (treaties are to be respected)   24

Palsgraf v. The Long Island Railroad Company   296, 310

Parentage Act of New Jersey   280, 289

"Pareto principle"   99, 108, 114, 115, 117

"Pareto superiority"   101, 115, 116, 184
Parrot v. Wells-Fargo Company   297, 299
Parsons v. Superior Court   340
particularity of natural law   17
"Path of the Law, The" (Holmes)   52
Patterson, Dennis   160, 161, 171, 172, 173, 174,
    175, 177, 183
Paul v. Consol. Fireworks Co.   297
PDA   144, 145
People v. Hobson   347
People v. La Fetra   390
People v. Thornton   214
Pemberton v. Pemberton   213
penal laws   33
Penniman's case   387
People ex rel. Twitchell v. Blodgett   396
Philosophical Investigations (Wittgenstein)   3, 160,
    160n. 1
Philosophy and Public Affairs (Altman)   121
philosophy of law   25, 26
Physics (Aristotle)   4, 17
Pierce v. Society of Sisters   414, 419
Planters Bank v. Sharp   386
Plato   8, 15, 409
    ethics of   130
Platonism   11
Plessy v. Ferguson   153
Ploof v. Putnam   358
Pohl v. State   407
Politics (Aristotle)   6, 7
Pollock on Torts   297, 302
Popper, Karl   105
Portee v. Jaffee   340
positive law   11, 26, 27, 190
"positive theory of economic analysis"
    (Posner)   104, 105, 108
positivism   3, 41, 65, 66, 67, 73, 74, 184
positivists   131
Posner, Richard   94, 95, 96, 97, 99, 104, 105, 108,
    109, 114, 118, 119, 176, 176n., 177, 182, 183
Powell, Justice Lewis   149
"power of speech"   7
"practical knowledge"   10
"practical reason"   16, 24
"practical reasonableness" (Finnis)   185
"practice of persuasion" (Patterson)   173
practice theory   160
pragmatism   86, 87, 90, 96, 113–114, 119
predestination   42
"prediction theory of law"   52
primal law   14
Principia Ethica (Moore)   42
Principles of Torts (Seavey)   310
private law doctrine   139
"private wrongs"   27
Problems of Jurisprudence (Posner)   96n. 1, 96n. 2,
    97, 99, 105, 109, 114, 119n. 1, 119n. 2
procedural due process 91
"productive knowledge"   10
property law   37, 62
Prosser's Law of Torts   306, 308, 310, 312, 317, 346
providence   29

proximate cause   299–305, 355
"prudential argument." *See* legal argument)
public interest   18, 19
"public wrongs"   27
Puffendorf, Samuel von   35, 208

Quine, W. V. O.   173, 174
Quintus   14, 15

racialism   110
Rastafarian faith   111
ratio decidendi   63
Rationale of Proximate Cause (Green)   299
rationalist tradition   24
rational nature   17
Ravo v. Rogatnick   346
Rawls, John   65, 76, 78
"Rawls' equilibrium technique" (in Dworkin)   79
realism   88, 120–124, 132, 140
realist analysis of legal indeterminacy
    (Altman)   120, 121, 122, 123, 124, 125, 131,
    132, 160, 184
reason   17, 28, 30
"reasonable annoyance" (Dworkin)   76
reasonable care   62
"reductionist," economics as (Posner)   107
Reed v. Moore   307, 318
"reflective equilibrium" (Dworkin)   82, 184
"regime of primary rules"   43
Rehnquist, Chief Justice William   147, 178, 235,
    236, 370
relativism   81
Republic (Cicero)   13
Republic (Plato)   15
res ipsa loquitor   355
Responsibility for Tortious Acts, vol. 3
    (Wigmore)   299
Restatement Second of Contracts   266, 269, 270,
    276n. 5
Restatement Second of Torts   346, 352
revelation   30, 31
Reynolds v. United states   413n. 4
Rhetoric (Aristotle)   11
Rhode Island v. Massachusetts   397
Richardson v. Ham   312
Richards v. Stanley   312
Riggs v Palmer   67, 72, 207
"right reason"   11
"rights of persons"   27
"rights of things"   27
risk contribution   353
Rizzo v. Goode   251
Robertson v. Methow Valley Citizens Council   255,
    256
Robert v. U.S.E.F. Corp.   298
Rodman v. State Farm Mutual Insurance   269, 272,
    273
"role of negation" (Finnis)   184
Roman law   11, 34, 52, 212, 213
Rowland v. Christoan   332, 341
"rule for conclusive identification of the primary
    rules of obligation"   46

"rule of action" 27, 28
rule of civil conduct 34
rule of interpretation 34
"rule of law" 187, 188, 189
"rule of recognition" 46, 48, 50, 51, 53, 54, 55
"rules of change" 47
Rutherforth, Thomas 208

Saint Francis College v. Al-Khazraji 145, 146, 152
Salmond on Torts 297, 300
*San Francisco Arts & Athletics, Inc. v. United States
    Olympic Committee* 373
Scalia, Justice Antonin 235
Schact v. United States 364, 368
Schenk v. United States 373
School of Economic Analysis of Law 95
Scott v. Shepard 299
Scott v. United States 276
"second order principles" 187. *See also* first or-
    der prinicples
Section 1981 (42 U.S.C. §1981) 145
Sees v. Baber 283, 286, 289
Seibert v. Lewis 387
self-interest 24
Shaare Tefila Congregation v. Cobb 145, 146, 152
Shadwell v. Shadwell 261
Shearman and Redfield on Negligence 297
Sheehan v. Sheehan 290
Sherman Act 71
sic utere tuo, ut alienum non laedas (use your own
    property in such a manner as not to injure
    that of another) 37–38
Sierra Club v. Morton 237, 239, 240, 244
*Simon v. Eastern Ky. Wlefare Rights Organiza-
    tion* 237, 238
Sindell v. Abbott Labs 344, 345, 346, 347, 348, 350,
    352
skepticism 81, 184
Slaughter House Cases 407
Slawson, W. 268
Sloane v. Southern California Ry. Co. 310
Smith, Adam 108
Smith's Commentaries 208
Smith v. Goguen 375, 376
Smith v. London & Southwestern Ry. Co. 300, 302
Smoot-Hawley controversy 237
"social and political life" 6, 7
social Darwinism
"social instinct" 7
socialism 113
society 17, 24, 30
Souter, Justice David 235, 244
South Caroline v. United States 396
Southern Ilinois Builders Assn. V. Ogilvie 220 n. 1
specific moral norms (Finnis) 198, 200, 201
"speculative reason." *See* "theoretical reason"
Spence v. Washington 363, 365, 369, 375
Sproles v. Binford 389
stare decisis 64
*Standard Form Contracts and Democratic Control of
    Lawmaking Power* (Slawson) 268
state 7, 33

"state of reflective equilibrium" (Rawls) 78
State Rubbish Collectors Assn. V. Siliznoff 313, 318
Statesman (Plato) 8
State v. Bartels 407
State v. Ferguson 271
State v. Houghland 271
State v. Mitchell 374
State v. Murray 271
State v. Royal 374
State v. Waterman 374
Statutory interpretation 207
Statutory Interpretation (Posner) 176n.
statutory law 108
Stevens, Justice John Paul 149, 150, 153, 235,
    246, 366
stoics 11, 22, 23
Street v. New York 375
strict liability 309
Stone v. Farmer's Loan and Trust Company 389
Stone v. Mississippi 388
Story on the Constitution 385
*Stuart v. School District No. 1 of Village of Kalama-
    zoo* 412
Studies in the Law of Torts (Bohlen) 297
Sturges v. Crowninshield 385, 386
subjectivism 184
Sullivan v. Dunham 297
Summa Theologica (Aquinas) 16, 19
Summers v. Tice 345, 346, 348, 352
Supreme Being 27, 28,
Supreme Court. *See* United States Supreme Court
supreme power 34
"surrogacy contract" 278–294
Surrogate Motherhood and the Baby-Selling Laws
    (Katz) 292
Sutherland, Justice George 394
symbolic speech 362, 365

Taft, Chief Justice George 164
Taking Rights Seriously (Dworkin) 74, 75, 77, 78
Talbott v. Stemmons 262
Talmage v. Smith 299
Taney, Chief Justice Roger 163, 164, 395, 401
Tarquinius, Lucius 14
Tarquinius, Sextus 14
taxation 26
Taylor, Charles 173, 173n.
Teamsters v. United States 223n. 5
"tender years doctrine" 283
Terminiello v. Chicago 366
Tertullian 22
Texas v. Johnson 361
Texas v. White 372
"textual perspective" 180
"theoretical knowldege" 11
"theoretical reason" 16, 24
"theory determination," idea of (Unger) 129
Thirteenth Amendment 112
Thomas, Justice Clarence 235, 236
Thomas v. Quartermaine 297, 299
Thompson v. Consolidated Gas Utilities 412
"thoroughly critical jurisprudence" (Unger) 128

Thucydides   22
Tinker v. Des Moines   364
Titian laws   15
Titius   31, 33
Title VII. *See* Civil Rights Act of 1964
Tort and Absolute Liability (Smith)   298–299
Touby v. United States   256
Touche Ross Co. v. Redington,   176
*Train v. Colorado Public Interest Research
     Group*   221
Traux v. Corrigan   408
Traux v. Raich   408
"treaties are to be respected." *See pacta sunt
     servanda*
True law   11, 13
Turpin v. Sortini   329
TVA v. Hill   236
Twinings v. New Jersey   408
Two Dogmas of Empiricism (Quine)   174

"unconscionable bargain"   275, 277
Unger, Roberto   119, 126, 127, 128, 129,   132,
     134, 140, 184
Uniform Commercial Code   275
United States Congress   71, 87, 165, 166, 176, 177,
     178, 179, 180, 181, 215, 215, 217, 218, 219,
     221–235, 372, 373, 376, 384, 399
United States Constitution   71, 114, 163, 164, 165,
     166, 168, 170, 171, 385, 396, 397, 398, 399, 400,
     401, 403, 405, 411, 412, 413, 414, 419
United States Express Co. v. Everest   297
United States Supreme Court   71, 140, 141, 143,
     144, 145, 146, 147–153, 157, 158, 164, 165, 166,
     167, 168, 176, 178, 179
United States v. American Trucking Assns.   221
United States v. Carroll Towing   101n. 1
United States v. Craig   217
United States v. Elevator Contractors   220n. 1
United States v. Fischer   216
United States v. Guthrie   372
United States v. O'Brien   363, 365, 365n. 2, 367
United States v. Public Utilities   Comm'n
     227, 228
United States v. Rutherford   225
*United States v. Students Challenging Regulatory
     Agency Procedures*   240
United States v. Union Pacific Railroad   217
United Steelworkers of America v. Weber   177, 178,
     179, 180, 181, 182, 219, 226
universality   17
universalizability principle (Finnis)   201

"unreasonable annoyance" (Dworkin)
     75
utilitarianism   82, 94, 95, 110, 112, 113, 115, 116,
     117

"validity of laws"   50, 51
*Valley Forge Christian College v. Americans United
     for Separation of Church and State, Inc.*   245
Vaughan v Taff Vale Ry. Co.   297
Vincent v. Lake Erie Transportation Company   356
Von Hoffman v. City of Quincy   385, 386

Walker v. Whitehead   385, 387
Warren, Chief Justice Earl   375
Warth v. Seldin   237, 238, 245, 246
"wealth maximization" (Posner)   96, 99, 101, 102,
     103, 105, 108, 109, 110, 111, 112, 113, 114, 116,
     117
Weber case. *See United Steelworkers of America v.
     Weber*
West Coast Hotel v. Parrish   293
West River Bridge v. Dix   388
West Virginia Board of Education v. Barnette   362,
     369, 416
West Va. Central R. Co. v. State   297
Wharton on Negligence   297
White, Justice Byron   145, 235, 236, 370, 376
White v. Hoyt   263
Whitmore v. Arkansas   237, 247, 251
Whitney v. California   370
Wickard v. Filburn   419
*Williams v. Walker-Thomas Furniture Com-
     pany*   274, 275
Williston on Contracts   270, 276n. 6
Wilson v. New   383
*Wimberly v. Labor & Industrial Relations Commis-
     sion,*   147, 148
Winterbotton v. Wright   313
Wittgenstein, Ludwig   3, 113, 160, 161, 171, 172
"women's experience" (Minow)   140
Woods v. Lancet   347
writ of *quod permittat prosternere*   39
wrongful life   330
Wyeth v. Cambridge Board of Health   408

Yick Wo v. Hopkins   407

Zafft v. Lilly & Co.   347
Zaleucus   15
"Zone of Danger"   307, 308, 311, 314, 3187, 320,
     321, 322, 333, 335, 338